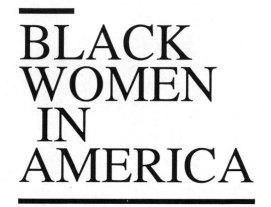

BLACK
WOMEN
IN
AMERICA

To Deborah G. Plant
a Louisiana Warrior Woman

BLACK WOMEN IN AMERICA

edited by

KIM MARIE VAZ

 SAGE Publications
International Educational and Professional Publisher
Thousand Oaks   London   New Delhi

For information address:

SAGE Publications, Inc.
2455 Teller Road
Thousand Oaks, California 91320

SAGE Publications Ltd.
6 Bonhill Street
London EC2A 4PU
United Kingdom

SAGE Publications India Pvt. Ltd.
M-32 Market
Greater Kailash I
New Delhi 110 048 India

Printed in the United States of America

Library of Congress Cataloging-in-Publication Data

Main entry under title:

Black women in America / edited by Kim Marie Vaz.
    p. cm.
    Includes bibliographical references and index.
    ISBN 0-8039-5454-9. — ISBN 0-8039-5455-7 (pbk.)
    1. Afro-American women—Social condiditons. I. Vaz, Kim Marie.
E185.86.B5418 1995
305.48'896073—dc20   94-31761

95 96 97 98 99 10 9 8 7 6 5 4 3 2 1

Sage Production Editor: Astrid Virding

Contents

**Part I. Black Women's Social History Through the Lens
of Their Activism**

Preface

I teach the course "Black Women in America" to university students every semester. Students often ask how I maintain my enthusiasm term after term. Without fail I tell them that this is my one chance to communicate directly to large groups a body of information from a Black woman's standpoint; the one place in the university setting where Black women's experiences are center stage, where it is permissible to affirm and value Black women's achievements as well as examine the wounds incurred from living in a racist and sexist society. It is the one place where over the course of several months I can discuss the various ways in which Black women have constantly reconstructed and transformed alien definitions of Black womanhood. Within the content of the material are pragmatic strategies for changing one's own life conditions. Hence, the nature of the subject matter acts as a personal and group energizer.

Through this anthology, I wish to share my approach to teaching about Black women in America. The collection offers an interdisciplinary study of Black women's historic activism, representation in literature and popular media, self-constructed images, and current psychosocial challenges. The contributors are an outstanding group of scholars representing a variety of disciplines. All of the chapters in this anthology are being published here for the first time. The original research of these scholars provides a wealth of knowledge that will be useful to professors, students, cultural workers, and all those interested in Black Studies and Women's Studies.

—KIM MARIE VAZ

Acknowledgments

This anthology benefited from a Research and Creative Scholarship grant from the Division of Sponsored Research at the University of South Florida and a grant from The Black Life Research Program sponsored by University of South Florida's Institute on Black Life. I would like to thank my colleagues at the University of South Florida for their support and encouragement, namely Juel Smith and the faculty and staff of the Department of Women's Studies and the Africana Studies Program. Marianne Bell's clerical assistance was invaluable. Dale Grenfell and Marquita Flemming at Sage Publications were unfailing in their enthusiasm for this project and I thank them. Kristin Bergstad proved to be an excellent and efficient copy editor. The anonymous reviewers' comments were very helpful to the contributors and I offer them our gratitude. My research assistant on the project, the insightful Gwynne Jenkins, generously gave more of her time than I could financially reward. Her commitment to the project accelerated the pace with which we were able to ready the manuscript for publication. I wish to thank the contributors to this anthology for their scholarly insights and forbearance.

Organization of the Anthology

KIM MARIE VAZ

⬚ I have organized the chapters in this anthology into four main sections: Black women's organizing activities, societal images of Black women, images Black women have constructed of themselves and each other, and, finally, contemporary psychosocial challenges.

A Legacy of Activism

In precolonial societies, gendered constraints on women's dietary habits, public decision making, and inheritance rights sought to subordinate women. Nonetheless, as Barbara A. Moss points out, African women were an integral part of their communities and often maximized their positions with resources gained by their own labor. Especially in matrilineal societies, individual African women could achieve high status as administrators in political systems and as spirit mediums in the religious arena. As part of the group, African women could band together to redress grievances against men and discipline male offenders. Enslaved African women passed on their legacy of resilience, resourcefulness, and spirituality to their African-American daughters who adapted these to confront and challenge the slave system.

One of the earliest forms of organized activism engaged in by Black women in the New World was female antislavery societies. Shirley J. Yee notes that all female organizations provided one arena through which free Black women could participate in the public domain and, at the same time, remain within acceptable boundaries of female behavior. Black women followed the practice of organizing separately from men and participating in specifically " 'female' activities, such as fund-raising in support of male leadership. . . . Yet, the existence of sex-segregated social activities was, ironically, as liberating as it was constrictive, for it helped sweep away the memories of slavery and create for Black men and women a sense of autonomy over their lives both inside and outside the home."

Black women's positions within precolonial African societies and New World Black liberation movements can be described as "constrained but empowered" (Collins, 1990). This is evident not only from Moss's and Yee's work but from Dorothy C. Salem's chapter on Black women in the formation of the National Association For the Advancement of Colored People, 1909-1922, and Mary C. Pruitt's findings on female civil rights activists in Minnesota. Salem's work reveals that Black women were pivotal to the development of the NAACP. They worked as mobilizers of antilynching campaigns, as investigators, as administrators, as branch directors, and as fund-raisers. Although they were overlooked by Black male and White leadership for years when key appointments were made, they persisted in assisting the NAACP to achieve its goals. Mary Toliver Jones and Josie Robinson Johnson are examples of the women Ella Baker could have been speaking about when she said that women outnumbered men in the Civil Rights Movement and the Movement was largely carried by them. Mary Pruitt interviewed these Minnesota women who signed up for a lifetime of commitment to working for social justice. Pruitt describes how these women acted out of an ethic of responsibility and from a perspective of social change as involving long-term struggle. The Civil Rights Movement provided opportunities for the development of women's leadership on the one hand and for the improvement of the quality of work lives for Black women on the other.

Deborah B. Carter explores the intersection of occupational changes and social change movements and their impact on African-American women. During World War II, African-American women were able to move from domestic and farm jobs into the manufacturing sector. For the first time, Black women were in a position to be organized by a trade union. In addition, the Civil Rights Movement framed class struggle in terms of the conflict between Whites and Blacks. The movement brought new leadership and strategies and a new ideology on the relationship between Black inequality and racial discrimination in the labor market. As a result large numbers of African Americans, particularly women in low-wage occupations, unionized.

M. Rivka Polatnick's case study of the liberation activism of poor Black women demonstrates that the issues they confronted were more broadly based than those of middle-class White women and activist Black men. The Mt. Vernon/New Rochelle poor women's group linked race, gender, and class inequality as reflected in their agenda: welfare rights, decent housing, the overthrow of capitalism, militant resistance of male supremacy while emphasizing the common struggle with Black men against racial oppression, and defense of birth control as positive technology. Unlike middle-class White women's groups, these poor

Black women valued mothering and family life and were alarmed about the implications of certain practices surrounding artificial reproduction. Polatnick concludes that White women did not "launch" nor do they "own" women's liberation activism; researchers and the general public must begin to think in less restricted ways about women's liberation. Polatnick's findings are reminiscent of Yee's in that Blacks defined abolitionist activity in more sweeping terms than did Whites. For Blacks, abolitionist activism entailed assisting runaway slaves, the establishment of literary societies to make up for the scarcity of schools for Blacks, opposition to recolonization, and the elimination of racism.

Many Black academic feminists strive to construct knowledge from the perspectives of Black working-class women. This can prove difficult if Black intellectuals adopt the stance of a "spectator-writer" as opposed to that of a "progressive, activist-writer." Joy James recounts the investigative activism of Ida Wells that incorporated dialogues with other activists and writers to divulge facts distorted or denied in White media. James analyzes the "narratives of conviction" of three Black feminists as they discussed the Central Park Jogger rape case. James cautions Black feminists against relying on White media exclusively, without considering Black and Hispanic coverage of situations affecting Black people. This, coupled with a lack of knowledge about Black women's antiracist and antisexist coterminous organizing, leads Black feminist writers to participate in the erasure of Black women's activism around issues of racial and sexual violence against women and fair trials for Black men and to reductive conclusions that Black women automatically subordinate sex to race.

Socially Constructed Images

Images of Black women that have been constructed by European and European-American leaders of religious, social, literary, cultural, and political institutions throughout the centuries have retained a pejorative characterization of Black sexuality. Baltasar Fra-Molinero rereads Old World historical texts and literary testimonies and discusses the practices of slavery as well as the literary representations of Black women in 15th and 16th century Spain. These ideas and customs eventually were exported to the New World, serving to create and justify Black women's marginality and exploitation. In the literature of that period, Black women were characterized as having bad tempers and loose sexual morals. The writers portrayed Black women as committing infractions, specific to their supposed perverse morality, that resulted in physical punishment by their White masters. These masters charged themselves with the responsibility of defending the "honor of their households." Mulatto women, on the other hand, escaped punishment and were exoticized by the largely White male writers of the era.

Yet, White women's fears of being cast aside as the object of affection by their husbands in favor of cunning and deceitful Black women also found its way into the literature, by at least one Spanish woman writer, to round out the negative characterizations of enslaved African women.

The actual sexual exploitation of Black women became a pervasive reality in the Old South and continued beyond emancipation. Madelin Joan Olds addresses the White Southern obsession with interracial sex in the postbellum period. Specifically, she explores the charge by White former slave owners that civil rights would encourage miscegenation. They reasoned that poor White men would be drawn to the beauty and wealth of affluent mulattoes, thereby producing children who could pass for White. Toward the turn of the century when Blacks made concrete progress, these former owners leveled the charge that Black men wanted to rape White women either because of Black equality or Black revenge. The revenge argument held that because of the concubinage relationship between White men and Black women, Black men were driven to rape White women. The equality argument proposed that it was the "New Negro," raised in freedom and granted political participation, that sought to terrorize White women. Nevertheless, it was Black women who were more frequently cited by White writers as being responsible for the so-called sexual immorality of the race, even as Black men were thought to be menacing White women. It was Black women who produced the unchaste daughters, bestial sons, and enticing mulattoes. The Black rapist theme, Olds concludes, served to protect race, class, and gender interests; that is, dominance of Whites over Blacks, rich over poor, and men over women, and to bolster as well as aggravate the sexual and power ambitions of White patriarchs.

The ideas of Black women's sexual immorality so meticulously crafted in Spain and carried through the postbellum South resurfaced in 1992 as Anita Hill accused the nominee for the Supreme Court, Clarence Thomas, of sexual harassment while she worked for him at two separate government agencies. In her chapter, Bridget Aldaraca reviews the attempts by Thomas supporters on the Senate Judiciary Committee to discredit Hill's testimony by establishing that she was not a reliable witness because she was "acting out a fantasy of unrequited love for a man who was her superior." Aldaraca notes that some Black writers on the subject also imbibed these ideas, suggesting that Thomas's remarks to Hill were simply Black male courting behavior.

Elizabeth Hadley Freydberg reviews the portrayal of Black women and Latinas in American Hollywood films. From this Eurocentric and androcentric industry flows the familiar societal stereotypes of both groups of women as prostitutes, whores, and drug addicts. Many contemporary male filmmakers, irrespective of race, retain this vision of Black women and Latinas, and these stereotypes continue to surface in modern films. Even though sophisticated and beautifully written works by women of color are readily available, Freydberg concludes that there is no indication that complex stories about Black women and Latinas will be emerging from Hollywood in the near future. Given the additional reality that women of color directors and producers remain on the margins of the industry, we will continue to be bombarded with derogatory images of Black women and Latinas.

Negative attitudes about the poor, Blacks, and women are not confined to popular media but are inscribed in the current welfare and housing policy, as well. These views held by many government policy makers reflect an unwillingness to come to grips with poverty and racism. Shirley M. Geiger addresses the ideological, racial, gender, and class factors that influence public policy decision making. She finds that instead of acting to relieve the economic and social hardships facing poor Black women who head households, U.S. public policy seeks to control the behavior of these women and their children. Geiger urges Black women not only to conduct research into the areas of public policy strategies that would enhance the lives of large numbers of Black women, but to monitor the voting habits of politicians from areas with substantial numbers of Black women solo parents.

Self-Expression

A Black woman is credited as being the first American woman political speaker to leave copies of her speeches and speak before a mixed audience of men and women. Maria W. Stewart delivered her first speech in 1832. Any woman daring to speak during this period had to contend with male hostility as it was delivered through the pulpit and through physical attacks by men during women's formal lectures. Charles I. Nero writes that although Black women have had a long history as public orators, public address anthologies—whether compiled by men, Black or White—have excluded their voices. White women also marginalize Black women as they reconstruct women's oratorical past. Another factor working to prevent the serious study of Black women's public address is the reliance on the model of great leaders. For men, women do not fit this model and for White women, Black women seldom figure as great women leaders. Moreover, those Black women whose speeches do find their way into print tend to be middle and upper class. Nero suggests that circumventing this class bias involves redefining public address to include a wide array of discursive practices, from poetry to naming behaviors.

Black women continually draw on institutions in the Black community to stretch the tight spaces they are assigned. It is to the African-American press that Linda D. Williams has turned to chronicle a wider range of images of Black women than ordinarily recorded in works on Black women. She debunks the lie about the absence of Black women athletes, managers, and owners in sporting activities as varied as swimming, golf, tennis, basketball, and track. Williams urges researchers to look beyond the image of Black women as victims—an image which suggests that only recent government and judicial decisions created opportunities for Black women to participate in local, state, and national sport competitions. Using institutions in the African-American community, Black women created opportunities for themselves before Althea Gibson and Wilma Rudolph made their marks and in spite of racism and sexism. The African-American weeklies chronicled the activities of Black women's athletics and even sponsored tournament play for women.

Beginning in 1948, Marion Cuyjet provided opportunities for brown-skinned Black girls to develop the theoretical and technical knowledge necessary to become successful ballet dancers. Melanye White-Dixon chronicles the development of Cuyjet's Judimar School and profiles four of her students (Judith Jamison, Delores Abelson, China White, and Donna Lowe Warren) who pursued performing careers with professional dance companies. Throughout her chapter, White-Dixon highlights the survival strategies that Black dancers developed to cope with the racism of the professional White American dance companies.

Women rap artists are asserting their voices in a musical genre whose male performers are often blatantly sexist. Robin Roberts suggests that much of women's rap should be considered "practical feminist criticism." Evidence of this comes through the women's clothing, mannerisms, posture, and physical stature and through their lyrics that declare that they are people deserving of respect, safe and pleasurable sex, and the right to be heard.

Psychosocial Challenges

The authors of this section warn activists, policy makers, researchers, and relatives of older Black women not to make assumptions about them. Because they are not a homogeneous group, Black women must be allowed to state their own needs and directions for liberation. Bernita C. Berry's chapter explores older Black women's perceptions of the meaningfulness of their lives in spite of social and structural constraints. She finds that Black women are certainly aware that discrimination exists based on age, race, and gender, but these have not prevented them from creating satisfying lives. Many of the women in her sample report having fulfilling lives stemming from their relationships with their families, jobs, and community involvement.

A self-help group for African-American women rearing their daughters' crack cocaine exposed children in Tampa, FL, has engaged in the process of defining their own needs. Drawing on his clinical work with these women, Aaron A. Smith recounts how through the group the women began to identify the manner in which these new and unplanned demands jeopardized their own economic, physical, and emotional survival. Even though these women were married they received virtually no support from their husbands, and adult children and relatives were often antagonistic. Having imbibed society's negative views of Black women and experienced strained familial relationships since childhood, coupled with poor educational histories and bleak employment records, these women are also faced with the task of defending their grandchildren against the destructive behavior of their daughters. Through the grandmothers' group the women were able to fend off feelings of isolation, cope with guilt about having failed as mothers, and learn to claim their legal rights as grandmothers and ultimately as Black women.

The two chapters in this final section serve as a reminder that Black women have an image of themselves that differs from those others impose. Collectively the authors of this anthology demonstrate that socially constructed images hide the complexities and ambiguities, the challenges and the joys experienced in the real lives of Black women.

Reference

Collins, Patricia Hill. (1990). *Black feminist thought: Knowledge, consciousness, and the politics of empowerment.* Boston: Unwin Hyman.

Introduction
Black Women's Lives and Cultural Contexts

KIM MARIE VAZ

🔊 Negotiating familial and environmental relationships that are structured in accordance with cultural mandates regarding gender, race, and class means dealing head-on with definitions of womanhood and the ensuing expectations about appropriate conduct and permissible aspirations for Black women. To explore the nature of the role Black women have been assigned within White society, I will draw on the 20th century's most popular literary and media event, Margaret Mitchell's *Gone With the Wind* (1936/1964). The novel is an embodiment of the social discourse that kept Black women enslaved, White women enthralled, and patriarchal power enshrined. An examination of the novel's subtext reveals a dialectic between social ideologies and capitalist production. The dialectic articulates the politics of race, gender, class, and culture that converge in a fiction of Black female identity designed to cast Black women as social ciphers and economic menials. *Gone With the Wind* provides a full contextual view of how negative images of Black women are created to satisfy the White imagination's idea of cultural supremacy and to justify European imperialism and economic exploitation and domination of Black women. The novel defines Black women as "the other," the subhuman counterpart in a wide array of social relationships. As Sandra Harding (1993) notes,

> the gender relations between men and women in any particular group [are not] shaped only by the men and women in that group, for those relations too are always shaped by how men and women are defined in every other race, class, or culture in the environment. . . . The femininity prescribed for the plantation owner's wife was exactly what was forbidden for the Black slave woman. (p. 18)

1

When published in 1936, *Gone With the Wind* was an immediate Book-of-the-Month Club best seller. At least one million copies of the book were sold when it was first published, and as late as 1980 about 40,000 copies of the book were sold annually. And, it is estimated that more than 90% of U.S. citizens have seen the 4-hour-long movie and most have seen it more than once (Pyron, 1983). The unprecedented and continuing success of this novel and film suggests how deeply entrenched in the American imagination are notions of patriarchy, European imperialism, and racial superiority and inferiority. Because the novel's epic sweep captures one of the most tumultuous periods in American history, it is a classic of the American literary tradition. This may account for its continued and current popularity. What may also account for the popularity of the novel and film is the propensity of the White imagination to indulge in deleterious fantasies of aristocratic privilege and to long for the idyllic days of antebellum America. That the wealth and welfare of a privileged few is contingent upon the subjugation and exploitation of the dispossessed and Black many hardly causes pause for consideration. Because this novel bespeaks the classic American mind-set, because it continues to generate destructive images of Black women that find the fantasies and longings for "bygone" days, and because these images and fantasies are transformed into pernicious politics and policies that affect the lives and quality of life of Black women, this classic novel demands meticulous examination. Although many have pondered the meaning of the popularity of the novel and film for various disciplines such as art and history and for various groups—Northerners, Southerners, White women, and "liberals" and "conservatives"—discussion of the book in relation to Black women is negligible. As a novel about women's culturally defined places and the place of Southern ideology in constructing a 20th-century American worldview, the meaning of the popularity paints a vivid picture of Black women's niche within the American sociocultural matrix.

Black Womanism and White Womanhood: Gender, Race, Class, and the Legacy of the Cult of True Womanhood

Alice Walker (1993) writes of Black women's disappointment and outrage when forced to realize that their definitions of feminism can greatly diverge from those held by White women. Walker offers a fictional account of a Black woman and White woman who planned a fund-raising ball in which guests were to come dressed as the feminist they most admired. The White woman came as Scarlett O'Hara. In confronting these competing feminist ideals, the Black woman coveys that her immediate visceral response to the woman's costume was related to the historic distrust between Black and White women. Scarlett certainly flouts the social and moral codes of the Old South: buying and running lumber mills, working while pregnant, working after giving birth, and driving her own buggy through "bad neighborhoods." Her husband, capitulating to social pressure, impregnates her and locks away her buggy. The community response to this ambitious woman is ostracism and contempt and the barriers she faces are unfortunately still current: threats of rape when traveling alone and the reluctance of men to work for a woman. Eve Sedgwick (1985) suggests that *Gone With the Wind* symbolized for White women the restrictions the female gender role imposed on them in terms of the obstacles encountered in realizing their ambitions and the alienation of their sexuality. Helen Taylor (1989) found that though White women readers did not necessarily like Scarlett's ruthlessness they admired her ability to "rise again," "do her own thing," and "make it in a man's world." For White women growing up in the 1940s in a society that was emerging from economic hardship, Scarlett was a survivor. She was a heroine who had not succumbed to the social and economic upheaval of her times. To those who grew up in the 1950s and 1960s, Scarlett was seen as a rebel who beat the establishment. Gina Berreca (1991) noted recently that in the 1950s many high school girls identified with Scarlett's nemesis, Melanie Wilkes. Wilkes conformed to all of the conventions required of White ladies, which included a belief in the racial inferiority of Blacks. According to Berreca, White teenagers currently identify with Scarlett. For young White women today, Scarlett is a career feminist, a successful upwardly mobile professional, a Yuppie (Taylor, 1989). Yet, Scarlett's privilege is consequent to the exploitation of enslaved Africans, poor Whites, and American Indians. Alice Walker (1993) writes that Scarlett is only one of many White women's heroines "whose real source of power, as well as the literal shape of their bodies, comes from the people they oppress" (p. 484). A most telling example of Scarlett's unabashed willingness to profit at the expense of the exploited is dramatized in her search for food at a plantation where the owners and those they enslaved have fled due to the victory of the Northern troops. "She knew every slave had his own garden patch and as she reached the quarters, she hoped these little patches had been spared" (Mitchell, 1936/1964, p. 427).

Although the position of the lady is made possible by the exploitation of people of color and poor Whites, Sedgwick (1985) observes that irrespective of race and class each female character in the novel "exists in some meaning-ful relation to the role of 'lady' " (pp. 8-9). As a White, monied woman who adhered to the four cardinal virtues—piety, domesticity, submissiveness, and purity—Melanie Wilkes is the undisputed "lady" of the novel. Belle Watling is White but not monied and as a prostitute, ladyship is far from her grasp. Mammy stands in awe of the social role of the lady, but can never be one because of her race. Mammy's existence is to service and support the true lady or the lady "wannabe." Scarlett strains to embrace the role even as she chafes under the force of its conventions. Having, however, no maternal yearnings, no desire to submit to patriarchal authority in the form of man or god, and no respect for conjugal fidelity or conventional sexual mores, she remains an unlikely candidate for ladyhood.

The role of the lady is constructed against a background of "otherness," consisting not only of Blackness and Black women, but also of poor White women and prostitutes (which are often tautological constructions in Mitchell's Old South vision). For example, Emmy Slattery serves as a receptacle of Scarlett's antipathy against poor White women.

> Emmie Slattery! The dirty tow-headed slut whose illegitimate baby Ellen [Scarlett's mother] had baptized, Emmie who had given typhoid to Ellen and killed her. This overdressed, common, nasty piece of poor white trash was coming up the steps of Tara, bridling and grinning as if she belonged here. Scarlett thought of Ellen and, in a rush, feeling came back into the emptiness of her mind, a murderous rage so strong it shook her like the ague.
> "Get off those steps, you trashy wench!" she cried. "Get off this land! Get out!" (Mitchell, 1936/1964, p. 537)

Where the character of Melanie Wilkes embodies the "idea" of the lady in its supreme form, other characters represent varying dimensions and nuances of the ideal. For instance, Aunt Pittypat is endowed with the essential quality of feminine dependency. Never able to make a decision and always in need of Scarlett, as well as the enslaved Peter, to make her feel safe, she is penned in puerile simplicity. Grandma Fontaine is the capitalist ideologue who reifies the astute, calculating mind of the lady who must be always cognizant of her situation. She instructs Scarlett in the politics of "rising again." She exhorts her in the expediency of exploiting those who are down as a means of individual economic growth and the necessity of rebuffing those same people once one's wealth is firmly reestablished.

Each woman is assigned a place within the social hierarchy based on her personal and economic attributes. Sexuality also figures as a major determinant of her position. Under patriarchy, White women's sexuality is denied, repressed, idealized, fantasized, and compromised. As Blacks are constructed as the objectified other whose raison d'être is to service Whites, so the White woman assumes the same position in White patriarchal imagination and ideological praxis. Her social constructions are designed to satisfy notions of White male virtue, chivalry, and imperiousness as they justify and rationalize his sexual appetite and unbridled lust to dominate, not only White women but other men less powerful than himself and all women. In *Gone With the Wind*, White men control women's bodies and use and dispose of them as they wish. Patriarchal ideology sanctions the O'Haras' overseer to honor or condemn the impoverished Emmy Slatterys as it condones Rhett Butler's marital rape of Scarlett.

At bottom of White men's privilege to proffer or withhold the honor of (White) women, to embrace or reject paternity, is their power to define sex, sexuality, womanhood, manhood, vice, and virtue. Out of the predominant patriarchal discourse emerges definitions of rape with clearly delineated images of "rapist" and "raped." For example, when Scarlett is robbed by a group of ruffians made up of Black men led by a White man, the community automatically determines the incident to be an act of sexual aggression though sex is not part of the assault. Propelled by the anti-free Black hysteria with its discourse of "Black man as rapist," even though the robbers' motive clearly is theft, the Ku Klux Klan is mobilized to defend "White women's honor." Many critics continue to read this scene as an attempted rape (Sedgwick, 1985). In White patriarchal constructions of womanhood, Black women function as the antithesis of the lady. Black women are never seen as victims/survivors of rape or as women compromised by White male objectification of them as sexual commodities. Where the issue of "mulatto" babies might have constituted the prevailing perception that Black women could not be raped, the patriarchal construction of the cult of *true* womanhood made it imperative that White women and men view Black women as wanton whores and their offspring as objects of jest.

> "Hah! They promised all the black wenches silk dresses and gold earrings—that's what they did. And Cathleen Calvert said some of the troopers went off with the black fools behind them on their saddles. Well, all they'll get will be yellow babies and I can't say that Yankee blood will improve the stock." (p. 449)

In contrast to this image of Black women as sexually lascivious is the asexual Mammy. Helen Taylor (1989) describes Mammy as the revered mother figure idealized by the White South as a fount of emotional and physical comfort for Whites. Mammy is passive, patient, and has no needs of her own. One is continually struck by the concern Mammy displays over the dietary habits of the O'Hara family, for example, but there is scarcely a passage in the novel in which she fixes something for herself to eat. Devoted to "her" White family, Mammy is hostile to poor Whites, rebellious Blacks, and Yankees. The novel brims with instances of faithful Black servants finding their identities caring for their enslavers. While Scarlett's mother, Ellen Robillard, grieved the loss of her true love, Pierre, she had also to decide whether to marry the middle-aged Gerald O'Hara. Mammy becomes distraught over the situation. Mammy

> cried herself out over her mistress' dark head, protested, "But, honey, you kain do dat!"
>
> "I will do it. He is a kind man. I will do it or go into the convent at Charleston . . ."

> So, Ellen, Ellen no longer Robillard, turned her back on Savannah, never
> to see it again, and with a middle-aged husband, Mammy, and twenty "house
> niggers" journeyed toward Tara. (Mitchell, 1936/1964, p. 54)

Mammy never makes any demands on the system, never asks for anything for herself, maintains a steady interest in the welfare of Whites, does not leave after emancipation, never gets sick, and never dies (Taylor, 1989). Taylor asserts that Mammy's image is comforting to Whites because she is content to subordinate her identity as a Black woman to whiteness. Mammy is a Black woman whom they can worship. Alice Walker (1993) speculates that the historic distrust between Black and White women stems in part from Black women's feelings that White women want them as slaves—a fear driven by White women's feelings of entitlement to some amount of servitude from Black women. Kesho Scott (1991) also has observed that in women's groups, Black women are expected to embody the slave role of Mammy by "protecting racists, sexists, and ethnocentrists from their own realities" (p. 156).

Language, Whiteness, Maleness, and the American Identity

Both the White characters in the novel and the real life readers respond to Black women's speech and communicative style in a similar manner. Much of the speech of faithful Black characters is mumbling performed within earshot of Whites.

> Her voice trailed off as she went down the long open passageway, covered
> only by a roof that led to the kitchen. Mammy had her method of letting her
> owners know exactly where she stood on all matters. She knew it was beneath
> the dignity of quality white folks to pay the slightest attention to what a darky
> said when she was just grumbling to herself. She knew that to uphold this
> dignity, they must ignore what she said, even if she stood in the next room and
> almost shouted. It protected her from reproof, and it left no doubt in anyone's
> mind as to her exact views on any subject. (p. 65)

Helen Taylor (1989) found that like herself, White readers skipped over Mammy's lines because deciphering them was too tedious. Audre Lorde (1983) has lamented a similar fate for her words in her epistle to Mary Daly. Black women's speech is often ignored not only by Whites, but also by Blacks. If Black women internalize this racist and sexist practice, it can lead to self-doubt of the kind expressed by hattie gossett's (1983) query: "who told you anybody wants to hear from you? you ain't nothin but a black woman!" (p. 175).

The indirect speech of Black women has been described as "fussin'." Gwendolyn Etter-Lewis defines *fussin'* as a Black woman's communicative strategy developed in response to racist and sexist communication rules (cited in Stanback, 1987). In both verbal exchanges and under their breath seemingly without a conversational partner, Black women "cuss people out." Etter-Lewis suggests this technique has developed as a result of being ignored and/or silenced. Because of racism and sexism, Black women often cannot freely express their ideas and opinions in nonconfrontational ways. Their speech is not taken seriously. What they say and their right to say it is not respected. Unless they fuss at or, as a last resort, cuss out husbands, children, employers, and White people generally, they are not heard (Stanback, 1987). In interracial settings, direct speech by Black women often results in their being labeled as "hostile" or a "troublemaker," someone who is too racially or sexually sensitive. This was Jill Nelson's (1993) experience as a reporter at *The Washington Post*. Speaking directly to the managing editor about the condescending attitude of her White feminist editor, Nelson became tagged as not only not Mammy, but part of Nat Turner's gang. Marsha Houston Stanback (1987) views racism, sexism, and classism as components of a dysfunctional communication system that structures White and Black speech styles and posits White communicative values as normative. Whites either fail or refuse to realize that sexist and racist communication comes "naturally" to them and that a conscientious effort to communicate in nonracist and nonsexist ways must be made. Hence, they often have limited communicative repertoires, which inhibits their capacity to adapt to the communicative styles of people of color. This system places Black women in a double bind, Stanback concludes, because their normal communication is interpreted as violating the rules for women's talk (i.e., talking like a "hostile Black") or capitulating to oppression (i.e., talking like a female Uncle Tom). Stanback identifies the speech acts of fussin' and the style of the so-called hostile Black female as Black women's communicative survival skills that should be retained until social and economic realities change.

In Mitchell's novel, the lines of Blacks are written in exaggerated Black dialect and White readers often find the lines comical (Taylor, 1989). Toni Morrison (1992) theorizes that Black speech in literature is "construed as an alien, estranging dialect made deliberately unintelligible by spellings contrived to disfamiliarize it" (p. 52). Morrison suggests that the aim is to reinforce class distinctions and otherness as well as to assert power and privilege. Mitchell as ideologue exemplifies Morrison's claim in that the novel's patriarch, Gerald O'Hara, is an adult immigrant who has retained a nonstandard Southern speaking style, yet his lines are not disfamiliarized. As European male immigrants constructed an American White male identity, they used color as a "reference for difference." Given the presence of an enslaved population, being White and male meant having a new sense of power, freedom, and absolute authority over others (Morrison, 1992). Gerald O'Hara symbolizes the wrestling up of an American identity in Mitchell's novel:

He liked the South, and he soon became in his opinion, a Southerner. There
was much about the South—and Southerners—that he would never comprehend; but, with the whole-heartedness that was his nature, he adopted its
ideas and customs, as he understood them, for his own—poker and horse
racing, red-hot politics and the code duello, State's Rights and damnation to
Yankees, slavery and King Cotton, contempt for white trash and exaggerated
courtesy to women. (p. 44)

As Morrison (1993) suggests, no matter what the ethnicity and nationality of the immigrant, in order to have status in American society, the
immigrant must adopt White society's negative appraisals of native-
born African Americans.

The Strong Black Woman

As the image of Mammy was constructed from White desire for
Black female subordination and control of Black female sexuality and
reproduction, the image of the strong Black woman was constructed to
fulfill Black people's need for a mythic nurturing figure. Asexuality
and complete devotion to family and community are the common
characteristics of these images. The strong Black woman image is
driven by what Black men and Black children want from their mothers.
In contrast to the Mammy, the strong Black woman is not loyal to
Whites, but dedicated to Black survival and liberation from White
domination. Kesho Scott (1991) describes the strong Black woman as
using her sassiness in defense of her family, accepting her subordinate
role to men, and committing herself to a life of service to others, all
while being expected to conform to Eurocentric standards of feminin-
ity. Donna Rushin's (1983) poem "The Black Back-ups" illustrates the
desire of Black children to have unlimited access to the emotional
sustenance and labor of their mothers and the resentment that occurs
because Black women have been required to devote these to White
families.

AuntJemimaonthepancakebox?
Auntjemimmaonthepancakebox?
Ainchamamaonthepancakebox?
Ain't chure Mama on the pancake box?
Mama Mama
Get off that damn box
and come home to me
And my Mama leaps offa that box
She swoops down in her nurse's cape
Which she wears on Sunday
And on Wednesday night prayer meeting
And she wipes my forehead

And she fans my face for me
And she makes me a cup o'tea
And it don't do a thing for my real pain
Except she is my Mama.
("The Black Back-Ups," by Kate Rushin from Barbara Smith's (ed.), Home Girls: A Black Feminist Anthology, p. 63, copyright © 1983. Used by permission of the author and of Kitchen Table: Women of Color Press. P.O. Box 908, Latham, NY 12110).

Artist Faith Ringgold's (1983) story quilt entitled "Whose Afraid of Aunt Jemima?" offers a Black feminist critique of the extent to which the Black family will go to enrich itself and raise its social status at the expense of the Black "dominant" mother figure. In this tale, Jemima's daughter's husband forbids interactions between Jemima and her grandchildren. Soon after Jemima is informed of his command by her grandchildren in an act designed to humiliate her, she and her husband die in an automobile accident. Jemima's daughter, her husband, and their "worthless chirun" end up owning the restaurant business that Jemima and her husband founded. In Toni Cade Bambara's (1971) short story "My Man Bovanne," Miss Hazel attends a neighborhood political party in which she is informed by her children that she is there to serve as an example of "the grass roots" (p. 4) and to organize the "council of elders" (p. 6). Miss Hazel is chastised by her adult children who judge her behavior at the party as unbecoming for a woman her age. They describe her close dancing with the local blind handyman, Bovanne, as characteristic of a female dog in heat. Their mother's drinking is perceived as excessive and her dress intolerably short. They heap their disapproval on her because she is living according to the values she holds dear: wearing synthetic wigs, sleeveless dresses, taking and getting rid of male lovers, and interacting with those whom many choose to belittle. Rather than conform to this infantile tyranny, Miss Hazel leaves the party with Bovanne, whom she intends to provide with some mother comfort in the form of a nice warm bath with jasmine leaves.

Visual artist Betty Saar's (see Cliff, 1982) construction of Aunt Jemima is similarly discordant. In Saar's "The Liberation of Aunt Jemima," Mammy holds a White baby, but also a pistol and a rifle. Michelle Cliff (1982) interprets Saar's juxtaposition of traditional elements symbolic of women's sphere (e.g., a baby and a broom) with nontraditional ones (e.g., a rifle) as a fusion of myth and reality—Black women's legacy of resistance to oppression. Reflecting on her own condescending treatment of the Black maids her family employed and the way they made her recognize their authority and humanity, Cliff has concluded that although everyone recognizes these images for what they are, the expectation that Black women will conform to them persists.

Afrocentric and Gynocentric
(Re)visions of Black Women's Behavior

Whereas Mammy mumbles under her breath about the welfare of Whites, Prissy clearly asserts her own needs directly to Whites. The African-based concept of trickster allows for a reinterpretation of Prissy, another principal Black character in Mitchell's novel. From the standpoint of the trickster figure, Mitchell's flat construction of Prissy as a lying, superstitious, incompetent, lazy imbecile becomes multifaceted. Mitchell's characterization of Prissy was hurtful to many Blacks, as this quote from Alice Walker (1993) suggests.

> Sometimes when I see movies that hurt me as a child, the pain is minor; I can laugh at the things that made me sad. My trouble with Scarlett was always the forced buffoonery of Prissy, whose strained, slavish voice, as Miz Scarlett pushed her so masterfully up the stairs, I could never get out of my head. (p. 481)

Numerous are the examples Mitchell narrates to delineate Prissy's recalcitrant acts. In matters of urgency to the White owners, Prissy, unlike the reliable Mammy or Uncle Peter, is a caricature of Black irresponsibility. As Melanie Wilkes's labor intensifies, Scarlett dispatches Prissy to find a neighbor to act as midwife. Prissy takes her time in returning to Scarlett.

> "Dey ain' dar, Miss Scarlett. Ah drapped in ter pass time of day wid Mammy on mah way home. Dey's done gone. House all locked up. Spec dey's at de horsepittle."
>   "So that' where you were so long! Whenever I send you somewhere you go where I tell you and don't stop to 'pass any time' with anybody." (Mitchell, 1936/1964, p. 353)

Shortly after this scenario comes the famous scene accompanied by the famous "Ah doan know nuthin' 'bout bringin' babies" line in which the Black woman is unmasked as liar (p. 365). After repeatedly claiming she knew how, Prissy continues, "Ah's lyin', Miss Scarlett! Ah doan know huccome Ah tell sech a lie" (p. 366).

Unlike Mammy, Prissy expresses her desires and her ideas about matters that have nothing to do with the ruling class. Though she is portrayed as stupid, Prissy takes her own needs quite seriously. As they approach Tara after fleeing Atlanta, Scarlett orders Prissy to get out of the rickety old buggy pulled by a sickly horse. Prissy retorts, "Miss Scarlett, Ah kain walk. Mah feets done blistered an' dey's thoo mah shoes, an 'Wade an' me doan weigh so much an'-" (p. 403).

Though constructed as the worst type of Black person a White could ever encounter because she does not put White people's ambitions before her own, Prissy is much more likely than the faithful old Black servant to listen to and act on her inner voice. Because Mitchell subscribed to ideas about White paternalism, she refused to conceive Black self-direction positively. Therefore, Prissy's behavior stemming from her own self-determination is always made to appear foolish. The message is clear and reinforced in numerous small and large ways that Black women who attend to their own feelings and intuitions (a) will not be taken seriously, (b) will be perceived as an obstacle to "legitimate" White institutions, and (c) will be threatened with a metaphorical selling down the river. In modern society this translates as bad evaluations and job terminations.

Helen Taylor (1989) notes that Prissy is a threat to the system because she cannot be ignored or left alone to carry out her tasks. Prissy, Taylor writes, is irritating to White readers because she is not Mammy. It was Black acceptance of such a negative and restricted view of Prissy that caused so many to cringe at her behavior upon reading the novel and/or viewing the film. Malcolm X's response is often taken as an illustration of this. "I was the only Negro in the theater and when Butterfly McQueen [cast as Prissy] went into her act, I felt like crawling under the rug" (X, 1965, p. 32).

Interpreting Prissy's character using the paradigm of the African trickster allows her behavior to be seen as consistent with accounts of enslaved women's resistance strategies. Paula Giddings (1984) notes that enslaved women often used tactics that did not incorporate brute force or direct confrontation. Rather, favorite methods of resistance included poisoning the master or burning the master's property. Narratives of ex-enslaved Black women differed from men's in that male narratives incorporated physical struggle against White slaveholders (Braxton, 1986). The narrative of the enslaved Harriet Jacobs (see Jacobs, 1987), Braxton asserts, probably speaks for many enslaved women. Because of size and strength, Jacobs—as many other women—could be overpowered physically by men and thus had to rely on wit and intelligence to beat her enemies. In the case of Harriet Jacobs lies an example of a woman who conceals from her master her literacy so she would not have to read his vile letters requesting her sexual favors. This is trickster behavior because the enslaved depended on Whites' perceptions of them as less intelligent as an important aspect of gaining success in their ongoing battle (Roberts, 1989). Jacobs also employed verbal posturing, specifically the strategy of "sass" to create distance between herself and her harassing master. Braxton (1986) points out that sass is associated with the female aspect of the trickster figure in Africa. In West Africa, sass was a form of medicine given to those suspected of not telling the truth. They had to drink buckets of it and if they threw it up, they were judged free of wrongdoing; if not, they died. So, sass is something that can kill. Metaphorically speaking, Jacobs makes her master drink the poison of her words. He loses his property and dies without ever recovering either his modest affluence or his bondwoman. Braxton observes that Jacobs used sass as a man would have used his fists.

Because of the harshness of their environment in terms of food production, natural disasters, and food scarcities resulting from them, many West African groups did not frown on behavior that incorporated cunning and trickery in well-defined instances. Moreover, given the hierarchal relationships that existed within African communities, individuals had to devise ways to gain what they wanted without bringing punishment on themselves and without disrupting the social order (Roberts, 1989). Roberts notes that in Africa, the trickster appeared in stories as a human or animal who skillfully obtained the material necessities of life, under conditions of austerity, through false friendship and deception. This story tradition continued among the enslaved Africans, and tales abound in which the trickster used "dissembling and manipulative behaviors to avoid work and other exploitative behavior of slave masters under the restrictive and economically unrewarding slave system" (p. 188). It was as a trickster figure that Prissy excelled. After delivering Melanie's baby,

> Prissy was beside her [Scarlett], chattering on in a pleased way.
> "We done right good, Miss Scarlett. Ah specs Maw couldn' a did no better."
> From the shadows, Scarlett glared at her, too tired to rail, too tired to upbraid, too tired to enumerate Prissy's offenses—her boastful assumption of experience she didn't possess, her fright, her blundering awkwardness, her utter inefficiency when the emergency was hot, the misplacing of the scissors, the spilling of the basin of water on the bed, the dropping of the new born baby. And now she bragged about how good she had been. (Mitchell, 1936/1964, p. 371)

The novel is replete with instances of Blacks contesting each other's statements in an effort either to curry favor with Whites or protect them from life's realities. From the perspective of Prissy as trickster, a Prissy-like position is an oppositional stance against the institution of slavery. The one departure in the novel in which a Black stands up for another Black and against a White takes place with Prissy center stage. After Scarlett bitterly criticizes Prissy's lack of knowledge about animal husbandry, Prissy's father comes to her defense.

> "A fine midwife your Prissy will make," Scarlett remarked caustically.
> "She said she [a cow] was bellowing because she needed milking."
> "Well'm Prissy ain' fixin ter be no cow midwife, Miss Scarlett," Polk said tactfully. (p. 423)

This momentary rebellion is so quick and subtle that it is easily missed, nonetheless it ranks as an instance of Black assertion and marks how problematic the system is for Prissy. Prissy is the first Black person Scarlett ever slaps (p. 366), the first she threatens to sell (p. 373), and the first whom she calls a "nigger" (p. 401). That Scarlett must rely on tactics of intimidation clearly positions Prissy as a threat to the slave system.

It is when we look only for White standards of behavior that are defined as exemplifying intelligent and nobel characteristics of Blacks, that we cannot see Blacks as positive cognitive agents. When we begin to look at the meanings of Black behavior from an Afrocentric and gynocentric standpoint, our understanding of human behavior is enlarged. The use of different standards and models allows for the identification of Black women's competence outside a White frame of reference.

In 1939 Black women representing the Neighborhood Councils of Washington, D.C., and the Phyllis Wheatley YWCA in Washington, D.C., wrote letters to Hollywood's Production Code Administration (a group that regulated the moral and social content of movies), protesting the perpetuation of racist lies about Blacks as lazy and shiftless, the representation of Black men as "rapists," and the use of derogatory expressions in the movie version of Mitchell's novel (Leff, 1984). Black women's continuous battle with images that are harmful to themselves and Black men has been ceaseless. Although I am not suggesting that Black women are victims of White racist ideology (for many Blacks crossed picket lines organized by Blacks to view the movie version of Mitchell's novel), at the same time it is imperative to understand that the controlling images of Black womanhood stemming from the White imagination have very real consequences in the lives of Black women. During 4 years of trying to fit in at *The Washington Post*, Jill Nelson (1993) lived with daily assaults on her integrity and sense of self meted out by a group of White people who felt themselves superior to her simply because of their skin color. The strain of White people interacting with her based not on who she was but their image of what she represented to them is evident from a passage in her autobiography in which she recounts a dialogue between herself and her therapist:

> At work I'm treated like a great big, intimidating Negress, so I spend half my time trying to make myself nonthreatening, even though I'm not *really* threatening, so the caucasians can deal with me—even though its not really me they feel threatened by, it's their *image* of me. I mean, actually, I'm really a softie. I wear my feelings on my sleeve. Is that so wrong? I feel like a criminal every day I go to work because I love myself and African American people. I really feel if I don't get away I'll go berserk, get a machine gun, go into the office and go off. (p. 231; italics in the original)

Paule Marshall (1966) aptly observed that few White writers have been able to extricate themselves from the national habit of thought of using the Black woman to embody "the fantasies that have little to do with her and much to do with the troubled and repressed conscience of the country" (p. 21). The construction of the Black woman as an exploitable other guides how Whites and Blacks behave toward Black women. The construction's long history is revealed by Alice Childress's (1966) overview of the socially and legally sanctioned exploitation of Black women's sexuality under enslavement, emancipation, and modern times. The concubinage of Black women by White masters and the forced breeding with enslaved Black men during enslavement; White men's legal abandonment of their offspring with Black women and the desertion by Black men after emancipation; and the 1960s' popular construction of Black woman as the emasculating wife/mother stripping Black men of their manhood characterized the Black woman's sexual alienation according to the historic patriarchal text. Childress concluded that "*Gone With the Wind* is not our story. And our history is not gone with the wind, it is still with us" (p. 16). As the continuing popularity of *Gone With the Wind* and the chapters in this anthology suggest, these images are not only prevalent in society, but are very damaging to the lives of Black women.

References

Bambara, T. C. (1971). *Gorilla my love.* New York: Random House.

Berreca, G. (1991, September 1). Television view: In celebration of the bad girl. *The New York Times,* pp. 21-22.

Braxton, J. M. (1986). Harriet Jacobs' Incidents in the life of a slave girl. *The Massachusetts Review: A Quarterly of Literature, the Arts and Public Affairs, 27,* 379-387.

Childress, A. (1966). The Negro woman in American literature. *Freedomways, 6,* 14-19.

Cliff, M. (1982). Object into subject: Some thoughts on the work of Black women artists. *Heresies: A Feminist Publication of Art and Politics, 4,* 34-40.

Giddings, P. (1984). *When and where I enter: The impact of Black women on race and sex in America.* New York: Bantam Books.

gossett, h. (1983). "who told you anybody wants to hear from you? you aint nothing but a black woman!" In C. Moraga & G. Anzaldua (Eds.), *This bridge called my back: Writings by radical women of color* (pp. 175-176). New York: Kitchen Table.

Harding, S. (1993). After the science question in feminism. In L. Richardson & V. Taylor (Eds.), *Feminist frontiers III* (pp. 12-20). New York: McGraw-Hill.

Jacobs, H. (1987). *Incidents in the life of a slave girl.* Cambridge, MA: Harvard University Press.

Leff, L. J. (1984). David Selznick's *Gone With the Wind:* "The Negro Problem." *The Georgia Review, 38,* 146-164.

Lorde, A. (1983). An open letter to Mary Daly. In C. Moraga & G. Anzaldua (Eds.), *This bridge called my back: Writings by radical women of color* (pp. 94-97). New York: Kitchen Table.

Marshall, P. (1966). The Negro woman in American literature. *Freedomways, 6,* 20-25.

Mitchell, M. (1964). *Gone with the wind.* New York: Macmillan. (Original work published 1936)

Morrison, T. (1992). *Playing in the dark: Whiteness and the literary imagination.* Cambridge, MA: Harvard University Press.

Morrison, T. (1993, Fall). On the backs of Blacks. In The new face of America: How immigrants are shaping the world's first multicultural society [Special issue]. *Time, 142*(21), p. 57.

Nelson, J. (1993). *Volunteer slavery: My authentic Negro experience*. Chicago: Noble Press.

Pyron, D. A. (1983). *Recasting Gone With the Wind in American culture*. Miami: University Presses of Florida, A Florida International University Book.

Ringgold, F. (1983). Who's afraid of Aunt Jemima?: Quilt and story [Exhibition: Faith Ringgold: Twenty years of painting, sculpture and performance, 1963-1983; April 8-September 4, 1984; The Studio Museum in Harlem].

Rushin, D. K. (1983). The Black back-ups. In B. Smith (Ed.), *Home girls: A Black feminist anthology* (pp. 60-63). New York: Kitchen Table.

Roberts, J. W. (1989). *From trickster to badman: The Black folk hero in slavery and freedom*. Philadelphia: University of Pennsylvania Press.

Scott, K. (1991). *The habit of surviving: Black women's strategies for life*. New Brunswick, NJ: Rutgers University Press.

Sedgwick, E. K. (1985). *Between men: English literature and male homosocial desire*. New York: Columbia University Press.

Stanback, M. H. (1987, November). *Claiming our space; finding our voice: Feminist theory and Black women's talk*. Paper presented to the Black and Women's Caucuses, 73rd annual meeting of the Speech Communication Association, Boston.

Taylor, H. (1989). *Scarlett's women: Gone With the Wind and its female fans*. New Brunswick, NJ: Rutgers University Press.

Walker, A. (1993). A letter of the times, or should this sado-masochism be saved? In A. M. Jaggar & P. S. Rothenberg (Eds.), *Feminist frameworks* (3rd ed., pp. 481-484). New York: McGraw-Hill.

X, Malcolm (1965). *The autobiography of Malcolm X*. New York: Grove Press.

PART I

Black Women's Social History Through the Lens of Their Activism

1. African Women's Legacy
Ambiguity, Autonomy, and Empowerment

BARBARA A. MOSS

🔁 "African-American women" conjure up images of strong, resilient women who have defied racist and sexist attempts to define and constrain them. The image of the Black woman "rock" is one of the most persistent images of Black women in America. The image has become "one of the staples of the culture: the dark all-knowing, all-seeing, all-understanding spiritual force that we can go to when all else fails us . . . one-part true, one-part national wish fulfillment" (Bogle, 1980, p. 75). The validity of the image is unimportant, the belief in it is. The actual women behind this image have consistently provided a reservoir from which African-Americans have sought relief and generally found it. Their resiliency has given rise to the notion that African-American women have unique qualifications by virtue of heredity, culture, or condition that prepare them for this role. In an attempt to discern the validity of this premise, this chapter examines women in precolonial African culture to examine the legacy that African women passed on to their descendants. Although Africa is a broad and diverse continent, cross-cultural examples will exhibit the commonality of African women's complex status in society.

Culture and Constraints

"There is a secret power in a woman by which she can send a king to fetch her a cooking stick" (Maranke, 1941, p. 165). Although a Shona saying, this adage succinctly conceptualizes the position of African women in many precolonial societies. It places women's power, real or imagined, well within the confines of the women's sphere and within easy reach of the very pinnacle of men's political power. Although ostensibly confined to the women's sphere, that amorphous domestic area encompassing procreation, nurturing, and husbandry, in actuality women traversed the breadth of their society. Using women's creative and spiritual talents, this sphere stretched past the fields into local and long-distance marketing networks. The domestic sphere was sufficiently expansive to encase even the political realm.

African women in precolonial societies occupied complex but often ambiguous positions. They were important as farmers, revered as mothers, respected as spirit mediums, yet restricted by gender-related taboos and silent in most public decision making. Although women in general occupied positions of importance and respect by virtue of their productive and reproductive roles, some women clearly wielded more authority than others socially, economically, and politically. We can say that women occupied more than one class. This perspective is not contrary to much of the feminist writings concerned with women and class, but adds a needed dimension to it (Robertson & Berger, 1986, p. 10). Although women did not share resources equally with men, they did accrue benefits from association with them. They were not a monolithic class. Some women were more privileged, more skillful, and thus more economically viable than other women. Through their association *with* men, not their dependence upon them, women gained access to the means of production in the domestic economy. Once within the system, women operated virtually on their own, accruing their own wealth or failing to do so. They achieved autonomy within a male-dominated society. This feat required skill, self-help strategies, and generally nonconfrontational approaches—thus the ambiguity of their position.

As individual women stepped from the privacy of the household and the compound to the public places in society such as the *dare* or male meeting place, hence from the proverbial women's to the men's sphere, women in general increasingly lost influence and power. As a group, women were recognized as essential because their procreative and productive labor helped fuel society, but they were often perceived as marginal in politics and public decision making.

Women possessed ambiguous positions within African societies, whether patrilineal or matrilineal. Patriliny created links between the father and his wife's sons, whereas matriliny created ties between the mother's brother and her children. Lineage did not provide for autonomous links between women of different generations (White, 1984, p. 55). Although women were recognized as essential to society, men sought to control women's status and minimize their influence through myths and biological constraints. W. D. Hammond-Tooke (n.d.) theorized that men must have a sneaking suspicion that "in fact women are perhaps more important than they are" (p. 131). Thus, in many societies women's importance was minimized with gender-specific restrictions. Among the Akan of Ghana, during menstruation even the queen mother could not perform religious rites for the ancestors, attend the chief's court, or associate with male functionaries in government (Aidoo, 1981, p. 68). Kikuyu folklore cited women's procreative responsibilities as the reason for restricting them from political activity (Clark, 1980, p. 360). A Burundi proverb belittled women's procreative abilities: "Woman is only the passive earth; it is the man who provides the seed" (Berger, 1976, p. 161). The Asante restrained aggressive women by criticizing them as *obaa-barima*, "he women" (Aidoo, 1981, p. 68). Women's deceit was emphasized in a Shona legend that blamed a woman for acquiring a ruler's powerful charms, which led to his downfall (Katsukunya, 1971, p. 77). Women were also psychologically held in check by restrictions on their diet. Among the Shona, they were prevented from eating eggs because it was thought that that would make them insane.[1] It was also feared that if a woman ate an egg she might become sterile through some antagonistic action on her own ova (Gelfand, 1971, p. 117). And among the Beti, women were prohibited from eating domestic animals, such as goat, sheep, and dog, although they were required to cook these foods. When cooking, they had to ask a man to test the seasonings or else taste the food and then spit it out. Certain kinds of highly valued yams were forbidden to nursing mothers (Guyer, 1984, pp. 28-29). These dietary restrictions served the function of continuously reminding women of their subordinate position in society.

Despite restrictions women were indeed a power to be reckoned with. Although not always seen, they were heard, in the privacy of their homes as aunts and mothers-in-law, and, as they advanced in age, increasingly in public places. A few women achieved a status almost equal to that of men—as rulers. These women were virtually honorary men and ruled as men did, but their status was often linked to their kinship affiliation. Biology as well as marital and domestic relationships determined how women fared in many precolonial societies. Within those constraints individual initiative and effort influenced women's life chances.

Gender and the Domestic Economy

Precolonial societies ostensibly took care of their people, especially women, providing extended families, close kinship systems, widow inheritance, and cohesive networks of associations. Inclusion in society afforded women access to land and animal husbandry. Women's ability to take advantage of these opportunities depended upon their membership in the community as daughters, wives, or mothers. Thus, most women were dependent upon relationships with men to gain entry into society at a productive level. Once recognized as members of the society, however, women operated independently within the constraints of the domestic economy. Enterprising women could invest the customary gifts that they received as wives, mothers, or mothers-in-law;

enhance their spiritual powers; or utilize their farming and craft expertise to their advantage.

The basic family unit was the household, which revolved around women and their children even in patrilineal societies. Women were the glue that bound society together and fueled the economically independent households. Women depended upon their own labor to maintain themselves rather than on the men to whom they were associated by birth or marriage. Self-reliance was a part of their culture; they were encouraged to be independent (Terborg-Penn, 1986, p. 198). Even in the Nguni military states of the Zulu and Ndebele the population did not depend upon raiding but upon the agricultural labor of women in independent households (Moss, 1982). Women produced their own food, housing, and other necessities (Henn, 1984, p. 4).

In patrilineal societies, kinship afforded women influence in their brothers' families, because the women's bridewealth enabled their brothers to marry. Among the Shona, the aunt assumed the title of *Semukadzi*, "the owner or controller of the wife." In fact she neither controlled nor owned the wife, but she advised her and her children. This relationship accorded her so much respect that it was said that "if she had had the proper 'tools' (male organs) she would have been a real father with full rights" (Holleman, 1969, p. 66). Her role was that of family lawyer and judge in household quarrels, inheritance disputes, and intrafamily relationships (Gandanzara, 1967, p. 12). Largely a domestic role, it was expanded in political families to influence political decisions.

Marriage served the economic function of providing access to land from which women could establish a household, the basic unit of production. Most societies had mixed economies based on livestock and agriculture. Women, as the principal farmers, cultivated the fields. Produce grown in their fields belonged to them, that grown in their husband's fields belonged to him. Wives had their own store-hut or granary from which they dispensed food for their family. The possession and disposal of property also came with marriage. Women could own movable property in their own right; they were entitled to the articles they brought to their husband's compound, such as cooking pots, baskets, and water pots. Women supplemented the food supply by hunting small animals and, seasonally, collecting flying ants, caterpillars, sand crickets, and beetles (Gelfand, 1971, pp. 168-171). These delicacies, snared at great expense of agricultural time and patience, provided protein for the diet. Conditions permitting, industrious women turned subsistence farming into economic security.

Although marriage generally brought economic stability, it did not always provide psychological well-being. Within a polygamous society, with few exceptions, every woman was assured a husband, thus no status accrued for the wife. Bridewealth conferred status on the woman within her own lineage because it made provisions for the marriage of her brothers, but not within her husband's. Once married the new wife had little real influence. Because she remained a part of her family's lineage and was thus protected by those ancestral spirits, her allegiance was somewhat suspect and she became a "stranger-wife." The new wife entered the rather closed community of her female in-laws at its lowest ranks, performing the most unpleasant chores in the household. Until the birth of her children she had little or no status within that lineage and her loyalty was often suspect. As one proverb warned, "To give a knife to a wife is to invite your death" (Hamutyinei & Plangger, 1974, p. 387). With motherhood, her condition improved.

Wives were important for their productive abilities but gained status for their reproductive abilities. Their status and trust grew with the birth and growth of their children and grandchildren. Another proverb proclaimed, "A girl is good once but great is a woman with a child" (Hamutyinei & Plangger, 1974, p. 377). Motherhood also brought potential economic empowerment. Women profited by the addition of their children's labor to the household as well as the marriage and the potential motherhood of daughters. As mothers-in-law they were generally accorded respect and provided with favors and gifts such as livestock that provided milk and offspring that could be used for transportation, sold, or traded. Whenever possible women allowed their livestock to increase. But family obligations, such as providing food for her children during times of scarcity, often required that the stock be slaughtered or traded. Women owning large herds were rare. Women disposed of their property as they saw fit, even providing bridewealth for members of their own lineage (Holleman, 1962, p. 182).

As in most societies, women generally outlived their spouse and upon the death of their husbands women were usually inherited by one of his kinsmen. They thereby remained within the household and continued to provide children for that lineage. Widows could use their dead husband's fields provided those were not inherited by one of his relatives (Gelfand, 1959, pp. 14-15). Women ostensibly had the right to refuse to be inherited or to state their preference for one of the kinsmen offered. But women of childbearing age preferred to be inherited because that afforded protection, continued access to land, and the ability to oversee their children's inheritance. Widows past childbearing age were not as likely to be inherited and had to rely upon adult sons for protection and support, working their late husband's fields, which were administered by their son. If married to their husband's kin, women retained his land in the same village and acquired additional land from their new spouse. Childless widows faced difficulties because there was generally no communal support for them and they had to rely upon family ties (Potash, 1986, p. 4).

As women aged and their children married, their influence increased within their lineage. Postmenopausal women were accorded increasing respect, performed duties in rituals, and achieved a status closely associated with that of aged men. Among the Asante, all the

known queen mothers who led their armies in battle had reached meno-
pause (Aidoo, 1981, p. 69). Although not legitimized in public, elderly
married women had considerable influence and power within both the
household and the village. Some accounts have estimated that they were
indispensable to decision making (Holleman, 1969, p. 206).

Much importance has been attached to women's domestic and agricultural responsibilities. Women performed the labor necessary to repro-
duce (feed, clothe, shelter, bear, and rear) the homestead and lineage.
These essential roles resulted in the empowerment of women as a group,
although as individuals their power was not recognized. The domestic
sphere was the basis of women's lives. From that vantage point they
interacted with members of the extended family, had access to land,
received cattle, and obtained recognition of their worth as procreative
individuals. In the religious realm, however, which permeated all
facets of society, women expanded upon their mundane positions as
wives and mothers and were truly empowered.

Maximizing Options Through Religion

According to precolonial African beliefs, spirits lived, possessed
individuals, and influenced the actions of the living, providing guidance and delivering retribution. By removing their protection from the
living they allowed sickness, drought, famine, and even death to take
place. Misfortune was not arbitrary, it was caused by a displeased spirit.
Ancestors were the intermediaries to God, who was perceived of as
omnipotent but distant. Those who could communicate with the spirits attained status in society. Religious ritual was thus an ear to God
and women did much of the whispering.

Regardless of their position in society, religion offered women an
opportunity for respect and empowerment. Women were an integral
part of religious ritual in many societies, for no other reason than that
they made the beer without which most ceremonies could not take place.
But more importantly, many intermediaries were women, although
they did not have a monopoly on this role. Within Nguni society 95%
of the diviners were women (Bryant, 1923, p. 48). Senior women, those
past childbearing, presided over rituals that were otherwise considered within the men's realm. Mang'anja women presided over household and community ancestral rituals, with the headman's eldest sister
directing rainmaking ceremonies and occupying a leading position
with men in the secret societies (Mandala, 1984, p. 143). Among the
Shona, the paternal aunt frequently performed rituals at funerals,
brewed beer for the ancestors, and interpreted family problems. It was
in the realm of religion that women held immutable power. As spirit
mediums, herbalists, diviners, and witches they bypassed society's restrictions. The role of religious specialists provided women with status,

respect, and social and economic security within their society because they provided necessary and important services.

Possession could provide economic security in exchange for treating leprosy, bilharzia, headaches, earaches, aching bones, and stomach trouble. When possible, women invested their earnings in livestock and garnered the respect of the village. Obed Mutezo remembered his grandmother, an herbalist, as

> a woman of real substance . . . the whole male population of that village . . . bowed before her like little things. She enjoyed not only chronological seniority over the male population but she also enjoyed the prestige that goes together with wealth. She paid brideprice for some of her sons and other near relatives, thus drawing even the wives of these men into the orbit of her powerful influence. (Sithole, 1970, pp. 51-52)

Women enhanced their prestige by giving gifts to their poorer clients. Willingness to redistribute their wealth earned them influence and power in their village (May, 1983, p. 30). Like headmen and chiefs, spirit mediums attained a loyal following.

Women were as likely as men to be selected as spirit mediums by the ancestral spirits. They were often concerned with illness, poverty, and infertility. Possessed women also had male spirits, taking on male roles, even in dance, to the amusement of those present (Bourdillon, 1976, p. 287). Yet they were hardly the helpless pawns of their spirits. A woman thus selected achieved heightened status within the family because the ancestors had chosen to speak to their children through her (Sithole, 1970, p. 44). Possession was a sign of admirable moral qualities and was an occasion for festivity.

Spirit possession cults not only provided women with higher social status but also relief from the frustrations of ordinary life, and addressed gender issues such as infertility, childbirth, and marital difficulties. Possession allowed women to demand food, clothing, or respite from domestic responsibilities (Harris, 1926). Evidence from some East African cults suggests that they may have been used to combat male domination and marital abuse. Women literally controlled their husbands during possession, demanding the banishment of a rival, protection from physical abuse, relief from heavy manual labor, and control of household goods (Berger, 1976, pp. 167-169).

Spirit mediums possessed the power to influence political authority significantly as well as wield political power in their own right, as in Rwanda during the 19th century. Male and female mediums chosen by the spirit of Nyabingi, a once powerful woman of royal lineage, gathered adherents into political units that survived for decades (Des Forges, 1986, p. 312). Mediums allowed them to function in the male sphere and acquire influence within their society. Where multiple mediums professed to speak for the same spirit, however, each with her own

interpretation, the outcome was generally determined by physical rather
than psychic forces, as among the Manyika in the late 18th century
(Ranger, n.d., p. 15).

Thought naturally to have more psychic powers than men, women
were believed to be witches more often than men. Men's powers were
said to have been derived from external magic (Douglas, 1970, p. xxix).
Women on the other hand were believed to have inherited witchcraft
from a vengeful mother or maternal grandmother. Here again is an
attempt to attribute negative characteristics to women. Nevertheless
the witch was taken as a necessary evil, acting as a focus for blame
when things went wrong. As an outsider she underlined the group's
solidarity by being the one who was "with us but not of us" (May, 1983,
p. 18). Her presence within the community was expected and even
accepted. A Shona proverb advised: "When you marry, marry a witch,
you will have somebody fighting on your behalf against a grudge"
(Hamutyinei & Plangger, 1974, pp. 146, 238, 281). The powerful witch,
despite her antisocial predilections, could be perceived as a desirable ally.

Despite dangers inherent in community reaction to their antisocial
deeds, some women actually confessed to being witches. According to
one informant, "To be feared had its advantages" (Crawford, 1967,
p. 60). Although young women rarely confessed, older women, already
cushioned by their status as mothers and grandmothers, could more
easily afford to make a confession when advantageous. Barren women
were saved from the stigma of childlessness by the status gained by
being a witch (Crawford, 1967, pp. 61-62). With the normal routes to
respect closed to them, desperate women, like the aged, barren, and
destitute, used the general fear of witches to enhance their status in
society by surrounding themselves with an aura of fear and grudging
respect. Women who were socially and economically secure within
their domestic position rarely professed to being a witch.

Women gained status through their association with spirits, even
those that were feared. Spirits were an affirmation that the ancestors
had not forgotten them. Through association with spirits women re-
versed the misfortune of infertility, poverty, or old age and achieved
economic security.

Women as Participants in the External Economy

Although not a prominent part of public decision making, women
were an important and integral part of the public economy, contributing
their labor to prevalent economic activities. While continuing to supply "necessary labor" to household economies, during various time
periods women were involved in such diverse activities as mining, salt
production, and local trade in pottery.

In southern Africa, women's involvement in mining evolved from their agricultural and domestic duties. Prospecting for gold and copper is believed to have been an outgrowth of a keen observation of vegetation rather than deliberate prospecting (Summers, 1969, p. 152). In fact, Portuguese travelers during the 18th century in Manyika recorded that women discovered lumps of gold while hoeing their fields (Bhila, 1982, p. 41). Food gathering also placed women in the position to discover mineral wealth. In the process of collecting termites it is possible that women noticed fragments of gold on the termite mounds (Summers, 1969, p. 162). Implements that women used in domestic duties were also used in mining. Hoes worn down by agricultural use were adapted for mine use. Cup and ball mortars, used in the milling of ore containing gold, were also commonly used in the household for grinding grains (Summers, 1969, pp. 169, 175).

Most of the gold washing was done by women. European travelers observed only women performing these labor-intensive tasks in some areas (Selous, 1893, pp. 281-282; Wood, 1893/1974, p. 101). Men were compelled to pan for gold only when their villages had been pillaged of women. In an attempt to obtain the necessary medium of exchange to replace kidnapped women, men temporarily took on these female chores (Burke, 1969, pp. 232, 235, 292). Once washed, the gold dust was packed into porcupine quills and men then traded it to the Portuguese for cloth, beads, guns, and women who had been raided from either their own or other villages (Beach, n.d., p. 3).

Involvement in the gold trade probably made life in general more difficult for women because panning gold was extremely time consuming and potentially dangerous, but it had its advantages. Even though this activity took women away from their main responsibilities—agriculture and the maintenance and care of children—it provided access to beads, cloth, and other items that were regarded as wealth, exchangeable for grain and cattle (Beach, 1980, p. 30). Women used the gold trade to maximize their economic opportunities whenever possible.

Women were also involved in the salt industry at the local and long-distance level. Because salt was obtained from the soil, its extraction, involving straining and boiling salty mud until a block of salt was produced, was well inside the women's sphere of activities. Blocks of salt were used as a medium of exchange in some areas (Bhila, 1973, p. 39). European trader Thomas observed that Shona women went long distances in search of salt (Thomas, 1872, p. 388). Through the salt trade women had access to livestock, iron implements, food in times of famine, and slaves (Mandala, 1984, p. 52). Pottery—also the preserve of women—was a skilled craft that produced pots for such household uses as cooking, beer brewing, and salt preparation.

Women participated in local and interregional trade involving agricultural surplus. They had a prevalent role in the local markets in West Africa. As European traders made their way into the hinterlands, they met men and women willing to trade a variety of items: agricultural produce, livestock, handicraft items. Traders and explorers routinely carried goods for trade for an expectant and seemingly eager market. As the number of European traders increased, Africans responded to their demands and increased agricultural output.

Women were an integral part of the trade relationship between Africans and Europeans beginning in the 15th century. In some areas women provided the link between African trading networks and European entrepreneurs as wives and trading partners. These liaisons produced generations of Afro-Portuguese who virtually controlled the trade for decades. Relatively independent in their own societies, these women were attracted by new economic opportunities. By the 18th century the *Signares* of Saint-Louis and Goree were an economic and political power, presiding over large households with many slaves (Brooks, 1976, pp. 22, 38).

Women were thus intricately involved in the wider economy of their society beyond the household. They adapted their lives to the changes in productive activity, taking on added responsibilities such as gold washing when it was feasible, while maintaining their basic agricultural duties. They augmented their resources with skills in pottery and salt trading. Yet for all their economic involvement, their ambiguous position in society also relegated many women to the status of commodities in times of economic and political upheaval.

Women as Commodities

Ironically women's procreative and productive labor was so highly valued that they were traded, paid as tribute, kidnapped, and hoarded. Their position as prized possessions did not increase their self-esteem or their rights. In the most extreme cases their economic value made them desirable as slaves. Most slaves in the domestic markets were women, who consistently brought higher prices (Robertson & Klein, 1983, p. 5). Prisoners of war were generally women and children; male prisoners were often executed. The Muslim slave market of the Arab world also absorbed mostly women and children (Robertson & Klein, 1983, p. 4). The principal reason for this demand centers around women's productive and reproductive abilities.

Although women were valued for their procreative abilities, slave women had lower fertility rates than free women. Douching with various preparations, they evidently registered their resistance to their condition by practicing abortion (Harms, 1983, p. 106). Their productive abilities were the main attraction. Slave women weeded rice or spun thread for male weavers' use. On Zanzibar, men picked cloves; women not only picked but separated and dried them. Women also mined alluvial gold and collected rubber and snails. Among the Gaza Nguni they

served as cultivators, maids, and porters. In Muslim societies slave women were especially desired; due to the seclusion of upper-class
women they were needed to do what was termed "women's work":
trading, farming, building homes, and porterage. Women slaves did
the same things that most free women did, which meant most of the
agricultural and virtually all of the domestic work (Robertson & Klein,
1983, pp. 8-11).

Some women, however, were able to turn slavery into a profitable
venture. Being the slave of a wealthy person provided more opportunity
for some women than being a free but vulnerable low-status woman.
Palace slaves in Dahomey were permitted to work for themselves as
well as for the king. Some women parlayed palace loyalty, hard work,
and astute political alliances into personal wealth. Some queen mothers rose from the ranks of slave women (Bay, 1983, pp. 363-364). Slave
women could also attain high positions, such as ward chiefs. Some women gained economic status from trading and became owners of other
female slaves. But the women who benefited most from the slave trade
were the wives and daughters of aristocrats and warlords, who enjoyed
the wealth from the trade and were relieved from domestic chores and
farming by the available slave labor (Afonja, 1981, p. 307).

Women were a valuable currency that all societies recognized. They
were used to reward soldiers as part of the booty of war, as payment
of fines, as repayment for a favor, and even as bridewealth. If a woman
committed a crime against a man she was always able to provide compensation: As a traditional saying explained, "A woman's fine is her
very self" (Hamutyinei & Plangger, 1974, p. 323). And during economic
crisis it was "customary" for women to be taken by force (Ranger, n.d.,
p. 6). They were also paid as tribute. Women, especially girls, served
more frequently as pawns than did boys (Robertson & Klein, 1983, p. 11).
In the 1880s the Portuguese forced the states of Rusambo and Chikanga
to pay tribute by threatening to seize their women (Wood, 1974, p. 319).
Women were also kidnapped to encourage labor recruitment (Beach,
n.d., p. 28). Like other valuable commodities, such as cattle, they were
also routinely acquired by raiding in times of scarcity. When the population was diminished by drought, disease, and warfare, the natural
recourse was to raiding or buying slaves. Periods of economic crisis
made women even more valuable as productive and reproductive laborers. Men obtained necessary capital by disposing of low-status women
(Wright, 1975, p. 819). Women were the leverage that made societies
productive.

Women were exchanged as commodities precisely because they were
valued for their productivity and reproductivity. That which empowered them once they were an integral part of society, as mother and
agriculturalist, made them vulnerable to raids in times of economic
scarcity. Their means of empowerment was subordinate to the higher
authority of male hegemony. But some resourceful women managed to

turn slavery to their advantage, utilizing their skills and relationships to make themselves indispensable.

Women in the Political Sphere

Women were involved at different levels in the political sphere. Their influence ranged from pawns to political actors. Although most women were not seen in public decision making, their opinions were heard in the household and, through kinship and friendship networks, made their way into formal decision-making bodies. Laws were local and ad hoc, developed to maintain order and settle disputes given the needs and nature of the entire community. Taking into account individual circumstances, they were extremely flexible, revolving around family obligations, bridewealth, the productive role of women, and spiritual intervention. Women thus played an integral part in the actual formulation of laws and administration of society. Among the Asante, political status was conferred by women even though most politicians were male. An Asante proverb reminded all that: "It's a woman who gave birth to a man; it's a woman who gave birth to a chief" (Aidoo, 1981, p. 65).

Nevertheless, in patrilineal societies women were often treated as subordinates in public decision making. Among the Shona, separate male/female spheres were clearly illustrated in the *dare* or male meeting place. This cleared space of ground was usually set up at the periphery of the village some distance from the living quarters. There men ate their meals, drank beer, and discussed matters of common concern among themselves. Women were excluded, although a woman could give testimony in an important case if she was the accuser or the accused (Gelfand, 1971, p. 65). Among the Igbo, however, the village assembly was open to all adults, but the men were more likely to speak than women. Older women frequently spoke out and were respected (O'Barr, 1975, p. 23). In matrilineal societies, women's participation was almost taken for granted.

Women were the means of cementing political alliances by the time-honored practice of political marriage. A chief giving a wife to another was considered "the most signal mark of honor the chief could bestow" on a potential ally (Bhila, 1982, p. 240). Such women provided rulers with a means of obtaining feedback from a potential rival. At this level of politics most women were little more than political pawns, unable to determine their alliances. Only the daughters of the elite fared better and could take advantage of their class status and maximize their standing by choice of marital alliance. Lower-class women had no such options. Some women, however, by virtue of kinship or political alliances were active participants in the public arena. As they took on the role of chief or "chieftainess," individual women took on the prerogatives of men.

Women were administrators in a number of African political systems. Even so, their involvement was usually due to class rather than gender. Within the Manyika political system, women were routinely appointed as ward heads. Both men and women were assigned by the king to administer a group of villages. The king was guided in his selection by the spirit medium of the clan, who was usually a woman. The spirit medium's decision to select women was not gender based, however, but was in response to instability within Manyika succession politics. It actually reflected the fact that women were not perceived as serious political contenders and were incapable of launching a successful coup. Utilizing the sexual prerogative of men, they were free to have relations with whomever they chose. Because of this freedom they were condemned by Europeans as having loose morals (Bazeley, 1940, p. 4).

Accorded all the rights and respect of a male chief, the Shona chief, Chikanga, was hardly representative of women in general. The paradox that she was a woman, mother, and chief created situations that required unique solutions. As European nurses Blennerhassett and Sleeman (1893) sat in bemused wonder in the presence of Chikanga, they noticed that "no other woman dared approach the 'council hut' " (p. 246). It was the preserve of men, yet as a mother, Chikanga was part of both the male and female domains. Chikanga's baby, which belonged to the women's sphere, was carried for her by one of her escorts and was kept outside of the council hut. The chief physically left one sphere for the other as she periodically left the hut to fulfill her duties as a nursing mother whenever the infant cried. Yet there were no contradictions in her identity. Her requests left no doubt that she considered herself at least an equal to men. She understood protocol and demanded her rights as any ruler, to be served "firewater." She was placated only with wine (Blennerhassett & Sleeman, 1893, p. 254).

There are no indications that women rulers' political decisions differed from those of male chiefs. Chikanga was involved in trade with the Portuguese and the British as it suited her own interests, as was her father, Chief Tendai Mutasa. She also responded to labor conscription with the same resentment as her male counterparts. Chikanga's refusal to supply laborers to the British South Africa Company resulted in an armed confrontation that left her husband, Fambisa, dead (Bhila, 1982, pp. 240-242). Other female counterparts, like Edwesohemaa Yaa Asantewaa, the Asante queen mother, also resisted European hegemony (Aidoo, 1981, p. 69).

Like their male counterparts, these women wielded considerable power. As intermediaries between the king and the local headmen, they governed all matters relating to witchcraft, theft, and murder. Their decisions could be appealed to the king and they could be dismissed or reappointed (Bazeley, 1940, p. 3). In many societies female rulers' authority rested on the good graces of the king or their hereditary legitimacy, rather than their gender. Among the Asante, the queen mother was a powerful political actor, yet her position did not rely upon a female constituency. Her hereditary royal position elevated her above other women, and she did not primarily represent women's interests (Aidoo, 1981, pp. 67-68). Because women were not their power base, their political agenda did not discernibly represent women's interests. In fact, the position of these elite women did not effectively change the condition of women in general. Fate or fortune had bestowed upon them the opportunity to become honorary men.

Even in the Zulu military state some women were influential and operated as honorary men. Shaka's mother, Nandi, was a dominant figure in society, as was his aunt, Mkabayi. In the royal praise poetry both women are addressed as men, Mkabayi is called "father of guile" and Nandi is referred to as "father of troubles" (Golan, 1990, p. 103). The Ndebele also frequently used women rulers. Mzilikazi appointed women in his family to preside over military outposts. They provided information on potential allies and enemies.

In contrast, among the Yoruba, the Iyalode was a chief with jurisdiction over all women in her town. She settled disputes in her court and articulated women's position on issues such as the declaration of war, the opening of new markets, or the administration of women at the local level (Awe, 1977, p. 147).

Some rulers were spirit mediums as well, which enhanced their authority. Another Shona chief, Muredzwa, was believed to have been more powerful than her sister Chikanga because she was a spirit medium. She had a Solomon-like wisdom, considerable wealth, many people working in her fields, and so many cattle that she could kill one at any time for meat for her people. But it was her spiritual powers that were renowned. It was said that whenever she left her house for Mtasa, rain would pour down to water her footprints so that enemies would be unable to follow her (Shepherd Machuma Files, n.d.).

Yet Muredzwa's life also provides insight into the ambiguities of even powerful women's lives. Despite the fact that, as a chief, she presided over territory, had great wealth in cattle, and commanded armies, as a woman she was powerless in the face of custom. She lost nine babies to the Shona practice of disposing of multiple births.

> After her first daughter Mukonyerwa, she had three sets of twins and followed by triplets, which brought the number to nine babies who were all thrown away being put in big pots. . . . If a woman would give birth to twins, she would be left alone kept in a hut which no one was allowed to enter, to go nearby or to talk to her till a witch doctor would be asked to come and give her some medicine which would make her not to give birth to twins anymore. (Shepherd Machuma Files; Mrs. Janet Choto, n.d.)

This particular custom affected women more heavily than men because they bore the responsibility for any problems in childbirth. Muredzwa's plight was echoed by other women from all levels of society who had the misfortune of giving birth to more than one child at a time. Aside from being treated as outcasts, custom also dictated that these women not grieve for their lost children, because public crying was taboo in such cases (Folta & Deck, 1988, p. 439). Thus even powerful women faced the ambiguity created by gender-related constraints in some societies.

Women as a group were recognized as important, even though individual women were often constrained. When women's perspectives were overlooked, many societies provided sanctioned means by which they could redress grievances and discipline male offenders. Among the Igbo, women expressed their disapproval and secured demands by public demonstrations including ridicule, satirical singing and dancing, and group strikes. This institutionalized form of punishment was known as "sitting on a man" (Van Allen, 1976). In Cameroon, Kom women had a similar mechanism for punishing and disgracing a man for offenses against women. This technique, known as *anlu,* sanctioned group action by women that included wild dancing, dressing in men's attire, polluting the offender's compound, and genital exhibition (Rogers, 1980, p. 23). These devices, recognized as legitimate within their societies, underscored women's authority and influence even though men publicly appeared to be the controlling forces. Organized women were a respected and often feared power in society.

Conclusion

African women occupied the breadth of their societies from powerful honorary men to women traded as slaves. Yet what emerges from these historical examples are women who consistently maximized their opportunities by empowering themselves. Molded by hard work and autonomy, they bequeathed to their descendants—some of whom were forcibly brought to the Americas—a legacy of resilience and self-reliance. They were women paradoxically "constrained but empowered" (Collins, 1990, p. 44).

Coming from societies in which they were never pampered or placed on a pedestal, they passed on the understanding that their labor often provided the pillars upon which family security rested. Working in the fields alongside men, slave women carried the same burdens, took the same beatings, and in addition performed gendered chores when they returned to the slave quarters. After emancipation the vast majority of African-American women were not privileged to be housewives but joined the workforce alongside their men, relegated to lower-paid labor-intensive employment by race and class. True to their agricultural roots, many also coaxed seeds into life on windowsills and in backyard gardens, keeping poverty at arm's length.

Like their African foremothers, African-American women were central to the family with the household revolving around them and their children. During slavery this essential role was given dubious validation by slave masters who traced lineage through slave mothers rather than slave fathers. After emancipation, Black women in female-headed households continued to shoulder family obligations by choice and by chance. Providing the energy in many self-reliant households, they were derisively labeled *matriarch* in a society that suppresses strong women.

It was an intrinsic understanding of their importance that gave African-American women leverage in their societies, even when they occupied subordinate positions in public. Just as their ancestors had made their voices known in the household and, when necessary, in public, they were that " 'something within' that shaped the 'culture of resistance' " (Collins, 1990, p. 142). Women who during their work hours bowed their heads and held their tongues, instilled in their children in the privacy of their homes the conviction that American society had to change. Filling the streets during the Civil Rights Movement, these women were fueled by a sense of their own legitimacy. In the tradition of Yaa Asantewaa, women like Harriet Tubman, Sojourner Truth, and Fannie Lou Hamer put themselves at the forefront of the struggle for independence. Grounded in their sense of justice, leadership was as natural for them as for anyone.

Outspoken; secure in their own legitimacy to act and express themselves; resilient, resourceful, and spiritual, African women were heard and affected change when they deemed necessary. True to the adage that, "Wise women never sit and wail their woes but presently prevent the ways to wail" (Sibisi, 1977, p. 177), African women were a force to be reckoned with. In America their descendants continue in this tradition.

Note

1. Mrs. Avis Chikwanha, interview with author, Harare, February 3, 1987.

References

Afonja, Simi. (1981). Changing modes of production and the sexual division of labor among the Yoruba. *Signs: Journal of Women in Culture and Society, 7*(2), 307.

Aidoo, Agnes Akosua. (1981). Asante queen mothers in government and politics in the nineteenth century. In Filomina Chioma Steady (Ed.), *The Black woman cross-culturally* (pp. 65-77). Cambridge, MA: Schenkman.

Awe, Bolanle. (1977). The Iyalode in the traditional Yoruba political system. In Alice Schlegel (Ed.), *Sexual stratification: A cross-cultural view* (pp. 144-159). New York: Columbia University Press.

Bay, Edna G. (1983). Servitude and worldly success in the palace of Dahomey. In Claire Robertson & Martin A. Klein (Eds.), *Women and slavery in Africa*. Madison: University of Wisconsin Press.

Bazeley, W. S. (1940). Manyika headwomen. *NADA: The Southern Rhodesia Native Affairs Department Annual, 17*(3), 3.

Beach, D. N. (n.d.). *Mapondera: The career of a hero of the northern Zimbabwean plateau, c. 1840-1904*. University of Zimbabwe History Department Seminar Paper No. 67.

Beach, D. N. (1980). *The Shona & Zimbabwe 900-1850: An outline of Shona history*. New York: Africana Publishing.

Berger, Iris. (1976). Rebels or status-seekers? Women as spirit mediums in East Africa. In Nancy J. Hafkin & Edna G. Bay (Eds.), *Women in Africa: Studies in social and economic change*. Stanford, CA: Stanford University Press.

Bhila, H.H.K. (1973). Trade and the survival of an African polity: The external relations of Manyika from the sixteenth to the early nineteenth century. *Rhodesian History, 3*, 11-28.

Bhila, H.H.K. (1982). *Trade and politics in a Shona kingdom. The Manyika and their Portuguese and African neighbours, 1575-1902*. London: Longman.

Blennerhassett, Rose, & Sleeman, Lucy. (1893). *Adventures in Mashonaland by two hospital nurses*. London: Macmillan.

Bogle, Donald. (1980). *Brown sugar*. New York: Harmony Books.

Bourdillon, M.F.C. (1976). *The Shona peoples. An ethnography of the contemporary Shona, with special reference to their religion*. Salisbury, Rhodesia: Mambo Press.

Brooks, George E., Jr. (1976). The Signares of Saint-Louis and Goree: Women entrepreneurs in eighteenth century Senegal. In Nancy J. Hafkin & Edna G. Bay (Eds.), *Women in Africa: Studies in social and economic change*. Stanford, CA: Stanford University Press.

Bryant, A. T. (1923, August). The Zulu family and state organization. *Bantu Studies, 22*, 47-51.

Burke, E. E. (Ed.). (1969). *The journals of Carl Mauch. His travels in the Transvaal and Rhodesia 1869-1872*. Salisbury: National Archives of Rhodesia.

Clark, Carolyn M. (1980). Land and food, women and power, in nineteenth century Kikuyu. *Africa, 50*(4), 357-370.

Collins, Patricia Hill. (1990). *Black feminist thought: Knowledge, consciousness, and the politics of empowerment*. Boston: Unwin Hyman.

Crawford, J. R. (1967). *Witchcraft and sorcery in Rhodesia*. London: Oxford University Press.

Des Forges, Alison L. (1986). "The drum is greater than the shout": The 1912 rebellion in northern Rwanda. In Donald Crummey (Ed.), *Banditry, rebellion and social protest in Africa* (pp. 311-331). London: James Currey.

Douglas, M. (Ed.). (1970). *Witchcraft confessions and accusations*. London: Tavistock.

Folta, Jeannette R., & Deck, Edith S. (1988, Autumn). The impact of children's death on Shona mothers and families. *Journal of Comparative Family Studies, 19*(3), 433-451.

Gandanzara, Nobath. (1967, May). [title not available]. *Umbowo, 50*(5), 12.

Gelfand, Michael. (1959). *Shona ritual with special reference to the Chaminuka cult*. Cape Town: Juta & Co.

Gelfand, Michael. (1971). *Diet and tradition in an African culture*. Edinburgh: E. & S. Livingston.

Golan, Dapha. (1990). The life story of King Shaka: Gender tensions in the Zulu state. *History in Africa: A Journal of Method, 17*, 95-111.

Guyer, Jane I. (1984). *Family and farm in Southern Cameroon*. Boston: Boston University Press.

Hammond-Tooke, W. D. (n.d.). The Cape Nguni witch familiar as a mediatory construct. *Man, 9*, 128-136.

Hamutyinei, Mordikai A., & Plangger, Albert B. (1974). *Tsumo-Shumo, Shona proverbial lore and wisdom.* Gwelo, Southern Rhodesia: Mambo Press.

Harms, Robert. (1983). Sustaining the system: Trading towns along the Middle Zaire. In Claire Robertson & Martin A. Klein (Eds.), *Women and slavery in Africa.* Madison: University of Wisconsin Press.

Harris, Grace. (1957). Possession "hysteria" in a Kenya tribe. *American Anthropologist, 59*(6), 1046-1066.

Henn, Jeanne K. (1984). Women in the rural economy: Past, present, and future. In Margaret Jean Hay & Sharon Stichter (Eds.), *African women south of the Sahara.* London: Longman.

Holleman, J. F. (1962). *Cash, cattle or women: A conflict of concepts in a dual economy.* Durban: University of Natal, Institute for Social Research.

Holleman, J. F. (1969). *Shona customary law with reference to kinship, marriage, the family and the estate.* Manchester, UK: Manchester University Press.

Katsukunya, V. (1971). Makate and Nehoreka. *NADA: The Southern Rhodesia Native Affairs Department Annual, 10*(3), 76-77.

Mandala, Elias. (1984). Capitalism, kinship and gender in the lower Tchiri (shire) valley of Malawi, 1860-1960: An alternative theoretical framework. *African Economic History, 13,* 137-169.

Maranke, Mrs. H. M. Titus. (1941). Rhodesia annual conference. *Official Journal of the Rhodesia Annual Conference of the Methodist Church,* p. 165.

May, Joan. (1983). *Zimbabwean women in customary and colonial law.* Gweru, Zimbabwe: Mambo Press.

Moss, Barbara A. (1982, November). *Women of the Mfecane.* Paper presented to History of Africa Seminar, Indiana University.

Murphy, H. H. Blackwood. (1926). The Kitui Akambo: Further investigation of certain matters. *The Journal of the Royal Anthropological Institute of Great Britain and Ireland, 56,* 195-206.

O'Barr, Jean F. (1975). Making the invisible visible: African women in politics and policy. *African Studies Review, 18*(3), 19-27.

Potash, Betty. (1986). *Widows in African societies. Choices and constraints.* Stanford, CA: Stanford University Press.

Ranger, Terence. (n.d.). *Women in the politics of Makoni District, Zimbabwe, 1890-1980.* Unpublished manuscript, University of Manchester.

Robertson, Claire, & Berger, Iris. (1986). Analyzing class and gender—African perspectives. In Claire Robertson & Iris Berger (Eds.), *Women and class in Africa.* New York: Africana Publishing.

Robertson, Claire, & Klein, Martin A. (Eds.). (1983). *Women and slavery in Africa.* Madison: University of Wisconsin Press.

Rogers, Susan G. (1980). Anti-colonial protest in Africa: A female strategy reconsidered. *Heresies: A Feminist Publication on Art & Politics, 3*(1), 22-25.

Selous, Frederick Courteney. (1893). *Travel and adventure in South-East Africa.* London: Rowland Ward.

Shepherd Machuma Files. (n.d.). *Historical Society 8,* Old Mutare Mission Archives, Old Mutare, Zimbabwe.

Shepherd Machuma Files; Mrs. Janet Choto. (n.d.). *Ishe Muredzwa's story.* Mtasa file, Old Mutare Mission Archives, Old Mutare, Zimbabwe.

Sibisi, Harriet. (1977, Autumn). How African women cope with migrant labor in South Africa. *Signs: Journal of Women in Culture and Society, 3,* 177.

Sithole, Ndabaningi. (1970). *Obed Mutezo: The Mudzimu Christian nationalist.* London: Oxford University Press.

Summers, Roger. (1969). *Ancient mining in Rhodesia and adjacent areas.* Salisbury: Trustees of the National Museums of Rhodesia.

Terborg-Penn, Rosalyn. (1986). Black women in resistance: A cross-cultural perspective. In Gary Y. Okihiro (Ed.), *In resistance. Studies in African, Caribbean, and Afro-American history* (pp. 166-209). Amherst: University of Massachusetts Press.

Thomas, Thomas Morgan. (1872). *Eleven years in Central South Africa.* London: John Snow.

Van Allen, Judith. (1976). "Aba Riot" or Igbo "Women's War"? Ideology, stratification, and the invisibility of women. In Nancy J. Hafkin & Edna G. Bay (Eds.), *Women in Africa: Studies in social and economic change.* Stanford, CA: Stanford University Press.

White, Luise. (1984). Women in the changing African family. In Margaret Jean Hay & Sharon Stichter (Eds.), *African women south of the Sahara.* London: Longman.

Wood, Joseph Garbett. (1974). *Through Matabeleland. The record of ten months' trip in an ox-wagon through Mashonaland and Matabeleland.* Bulawayo: Bulawayo Books of Rhodesia. (Original work published 1893)

Wright, Marcia. (1975, December). Women in peril: A commentary on the life stories of captives in nineteenth century East-Central Africa. *African Social Research, 20,* 800-819.

2. Organizing for Racial Justice
Black Women and the Dynamics of Race and Sex in Female Antislavery Societies, 1832-1860

SHIRLEY J. YEE

In February 1832 a group of free Black women in Salem, MA, organized the Female Anti-Slavery Society of Salem. This all-Black organization espoused the broad objectives of Black abolitionism by pledging to work for "mutual improvement, and to promote the welfare of our race."[1] Antislavery, anticolonization, antiracism, and the development of a self-reliant Black community were explicit parts of the agenda. In support of these goals, the women promised to raise money to help finance *The Liberator*, the Boston-based newspaper that demanded both the immediate end of slavery through the moral persuasion of slaveholders and the achievement of racial equality. Two years after its founding, the members reconstituted the society into a racially mixed organization and renamed it the Salem Female Anti-Slavery Society.[2] Although noted as the first female antislavery society, the Salem organization represented the continuation of a long tradition of activism among free Black women.

In this chapter I examine Black women's participation in organized abolition between 1832 and 1860. A number of themes emerge in this study: the vitality of the northern free Black community during the antebellum period; the centrality of kinship/friendship ties and Black institutions in providing avenues for participation in organized antislavery; and, Black women's responses to the contradictions and tensions regarding racism and sexism within the movement.

Community institutions, such as churches, shops, and boarding houses, were important avenues through which Black women and men participated in social activism. In addition to providing spiritual or material sustenance, they served as places where people could gather, discuss the news of the day, and pass on information about employment opportunities and social and political events. Black abolitionists Lewis and Harriet Hayden of Boston, for example, operated a clothing store that was both a business that catered to a racially mixed clientele and a place to clothe and house runaway slaves. Women's charitable and reform organizations were also familiar features in Black neighborhoods and provided a variety of services for needy members of the community, particularly widows, orphans, and fugitive slaves.[3]

The motivations for forming exclusively Black organizations varied. Prevailing racism was a contributing factor. Black men formed fraternal associations, such as the Odd Fellows and Masons, as a result of their exclusion from White Masonic and fraternal orders. The particular needs of the free Black community, however, also inspired Black activists to organize separately. Black-run Vigilant Committees in New York, Philadelphia, and Boston, for example, helped provide runaway slaves with clothing, food, and temporary shelter from slave catchers.[4] Men's and women's literary societies helped make up for the dearth of adequate schools available to Blacks and the outright exclusion of Black men and women from institutes of higher learning.

These activities for mutual aid, self-improvement, and the elimination of racism reflected a broader vision of "abolitionism" than that which existed among many of their White colleagues. Black leaders had espoused these objectives more than a decade before White abolitionist William Lloyd Garrison emerged in 1831 as the "leader" of radical abolition. Unlike many Blacks, Garrison and other White abolitionists had previously allied themselves with the American Colonization Society (ACS), a group of prominent Whites who had organized in 1816 to send Blacks to Africa.[5] The movement flourished in the 1820s, but by the end of the decade a small faction of colonizationists, including Garrison, had grown disillusioned, arguing that the plan had never been for the benefit of Blacks, but was simply a way to rid the country of a group that Whites considered undesirable. By 1830, Garrison's group had extricated itself from the colonizationists, denouncing the movement as racist and advocating a more radical scheme for eliminating slavery and racism in American society. Garrisonians eventually made up a small, albeit vocal, contingent of those White Americans who supported both antislavery and racial equality.[6]

Black leaders had repudiated colonization from the beginning. On a cold January day in 1817, one year after the formation of the ACS, Philadelphia free Blacks crowded into "Mother" Bethel Church where they formally denounced the scheme and began formulating a strategy for launching a Black-initiated abolition movement.[7] The Philadelphia meeting served as an important catalyst, for Black abolitionism emerged in other northern cities and towns as well, such as Boston, New York, and Cincinnati, where sizeable Black populations resided and Black activism flourished. The predominantly male leadership, many of whom were members of the clergy or prosperous businessmen and tradesmen,

brought the interests of free Blacks and slaves together on one agenda,
maintaining that ending chattel slavery in the South was only part of
the larger vision for freedom, and that all racial barriers to Black achievement in employment, education, and politics should be eliminated as
well. To this end, Garrisonians and Black abolitionists were in agreement
and attempted to build an interracial coalition.

Black men, in fact, had been instrumental in the formation of the
American Anti-Slavery Society (AAS), the interracial national antislavery
organization. In 1831, 2 years before its founding, Black leaders held
the First Annual Convention of People of Color in Philadelphia, where
they discussed the possibility of establishing a national society and had
invited Garrison and several other White radicals as guests. Radical
abolitionists continued to challenge the custom of racial segregation.
The New England Anti-Slavery Society, Garrison's group, had even
admitted Black men as members.[8] Lasting friendships developed between many Black and White activists out of this working relationship.
But, regardless of such daring attempts to bridge racial barriers, the
unequal treatment and prejudice Blacks often experienced from their
White colleagues were well known. For example, whether to extend to
Blacks membership in predominantly White antislavery societies and,
hence, acknowledge racial equality, remained controversial on both the
state and local levels.

Addressing Racism and Sexism in the Movement

For free Black women activists, racism and sexism intertwined to
shape their modes of activism and their vision of freedom. On the one
hand, the focus of their antislavery societies was to raise funds in support of the movement; in particular, the antislavery newspapers and
traveling lecturers. Like White women, Black women also followed the
custom of sex-segregation in organized public activism and accepted
their supportive role to male leadership. Their societies functioned as
auxiliaries to local male organizations and, ultimately, to male-led state
societies and the AAS.[9] On the other hand, the situation of Black women
differed fundamentally from that of White women. Black women had
a long history of working together with the men of their race against
racism and for the advancement of their community. Like Black men,
Black women participated in the formation and operation of mixed-race
and all-Black antislavery organizations and, at the same time, were
actively involved in activities such as temperance, moral reform, education, and benevolence in their communities.

The particular role Black women played in organized antislavery
was shaped by the community's notion of freedom and by the rise of
White middle-class urban ideas about appropriate sex roles. As James O.
Horton has pointed out, dominant middle-class ideas promoting sepa-

rate spheres also permeated the antebellum free Black community. The most powerful institutions in free Black society, the churches, schools, and the press, championed men's "proper" roles as heads of households and sole providers for their families. Women were instructed to live up to contemporary notions of "true womanhood," in which they were to pursue a domestic education that taught them to "manage a house, and govern and instruct children."[10] Even Frederick Douglass, a long-time supporter of women's rights, once argued that a well-trained wife and mother should operate a "well regulated household . . . one of women's brightest ornaments—a source of happiness to her and to those who are dependent upon her labors of love for the attractions of home and its endearments."[11] This ideology also sanctioned specific forms of female participation in activities outside of the home by encouraging wives to extend their moral responsibilities into the public realm. The priority of the "true" woman, however, was to stay at home and create a comfortable and nurturing atmosphere for her husband and children.[12] In slavery, such autonomy had been difficult, for daily life and labor had been structured and controlled by masters. Women, as well as men, labored long and arduously for the slaveholding economy and suffered under the lash as men did. Slave women, however, were also in constant danger of rape by White masters and overseers and served as breeders for the slave system. The slave quarters were the only places in which men and women could find refuge and forge autonomous social roles for themselves. Thus, to many Blacks, separate social roles for men and women held special importance as a symbol of free status and a rejection of slave life.

But, harsh economic realities prevented many Blacks from attaining these ideals. Racism had barred many free Black men from well-paying jobs. As a result, women of all ages were forced to earn a wage, usually in some type of domestic work, as live-in servants in White households, day servants, or by taking lodgers, sewing, and laundry into their homes. A report on the status of Blacks in Philadelphia during the 1830s noted that Black women could also be found as school mistresses, cake bakers, shopkeepers, and carpet makers.[13] Others were street sellers, prostitutes, or rag pickers.[14]

Participating in social activism was difficult when one had to earn a wage. Nevertheless, free Black women who entered into organized antislavery work came from a range of socioeconomic positions, although financial circumstances shaped the extent to which they could devote their time and energy to the movement. Harriet Hayden, for example, participated in the Boston Female Anti-Slavery Society (BFASS) activities whenever she could. Yet, her many responsibilities, which included helping in her husband's store and running a large household, limited her involvement in the BFASS. In a letter to White colleague Maria Weston Chapman in 1843, she expressed her regrets at being unable to participate in the annual fair:

In the accompanying article you will find that I have made a faint and trifling
response to the call. It is the hasty production of a very short period of leisure
. . . I have been spending the last week in working for the Mass. fair, I want
very much to do a great deal but time & circumstances forbid.[15]

Class Stratification in the Free Black Community

The women of the Forten, Smith, and Whipper families fared differently than working-class women like Hayden, for their families counted
among the most prosperous Blacks who donated a great deal of time,
energy, and material resources to the movement. Unlike most free Black
women, these women were not forced to earn a wage: Their husbands
were prominent businessmen whose earnings were more than enough
to support their families. Freed from the hardships that most women
faced, well-to-do Black women could devote much of their time to social
reform. Charlotte Forten was a founder in 1833 of the interracial Philadelphia Female Anti-Slavery Society. Her husband, James, had amassed
a fortune as a sailmaker and inventor on the Philadelphia docks. They
lived with their five children in a three-story brick residence on Lom-
bard Street. In this home, which they opened to abolitionist friends,
their children grew up in an atmosphere in which social activism was
virtually part of their daily routine. The Forten daughters, Harriet,
Margaretta, and Sarah Louise, were active in the movement. All three
had taught school and attended PFASS meetings. Harriet had married
Robert Purvis, the wealthy son of a slaveholder and a slave woman,
and hosted abolitionists at their home in Byberry; Margaretta regularly served as Recording Secretary of the PFASS; Sarah Louise wrote
antislavery poetry for *The Liberator*.

Harriet Smith and Mary Ann Whipper were also active abolitionists who often served as delegates to antislavery conventions. Their
husbands, Stephen Smith and William Whipper, were co-owners of a
successful lumber company in nearby Columbia, PA.[16]

Other Black activist women came from less prosperous circum-
stances but enjoyed comfortable lives as long as all adults in the family
earned a regular wage. The Douglass family is a case in point. Grace
Bustill Douglass had come from a long line of activists. Her mother
was Elizabeth Morey, the daughter of an Englishman and a Delaware
Indian woman. Yet, Grace's family identified with the Black community.
Her father, Cyrus Bustill, was a baker and Revolutionary War veteran.
His relatives were Black Quaker abolitionists who had settled in Little
Egg Harbor, NJ, and Philadelphia.[17] A devout Quaker herself, Grace
Douglass attended the predominantly White Arch Street Meeting, even
though she had been discouraged from seeking membership and was
required to sit in the segregated pew. She and her husband, Robert
Douglass, were active in Philadelphia Black society. He was a founder

of the First African Presbyterian Church and she was a respected founding member of the PFASS. Grace's only daughter, Sarah Mapps Douglass, sometimes served as the Society's librarian in addition to teaching school. Grace's sister, Mary Bustill, and several female cousins were also familiar figures in the community.

In addition to her active participation in the PFASS, Grace Douglass was a vital source of economic support for the family. Until her death in 1842, she operated a hat shop next door to her father's bakery on Arch Street. When she died, the family faced serious economic difficulties. Much of the responsibility for keeping the family afloat fell to Sarah, who was 36 years old at the time of her mother's death. Sarah, who went on to teach for 40 years in the Philadelphia Black community, brought in a small income, but it was necessary for her family's survival. After her mother's death, Sarah's health was so delicate that her physician advised her to stop teaching, yet the Douglass's situation required her to continue. Domestic work was apparently not an option, given Douglass's health, the low status of domestic labor, and the elevated social position of the Douglass family in the free Black community. According to Douglass's own account, tears filled her eyes when a White Quaker woman in New York, where Douglass was teaching briefly, assumed she was a servant.[18] White friend and colleague Sarah M. Grimke observed that domestic service "would neither suit [Douglass's] disposition or inclination."[19]

In Boston, Susan Paul faced similar hardships. The Pauls were well known among both White and Black abolitionists, yet their financial situation was precarious. Susan's father, the Reverend Thomas Paul, was a Black Baptist minister who enjoyed the love and respect of Black Bostonians. When he died, his daughter Susan carried the burden of supporting the family, which included her widowed mother, several siblings, and nieces and nephews. The family's economic circumstances worsened as Susan, ill with consumption, struggled to make ends meet through teaching and seamstressing. Her connection to the abolitionist community was instrumental in her attempt to keep the family together as long as possible. Yet, despite her efforts, the family eventually fragmented. When Susan Paul died in 1841 at age 34, the younger children under her charge were taken in by various friends.[20]

Paul's activism in the movement had included the education of Black children, serving as secretary of Boston's Black temperance society, and membership in the racially mixed Boston Female Anti-Slavery Society.[21] In her primary school she combined religious instruction with general education and had organized the Garrison Junior Choir, a Black youth group that frequently performed in public. Leading White and Black abolitionists such as Garrison and James G. Barbadoes supported her efforts and linked her concerts with the movement. As Garrison noted in 1834, Paul's concerts had "a powerful tendency

to beget sympathy, to excite admiration, and to destroy prejudice."
Garrison provided advertisements in *The Liberator,* and Barbadoes and
James Loring, another prominent White abolitionist, sold tickets to her
concerts at *The Liberator* office for 25 cents apiece.[22] In addition to her
work in Black education, Paul was active in the BFASS. In 1837, she was
one of two Black women chosen as delegates to the Anti-Slavery Convention in New York as a "favourable specimen" of her race.[23]

Interracial Cooperation

The Boston and Philadelphia societies to which the above group of
women belonged, began as interracial organizations in 1833. In a Philadelphia schoolroom, in February of that year, a group of Black and
White women met "to take into consideration the propriety of forming
a Female Anti-Slavery Society." Most of the White members of the PFASS
and at least one Black member, Grace Douglass, were Quakers. Given
the long history of Quaker agitation against slavery and the egalitarian
philosophy of Quakerism, it is not surprising that the Philadelphia
organization began as a racially mixed enterprise.[24] In addition to the
Forten and Douglass women, the Black women who attended the organizational meeting included Sarah McCrummell, wife of abolitionist
James McCrummell, and Hetty Burr, whose husband, John, was an agent
for *The Liberator*.[25] In an effort to combine antislavery with community
action, the founding committee agreed to "propose such measures as
will be likely to promote the Abolition of Slavery and to elevate the
people of colour from their present degraded situation, to the full
enjoyment of their rights and to increased usefulness in society."[26]

Black and White members of the PFASS cooperated on a number of
issues that Black activists considered of vital importance: the abolition
of racial prejudice and slavery, and assisting in Black community projects
such as education and the Underground Railroad. Hetty Reckless and
Sarah Douglass were especially instrumental in ensuring that the Society
address the practical needs of the free Black community. In the area of
education, the Society devoted a great deal of resources to the improvement of schooling for Philadelphia Blacks. Douglass's involvement in
the PFASS Education Committee enabled her to operate and sustain a
school for Black children and at the same time ensure that the priorities
of the Black community remained an integral part of the PFASS agenda.
Four years before Douglass joined the committee in 1840, other members had supported her efforts by pledging that the Society assume
responsibility for establishing her school. In 1838 the Society received
approval from the male-led parent organization, the Pennsylvania Abolition Society, to provide financial assistance after several members

learned of the difficulties Douglass faced in keeping the school heated and adequately supplied.

By 1840 the Society began monitoring the education of Black children in the city, which included visiting the homes of parents to convince them of the necessity of education. Each member also was assigned to particular schools to "advise & instruct teachers and report to the Committee the state of that school." Apparently, monitoring was inconsistent. Critics chastised the committee, noting that, "had the proposed plan been pursued by an *efficient* Committee, it might have been productive of good results, but many have been so neglectful that the report of the Condition of the schools cannot be (so full) as it might have been."[27]

Despite such criticism, Douglass believed that the Society had actually eroded her autonomy and in March 1840 requested that the Society relinquish its control over the school. Although the Board members expressed regret over her request, they left no indication of hard feelings toward Douglass or her school. White member Mary Grew's resolution illustrates the support that still existed: "Resolved, That this society deeply regret[s] the withdrawal of the school taught by S. M. Douglass from their charge," adding that, "the supervision & maintenance . . . has been a source of pleasure to them, & that they wish for it a continuance of prosperity & usefulness under her care."[28]

Despite its separation from the school, the Society continued to provide economic assistance. At the 1840 meeting the Board allocated an annual sum of $125 for rent and supplies.[29] The following year, in exchange for providing her with funds to maintain a decent schoolroom, Douglass agreed to allow the Society to hold its regular meetings there.[30] In 1847, the Society agreed to purchase a stove for the schoolroom. The Society continued to pay for rent and supplies until 1849, even during periods of declining enrollment.[31]

In addition to supporting Black education, the PFASS assisted benevolent and reform organizations in the free Black community, including the Underground Railroad. Hetty Reckless (sometimes listed as Hester or Esther Reckless) was instrumental in strengthening the connection between the Society and the Black community. Little information exists on this energetic woman, except that she was a regular member of the PFASS and participated in a variety of community projects. For Reckless, as for many free Black women, community activism was tied to antislavery. In 1841 Reckless encouraged the Society to provide financial assistance to the Sabbath schools that Blacks had established in the city. She was also an active proponent of antiprostitution. In 1847, at the same meeting at which members allocated money for Douglass's stove, they donated $25 to the Moral Reform Retreat, a boarding house that Reckless had established to serve as alternative lodging for prostitutes.[32] The year before, she had spearheaded a drive to ally the PFASS with the predominantly Black Female Vigilant

Committee in Philadelphia. This committee had been in existence since 1838 and served as an auxiliary to the male Philadelphia Vigilant Association. Reckless's dual membership with the Vigilant Committee and the PFASS provided her with the opportunity to convince other members of the Society to pledge financial assistance to the Black community. In September 1841 she urged her colleagues to invoke their "sympathy and pecuniary aid" and reported that the Committee had helped 35 slaves "in their escape to a land of liberty" since the last monthly meeting. The members resolved to "more efficiently . . . bear in mind the wants of the Vigilance Committee."[33] Yet, the Society's funds were limited. In spite of its verbal support for the Underground Railroad, the Society refrained from allocating a fixed sum to the Vigilance Committee, deciding instead to provide funds on a case-by-case basis. Nevertheless, Reckless persisted. Four years later, she reported difficulties in securing money to assist the large numbers of fugitives arriving in the city annually. In June 1845 the Society donated $10 to Reckless for "the benefit of fugitive slaves."[34]

The decision to limit aid to fugitive slaves in part reflected different interpretations of the Society's function. Lucretia Mott, an influential White member of the PFASS and of Philadelphia Quaker society, expressed in 1856 that although helping destitute runaways was important, those born into slavery far outnumbered the slaves who escaped. According to Mott, such assistance was "not properly antislavery work," but extraneous to the real purpose of the Society—to eliminate slavery "root and branch."[35]

Mott's view differed substantially from Black abolitionist ideology, which had embraced a more inclusive vision of activism in antislavery societies, as exemplified through the work of Sarah Douglass and Hetty Reckless. Views on the goals of abolition, however, did not always divide neatly along racial lines, for some White women also seem to have supported the larger agenda. The resignation of Esther Moore, the first president of the PFASS, apparently jolted the members into discussing seriously the difference between the "mere branches" of the movement and "real" antislavery work. Moore had resigned from the Society in 1846 in order to lend greater support to the Vigilant Committee.[36] Clearly, though, the active presence of Black women like the Douglasses, Fortens, and Reckless also forced the more conservative members of the PFASS to reconsider the breadth of the Society's agenda.

In Boston, Black women had been actively involved in BFASS activities since its founding. Like the Philadelphia Black women, the Black members of the Boston society participated in both organized abolition and community activities. Some information exists on these women. Eunice R. Davis, Margarett Scarlett, Eliza Ann Logan Lawton, and Anna Logan worked together in the fight against public school segregation in Boston. Davis, Logan, and another BFASS member,

Caroline F. Williams, belonged to the Zion church and participated in various church functions. More notable members of the Society included Susan Paul, Nancy Gardner Prince, Louisa F. Nell, mother of Black abolitionist and writer William Cooper Nell and wife of William G. Nell, and Anna Murray Douglass, first wife of Frederick Douglass.[37]

Tensions over the prospect of breaking racial customs, however, seemed greater in this society than in the Philadelphia organization, where the Quaker influence resulted in a greater degree of egalitarianism. At BFASS meetings Blacks and Whites were seated in separate sections of the hall. One prominent White member, Elisha Blanchard, admonished Black colleague Charlotte Coleman for sitting in the White section, pointing out that although White members were willing to help Blacks, "traditions must not be violated." She added, however, that despite Coleman's indiscretion, most Blacks were "very well in their place."[38]

Some members of White female antislavery societies engaged in heated debates over whether to allow Black women to join their organizations. In Fall River, MA, the female society almost disintegrated when a member extended membership to three young Black women who had been attending meetings. The Society eventually admitted the women.[39] In New York, the New York Ladies Anti-Slavery Society (NYLASS) opposed social mixing between the races and excluded Blacks from membership. Although the constitution did not explicitly forbid Blacks from joining, the membership fee was $25, high enough to discourage working-class women, both Black and White. Race prejudice, however, probably manifested itself in less tangible ways, enough so that such attitudes became well known in abolitionist circles. In 1836 Anne Warren Weston expressed her frustration with Abigail Ann Cox, a leader of the NYLASS: "Mrs. Cox is the life & soul of the New York Society and she is in a very sinful state—full of wicked prejudice about colour; they do not allow any coloured women to join their society." Weston added that such attitudes were debilitating, referring to colleague Lydia Maria Child's description that the New York society was "very lifeless." The racial attitudes of women like Cox had apparently caused a rift in the Society. Weston defended members of the organization who disagreed with Cox, declaring that Juliana Tappan and her family had "none of this prejudice," and that Cox and Tappan were "hardly on speaking terms."[40]

Despite the exclusionary practices of the NYLASS and the racist attitudes of its members, Black women in New York City were active participants in organized antislavery. In Manhattan, for example, Black women formed a female antislavery society that included a few White members. One of these members was Abby Hopper Gibbons, who once noted, "Here I am, the only white female member of the Manhattan Anti-Slavery Society."[41]

Challenging the Order

Weary of the racism that existed in White and racially mixed anti-slavery societies, disillusioned with Garrison's leadership and the strategy of moral persuasion, and eager to address more directly the practical needs of free Blacks, a number of Black leaders like Frederick Douglass and Martin Delany pushed for independence from White abolitionism and a greater emphasis on Black nationalism. Many Black women answered Douglass's call for Black unity. The formation of the Women's Association of Philadelphia in 1849 is a good example of the way Black women abolitionists organized in support of these goals.

Several founding members of the Association, Sarah Douglass, Hetty Burr, Harriet Smith, and Amy Matilda Williams Cassey, still maintained their ties with the PFASS. The dual membership these women held suggests that although they supported Douglass, they had not given up on the idea of interracial cooperation, especially after 16 years of activism in the PFASS.[42] Other Black women may not have held such close ties with the interracial Society. Association members who did not hold membership in the PFASS included Mary, Hester, and Lydia Ann Bustill, cousins of Sarah Douglass, as well as Rachel Lloyd, Mary Barrott, Louisa Bristol, Helen Johnson, and Charlotte Mills.

The purpose of the Association was to support, through fund-raising, Frederick Douglass's newspaper, the *North Star*, devoting themselves to the "Elevation of the Colored People in the United States by Self-Exertion."[43] The founders hoped that this organization would meet the needs of the community, for, apparently, the PFASS alone had been insufficient for mobilizing Black women. In their constitution they declared that, "The Necessity of an efficient organization for the support of our cause has long been apparent and its absence deplored." Like the other female antislavery societies, the Women's Association of Philadelphia organized colorful fairs in order to raise money. In its advertisement, the members of the fair committee urged Blacks to have confidence in Frederick Douglass's "talents and correct principles."[44]

But even though free Black women worked diligently alongside Black men, a number of women raised the so-called Woman Question in Black abolitionist organizations. Such demands occurred during a period in which challenges to women's "proper" place in public activism had come to a head. Since the mid-1830s, radical-minded Black women such as Sojourner Truth, Maria Stewart, and the White Grimke sisters questioned the assumption that women should play a limited role in the movement and avoid areas that were considered traditional male domains, such as public speaking and political writing. A number of Black feminists had been original members of antislavery societies. Harriet Forten Purvis and her sister Margaretta Forten, for example, both identified with women's rights and had been part of the first generation of members of the Philadelphia Female Anti-Slavery Society.[45]

Members of female antislavery societies apparently did not challenge their auxiliary status within the hierarchy of state and local societies, probably because women's organizations exercised a fair amount of autonomy over daily business and internal decision making. Many members of female antislavery societies, however, supported women's rights at the same time that they worked in auxiliary women's organizations and challenged the restrictions placed on women within the national organization. The groundbreaking, yet controversial, decision occurred at the anniversary meeting of the AAS in May 1840 in which Abby Kelley Foster, a White woman, won a seat on the executive committee. The decision had several consequences: It gained for women an equal voice with men in the AAS and in the state and local societies, but it also was the final straw that led to the official split in the national organization. Dissenters, led by the Tappan brothers of New York, left the meeting to form the American and Foreign Anti-Slavery Society, whose members considered the Woman Question as well as other issues separate from abolition.[46]

The victory in the AAS was significant, for 8 years later a predominantly White middle-class contingent of feminists held the first national women's rights convention at Seneca Falls, NY. There, the delegates presented a list of demands that included the right to divorce, child custody, access to the professions and higher education, and the right to vote.[47] Out of a total of 240 people (200 women and 40 men), the only Black person who attended was Frederick Douglass.

Black women's absence at Seneca Falls was revealing. First, it reflected the growing divergence between Black and White women over the meaning of women's rights. For Black abolitionist women and the rising generation of Black feminists after the Civil War, women's rights included the elimination of racism as well as sexism, a position that often placed them at odds with many White feminists who viewed the issues separately and had pushed for the separation of women's rights from abolition since the 1840s. Second, Black women may have considered their multiple responsibilities to home and community of more immediate importance, although they may have supported the demands of the Seneca Falls meeting.

The Black conventions, which had excluded women from having a voice in the proceedings, became the focus of Black women's agitation for equality. At the conventions, the debate shaped up similarly to the predominantly White-male-led AAS. While White women were busy at Seneca Falls, a number of Black women were organizing a collective protest at the annual meeting of the National Convention of Colored Freedmen in Cleveland, OH. There, they presented their first official demand for equality. Frederick Douglass and Martin Delany, together with one Black woman, motioned to allow women to participate as full members, to speak and vote in the proceedings as the men did. After much debate, the business committee approved the proposal.[48] The following year a group of Black women who attended the Ohio State Convention in Columbus threatened to boycott the convention unless they were allowed equal status with men at the proceedings. The resolution they submitted to the business committee maintained that the exclusion of women was "wrong and shameful," and that unless women were granted equal privileges with men, they would "attend no more after tonight." After some debate the committee adopted the resolution.[49]

Change, however, came slowly and inconsistently. Decisions about women's "proper" role in the conventions varied from state to state. Almost a decade after the Ohio conventions, only a few Black women could be found in decision-making positions. By this time many opponents had adopted the position of separating the issue of sex equality from racial equality. In 1855 a Black woman was expelled from a convention in New York "for no other reason than her sex." That same year in Philadelphia, delegates at the National Convention of Coloured Men excluded women from membership, voting 23 to 3 against admitting Mary Ann Shadd as a member, despite Frederick Douglass's support of Shadd's candidacy. As one observer noted, "a few men of sense" protested her candidacy, arguing that the meeting "was not a Women's Rights Convention."[50]

Despite the sexism and racism they encountered in the movements for abolition and women's rights, Black women carried on the struggle for equality throughout the remainder of the 19th century. For Black women, antislavery societies had provided a forum through which they could address the existence of racism and sexism, for the antislavery movement had the potential for undermining both systems of oppression. On a daily basis, Black women struggled to maintain a balance between their commitment to women's rights and to the welfare of their race. This early generation of free Black women initiated the discussion and subsequent generations of Black feminists sustained it.

Conclusion

The study of Black women's participation in the formation and operation of female antislavery societies offers an illuminating glimpse of Black women's organizational patterns during the antebellum period and the dynamics of gender and race both in abolitionism and in the emerging women's movement.

Black women abolitionists were a diverse group. As the experiences of many of these women attest, economic circumstances and occupational and family responsibilities shaped the degree to which they could devote themselves to the movement. Free Black women who came from wealthy families could devote a great deal of their time to the movement and, as a result, tended to form the leadership among Black members of antislavery societies. Those women who did not come from well-to-do families juggled their time between earning a wage and caring for their own families and needy members of the community. But, regardless of their economic circumstances, Black women's participation in public activism was considered an extension of their domestic and moral responsibilities to the community, which fulfilled their duties to their sex and their race. In so doing, they found themselves enmeshed in the emerging debates over customs that had for so long dictated the "proper" behavior of women and Blacks. The multiple forms of activism that so closely touched both their personal lives and their communities challenged the notion that the private and public spheres remained separate entities in women's lives. For free Black women, these spheres were inextricably connected.

Female antislavery societies served as one of many avenues through which free Black women could participate in the public arena and, at the same time, remain within acceptable boundaries of female behavior. Black women maintained the custom of organizing separately from men and participating in specifically "female" activities, such as fundraising in support of male leadership. The result was the reinforcement of patriarchy. Yet, the existence of sex-segregated social activities, ironically, was as liberating as it was constrictive, for it helped sweep away the memories of slavery and create for Black men and women a sense of autonomy over their lives both inside and outside the home.

As members of female antislavery societies, Black women abolitionists provided a crucial link between the practical needs of the community and the ideology of the movement. Their presence in formulating the agenda and disbursing funds was particularly important in interracial societies, in which White members were often unaware of the particular needs of the Black community. In these societies, Black members helped focus support on projects that were considered vital to the survival and advancement of the Black community.

The existence of both segregated and interracial antislavery societies, however, illustrates the tenuous alliance that existed between Black and White abolitionists. Many Black and White women saw a value in working together, despite objections to social mixing between the races. But, women of both races were soon made painfully aware that although their organizations presented a rare opportunity to challenge racism, they were also centers of conflict that revealed the limits of cooperation by either consciously or unconsciously replicating the racism that existed in the society at large. In an effort to avoid racism from their White colleagues and to meet the needs of their Black neighbors more effectively, Black women also gathered together to form all-Black societies.

Nevertheless, Black women's organizational patterns were not simply responses to the actions of others. As activists in either all-Black or interracial antislavery societies, their activism reflected a long-standing devotion to the cause of freedom and equality.

Notes

1. *The Liberator* (November 17, 1832), p. 183.

2. *The Liberator* (November 17, 1832), p. 183.

3. The exact numbers of these societies is difficult to ascertain, for many were short-lived and left few records. See Daniel Perlman, "Organizations of the Free Negro in New York City, 1800-1860," *Journal of Negro History, 56* (July 1971), pp. 181-182.

4. For excellent studies on Black community organizations and institutions, see Gary B. Nash, *Forging Freedom: The Formation of Philadelphia's Black Community, 1720-1840* (Cambridge, MA: Harvard University Press, 1988); Leonard P. Curry, *The Free Black in Urban America, 1800-1850: The Shadow of a Dream* (Chicago: University of Chicago Press, 1981); James O. Horton & Lois E. Horton, *Black Bostonians: Family Life and Community in the Antebellum North* (New York: Holmes & Meier, 1979); Lois F. Horton, "Community Organization and Social Activism: Black Boston and the Antislavery Movement," *Sociological Inquiry, 55* (Spring 1985), pp. 182-199; David M. Katzman, *Before the Ghetto: Black Detroit in the Nineteenth Century* (Urbana: University of Illinois Press, 1973); Jane Pease & William H. Pease, *Black Utopia: Negro Communal Experiments in America* (Madison: State Historical Society of Wisconsin, 1963); Daniel Perlman, "Organizations of the Free Negro in New York City, 1800-1860," *Journal of Negro History, 56* (July 1971), pp. 181-197; and Robin Winks, *The Blacks in Canada* (Montreal: McGill-Queen's University Press, 1971).

5. There are numerous books on this subject. See Merton L. Dillon, *The Abolitionists: The Growth of a Dissenting Minority* (New York: Norton, 1974); James Brewer Stewart, *Holy Warriors* (New York: Hill & Wang, 1976).

6. See Dillon, *The Abolitionists*.

7. Benjamin Quarles, *Black Abolitionists* (New York: Oxford University Press, 1969), pp. 3-5.

8. Dillon, *The Abolitionists*, p. 53.

9. In December 1833, delegates from three major antislavery contingents in Philadelphia, New England, and New York met at a convention in Philadelphia to form the American Anti-Slavery Society. See Dillon, *The Abolitionists*, p. 54.

10. Charles B. Ray, "Female Education," *Colored American* (March 18, 1837), *Black Abolitionist Papers*, Reel 1, fr. 1008.

11. *North Star* (March 17, 1848).

12. See Barbara Welter, "The Cult of True Womanhood, 1820-60," *American Quarterly, 18* (Summer 1966), pp. 151-174.

13. *A Statistical Inquiry Into the Conditions of the People of Color of the City and Districts of Philadelphia* (Philadelphia: Kite & Walton, 1849), p. 18.

14. Lorenzo Greene & Carter G. Woodson, *The Negro Wage Earner* (Washington, DC, 1930), pp. 3-5. See also Dorothy Sterling, ed., *We Are Your Sisters: Black Women in the Nineteenth Century* (New York: Norton, 1984).

15. Harriet Hayden to Maria Weston Chapman, New York, November 27, 1843, *Black Abolitionist Papers*, Reel 4, fr. 0705.

16. Martin R. Delany, *The Condition, Elevation, Emigration, and Destiny of the Colored People in the United States* (Philadelphia, 1852; reprint ed., New York: Arno Press, 1968), pp. 95-96.

17. Dorothy Sterling, ed., *We Are Your Sisters*, p. 103.

18. Sterling, *We Are Your Sisters*, p. 131.

19. Sarah Grimke to Gerrit Smith & Mrs. (Ann Carroll Fitzhugh) Smith, Belleville, NJ, July 11, 1842. Gerrit Smith Papers, Reel 10.

20. Anne Warren Weston to Mr. & Mrs. H(enry) G. Chapan, Weymouth, May 18, 1841, Boston Public Library; Lydia Maria Child to Jonathan Phillips, January 23, 1838, Schlesinger Library.

21. Quarles, *Black Abolitionists*, p. 94.

22. *The Liberator* (January 4, 1834), p. 3.

23. Anne Warren Weston to Deborah Weston, Boston, April 18, 1837, Boston Public Library.

24. Amy Swerdlow, "Abolition's Conservative Sisters: The Ladies New York Anti-Slavery Society, 1834-40." Paper presented at the Third Berkshire Conference on the History of Women, Bryn Mawr College, June 1976.

25. Sarah McCrummell's husband was James McCrummell, a barber and dentist, who was one of the three Black men to take part in the proceedings to form the AAS; Hetty Burr's husband, John P. Burr, was a Black merchant.

26. PFASS, minutes, Pennsylvania Abolition Society Papers (PASP), Historical Society of Pennsylvania (HSP).

27. PFASS, minutes, January 1, 1840. Sixth Annual Meeting.

28. PFASS, minutes, March 12, 1840.

29. PFASS, minutes, March 12, 1840.

30. Edward T. James, ed., *Notable American Women*, Vol. 1 (Cambridge, MA: Harvard University Press, 1971), p. 511; PFASS, minutes, September 29, 1836 and April 19, 1841.

31. PFASS, Education Committee, minutes, 1841.

32. PFASS, minutes, January 14, 1847.

33. PFASS, minutes, September 9, 1841.

34. PFASS, minutes, June 12, 1845.

35. PFASS, minutes, April 10, 1856.

36. PFASS, minutes, October 8, 1846.

37. Delany, *Condition*, p. 123. Nancy Prince was an evangelical reformer who had lived in the courts of Czars Alexander I and Nicholas I with her husband, a footman of the court. She later returned to Boston as a widow and directed her reform activities to improving the condition of Blacks in Jamaica. While in Boston, she raised money for her Jamaica project in addition to attending BFASS meetings. See Nancy Prince, *A Black Woman's Odyssey Through Russia and Jamaica: The Narrative of Nancy Prince*, with an introduction by Ronald G. Walters (New York: Marcus Wiener, 1990).

38. James O. Horton & Lois F. Horton, *Black Bostonians*, p. 94.

39. Malcolm Lovell, ed., *Two Quaker Sisters: From the Original Diaries of Elizabeth Buffum Chace and Lucy Buffum Lovell* (New York: Liveright Publishing, 1937), pp. 118-119.

40. Anne Warren Weston to Deborah Weston, October 22, 1836, Boston Public Library.

41. Sarah Hopper Emerson, ed., *The Life of Abby Hopper Gibbons Told Chiefly Through Her Correspondence*, (New York: G. P. Putnam, 1896), vol. 1, p. 99.

42. Amy Matilda Williams Cassey hailed from a distinguished activist family. Her father, the Reverend Peter Williams, was a respected Episcopal clergyman from New York and her first husband, Joseph Cassey, was a Black businessman and community leader in Philadelphia. Upon his death, she married Charles Lenox Remond of the respected Remond family from Salem, MA. See Julie Winch, *Philadelphia's Black Elite* (Philadelphia: Temple University Press, 1988), and Delany, *Condition*, pp. 94-95.

43. *North Star* (March 3, 1849).

44. *North Star* (July 13, 1849); *Black Abolitionist Papers*, Reel 6, fr. 0044.

45. Sterling, *We Are Your Sisters*, 410n.

46. The "woman questions" was not the only issue that divided the abolitionists. Dissenters also disagreed with Garrison's condemnation of the churches and his universalist approach to social reform. See Dillon, *The Abolitionists*.

47. See Ellen C. Dubois, *Feminism and Suffrage: The Emergence of an Independent Women's Movement in America, 1848-69* (Ithaca, NY: Cornell University Press, 1978).

48. Willie Mae Coleman, "Keeping the Faith and Disturbing the Peace," unpublished doctoral dissertation, University of California, Irvine, 1982, p. 18.

49. Colored Citizens of Ohio, State Convention, Columbus, January 10-18, 1849, minutes and addresses, p. 15.

50. British Banner, November 20, 1855, in *Black Abolitionist Papers*, Reel 9, fr. 0938.

3. Black Women and the NAACP, 1909-1922
An Encounter With Race, Class, and Gender

DOROTHY C. SALEM

Modern racial reform movements emerged during the last decade of the 19th century when the system of racial segregation materialized in explicit laws and racial ideologies received popular, scientific, and political support. Social reformers went against the predominant legal and ideological trends as they established organizations to improve the legal, political, economic, and social conditions of African Americans. Yet, most of these social reformers carried some prevailing racial, class, and gender attitudes into their mission to help African Americans. The presence of Black women in social reform organizations during this period depicted the complex interrelationships of race, class, and gender. This is a case study of Black women in the NAACP during the initial years of its formation as they encountered and responded to issues of race, class, and gender.

The late 19th- and early 20th-century era was ripe for reform. Lynching was becoming increasingly cruel and barbaric. Race riots in New Orleans in 1874; Wilmington, NC, in 1898; Statesboro, GA, in 1904; Atlanta in 1906; and Brownsville, TX, in 1906 reflected the racial conflict in the South. In New York and Philadelphia the increasing number of attacks on Blacks by crowds of White males demonstrated the racial hatreds of northern urban residents. Twenty years after the end of Reconstruction, Blacks earned their living through domestic or personal service and agriculture, most as tenants or sharecroppers. Their children were less likely to attend school and six times more likely to be illiterate than their White counterparts. Per capita expenditures per pupil and teacher were less for all levels of education of the race.

This context pressed leaders into action. Lacking financial resources and political rights, leaders echoed the values of self-help and racial solidarity. They formed the Afro-American League/Council (1890), the National Association of Colored Women [NACW] (1896), and the Niagara Movement (1905) as national attempts to protect their rights and improve conditions. Ultimately both male-led attempts at national racial solidarity failed due to lack of mass support and funds and to factionalism, isolation from the White power structure, and inexperience of the leadership. The NACW, however, continued to expand in numbers and in influence as women increasingly tapped the resources of the community and as the era encouraged women into active reform. The failures served as learning experiences. When faced with worsening conditions, the leaders saw the importance of interracial cooperation with the White social reformers of the Progressive era.

These White reformers were upper-middle-class patricians, many of whom had devoted their lives to improving conditions for Blacks, immigrants, and the poor. Although less likely to experience the fears and prejudices of lower-class Whites, who competed with these groups for jobs, housing, and services, the patrician reformers were not totally free from prevailing stereotypes and attitudes about race, class, and gender.

The National Association for the Advancement of Colored People was founded as a reaction of these White reformers to racial injustice. When a bloody race riot gripped the city of Springfield, IL, in August 1908, a small group of White reformers issued a call for "all believers in democracy to join in a national conference for the discussion of present evils, the voicing of protests and the renewal of the struggle for civil and political liberty."[1] Sixty prominent men and women signed "The Call," which appeared in Oswald Garrison Villard's New York *Evening Post*.

Founding Mothers

The initial group of signatories included many women, a reflection of an era that increasingly utilized the time and talents of women, whose morality was thought necessary to reform society. One third of the signatures belonged to women representing leadership in suffrage, settlement-house work, prison reform, labor unionism, pacifism, and child labor activism. The majority of the male and female signatories had careers in reform and charity causes and represented upper-middle-class patrician family backgrounds.

Black female participation during the early years of the NAACP served as an example of the difficulties faced when well-meaning White, upper-class reformers work with minority men and women, most of whom lacked the special privileges of their White counterparts. Only two of the women signatories represented the Black community, Ida B. Wells-Barnett of Chicago and Mary Church Terrell of Washington, DC.

Both women had national reputations as speakers or organizers for racial and gender issues.

Wells-Barnett and Terrell had many interests in common yet differed in background, leadership style, and organizational tactics. Wells-Barnett was born in Holly Springs, MS, where she attended the segregated Rust College. After attaining a teaching position in Memphis, she purchased a first-class ticket for her journey. Due to the Jim Crow policies in public transportation, the conductor tried to eject her forcibly from her seat in the first-class car to ride in the Jim Crow car. Always the fighter, Ida Wells physically fought her removal. When that failed, she endured her humiliation, later bringing suit against the railroad company for the racial discrimination. Once in Memphis, she combined her teaching with journalism. Outspoken on issues of racial and class discrimination against and within the Black community, Wells soon found such views threatened her job. The lynching of three middle-class Black men launched her career in the antilynching movement and in journalism and brought her into closer contact with social reformers of the women's movements for suffrage and temperance.

Mary Church Terrell also called Memphis home as the daughter of the first Black millionaire, Robert Church. Her privileged, interracial education at Oberlin College and in Europe prepared her to enter reform activities on an equal footing with her White counterparts. After completing her education, Terrell encountered the gender and class biases of her own father, who threatened to disinherit her for accepting a teaching position to share her privileged education with her race, an action that went against his belief that "ladies" should not work outside the home. Although they shared race and class perspectives, gender ideals provoked conflict within her father's home.

Both Wells and Terrell combined race, class, and gender in their activities. Both actively participated in the national efforts for racial reform in the Afro-American Council and the National Association of Colored Women as leaders, speakers, and liaisons with local reform organizations. Both were active in interracial organizations. Terrell was one of the charter members of the Constitution League founded by John Milholland, White reformer and philanthropist, to protect the constitutional rights of Black Americans. She was also a frequent participant and speaker in the New York Social Reform Club and the National American Woman Suffrage Association. A speaker on the Chautauqua circuit, Terrell was well known to White audiences, as was Wells known as a speaker against lynching.

After her marriage to Ferdinand Barnett, a Chicago attorney, Ida B. Wells-Barnett received criticism from Susan B. Anthony, the White leader of the woman's suffrage movement. Anthony felt Wells-Barnett was particularly skilled and suited for her role in the antilynching movement. This "calling" would undoubtedly be compromised by the responsibilities of marriage and family. But Wells-Barnett proved

Anthony wrong. Instead of international travel, she remained close to her family and focused her activism on local reform with such White Chicagoans as Celia Parker Wooley, Jane Addams, Florence Kelley, and Sophinisba Breckinridge in the Frederick Douglass Center. She participated in the National American Woman Suffrage Association and occasionally stayed at the home of Susan B. Anthony while traveling on the antilynching lecture circuit.

Although both women married lawyers, their husbands' careers followed different paths and political affiliations. Ferdinand Barnett joined his wife in criticizing Booker T. Washington through the columns of their newspaper, the Chicago *Conservator*. Robert Terrell, in contrast, received direct benefits from Washington's influence on his federal appointment as municipal judge in the District of Columbia. Yet, Mary Church Terrell became more open in her criticism of Washington's leadership as race relations deteriorated. These Black women joined wealthy White signatories in extending an invitation to a thousand leaders to attend the first national conference in New York.[2]

The White women signatories represented families of wealth and social concern. These women included Jane Addams, founder of the Hull House Settlement in Chicago and a female reform network of full- and part-time residents; Florence Kelley, founder of the Consumer's League; Julia Lathrop, lecturer at the Chicago School of Civics and Philanthropy; Sophinisba Breckinridge, Edith Abbott, and Grace Abbott, social service activists; Ellen Gates Starr, cofounder of Hull House; and Alice Hamilton, public health crusader. Leaders of the Women's Trade Union League, such as the director of the University of Chicago Settlement, Mary E. McDowell, and Margaret Dreier, Leonora O'Reilly, Kate Claghorn, and Helen Marot, joined with New Yorkers Jane E. Robbins, a public health physician and director of New York's College Settlement; Lillian Wald, founder of the Henry Street Settlement; and Mary White Ovington, leader in the Consumer's League, Social Reform Club, and founder of Greenpoint Settlement, to influence other Americans to attend the conference focusing on racial injustices. Leaders in women's education, such as Mary E. Wooley, president of Mount Holyoke College, joined with wealthy White social researchers Susan P. Wharton and Mrs. Rodman Wharton of Philadelphia and Helen Stokes of New York to discuss ways to improve urban conditions and injustices. Together these women used their reform networks to organize for racial protection.

Class and Gender Converge

The class nature of the founding meeting was evident in the list of signatories and in those invited.[3] Because most Black leaders were tied to jobs as teachers, lecturers, journalists, or ministers, the time and expenses for travel limited the participation of most Black women, who possessed "no entrenched and comfortable security in even their achieved class status."[4] Jane Addams organized a fund-raising committee to raise money to cover the travel expenses of Ida B. Wells-Barnett. Hence, the time and travel costs resulted in a Black presence that reflected the Northeast in general, and the New York-Brooklyn area specifically.

As the National Negro Committee met from May 31-June 1, 1909, a subcommittee compiled a list of people to serve on the Committee of Forty on Permanent Organization. Only three Black women made that list: Wells-Barnett, Terrell, and Maria Baldwin. Baldwin had less national recognition but her prominence in Boston, a center of radical agitation, provided influence with leading Black and White reformers. As the head of the Agassiz School for children of the White elite, Baldwin held the "most distinguished position achieved by a person of Negro descent in the teaching world of America."[5] She was known to White reformers in New York and Boston through her addresses to prominent audiences in those cities and through her ties to the Boston Black leadership with a history of interracial cooperation and "elitist militancy."[6]

These three Black women used their racial and gender awareness to influence the representation on further committees. The Committee of Forty on Permanent Organization recommended that a National Committee of One Hundred elect an Executive Committee of 30 members from its membership. Thereafter, Black women gained influence through the service of New York clubwomen Frances R. Keyser and Maritcha R. Lyons on the Committee of One Hundred and on its subcommittee to select 16 people to fill vacancies on the Committee of One Hundred. Keyser and Lyons selected sister clubwomen from other areas of the country: Josephine Silone Yates, club leader from Kansas City, MO; Carrie Clifford, club leader from Cleveland prior to the Washington appointment of her husband, H. H. Clifford; and Mary B. Talbert of Buffalo, president of the New York State Federation of Colored Women. Through the club network, Keyser and Lyons expanded the representation of Black women.[7] Talbert, for example, was not even known to W.E.B. Du Bois, a frequent consultant about appointments. When asked about Talbert in a letter, he recommended a White reformer for the post, indicating no information about Talbert, who eventually went on to the presidency of the National Association of Colored Women (NACW) and became one of the most active organizers in the NAACP and a recipient of the Spingarn Award. Du Bois did know Clifford through her role in the auxiliary of the Niagara Movement.[8]

By the middle of 1910 the Black female presence was apparent. Frances Keyser, Terrell, and Wells-Barnett served on the 21-member Executive Committee with 5 White women. The 66-member General Committee included Baldwin, Lyons, Talbert, and New Bedford club leader Elizabeth Carter. This female reform network continued to expand

Black female involvement, which, in turn, spread the philosophy, raised money, and increased membership of the NAACP. In so doing, Black women played a significant role in tying the NAACP to the communities and, in turn, created a Black-led NAACP.[9]

Gender Roles Emerge

Black women served in traditionally female roles as proselytizers and fund-raisers for the NAACP. Mary Talbert had the Buffalo Phyllis Wheatley Club sponsor lectures by NAACP leaders Mrs. Henry Villard and W.E.B. Du Bois, and served as a speaker for the National Convention of Odd Fellows in Baltimore. Maritcha Lyons described the NAACP goals to the Northeastern Federation of Colored Women's Clubs. Delegates to the National Association of Colored Women biennial in Louisville heard speeches by Wells-Barnett and by Frances Blascoer, White executive secretary of the NAACP. In a 1910 fund-raiser at the Berkeley Theatre, Mary Church Terrell lectured and soprano Madame Azalia Hackley entertained to produce what Du Bois called a financial and propaganda success. To expand both political and fund-raising potential, the women went beyond the Black community to tap the White reform networks. Terrell joined Brooklyn YWCA leader Addie W. Hunton in lectures to the Society of Friends and the Society of Ethical Culture. Bostonian Mary Wilson traveled in the Northeast giving speeches to interested White audiences.

The Black women used the columns of *The Crisis* to expand reader awareness of racial and gender issues. Addie Hunton initiated a regular column entitled "Women's Clubs" in May 1911 to chronicle the social services of Black women in the communities. Hunton joined such other Black women contributors as Mary Church Terrell, Carrie Clifford, Mary Talbert, and Adella Hunt Logan, member of the National Women Suffrage Association and wife of Tuskegee Institute's treasurer, Warren Logan. In these columns, the Black women criticized the subtle and overt forms of racial discrimination in White reform movements and persuaded African Americans to take on a more active role in woman's suffrage, the war effort, and other reforms.[10]

The impact of Black female participation during these early years was of primary importance in the organization of NAACP branches. Mary White Ovington felt this role so important she said, "Our Advancement Association would be a mere National Negro Committee but for the organized work of the women in the branches."[11] From 1910 to 1915, they reflected sex roles typical of grassroots organizations in other social movements[12] in that they built the organization and membership through their participation as active, voluntary, and unpaid field-workers. After a solid support base was created in the Black communities, the official positions then went to men of the race, who had greater access to skills and networks restricted to women. Analysis of this initial organizing role provides an explicit view of the complex interconnections of race, class, and gender.

Black female field-workers traveled throughout the major urban areas, supported by commissions received from enlisting members and selling subscriptions to *The Crisis*. They often combined agendas in these travels. For example, Mary Talbert combined her organizing activities for the National Association of Colored Women with her NAACP organizing. The "first field worker,"[13] Kathryn Johnson, a public school teacher, started in Kansas City as an agent of *The Crisis*. Although her commissions on branch memberships and subscriptions barely covered her expenses, her commitment to the NAACP ideals spurred her on. Through Texas and Louisiana, Johnson encountered threats of violence and community ignorance about the NAACP. The nurturance of hope and pride became preconditions for branch development in these areas.

Johnson's success in the Northeast and Midwest led to concentration in these areas and to the exposure of class biases by the Black and White women of the NAACP. In the Midwest, Johnson relied on Black women and Black institutions. In 1914 she organized a branch at the Lincoln Colored Home, founded and managed by the Black women of Springfield, IL. At this branch, all the officers were women, a reflection of their institutional leadership.

Black institutions established links with the communities. Johnson spoke to organizations of pullman porters, teachers, mail clerks, and neighborhood activists. Due to her successes in Illinois, Missouri, and Iowa, she became a "reimbursed" field agent in February 1915. Her commissions on memberships and subscriptions had been enhanced by the NAACP's payment of expenses—one dollar per day.

By summer 1915, Johnson had organized eight branches, most of which had White members, a strongly encouraged goal of the national office. Johnson tried to adjust goals and methods to fit individual community contexts, however. Her experiences had taught her that each branch had to assume its own form and direction. In cities such as Philadelphia, Black communities did not want Whites as their leaders. In other cities, only White leadership would produce a following. Therefore, Johnson felt that Whites should not be "forced" into branches where Blacks neither wanted them nor trusted them.[14] By fall 1915, Johnson received commendation for her fieldwork; another field agent, Nettie Asberry, newspaper editor in Tacoma, WA, had not yet reported success in the Northwest.

Class Conflicts Arise

The steady growth of Black female influence, however, did not prevent conflict within the NAACP. Occasionally the class biases of both Black and White leadership became apparent. Depending on the individual personality of the woman encountering these biases, responses ranged from head-on conflict to endurance while forging on toward the goal. As time went on, many women used the NAACP as a vehicle for attacking these biases in an organized fashion. But first, the women created a strong Black membership to serve as a foundation for moving Black leaders into place. Once in place, the Black leaders increasingly called attention to the problems both within the NAACP and in the overall social environment.

The difficulties encountered by Kathryn Johnson in 1915 demonstrated the overt class biases in the NAACP leadership. During the remainder of the year, Johnson worked with Mary Wilson, wife of Boston branch president Butler Wilson. Johnson's success at organizing Blacks, combined with her frank appraisals of people and situations, conflicted sharply with the diplomatic talents and interracial abilities of Mary Wilson. Although Johnson had little faith in White direction of a Black movement, Wilson's experiences in the interracial Boston community produced a woman accustomed to working with White leaders and reared in the ideology of full equality. Her branch organizations throughout Pennsylvania, Ohio, and New York relied upon church organizations and interracial leadership. Her work was so effective that May Childs Nerney, the White secretary of the NAACP, called on Wilson to revitalize the branch in Orange, NJ.

The impact of female participation as field-workers and branch participants did not lead to greater influence in the national headquarters. Mary Church Terrell served on the Board of Directors in 1912-1914. When White journalist Mary D. Maclean died in July 1912, Brooklyn physician Dr. Verina Morton Jones completed Maclean's term and received reappointment until 1918. Despite little representation in the boardroom, Black women nevertheless received recognition for their organizational and leadership roles in the communities. The growth of Black branch membership stimulated a move for greater visibility in leadership. By the time the NAACP held its annual meeting in January 1916, May Childs Nerney reported on the progress of branch organization and expressed hopes that soon the "whole burden"[15] might soon be carried by the "victims" themselves. She recommended the NAACP appoint a full-time field organizer to assume some of the burdens of the secretary. Before resigning, Nerney recommended Jessie Fauset and others for that position. The timing seemed conducive for a Black woman to move into that position, based on their successful careers in field organization and branch leadership.

Several Black women qualified for national leadership roles. For her successful fieldwork, Kathryn Johnson received commendation at the annual meeting. Other organizers such as Bostonian Mary Wilson; Susan Elizabeth Frazier of the Brooklyn branch; Sarah Brown, representative to the Baptist Women's District Convention; and Nannie

Burroughs, founder of the National Training School for Women and Girls in Washington, received the praises of White leaders for their proselytizing and fund-raising skills on the part of the NAACP. The efforts of these Black women reflected the crucial needs for White support, and more importantly, the traditional reliance of emerging organizations on women for organizing and fund-raising.

Because the position of national field secretary required an ability to court White favor, present a favorable image to audiences of both races, and behave diplomatically in a variety of political and social contexts, the choice of the NAACP was extremely important to the fledgling racial advancement organization. Mary White Ovington, founding member and Acting Secretary of the NAACP, joined with Mary Wilson to advise the new national secretary, Royal Freeman Nash, that Kathryn Johnson lacked the "Personality and intellect to interest either the more cultured members of the colored race or the white friends"[16] of the NAACP. Ovington continued her persuasive critique of Johnson, saying the NAACP needed a field-worker "whose personality is big enough to get our propaganda across before just the audiences which [denied Johnson] . . . a hearing."[17] Nash confirmed the assessment after hearing Johnson speak in Cleveland, where her favorable audience response was attributed to "the almost exclusive blackness of those audiences [with only] . . . two or three strong white members."[18]

Johnson's reliance on the Black community, her conflicts with the Black elite, and her direct style of communication led to her demise in the NAACP. Unlike Wilson, Hunton, Clifford, Terrell, and Talbert, Johnson was unable or unwilling to put on the "mask" to gain cooperation from the Whites in the organization or in the communities. Coming from a segregationist town, Johnson lacked the cosmopolitan skills needed by the NAACP. She issued a defensive series of letters to Royal Nash in which she accused such elite Black women as Mary Wilson, Mary Talbert, and Addie Dickerson, Philadelphia club leader, of undermining her position and accomplishments. Her success with ordinary Black community people and refusal to bow to White leaders had led to her downfall. By the end of the summer, Kathryn Johnson's dismissal was final.

James Weldon Johnson: Bridge Builder

The NAACP's decision on the choice for the National Field Secretary position reflected race, class, and gender concerns. Nash acknowledged five candidates under consideration for the position, three of whom were specifically named: William Pickens, graduate of Yale University, dean of Morgan College, and former president of the Talladega College branch of the NAACP; fellow Black academician John Hope,

president of the Atlanta Baptist College (Morehouse); and Elizabeth
Freeman, a White, women's suffrage leader and the investigator of the
Waco lynching. The other two candidates were not mentioned, but
probably included the names of the candidate selected by the NAACP's
Nominating Committee, Mary E. Jackson, and the successful candi-
date, James Weldon Johnson.

Although the official committee had selected a Black woman for
the position, the decision process that resulted in the appointment of
James Weldon Johnson embodied the race, class, and gender politics of
both the NAACP and the societal context within which the organization operated. The NAACP assembled a national gathering of Black
leaders at the Amenia, NY, estate of the chairman of the NAACP Board
of Directors, Joel Spingarn. From August 24 to 26, 1916, the Amenia
Conference provided a forum for the discussion of racial problems and
solutions. The conference sought productive discourse made easier
following the death of Booker T. Washington in 1915. Mary Terrell, a
leader with a foot in both the Washington and the radical camps, felt
the meeting responded to the need for "colored people of all shades and
varieties of opinion to thrash out their differences and unite on some
definite programs of work."[19]

Although Black women received recognition for their efforts, the
NAACP did not offer the position of National Secretary to a woman.
W.E.B. Du Bois, editor of *The Crisis,* recognized the importance of the
women, saying, "We had the women there to complete the real conference."[20] Those visible in attendance included Mary Terrell, Mary Talbert,
Addie Hunton, Mary Wilson, Nannie Burroughs, Dr. Verina Morton
Jones, and Lucy Laney. Visibly absent were the female field-workers
and branch leaders: Kathryn Johnson, still battling to save her job;
Nettie Asberry, the Northwest organizer; Agnes Adams, Boston branch
leader; Carrie Clifford, Washington branch leader; and the choice of
the nominating committee, Mary E. Jackson.

At the Amenia Conference, James Weldon Johnson impressed the
Chairman of the Board, Joel Spingarn, with his speaking and negotiating skills. Johnson's performance on the panel, "A Working Programme
for the Future," demonstrated his value to the NAACP. Johnson had
lived in the South and had established a career in New York. The
NAACP's goal to increase the Black membership and branches in the
South could be well served by a man from the South. Also, the need
was for a person comfortable with government, legal, artistic, and church
leaders. Instead of rewarding an experienced field-worker, the White
male leadership of the NAACP chose Johnson, a man for all situations.

For Johnson to ascend to the position, a Black woman had to be
denied the position—creating an awkward exercise of power politics.
The December meeting of the board of directors heard the "Report of
the Committee on National Organizer." Mary White Ovington, chairman of the committee, read the report, which recommended Mary E.

Jackson for the position to begin January 1917 with a salary of $2,000 a year plus expenses. The selection of Jackson reflected the influence of Black female elites within the NAACP. Jackson had well-established contacts in the national club movement, the YWCA, and White reform circles. Her work with the Labor Department in Rhode Island had established her experience with government. Almost certainly her close friendship with Mary Wilson provided the necessary access through which the Black female elites were able to influence the White women leaders at the national headquarters.

Not all White men opposed the appointment of a Black woman. Board members Paul Kennaday and William Sinclair moved for the approval of the report. But the outcome had already been decided. After discussion, their motion lost. Charles H. Studin moved, was seconded, and voted that James Weldon Johnson be appointed. The Chairman (Spingarn) and one other (Nash) were empowered to negotiate a contract with Johnson. Only one dissenting vote (probably Ovington's) opposed the move to negate the recommendations of the official nominating committee and put in the candidate personally selected by the chairman of the board of directors at the Amenia Conference. In fact, James Weldon Johnson had already accepted the position in a letter to Spingarn dated November 5, 1916. The power of White males overruled the power of the White female chairman of the nominating committee, Mary White Ovington. A Black male leader was preferable to the nominating committee's selection of a Black female.[21]

The selection of a male leader of Johnson's breadth was predictable. The women of the NAACP were hampered by the multiple role expectations and responsibilities that restricted women of their era. Priorities of husbands, homes, and other reform interests competed for the time and energy devoted to the NAACP. Mary Wilson aided her husband in the Boston branch while fulfilling her reform and fieldwork responsibilities. Nettie Asberry combined home and club responsibilities with that of editor of a Tacoma newspaper and NAACP Northwest field organizer. Her geographical isolation from the New York national headquarters made even occasional visits an unrealistic drain on time and personal finances. Mary Church Terrell, an accustomed, frequent traveler of substantial financial circumstances, had to limit her activities in the NAACP to help her husband survive as the only Black judge of the municipal court in Washington, DC, during the political nadir of the Wilson years. Even New York residents Mary Talbert and Addie Hunton admitted to home conflicts with their active field organizing. Both women were active in other organizations, such as the YWCA, NACW, and local charities, which lessened their available time. Addie Hunton was able to expand her NAACP role only after resigning her YWCA role and her husband's death. Talbert, too, took on more responsibilities after fulfilling her presidency of the

NACW. By 1920, both women ascended to higher positions in fieldwork in the NAACP.

Although James Weldon Johnson received the "star" position as National Field Secretary, Black women continued their strong role. Johnson focused on branch development in the Dixie District, as Mary Talbert developed branches in the Southwest. In 1916, 68 branches existed in the North and West, but only 3 in the South. By 1919, of 310 branches, 131 were southern. Talbert's 1918 report to John R. Shillady, the newly appointed secretary of the NAACP, illustrated the dedication and commitment of the female field organizer. Talbert's 87-day trip carried her 7,162 miles, resulting in the formation of nine new branches in Texas and Louisiana, six campaigns to increase branch membership, and lectures to 57 local groups, 19 universities and schools, and three state conventions. Using the existing female support network to advertise the NAACP, Talbert worked through the NACW, Women's War Councils, and the YWCA to get membership and influence in the community. Talbert likewise used her "other" activities as a guise through which she might gain information for the NAACP in the South. During her travels to raise money for the Liberty Loan Drives during World War I, Talbert gathered evidence for the NAACP about railroad accommodations and conditions of travel for Blacks.[22]

Other women of the NAACP used their war roles to enhance the information and goals of the NAACP. During spring 1919, Kathryn Johnson, Addie Hunton, and Helen Curtis, wife of the minister to Liberia, went to France to attend to the needs of the 200,000 Black troops. Hunton and Kathryn Johnson recorded for the NAACP the discrimination against Black soldiers—their confinement to camps to prevent contact with French women, the slander by White officers, and the American-originated propaganda about the Black male anatomy. Hunton and Talbert used their affiliation with the YWCA to attend and report back to the NAACP on the Pan-African Congress in Paris, February 21, 1919, and to "tell of our treatment over here."[23] The International Congress of Women in Zurich, May 13-17, 1919, provided the platform for Mary Church Terrell to bring to a global forum of female representatives reports about the racial difficulties in the United States.

New Woman and New Negro:
Postwar Prime Movers

When the women returned to the United States, demobilization had hastened social and economic tensions into the Red Summer of 1919. By year's end, 77 Blacks had been lynched, including 11 soldiers. The war not only developed a heightened racial consciousness, but also enabled Black women to extend their organizational networks. The armistice allowed the Black women to refocus their attentions on the chronic American problem of lynching. In May 1919 the NAACP sponsored a National Conference on Lynching that drew more than 2,500 men and women to Carnegie Hall to hear speeches by Black and White leaders. Before disbanding, the conference prepared "An Address to the Nation on Lynching," signed by leading citizens including an ex-president of the United States, an attorney general, seven state governors, a university president, and leading reformers.[24]

Talbert became the guiding force behind the postwar mobilization of Black women against lynching. She relied on the extensive club structure to extract personnel, imagination, money, and volunteer activity to spread the information and create a political cadre for the NAACP. Through the NAACP, Black women raised money to fund investigations, generate publicity, and sponsor public meetings to increase public support for the Dyer federal antilynching bill. Within a few years, Talbert mobilized Black women into an ad hoc group for fund-raising and publicity. Known as the Anti-Lynching Crusaders after July 15, 1922, the women worked with religious fervor in their crusade to unite one million women in the suppression of lynching. The staff received no pay; every cent went for antilynching activities. With the help of supportive White female reformers, the Black women created the foundation for a movement against lynching and racial violence that finally came to fruition in the 1930s with the founding of the Association of Southern Women for the Prevention of Lynching.[25]

During this period, the emergence of both the New Negro and the New Woman influenced the role of women in the NAACP. Women continued to organize branches throughout the Northeast, Midwest, and Southwest. Their importance to branch development and as regional organizers led to the NAACP's reward of appointments to offices. During the postwar era, both Nannie Burroughs and Mary Talbert served on the Board of Directors. Talbert became one of the six vice presidents of the NAACP and winner of the Spingarn medal. By 1920, James Weldon Johnson had assumed the position of acting secretary of the NAACP. As Johnson moved into that role, a Black woman, Addie Hunton, assumed his former position as national field organizer. Mary White Ovington's advice to include more Black women in leadership positions fell on receptive ears. The field organizer position passed from Hunton to another energetic proselytizer for the NAACP, Daisy Lampkin, who served as the Regional Field Secretary (1930-1935) and National Field Secretary (1935-1947). In the NAACP, similar moves of Black men into leadership positions brought women along in their ascent. When the Reverend R. W. Bagnall, formerly the leader of the Detroit branch, took over as the director of branches in 1920, Catherine Lealtad, a young woman with experience in the YWCA, became the assistant director of branches.

In the NAACP, Black women maintained a tradition as prime movers. Overlooked at first by the White patricians and by the Black male leadership, Black women active in the NAACP slowly expanded the participation of their sisters through a methodical attempt to include Black women from various points of the country. They in turn brought others into the fold. At first they received no salaries to travel throughout the country, organizing branches and obtaining subscribers to *The Crisis*. Their initial commitment to the ideals of the NAACP produced results that eventually pushed the predominately White-led organization to begin appointing Black leaders. Although a Black woman failed to receive the office of National Field Secretary in 1916, by 1920 that position did go to a Black woman. Black women have continued effective leadership in that role. Their leadership as the mobilizers of antilynching campaigns, as investigators, as administrators, as branch directors, and as fund-raisers made the NAACP organizationally dependent on their energies and abilities. The dynamics of race, class, and gender, though influential in the early years, failed to thwart Black women in their attempt to achieve the goals of the NAACP. As extensions of the Black community, the Black women helped the NAACP become *the* advancement organization for the race, and, in turn, the organization provided recognition for their efforts. Their leadership lessened the presence of race, gender, and class insensitivities by including leaders who had experienced such double and/or triple discrimination. The consciousness of Black women helped to raise the level of sensitivity within the NAACP.

Notes

1. Charles Flint Kellogg, *NAACP: The National Association for the Advancement of Colored People* (Baltimore, MD: Johns Hopkins University Press, 1967), p. 298.
2. For the most helpful information about the role of Black women in early racial advancement organizations, one must turn to contemporary sources. W.E.B. Du Bois's books *The Autobiography of W.E.B. Du Bois* (New York: International Publishers, 1968) and *Darkwater: Voices From Within the Veil* (New York: Schocken, 1920) and his articles in *The Crisis* demonstrate his philosophical support of an active role for Black women within the social reforms. His correspondence in the Du Bois Papers (University of Massachusetts, Amherst) also demonstrates a consistent interaction and support for leading Black women. Mary White Ovington's *Portraits in Color* (New York: Viking, 1927), *The Walls Came Tumbling Down* (New York: Harcourt, Brace (reprint ed., Arno Press, New York, 1969), and *Half a Man: The Status of the Negro in New York* (New York: Longmans, Green, 1911) contain vignettes, insights, and organizational information not found in other biographical or organizational works. Ovington's papers at Wayne State University (Detroit, MI) provide further information.

The autobiographies of Black women provide other insights. Alfreda Duster, ed., *Crusade for Justice: The Autobiography of Ida B. Wells* (Chicago: University of Chicago Press, 1970) is useful for a critical perspective of White and Black leadership from Wells-Barnett's point of view. Wells-Barnett had great difficulty working within any organized group, so her viewpoints have to be weighed with consideration to her other conflicts. Her autobiography contains many errors in dates of events. Her accounts of these events frequently are quite different from those of other participants and should not be automatically accepted without cross-checking with other accounts. Mary Terrell's autobiography, *Colored Woman in a White World* (Washington, DC: Ransdell Press, 1940) is much more even in treatment but frequently smooths over interorganizational conflicts. Charles Flint Kellogg (*NAACP*, 1967) seldom mentions the Black female role except in footnotes, and even then women's names are often misspelled or incomplete—or not identified as Black women's.

Stephen R. Fox, *The Guardian of Boston: William Monroe Trotter* (New York: Atheneum, 1971), Nancy Weiss, *The National Urban League* (New York: Oxford University Press, 1974), and Robert L. Zangrando, *The NAACP Crusade Against Lynching, 1909-1950* (Philadelphia: Temple University Press, 1980) provide a few references to Black women within the Boston reform community, the Urban League, and the antilynching movement.

3. Sources differ as to numbers of signers and women. Fox, *Guardian of Boston*, cited more than 50 and 7 Blacks. "The Call," reprinted in Kellogg, *NAACP*, pp. 297-298, has 60 signers with 7 noted Black leaders including Mary Terrell and Ida Wells-Barnett. Wilson Record, "Negro Intellectual Leadership in the National Association for the Advancement of Colored People: 1910-1940," *Phylon*, 18 (Fall 1956) said, "Only one Negro woman of note, Ida Wells Barnett, was among the signers of the call" (p. 380). Apparently, Record did not know about the significance of Terrell or was not aware of her identity. The White women who signed the call represented reform leadership within the suffrage, settlement-house, child labor, labor, prison reform, pacifism, and educational reform movements: Jane Addams, Harriet Stanton Blatch, Kate Claghorn, Mary E. Dreier, Florence Kelley, Mary E. McDowell, Leonora O'Reilly, Mary White Ovington, Jane Robbins, Anna Garland Spencer, Mrs. Henry Villard, Lillian Wald, Susan P. Wharton, Mary E. Wooley, Helen Stokes, Mrs. Rodman Wharton, and Helen Marot. For information about the individual women, see Edward T. James, Janet Wilson et al., eds., *Notable American Women, 1607-1950* (Cambridge, MA: Belknap Press, 1971) and further updated editions of the collection.

4. Hallie Q. Brown, *Homespun Heroines* (Xenia, OH: Aldine Press, 1926; reprint ed., Freeport, NY: Books for Libraries Press, 1971), p. 183.

5. Benjamin Brawley, *Negro Builders and Heroes* (Chapel Hill: University of North Carolina Press, 1937), pp. 278-279; Margaret Murray Washington, "Club Work Among Negro Women," in J. W. Gibson, ed., *Progress of the Race* (Naperville, IL: J. L. Nichols, 1920), pp. 186-189; Brown, *Homespun Heroines*, pp. 182-183; *The Crisis*, 13 (April 1917) p. 281; and Kellogg, *NAACP*, pp. 298-301.

6. Fox, *Guardian of Boston*, p. 25.

7. For information about the women in the club movement, see: Dorothy Salem, *To Better Our World: Black Women in Organized Reform, 1890-1920* (Brooklyn: Carlson Publishing, 1990); Elizabeth Davis, *Lifting as They Climb* (Washington: National Association of Colored Women, 1933), pp. 236-239; Dannett, *Profiles*, p. 309; Brown, *Homespun Heroines*, p. 151; St. Clair Drake, *Churches and Voluntary Associations in the Chicago Negro Community* (Chicago: Works Progress Administration Report, 1940), pp. 21-22; "Some Chicagoans of Note," *The Crisis*, 10 (September 1915), pp. 237-242; Fannie B. Williams, "Colored Women of Chicago," *The Southern Workman*, 43 (1914), p. 566; Charlotte Martin, *The Story of Brockport for 100 Years, 1829-1929* (Brockport, NY: Local History, Seymour Library, 1964), pp. 21, 36-37; Duster, *Crusade*; Dannett, *Profiles*, pp. 327, 269, 221; Clement Richardson, *National Cyclopedia of the Colored Race* (Montgomery, AL: National Publishing, 1919) p. 143; Bert Loewenberg and Ruth Bogin, eds., *Black Women in Nineteenth-Century American Life: Their Words, Their Thoughts, Their Feelings* (University Park: Pennsylvania State University Press, 1976), pp. 263-264; Gertrude Mossell, *The Work of Afro-American Women* (Nashville, TN: Fisk University Press, 1894, reprint ed., Freeport, NY: Books for Libraries Press, 1971), p. 112; Allan H. Spear, *Black Chicago: The Making of a Negro Ghetto, 1890-1920* (Chicago: University of Chicago Press, 1967), pp. 50-70.

Drake (p. 125, cited above) claimed the Chicago middle class was not "caught on the horns of the Du Bois-Washington dilemma." The records of the national office of the NAACP continually reflect the need to motivate the Chicago branch, which the NAACP administration felt was in the hands of the conservatives. Duster also calls attention to the disagreements between the radical and conservative camps. For further discussion about the factionalism see, Kellogg, *NAACP*, pp. 124-125.

8. The correspondence in the Du Bois Papers demonstrates the women with whom Du Bois corresponded and had knowledge of careers or families. Talbert was not known to Du Bois at the time of her appointment.

9. For further information see chap. 5 of Salem, *To Better Our World*; Salem, *The Crisis*, 1 (November 1910), p. 122; Davis, *Lifting as They Climb*, pp. 169-170; and Dannett, *Profiles*, p. 231.

10. Mrs. John E. Milholland, "Talks About Women," *The Crisis*, 1 (December 1910), p. 28. Minutes, Executive Committee, January 3, March 7, April 11, and June 6, 1911, Board Minutes, NAACP Papers; Mary Talbert to M. Nerney, January 14, 1913, Mary Wilson to M. Nerney, March 10 and December 23, 1914, in NAACP Papers. Program for Mass Meeting of NAACP, Young's

Casino, January 12, 1913, in Archibald Grimke Papers, Howard University; Addie Hunton to M. Nerney, November 25, December 3, and 14, 1912, and April 19 and May 25, 1913, in Special Correspondence, NAACP Papers. For further delineation of this role see the periodic correspondence 1912-1913 between Hunton and Mrs. Butler Wilson in Special Correspondence Files, NAACP Papers.

11. Ovington, *Walls Came Tumbling Down*, p. 167.

12. Ronald Lawson and Stephen Barton, "Sex Roles in Social Movements: A Case Study of the Tenant Movement in New York City," *Signs: Journal of Women in Culture and Society, 6* (Winter 1980) pp. 230-247, provides an analysis of women's roles in an urban social movement. A similar role existed for the Black women in their grassroots organizational work during these early years of the NAACP.

13. This designation is cited in *The Crisis, 8* (July 1914), p. 142; Kellogg, *NAACP,* p. 131; and Kathryn Johnson to Roy Nash, August 19, 1916, Administrative Files, NAACP Papers.

14. For greater understanding about Johnson's feelings and tactics see: *The Crisis* 8 (July 1914), p. 142; Kellogg, *NAACP,* p. 131; Kathryn Johnson to Roy Nash, August 19, 1916, Administrative Files, NAACP Papers. Kathryn Johnson to May Nerney, January 6, 1914; Board Minutes, January 13 and February 2, 1915, NAACP Papers. Kathryn Johnson to May Nerney, August 13, 1915, Administrative Files, NAACP Papers. Wheatley YWCA, *Report,* to May Childs Nerney, September 11, 1915, in Administrative Records, NAACP Papers. Kathryn Johnson to Roy Nash, July 11, 1916, Administrative Files; Board Minutes, May 10 and June 14, 1915, NAACP Papers. Kathryn Johnson to May Nerney, September 17, 1915, Administrative Files, NAACP Papers.

15. Minutes, Annual Meeting, January 3, 1916, in Board Files, NAACP Papers.

16. Roy Nash to Kathryn Johnson, August 16, 1916, Administrative Files, NAACP Papers.

17. Roy Nash to Kathryn Johnson, August 16, 1916, Administrative Files, NAACP Papers.

18. Roy Nash to Joel Spingarn, October 27, 1916, Joel Spingarn Papers, Howard University.

19. Terrell, *Colored Woman,* p. 195.

20. W.E.B. Du Bois, *The Amenia Conference: An Historic Negro Gathering* (Amenia, NY: Troutbeck Leaflet No. 8, September 1925), copy in Mary Terrell Papers, Library of Congress.

21. For information about the women and the context in which James Weldon Johnson was chosen, see: Roy Nash to Kathryn Johnson, January 17, 1916; Kathryn Johnson to Joel Spingarn, July 21, 1916; Kathryn Johnson to Roy Nash, August 15, 1916; Administrative Files, NAACP Papers, show that Johnson continued to direct letters to defend herself throughout August. Defensive in tone, her letters met the charges by Mary Wilson and continued to accuse other Black women of undermining her. Mary Talbert and Addie Dickerson were specifically mentioned. The once proud Johnson then stooped to sympathetic appeals claiming she would have no money to survive if the NAACP went forward with her dismissal. For Johnson, the NAACP rejection seemed to symbolize the difficulties of interracial organization during that time.

For sources dealing with the candidacy of Black men and women see: Roy Nash to Kathryn Johnson, August 16, 1916, Administrative Files, NAACP Papers; Roy Nash to Joel Spingarn, October 27, 1916, J. Spingarn Papers; Kellogg, *NAACP,* n. 61, p. 132; and James Weldon Johnson, *Along This Way: An Autobiography of James Weldon Johnson* (New York: Viking, 1933), p. 314; Cleveland *Gazette,* July 22, 1916; Kellogg, *NAACP,* p. 218. These sources only verify the candidacy of Elizabeth Freeman, William Pickens, and John Hope. Other possible candidates could have included such field-workers as Martha Gruening or Nettie Asberry.

22. For further information about the conflict, see: Mary Terrell, *Colored Woman,* p. 195. W.E.B. Du Bois, *The Amenia Conference,* copy in MCT Papers, LC. Categories used by Fox, *Guardian of Boston,* pp. 31-41. Trotter's name appeared on the list, but according to Fox, Trotter did not attend. See Fox, pp. 202-231, Program, The Amenia Conference, August 24-26, 1916, copy in MCT Papers, LC. Minutes, December 11, 1916, and January 8, 1917, Board Files, NAACP Papers.

The Minutes of the Meetings of the Board of Directors, December 11, 1916 and January 8, 1917 present a puzzling set of events. At the December meeting the Report of the Committee on National Organizer was read by Mary White Ovington, the chairman of the committee. She reported the committee recommendation for the position of National Organizer as Mary E. Jackson, a Black woman from Providence, RI. Jackson's contract was to begin January 1, 1917 for a period of one year's probation, 3 month's notice if terminated, and include a $2,000-a-year salary plus expenses when doing fieldwork. Ovington recommended changing the title to "Field Secretary and Organizer" due to the type of work Jackson would have to carry out. Board members Paul Kennaday and William Sinclair moved that the committee report be approved. Discussion followed and that motion lost. Dr. Sinclair then moved for the matter to be laid on the table until the next Board meeting. His motion also lost. Much of the interceding discussion is not officially recorded in the Minutes, but suddenly a Mr. Studin made a motion, which was seconded and carried, that Mr. James Weldon Johnson be appointed as Field Secretary and Organizer and that a committee consisting of the Chairman (Spingarn) and one other be empowered to place Johnson under contract. Studin's motion carried with one dissenting vote (no names were mentioned, but those attending the meeting included Du Bois, J. Spingarn, Studin, Ovington, Sinclair, Kennaday, Dr. Holmes, Dr. Bishop, Mr. Crawford, Dr. Jones, Arthur Spingarn, Mr. Wilson, and Mr. Russell. From this list, I assume the dissenting vote was Ovington's. Joel Spingarn appointed Roy Nash to serve on the Committee to obtain Johnson. At the next meeting, January 8, 1917, James Weldon Johnson was present in the role of National Organizer and Field Secretary. Joel Spingarn appointed his brother, Arthur Spingarn, and Studin to a committee charged with working with James Weldon Johnson. The Nominating Committee's recommendation of Mary Jackson is puzzling. Because Jackson lacked prominence within NAACP records and literature, her choice is difficult to understand, especially when coupled with the knowledge held by several members of the Board that James Weldon Johnson had already accepted the position in his letter to Spingarn, November 5, 1916 (Joel Spingarn Papers, Howard University). The discussion of Johnson's appointment had been discussed since the Amenia Conference when Johnson impressed Spingarn with his abilities.

See the following correspondence for further information about the Johnson appointment: Roy Nash to Joel Spingarn, October 27, 1916, Spingarn Papers, Harvard University [HU]; Joel Spingarn to James Weldon Johnson, October 28, 1916, in Oswald Garrison Villard Papers, Houghton Library, HU; for Ovington's change in perception see Mary White Ovington to Joel Spingarn, September 26, 1917, in Spingarn Papers, HU. Johnson's appointment demonstrated the weakness of female powers within the central administration of the NAACP. The fact that Sinclair and Kennaday moved for Ovington's recommendations shows that not all of the men on the Board were in on the tactic to overrule the committee's recommendation. Jackson's nomination also showed the impact of female fieldwork. Jackson was a close friend of Mary Wilson, wife of Butler Wilson. May Nerney sent Wilson's mail in care of Jackson during January 1915. As a National Organizer for the NACW, Jackson had skills and contacts within the Black female network. Within a few years, Jackson went on to leadership within the YWCA as the National Industrial Secretary of the YWCA Colored Work.

For information about Mary Talbert, Mary Wilson, Nettie Asberry, Mary Jackson, Agnes Adams, and Kathryn Johnson, see Mary Ovington, "The National Association for the Protection of Colored People," pp. 107-116; Fox, *Guardian of Boston*; Dannett, *Profiles*; Brown, *Homespun Heroines*; and special sections of *The Crisis*, such as "Women's Clubs" or "Men of the Month" [e.g., Maria Baldwin is discussed in the *The Crisis*, 13 (April 1917) p. 281]; "Votes for Women," 10 (August 1915), pp. 178-192, mentions several women. For Mary Terrell's role, see Terrell, *Colored Woman*; Sammy Miller, "Woodrow Wilson and the Black Judge," *The Crisis*, 74 (February 1977), pp. 81-86; and "Robert H. Terrell: First Black D.C. Municipal Judge," *The Crisis*, 73 (June/July 1976), pp. 209-210; *The Crisis*, 13 (January 1917), p. 119; Dannett, *Profiles*, p. 317; Nannie Burroughs, "A Great Woman," (n.d.), speech about Mary Talbert, copy in Nannie Burroughs Papers, Library of Congress; Mary Talbert to John Shillady, January 2, 1919 and May 15, 1920, Administrative Files, NAACP Papers; Mary White Ovington, Office Diaries, April 19, 1920, NAACP Papers; Addie Hunton to Du Bois, January 26, 1918, in Du Bois Papers, UM. Johnson, *Along This Way*, p. 316. Mary Talbert to John Shillady, December 23, 1918, Administrative Files, NAACP Papers. Mary Talbert, Report, in Talbert to Shillady, December 23, 1918; Mary Talbert to James Weldon Johnson, January 9, 1919 and February 25, 1919; Mary Talbert to John Shillady, May 16, 1919, Administrative Files, NAACP Papers. Mary Talbert to James Weldon Johnson, February 12, 1919, Administrative Files, NAACP Papers. Mary White Ovington, Office Diaries, April 7, 1919, Branch Files of Charleston, SC, May 10 and December 17, 1917, all in NAACP Papers.

23. Talbert to Emmet [sic] Scott, January 14, 1919, and Talbert to James Weldon Johnson, January 9, 1919, both in the NAACP Papers.

24. Du Bois, *Dusk of Dawn* (New York: Harcourt, Brace, 1940) pp. 265-266; James Weldon Johnson, *Along This Way*, pp. 339-340; and Kellogg, *NAACP*, pp. 233-235.

25. For further information see notes 12-20 in chap. 8 of Salem's *To Better Our World*.

4. Racial Justice in Minnesota
The Activism of Mary Toliver Jones
and Josie Robinson Johnson

MARY C. PRUITT

🔰 Mary Alice Toliver Jones, born in 1904, came of age as a community leader at the settlement called the Hallie Q. Brown Community House in the Negro neighborhood in St. Paul, MN. When she graduated from Mechanic Arts High School and applied for college, the University of Minnesota barred her from their Nursing Department. Mary Jones had learned at home to prize education and to take personal responsibility for making this a fairer world. Her solution: She pioneered on behalf of her race in the Home Economics Department.

Mary Toliver married postal worker and businessman Robert Archie Jones. The *St. Paul Recorder* captioned a portrait of the family in the Negro newspaper: "Future builders of the St. Paul community." Mary Jones devoted herself to her husband and six children.

As her children grew, Jones practiced her artistry with food at community suppers for the organizations she believed in: the National Association for the Advancement of Colored People (NAACP), the Urban League and its Women's Auxiliary, and Pilgrim Baptist Church. Jones focused her work on pragmatic Negro community organizations. Her preference for a name for her people reflected her generation. Negro, not Black, Jones believed, was the most dignified title.[1]

Josie Robinson Johnson came of age as a leader in the 1960s in the Civil Rights Movement. She adopted the community name Black, reflecting her generation. Born in Houston in 1930, Johnson graduated in 1951 as a sociology major from Fisk University. In Houston and Minneapolis she pursued graduate training and a teaching career. She married engineer Charles W. Johnson, and they had three daughters. Johnson moved to Minneapolis in the early 1960s.

Like Mary Jones, Johnson was a child of Black institutions, and this training showed in her volunteer and professional careers. Johnson served as an officer in the Minneapolis NAACP and the children's service organization, Jack and Jill. Johnson worked with racially exclusive groups as well as racially mixed groups. She pioneered for her race in an institution central to politically active women in Minnesota, the League of Women Voters. In the early 1960s, the League worked in coalition with Black and Jewish neighborhood associations to secure Fair Employment Practices Commissions in Minneapolis, St. Paul, and Minnesota. In 1968 Johnson became the first Black woman to serve on the National Board of the League of Women Voters.[2]

Mary Jones's father forbade her to go South in the first two decades of the century. In the early 1960s the Student Non-Violent Coordinating Committee and National Council of Negro Women demanded the right of travel to the dangerous Deep South. In 1964 Josie Johnson journeyed to Mississippi with an interfaith delegation of Minnesota women to participate in the Freedom Summer campaign. Catholic, Jewish, and Protestant White women visited interracial programs in the capital city of Jackson. Minnesota Black women visited a Freedom School in Vicksburg, MS.

Josie Johnson was best known for her role as the first Black appointed to the Board of Regents at the University of Minnesota, in 1971. When the Minnesota Student Mobilization Committee staged an anti-Vietnam War rally at the university in 1973, Regent Josie Johnson delivered an eloquent call for justice at home and abroad. "Young people," Johnson concluded,

> I beg of you, from a very personal sense, of a need to be committed for a long period of time, to . . . continue your spirit of concern long enough to make the kinds of substantive changes that have to be made in our society if every man is indeed going to be free and equal.[3]

Josie Johnson's plea for justice appeared in the University of Minnesota's student newspaper, the *Minnesota Daily*. The University of Minnesota Archives kept a file on Regent Johnson. The Minneapolis Room of the Minneapolis Public Library also collected clippings from the *Minneapolis Tribune, Minneapolis Star* and the *St. Paul Pioneer Press* about Johnson's leadership. Those resources inform this chapter.

Mary Jones and her family appeared in the Negro community newspapers, the *St. Paul Recorder* and the *Minneapolis Spokesman*, where her husband worked as advertising manager. In the Negro press I also found more of Mary Jones's ideas when I followed her friends and colleagues in women's associations, the NAACP, the Urban League, and the Urban League Auxiliary.

Both Jones and Johnson devoted their lives to the struggle for racial, social, and economic justice. Each participated in lengthy oral history interviews. The interviews added to the written sources the elements of strategy, emotion, and intellectual purpose.

Mary Toliver Jones: "We Backed Anything That Involved the Civil Rights Movement"

Born in 1904 in Rock Island, IL, Mary Toliver came with her parents to St. Paul's Negro community when she was 5 years old. From childhood she felt an identification with the female-defined leadership in the Civil Rights Movement. Her mother was born of free people in Tuscumbia, AL. On her mother Julia Terrell's side of the family they were distantly related to the distinguished Mary Church Terrell, an Oberlin College graduate and first president of the National Association of Colored Women.[4]

Jones's father's family were slaves, escaped to Kentucky, where her father was born. James Toliver brought his young family to St. Paul for the same reason that hundreds of Negroes migrated to Minnesota: The commissary for the Great Northern Railroad and the railway stations had jobs and a Negro-identified union, the Brotherhood of Sleeping Car Porters. James Toliver was a Red Cap and Julia Toliver was a homemaker.

Mary Jones grew up in the neighborhood called Rondo, just west of downtown St. Paul. When she married and raised her family, they lived on Rondo Avenue. Rondo was the main east-to-west thoroughfare between University Avenue on the north and Selby Avenue on the south. Evelyn Fairbanks, author of *Days of Rondo, A Warm Reminiscence of St. Paul's Thriving Black Community in the 1930s and 1940s,* recalled Rondo as a "colored neighborhood" but also as an immigrant neighborhood of Swedish Lutherans, Irish Catholics, and Russian Jews.[5]

In our interview, Mary Jones described many eras of her life in relation to friends who were Negro leaders in St. Paul. As a child she went to church with Roy Wilkins, his sister Armeda, and brother Earl. "I wanted to go to school like they did," she recalled. Roy Wilkins's family came to St. Paul the year Jones was born, 1904. He put himself through the University of Minnesota by working as a Red Cap, a Pullman car waiter, and a meatpacker. Wilkins edited the *Minnesota Daily* and the Negro paper *The Appeal* and was the executive secretary of the NAACP between 1955 and 1976.[6]

Anna Arnold Hedgeman also played a leading role in the drama of civil rights. Wilkins and Hedgeman helped to organize the March on Washington in 1963. Hedgeman, born in Anoka, just north of Minneapolis, was the first Negro graduate of St. Paul's Hamline University. She pioneered for her race at the YWCA in New York City and on the national YWCA board. In the 1940s, Hedgeman served as Executive Director of the National Campaign for a Permanent Fair Employment

Practices Commission. In 1949 the Truman administration appointed
her as assistant to the director of the Federal [Social] Security Agency.[7]
The progress of her heroes marked touchstones of racial progress for
Mary Jones.

Mary Jones attended Girl Reserve programs at the YWCA, although racial restrictions barred her from YWCA camp. Nearly 60
years later, in our interview, Jones reflected, "That was terrible. The
Y W *Christian* Association!" The YWCA sponsored some Negro programs in St. Paul and held some joint programs. But they were not
fully integrated until after 1946, when a Minnesota woman led the
national YWCA to accept an Interracial Charter. Helen Jackson Wilkins
[later Claytor] attended Girl Reserves as a child and may have met
Mary Jones there. She graduated with honors from the University of
Minnesota in 1928, worked for the YWCA, and married Earl Wilkins.
In 1946, with Julia Bell, she wrote the Interracial Charter, introduced it
to the national YWCA convention, and saw that the convention passed
it. The charter and the work it engendered made the Y, as Mary Jones
dreamed, a more "Christian" place. The charter pledged:

> Wherever there is injustice on the basis of race, whether in the community, the
> nation or the world, our protest must be clear and our labor for its removal
> vigorous and steady. And what we urge on others we are constrained to practice
> ourselves.[8]

Not only in response to discrimination, but also out of race pride,
the Negro community created rich cultural and social services resources.
Mary Jones was proud of being a charter member of the Book Lovers
Club. Her father loved to shop for and listen to operas and her uncle
was a student of Shakespeare. Jones recalled, "Father insisted that we
read." Every Sunday afternoon, after church at Pilgrim Baptist, the
Tolivers attended Vespers at church where they heard speeches, music,
and poetry by local and national Negro leaders. Jones looked forward
to socials at her father's lodge, Local 516 of the Brotherhood of Sleeping Car Porters. Perhaps her mother belonged to the Women's Auxiliary of 516.

Jones attended McKinley Grade School and Mechanic Arts High
School, integrated schools in St. Paul. Elementary school children got
along most of the time. Teachers were strict and the quality of education good at McKinley and Mechanic Arts. By high school, children
recognized racial and ethnic differences and sometimes Negro students were harassed.[9] Mary Jones remembered feeling sorry for the
Jewish children, who were called "kikes" and other racist names. Her
best friend in school was Jewish, her chemistry laboratory partner
Jennie. Both shut out of the middle-class White institutions, they looked
to female-run culturally grounded settlements for activities after school:

the Hallie Q. Brown House for Mary and Central Community House for Jennie.

The Negro community was very protective of its young women who, like Jones, lived at home before marriage. Jones recalled that dances and parties for teenagers were confined to private homes, where the parents simply rolled up the rug. After Hallie Q. Brown House opened, teenagers socialized in the Lounge.[10] In response to constant vulnerability, club women acted aggressively on behalf of Negro youth. The portraits of Negro women's clubs in the 1924 classic, *Who's Who Among Minnesota Women*, reflected this tension between uplift and vulnerability.

The Federation of Colored Women's Clubs

The Minnesota Federation of Colored Women's Clubs, located in Minneapolis, St. Paul, and Duluth, supported civic causes and sponsored scholarships and charity drives. The Colored Women's Federation ran a legal aid service. *Who's Who* reported that the "legal department of the state federation has done good work, one young girl being pardoned through its efforts in 1915."[11] Mary Jones was 11 years old in 1915. Like young Negro men, girls were vulnerable to scapegoating in any unpleasant social situation with Whites. Cecil E. Newman, publisher and editor of the Twin Cities Negro press, explained the problem this way: "If you are a Negro and are arrested, it is proof of your guilt."[12]

Mary Jones's father would not allow her to go South when she was young. After high school she received a job offer in Mississippi, but her father forbade her to accept. James Toliver did not fully explain his fears for Mary but the Negro community knew: Threats of physical violence were a daily presence to Negro citizens in the South. Women and children were not immune. Nevertheless, Negro women called upon their heritage of resistance and did what they could to fight violence. Contemporary journalist and historian Paula Giddings chronicled the female-directed antilynching movement in *When and Where I Enter: The Impact of Black Women on Race and Sex in America*. Ida B. Wells led the first national antilynching campaign in 1892. Jones's relative Mary Church Terrell began her public career in that struggle.[13]

In 1921 the NAACP opened a new chapter in the antilynching campaign when the executive director of the NAACP convinced the U.S. Representative from St. Louis, L. C. Dyer, to introduce an antilynching bill. The National Association of Colored Women responded with their Anti-Lynching Crusade. They set a goal to raise one million dollars and recruit one million women to support NAACP legislative efforts. Although the antilynching bill did not pass Congress, Paula Giddings concluded: "the publicity and ideas generated by the Black women may have been partly responsible for the decrease in lynchings from

301 between 1919 and 1923 to 100 between 1924 and 1928." By 1930 the annual count of lynchings was 20.[14]

The National Association of Colored Women boasted that it had female legislative contacts in many states.[15] Mary Jones's heroine Nellie Francis sat on their national board and served as president of the Minnesota Federation of Colored Women's Clubs. She could have been Minnesota's appointed lobbyist. This coordinated effort from nation-wide to grass roots was typical, not atypical, of the skill and strength of early 20th-century women's associations. What that meant to Mary Jones was a modeling of the importance of women's work, not only at the national and state level but also at the community level, where Mary Jones stood.

Minnesota passed one of the first antilynching laws in the country. A member of the first class of Minnesota women legislators, Farmer-Labor Party leader Myrtle Cain, carried the bill.[16] Nellie Griswold Francis authored the bill. Francis held office in all the major Negro associations, including: the Colored Women's Clubs, the Big Sister Department, Tri-State Women's Baptist Convention, NAACP, Urban League, and Everywoman's Progressive Council. Francis also earned respect as a bridge-builder to other communities. She worked with the local National Defense, Ramsey County Republican Women's Club, Schubert Club, and the Women's International League for Peace and Freedom. Nellie Francis parlayed the goodwill that she had built into an interracial coalition. It was from that base that Francis directed the campaign for a bill against racial violence.

In *Who's Who Among Minnesota Women*, journalist Mary Dillon Foster chronicled the leadership of Nellie Francis and the Every-woman Progressive Council of St. Paul. "Propaganda has been contin-ued against sensational publicity of petty negro crime in public press and to promote publicity for progressive negro events. The council arranged a mass meeting with members of [1923] state legislature for state Anti-Lynching bill, which passed."[17]

The threat of violence against her race probably was not unknown to Mary Jones, because Nellie Francis was her favorite heroine and the antilynching crusade occurred in Minnesota when Jones was in her late teens. During our 1983 interview Jones proudly recalled that she had been among a select group of young people to be invited to Nellie Griswold Francis's home for special events.

Violence against women sometimes took subtler forms than the threat of direct physical violence. The experience of Mary Jones's famous relative, Mary Church Terrell, illustrated another way that Negro women were vulnerable. At age 28, after graduating from Oberlin College, studying in Europe, and a teaching career, Mary Church married Robert Terrell. When they tried to start a family, the only Southern hospital that would accept her was an understaffed, outdated facility.

Giddings wrote in *When and Where I Enter* that Terrell "underwent the heart-wrenching experience of losing three babies within days of their birth in a span of five years." She went North for the successful birth of her daughter.[18]

Negro citizens were targets in Minnesota. In 1920 in Duluth a mob broke into jail, captured three Negro circus roustabouts, and hung them from lamp posts. The NAACP found that the young men had committed no crime. It took the NAACP 6 months to arrange the release from jail of 40 other Duluth Negro men who had been plucked out of their homes by the mob and wrongly accused.[19] Others who threatened "White supremacy" also found themselves to be targets in Minnesota, particularly Jews, Catholics, recent immigrants from Southern and Eastern Europe, and labor militants.[20] The North was bad enough— Mary Jones obeyed her father's wishes not to go South as a young woman. She did not leave the North until she was nearly 60 years old: In the 1960s her son Robert, Jr., invited her to his home in Atlanta.

Mary Jones's Role Models: The Intellectual Tradition of Negro Women Artists and Politicians

The Toliver family lived in modest circumstances, but because of James Toliver's steady job as a Red Cap, Mary was able to plan a future. Mary finished high school at Mechanic Arts High School in the evening while working days in a department store stockroom. Custom prevented her from applying for higher paid clerk positions where she would have had contact with customers. In the Civil Rights Movement of the 1950s and 1960s this right to clerical, waitress, receptionist, and secretarial jobs was an important female-centered demand. Jones did recall being proud of her earnings and of buying her own clothes and, for her mother, a dining room set. Dreaming of a more satisfying career, Jones studied psychology, algebra, and geometry to prepare for college. Between high school graduation in 1924 and college in 1930 it was the female-run settlements and clubs that broadened her horizons.

The Hallie Q. Brown settlement house, called Hallie Q. by the community, was founded in 1929 by the Urban League and other neighborhood groups.[21] Mary Jones spent so much time there that her mother called her "my little volunteer." The talented social worker I. Myrtle Carden encouraged her to teach nutrition and home economics to teenagers. I. Myrtle Carden led Jones's list of mentors. Others were Lena O. Smith, her sister Frances Smith Brown, and Ethel Maxwell Williams.

The recent work by Patricia Hill Collins, *Black Feminist Thought: Knowledge, Consciousness and the Politics of Empowerment*, celebrated the community-focused work of women like Mary Jones and her heroines. Collins wrote:

African-American women not commonly certified as intellectuals by academic institutions have long functioned as intellectuals by representing the interests of Black women as a group and fostering Black feminist thought. Without tapping these so-called nontraditional sources, much of Black women's intellectual tradition would remain "not known and hence not believed in."[22]

Lena O. Smith and Frances Brown were prominent politicians in civil rights work. Lena O. Smith, who was single, practiced law and headed the NAACP Legal Redress Committee. Cecil E. Newman editorialized in the *Minneapolis Spokesman* in 1941: "Minneapolis lawyers dread opposing Miss L. O. Smith . . . Twin City lawyers call her the best attorney among women members of the bar in the Northwest."[23]

L. O. Smith worked more closely than her sister did with the socialistic Farmer-Laborites and the labor-identified Communist Party. Her work as chronicled by the *Spokesman* proved that race-identified organizations were her priorities; however, Smith spoke at a mass rally, organized by the Communists, to raise money and publicize the cause of the Scottsboro Boys in 1936.[24]

In the 1930s Minneapolis labor leader Nellie Stone Johnson pioneered for her race and sex as vice president of her union. She found common cause with Minnesota Communists throughout the 1930s and 1940s because they fought for jobs for Negro workers, particularly through her union, Miscellaneous #665, Hotel and Restaurant Workers.[25]

Frances Smith married the prominent Negro physician W. D. Brown. Frances Smith Brown was the fund-raiser for the NAACP and the Urban League who tapped Minneapolis elites, like Mayor, later Senator, Hubert H. Humphrey, for the yearly membership dollar. Brown was also an artist with words. Mary Jones recalled hearing her recite "The Raven" at Hallie Q.

Brown played a part in the integration of the YWCA, serving first on the interracial committee. In 1945 she was reelected to the Minneapolis Y Board. Her election showed the courage of Y members in supporting the integration of the swimming pool and other programs. Helen Jackson Wilkins's Interracial Charter sparked change in Minneapolis, too.[26]

The Smith sisters were careful to spend some time mentoring the next generation. University of Minnesota students, including cartoon artist Myrtle Wormley and *Spokesman* journalist Nellie Dodson, were among the college women of the Alpha Kappa Alpha sorority. They met at Frances S. Brown's home and L. O. Smith delivered an address.[27]

Another prominent heroine of Mary Jones's was Ethel Maxwell Williams, who earned a master's degree at the University of Minnesota School of Social Work. When a St. Paul employee at a luncheonette was assigned a segregated dressing room, Williams was among the Urban League activists who protested. It was Mrs. Williams whom the plant vice president called with an apology.[28]

In 1945, during the campaign to pass a permanent Fair Employment Practices [FEPC] bill, Ethel Williams traveled with an interracial
delegation from the Twin Cities to lobby in Washington, DC. The delegation caucused with Anna Arnold Hedgeman, Executive Director of
the National Campaign for a Permanent FEPC. Hedgeman helped
arrange the prize of the trip: a 45-minute audience with Eleanor
Roosevelt, who supported FEPC legislation.[29]

When Hedgeman came to Minneapolis in 1945 to speak about her
work on the drive for a Permanent FEPC, 450 persons heard her address
at Hallie Q. Brown. Dignitaries in the audience were philanthropist
Louis W. Hill; representatives of St. Paul industrial firms; religious
leaders of the Catholic, Jewish, and Protestant faiths; a representative
of the Asian-American community, Miss Fuigi Shegawa; and Ruth
Gage Colby of the Women's International League for Peace and Freedom. Hedgeman asserted that the filibuster against FEPC had to be
broken, "because if it is successful it will surely become the pattern for
future attacks on bills of equal importance to all the people." Looking
to the opening conference of the United Nations, Hedgeman concluded: "It is especially important the bill be passed now so the United
States may come to the San Francisco conference with clean hands and
courage."[30]

Scholar Patricia Hill Collins emphasized the intellectual contribution to community uplift by artists and political activists:

> [they] are typically thought of as nonintellectual and nonscholarly, classifica-
> tions that create a false dichotomy between scholarship and activism, between
> thinking and doing. Examining the ideas and actions of these excluded groups
> reveals a world in which behavior is a statement of philosophy and in which
> a vibrant, both/and, scholar/activist tradition remains intact.[31]

Mary Jones's Calling: Marriage and Family

Mary Jones's intellectual and activist training was grounded in
women's and community associations. Her lifelong study of civil rights
pioneers was not conducted in a college but through hearing Anna
Hedgeman and L. O. Smith speak and by reading their words in the
Recorder. Jones recalled how proud she was of Anna Hedgeman for
being the first Negro graduate of Hamline University in St. Paul and
for her leadership in breaking down racial barriers at the YWCA.

From after high school graduation in 1924 until 1930, Jones went to
night school, preparing herself for study at the University of Minnesota.
She aspired to training in nursing, but that department rejected Negro
applicants. In home economics, her second choice, the mature and
dignified 26-year-old pioneered for her race. Then she found herself
barred by racial restrictions from participating in the residential program

at the Home Management House. Jones practiced the art of human relationships. She negotiated a compromise with the Home Economics Department to complete a one-month internship in nutrition, her major. Mary Jones, the first Negro to complete a home economics internship at the University of Minnesota, has a place on the honor roll of anonymous soldiers in the Civil Rights Movement.

In 1932, after 2 years in college, she fell in love and married a fellow student, journalist and post office worker Robert Archie Jones. Robert Jones worked two and sometimes three jobs most of his life, but he did not want Mary to work outside the home. Mary Jones and her husband had six children born between 1934 and the late 1940s: Julia Elizabeth, Roberta Alyce, Marion Carol, Robert, Jr., Harvey Cecil, and Diane Marie. Maintaining a family meant for Robert Jones working as a post office worker for 45 years. Despite this commitment, Jones's heart was in his job as advertising sales manager for the Negro paper, the *Recorder*, which he had helped Cecil E. Newman to found in 1934.

Robert Jones developed a commitment to civil rights as a young man. Mary Jones explained, "Robert was a cadet [in a military preparation program] in Dunbar High School in Washington, DC during World War I. President Wilson would look the other way when Negroes marched." In spite of the indignities of racism, Mary Jones agreed with her husband, who often said, "When someone is on your neck, you work harder." Mary Jones remembered, "My husband was very proud, very dignified. He met businessmen man to man."

Whereas Robert Jones and his family supported the race-conscious *Recorder* and *Spokesman*, Mary Jones's distant relative Mary Church Terrell fought to eliminate segregation in the nation's capital. From 1907 through 1949, Terrell's suit was in the courts; it opened Washington restaurants, if not other public accommodations, to Negro citizens.[32] From 1950 through 1953 Terrell and union activists from United Cafeteria and Restaurant Local 471 picketed and raised funds to open all public accommodations in Washington, DC. Mary Terrell was 90 years old in June 1953 when the Supreme Court ruled in her favor. President Eisenhower tried to take credit for desegregation of the capital, but labor journalist Annie Stein insisted, "people knew who had really done the job."[33]

Mary Jones's name appeared in the Negro papers most typically in the context of her family. In the December 1949 family portrait, Mary Jones was holding baby Diane Marie on her lap.[34] The *Recorder's* caption for the portrait, "Future builders of the St. Paul community," illustrated how important the Jones family was to the *Recorder*. The Jones children spent many hours at the paper, getting help with homework and helping out on the paper when deadlines approached. Robert Jones's skill as the advertising manager kept the paper on an even keel.

Mary Jones raised a big garden each year, making jelly and canning five bushels of tomatoes. Often, she recalled, "My husband worked right along with me." From her marriage in 1932 to the late 1970s, Mary Jones's second career was the Urban League Auxiliary. There she practiced her artistry with food by creating countless dinners and bake sales. Her work funded scholarships and lobbying efforts by the Urban League and the Council of Negro Women. Mary Jones saw herself as a player in the community ensemble for racial justice. "We backed everything that involved the civil right movement," she said.

The Women's Auxiliary of the Urban League

Most items in the February 17, 1935, *St. Paul Recorder* "Society News" were routine. The Adelphi Club made plans to increase their student loan club, supporting the aspirations of more Negro students to high school or college. Someone took ill. Another recovered. Guests enjoyed "a delicious lunch" and a Saturday dance. Club women expanded the spaces where they could walk. The arts and crafts club of Hallie Q. Brown settlement house mounted an exhibit at the predominantly White YWCA.[35]

But one item in February 1935, "St. Paul Society News," represented an action for community uplift that was bolder than most. The comment was subtle, the action nonthreatening. "Urban League Auxiliary Notes" announced that 35 members and friends "toured the Zinsmaster Bakery on last Friday night." Then the women retired to Hallie Q. to play cards, compete for prizes, and have a "delightful lunch." At first glance this story sounded much like other women's association reports: friends and guests, a program, card games, and a meal. But the auxiliary's action took on added meaning between 1935 and 1940 when the Urban League and the *Spokesman* and *Recorder* led a campaign for jobs in breweries and bakeries.[36]

After the Auxilliary's tour of the Zinsmaster Bakery, Cecil E. Newman criticized the bakeries of the Twin Cities for not employing any Negro workers.[37] But the newspaper did not comment on the actions of the Urban League Auxiliary. Was their style too subtle to gain attention? I think the women chose the subtle style because women's work within mixed-sex organizations was defined by male-directed institutions as support, or auxiliary, to the main event, action by men. The women's affiliations were vulnerable to criticism about their leadership strategies, and small, local women's groups did not have a press of their own to express their point of view.[38] That vulnerability did not deter the auxiliary from choosing, planning, and carrying out a public action.

Thirty-five Negro women toured the plant. Were they dressed up in hats and gloves, fine stockings, and heels, as women did in the 1930s for a public occasion? Or were auxiliary members dressed in a best housedress with a flower pinned to each collar? The Negro women would have looked very much like the wives of the workers at the plant looked when they went out to a meeting. How different, then, might Negro men look than the husbands, fathers, or brothers working at the bakery? The auxiliary created a visual image of disciplined, polite, and well-spoken citizens—who happened to be Negro. If the management of the bakery decided to break racial barriers and employ Negro workers, this image of Negro women could have deflected some racial tension.

On May 24, 1935, the *Spokesman* and the *Recorder* published a cartoon, one in a series, by University of Minnesota art student Myrtle Wormley. Front and center on page 1, the cartoon was labeled "The Brewery Situation." "Two Pictures" contrasted a Negro waiter, in formal attire, telling a customer, "Yes, m'am, Twin City beers are the best." The second panel showed a dejected Negro man and woman being turned away by a brewery employment officer. A sign on his desk declared, "No Colored Help Wanted." Cecil E. Newman crowed that the brewers were on the defensive: "In an interview with two of the leaders of the brewing business the editor was severely taken to task for ingratitude and forgetfulness." Newman had made the point to brewery owners that Wormley's cartoon made: Negro business owners, waiters, porters, and hotel keepers bought, sold, recommended, and consumed Twin Cities beers. But, "for years on end our people have spent many thousands of dollars without even thinking of asking anything in return." The Great Depression was "pinching too hard," Newman concluded. "Work is too scarce. We must find employment."[39]

The following month, the *Spokesman* boasted that the Gold Medal Brewery "Bottling Company Has Colored Salesman." In July, Engesser Distributors hired a colored driver and Yankee Beer hired Sam Davis as a salesman-driver.[40] Yankee Beer gained an order for six kegs of beer when a committee of the African American Episcopal Church cancelled their order with Hamm's Brewery, who refused to hire Negro workers.[41] Community action also realized jobs for women. These articles appeared in 1941 and 1942: "Urban League Places Negro Girl at Donaldson's [department store]" and "Group Finally Gets Place on Anker [hospital nursing] Staff."[42]

The Urban League Women's Auxiliary of St. Paul earned a front page article in the *Spokesman* and *Recorder* when, escorted by a tour guide, 40 members and friends toured the unyielding Hamm's Brewery. Twice in the five-paragraph article the press noted that the company served refreshments to the women. Integrated dining was not yet the rule in public in Minnesota, nor was integrated housing. At the University of Minnesota in 1935 the Regents rejected a petition by the All-University Council of students to allow Negro students to live in Pioneer Hall on campus.[43]

The St. Paul Women's Auxiliary of the Urban League led at least one more tour to lend their subtle pressure in a jobs campaign. In January 1940 the women toured the Swift packinghouse plant.[44]

While Robert Archie Jones served on the board of the Urban League, Mary Alice Jones ran the fund-raisers that financed actions such as the bakery and brewery jobs campaign. As she put it, "I never wanted to be up front." After Robert Jones's death in 1971 she held her only wage-earning job since her marriage. With then-publisher Mary Kyle's encouragement, Mary Jones took over her husband's advertising books at the *Recorder*.

Josie Robinson Johnson: "My Family Had Been an *Outreach Family* Forever": *A Child of Black Institutions*

Josie R. Johnson knew the strengths of the Black family and of Black institutions, for she was a child of the NAACP, the Brotherhood of Sleeping Car Porters, and the community centers of her grandmother's drugstores and her mother's open-door home. Born in 1930, Josie R. Johnson was of the generation of Mary Jones's daughters, one of whom, Marion Jones Kennon, became Johnson's colleague in civic work.

Josie Johnson grew up in Houston, TX, in an extended family of strong community leaders. One of young Josie's closest friends was her maternal grandmother Ida Irene McCullough Leonard Jones, who married at 15. She was a beauty operator and a private consultant on cosmetology. Ida Jones entered the drugstore business with her second husband, a pharmacist. She retired at 70 after working 30 years, 7:00 a.m. to 7:00 p.m., 7 days a week. In return for clothes and school expenses, Josie Johnson worked for her grandmother in the Leonard Drug Stores on Houston's West Side during summers and school holidays. Also close to Josie were her grandmother's sisters, Josie and Neni, who ran boarding homes and owned real estate in Houston. Aunt Josie helped Josie's mother, Josie Bell McCullough Robinson, when she was going to college. Johnson rejoiced in her heritage, as she put it, "of wonderfully strong, hard-working, independent women."

In her recent *Black Feminist Thought*, contemporary scholar Patricia Hill Collins reclaimed a heritage of strong women and outreach workers like the women of Josie Robinson Johnson's family. Collins explained that Black women's activism "has occurred along two primary dimensions." The first dimension has been the struggle for community survival. This struggle required "vigilant action" to clothe, nourish, house, and do everything necessary to keep the next generation alive. The second dimension has been training the next generation in race consciousness and resistance. Collins wrote: "Black women's actions to maintain community integrity through the struggle for group survival is both conservative and radical."[45]

One of the few privately owned homes in the Black neighborhood, the Robinson's was always open to neighbors in need. In her interview, Johnson said of her mother: "She did some of everything—nursery school, social work. She expected nothing in return; she *shared* her resources. . . . My family had been an *outreach family* forever." Mrs. Robinson calculated how best to spend her time and energy. She held a bachelor's degree in education and she used that skill to earn extra money to support her outreach household.[46] Mrs. Robinson privately tutored White middle-class students. When they came to her discreet school, they were often illiterate. Johnson called her mother an "unlicensed social worker" and "community confessor" who made their home the center of the Black community. She explained, "My mother reared me with a philosophy that suggested: There but for the grace of God go I."

Her father, Judson Robinson, counted on her mother's support in his endeavors. Both college graduates, Johnson's parents met in 1926. Judson Robinson put himself through college as a dining car waiter on the Southern Pacific Railroad. He was a union activist under Asa Phillip Randolph's leadership in the Brotherhood of Sleeping Car Porters. Like the Jones children who visited Cecil E. Newman's newspaper office, Johnson remembered, "I used to go down to the office with my father." He worked for the railroad until 1947, when he opened a real estate business, Judson Robinson and Sons. His daughter was his first secretary.

Judson Robinson also acted on an ethic of service to the Black community. His father, a college graduate, had been a teaching minister, traveling the backwoods of Texas. Josie R. Johnson remembered her father as "very involved in politics. I think that's where I got my interest." Both staunch Democrats, her parents did civic and political work, not, Johnson emphasized, purely social activism. Before the Voting Rights reforms of the 1960s, Southerners had to pay poll taxes; in a cash-poor community plans had to be carefully thought out in advance. Johnson remembered "making sure that people paid their poll tax. We worked the precincts very thoroughly." Southern civil rights workers like the Robinsons could count on some donations from Northern unions. Labor leader Nellie Stone Johnson recalled that Black and White workers in Minneapolis Hotel and Restaurant Union #665 collected money for poll taxes, sometimes by walking to work and sending their carfare money South.[47]

After graduating from St. Nicholas Catholic High School, Josie Johnson earned a B.A. in sociology from Black-identified Fisk University in Nashville, TN, in 1951. She soon married Charles W. Johnson, an engineer. After the birth of their first daughter, Partice Y. Johnson, she did graduate work and earned a Teacher's Certificate at Texas Southern University. They moved to the Minneapolis suburb of Bloomington in 1956. Daughters Norreen E. and Josie I. Johnson were born in 1956 and 1958.

Service in the Minneapolis Black Community

In the early 1960s when her girls were young, Johnson served as program director for Jack and Jill, a community group that she described as bringing "parents and children together in a planned organizational format of education and culture in the community." From 1962 to 1965 she led the Women's Service League, an Urban League project for Black junior high school girls. Adult volunteers established groups in the schools, Johnson wrote, to "discuss their problems, assist in eliminating frustration and encourage achievement."[48]

Johnson developed close friendships with other energetic Black activists. At The Way, a drop-in center style settlement house, she worked with Gwen Davis Jones and Syl Davis. Johnson appreciated their skills: "speaking, planning strategy, mapping problems, identifying demands. [The times] required organization and skill and the ability to communicate. . . . We had to redirect the issues and to save our children."[49]

Josie Johnson found an abiding interest in the Black family. North Minneapolis's Phyllis Wheatley settlement housed one of her best projects. Titled ENABLE, the program was sponsored by the Equal Employment Opportunity Council, Family and Children Services, the Jewish Community Center, and the Urban League. Under ENABLE Johnson designed and taught a course, "Black Families in White America." The curriculum focused on the impact of welfare on families and, Johnson recalled, "what aspects of a community caused tension. By looking at the *whole* family, not just in the schools" it was designed, among other things, to "get people off [public] support." The revolutionary potential of the program lay in its grassroots base.

Researcher Judith Rollins, in her eloquent text *Between Women, Domestics and Their Employers*, located the self-concept of Black community-focused women not in their occupation but in their standing in the community. Rollins wrote that domestic workers created "a way to retrieve their dignity by altering definitions and operating on the basis of different values." Domestics forged a coping strategy, Rollins found, in "their value system, which measures an individual's worth less by material success than by 'the kind of person you are,' and by the quality of one's interpersonal relationships and by one's standing in the community."[50]

Community-centered values held North Minneapolis's ENABLE together. Neighborhood workers were appreciated for their talents. And, while addressing the daily-life problems of its ordinary citizens, ENABLE also opened windows on the wider world of the national civil rights movement.

Across the nation local conditions provided the inspiration for protest. NAACP organizer Ella Baker directed civic protest in New York City and in the South. Paula Giddings judged that Baker was the midwife for the church-identified Southern Christian Leadership Conference (SCLC) and the youth-identified Student Non-Violent Coordinating Committee (SNCC). Baker put it best: "I was only interested in seeing that a leadership had a chance to develop. . . . My theory is, strong people don't need strong leaders."[51]

Projects like ENABLE in Black and other ethnic communities won funds from the federal War on Poverty. As Martin Luther King, Jr., wrote in 1963 in the now classic document of protest, *Letter From Birmingham Jail,* the spirit of these years created a sense of intense urgency.[52] A new generation of students protested throughout the South at lunch counters, swimming pools, and schoolhouse doors. In 1960 the Minneapolis Youth Council of the NAACP acted in solidarity with their Southern brothers and sisters. They protested at the Woolworth store on Nicollet Avenue, reminding Minneapolis that the chain store discriminated at lunch counters in the South. The public and the police accepted the peaceful protest.[53]

But the backlash had begun. The federal bureaucracy resisted change and rejected Black-identified values. In St. Paul the bulldozers of "urban renewal" and a new freeway took the exact path of Rondo Avenue, crushing the center of the Black community. In Minneapolis, despite the fact that ENABLE was a very successful program, the government found it too comprehensive and cut the program. Later Josie Johnson was selected Woman of the Year for her work with the Black family by the professional Black women's affiliation, Iota Phi Lambda Sorority. When selected, Josie R. Johnson stated she would rather have been awarded a continuation of ENABLE.[54]

In an effort to communicate what was happening in her community, Johnson forged links with White-dominated groups. In the League of Women Voters, Johnson served as Membership Chair, sat on the state board, and became the first Black woman on the national board from 1968 to 1970. Johnson said she hoped to "try to bring them along," to give the League information from her community, and to bring her community to a training ground for action. She explained:

> My role was quite clear—to recruit Black people and get them involved in the League. Self-definition and realism were required. I did not pretend that the world was different than it was . . . I felt pretty much in control of my own destiny. I did not join groups to become separate from my community.

Across the country Black female activists of Johnson's generation were leading cross-cultural women's groups. Poet Kate Rushin honored women like Johnson, and Nellie Francis before her, with "The Bridge Poem." Being a human bridge was weary work. Rushin wrote,

Nobody
Can talk to anybody
Without me
Right?
I explain my mother to my father my father to my little sister
My little sister to my brother my brother to the white feminists
The white feminists to the Black church folks the Black church folks
To the ex-hippies the ex-hippies to the Black separatists the
Black separatists to the artists the artists to my friends parents . . .
I must be the bridge to nowhere
But my true self
And then
I will be useful

(The Bridge Poem, by Kate Rushin, in The Black Back-Ups
[Ithaca, NY: Firebrand Books, 1993].
Copyright © 1993 by Kate Rushin. Used by permission.)

Some White social service workers did not want to walk across bridges to other cultures. That hard-heartedness was fresh in Johnson's memory during our interview nearly two decades later. At a meeting at the YWCA, Johnson chose a seat in a row of folding chairs. When Johnson sat next to a White woman, a person active in the women's social service community, the White woman got up and moved away.

In White neighborhoods across Minnesota in the 1960s many publicly minded women worked for civil rights. In the Minneapolis suburb of Golden Valley, Peggy Spector designed and taught an antiracist curriculum in her daughter's primary school. In South Minneapolis, Carol Johnson Flynn, now a Minnesota state senator, worked on the Field-Hale School plan, which paired a White and a Black grade school. In Zumbrota, near Rochester, Sue Rockne fought for economic justice for Native Americans of the Mdewakanton Dakota community. Rockne also lobbied at the legislature and for better housing for persons of color in the city and the Dakota in the countryside. In St. Paul, Carol Connolly opened her home for fund-raisers for the American Indian Movement and Parents for Integrated Education.[55] Spector, Flynn, Rockne, and Connolly represented the Jewish, Swedish Lutheran, small-town Protestant, and Irish Catholic communities of Minnesota.

Direct Action and a New Generation

In July 1964, 140 teams of youth groups canvassed Minneapolis and suburban neighborhoods, reaching an estimated 300,000 homes and raising $21,000 to send to the Mississippi Freedom Summer Campaign. Liberal established churches and service organizations like the YWCA sponsored the youths' campaign. The *Minneapolis Spokesman* called them "salesmen for racial justice." They sold buttons for 50 cents each, picturing a Black and White handshake. The money was sent to Jackson, MS, to the Council of Federated Organizations, representing the NAACP, SCLC, SNCC, the Congress of Racial Equality, and the National Council of Churches. The *Spokesman* proudly announced that the Field House at St. Paul's St. Thomas College was packed, as "Over 2,600 Young Folks Cheer Results of Fund Drive." We can assume that the women who were the backbone of the churches in the community volunteer corps did the lion's share of the coordination and the chauffeuring. Most canvassers were high school age, and, the *Spokesman* emphasized, "representing all religious faiths and many races." An adult leader from suburban Bloomington "was heard to state jubilantly at the rally: Mississippi will not profit half as much from this operation as will Minnesota."[56]

When 17 Minnesota college students went to Mississippi for the summer project, the *Spokesman* voiced enthusiasm for their idealism: "The Mississippi Summer Project is a beginning of human contacts at a level of mutual respect which [is] our only hope of achieving" communication and justice.[57] The student volunteers were from the University of Minnesota, Carleton College in Northfield, St. John's University in Collegeville, St. Mary's in Winona, and St. Cloud State.[58]

The Minnesota legislature was not as responsive as the youth of the state to the imperative of racial justice. In spite of strong ecumenical support from the religious community,[59] in 1961 the initial state fair housing law, Josie Johnson remembered, "barely passed." Although she was discouraged, Josie Johnson felt the need for another organization to engage the Black community who mourned the loss of ENABLE. More activism was Johnson's solution. Like Nellie Griswold Francis who created the antilynching coalition in 1923, in 1963 Josie Johnson had positioned herself for leading an interracial team of community-focused women.

An organizational umbrella was at hand. Josie Johnson had already galvanized community-oriented Black women into the first Minneapolis section of the National Council of Negro Women (NCNW). Writing in 1968, a Minneapolis member recalled the NCNW as "probably *the outstanding* voluntary, non-profit national organization in the forefront of the Negro drive for equality and citizenship in this country." The Minneapolis NCNW offered energetic programs for delinquent girls, leadership training, housing information and advocacy, job training referral, and consumer protection. To support their work with prison inmates they held an art show of paintings by Black artists.[60] A member described the Minneapolis NCNW's Workshops in Mississippi, which twice won the Lane Bryant award from the NCNW in the mid-1960s: "Taking the role of advocacy [Wednesdays in Mississippi] uses workshop methods to close the communication gap between rural and urban poor, government and civic personnel, [by] working on a wide range of economic and civil rights abuses."[61]

Minnesota Women
at Mississippi Freedom Summer

In 1964 Josie Johnson worked out of a sense of urgency. She felt it was critical to keep doors of communication open to White liberals and to disaffected Blacks. With the NCNW program Wednesdays in Mississippi Johnson led a coalition of community-minded Minnesota women to the Deep South.

In a movement that was routinely greeted with attack dogs and riot police and fire hoses, 1963 was the most violent year. In Jackson, MS, an assassin gunned down NAACP leader Medgar Evers in his own front yard. In Winona, MS, grassroots voting rights leaders Fannie Lou Hamer and Annelle Ponder endured brutal beatings—Ponder for hours—with leaded leather straps. Both took months to recover; Hamer's injuries troubled her for the rest of her life. Hundreds of anonymous martyrs went unheralded outside of their communities. To restore community women's heroism to the public consciousness, Paula Giddings chronicled their work in *When and Where I Enter*.[62]

In 1963 Anna Arnold Hedgeman was an executive in the National Council of Churches. She opened her memoir with her visit that year to Birmingham, AL. An interracial team of workers from the National Council of Churches came for the funeral of Addie Mae Collins, Carol Denise McNair, Carole Robertson, and Cynthia Dianne Wesley—ages 14, 11, and 10. They died in a bomb explosion while putting on their choir robes in the Sixteenth Street Baptist Church, the meeting place of the Birmingham civil rights protests.

When she entered the church, Hedgeman wrote, "Bits of glass peppered the floor amid scattered Sunday school books; Bible verses were still on the blackboards." A shattered glass window of Jesus Christ reminded her that Black citizens were today living out the Crucifixion story. To Hedgeman, demonstrations against injustice in Montgomery, Little Rock, Jackson, Birmingham, Chicago, Detroit, and New York reflected modern sacrifices and courage. Hedgeman wondered, why should Whites be surprised at "the so-called Negro Rebellion?"

In Birmingham in 1963 Anna Hedgeman alternated between hope and despair. "Could these four crucified children and the broken figure of Jesus so reach into the souls of all of us that the potential of the Resurrection might again be comprehended in our living?" Hope changed to despair when the mourners walked a gauntlet of Alabama State police, "with guns trained not on the guilty white community but on the funeral procession and on the . . . little white caskets."[63]

Historian Harvey Sitkoff believed that the "orgy of racist violence" in 1963 "aroused the dormant conscience of millions of white Americans. . . . Dozens of student associations, labor unions, and religious organizations provided financial and political backing." Greater protest was then possible.[64] But the South was ready. In 1964, White

Mississippi armed the state to intimidate and to control the volunteers in the Freedom Summer project. The state Highway Patrol grew from 275 to 475 men, and Jackson's police force doubled. The ordinary Black citizens of every little town who did any one action on behalf of civil rights literally risked their lives.

Sitkoff commented that President Johnson dithered about what to do while "white terrorists bombed another thirty homes, burned thirty-five more churches, assaulted at least eighty [movement] workers, and shot at some thirty civil rights workers."[65] Cecil E. Newman also alternated between hope and despair. In mid-July he warned readers of the *Spokesman* and the *Recorder*, both White and Black, to stay out of the Deep South in the summer of 1964.[66]

Josie Johnson led Minnesota women to Jackson and to Vicksburg, MS, where they visited a Freedom School. The Freedom Schools did what Hallie Q. Brown and Phyllis Wheatley settlements, the Federation of Colored Women's Clubs, and the Urban League Auxiliary did in Minnesota: taught history and race pride and a culture of resistance.[67]

Josie Johnson's call, "to save our children," was heard by organized White women from the YWCA, the Protestant group Church Women United, and the Minneapolis Council of Jewish Women. In a radical identification with the parents and the children in the Black Deep South, White Minnesota women joined the Minneapolis Council of Negro Women in a visit to the state capital, Jackson, MS, where so much of the civil rights protest—and the White backlash—took place. The Black women also visited a Freedom School in Vicksburg, MS, the county seat of Warren County, 40 miles west of Jackson and situated along the Mississippi River.

At Freedom Schools the teachers, librarians, and local project staff were mostly women.[68] Paula Giddings emphasized that Black women acted as project directors, and some were in the inner circles of leadership of SNCC. Giddings wrote: "All of this was not to say that there was no sexual discrimination in SNCC—James Foreman himself admitted there was—but it was not perceived to be as 'crippling' as other problems." And on the local level, in rural areas where Black protesters were so vulnerable, Giddings documented that, "It was Black women who represented both the moral and social authority when controversial decisions had to be made."[69]

Josie Johnson testified that in Freedom Summer she had forged a closer identity with ordinary Black Southern women who were important because of what they did and the kind of persons they were. Johnson recalled Fannie Lou Hamer, and said we must put names to the anonymous terror and to the anonymous heroes. "If we don't *learn* from our history," Johnson said, "we're bound to repeat it." Here is her summary of the Minnesotans' pilgrimage:

It was an integrated group of women from the National Council of Negro Women, the Council of Jewish Women, United Church Women and the YWCA. And I was a part of a select team that went to Jackson to get some first hand information on the condition of women and girls in the civil rights struggle.

We left from Minneapolis as an interracial team, and then we went our separate ways in Jackson. . . . The White women visited White churches who were supportive of the movement; they also attended a NAACP rally.

The night we got there we went to a Black church where there was a mass meeting of the NAACP. And I will never forget, there were people patrolling the church with shotguns to try to keep the church from being attacked. It was *very* troubling times.

The Black delegates [from Minnesota] went to see a Freedom School in Vicksburg, Mississippi, and the next day after we left the school was bombed. There were stacks and stacks of books, and White people working too with our children in Vicksburg. Just a *mean* community, Jackson, Mississippi.[70]

Other women's associations acted, if not in Mississippi, in support efforts at home. The Women's International League for Peace and Freedom hosted Black Southern speakers and supported voting rights.[71] Democratic Farmer-Labor Party [DFL] women, like women of the Farmer-Labor Association before them, organized intercultural and interracial work. In the 1960s DFL women lobbied for fair housing legislation and for the FEPC.[72]

In 1963, the *Minneapolis Spokesman* announced that a broad-based coalition of Minnesota women had come together in the Women's Committee on Civil Rights. At the 1964 meeting 200 delegates heard an address by Dr. Dorothy Ferebee, past president of the NCNW. These women's associations staffed planning committees and sponsored the meetings: the National Council of Jewish Women, Business and Professional Women's Clubs, the Minnesota League of Women Voters, the Minnesota Nurses Association, Democratic and Republican National Committeewomen, the St. Paul Archdiocese of Catholic Women, the Protestants of Church Women United and, of course, the YWCA.[73]

In 1963, 1964, and 1965 the NCNW, YWCA, and organized Jewish, Catholic, and Protestant women worked together to create the Minnesota Women's Committee on Civil Rights. They stood on the cutting edge of change. Workshops on Justice, Education, Community Education, Employment, and Housing sought to take this activist audience beyond education and into action. The Committee announced their challenge: "How can women's organizations work against discrimination?" One conclusion is clear: At least in those 3 years, Black and White Minnesota women tried to make change together.

The coalition lasted 3 years. Then a statewide and a national effort called the Commission on the Status of Women tried to continue that cooperation. Josie Johnson served on the Minority Women committee. The 1965 Commission on the Status of Women (CSW) published a lengthy report by and about women of color in Minnesota. Native American women were represented by Ada Deer of the Menominee nation.

Dorothy Height, president of the NCNW, and Minneapolis's Viola Hymes, president of the National Council of Jewish Women, served on the President's CSW. They made sure that minority women's voices were heard in that national forum.[74] Nevertheless, Black women were not on such equal footing with White women as they were in the Women's Committee on Civil Rights.

When the NCNW led a women's coalition they worked hard to draw all the participants into a true partnership. The Wednesdays in Mississippi workshop forced a radical identification by Black and White women with families and communities very unlike themselves. The Mississippi trip did what the NCNW wanted: to force Black and White, rural and urban Americans to talk, *face to face*, about achieving social justice. How much good it did in the long run was what Josie Johnson worried about.

Social Justice Demands a Lifetime Commitment

Josie Johnson spoke at the University of Minnesota at an anti-Vietnam War rally organized by the Minnesota Student Mobilization Committee in 1973. As Mary Jones would have done, she pleaded with students to sign up for life in the social justice struggle. Josie Johnson used the prestige of her Regent's position to argue on behalf of those less fortunate than herself. She said,

> The charge . . . I would like to make to those of you who are taking time now is to consider the larger question, which is the moral climate of our society. If . . . that doesn't become a continued concern, and one that you sense not only in a moment of crisis . . . if these questions aren't for your consideration and for surface discussion all the time, then history will continue to repeat itself, and you'll find you or your children, or your grandchildren assembling at any one moment of history to try and correct that ill . . . those in power who see themselves as superior will continue to have their own way in Africa, Asia and Latin America as well as at home, threatening other people's right to be free and equal as well as different. Try to find out how you can extend this momentary concern about the moral issue of war, how that can be extended to the moral issue of peoples who may very well be different and who need to have you concerned not for four years, and not for a moment of fadism, and not at a time that is highly acceptable, but for [the long run] . . . enough to draw some conclusions for the direction that this society shall take.
>
> Young people, I beg of you, from a very personal sense, of a need to be committed for a long period of time, to think about our society, to try and determine where you fit in it, and try to figure out if you can make a contribution that is significant . . . continue your spirit of concern long enough to make the kind of substantive changes that have to be made in our society if every man is indeed going to be free and equal.[75]

Notes

1. Mary A. Toliver Jones, interview by author, tape recording, St. Paul, MN, November 3, 1983. Unless noted, all other information about Mary Jones is from the interview.

2. Josie R. Johnson, interview by the author, tape recording, Amherst, MA, April 11, 1984. Unless noted, all other information about Josie Johnson is from the interview. Josie R. Johnson, *Personal Data and Experience*, University of Minnesota Archives [U of MN], September 19, 1973.

3. "Protest Analyzes Postwar Thinking," *Minnesota Daily*, January 22, 1973, U of MN. "Partial Text of Mrs Johnson's Remarks," *Minneapolis Star*, p. 26, January 1973. Reprinted with permission of the Star Tribune, Minneapolis-St. Paul.

4. Paula Giddings, *Where and When I Enter: The Impact of Black Women on Race and Sex in America* (New York: Bantam Books, 1984), pp. 93, 109.

5. Evelyn Fairbanks, *The Days of Rondo: A Warm Reminiscence of St. Paul's Thriving Black Community in the 1930s and 1940s* (St. Paul: Minnesota Historical Society [MHS] Press, 1990), pp. 1, 150.

6. Roy Wilkins Special, WCCO-TV, Minneapolis, MN, September 7, 1981. Dr. James Shannon, "The Pilgrim Church," *Minneapolis Tribune*, April 11, 1978.

7. Giddings, pp. 245, 313-314. "Anna Arnold Hedgeman to Speak at Hallie," *Spokesman*, March 9, 1945. "Hedgeman Gets Top Post From Democrats," *Spokesman*, December 30, 1949.

8. Susan Lynn, *Progressive Women in Conservative Times, Racial Justice, Peace, and Feminism, 1945 to the 1960s* (New Brunswick, NJ: Rutgers University Press, 1992), pp. 45-47.

9. Fairbanks, pp. 150-151.

10. Fairbanks, pp. 138-139.

11. Mary Dillon Foster, *Who's Who Among Minnesota Women*, St. Paul, 1924, pp. 101, 205. Only available on reserve at the Minneapolis Public Library and Wilson Library, U of MN.

12. Foster, pp. 101, 205. Madge Hawkins, Undated Notebook, Vol. 6, Box 11, Oscar Hawkins Papers, MHS.

13. Giddings, pp. 17-31.

14. Giddings, pp. 177, 206.

15. Giddings, p. 177.

16. Myrtle Cain, Resume of Experience, January 13, 1949, Myrtle Cain Papers, MHS.

17. Foster, pp. 101, 111.

18. Giddings, pp. 19, 22.

19. *The Crisis*, August 20, 1920; September 20, 1920. For other violence against farm protest, union protest, and "non-patriotic" immigrant groups during World War I see Carl H. Chrislock, *Watchdog of Loyalty, The Minnesota Commission of Public Safety During World War I* (St. Paul: MHS Press, 1991).

20. Robert L. Duffus, "The Ku Klux Klan in the Middle West," *World's Work*, XLVI, 1923.

21. Fairbanks, p. 139.

22. Patricia Hill Collins, *Black Feminist Thought: Knowledge, Consciousness, and the Politics of Empowerment* (New York: Routledge, Chapman, Hall, 1991), p. 15.

23. Cecil E. Newman, Editorial, *Spokesman*, p. 2, May, 23, 1941.

24. "United Behind the Defense of Menaced Scottsboro Boys," *Spokesman*, June 24, 1936

25. Nellie Stone Johnson, interview with author, tape recording, Minneapolis, MN, March 16, 1983. I am working on a biography of Johnson based on interviews and archival materials at MHS. At great personal cost she stayed with the Communist Party until 1950 because they remained the political group most willing to work for racial justice (Fairbanks, p. 92).

26. "Mill City Branch NAACP Begins Drive," *Spokesman*, May 2, 1941; "Hubert H. Humphrey Renews Mpls. Urban League Annual Membership Fee," *Spokesman*, January 13, 1950; "YWCA Annual Meeting in Mpls. Tuesday," *Spokesman*, January 26, 1945.

27. "Youth Clinic Great Success," *Spokesman*, August 30, 1940; "Speaker at Hallie Q," *Spokesman*, January 24, 1936; "Annual Celebration AKA College Women," April 17, 1936; "Frederick Douglas Civic League," *Spokesman*, April 24, 1936.

28. "Ordanance [sic] Plant," *Spokesman*, November 6, 1942; "Form Civilian Defense," *Spokesman*, December 19, 1941; "Charges of Segregation of Women Workers," February 2, 1945.

29. "Twin City Delegation Invades D.C." *Spokesman*, March 2, 1945; "Highlights of the Trip," *Spokesman*, March 9, 1945,

30. "Hallie Annual Hears Mrs. Ann [sic] Hedgeman," *Spokesman*, p. 2, April 6, 1945. Anna Arnold Hedgeman, *The Trumpet Sounds, A Memoir of Negro Leadership* (New York: Holt, Rinehart & Winston, 1964), pp. 13-17.

31. Collins, pp. 15-16.

32. Mary Church Terrell, "What It Means to Be Colored in the Capitol of the United States," Gerda Lerner, ed., *Black Women in White America: A Documentary History* (New York: Vintage, 1973), pp. 378-382.

33. Annie Stein, "A Woman Fights and Jim Crow Bites the Dust," *March of Labor*, July 1954, Arthur Le Sueur Papers, Box 14, MHS.

34. "Baby Girl Arrives," pp. 2-3, *St. Paul Recorder*, August 10, 1934; "The Family, An American Institution," *St. Paul Recorder*, December 28, 1949.

35. "St. Paul Society News," *St. Paul Recorder*, February 17, 1935, p. 3.

36. "Urban League Auxilliary Notes," *Spokesman*, February 17, 1935.

37. Editorial, *Spokesman*, February 22, 1935.

38. "Dr. Mary Waring Attends Women's State Meeting" [Editorial], *Spokesman*, June 26, 1936. Cecil E. Newman, Editorials, *Spokesman*, November 30, 1934, and February 23, 1945. Cecil E. Newman, "Women Leaders In Minnesota State Politics," *Spokesman*, October 2, 1936. See Angela Davis's and Anna Hedgeman's reports of contravention of women's work in the 1960s, in Giddings, pp. 313, 316.

39. "Two Pictures: The Brewery Situation," Cecil E. Newman, *Recorder*, May 24, 1935, p. 2.

40. "Bottling Company Hires Colored Salesman," *Spokesman*, June 7, 1935; "Proof of the Pudding," *Spokesman*, July 5, 1935, p. 2.

41. "Hamm's Brewery Loses Picnic Beer Order," *Spokesman*, July 21, 1935.

42. "Urban League Places Negro Girl at Donaldson's," *Spokesman*, October 9, 1942, p. 1. "Group Finally Gets Place on Anker Staff," *Recorder*, February 7, 1941, p. 1.

43. "Negro Bar In 'U' Housing Upheld by Regents," and Editorial, *Spokesman*, October 25, 1935.

44. "Women's Auxiliary Notes, Urban League," *Spokesman*, June 21, 1935, p. 3. "Urban League Women Tour Swift Plant," *Recorder*, January 12, 1940.

45. Collins, pp. 141-143. That was also the main point of the classic essay that Angela Davis wrote in prison in 1971, "Reflections on the Black Woman's Role in the Community of Slaves," *Black Scholar*, December 1971.

46. "Portrait, Josie R. Johnson," KTCA TV, St. Paul, MN, February 16, 1992.

47. Nellie Stone Johnson, interview with author, tape recording, Minneapolis, MN, November 16, 1983.

48. Johnson, *Personal Data and Experience*.

49. J. R. Johnson, *Personal Data and Experience*.

50. Judith Rollins, *Between Women, Domestics and Their Employers* (Philadelphia: Temple University Press, 1985), pp. 161, 213.

51. Ellen Cantarow, with Susan Gushee O'Malley and Sharon Hartman Strom, *Moving the Mountain: Women Working for Social Change* (Old Westbury, NY: Feminist Press/McGraw-Hill, 1980), pp. 53, 86. Giddings, pp. 274, 275.

52. Martin Luther King, Jr., *Letter From Birmingham Jail*, American Friends Service Committee Paper, May 1963. This 15-page pamphlet is the full, original document. It is a more compelling document.

53. Earl Spangler, *The Negro in Minnesota* (Minneapolis: T. S. Denison, 1961), p. 158.

54. Johnson, *Personal Data and Experience*.

55. Peggy Spector, interview with author, St. Paul, Mn., 31 May 1984. Carol Johnson Flynn, interview with author, St. Paul, Mn., 6 June 1984. Sue Rockne, interview with author, St. Paul, Mn., 28 Dec. 1983. Carol Connolly, interview with author, St. Paul, Mn., 13 Feb. 1985.

56. "Over 2,600 Young Folks Cheer Results of Fund Drive," and "Twin City Area Gives Good Support to Mississippi Project," *Spokesman*, July 23, 1964, pp. 1, 4; "Minnesota Task Force For Mississippi Project Expands State Program," *Minneapolis Spokesman*, August 6, 1964, pp. 1, 4.

57. "Twin City Mayors Join in Support of Mississippi Summer Project," *Minneapolis Spokesman*, July 16, 1964, pp. 1, 4.

58. "Four Minnesota Colleges Represented in Mississippi Rights Summer Project," *Minneapolis Spokesman*, July 30, 1964; "Packing Up Clothes for Mississippi Families," *Minneapolis Spokesman*, August 20, 1964.

59. "We Have A New Law," Box 5, #11,961, Democratic Farmer-Labor State Central Committee [DF-LSCC] Papers.

60. "The National Council of Negro Women," *Minneapolis Negro Profile*, 96, Minneapolis Room, Minneapolis Public Library.

61. "The National Council of Negro Women."

62. Giddings, pp. 267-290.

63. Hedgeman, pp. 3-4.

64. Harvey Sitkoff, *The Struggle for Black Equity, 1954-1980* (New York: Hill & Wang, 1981), pp. 150-152.

65. Sitkoff, pp. 172, 176.

66. Cecil E. Newman, "Publisher's Corner," *Minneapolis Spokesman*, July 16, 1964.

67. Fairbanks, 141-142. "Urban League to Present Negro History Program," *Spokesman*, January 18, 1935.

68. Sara Evans, *Personal Politics: The Roots of Women's Liberation in the Civil Rights Movement and the New Left* (New York: Knopf, 1979), p. 77.

69. Giddings, pp. 284, 302-303.

70. Johnson interview.

71. "WILPF Speaker," *Minneapolis Spokesman*, June 4, 1964. Madge Hawkins, Undated Notebook, MHS.

72. Mary C. Pruitt, *"WOMEN UNITE!" The Modern Women's Movement in Minnesota*, chap. 5, unpublished doctoral dissertation, University of Minnesota, 1987.

73. "MN Women Plan Rights Workshop Nov. 14, Ambassador Hotel," *Spokesman*, November 16, 1963; "Dorothy Height to Address Minnesota Women's Civil Rights Group," *Spokesman*, September 24, 1964; "Minn. Civil Rights Group to Hear Dr. Dorothy Ferebee," *Minneapolis Spokesman*, January 7, 1965.

74. *Minnesota Women, Report of the Governor's Commission on the Status of Women, 1965*, St. Paul, MN, 1965.

75. "Protest Analyzes Postwar Thinking," "Partial Text of Mrs. Johnson's Remarks," *Star*.

5. The Impact of the Civil Rights Movement on the Unionization of African-American Women
Local 282-Furniture Division-IUE, 1960-1988

DEBORAH BROWN CARTER

🔊 Since the 1950s the number of women who are labor union members has increased, with growth especially pronounced among African-American and Hispanic women. Although a decline is evident in recent years, approximately 22% of African-American women were union members in 1988 (U.S. Bureau of the Census, 1989). The explanation for the unionization of African-American women can be found in the changing occupational distribution of women of color (Fredrickson, 1985) and the Civil Rights Movement. The movement of Black women out of agriculture and domestic employment into manufacturing positioned them to be organized. The Civil Rights Movement then provided the leadership and resources, and defined union organization as one strategy to alleviate racial inequality.

In this chapter I will explore the experiences of one group of African-American women organized by Local 282-IUE, located in Memphis, TN, between the years 1960 and 1988. Local 282 exemplifies how social structural change interacted with cultural change to transform the local union's membership. Although in 1960 a little less than half of Local 282's membership was female, in 1988 more than 90% were women. The feminization of Local 282 is also significant because of the implications for theories of unionization. The feminization of the labor movement invites a look beyond strictly structural explanations for union growth—such as unionism as a function of the levels of employment, wages, or prices—to a more dynamic analysis that views unionization in the context of the conflict between labor and capital over

AUTHOR'S NOTE: This chapter is from the author's unpublished doctoral dissertation, *The Local Labor Union as a Social Movement Organization: Local 282-IUE, 1943-1988,* Vanderbilt University, 1988.

Table 5.1 Local 282 Membership and Percentage Change in Membership, 1950-1980

Year	Membership	Additional Members	Percentage Change From Previous Period
1950	245		
1960	797	552	230
1970	1,726	929	116
1980	2,313	587	29

working conditions and wages. The class struggle, for women of color, must be understood as occurring alongside and overlapping with the struggle against racism and gender exploitation. To understand fully the unionization of this group we must appreciate the interaction of race, class, and gender.

Local 282: Background
and Role as Organizing Agent

Located in Memphis, TN, Local 282 was incorporated in May 1943 as a local union affiliated with the United Furniture Workers-Congress of Industrial Organizations (UFW-CIO) (*Furniture Worker's Press*, 1943). The UFW had been formed in 1939 as part of the CIO industrial union drive that sought to unionize workers excluded by the craft-oriented American Federation of Labor. In 1986, the United Furniture Workers of America merged with the International Union of Electrical Workers (IUE). The UFWA is now the Furniture Division of the IUE. The Furniture Division organizes workers in the furniture and wood-products industry.

Local 282 was very small when first chartered, but slowly grew until at its zenith it organized 2,200 workers, with the greatest period of growth occurring between 1960 and 1980. Between 1960 and 1970 the local union's membership doubled; it increased by one third between 1970 and 1980 (see Table 5.1). This fact is significant given that the UFWA and the labor movement as a whole experienced declining membership. The general labor movement dwindled from 35% of the workforce after World War II to less than 22% in 1980 (U.S. Bureau of Census, 1989), whereas UFWA membership declined by 36% between 1970 and 1984 (Cornfield, 1989).

Local 282 is one of a few local unions within the IUE that directly organizes workers. The organizing function is usually undertaken by the Organizing Departments contained within international unions. These bear the primary responsibility for recruiting new members. International Representatives or business agents are dispatched by the international union to assist local unions in organizing campaigns. They conduct an organizing campaign at a nonunionized plant, which culminates in a representation election in which workers vote yes or no for union representation. The election itself is directed by the National Labor Relations Board as stipulated by the 1935 National Labor Relations Act. This type of organizing can be called *new plant organizing*. Once a plant is unionized, it forms a separate local of an international union. Therefore, the typical local union membership is drawn from one plant. After the local union is established, the only recruiting activity is directed to new hires. This type of organizing may be termed *in-plant organizing*.

Local 282 is an amalgamated local union, however, one in which membership is based in more than one shop or plant. The amalgamated union is comparable to the Organizing Department of the International union in that it organizes new plants. Once a plant is unionized, it becomes a shop within the local union. In this type of local union, organizing, contract enforcement, collective bargaining, and strikes are the responsibility of International Representatives headquartered at that local, and elected union officials. Local 282 has always been an amalgamated local union.

Theoretical Background

A traditional lament of scholars of the working class is the alleged lack of class consciousness within the American working class (Bell, 1973). Singled out are racial, ethnic, and gender divisions that split the workers, and the tendency of employers to exploit these divisions to reduce solidarity. Decrying the lack of solidarity between Black and White workers and men and women has oftentimes meant that when people have joined together to behave in class-conscious ways, their actions are overlooked or underemphasized (Fantasia, 1988). Such is the case with low-wage unionism.

Jack Barbash (1973) noted the emergence of a new form of unionism in the 1960s: the organization of workers in low-wage jobs, many of whom were African-American and Hispanic women. Although the overall number of labor union members in the 1960s grew only 12%, unions that organized low-paid workers expanded. For example, Service Employees International Union (SEIU), which organizes workers in low-wage service jobs, increased its membership by almost 60%. Low-wage unionism was attributed to changes in the union proneness of low-wage workers: the inclination of workers to join labor organizations. Barbash proposed that this tendency was enhanced by the increasing size of low-wage employers, and most importantly resulted from the unifying effect of the Civil Rights Movement on poorly paid workers. The Civil Rights Movement was so important that Barbash argues that during the 1960s there was an "interlocking of trade union-ism and civil rights" that led to significant union gains.

Since Barbash's work, little theoretical attention has been directed to low-wage unionism, despite the fact that it is indicative of union growth within the widespread decline of the American labor move-ment. The development of this new form of unionism has important theoretical implications for scholars of the union movement and pro-vides clues as to the distribution and makeup of the American union movement in the future.

One of the most important observations is that the vast majority of new union members were African Americans and substantial numbers were African-American women. There are, however, few studies in the unionization literature that focus exclusively on the unionization of African-American women. Cornfield (1991) maintains that union studies have neglected the empirical study of the propensity of subgroups to organize themselves into unions, particularly what he terms "the ef-fects of class identification on the propensity to unionize" (p. 32). In other words, we know little about the identification of people with class groupings and how this identification factors in the unionization decision.

When seeking to decipher union growth and decline, the most popu-lar interpretations rely on changes in social structure as the explanation for changes in union membership. For example, Daniel Bell's (1973) saturationist view is a structural perspective that proposes that unioni-zation is a function of the structure of the U.S. economy. The dramatic declines in the manufacturing sector and the advent of the postindus-trial economy have meant equally dramatic declines in labor union membership as unions have suffused their potential base of support. Union membership is thus a function of the size of the manufacturing sector. Other structural explanations tie unionization to the levels of prices, wages, and employment (Cornfield, 1991; Heneman & Sandever, 1983).

To grasp the significance of low-wage unionism, however, we must understand the interaction of class, gender, and race and how this inter-action affects the propensity to unionize. The analysis is an attempt to interject a dynamism in static structural explanations because, as Fantasia (1988) argues, class is "an expression, the lived experience . . . an experience shaped by the interaction of collectivities in opposition to each other" (p. 21). Unionization is thus conceptualized as class strug-gle in which both objective factors—that is, the structure of the female working class—is considered, as well as subjective factors, meaning the development of class consciousness, and both are viewed as neces-sary for union growth.

Low-wage unionism informs us that class and class consciousness oftentimes take on varied forms. During the Civil Rights Movement, large numbers of African-American women unionized. They unionized because the class struggle was framed in terms of the conflict between Blacks and Whites. African Americans identified themselves as both Black and working class, and this dual identification led to collective action within the workplace. Further, the Civil Rights Movement brought resources not available to the labor movement before this time. The movement provided leadership and new strategies for organizing workers. Even more importantly, it provided a new ideology that defined economic inequality as a component of racial inequality. The result was an intensification of both racial and class consciousness among African-American women.

In the first phase of the Civil Rights Movement in the South, the primary goal, as articulated by Martin Luther King, Jr., and other civil rights leaders, was to break the pattern of racial segregation in public facilities such as schools, restaurants, and transportation. This goal fueled the bus boycotts, freedom rides, and sit-ins. Many civil rights leaders, however, began to recognize that the desegregation of public facilities was only part of the struggle for Black equality. The exclusive focus on segregation did not attack the root causes of Black inequality: racial discrimination in the labor market in the form of two-tiered job structures and lower wages for Black workers. They argued that the movement needed to turn its attention to the miserable economic condition of Black workers.

One strategy used to move this agenda was to ally the Civil Rights Movement more closely with the labor movement. The strategy called for the civil rights leadership to support union organizing, drives, and strikes. King aided the organizational campaigns of District 65 of the Distributive, Processing and Office Workers Union and Local 1199, Drug and Hospital Employees when they attempted to mobilize Black and Puerto Rican women in the Northeast in the mid-1960s (Foner, 1980). The support given the labor movement by King and other civil rights leaders is representative of the interlocking of trade unionism and civil rights. As a result, the class struggle in the 1960s largely assumed the form of racial conflict between White male employers and women of color.

In the following sections, I discuss how the changing occupational structure positioned African-American women to be unionized; second, how the Civil Rights Movement raised class consciousness among them; and finally, why Black women were amenable to the social changes sought by the movement.

The Occupational Structure
of Black Women in Memphis, 1940-1988

Any discussion of the relationship between labor and capital in the South before the 1960s must begin with the impact of the racial caste system on those relations. Capital not only had the unqualified support of the political system in its exploitation of workers, it also had the advantage of a working class cleaved in two (Marshall, 1967). The caste system subordinated Blacks to the lowest rungs of the occupational ladder. For African-American women this meant employment as domestics and farm laborers (Fredrickson, 1985; Terborg-Penn, 1985).

Beginning with World War II, with the shortage of White male workers, manufacturers turned to groups that theretofore had been excluded from the factories: African-American women. In the furniture industry, the industry organized by Local 282, the percentage of African-American women workers was only 3.3%. In 1950, this had risen to 22.7% and by 1970 was 30.7% (U.S. Bureau of the Census, 1952, 1963, 1973). For African-American women, employment in furniture manufacturing meant a slight move up the occupational ladder and a somewhat higher wage. The change was only slight because Southern furniture manufacturers paid very low wages. Government figures reported that the average annual wage for White workers in U.S. manufacturing industries was $2,841, and it was only $1,295 for Blacks (U.S. Bureau of the Census, 1951). But the average wage for all workers in the Memphis furniture industry was only $1,256. We can assume that the average wage for African-American women was much lower than this, given racial and sexual discrimination in wages.

The switch from domestic and agricultural employment to manufacturing positioned African-American women to be organized by the trade union movement, which has consistently focused its attention on manufacturing. Further, the concentration of women in the factory brought women together, removing another obstacle to unionization: their isolation in single households and on farms. This has been one of the main impediments to the unionization of African-American women (Fredrickson, 1985). Simply being in a position to organize was not enough, however. What was needed were resources and new definitions of the situation to provide the impetus to action. These were provided by the Civil Rights Movement.

The Impact of the
Civil Rights Movement on Local 282's Growth

The 1960s have been described as one of the most turbulent periods in American history, because within this decade we see the awakening of a number of social movements. The premier social movement of the 1960s was the Black struggle for equal rights; this movement provided a model for the others that emerged. "Within each historical era there are typically one or two movements that color the preoccupations and social change affected during the era" (Turner, 1988, p. 391). Sara Evans (1979), in discussing the influence of the Civil Rights Movement on the women's movement, states, "twice in the history of the United States the struggle for racial equality has been midwife to a feminist movement. . . . Working for racial justice, [women] gained experience in organizing, and in collective action, an ideology that described and condemned oppression analogous to their own, and a belief in human rights that could justify them in claiming equality for themselves" (p. 24). Few scholars, however, have assessed the impact of the Civil Rights Movement on the labor movement.

To begin to comprehend how the Civil Rights Movement affected the labor movement, we must understand that social movements are usually embedded within historical cycles of protest. These cycles have occurred regularly in the American experience—the 1870s, 1890s, 1930s, and the 1960s. Cycles are characterized by two features: "new technologies of protest that spread from the point of origin to other sectors of protests; and redefinitions of cultural values and beliefs to apply to new situations" (Turner, 1988, p. 392). The Civil Rights Movement developed both new technologies of protest and a new definition of events that were adopted by other movements. These new technologies included direct action tactics—boycotts, marches, demonstrations, and sit-ins—and new strategies such as a greater dependence on coalitions with churches, students, and other unions to achieve movement goals. Even more importantly, the ideology of the Civil Rights Movement, its focus on racial injustice and human rights, spoke to the concerns of many dispossessed groups.

No social institution in the United States escaped the implacable tide of the Civil Rights Movement as it swept over the country beginning in the late 1950s. As the movement spread, every part of society was forced to confront the specter of institutional racism, including the labor movement. Black labor union members called attention to segregated local unions in the South, the deficit of Blacks in leadership positions in the international unions and the local unions, and the exclusion of Blacks codified in the constitutions of some of the international unions (Foner, 1982).

Pressure for change at Local 282 came from the membership in the late 1950s, a substantial minority of whom were Black workers. They complained that the International Representative assigned to the local union was insensitive to the concerns of Black members. In response to those complaints, the General Executive Board of the UFWA, in 1960, replaced the White male International Representative with LeRoy Clark (interview of LeRoy Clark, October 1987).

LeRoy Clark, who is Black and a civil rights activist, was hired by the UFWA after World War II and was assigned to several local unions in Winston Salem, NC; Chicago; and New York. As one of the few Black organizers on the UFWA's staff, Clark became a spokesman for Black interests within the UFWA. At the 1970 UFWA Convention, Clark was elected Southern Vice-President, the first Black to hold the position of vice president, and also was appointed director of the newly created UFWA Office of Civil Rights (*Furniture Worker's Press*, 1970). As a civil rights activist, Clark is a long-standing member of the National Association for the Advancement of Colored People and served as president and vice president of the Memphis branch in the late 1960s and early 1970s.

Clark's appointment had a far-reaching impact on Local 282. First, it meant that members and potential union recruits had someone with whom to identify, who understood worker concerns regarding racial discrimination in the workplace. Union activists believe that worker response to appeals for solidarity are more effective when they emanate from organizers who have had experiences similar to those of the workers (interview of LeRoy Clark, October 1987; interview of Willie Rudd, October 1987; interview of Carl Scarborough, August 1986).

Clark was responsible for two important changes that increased resources in the form of organizers at Local 282. First, he urged that the part-time position of president become full time. The General Executive Board (GEB) decided to remit part of the per capita payments back to the local union for the president's salary and travel cost. Carl Scarborough was elected as Local 282's first full-time president. But even more importantly, Clark hired Black female organizers for the first time in Local 282's history, Myrtle Thornton and Alzadea Clark (*Furniture Worker's Press*, 1962).

Clark and the African-American women organizers, drawing on the themes of the Civil Rights Movement, began to tie the goals of the labor movement to those of Civil Rights Movement. In organizing campaigns, they emphasized that low wages and unsafe working conditions could be tied to racial discrimination by management. They argued that the only way to improve wages would be to join the union. As early as 1962, union leaders negotiated clauses in union contracts that forbade discrimination on the basis of race (*Furniture Worker's Press*, 1962).

What was significant about these women is that they were recruited from within the shops organized by Local 282. These women had familial and friendship ties with workers in other plants, to whom they could reach out. The result was that during this period of Local 282's history, an unprecedented number of organizing campaigns took place. Over the 12-year period from 1963 to 1975, there were 48 organizing campaigns. This is in contrast to 58 campaigns in the previous 20 years of the local union's establishment.

Not only did the number of organizing campaigns increase, but the local initiated a strategic change that added even more members: *general unionism.* General unionism refers to organizing outside the jurisdiction of a particular union, which in the case of Local 282 was furniture and wood-products manufacturers. In the 1960s, Local 282 began to organize manufacturers in such disparate industries as air-conditioning and food. In fact, 30% of the campaigns between 1963 and 1975 were outside the traditional jurisdiction of the Furniture Workers.

Local 282 also changed its organizing tactics in the early 1960s, utilizing those popularized by Civil Rights Movement. The Civil Rights Movement had been very effective by this time in employing direct action techniques such as sit-ins, marches, and demonstrations. Local 282 leaders escalated the local union's commitment to direct action through strike activity. Between 1943 and 1963, Local 282 used the strike only 5 times. But between 1963 and 1980, there were 23 strikes.

The strategic change that was most striking, however, was the union's alliance with the local and national Civil Rights Movement. The local union sought ties with the movement to aid in organizing campaigns and strikes. Coalitions of civil rights groups are another hallmark of the Civil Rights Movement, and this strategy was adopted by not only Local 282, but other unions. Probably the most effective and most tragic of these alliances was the one that won the Memphis Sanitation Worker's Strike in 1968, and that ended with the assassination of Martin Luther King, Jr. Local 282 members were deeply involved in the strike, providing its headquarters and collecting weekly donations.

The lessons learned by the Sanitation Worker's Strike were invaluable: Local 282 leaders and organizers used the strike as a model for conducting organizing campaigns and strikes. The local union utilized a coalition of labor, church, civil rights, and student groups to win one of its largest organizing campaigns in 1977 and 1978—Memphis Furniture.

The struggle to organize Memphis Furniture represents the new working-class conflict in the South that pits White male employers against a predominately Black female labor force. At Memphis Furniture, which also had two plants in Arkansas, there existed a racial division of labor in which Black females were assigned the dirtiest, lowest paying jobs within the plants. Wages were so low that most of the workers qualified for welfare and food stamps. Workers had no job protection: They were oftentimes dismissed from their jobs arbitrarily during the summer and over Christmas vacations, only to be rehired later at the starting wage. The part of the plant where White workers were concentrated was air-conditioned, but Black workers had to toil in sweltering Memphis summers (Rudd, 1987).

The UFWA had attempted to organize the plants many times in the past. Organizational efforts were unsuccessful because of the tremendous resources the company brought to bear against them. They were willing to use any device, legal or illegal, to keep their plants nonunion. Company officials never hesitated to fire union sympathizers. The race issue was constantly being used to divide workers. They also hired union-busting lawyers who used sophisticated tactics such as captive-audience meetings. They also were not adverse to using the Memphis police to harass strikers on the picket lines and even in their own homes (*Furniture Worker's Press*, 1945).

Willie Rudd, who was president of Local 282 at this time, said that the only way to organize such a powerful employer was to bring local and national attention to the organizing campaign and to use all the resources at the union's disposal. Rudd and other organizers first called upon the national AFL-CIO's Industrial Union Department [IUD]. The IUD surveyed the plant for the UFWA. The purpose of the survey was to analyze the company's financial position to determine if it could afford to give workers higher wages and benefits. Obviously if a company had a tremulous financial position, a union organizing campaign would be almost useless. The survey was also undertaken to assess the wage and internal labor market of the plant so that union organizers might better understand the conditions that gave rise to worker grievances.

Rudd then turned to political activists within the community. Workers were addressed by African-American Congressman Harold Ford, who represented Memphis in the U.S. Congress, and also by the leader of the Memphis State, County and Municipal Employees Union—the union to which the Sanitation Workers belonged.

Nationally known members of the Civil Rights Movement also assisted when Bayard Rustin was asked to help with the campaign. Rustin was the major organizer of the 1963 March on Washington. At Rustin's request, Coretta S. King came to Memphis where she addressed an organizational rally. Mrs. King's visit was very significant because it was the first time she had visited Memphis since her husband's assassination 9 years before.

The alliance between the two movements was crucial for Local 282's growth. The Memphis Furniture campaign added more than 600 members to Local 282, which increased membership in the local union by one third. This alliance was used in several organizing campaigns and strikes, and thus the interlocking of trade unionism and civil rights was a successful strategy for Local 282.

Implications of the Interlocking of Trade Unionism and Civil Rights for the Organization of African-American Women

The joining of the Civil Rights and the labor movements was significant for the organization of Black women for three reasons: (a) it was a continuation of the historical tradition of collective organization among African-American women based on family and kin networks as a bulwark against racial and class oppression; (b) because of the role

played by the Black church in providing economic, social, and ideological support for unionization; and (c) the ideological substance of
the movement that spoke to concerns larger than the narrow economic
self-interest ideology of American trade unionism.

One of the most important reasons that Black women were so willing
to join Local 282 is the heritage of collective action within the Black
community. The precariousness of economic and political life has led
African-American women to pursue collective solutions to a variety of
problems (Stack, 1974; Terborg-Penn, 1985). This collective organization took the form of networks of reinforcing support based on kin and
friends. In the 1960s, as I emphasized above, African-American women
were recruited into the ranks of union organizers. These women served
as role models and resources for other women who sought to improve
their economic condition. In organizing campaigns and strikes, these
networks within which women were embedded provided financial
support and transmitted information about unionization. In fact:

> more recently . . . the leadership in southern union organizing efforts has
> come increasingly from Black women. Brought up in opposition to White author-
> ity and trained in the Civil Rights Movement, in many southern mills Black
> women have been the workers most responsive to seeking cooperative solu-
> tions to work situations. (Fredrickson, 1985, pp. 173-174)

A second reason that the interlocking of trade unionism and civil
rights led to organization of Black women was the role played by the
church. Although the Black church is led by men, women form the majority of its members (Lincoln, 1984). It is difficult to assess the impact
of church support for the labor movement. The church provided and
continues to provide money and meeting places for union organizing
campaigns and strikes. But just as important has been the moral support. Martin Luther King, Jr., as a minister, believed that union organization was one important technique for decreasing economic inequality between African Americans and Whites, and believing so, civil
rights leaders became union organizers. King time after time lent support
to organizing campaigns and strikes. This support legitimated, in the
eyes of African-American women, the trade union movement.

The ideology of the Civil Rights Movement, more importantly,
spoke to the experiences and values of African-American women. Snow
and Rockford (1988) argue that people will join a movement only
when that movement is framed in the language of their own experiences; it must speak to the central life experiences of those it seeks to
recruit. LeRoy Clark stated that he believed the most important contribution of the Civil Rights Movement to the labor movement was to
make workers aware of their rights and convince them that they must
take action to achieve them (interview of LeRoy Clark, October 1987).

Freeman and Medoff (1984) argue that after World War II an implicit compact developed between labor and capital. In exchange for labor peace, employers were not as averse as they might have been to unionization. The ideology undergirding this compact was one that de-emphasized class differences, paid no attention whatsoever to racial and sexual discrimination in the workplace, and underscored the benefits to individual workers of cooperation between management and labor.

The labor movement influenced by the Civil Rights Movement, however, refocused attention on racial inequality and accentuated class differences and antagonistic relationships between labor and capital. This refocusing spoke directly to the experiences of African-American women, who have always occupied the lowest positions within the occupational structure because they are both Black and female. By highlighting racial and class differences between women workers and male employers, the labor movement demonstrated to women a concern for their grievances in the language of their experience.

Conclusions

Theories of unionization that rely on structural change to explain union growth and decline are remiss because they ignore the role of consciousness, particularly how class and ethnic identification lead people to join labor organizations. It has been demonstrated in this chapter how the Civil Rights Movement redefined economic inequality as part and parcel of racial inequality. This raised awareness among African-American women of the dual nature of their oppression. This expanded awareness led to unprecedented growth in the labor movement as African-American women realized that they were the victims of both racial and economic exploitation.

During the 1960s the labor movement demonstrated its continued tenacity, despite setbacks in its overall strength, as workers previously out of the union orbit were brought into it: African-American women. These women became union members because they moved into the traditional jurisdiction of American trade unionism and because of the Civil Rights Movement. The movement galvanized these women by providing resources to help them organize and—more importantly—it redefined union organization as part of the larger struggle to liberate Black America. Without the Civil Rights Movement many of these workers would have remained unorganized. The interlocking of Civil Rights and the labor movement gave Black women an opportunity to improve their economic position and infused them with a new sense of their own efficacy, a belief that they could make a difference in their own lives and the lives of others.

References

Barbash, Jack. (1973, December). The emergence of low-wage unionism. In *Industrial Relations Research Association proceedings*, 26th Annual Winter Meeting, New York.

Bell, Daniel. (1973). *The coming of post-industrial society.* New York: Basic Books.

Cornfield, Daniel. (1989). *Becoming a mighty voice: Conflict and change in the United Furniture Workers of America.* New York: Russell Sage.

Cornfield, Daniel. (1991). The US labor movement: Its development and impact on social inequality and politics. *Annual Review of Sociology, 17,* 27-49.

Evans, Sara. (1979). *Personal politics: The roots of women's liberation in the civil rights movement and the new left.* New York: Vintage.

Fantasia, Rick. (1988). *Cultures of solidarity: Consciousness, action and contemporary American workers.* Berkeley: University of California Press.

Foner, Phillip. (1980). *Women and the American labor movement: From World War I to the present.* New York: Free Press.

Foner, Phillip. (1982). *Organized labor and the Black worker: 1619-1981* (2nd ed.). New York: International Publishers.

Fredrickson, Mary. (1982). Four decades of change: Black workers in southern textiles, 1941-1981. *Radical America, 16*(November-December), 27-44.

Fredrickson, Mary. (1985). I know which side I'm on: Southern women in the labor movement in the twentieth century. In R. Milkman (Ed.), *Women, work and protest* (pp. 157-175). Boston: Routledge & Keagan Paul.

Freeman, Richard, & Medoff, James. (1984). *What do unions do?* New York: Basic Books.

Furniture Worker's Press. (1940-1988). [Various issues; monthly newsletter of the United Furniture Workers of America.]

Furniture Worker's Press. (1943, May). [Newsletter of the United Furniture Workers of America.]

Furniture Worker's Press. (1945, July). [Newsletter of the United Furniture Workers of America.]

Furniture Worker's Press. (1962, January). [Newsletter of the United Furniture Workers of America.]

Furniture Worker's Press. (1970, October). [Newsletter of the United Furniture Workers of America.]

Heneman, Herbert, & Sandever, Marcus. (1983, July). Predicting the outcome of union certification elections: A review of the literature. *Industrial and Labor Relations Review, 36,* 550-570.

Lincoln, C. Eric. (1984). *Race, religion and the continuing American dilemma.* New York: Hill & Wang.

Local 282 Organizational Files, 1975-1986. [Local 282-IUE, 1254 Lamar Ave., Memphis, TN 38104]

Marshall, F. Ray. (1967). *Labor in the south.* New York: John Wiley.

Rudd, Willie. (1987). *The real Memphis furniture story.* Pamphlet. [Available from Local 282-IUE, 1254 Lamar Ave., Memphis, TN 38104]

Snow, David A., & Rockford, E. Burke. (1988). Frame alignment processes, micromobilization and movement participation. *American Sociological Review, 51,* 464-481.

Stack, Carol. (1974). *All our kin: Strategies for survival in a Black community.* New York: Harper & Row.

Terborg-Penn, Rosalyn. (1985). Survival strategies among African-American women workers: A continuing process. In R. Milkman (Ed.), *Women, work and protest* (pp. 139-155). Boston: Routledge & Keagan Paul.

Turner, Ralph. (1988). The theme of contemporary social movements. *British Journal of Sociology, 20,* 390-405.

U.S. Bureau of the Census. (1951). *County business patterns, Tennessee: 1950.* Washington, DC: Government Printing Office.

U.S. Bureau of the Census. (1952). Table 83—Race and class of worker and of employed persons, by industry and sex, for the state and for standard metropolitan areas of 100,000 or more: 1950. In *United States census of the population: 1950, Vol. 2: Characteristics of the population, part 42: Tennessee* (pp. 291-295). Washington, DC: Government Printing Office.

U.S. Bureau of the Census. (1963). Table 129—Industry of the employed by race and class of worker, and of the experienced civilian labor force by color, by sex, for the state and for standard metropolitan statistical areas of 250,000 or more: 1960. In *United States census of population: 1960, Vol. 1: Characteristics of the population, part 44: Tennessee* (pp. 530-539). Washington, DC: Government Printing Office.

U.S. Bureau of the Census. (1973). Table 186—Industry of employed persons by class of worker, race, and sex: 1970. In *United States Census of the population: 1970, Vol. 1: Characteristics of the population, part 44: Tennessee* (pp. 816-837). Washington, DC: Government Printing Office.

U.S. Bureau of the Census. (1981). Table 184—Labor force characteristics by race and Spanish origin for the counties: 1980. In *United States census of the population: 1980, Vol. 1: Characteristics of the population, Ch. C: General Social and Economic Characteristics, part 44: Tennessee* (pp. 478-492). Washington, DC: Government Printing Office.

U.S. Bureau of the Census. (1989). *Statistical abstract of the United States: 1989* (109th ed.). Washington, DC: Government Printing Office.

6. Poor Black Sisters Decided for Themselves
A Case Study of 1960s Women's Liberation Activism

M. RIVKA POLATNICK

🖹 Writers on the 1960s' rebirth of feminism typically discuss why middle-class Whites launched a women's movement, and why Black[1] women did not join it. Other women of color, and working-class and poor women, also are portrayed as absent from the early movement. Though these characterizations contain a measure of truth, basically they are misleading.

With regard to Black women, it is true that few in the sixties saw themselves as part of the women's movement—either of its liberal "women's rights" or radical "women's liberation" wings. Some Black women did participate and even play leadership roles.[2] But women's movement organizations were predominantly White, and White-dominated.

However, if we look only at activists within the self-defined women's movement, we leave out women who fought for the cause in other contexts. Some Black women in the 1960s battled male supremacy in Black or community organizations. Some formed separate women's groups that were antisexist, but these groups typically did not consider themselves part of the White-dominated "women's movement." All these women were part of the 1960s' wave of women's rights/ liberation activism. Studies that cover only the narrowly defined women's movement build the impression that Black women did not take up the cause.[3]

AUTHOR'S NOTE: First and foremost, I want to thank the women I interviewed, whose help and insights made this study possible. The research was supported in part by the Mabelle McLeod Lewis Fund. On earlier versions of this material I received helpful feedback from Beatriz Pesquera, Sandra Uyeunten, Isabel Tirado, Bob Blauner, Arlie Hochschild, and Barbara Christian, and on a draft of this chapter, from Elaine Bell Kaplan, Lois Helmbold, Nancy Grey Osterud, and Patricia Guthrie. I also thank Kim Vaz for her interest in my research, Barbara LaRocca for her encouragement, and Esta J. P. Grill for her understanding and love.

From the start of the contemporary women's movement, women of different racial/ethnic groups and economic classes were "in motion" for the women's cause. Women of color and working-class women took up the cause in their own ways, just as White women and middle-class women took up the cause in *their* own ways.

In the late 1960s, many White women who advocated women's liberation began to make it their central or even exclusive political focus, whereas most women of color who advocated women's liberation tended to spread their efforts among racial, class, *and* specifically women's issues. The political strategy of building an independent women's liberation movement was developed and pursued largely by White women. If pursuing that strategy becomes the sole model of women's liberation activism, we wipe most women of color off the record of contributors to the cause.[4]

This chapter describes a pioneering 1960s' group of Black and mainly poor women, the Mount Vernon/New Rochelle group,[5] who were outspoken critics of women's oppression and militant advocates of women's liberation. The 1960s' radical women had particular impact through their writings, and this group's papers were widely distributed and frequently published, including in three major 1970 mass market anthologies (Cade; Morgan; and Tanner). Yet I never have seen this group mentioned in any study of the contemporary women's cause.[6]

What follows is a "herstory" of this remarkable group. My account is based on primary written sources from the 1960s through early 1970s—the group's published and unpublished writings, transcripts of group meetings—and on my 1983 interviews with six women who were core members.[7] The group consisted of two networks of lower working-class women in the neighboring cities of Mount Vernon and New Rochelle (near New York City), and a middle-class Black social worker who played a key catalyst role. Because little has been written on why Black women took up the women's cause in the 1960s, I give background on how the group originated. The two networks developed independently, so I tell their separate stories first, and then discuss their joint efforts. In the conclusion, I come back to the issue of the different forms of 1960s' women's liberation activism.

The Mount Vernon Branch

The Mount Vernon branch of the group goes back to 1960, when Pat R.[8] came to the poor neighborhood there as a "volunteer visitor" for Planned Parenthood. Pat was a radical social worker in her thirties, living with her husband and three small children in New Rochelle. From a prominent Black family in Baltimore that owned a newspaper chain, Pat had gravitated toward the leftist influences in her environment and had numerous connections to Black and other radicals. She had developed a keen interest in the psychology of oppression.

In 1960, the local Planned Parenthood organization was worried about a sharp rise in births among poor Black teenagers. Girls had been giving birth as young as 12 or 13, and by their early twenties, might have six or seven children. Many of these girls had grown up in the rural South. When they moved north, they encountered harsh ghetto conditions and schools they found extremely alienating, and their prospects for employment were bleak. Northern-born Blacks looked down on them. In this inhospitable environment, Pat comments, "their only outlet was getting pregnant."[9] Usually they ended up without a stable male partner and with welfare as their means of support. Planned Parenthood wanted someone who could bring birth control advice to this community.

Pat decided to take on the task. She saw birth control as an important tool for women to gain some control over their lives:

> My generation was not allowed birth control. We were extremely vulnerable to pregnancy and birth. In adolescence there was always a great fear and foreboding about getting pregnant, which had a very negative effect on relationships with men. You could only get birth control if you were married and middle class, able to afford a doctor.

The women who would become part of a politicized network in Mount Vernon ranged from grandmothers to teenagers. Those who were employed had low-paying factory jobs or did domestic work in the homes of affluent Whites. Many of the women were mothers on welfare.

When Pat began going door to door in the slum buildings, she decided to expand her focus beyond birth control. Women were telling her, over coffee in their kitchens, about hassles with landlords, schools, hospitals, and the Department of Welfare. Pat began talking with them about how these daily problems fit into the larger picture of national and world politics. She also discussed Black history and the Black movement, about which the women had heard little.

The women began opening up about their personal lives. "Under conditions of poverty," Pat saw, "the family becomes an arena of power struggles of enormous proportions." The women were especially eager to discuss their problems with men. Individual conversations evolved into group sessions.

Joyce H., then a domestic worker in her twenties, was suspicious at first of this middle-class "good-doer," but she explains why she became involved in the developing group:

> We had so much fun talking. [Pat] opened your eyes to see these things that you don't pay any attention to. She was talkin' about the President and the different

parts of government, and what-not. And when she said these things you went
to the paper and actually started reading and listening to the news.

Joyce recalls a sense of waking up to the environment around her
and questioning old assumptions. For example, having always worked
to support herself, she would "get ticked off" about mothers on welfare who "had these men and kept havin' these babies." After talking
with Pat about welfare recipients, "I started really looking at them.
And then I got this opinion there are some women who need welfare,
should have it, and I'd gladly help, though there was others I didn't
want to give a penny to." With Pat's prodding, the women were asking
more questions about the larger social system: *Why* were so many mothers on welfare?[10]

As the women expressed interest in various subjects, Pat brought
articles and books for them to read. Over time, she encouraged them
to write down their thoughts and observations. She talked with the
children, too, and began tutoring them after school.[11]

When it seemed appropriate, Pat did discuss birth control. She
encouraged women to use diaphragms, but they were "horrified" at
having to "handle [their] genitals and insert a mechanical device."[12]
Many of the women felt pressured by their men to have sex without
precautions. As Joyce remembers, "The men still had that thing of keep
them with stomachs big, and barefooted, you know, that macho thing.
. . . Pat was trying to get those women to wake up that it didn't have
to be that way."

Pat argued strongly for legalizing abortion. New York State law at
the time allowed it only to save the mother's life. Some Mount Vernon
women were personally opposed to abortion, but discussing the issue
heightened awareness of the constraints on women's lives. Joyce explains, "Pat had to break it down to women: Why should you have a
baby you don't want and you can't take care of?"

At this very juncture in the early 1960s, the women began hearing
about the new birth control pill. Like many women, the Mount Ver-
nonites were afraid of it at first: What would it do to them? But as more
and more favorable publicity came out, they began to warm up to it,
feeling its tremendous promise. Some took the pill early on. Most waited
2 or 3 years, until the mid-1960s. That was when, as Pat put it later, "they
began to revolt. . . . That Black woman began popping those pills into
her mouth and telling her husband and lover what she thought. . . . She
had made an interior decision to control her own destiny."[13]

Most of the Mount Vernon women, living in unrelenting poverty,
felt little connection to the Black civil rights movement. Joyce remembers conversations with Pat about:

the so-called Black leaders, King, Whitney Young, Randolph, and all of 'em. I
used to say, "What are you talkin' about? He ain't my leader!" And Pat would
crack up. I'd say "Don't you know that man hasn't done nothin' for me!"

Pat spoke with the women about social change movements around
the world, and brought them all kinds of readings from the left. Some
of the women had only grade school educations and had to work hard
at the reading. But they wanted to learn more. "We had never had any
experience with anyone who had faith in us, had faith . . . that we
could change our lives."[14]

Confrontations: "The Welfare,
the Landlord, the Black Male"

Poor mothers in Mount Vernon always had had their troubles with
the Department of Welfare. Many found it hard to get the full amount
of money to which they were entitled by law. Most felt their dignity
affronted by welfare procedures. In 1964, the year major riots were
erupting in urban Black ghettos, some local welfare recipients turned
to violence too, attacking a caseworker and supervisor. Soon after these
incidents, the Welfare Department gave everyone an extra allowance.

The Mount Vernon network was quite aroused by these developments. Primed by their political education, they began to take action
against the oppressive conditions of their lives. Rita V. organized a
welfare mothers group that fought for welfare rights. Several women
decided to undertake a rent strike. They were facing a rent increase in
a building without adequate heating and infested with rats and roaches.

Middle-class feminists may recognize welfare rights as a "women's
issue," but for the Mount Vernon women, decent housing was too. The
women were the ones maintaining family life (men being more marginally involved). The women had the primary responsibility for providing housing for their families.

As the women began organizing the rent strike, they confronted a
painful reality: "The first enemy was not the landlord, was not the
welfare, but the Black male!"[15] The men in their lives did not want the
women stirring up trouble. When the women went ahead anyway, some
of their men began beating them up. Pat recounts,

> Soon I was being called into the ghetto . . . to wipe up the blood and take care
> of children because a woman had gone to jail because she had killed her man.
> Three deaths came in a very short time. The violence of the women was a
> reaction to the equivalent violence of the men. It was a revolutionary confron-
> tation fought out in ghetto apartments. This awakened me, forced me into
> seeing the woman's revolution. It was unfolding before my eyes.[16]

The women lost their battle with the landlord; he managed to evict
them. Some of the women felt defeated, momentarily, but soon they

could sense how much the experience had strengthened them. "We were mad now and we were not taking shit from anybody."[17]

During these confrontations, the group began defining their allies as those women who "put children first"—that is, who gave priority to the needs of family and community—versus the "dick-happy sisters" who neglected their children and always put a man first.

Freedom School

By 1966, the Mount Vernon women were taking a stand against the war in Vietnam, which they had decided was "a war against people like us." They argued with men in their community who wanted to enlist.[18]

That same year, the women launched a project that would be a central focus through the early 1970s. Pat had been tutoring children individually and in groups, and they were flourishing in a way they never had in their schools. A number of the mothers wanted to make things more organized, and bring in more children. The group decided to create a "Freedom School," which met on Saturday afternoons at Joyce H.'s apartment. It grew at its peak to 35 children, ranging in age from 2 to 14.[19]

The Freedom School went beyond traditional academics. The children studied African and African-American history, and learned self-pride. They developed their consciousness about racial, class, women's, and children's oppression. And they discussed how to confront these issues in their own lives.

Providing an effective education for children also must be seen, in the context of this community, as a "women's issue." Mothers shouldered most of the parental responsibility for children's learning. The Freedom School collectivized a primarily female job and carried it out better than the individual mothers could.

The Debate With the Nationalists

By 1966, Black movement ideology was shifting toward nationalism. The Mount Vernon women disagreed with the politics of "Black unity" and "Black power." They saw the nationalist leaders as middle-class men trying to get power for themselves, on the backs of the Black poor. They were further alarmed when some nationalists began telling Black women to "get behind" their men, so the men could take their rightful place as the leaders. The Mount Vernon group became outspoken critics of this line.

Some nationalist women took a different tack concerning sexual politics: They portrayed the African past as sexually egalitarian or even matriarchal, blaming Western culture for subordinating women. Pat debunked these visions, talking about hierarchical structures in the old Africa with the masses of women on the bottom and only a few "queens" sharing some privileges of the ruling males. The Mount Vernon group concluded that nationalist women wanting to be "African queens" did not have poor women's interests at heart.

The group engaged in heated ideological exchanges with nationalist women, exposing the contradictions of sex and class within the Black community. They circulated their writings to other poor women.

"Poor Black sisters decide for themselves whether to have a baby"

In 1968, the Mount Vernon women were noticing material in the Black Muslim newspaper and other Black publications that was anti-birth control. That summer, Pat R. received a statement by the Black Unity Party of Peekskill, NY, entitled "Birth Control Pills and Black Children." It began, "The Brothers are calling on the Sisters not to take the pill. . . . To take the pill means contributing to our own *GENO-CIDE.*" The Unity Party said White supremacists were pushing birth control on Black women as the latest means of "Race Control." Blacks should view procreation as highly positive, they asserted. "When we produce children, we are aiding the REVOLUTION in the form of NATION building."[20]

The sisters of Mount Vernon decided they had to write a response (September 1968), which they addressed to "Dear Brothers." "Poor Black sisters decide for themselves whether to have a baby or not to have a baby," they declared. They attacked poor Black men bitterly for failing to help them raise the children. The pill meant that "men could no longer exploit us sexually or for money and leave the babies with us to bring up." The women agreed that "whitey" had genocidal motives. But the pill, they argued, gave them "freedom to fight genocide of Black women and children. . . . Having too many babies stops us from supporting our children, teaching them the truth . . . and fighting Black men who still want to use and exploit us."

The women closed by challenging the motives of the "Black unity" people: "You want to use poor Black women's children to gain power for yourself. You'll run the Black community with your kind of Black power—You on top! The poor understand class struggle!"[21]

When the group decided to distribute their statement beyond their own community, a domestic worker suggested that Pat as an educated intellectual should write an accompanying piece, because many people would dismiss the words of poor women. Pat's essay "Poor Black Women" depicted the process of awakening from oppression. She wrote that the poor Black woman at first saw her problem as

oppression by the Black man. But awareness in this case has moved to a second phase and exposes an important fact in the whole process of oppression. It takes two to oppress, a proper dialectical perspective to examine at this point in our movement.

This idea of "it takes two" had become a central concept of the group's thinking. Pat explained that oppressors need "the cooperation of the oppressed," and secure it in the long term "by psychological manipulation and seduction." The oppressed come to believe in their masters' superiority. In the case of woman and man, she also gives him "the surplus product of her body, the child, to use and exploit."

But the poor Black woman was breaking through the illusion of being inferior, and moving toward rebellion. Conditions in the United States had forced her to raise the children herself, which weakened "male authority." Now she was inspired by the "revolutionary struggles" of "the have-nots in the wider world." She did not want her children used as soldiers to suppress those struggles. She "has begun to question aggressive male domination and the class society which enforces it, capitalism."[22]

These two papers circulated through radical networks around the country, and appeared in women's movement, New Left, and then mass market publications. The Mount Vernon group had become a national political presence.

The New Rochelle Branch

The group of New Rochelle young women who would join forces with the Mount Vernon network numbered 6 to 10 at the core, and up to 20 counting marginal members. They grew up together in a low-income housing project, where the city's Black population was concentrated. Many of their mothers worked as domestics or as cleaning women in local hospitals; a few were typists or nurse's aides. Most of their fathers had worked in factories in the early 1950s, but had lost those jobs when the economy went into a slump. The mothers and fathers blamed each other for their problems, and many of the fathers drifted away from their families.[23]

Just entering adolescence in the early 1960s, Carrietta G., Maureen W., Linda Landrine,[24] and friends experienced some of the racial struggles spearheaded by the civil rights movement. In 1960-1961, their parents helped fight a successful campaign to integrate New Rochelle's schools; as sixth graders the girls were thrust into the hostile environment of White schools in the affluent part of town. In 1964, when a White policeman brutally clubbed a young Black man outside their housing project, the girls took part in angry protests by project residents.[25]

As high school students in the middle to latter 1960s, some of these young women were tutoring children, to "uplift" the educational level of their community. Some also joined a co-ed drum corps, which had a strong impact on their thinking about women and men. Maureen W. recounts:

> We had to march fifty blocks just like the guys marched fifty blocks. I was carrying rifles, sabers, right?—men's flag poles because we couldn't afford to get the lighter weight for women. We marched in the rain, dirty, sweaty, right along with [the guys].

Later these young women would resist suggestions that "you can't do as much as I can."

The Sisters in BRO

The assassination of Martin Luther King, Jr., in April 1968 galvanized many Black students at the high school into political action. They launched an organization, Black Radicals Onward (BRO), which grew to several hundred members. BRO aimed to serve and protect the Black community and to promote Black unity and pride. Its community services included baby-sitting, tutoring, helping old people with shopping, and running weekend recreation programs. BRO published a weekly paper, established a freedom school and a theater group, and fought successfully for high school Black Studies classes. BRO also created evening "community patrol" groups to prevent mugging and vandalism and break up drug traffic.[26]

Within BRO was a core of young women used to speaking up and used to standing up for themselves. When the group first adopted the name Black Radicals Onward with its acronym BRO (the widely used short form of "brother"), one woman objected that this slighted the sisters. But the others let the issue pass. Carrietta recalls that, "as an individual I wouldn't let no one suppress me, but I wasn't thinkin' about it on that level."

But other female/male issues arose soon that these women did not let pass. One involved leadership positions in BRO. The women "found out there was a clique within the organization which was all males—about three or four who were making decisions." When the group established formal leadership roles—"ministers"—the women insisted on having "ministresses" too, to ensure females would be represented. Who participated in the evening community patrols became another issue. At first only the men went out, but the women objected and joined the patrols.

At a community meeting held by BRO, the young women met Pat R., who became a source of support and information on the women's liberation issue. The women had periodic group meetings with Pat, and also a lot of one-to-one exchanges. "Pat came in with the theory," Carrietta and Linda relate. "We knew there was an antagonism between men and women. Pat would help us analyze why. She would bring in the history, and put it in the right perspective." Maureen W. recalls learning about women's participation in revolutionary movements: "In Cuba, they had a similar struggle [to ours] with the men, when they were in guerrilla warfare with Castro. They also could not be on the front, until [there was] a male shortage and they [were] needed."

As the young women got more intimate with Pat, she backed them in their struggles with husbands and boyfriends too. One of the women describes such a situation:

> [Pat] saw where we was having that power struggle between the two of us because he wanted that power that I wouldn't give him over me. So we were constantly bickering back and forth, but we weren't using the terms "You're oppressing me." I was just letting him know "Hey, no, I don't want to do it that way," or "I don't like it that way, so just because you said it that way, don't mean it has to be that way." But we weren't able to define it the way Pat was, and then Pat, like, came in. She was like the intermediary. "That is a form of oppression!"

Among the 10 to 15 women taking part in sessions with Pat were some whom the militants labeled "apolitical": "they weren't able to follow through, weren't strong enough." The militants started seeing these others as "phonies," who

> really wanted men to dominate them, though they would say they didn't around Pat. We was telling Pat it was very hard to deal with our males when we got these other women counteracting us. If you have the other women that they can easily go to, then it was hard.

Despite their readiness to attack male domination, even the militants remained close with men in BRO. "There was not that much separation," Maureen W. remarks. "The struggle for us was common: for all Black people. That overshadowed it. [The men] definitely weren't our enemies."

"Renegade Women": Sisters, Muslims, Panthers

By fall 1968, BRO members were feeling a strong influence from two other Black organizations: the Black Muslims and the Black Panthers. A number of BRO brothers had become followers of Elijah Muhammad. "They wanted all of us to come in there and wanted the women to put something on their head and wear long dresses," Carrietta recalls. "We was like, 'No, now you're crazy.' " The few BRO women who did join the Muslims, Linda Landrine comments, "wanted the man to be over them anyway, because the whole idea of the religion itself was that the woman should stay in the background."

Those who remained in BRO gravitated toward the Black Panthers. "At the time," Linda and Carrietta remember, "we felt we had to destroy the system. The Muslims were saying we're gonna build our own empire. Those that fit with the Muslims still wanted to be part of the system." BRO adopted much of the Panther Party program and built ties with Panthers in Harlem.

Some of those Panther men had yet another conception of women's role. "They felt that by us being in the movement meant that we had to go to bed with them." Carrietta remembers her reaction: "I jumped up on the table and I was telling 'em, 'Uh uh, that's our bodies. We control that. We say what we want to do. You all don't come here and tell us what we got to do. You're going a little too far!' "

Some men in BRO tried taking this same stance, Maureen relates. "We had a big meeting among ourselves and they said, 'We feel if we want to have sex with any woman in the group, we can.' And we just said, 'Wait, no, this is it!' We purged it."

The women saw their men picking up from New York Panthers other ideas about what women's role should be: "to provide meals, a big social function. But we weren't to have weapons or be on the front line—just stay in the background." The women had been "doing okay" with the BRO men till this point, but as Maureen explains it,

> I guess the fellows felt like that somewhere inside them. I think they even went down there to get some [idea] how to put us in [our] place, really, from the Panthers. These renegade women, that's what they called us, renegade women, down there.

These New York Panthers "said [women's liberation was] a reactionary White women's movement, that didn't have a place for Black women in it. Something created to cause friction between the Black male and the Black woman." (Some months later, the Panther Party announced from their national headquarters that they supported women's liberation.)

From the combined influence of the Muslims and Panthers, men in BRO began taking a more protective attitude toward women. They insisted they had to walk women home after meetings. Linda got furious: "Nobody ever walked me before, and you're not gonna do it now." Carrietta remembers a "big argument" afterward with the less militant women:

> [They] was sayin', "I don't want him to oppress me, but I want to be able to depend on him for walking me home." I'm sayin,' "What in the fuck do you mean you got to have a man walk you here, walk you there? You've been walking all your life! What are you talking about? You know, don't use—," cause they was using what the Panthers was saying for their benefit, because they wanted to try and get one of them men that was involved.

When the BRO women visited the Panthers in New York, they tried talking to the Panther sisters "about their womanhood." But what the BRO women said contradicted the prevailing anti-women's liberation line, and this "caused a lot of confusion between the two of us." Eventually the BRO women "busted up even having any relationship with them."

Black Women's Liberation,
White Women's Liberation

In the last months of 1968, the New Rochelle women were hearing more about "White women's liberation." They perceived "the White women's struggle" as different in important ways from their own. "Women's liberation for White women was their way to get out of the home. We never was house women. We was always out there. We couldn't afford not to work." The White women, they believed, wanted to compete with men. "All we were saying was treat us like human beings."

In attempting to build an understanding of "Black women's liberation," the New Rochelle group encountered much resistance from those around them. Their Panther acquaintances were not the only ones denying the relevance of the issue to Black women's lives. "Touchy problem, you know. We got backlash from community organizations because they said the struggle was Black and White and 'we don't have these problems.'" Many women in the community felt they had nothing to be liberated from, because they headed their own households, like their mothers before them. But the New Rochelle group contended that "even being the head of the household, you're still oppressed, and you still have a man somewhere, with his foot on your neck."

Women living with a man, the group thought, had problems similar to those the White women talked about: "whose role is what role?" They saw a lot of these women "oppressed within the home, not knowing how to get him off their back. Instead of dealing with the husband, they'd run off to church and deal with Jesus."

The New Rochelle women had to challenge the popular belief that in the paid labor force, Black women fared better than Black men. Pat R. provided statistics from the Department of Labor showing that the women (working full time) earned less than the men, within every educational level and for all types of work except professional and managerial. The data also revealed substantially higher unemployment rates for the women.[27]

The group strove to get historical perspective on Black female/male relations. Carrietta describes the broad pattern they perceived:

> From slavery, we was able to get by a little more than the men. So we put the men on a pedestal, tryin' to build them up. They took it out of proportion, and started being a slavemaster, sayin' all women is for is cleaning, cooking,

having babies. The Black man wanted to oppress us. It was the only way he
could feel like he was something.

Because Black women's lives had been hard, many "wanted to have
someone to depend on." Too often, they became dependent on welfare
instead—"welfare is the man too, any way you look at it."

In the New Rochelle group's personal experiences as young Black
women emerging into adulthood, three areas of struggle stood out the
most. First, they had known and rebelled against the tight constraints
put on girl children by anxious parents. "Our liberation was breaking
away from the family." Second, some now faced the discrimination of
the job market, "still as real as it had been for our Black mothers. We
either took those minor office jobs or went back to momma's job at
Miss Anne's or into the hospital scrubbing floors or carrying meal
trays."[28] Third, some were already in marriages or relationships with
men, and fighting for equality there.

In relationship struggles, one factor they saw affecting Black
women was the "shortage" of Black men. This made it difficult to make
demands on a mate. Linda recalls that

> one thing the older women taught us, you never ask a man where he's goin'
> and never ask him where he's been, as long as he's takin' care of the house,
> because they gonna do what they gonna do.

The group hoped they could get men to behave differently, Linda
explains, by helping them "understand the system and its dynamics."
The group was very concerned about the heavy competition the male
shortage generated among women.[29]

Finding themselves as Black women's liberationists a "minority
within the minority," the New Rochelle young women were heartened
when Pat began bringing them together with the like-minded women
of Mount Vernon.

Joint Efforts

In 1969, Pat R. and Mount Vernon and New Rochelle women
cooperated on several ventures. First, they produced "A Historical and
Critical Essay for Black Women in the Cities." This sweeping theoretical analysis dated male domination back to an early overthrow of
women by men, motivated by men's fear of women and their "inner
and reproductive powers." Men then created cultures based on "suppression of the female" and of "things having to do with the body."
The group described also the historical subjugation of Black people,
and the "alienation" of the lower class from the "products of their labor."
Together these processes had produced contemporary Western culture.

The essay addressed the current impact of race, class, and sex oppression on Blacks in the United States. The men vent their frustrations violently on the women, and the women strike back. "The cycle continues as both are unable to bring the contradiction to its logical explosive conclusion and synthesis—confrontation with THE MAN."

Meanwhile the White male elite was moving toward new levels of power, including control of reproduction. "He struggles to perfect artificial insemination and a machine host for the human fetus."

The women invoked "our fearsome but inevitable historical duty to overthrow oppressive male authority and its system." It was time to "vomit up" the "dying myths" of White and male supremacy. Revolutionaries, they concluded, "dare to dream of a utopia, a new time of equilibrium and synthesis."[30]

During the writing of the "Historical and Critical Essay," the Mount Vernon women were invited to meet with three Vietnamese revolutionary women in Canada. A Canadian women's peace group was sponsoring the visit of the Vietnamese, so that U.S. and Canadian women could talk with them about ending the war. Pat asked some New Rochelle young women to go, Carrietta G. recalls,

> because of the women's liberation thing, and what we was struggling with. She was showing how they were liberated, how they were fighting on the battlefield, and she wanted us to find out how did they get from underneath the man to actually do this.

At the July 1969 meeting, the Vietnamese women spoke of having "struggled with their families in order to take an active part in the war movement."[31] But they also

> said there's no such thing on a battlefront as women's liberation. They said, "I don't have time to think I'm a woman. We're all one. Little children too pick up the gun and fight. The whole country is in struggle, everybody."

The Vietnamese women told the gathering "that in an outright revolution, you have to give it all. You can't fear death." The New Rochelle women were moved to take a more searching look at their own commitment.

Carrietta: I'm questioning myself as an individual: Are you willing to do this? Put your life on the line? I thought if they can do it why don't we? But there was only a handful of us. We realized we weren't strong enough.

Maureen: I think after Malcolm and Martin [were killed], we knew we wasn't gonna die, cause no one would be here to teach. You weren't gonna change anything now. I think we were starting to come to that. Self preservation.

That fall (1969), Pat R. and others composed a "Letter to a North Vietnamese Sister From an Afro-American Woman." Women of both networks had been experiencing harassment from U.S. intelligence agents, local authorities, and right-wing organizations. "We wanted to send the letter as like a last testament if anything happened," Pat explains.

This letter predicted a period of increasing repression in the United States. The women hoped it would "increase revolutionary rage and fervor across class and ethnic lines," creating "a base for a real revolution."

They reported that North American women were being "moved by historical forces and exalted out of their slave mentality." Black and White women were developing their own analyses of capitalism. "The middle-class White female sees the oppressor as maleness gone mad. . . . This is the warfare state, a dynamic capitalist power requiring periodic wars to survive." Poor Black women were fighting daily oppression by Black males

> in a silent warfare of guerrilla wits and homemade weapons. . . . A few are beginning to see their oppressors as those who mean to keep them barefoot, pregnant, and ignorant of male oppression. . . . Some have begun to move toward smashing the myth of Black female social and economic dominance over the Black male.

The group wrote that they had joined "the oppressed throughout the world" in "the struggle for a new world and a new people." Ultimately that meant destroying capitalism and imperialism. They signed off, "Onward to the world revolution."[32]

Postscript: Into the 1970s

In the early 1970s, the Mount Vernon/New Rochelle group, with some Freedom School children and sympathetic men, put together a powerful book based on their experiences and writings over the years: *Lessons From the Damned: Class Struggle in the Black Community* (The Damned, 1973/1990).[33]

Lessons instructed "revolutionary brothers and sisters" to aim in the long term for the overthrow of capitalism. But directly ahead was a period of fascism, the final stage in capitalism's decay. This stage might last for many years, as the fascists try "to hold back by brute force the new woman, the new man, and a new world with new social and economic relationships."

Revolutionaries should help people understand capitalist development and class struggle. They needed to "break down these big issues to the smaller issues of daily life." Revolutionaries had to "learn to think dialectically, analyzing the movement and interaction of opposites." Crucial to a dialectical understanding was to see how the oppressed— women included—cooperated in their own oppression:

> We must go deeper into our class and racial experience, and the women and youth into their need to subordinate themselves to men and adults. We must learn why we have loved our chains and not wanted to throw them off. Only we, the politically conscious oppressed, can find out how we were molded, brainwashed, and literally produced like any manufactured product to plastically cooperate in our own oppression. This is *our* historical responsibility.[34]

After finishing their book, the *Lessons* team fell apart (as BRO had already). In 1973, the Freedom School folded. A few Mount Vernon and New Rochelle women continued individual activism, for example in welfare rights. But by 1974-1975, both networks were coming apart. Pat sees the "economic depression" then as a contributing factor, diverting and draining people's energies.

Most of the New Rochelle young women married and had children. They put more energy into families.

Maureen: We went backwards. For the patience, because you figure your kids and your family would keep you from gettin' killed out there, slow you down. Because we was movin' too fast.

Carrietta: We was movin' too fast, ahead of our time.

Maureen: There were things we left undone so we could dedicate ourselves to the struggle. And they had to be dealt with within us.

Carrietta: But those of us who was aware, you could never lose that anyway. We always kept on top of what was goin' on. It's just that we wasn't as active.

Conclusion

The 1960s' women's liberation activism of poor Black women took its own particular forms.[35] What, then, were the distinctive features of the Mount Vernon/New Rochelle group's approach? How did their activism compare with that of White and middle-class women in this period?

First, this group consistently linked the issues of racial, class, and sex equality. Their action and writing projects addressed their concerns as Black and poor people, as well as their concerns specifically as women. The Mount Vernon branch's longest-term project, the Freedom School, educated children to confront all those forms of oppression.

In taking action to improve the conditions of their lives, the Mount Vernon women did not stop to decide what was a "women's issue" and what wasn't. Consider again their initial political actions: for welfare rights and for decent housing. In both cases they were fighting to provide basic needs—income and shelter—for themselves and their children. White middle-class feminists (usually) define the former as a women's issue, but rarely the latter.[36]

Over time, the Mount Vernon/New Rochelle group came to see class as in some senses the primary contradiction, and the overthrow of capitalism as the essential means for creating a society based on equality. Thus they considered themselves part of a broad anticapitalist movement, not part of the women's movement per se. But their ultimate emphasis on class struggle did not mean downplaying the women's cause or putting it on a back burner. They continued to attack male supremacy militantly.

A major aspect of their fight against male supremacy was their insistence on being "in the front lines" of the Black struggle, and their resistance to the idea that men should be the leaders. In the latter 1960s, White women too were battling male domination in social change movements, but Black women had to contend with the added charge that they had been too dominant in their families and communities, and had helped emasculate their men.[37]

Though the group did not hesitate to condemn abusive or exploitative behavior by Black men, they also emphasized their bond with their "brothers," reinforced by common struggle as an oppressed racial minority. Over time, the group moved toward a more sympathetic understanding of how the social and economic system drove the men to take out frustrations on the women. In the larger picture, Black men "weren't our enemies." The group also took pains to differentiate between oppressor "fathers" and revolutionary "sons," expressing their hope that the youth could be educated to reject patriarchy. In broad comparison, White women's liberationists in this period differentiated less among categories of men, often lumping all men together in statements about male behavior and male power. Many of them moved toward political separatism from men, launching a women's liberation movement independent of the New Left.

The Mount Vernon women's defense of birth control was another key part of their women's liberation activism. Like their middle-class White sisters, they saw reproductive self-determination as crucial to women's freedom. For the Whites, the cutting edge of this fight was legalizing abortion. For poor Blacks, it was taking a women's liberation stand on the racial and class issue of birth control as genocide.

Although the group favored the birth control pill, as technology *they* could control, they sounded an early alarm about developments toward artificial reproduction, which they could perceive only as a tool of White male control. Some White women radicals in this period argued that alternative reproduction could prove liberating for women.[38]

In marked contrast to most of the White women's liberationists, this group had a positive view of motherhood. Their lives revolved around kin and neighborhood networks in which mothers were the key figures. In these women-centered networks, child-rearing responsibilities were shared. With few other life options, women commonly got their main sense of accomplishment from mothering—whether their own or other women's children.[39] For young middle-class White women in this period, other opportunities were opening up, and they tended to view motherhood as a burden. To them it meant being isolated in a nuclear family and having sole responsibility for the child rearing. The disparate realities of the two sets of women colored their political theories. The poor Black women considered motherhood a source of power; the middle-class Whites saw it mainly as a source of oppression.[40]

The Mount Vernon/New Rochelle group's positive attitude toward motherhood ties in with a final significant feature of their activism: their focus on working with children. They placed great importance on their role as socializers and educators of the young. To middle-class Whites, the group's theme of "putting children first" might smack of traditional female socialization for self-sacrifice. But for these women held down so strongly by racial and class oppression, the children would have to carry on their hope for "the new woman, the new man," and "new social and economic relationships."

The Mount Vernon/New Rochelle group provides an inspiring example of women empowering each other to fight racial, class, and sex inequality. The fact that they linked these issues and fought on all these fronts by no means should exclude them from the record of contemporary women's liberation struggles. Indeed, as bold pioneers in confronting the complex interactions of race, class, and sex, they deserve a place of honor in that record.

If we recognize the different forms women's liberation activism has taken, and discard the idea that only middle-class White women launched and "own" this cause, we have a sounder basis for building alliances. Those alliances must be grounded in a commitment to fighting racial and class inequality.

Notes

1. Although in the 1990s *African-American* has become the preferred term, in writing about the 1960s I use the preferred term of that period, *Black*.

2. For example, in the New York City area, where I did my research, civil rights lawyer Flo Kennedy was an early member of the New York chapter of NOW (National Organization for Women) and a leader in women's movement circles. Cellestine Ware helped found New York Radical Feminists in 1969.

3. Major studies of the early movement include: Cellestine Ware, *Woman Power* (1970); Judith Hole and Ellen Levine, *Rebirth of Feminism* (1971); Jo Freeman, *The Politics of Women's Liberation* (1975); Barbara Deckard, *The Women's Movement* (1975); Redstockings, *Feminist Revolution* (1975, 1978); Sara Evans, *Personal Politics* (1979); Alice Echols, *Daring To Be Bad* (1989). Ware says most about Black women's relation to the cause, but focuses on why they were not attracted to the movement. An excellent relevant study is bell hooks, *Ain't I a Woman: Black Women and Feminism* (1981), but she too focuses more on critiquing racism and classism in the early women's movement than on discussing Black women's antisexist activism in that period.

One significant Black group that has been ignored or mentioned only in passing in accounts of the early women's liberation cause is the Black Women's Alliance. It developed from the Black Women's Liberation Committee of SNCC (Student Nonviolent Coordinating Committee), and then in 1971 became the Third World Women's Alliance.

4. These points are developed more fully in M. Rivka Polatnick, "Will the Real Feminist Activists Please Stand Up: Issues of Exclusion in Conceptualizing the Women's Movement" (unpublished manuscript, Women's Studies Program, San Jose State University, San Jose, CA 95192-0123).

5. The group, really a loose network of women from two neighboring communities, did not have an official name. Their writings were published under several names, including "Pat Robinson and Group" and "Black Women's Liberation Group, Mount Vernon, New York." In consultation with the members I interviewed, I chose to use "Mount Vernon/New Rochelle group," which recognizes the group's two branches and acknowledges collective effort rather than a single individual. The group members felt strongly about the latter point (see Note 8).

6. As I began researching this group, I myself—a middle-class White women's liberation activist since the 1960s—had to struggle with my reaction, "Is this *really* a women's liberation group?" Because they did not fit my mold from White radical feminism—which focused predominantly on sex oppression and only secondarily on racial and class oppression—I found it challenging to write about them as women's liberation activists. This project continued to shake up my own limited definitions of the women's cause.

7. The research was done for my dissertation, *Strategies for Women's Liberation: A Study of a Black and a White Group of the 1960s* (1985), which I am revising for publication.

The only account of the Black group in print is their self-account, "The Revolt of Poor Black Women," in The Damned, *Lessons From the Damned* (1973/1990), pp. 89-111. Pagination of the body of the book is the same in both editions.

I interviewed two women from the Mount Vernon branch, three from the New Rochelle branch, and Pat R., the social worker and psychotherapist who brought the branches together.

8. The group members asked me to use first names and last initials only, except Linda Landrine, who wanted her full name used. The introduction to *Lessons From the Damned* explains their viewpoint: "Please let our individual names pass away and be forgotten with all the nameless like us—and those too who went before and yet in reality made it possible for us to speak today" (p. 9). In my text, I honor the group members' request, but in citing their writings, I use full names if the original source did.

9. Pat R., interviews with author, New Rochelle, NY, September 7 and 28, 1983. *Subsequent information and quotations from Pat R. are from these interviews,* unless otherwise indicated.

10. Joyce H. and Catherine H., interview with author, Mount Vernon, NY, October 8, 1983. *Subsequent information and quotations from Joyce H. are from this interview. Subsequent information about the Mount Vernon branch is integrated from this interview and the Pat R. interviews,* unless otherwise indicated.

11. At first Pat was an unpaid volunteer for Planned Parenthood. Eventually she got some pay for her birth control education work. Throughout the 1960s, she spent as much time in the Mount Vernon community as she could, given her responsibilities as a mother of three and the other paid counseling and teaching work she took on later.

12. Patricia Robinson, "Revolt of the Black Woman," interview by Dan Georgakas, New Rochelle, April 1967 (unpublished manuscript), personal files of Patricia Robinson, p. 7.

13. Robinson, "Revolt of the Black Woman," p. 7.

14. The Damned, *Lessons,* p. 90.

15. Robinson, "Revolt of the Black Woman," p. 1.

16. Robinson, "Revolt of the Black Woman," p. 2.

17. The Damned, p. 92.

18. The Damned, p. 93.

19. The Damned, p. 124. See also pp. 93, 113-120, 124-128.

20. Black Unity Party (Peekskill, NY), "Birth Control Pills and Black Children," in *Lilith* [Seattle], Fall 1968, p. 7.

21. [Mount Vernon Group], "The Sisters Reply," in *Lilith,* Fall 1968, p. 8. (Published elsewhere later; see References.)

22. Patricia Robinson ["Poor Black Women"], *Lilith,* Fall 1968, pp. 9-11. The article was untitled in *Lilith,* and given slightly varying names when reprinted elsewhere (see References).

23. Interview with Maureen W., Carrietta G., and Linda Landrine, New Rochelle, NY, October 23, 1983; The Damned, pp. 103-105.

24. See Note 8 about the women's names.

25. Interview with Carrietta G. and Linda Landrine, New Rochelle, NY, October 9, 1983; The Damned, pp. 108-109. In the rest of my treatment of the New Rochelle branch, *the information and quotations are from the 1983 interviews or from a January 26, 1985 supplementary phone interview with Linda Landrine*, unless otherwise indicated. In the 1983 interviews, the women often spoke in tandem, adding to each other's comments. That is why some quotations are not attributed to a single individual.

26. Black Radicals Onward, *Harambee* (New Rochelle), April 19, 1969 (personal files of Patricia Robinson); interviews.

27. U.S. Department of Labor, Citizens' Advisory Council on the Status of Women, Statistics sheet, August 1969 (personal files of Patricia Robinson); interviews.

28. The Damned, p. 109.

29. People attribute the "shortage" of Black men to several factors: They have a high death rate, including from homicide; many are away in the military and in prisons or other "correctional" institutions; some have been incapacitated by prolonged unemployment, and/or drugs and alcohol; more Black men are in interracial relationships than Black women.

30. Pat Robinson and Group, "A Historical and Critical Essay for Black Women in the Cities, June 1969," in Toni Cade (Ed.), *The Black Woman*, pp. 198-210. A second, slightly different version was published elsewhere; see Haden, Middleton, and Robinson (1970) in the Reference section.

31. Patricia Robinson, "NFL, N. Viet Women Tell Peace Desires, How They Help Fight," *The Afro-American*, July 19, 1969, p. 15 (personal files of Patricia Robinson). Reprinted with permission of the Afro-American Co. of Baltimore City, Inc. and the Afro-American Newspapers. All other quotations about the meeting with the Vietnamese are from my interviews. The experience also is described in The Damned, pp. 96, 101-102.

32. Pat Robinson and Group, "Letter to a North Vietnamese Sister From an Afro-American Woman," Fall 1969, in Cade, pp. 189-194. Cade includes the mistaken date September 1968 in the title.

33. The 1990 edition is identical to the original except for a new Foreword and Introduction.

34. The Damned, pp. 145-153.

35. A frequent reaction to my research has been: Was this group unique or were there others like it? A second related question concerns the role of middle-class Pat R.: To what extent were the group's ideas and writings really coming from her?

I am not arguing that groups like this were common in the 1960s; this was a pioneering group, and more militant on the women's liberation issue than most 1960s Black women's groups. However, there certainly were other pro-women's liberation writers and activists among Black women in the late 1960s. See, for example, articles by: Kay Lindsey, Toni Cade, and others in Cade (Ed.), *The Black Woman*; Mary Ann Weathers in Leslie B. Tanner (Ed.), *Voices From Women's Liberation*; Frances M. Beal and Eleanor Holmes Norton in Robin Morgan (Ed.), *Sisterhood Is Powerful*; Mabel Hobsen in *Liberation Now!: Writings From the Women's Liberation Movement*. See also Gloria Martin's 1967 speech excerpted in Redstockings, *Feminist Revolution* (1978 abridged ed.), p. 18.

I would argue that the sentiments and concerns expressed by the Mount Vernon/New Rochelle group were not uncommon among poor Black women, but the group's level of political sophistication was unusual and the result of Pat. R.'s involvement (more so for the Mount Vernon branch than the New Rochelle branch). The group's process of developing ideas and writings was interactive and synergistic. Distrustful of middle-class Black women, the Mount Vernon women would not have responded to Pat R. with the heartfelt enthusiasm they did, had she been imposing alien views on them rather than helping them develop and articulate their own understanding of the world. The group's politics were rooted in the realities and perspectives of poor women.

36. I was pleased to see housing listed as one of 16 issues on the National Organization for Women's "Political Initiatives Action Ballot" I received in January 1992.

37. For an in-depth analysis of this issue, see bell hooks, *Ain't I A Woman*, pp. 70-83.

38. In recent years, White feminist attitudes have shifted toward the Mount Vernon/New Rochelle group's view.

39. See Patricia Hill Collins, "The Meaning of Motherhood in Black Culture and Black Mother/Daughter Relationships," in *Sage: A Scholarly Journal on Black Women*, 4(2) (Fall 1987), pp. 3-10, and Chapter 6 "Black Women and Motherhood" in her book *Black Feminist Thought* (1990).

40. This comparison is developed further in M. Rivka Polatnick, "Diversity in Women's Liberation Ideology: How a Black and a White Group of the 1960s Viewed Motherhood" (unpublished manuscript, Women's Studies Program, San Jose State University, San Jose, CA 95192-0123).

References

Note: [PR] = from personal files of Patricia Robinson.

Black Radicals Onward. (1969, April 19). *Harambee* (New Rochelle). [PR]

Black Unity Party (Peekskill, NY). (1968, Fall). Birth control pills and Black children. *Lilith* [Seattle], [1st issue], p. 7. [*Lilith* is available from Redstockings Women's Liberation Archives, Archives Distribution Project, P.O. Box 2625, Gainesville, FL 32602]

Cade, Toni. (Ed.). (1970). *The Black woman*. New York: Signet.

The Damned. (1990). *Lessons from the damned: Class struggle in the Black community*. Ojai, CA: Times Change Press. [Original work published 1973]

Haden, Patricia, Middleton, Donna, & Robinson, Patricia. (1970). A historical and critical essay for Black women. In Leslie B. Tanner (Ed.), *Voices from women's liberation* (pp. 316-324). New York: Signet.

Morgan, Robin. (Ed.). (1970). *Sisterhood is powerful: An anthology of writings from the women's liberation movement*. New York: Random House.

[Mount Vernon Group]. (1968, Fall). The sisters reply. *Lilith* [Seattle] [1st issue], p. 8. [Reprinted by New England Free Press; anthologized as "Statement on birth control" in Robin Morgan, ed., *Sisterhood is powerful*, pp. 360-361]

Robinson, Patricia. (1967, April). Revolt of the Black woman. Interview by Dan Georgakas, New Rochelle. Unpublished manuscript. [PR]

Robinson, Patricia. (1968, Fall). [Poor Black women]. *Lilith* [Seattle] [1st issue], pp. 9-11. [Reprinted by New England Free Press; anthologized as "On the position of poor Black women in this country" in Toni Cade, ed., *The Black woman* (New York: Signet) pp. 194-197]

Robinson, Patricia. (1969, July 19). NFL, N. Viet women tell peace desires, how they help fight. *The Afro-American* (Baltimore), p. 15. [PR]

Robinson, Pat, & Group. (1970). A historical and critical essay for Black women in the cities, June 1969. In Toni Cade (Ed.), *The Black woman* (pp. 198-210). New York: Signet.

Robinson, Pat, & Group. (1970). Letter to a North Vietnamese sister from an Afro-American woman. In Toni Cade (Ed.), *The Black woman* (pp. 189-194). New York: Signet.

Tanner, Leslie B. (Ed.). (1970). *Voices from women's liberation*. New York: Signet.

7. Searching for a Tradition
African-American Women Writers, Activists, and Interracial Rape Cases

JOY JAMES

This chapter explores the politics of African-American women's writings on interracial rape cases, lynching, and fair trial activism. Beginning with the political thought of Ida B. Wells-Barnett, with references to her peers Florida Ruffin Ridley and Mary Church Terrell, I examine the connections between the historical writings of women antilynching activists, contemporary Black feminist revisionism, and Afra-American writings on and fair-trial activism surrounding the 1989 Central Park Case.

Ancestor Mothers and Antiviolence Campaigns

To justify their own barbarism they assume a chivalry which they do not possess. True chivalry respects all womanhood, and no one who reads the record, as it is written in the faces of the million mulattoes in the South, will for a minute conceive that the southern white man had a very chivalrous regard for the honor due the women of his own race or respect for the womanhood which circumstances placed in his power. That chivalry which is "most sensitive concerning the honor of women" can hope for but little respect from the civilized world, when it confines itself entirely to the women who happen to be white. Virtue knows no color line, and the chivalry which depends upon complexion of skin and texture of hair can command no honest respect.[1]

African-American feminist Joanne Braxton in *Black Women Writing Autobiography: A Tradition Within a Tradition*[2] describes how she first met

AUTHOR'S NOTE: Parts of this chapter were published in Z (February 1992). I thank Chris Selig and Katarina Gruber for their research assistance; and Ernest Allen, Jr., for editorial suggestions for this chapter.

the outraged mother or ancestor mothers "in search of a tradition to claim them," while reading autobiographies of Afra-American women such as Ida B. Wells-Barnett.[3] According to Braxton, African-American women have historically been "carriers of tradition" as well as "values of care, concern . . . protection, and, most important, the survival of the race."[4] In autobiographies such as *Crusade for Justice: The Autobiography of Ida B. Wells*,[5] Braxton maintains that the Afra-American "autobiographer incorporates communal values . . . to function as the 'point of consciousness' of her people."[6] The life of Ida B. Wells exemplifies courageous commitment to communal values. Wells's political activism and writing popularized critical, radical thinking to counter racial-sexual violence in the United States. Her written legacy includes *Crusade for Justice*; the pamphlets *Southern Horrors: Lynch Law in All Its Phases* (1892), *A Red Record: Lynchings in the U.S., 1892, 1893, 1894* (1895), *Mob Rule in New Orleans* (1900); as well as numerous newspaper articles and editorials.

In addition to Ida B. Wells-Barnett, Afra-American antilynching activists such as Florida Ruffin Ridley, and Mary Church Terrell established a political language and critique of U.S. racial-sexual politics that demystified the moralism of the press, courts, and police.[7] Their uncompromising demands for justice challenged the U.S. "Red Record" of African Americans disproportionately sentenced, brutalized, imprisoned, and murdered at the whim of Whites. Skeptical that media, court, or mob prosecution was motivated by the desire to end sexual violence, these women created a legacy of investigative reporting to ascertain facts distorted or denied by racist institutions. As activists they inherited, shaped, and passed on an even broader legacy of political consciousness. Their analyses established the foundations for both antiviolence and pro-democracy campaigns as the greater context for ending lynching.

Lynchings—the murders of African Americans for (often alleged) crimes against property and people—constituted attacks on entire communities. "Crimes" included "talking back" to Whites and just being "in the wrong place at the wrong time." Punishment could be collective, including the destruction or appropriation of property and extending to group lynchings of family or community members.[11] Although the majority of victims were men, African-American women and children were lynched as well.

The year 1892, which witnessed the greatest number of reported lynchings—241, to be exact—was a pivotal one for the antilynching campaigns.[8] Among the victims of these atrocities were 160 African Americans, 5 of whom were women or girls.[9] Also, in Memphis that year, Thomas Moss, Calvin McDowell, and Will Stewart were lynched for competing with White businesses by opening the "People's Grocery Company" and for defending themselves when attacked by unidentified, armed White men.[10] Moss, McDowell, and Stewart were all personal friends and associates of Ida B. Wells, then an editor and co-owner of Memphis's African-American paper, the *Free Speech*. Outrage at their murders transformed Miss Wells into an antilynching crusader. A platform was provided her later that year when African-American women convened a testimonial for her in Brooklyn—the largest gathering of Club Women to that date. The gathering raised funds ($500) for the publishing of *Southern Horrors* and the underwriting of a speaking tour for Miss Wells in the United States and England.

Ida B. Wells's fierce denunciations and her ability to critically depict a society that condoned such violence were key features of her public speaking and political writings. Appealing to both morality and political insight, her critiques focused on the racial-sexual politics of interracial sex and the duplicity of the legal system's double standards and its complicity in lynchings. An analysis of the politics of lynching appeared in one of her news dispatches, excerpted below:

(1) First: That all the machinery of law and politics is in the hands of those who commit the lynching; they therefore have the amending of the laws in their own hands; and that it is only wealthy white men whom the law fails to reach; that in every case of criminal procedure the Negro is punished.

(2) Second: Hundreds of Negroes including women and children are lynched for trivial offenses on suspicion and in many cases when known to be guiltless of any crime, and that the law refused to punish the murderers because it is not considered a crime to kill a Negro.

(3) Third: Many of the cases of "Assault" are simply adulteries between white women and colored men.[12]

Discrediting apologias for lynchings,[13] Miss Wells critiqued the "law and order" rationalizations of the postbellum South. Lynching advocates claimed that lynchings were a response to "race riots"; but these African-American led "race riots," she observed, never materialized. Another claim was that terrorism prevented "Negro domination" of Whites through the vote; by the late 1800s, however, African Americans had been so effectively persecuted that they posed no serious electoral "threat."[14] Increasing awareness of the invalidity of these rationalizations, according to Ida B. Wells, led to still another justification for racist violence:

> Brutality still continued; Negroes were whipped, scourged, exiled, shot and hung whenever and wherever it pleased the white man so to treat them, and as the civilized world with increasing persistency held the white people of the South to account for its outlawry, the murderers invented the third excuse— that Negroes had to be killed to avenge their assaults upon women. There

could be framed no possible excuse more harmful to the Negro and more
unanswerable if true in its sufficiency for the white man.[15]

Although as specious as the other rationalizations, the accusation of
sexual assault against a White woman by an African-American man
proved to be the most incendiary and tenacious of charges. Raised in
only a fraction of lynchings, this accusation nevertheless became the
general rationalization for racist violence in that era. Legitimizing and
mobilizing support for lynching, this charge led to the acquiescence to
lynching, even by those who considered themselves above the mob.

Lynchings embodied the antithesis of rape prevention or prosecution. Given their inherent sexual politics, such acts functioned as exor-
cisms to entertain as well as pacify the White mind haunted by Black,
sexual demons. Lynchings were sites of sexual violence and sexual
mutilations. Demonized African Americans were tortured, hung,
quartered, burnt alive, their body parts and genitalia taken home as
souvenirs. The overwhelming connection between most interracial
rape cases and lynching was, as Ida B. Wells documented in *Southern
Horrors* and *A Red Record,* that African-American women and children
were raped prior to and during lynchings; they were also lynched
along with African-American men who assisted or defended them, for
resisting rape by White men. A rare phenomenon for White women,
interracial rape was an everyday reality for African-American women.
The vast majority of sexual violence against White women, and a
significant amount directed against African-American women at the
time, stemmed from White men. Legal and social institutions tended to
deny White men's sexual violence against White women, African-
American women, and men, and ignored African-American men's
sexual assaults against African-American women as well. Logically, if
a rational connection between lynching and the prosecution of sexual
crime existed, the majority of lynch victims would have been White
men, who, as a caste, were the moral and legal prosecutors of sexual
violence, yet the least prosecuted and censured for sexual violence.[16]

To demystify the belief that White men enforced written or unwrit-
ten laws for the protection of White women, Miss Wells engaged in a
radical critique of lynching apologias, exploring their basis in psy-
chosexual mythology. Ida B. Wells's critique of the sexual politics of
lynching proved relentless. Her demystification of "rape," controversial a century ago and remaining so today, was the cornerstone of
moral and political resistance to racist violence justified as the vindi-
cation or prevention of sexual violence. In her memoir Miss Wells
recalled her initial belief in European-American assertions that lynching was a preventive measure to protect White women's virtue and
restrain the sexual savagery of African-American men. The lynchings
of her associates and her subsequent investigative reporting taught her
otherwise. In May 1892, after more lynchings followed the deaths of

her friends, Ida B. Wells wrote an editorial ridiculing the charge of "rape" as justification for violence. In response, Memphis's White citizens burned down the *Free Speech* and threatened to lynch the writer; the bounty they placed on Ida B. Wells's head exiled her from the South for decades. Her editorial reads in part:

> Eight Negroes lynched since last issue of the *Free Speech*. Three were charged with killing white men and five with raping white women. Nobody in this section believes the old thread-bare lie that Negro men assault white women. If Southern white men are not careful they will over-reach themselves and a conclusion will be reached which will be very damaging to the moral reputation of their women.[17]

Despite this polemic, Ida B. Wells did not categorically deny that African-American men assaulted European-American women. The body of her writings, in which the word *many* is generally used to describe false accusations of rape, make it clear that she makes no assertion of universal innocence. (Her memoir's reprint of a 1894 letter by Florida Ruffin Ridley, excerpted below, best reveals her position.) She did demand, however, that White society recognize that actual rape had very little to do with the lynching of African Americans:

> With the Southern white man, any mesalliance existing between a white woman and a colored man is a sufficient foundation for the charge of rape. The Southern white man says that it is impossible for a voluntary alliance to exist between a white woman and a colored man, and therefore, the fact of an alliance is a proof of force. In numerous instances where colored men have been lynched on the charge of rape, it was positively known at the time of lynching, and indisputably proven after the victim's death, that the relationship sustained between the man and woman was voluntary and clandestine, and that in no court of law could even the charge of assault have been successfully maintained.[18]

Voluntary sexual relationships between European-American women and African-American men were defined by Whites as "sexual assaults"; consensual relations were reconstructed as the "rape" of White women. Such voluntary, interracial associations were punishable by the death of the African-American man involved. Although there were instances of White women being ostracized, institutionalized, and beaten for engaging in such alliances, a repudiation of the relationship through the "rape" accusation brought absolution. African-American men had no such "escape clause," which explains Ida B. Wells's assertion that these liaisons were often voluntary only on the part of the White woman involved. In the reconstruction of "rape" under White supremacy, European-American women, particularly those from the propertied classes, were conceived as "inherently virtuous" and absolved of sexual promiscuity and miscegenation; European-American men, again, particularly of the propertied classes, were considered "inherently chivalrous" and absolved of sexual violence. African-American men, on the other hand, were identified as "rapists"; defined as "inherently promiscuous," African-American women by definition could not be "violated" because they were without "virtue." The moral and social "legality" of lynching was thus based on racial-sexual mythology and a White code of chivalry.

This code of chivalry featured a macabre duet played in bipolar stereotypes of White knights and ladies; Black sexual brutes and savages. A White man, by definition a "gentleman" in comparison to African Americans, would not rape a "lady" (White woman) and could not rape an object (Black woman). (Intra-class rape of White women, including incest, was usually represented as the "seduction" of the White adult male). A White woman, by definition a "lady" in comparison to Black women, could not desire a "brute"; nor would she join in coalitions with "sexual objects," who argued that lynching's mythology of Black (sexual) pathology functioned as the apologia for rape in a society where alleged and actual assaults against Whites were prosecuted but the prosecution of sexual violence against Black women was an anomaly.

Afra-American antilynching activists rejected the dominant culture's delusions concerning sex and violence. With no control over how White men treated White women, through the Negro Women's Club Movement, Afra-American women organized against their sexual exploitation and assault by both European- and African-American men. These activists-writers did not sever the issues of gender and sexual violence from race politics. For decades women such as Ida B. Wells-Barnett urged U.S. White women to respond to the political use of the "rape" charge in lynchings, recognizing the connections between resistance to sexual and resistance to racial violence: Neither for White nor especially for African-American women was there prosecution of rape, as a nonconsensual act, under lynch law. Women in the antilynching campaigns resisted racial violence, protesting White supremacist terror and sexual violence against African-American women, children, and men. Women in the antilynching campaigns could not realistically sever instances of racist and sexual violence, for race was "sexualized" and sex "racialized." The dual realities of the assaults against African Americans did not permit prioritizing "race" before "sex."

Antilynching Activism as "Counter-Feminism"

[An] error on the subject of lynching consists of the widely circulated statement that the moral sensibilities of the best negroes in the United States are so stunted and dull, and the standard of morality among even the leaders of the race is so low, that they do not appreciate the enormity and heinousness of rape. . . . Only those who are densely ignorant of the standards and sentiments of the best negroes, or who wish willfully [sic] to misrepresent and maliciously slander a race already resting under burdens greater than it can bear, would accuse its thousands of reputable men and women of sympathizing with rapists, either black or white, or of condoning their crime. (Mary Church Terrell, National Association of Colored Women, 1904)[19]

Among contemporary revisionists, Ida B. Wells-Barnett has gained notoriety for being "indifferent" to sexual violence against White women and for "sympathizing with [Black] rapists." Such criticisms may be traced to her editorializing on the "old thread-bare lie"; however, one can only reconstruct Wells-Barnett as a woman of stunted moral sensibilities by erasing or distorting the political praxis of the antilynching movement.

In the absence of historical investigation, such constructions are put forth. For example, in "Split Affinities," Black feminist Valerie Smith focuses on African-American women's perspectives on interracial rape cases to present an argument for Ida B. Wells as a "counter-feminist."[20]

Smith posits that the divided loyalties of African Americans leads to "split affinities" in interracial rape cases:

> Within a context in which rape charges were often used to justify lynching or legal execution, black men and women often perceive an accusation of rape as a way to terrorize innocent black men. This kind of reasoning may lead to the denial of the fact that some black men do rape.[21]

Supporting her thesis on "split affinities," Smith analyzes representations of interracial rape in contemporary "journalistic discourse" and a short story by Alice Walker, "Advancing Luna"—and Ida B. Wells. Smith's narrow reading of Walker's fiction informs her reconstruction of Wells-Barnett as counter-feminist, blurring the distinctions between fact and fiction (historical research, rather than taken as Walker's creativity, is a more accurate guide for assessing the politics of Afra-American antilynching activists).[22]

Smith expands her insights into reductive generalizations. Without references to historical research on lynching or Wells's pamphlets, Smith writes that Ida B. Wells-Barnett's "opposition to lynching as a practice requires her effectively to deny the veracity of any white woman's testimony against a black man." Smith's interpretations of passages from Wells-Barnett's autobiography, and an act of ventriloquism, allow her to claim that a logical reading of Wells's sentences reveals her "effectively blaming white women for the lynching of black men" (pp. 273-274). This reading, of an autobiography in which Wells-Barnett also writes that, until the lynchings of her friends, she had accepted the apologia of lynching as the extralegal execution of Black male rapists, crassly simplifies Ida B. Wells-Barnett's politics.

Valerie Smith's portrait of Ida B. Wells-Barnett as indifferent to sexual violence against White women suggests that Wells-Barnett held a profound disregard for White women. Yet, Wells-Barnett had working relationships and personal friendships with prominent White feminists such as Susan B. Anthony; in addition, English and European-American women joined her and other African-American women in suffrage activism and the establishment of "halfway houses" for single women, as well as antilynching organizing.

Credible historical accounts depict Ida B. Wells-Barnett as a radical antiracist, not anti-White. Public hostility to lynchings rather than personal hostility toward White women motivated activists such as Ida B. Wells-Barnett. In fact, if she were contemptuous of sexual violence in White women's lives, as Smith implies, she would have alienated most of her White female supporters. Joanne Braxton maintains that Ida B. Wells provided leadership for both Black and White women:

> Despite the enormity of her task, Wells forged a legitimate black feminism through the synthesis of black nationalism and the suffrage movement, providing a useful model with race, not sex, as a point of departure. Her work established not only the ideological basis for later antilynching work by the NAACP but also for similar work done by the Association of Southern Women for the Prevention of Lynching, a white group headed by Texas feminist Jessie Daniel Ames.[23]

Only through indifference to the historical record can one reconstruct Wells-Barnett as a counter-feminist antipathetic to White women. Smith's lack of research limits her critique of the historical figure she appraises as well as antilynching activism.

Revealing its weaknesses, Smith's analysis uses the terms *accusations* and *instances* interchangeably when referring to interracial rape, rendering accusations synonymous with facts. Smith likewise confuses the prosecution of rape with the crime of rape, writing: "Wells' formulations which 'subordinate' sex to race means that the crime rape can never be read solely as an offense against women's bodies" (p. 274). In another passage Smith describes how women's "bodies" are hierarchically valued in society because of racism, classism, and (hetero)sexism.[24] Given this reality, the prosecution of rape is never "read solely as an offense against women's bodies." But a century prior to the appearance of Smith's essay, antilynching activists, such as Ida B. Wells, Florida Ruffin Ridley, and Mary Church Terrell, recognized that the prosecution of rape was determined by the social status of the woman assaulted as well as that of the accused. Valerie Smith fails to see that progressive, contemporary analyses, including Black feminism, are rooted in and indebted to the earlier analysis of African-American women.

In addition, one cannot infer a uniform practice of subordinating sexual oppression to racial oppression in African-American women's challenges to lynching (although it would be useful to examine with specificity how, and under what conditions, Afra-Americans subordinate sex to race and vice versa). In antilynching organizing, it was impossible for Black women to make sexual/gender issues "subordinate" to racial issues, given the interrelatedness of racial and sexual violence. As noted earlier, the historical antilynching campaigns were also waged as anti-sexual-violence campaigns; political wisdom dictated that ending lynchings, as well as false and illegal prosecutions, increased the likelihood of legitimate and legal prosecutions of rape. (Afra-Americans active in the antilynching and the Club Movement also worked to end sexual violence/exploitation within African-American communities.[25])

Ignoring historical research to ascribe a binary-opposition to African-American women writer-activists dismisses the possibilities of their having developed an integrated political analysis. Braxton explores the intersections of issues in Ida B. Wells's politics, obscured by Smith:

> Wells's involvement in the black women's club movement should not be diminished, for it involved the active fusion of powerful influences: black feminism and black nationalism. The result of this fusion was the development of a race-centered, self-conscious womanhood in the form of the black women's club movement. . . . For an Ida B. Wells or a Frances E. W. Harper, a blow at lynching was a blow at racism and the brutally enforced sexual double standard that pervaded the South. It was a defense of the entire race.[26]

Organizing against racist violence created a "womanhood" formed by race, gender, and class (the impact of "class" on African-American women's experiences of race, sex, and interracial rape cases requires additional investigation).[27] Unaware of the historical roots of her own feminism, Smith advocates a multitextured Black feminism over a mono-dimensional Eurocentric one, describing the former as a more competent framework for analysis: "black feminism presumes the 'intersectionality' of race and gender in the lives of black women, thereby rendering inapplicable to the lives of black women any 'single-axis' theory about racism or sexism."[28] This "new" analysis, however, is based on a paradigm articulated more than a century ago by African-American women antilynching activists. Their political thought might prove more effective in demystifying current social violence than the critiques of some contemporary Black feminism. Race and gender, after all, intersect (with class and sexuality) not only in African-American women's lives but in European-American women's lives as well. Delineating the impact of race in White women's lives and their complicity in White supremacy as well as racial-sexual violence, Ida B. Wells applies this "intersectionality" more consistently than Valerie Smith, who provides no analysis of White women's complicity in lynchings.

Given for the historical record, Smith's criticisms of Ida B. Wells's "focus on the unreliability of White rape victims" are questionable. Valerie Smith herself observes that false rape accusations by White women against Black men shaped the history of lynchings. Ida B. Wells, moreover, did not view White women in lynchings collectively as "rape victims." Her investigative reporting, documented in *A Red*

Record and elsewhere, reveals that many who claimed to be "rape victims" in order to sanction lynchings, were not sexually assaulted or, if assaulted, their assailants were not Black men. To state as Wells did that *consensual* relationships between White women and African-American men were designated and punished as "rape," whereas sexual violence by Whites against Blacks was not, is not in itself a suggestion that Black men do not assault White women or that sexual violence against White women is irrelevant.

Silence about the intellectual dependencies of contemporary thinkers on their predecessors posits historicism. According to this historicism, evolution has elevated contemporary thinking to a plateau above the political thinking of our foremothers. When ahistorical and revisionist, feminism may shape a discourse that promotes obscurantism concerning historical and contemporary political women's struggles. Maintaining that her predecessors, the women who pioneered the antilynching campaigns, left no suitable, gender-progressive legacy on interracial rape cases, Valerie Smith (mis)reads the past to build narratives on contemporary interracial rape cases, such as the Central Park Case.

For example, "split affinities" notes that African-American women's "identification with white women is problematic" given society's greater indifference to violence against Black women. According to Smith, African-American women, as "members of communities under siege . . . may well sympathize with the black male who stands accused . . . as women they share the victim's sense of violation" (p. 275). These insights into the psychological mind-sets of African Americans concerning interracial rape cases are not totally representative of African-American women's responses to interracial rape; nor can they be critically superimposed onto historical African-American women's responses to interracial rape cases and lynching. Moral and political judgments may lead to actions that might diverge from the original empathic and/or antipathetic feelings. Afra-American women, whatever their emotional sentiments, may organize based on their perceptions of political or moral responsibilities, even where these felt obligations diverge from their sympathies.

Smith's focus on Afra-Americans torn by "split affinities" and/or defensively supportive of Black defendant(s) fails to acknowledge that some African Americans prove highly unsympathetic to accused Black males whom they believe guilty (particularly because African-American men are the primary source of sexual violence against African-American women). Still others, outraged by the sexual violence as well as the racist prosecution of the accused, may identify with both survivor and defendant(s), embracing dual rather than split identities. These various perspectives characterized African-American women's responses to the Central Park Case. Smith discusses this case, one of the most sensationalist of contemporary interracial rape trials, without taking into account the diversity of African-American responses.

Black Feminist "Narratives of Conviction" and the Central Park Case

Black feminists Valerie Smith, bell hooks, and Barbara Smith offer important critiques of sexism and misogyny among African Americans within the progressive frameworks of their larger works. These authors' various essays on the 1989 Central Park Case, however, construct different "narratives of convictions" within frameworks that subordinate not race to sex, but specificity and investigative research to symbolism and antiviolence rhetoric. In order to condemn sexual violence, each writer depicted the defendants, as well as the survivor, in symbolical terms, forgoing the specific events of the case; dismissing critical counter-discourse, they privileged instead the accounts of the White, mainstream media. This media, which has no salient history of antiracist politics or racially neutral objectivity, especially concerning interracial rape cases,[29] presented fair-trial advocacy as misogynist, demonized the defendants, and transformed the survivor into an icon. Of the feminist essays cited below, the works of bell hooks and Valerie Smith acknowledge the racist aspects of media coverage; yet none of these three essays suggested the existence of a progressive African-American women's tradition linking anti-sexual violence with fair-trial advocacy for interracial rape cases.

In "Split Affinities," Valerie Smith presents a narrative on the Central Park Case that explicitly argues against the existence of such a tradition. In the same way that sexual violence cases involving African-American female victims tend to receive the least attention, Smith accords least importance and least legitimacy to antiviolence organizing led by African-American women. Although African-American women's organizations have, on their own initiative, organized and educated against sexual violence, Smith's language deflects from the leadership of Black women in organizing to counter sexual violence.[30] Soon after the Central Park assault, African-American women at Medgar Evers College in Brooklyn called a press conference to announce their formation of a new organization—WAVE (Women Against Violence Everywhere); although notices were sent to virtually all New York City media, the meeting received basically no press coverage. Its absence from coverage of city responses to the assault and impending trial indicated that those who relied solely upon mainstream media for their information concerning this or other interracial rape cases would be unaware of the existence of anti-sexual violence organizing by African-American women; as well as women's fair-trial activism discussed below.

Smith restricts her analysis of "journalistic discourse" concerning the Central Park Case to the White media, providing no coverage from alternative sources such as African-American or Spanish-language media (the former was skeptical whereas the latter was largely uncritical of the prosecution). Smith offers no explanation for privileging White press accounts. Written before the 1990 Central Park trial, "Split Affinities" does not permit the defendants the right of presumed innocence until proven guilty. Assuming and projecting the impartiality or objectivity of the dominant media leads Valerie Smith to assert pretrial media "convictions" or judgments (particularly those of *The New York Times*) as indicators of factual guilt, writing: "[t]o review the details [of the case]: on the night of Wednesday, April 19, 1989, a young white woman jogger was raped repeatedly and severely beaten in Central Park in Manhattan by a group of black and Puerto Rican adolescent males between the ages of 14 and 17" (pp. 276-277). The words of police and the White media are presented uncritically as "fact." The "narratives" of activists and writers critiquing the prosecution, not designated as significantly newsworthy by *The New York Times*, do not appear. Most importantly, there is no attempt to analyze conflicting reports or deconstruct media accounts with reference to the known, specific facts pertaining to the case that rendered it problematic. For example, even within mainstream conviction narratives, media acknowledged the factuality of retracted incriminating statements, the lack of witnesses, and absence of material evidence. Analyses of journalistic accounts of interracial rape cases need to explore the ways in which narratives may blur the distinctions between fictive and factual guilt, and the presence or erasure of physical evidence in the construction of media narratives.

bell hooks's writing on the Central Park Case, "Reflections on Sex and Race," similarly mirrors the conviction narratives of the mainstream media and "Split Affinities."[31] Like Valerie Smith, hooks assumes the guilt of the accused prior to the trial and without evidence. Despite her shrewd observations about the racist coverage of the case—"Images of black men as rapists, as dangerous menaces to society, have been sensational cultural currency for some time . . . the media has played a major role in determining public response" (p. 60)—she unquestioningly accepts police statements conveyed through the mainstream media as factual. Influenced by *media* convictions, she depicts critics of the convictions as a monolith complicitous in sexual violence. Little indication is given that African-American communities are capable of their own shrewd and subtle critiques of racism and sexism. Echoing hooks's argument, Barbara Smith also disavows the existence of a humanist African-American political tradition concerning interracial rape cases where the accused is Black and the survivor/victim White.

In "Black Feminism Divorced From Black Feminist Organizing," a critique of bell hooks's *Ain't I A Woman: Black Women and Feminism*,[32]

Barbara Smith raises important and critical issues concerning the relationship of African-American feminism to political organizing. "Theory and analysis are not merely the listing of opinions,"[33] she asserts. In "Jogger Rape: Ask a Black Feminist,"[34] Barbara Smith expresses strongly held opinions in response to Sally O'Brien's "Jogger Verdict Pains, Angers Black Community"[35] (both articles appeared within several months after the trial in the progressive, White weekly *Guardian*, based in New York City). Barbara Smith begins her article by identifying herself as a "Black socialist feminist" who is "shocked to discover that [a White, Communist feminist's] overriding concern was that the Black and Latino teenagers who had been arrested get a fair trial." Smith explains why she finds fair-trial concerns "shocking": "I am a member of the Black community and I am far more pained and angry that O'Brien sees fit to portray the entire African-American community as indifferent to the realities of sexual violence and misogyny than I am at the jury's guilty verdict." O'Brien's article consisted of interviews with African-American leaders who questioned the validity of the August 1990 convictions. Restricting her interviews and reporting to community leaders intimate with the details of the trial and the media coverage, O'Brien neither presents nor constructs a monolithic African-American community. She begins her article, writing: "While many believe the verdict was just, many others, particularly in the African-American community, responded with shock and anger."

O'Brien's article is composed almost entirely of quotes from well-known African Americans: activist-educator Nomsa Brath; Father Lawrence Lucas, then pastor of Harlem's Resurrection Catholic Church; East Harlem Democratic District leader William Perkins; and the editors of the Brooklyn-based weekly, *The City Sun*. Avoiding any dialogue with the African-American community, Barbara Smith instead attacks O'Brien, a non-African American. Neglecting to ground the case in research or interviews, she uses symbols and antiviolence rhetoric to argue that rejecting the validity of the prosecution is equivalent to invalidating "the realities of sexual violence and misogyny." Like Valerie Smith, Barbara Smith will not allow a distinction between the horrific crime itself and its prosecution: to be "pro-survivor" one must be "pro-prosecution." A pro-prosecution stance is not synonymous with support for a just or fair trial; although a fair trial is indispensable in obtaining justice for survivor and the accused.

Barbara Smith's persistence in claiming a universal wasteland of gender-progressive African-American politics leads her to the following conclusion: "What the Central Park rape points out more than anything else, especially its treatment in the media, is how insignificant the voices of Black women are in determining the meaning of events that directly affect our lives." This assertion (also made by Valerie Smith) that African-American women, and particularly Black feminists, are never asked what "all of this means to us," is somewhat misleading. It is unclear to whom the statement itself is addressed (perhaps it is primarily directed at Whites). In fact the African-American weekly, the *Amsterdam News,* eventually turned over major parts of its coverage of the case to Black women. African-American women journalists from NYC radio stations WBAI-NY and WLIB-NY, writers for NYC's African-American press, the *Amsterdam News* and *City Sun,* as well as activists belonging to the New York chapter of the NAACP, and women's groups such as Motherlove and the International Working Women's Day Committee (IWWDC), all took public positions as fair-trial advocates in the Central Park Case. Given their diverse political views, including pro-feminist politics, it is impossible to dismiss these African-American women as uniformly counter-feminist or indifferent to sexual violence. None of the Black feminist writings reviewed here referred to coverage by African-American media as a possible source for other progressive perspectives on the case. Failures to report and critique the various Afra-American perspectives on the Central Park Case and trials "silences" the diversity of women's voices. Most media censured and censored those who spoke against both racial and sexual violence. Pro-woman/feminist fair-trial advocacy by some journalists, as well as organizing by multiracial women's groups/coalitions, went unrecognized. This silence surrounding progressive/radical women's activism splinters off new meanings of "split affinities." Such silence allows symbolism to replace specifity and the problematic aspects of media/state representations in interracial rape cases to be obscured.

Women and Progressive
Fair-Trial Activism on the Central Park Case

We know positively of case after case where innocent men have died horrible deaths. We know positively of cases that have been made up. We know positively of cases where black men have been lynched for white men's crimes. We know positively of black men murdered for insignificant offenses. All that we ask for is justice—not mercy or palliation—simply justice. Surely that is not too much for loyal citizens of a free country to demand. . . . We do not pretend to say there are no black villains. Baseness is not confined to race. We read with horror of two different colored girls who recently have been horribly assaulted by white men in the South. We should regret any lynchings of the offenders by black men but we shall not have occasion. Should these offenders receive any punishment at all, it will be a marvel. (Florida Ruffin Ridley, Boston's Women's Era Clubs, 1894[36])

On April 20, 1989, at 1:30 a.m., two men found a brutally beaten unconscious woman in a muddy ravine in Central Park.[37] During the night of April 19, this woman was violently assaulted while jogging in Central Park. That same night approximately 50 African-American and Puerto Rican youths had assembled at about 9 p.m. and entered the park, scattering in groups of various sizes. Some African-American and Latino youths assaulted several men in the park and threatened others. Youths were detained while exiting the park around 10 p.m. and those picked up for questioning in the following days became suspects in whatever crimes occurred in Central Park that night; these youths were dispersed, like others who entered the park that night, at different locations and exited at different times.[38] Within several days, *The New York Times*[39] and other mainstream, White media, dubbed the survivor, an upper-class European American woman who worked as an investment banker for Solomon Brothers, the "investment banker" or "the jogger" and the detained African-American and Latino male teens the "wolfpack"; this media also denounced the suspects as guilty. The first *New York Times* article to cover the assault appeared April 21. Written by Craig Wolff and relying on uncorroborated police statements for its information, the article ran under the headline, "Youths Rape and Beat Central Park Jogger." All subsequent *New York Times* coverage was consistent with the tone and conviction of this first article. In this climate, the claims by New York City's African-American press and some activists that these (media) convictions created a "legal-lynching" were easily dismissed as "misogynist" or "racist." Because the case had assumed the mythic proportions of a "morality play,"[40] police and assistant district attorneys played to racial-sexual myths and imagery. By promoting and then appending themselves to the reconstruction of the survivor as an icon, police and ADAs came to represent all that was "good," or at least safe, whereas the youths represented "Clockwork Orange" criminality.[41] Generally, the issue of a fair trial to establish guilt appeared "news-worthy" only to the African-American media and individuals skeptical of most media reporting on such issues.

Arguments for presumed innocence until the youth were proven guilty (arguments which some still construe as a case against conviction) contained information largely unknown or ignored, given media coverage that presented accounts critical of the prosecution sporadically and only within narratives of conviction. Information problematic to the Central Park Case convictions disturbed a social equilibrium poised on the image of the youths' savagery. Given the absence of evidence and sensationalist pretrial judgments, progressive activists argued that the willingness to critically reexamine the Central Park Case convictions was tied to demystifying the racial-sexual stereotypes shaping most media representations of this interracial rape case as well as suspicion of media, police, and court activity surrounding the trial. In its racist, rhetorical, and selectively sincere opposition to the epidemic of sexual violence and abuse of women, some argued that most media/police traded in a just judicial process in order to cloak themselves in chivalry. This chivalry was apparently reserved for upper-class, White women: The White media paid little attention to the reported rapes, brutal beatings, or murders of 25 women of color the week of the Central Park assault.

The reluctance of some women and men to accept the prosecution's or state's narrative for the Central Park Case stemmed in part from the questionable aspects of police activity on the case. Most media, even those whose pretrial judgments made the possibility of a fair trial in New York City nil, observed that convictions would be difficult in the absence of a physical case against the youths. Police had obtained neither witnesses nor evidence (blood, semen, hair, soil, fingerprints, footprints, or skin tissue) to connect any of the defendants in the first trial to the scene of the crime. Still, in spring 1989, without corroborating physical evidence or witnesses, the media "convicted" the youths. The basis of those and later jury convictions [42] rested on "confessions," the video-taped and written statements taken from the youths during police interrogation. Some defense attorneys maintained that police physi-cally assaulted several of the youths during interrogation and de-tained others for long hours without food or sleep.

The continuous pretrial replay of videotapes on television and in print gave them a reality independent of their correspondence to physi-cal reality; in some videotaped statements, youth(s) told the wrong location of the assault, described holding down the arms of the survi-vor who was found bound and gagged, and misidentified her attire.[43] Along with the video statements, the youths' contradictory, inconsis-tent, and factually incorrect written statements were conveyed in a language that was unbelievable to some. *Newsday*, among the White New York dailies the most critical of the prosecution, ran several stories questioning the validity of a case built on these statements. In "Salaam's Mom Also Waits for Evidence," Carole Agus wrote:

> A detective read a supposed "confession" of Raymond Santana . . . it sounded like coptalk in its purest form. There never was a 14-year-old working-class kid that ever talked the way Santana is supposed to have talked to the police that night: *"We met up with an additional group of approximately 15 other males who also entered Central Park with us. . . . We all walked southbound in the park in the vicinity of 105th Street."*
>
> We who are watching this trial all have more than we think in common with [Ms.] Salaam. We are waiting to see if there is any believable evidence that will connect these kids to the crime. So far, we haven't heard any.[44]

Unlike Santana and McCray, Sharomme Salaam's son, Yusef, gave no statement. He also passed a lie detector test soon after the assault supporting his assertions that he was never at the scene of the crime. The collective trial proved particularly prejudicial for him. (Presiding Judge Galligan, known as a "hanging" judge and allegedly specially selected for the case by District Attorney Robert Morgenthau, had mandated collective trials.)[45] An "unsigned confession" attributed to Salaam was in fact written by Detective Thomas McKenna 2 days after his interrogation of the former and included more information than that found in McKenna's notes taken on April 20, the night Salaam was detained by the police. McKenna in fact admitted that in order to induce Salaam to confess, he lied to him during the interrogation, telling Yusef that his fingerprints had been found on the survivor's clothing. Although Salaam states he told McKenna he had not been at the scene of the crime and knew nothing of the assault, most media legitimized McKenna's actions with the rationale that because the detective publicly acknowledged lying to the 15-year-old, he thereby retained his integrity and his credibility as a police officer. Because there were no eyewitnesses or corroborating witnesses to testify that the youths on trial attacked the survivor, the only witnesses against the youths concerning the attack[46] were police and ADAs who could testify solely to the validity of the incriminating statements they obtained during interrogations.[47] The refusal to uncritically accept statements by the police or ADAs, as well as the belief that everyone is entitled to a just trial, led to progressive fair trial activism. (I distinguish here between progressive fair trial activism that critiques sexual violence as well as researches specific facts concerning the case, and reactionary fair trial activism that presents a misogynist defense of the youth or denies the reality of the assault; both types of activism existed around the Central Park Case, however, usually the latter was privileged in mainstream media accounts.)

Motivated by their criticisms concerning the prosecution's case, during the first collective trial, women in Motherlove and the International Working Women's Day Committee (IWWDC) called a citywide meeting to build nonsexist/nonracist activism for a fair trial. Motherlove, a small Harlem-based women's group created to support the mothers of the defendants and the youths' right to a fair trial, had organized community forums and meetings on the trial in the Harlem community. IWWDC, as a New York-based group of African-, Latin-, and European-American women activists, organized educational events on March 8 celebrating women's contributions to liberation movements. At the suggestion of Motherlove, IWWDC issued an "open letter to the community." Through progressive media, such as African-American journalist Rosemari Mealy's WBAI-NY radio shows with guests Nomsa Brath, an organizer for Motherlove, Esperanza Martell, and flyers, IWWDC invited representatives from women's and social justice organizations to attend an "Educational Forum on the Central Park Case" on July 19, 1990, at the Martin Luther King Labor Center (Local 1199) in Manhattan. That night, lawyers, journalists, and activists, representing different political views, spoke to the packed meeting room, mostly filled with African-American, Latina, and European-American women.

The key presentation came from IWWDC. Citing the tradition of legal lynchings in U.S. courts, IWWDC linked the Central Park Case to: the Scottsboro Case in the 1930s; New York City's Harlem Six and George Whitmore cases in the 1960s (Whitmore signed a 61-page false "confession" during police interrogation); and more recently, Boston's Carol Stuart case. In all of these cases innocent African-American men were imprisoned for crimes against White women. Because the innocence of the Central Park Case defendants, presumed guilty in most public and media discourse, could not be proven without a doubt, these previous cases were used to emphasize the flaws and racial-sexual biases of the judicial system.[48] They also served as an intellectual and moral foundation for those demanding a fair trial and further investigation. Forum organizers continuously urged people to investigate for themselves the legitimacy of the prosecution's case by attending the trial; develop antiracist and antisexist coalition work; and recognize that the denial of the democratic right of a fair trial to anyone was a dangerous precedent for everyone.

IWWDC devoted most of its program to confronting the mythic proportions of the Central Park Case. The program's primary speaker was Suzanne Ross, a European-American activist and IWWDC member. Ross used Angela Davis's essay, "The Myth of the Black Rapist" from *Women, Race, and Class* to analyze the historical, political aspects of press coverage and the survivor's exploitation as a racial-sexual icon by the White media.[49] Those present heard the historical arguments that demystifying the "myth of the Black rapist" decreases social indifference to lynching and sexual violence. Ross connected Davis's critique of the White obsession with African-American men as rapists with an analysis of how myth both rendered the prosecution of sexual violence against women of color a legal aberration and obscured sexual violence in White women's lives and their complicity in this obscurantism. Current FBI statistics report that more than 90% of reported rapes are *intraracial*, that is, occur within the same racial or ethnic group. Because those survivors tend to report sexual assaults only when they are likely to be considered "believable" (i.e., when their assailant conforms to the stereotype of "rapist"), sexual violence is grossly underreported. Just as antilynching activists had done in the 19th century, IWWDC argued that unexamined racial-sexual mythology, as the cultural and social backdrop for interracial rape cases, increased the likelihood of lynching and social indifference to lynching.[50] They also maintained throughout their activism that legal lynchings legitimize violence as well as the state's refusal to prosecute sexual crimes seriously; and that the abrogation of the legal rights of anyone jeopardizes the rights of everyone.

Demands for justice in the Central Park Case were often condemned as calls for mitigation and a condoning of sexual violence. Activists who argued that racism and classism created an unfair judicial process and that violence against women was unacceptable, were critized by media depicting all fair-trial organizing as anti-White and antifemale. African Americans who made misogynist and sexist statements throughout the case were portrayed by influential media as representative of the reactionary politics of African Americans in general and fair-trial activists in particular. This selective focus on misogyny, and the general social outrage that accompanied such reports, enabled mainstream media conviction narratives to ignore or obscure the weaknesses of the prosecution's case, erasing the distinction between the brutal assault on the one hand, and the prosecution of the youths on the other. Without that critical distinction, given the emotionalism and media hype surrounding the case, criticism of the prosecution was portrayed uniformly as criticism of the survivor, and support for the youths' right to a fair trial became "sympathizing with rapists." The possibility of being outraged by both the violent assault against the survivor *and* the pretrial conviction and police malfeasance became a public anomaly. The dominant media mandated, as it had a century ago, that no context existed for simultaneous organizing against sexual and racist violence, ensuring that most of the public equated progressive organizing with reactionary denials—denials that the assault was horrific, that African-American men assault White women, that sexual violence is a deadly epidemic.

Stigmatized as counter-feminist or misogynist, fair-trial activism was rarely recognized as part of a discernible radical Afra-American tradition of antiviolence organizing. Even Black feminists writing for White publications further obscured the complexities of the case and organizing, allowing only narratives of conviction to bear the respectability of feminism and moralism. As respectability became based on one's distance from fair-trial activism, criticism of the state's (media, police, courts) prosecution by racial-sexual ideology was transformed into indifference to sexual violence. The desire to distance from critiques of the prosecution stemmed from the unpopularity of such critiques given the pretrial media publicity which depicted the youths as guilty; it also was connected to another desire, not to be identified with the misogynist or anti-survivor statements made by African Americans. Both these desires worked to discourage investigative research and critical thinking. (Ironically, in the absence of critical thinking and judgment, those supporting and those condemning the prosecution shared certain similarities.) The multiplicity of responses among African Americans concerning this interracial rape case ranged from an inflexible certainty in the youths' guilt which precluded any critical study of the prosecution's case as well as considerable hostility toward the courts, police, and White media, a hostility which for some extended to the survivor as well. Although some African Americans vilified the survivor, others, specifically those engaged in progressive politics, expressed concern for the survivor as well as abhorrence of sexual violence. For instance, Harlem District Leader William Perkins and activist the Reverend Herbert Daughtery questioned the legitimacy of media "convictions" and organized a prayer vigil for the survivor soon after the attack in 1989; New York City leaders, including White feminists, spoke at this vigil. Most progressive acts for critically rethinking the case, particularly political actions by African-American women, were usually minimized, ignored, or derided in mainstream media.

Conclusion

Disavowals of the existence of a humanist African-American political tradition concerning interracial rape cases diminish the historical and contemporary contributions of radical activism. Acknowledged or unacknowledged, the political thinking of ancestor mothers on interracial rape cases, lynching, and activism reappears in the work of contemporary African-American women. The legacy is a contested one—both repudiated and claimed, it is depicted as either antiquated and denial-ridden or as valuably instructive for contemporary antiviolence campaigns.

In a culture profoundly ignorant of and adept at ignoring the contributions of Afra-Americans, it is easy to misrepresent African-American women's politics on interracial rape cases and lynching as counterprogressive. Revisionist writing that depicts African-American civil rights/liberation movements as uniformly sexist deflect from progressive, political African-American women's traditions coexisting with and within patriarchal traditions; for example, women-led African-American movements such as the antilynching campaigns. Black feminist critiques of African-American sexism and misogyny are indispensable. If marred by reductionism and the erasure of women's progressivism, these critiques can obscure the complexity of racial-sexual politics and human rights activism. Minimizing the links between contemporary feminist politics and historical Afra-American protest and resistance increases the likelihood of matraphobic paradigms. Matraphobia, the fear of becoming what our (fore)mothers were,[51] engenders misrepresentation, distorted memories, and political amnesia. Perhaps the disassociation stems from our aversion to the weaknesses of ancestral mothers or arises from our fears of inheriting the dangers and risks of their powerful radicalism confronting an oppressive state. At its most debilitating, matraphobia diminishes our political resources and options.

Historically, in interracial rape cases, women engaged themselves in independent, investigative research to determine the facts of the case independent of state information. Their dialogues with other activists and writers and journalists in the African-American press created a counter-discourse and a skepticism for critically reviewing events that challenged hegemonic interpretations of racial and sexual violence. The presence or absence of these and similar political strategies today determines the distance between the progressive spectator(-writer) and the progressive activist(-writer). The difference between being a critic of, and being in opposition to, oppressive practices sometimes manifests as the distance between political rhetoric and radical struggle for social change. This dilemma or divide in contemporary Black political life appears not to have been so critical for historical women, such as Ida B. Wells-Barnett, who were both activists and writers.

Today, in order to bridge an emerging chasm, African-American writers may seek to initiate and sustain a greater dialogue between activists and academics. Analyzing the relationship between commentary and organizing strengthens critical writing, research, and activism. Or, as Cornel West notes: "Local activists must become more and more at the center of how we think about the condition for the possibility of social motion and social movement."[52] This seems particularly true in interracial rape cases where racism and sexism violently converge and mythology shapes cultural meanings and social and legal prosecution.

Studying and critiquing the political practices and thinking of ancestor mothers—and activist sisters—furthers a productive dialogue. Documented in their writings, the antiviolence activism of African-American women provides a framework for (re)examining interracial rape cases and our approaches to racialized sexual violence. Exploring the dynamics of racial-sexual politics and political resistance, we may note state complacency toward sexual and racist crimes and social indifference to sexual violence that does not "violate" or cross class and race hierarchies or lines. (This greater indifference to intraracial sexual violence is evident among African Americans, given the divergent responses in Black communities to the Tawana Brawley and the Mike Tyson cases.) Women's complicity in the nonprosecution of sexual violence and their validation of mob violence and state malfeasance as "prosecution" and "protection" remain critical issues for examination.

Addressing these issues we may find that the political traditions of ancestor mothers such as Ida B. Wells-Barnett are now, as in her era, too radical to be claimed by more than a few. Still, we are indebted to the work of our ancestor mothers. Standing on the ground they fought for, we cannot suppress indefinitely their memories and legacies. Perhaps the best way to honor them, and the political analyses and protest traditions of all who resisted racial-sexual violence, is to continue to struggle with our inheritance.

Notes

1. Ida B. Wells, *A Red Record: Lynchings in the United States* (Chicago, Donohue & Henneberry, 1895; reprinted in Ida B. Wells-Barnett, *On Lynchings* (Salem, NH: Ayer, 1990).

2. Joanne Braxton, *Black Women Writing Autobiography: A Tradition Within a Tradition* (Philadelphia: Temple University Press, 1989). According to Braxton, a balance between the "confessional narrative and the historical memoir" allows Miss Wells to relate both her public and private

"duties" as well as "demonstrate her development as a political activist and as an outraged mother." For Braxton, *Crusade for Justice* "looks forward to the modern political autobiographies of Ann Moody, Shirley Chisholm, and Angela Davis . . . [and] represents an important link between the old and the new, part of the 'lost ground' of Afro-American literary tradition" (Braxton, p. 138).

Despite her remarkable achievements, Ida B. Wells was not flawless. When her *Free Speech* editorials exposed the sexual relationships of semi-competent African-American women teachers with corrupt White male members of the school board, Ida B. Wells showed little compassion for the African-American woman who committed suicide after Wells publicized her "mesalliance." After the White school board, angered at the exposure of its corruption, fired Miss Wells, she became a journalist. Braxton also notes Ida B. Wells-Barnett's autobiography claims that Frederick Douglass believed African-American men's proclivity to rape (*Crusade*, pp. 72-73) although there seems to be no record of this as his position. Wells may not have fully acknowledged the extent to which Frederick Douglass influenced her politics.

3. Braxton, p. 2.

4. Braxton, p. 3.

5. Ida B. Wells-Barnett, *Crusade for Justice: The Autobiography of Ida B. Wells,* Alfreda Duster, ed. (Chicago: University of Chicago Press, 1970).

6. Braxton, p. 12. Alfreda Duster spent 35 years finding a publisher for her mother's autobiography and 3 additional years working with historian John Hope Franklin to research and verify Ida B. Wells-Barnett's accounts of historical events. Braxton finds that Duster's role "represents one of the central paradoxes of *Crusade for Justice,* the dependence of the deceased mother on the living daughter for the revelation and publication of her autobiography" (Braxton, p. 107). I suggest that rather than paradox it reveals the interdependency of ancestors and progeny.

7. For additional analyses on sexual violence and lynching, see: Estelle Friedman & John D'Emilio, *Intimate Matters* (New York: Harper & Row, 1988); Angela Davis, *Women, Race and Class* (New York: Random House, 1981); Gerda Lerner, ed., *Black Women in White America: A Documentary History* (New York: Pantheon, 1972).

8. According to Wells's *A Red Record,* most of these lynchings were committed in Tennessee, Alabama, Arkansas, Georgia, and Mississippi. August Meier's preface to *On Lynchings* (reprint ed., 1990), a collection of Miss Wells's three pamphlets, states that the numbers of African Americans reported lynched averaged more than 100 a year during the 1880s and the 1890s, with lynching "peaking" in 1892 when 161 women and men were lynched. *Intimate Matters* reports that between 1889 and 1940 at least 3,800 men and women were lynched in the South and its bordering states, citing an average of 200 lynchings per year during the 1890s. D'Emilio refers to Whites as well. Prior to the Civil War the majority of lynching victims were White, yet during and after Reconstruction lynching became synonymous with violent assaults on African Americans.

9. Meticulous in her research, Miss Wells uses the lynching or murder numbers reported in the White press, believing them to be an undercount but that Whites could not argue that their own numbers were exaggerated. Concerning her pamphlet, *Southern Horrors: Lynch Law in All Its Phases,* historian Rosalyn Tergborn-Penn notes: "She knew that if she wasn't meticulous people would question her. . . . She often used the white newspapers so people could not say she was making it up" ("Ida B. Wells: A Passion for Justice")

Not assuming guilt in the absence of just court trials and evidence, Ida B. Wells lists the reasons given for the reported lynchings of 1892:

> Rape, 46; murder, 58; rioting, 3; race prejudice, 6; no cause given, 4; incendiarism, 6; robbery, 6; assault and battery, 1; attempted rape, 11; suspected robbery, 4; larceny, 1; self defense, 1; insulting women, 2; desperadoes, 6; fraud, 1; attempted murder, 2; no offense stated, boy and girl, 2. . . . In the case of the boy and girl . . . their father, named Hastings, was accused of the murder of a white man; his fourteen-year-old daughter and sixteen-year-old son were hanged and their bodied filled with bullets, then the father was also lynched. This was in November, 1892, at Jonesville, Louisiana. (*A Red Record,* p. 20)

Wells continues: "During the year 1894, there were 132 persons executed in the United States by due form of law, while in the same year, 197 persons were put to death by mobs who gave the victims no opportunity to make a lawful defense" (*A Red Record,* p. 15).

10. Ida B. Wells was the godmother of Thomas and Bettye Moss's infant daughter Maurine. See *Crusade*, pp. 47-52.

11. Anne Moody's autobiography, *Coming of Age in Mississippi* (New York: Dell, 1968), describes collective punishment in her hometown in the 1950s, where Whites firebombed the home of an African-American man having an affair with a White woman; his family was killed in the fire.

12. *Crusade*, pp. 136-137. This passage, a response to lynching apologists, appeared in a special correspondence from Liverpool for the *Inter-Ocean*, April 9, 1894.

13. Ida B. Wells's critique of three rationalizations for terrorism against African Americans in the postbellum South is similar to that of Frederick Douglass, who wrote:

> the justification for the murder of Negroes was said to be Negro conspiracies, Negro insurrections, Negro schemes to murder all the white people, Negro plots to burn the town . . . times have changed and the Negro's accusers have found it necessary to change with them. . . . Honest men no longer believe that there is any ground to apprehend Negro supremacy . . . altered circumstances have made necessary a sterner, stronger, and more effective justification of Southern barbarism, and hence we have . . . to look into the face of a more shocking and blasting charge. (Frederick Douglass, quoted in *Intimate Matters*, p. 218)

14. Wells writes: "The white man's victory soon became complete by fraud, violence, intimidation and murder. The franchise vouchsafed to the Negro grew to be a 'barren ideality' and regardless of numbers, the colored people found themselves voiceless in the councils of those whose duty it was to rule" (*A Red Record*, p. 10).

15. *A Red Record*, p. 10.

16. Angela Davis argues this point in "Rape, Racism and the Capitalist Setting," *The Black Scholar*, April 1978.

17. *Crusade*, pp. 65-66.

18. *A Red Record*, p. 11.

19. This quote appears in *Black Women in White America*, p. 205.

20. Valerie Smith, "Split Affinities," in *Conflicts in Feminism*, Marianne Hirsh and Evelyn Fox Keller, eds. (New York: Routledge, 1990).

21. V. Smith, p. 275.

22. V. Smith shapes the story to support her thesis that African-American women activists' pained and confused politics on interracial rape lead them to support Black male rapists rather than their White female victims. Through highly selective, at times out of context, quoting of Walker's short story, Smith imputes to the Black woman narrator a hostility for Whites and White women that does not exist in Walker's text. Walker's story is more ambiguous and more complex and does not support the Black female sexist-villain and White female feminist-heroine thesis of "Split Affinities."

23. Braxton, pp. 137-138.

24. V. Smith compares White media coverage of the Central Park Case with its coverage of the March 22 rape of a young White woman with a broomstick handle and a miniature baseball bat by five middle-class White teenage football players:

> The reporting of these two cases must prompt us to ask why the rape of a brilliant, middle-class investment banker by a group of young black men is constructed to seem more heinous than the rape of a 'mildly retarded' young white woman by a group of young white men. Rape here is clearly not represented as a violation of a woman's body alone. Rather, in the terms of interlocking issues of race, class, and gender, these crimes suggest that certain women's bodies are more valuable than others. (Smith, p. 278)

25. *Crusade for Justice*.

26. Braxton, p. 122.

27. *Crusade for Justice* suggests that upper- and middle-class African Americans tend to be more protected from, and therefore indifferent to, lynchings whose victims stem from the poorer

classes. Clenora Hudson's "The Unearthing of Emmett Till: A Compelling Process" (*The Iowa Alumni Review*, October 1988) also supports this interpretation.

28. V. Smith, p. 272.

29. European- and African-American journalists critiqued the police malfeasance and media pretrial convictions that dominated coverage in *The New York Times* and the *New York Post*.

30. Presenting the "anti-rape movement" as led by White women, Valerie Smith writes that African-American women fail to "find common cause with white women in the anti-rape movement" because of our "invisibility as victims within the movement, and a perceived indifference within the movement to the uses to which the fraudulent rape charge has been put" (Smith, p. 276).

31. bell hooks, "Reflections on Sex and Race,"

32. bell hooks, *Ain't I A Woman: Black Women and Feminism* (Boston: South End Press, 1983).

33. Barbara Smith, "Black Feminism Divorced From Black Feminist Organizing," *The Black Scholar* (Vol. 14, No. 1, January/February, 1983), p. 45, special issue on "Black Community Issues." According to B. Smith, hooks ignores or minimizes Black male oppression during slavery and overestimates the extent to which Black men were spared sexual abuse and humiliation. Barbara Smith writes: "If the system protected Black male sexuality so thoroughly, what in the world is the history of lynching all about?" (p. 39).

34. Barbara Smith, "Jogger Rape: Ask a Black Feminist," *Guardian*, New York City (November 7, 1990).

35. Sally O'Brien, "Jogger Verdict Pains, Angers Black Community," *Guardian*, New York City (September 12, 1990).

36. Quoted in *Crusade for Justice*.

37. The two collective trials in 1990 for the assault ended with the convictions of six African-American and Latino youths. This chapter focuses on the first collective trial where, in August 1990, Antron McCray (16), Yusef Salaam (16), and Raymond Santana (15) received (and are now serving) the maximum youth sentence for rape and assault: 5-10 years in prison. Their appeal attorneys include William Kunstler for Salaam and Vernon Mason for McCray.

38. Rick Hornung's thoroughly researched account of the arrests is used in this discussion of the first trial. See Rick Hornung, "The Case Against the Prosecution," *Village Voice* (February 20, 1990) for an in-depth discussion of the arrests.

39. Craig Wolff, "Youths Rape and Beat Central Park Jogger," *The New York Times* (April 21, 1989) p. B1.

40. European-American Michelle Hammer describes the "callousness" of the mythology objectifying the survivor:

> How many times have we heard the word miraculous, as though the gods themselves were on her side? This miraculous recovery has been expressed as a triumph of good over evil, her extraordinarily good attitude—the result, as the myth would have it, of good breeding, good family, good schools, a good job—has made medicine itself seem almost superfluous. Her good attitude has prevailed over bad boys, from bad families, who do bad things (including live) in that bad part of town where the good jogger somehow strayed. In the stiff and demanding morality of this myth, only a miraculous recovery will do, because her recovery is not only her reward for being good, but also proof that she is good. As an '80s morality tale this made perfect sense, since having the goods in the '80s made you good. Hence, the apotheosis came when Salomon [Brothers], named her a vice president. It was as if to say, not only had she not lost ground, she had gained. And gains could be made only by getting ahead, not by wavering. (Hammer, "Memory, Myth and the Jogger," *Newsday*, June 21, 1990, pp. 72, 74)

41. Consistent with the symbolism in the prosecution's case, necessitated by the absence of either witnesses or evidence, ADAs Elizabeth Lederer and Linda Fairstein, as White women, became simultaneously the avengers and symbols of victimized (White) women—the former by assuming the "male" roles of state prosecutors, the latter by appropriating the body and voice of the survivor. Their highly visual presence also allowed the state's role to be feminized.

When the survivor testified for 15 minutes in the August 1990 trial, it was to detail her recovery from the brutal beating. This account was used as testimony against the youths, although she failed to identify any of them as her assailants. Lederer and Fairstein were the only

(White) women who claimed in court that the youths had sexually and physically assaulted anyone. With repeated displays of medical photographs of the survivor's battered and partially nude body taken soon after the assault, and by having the survivor "testify," despite her being afflicted with amnesia, Lederer introduced the woman's "body" as evidence of the youths' guilt. Only words—those of Lederer, Fairstein, and the police, as well as the youths' (Salaam excepted) own incriminating, contradictory, and repudiated statements—connected the youths to the "body." The Manhattan District Attorney's office lists the file of the Central Park Case as "closed," although ADA Lederer publicly acknowledges that there is still a "rapist[s] out there" connected to the April 1989 assault; even though physical evidence existed, police never attempted to find the male(s) whose semen matched that found on the survivor. (See: Transcript #3034, *Phil Donahue Show*, September 14, 1990, "Crime and Punishment: Was the Jogger Defendant's Sentence Fair?")

42. Timothy Sullivan describes troubling aspects of jury deliberations: jurors who already believed the youths guilty reconstructed reality: "[Juror] Brueland . . . believed he could read the lips of one defendant on videotape [tapes were redacted] and discern Salaam's name. . . . In fact, neither McCray nor Santana names Salaam anyplace on the tapes." (Timothy Sullivan, "Jogger Juror Threatened to Block Verdict," *Manhattan Lawyer*, 3(21), October 1990, pp. 1, 25-27.)

43. Inconsistencies in the prosecution's case are reported in: Elombe Brath, "The Media, Rape and Race: The Central Park Jogger Case," *NOBO: A Journal of African American Dialogue* (Winter 1991); Timothy Sullivan, "Jogger Juror Threatened to Block Verdict," *Manhattan Lawyer*, 3(21), October 1990, pp. 1, 25-27. Brath argued that, due to the inconsistencies in the statements and the questionable conditions under which they were taken, it was more accurate to refer to the video and written statements by the youths as "self-incriminating statements" rather than "confessions."

44. Carole Agus, "Salaam's Mom Also Waits for Evidence," *Newsday* (July 18, 1990), pp. 3, 25.

45. *The New York Times* reported in August 1990 that Galligan's offices were charged with anti-Black bias by NAACP legal counsel on issues unrelated to the Central Park Case.

46. Other attacks against male joggers or cyclists occured in the park that night. The ADA had a stronger case against some youths concerning these attacks.

47. Detailing police admissions to breaking the law in order to obtain incriminating statements, *Village Voice* writer Rick Hornung predicted: "The police engaged in . . . conduct so improper that it . . . will undoubtedly be the grounds of a strong appeal even if the defendants are found guilty." According to Hornung, the pretrial hearings revealed that police violated: state laws protecting juvenile rights by separating all the children from their parents; Fifth Amendment and Sixth Amendment rights of at least three defendants by failing to inform them respectively of their rights to remain silent and to consult an attorney; Fifth Amendment right against compelled self-incrimination (accompanied by ADA Linda Fairstein, police transported several of the youths involved in the second trial to the scene of the crime, without defense lawyers or parents, in order to have them "put themselves in it" more convincingly. (See Rick Hornung, "The Case Against the Prosecution," *Village Voice*, February 1990, p. 32.)

The need to prove innocence in order to mobilize for a fair trial is an inversion of the U.S. justice system where, in theory, only guilt beyond a reasonable doubt must be proven must be proven guilty. In the absence of virtual certainty of the youth's innocence, people acquiesed to police malfeasance and the possibility of an unfair trial; or as one African-American man opined: "They railroaded the right guys."

49. Erica Munk's "Body Politics at Its Worse [sic]" (*Village Voice*, July 31, 1990) reported the July 19, 1990 organizing session as an "anti-survivor" event. Her article failed to note that the key address at the forum advocating fair-trial activism was given by a White woman, Suzanne Ross. Munk, who argued that the youths were guilty (based on her experience as a theater critic, which gave her insight into the veracity of the videotaped confessions) identified by name African-American women who were minor speakers or moderators, depicting them as uniformly hostile to White women. In fact, an African-American woman strongly criticized a Black lawyer for his harsh rhetoric concerning the defense lawyers' refusal to cross-examine the survivor. See Joy James, "The Myth of the Black Rapists," Letters to the Editor, and Munk's reply, both in the *Village Voice*, August 14, 1990.

50. Loretta Ross, "Rape and Third World Women," *Aegis* 1983, Washington, D.C.

51. Braxton, referring to biological mothers, attributes this term to Margaret Homans (see Braxton, p. 3). I use *matraphobia* here to refer to ancestral, not biological, mothers.

52. Cornel West. "We Socialists," *Crossroads* (July-August 1991), No. 12, p. 4.

PART II

Image Wars: Literary
and Popular Constructions
of Black Women

8. The Condition of Black Women in Spain During the Renaissance

BALTASAR FRA-MOLINERO

In *The Supper at Emmaus*, by the Spanish painter Diego Velázquez (1599-1660), a young Black woman is portrayed in a scene of domestic life. She is in the kitchen, but she seems to have stopped working. Amid pans and earthen jars, leaning against a table, this woman, an adolescent, has her head slightly bent toward a window, a gesture that suggests that she is listening, or maybe eavesdropping. Through the window we can see the object of her interest: In the background Jesus Christ is sitting and talking to his disciples.

Placing a Black woman in the center of a religious painting had for Velázquez and his contemporaries a refreshing effect of verisimilitude and a powerful evangelical force. The word of God reaches everywhere and everyone, "even" a Black slave in the kitchen. Thus the painting speaks of two worlds, two environments that existed in Spanish society at the time: the world of the kitchen and the world of the dining room. In the case of Seville, Velázquez's hometown, women, especially Black women, belonged in the kitchen. This Black woman was being excluded from certain company and from the place where decisions about everything—including herself—were made. The dining room was the place of her owners, White and mostly male.

In the present chapter I study the attitudes toward Black slave women in Spain during the 16th and 17th centuries. Historical evidence will be combined with other testimonies—especially literary ones—to build a case for the way in which Spanish society came to construct the concept of "blackness" as synonymous with "slavery" and how Spain, as a society, combined gender and race in the development of stereotypes about Black women that in time would travel across the Atlantic and can be identified in the Western hemisphere even today.

Slave women in Renaissance Spain were of several different origins, and the process by which they became slaves depended on factors related to geography, religion, skin color, and political and economic circumstances. Legal records of wills, sales, and other transactions often classify a slave as "White Moor" or "Black Moor," or simply "White" or "Black." The pervasiveness of these descriptions indicated a need to associate the institution of slavery with the notion of racial boundaries. The slaves from the Canary Islands were considered "White," to distinguish them from "Blacks" and "Guineans." These documents reveal distinctions made between a *negra mora* (a Black Moor woman), a *negra* (a Black woman), and a *negra de Guinea* (a Black woman from Guinea). Yet, the classification of slave women consisted of fewer classes when compared to those used for slave men. Color, religion, and ethnic origin were clearly specified in documents concerning men slaves much more frequently and in more detail than in the case of women.[1]

Racial classifications based on skin color were not new to Spanish society. At the beginning of the 16th century, slaves of mixed race were called *loros*, a term used during the Middle Ages. Only later did they start receiving the name of *mulatos*, the term from which the English *mulatto* comes.[2] This term was applied in a discriminatory manner. Muslim slaves from North Africa did not have their mixed-race children, whose fathers were Christian Whites, dubbed in any particular way. But as the 16th century advanced, color started being more important than religion or ethnic origin.

By the time of the Columbian expedition to America, slavery was becoming a thriving institution in the Iberian Peninsula and the Canary Islands. Entrepreneurs immediately carried it across the Atlantic. Legislation from the *Siete Partidas*, the Medieval Castilian code of jurisprudence, was at the base of most legal practice during the Spanish Empire. Yet the legal frame quickly accommodated to the new aspects of slavery in places like Peru, New Spain (Mexico), or Hispaniola.[3] Instrumental in the colonization of the "New World" was the massive use of slaves on sugar and cotton plantations and in mining (Greenfield, 1979, pp. 114-116). Spain became a colonial empire and a slave society more or less at the same time. The choice of slave peoples over colonized peoples was the direct result of a policy that considered sub-Saharan Africa off limits for territorial expansion, while at the same time thought of the discovered territories in America, the Canary Islands, and the Philippines as "natural" prolongations of the kingdom of Castile. Indians, Guanches (natives of the Canary Islands), and Filipinos were to be "subjects," whereas sub-Saharan Africans—Blacks—were to be slaves.[4]

Spain was not a unified country by the time Columbus sailed to America in 1492. Different kingdoms were more or less united by the Catholic monarchs, Ferdinand and Isabella. They created a common foreign policy but internal legal systems among them remained quite separate. Thus, in Renaissance Spain, attitudes toward Blacks were shaped by different experiences and practices of slavery. Rather than *slavery*, we should be talking of *slaveries*.

Slavery had been a common practice throughout the Middle Ages in Spain, especially in the eastern kingdom of Aragon and in the Muslim kingdoms of Al-Andalus. It was a social phenomenon that affected a variety of people of different ethnic and religious backgrounds. Muslims captured in wars by Christian overlords were reduced to slavery; Slavic people (from whom the word *slave* is derived; *esclavo* in Spanish, *sclau* in Catalan/Valencian) were also bought in significant numbers. Records from the late 15th century and early part of the 16th show little difference in the price of Black slave women in comparison with their "White" counterparts. This would change in the course of the century when slavery became more specialized and sub-Saharan Africans became the favorite victims of the trade. But by the middle of the 16th century it was becoming quite clear that the majority of slaves were coming from sub-Saharan Africa.[5]

"White" slaves became synonymous with Muslim North African slaves. Their value was connected with the possibility for their owner to obtain ransom money from their relatives in North Africa. In the case of a Muslim slave woman, her chances of being ransomed were slim. Muslim slaves, on the other hand, always had the possibility of taking refuge among the *moriscos*, the Muslim minority that remained in Spain after the conquest of Granada in 1492, and thus cross the sea back to freedom. Aware of this, the Cortes of Castile, or Parliament, asked King Philip II in 1560 to forbid the *moriscos* of Granada from owning slaves, especially Black ones. If the condition of slaves became more and more circumscribed to the ethnic/racial group of Black Africans, owning slaves became the exclusive privilege of Christian Whites.

Just as the guitar used in the blues can be traced back to Muslim Andalucía in southern Spain, so can slavery. Black slaves had existed in Muslim Spain ever since the conquest of the old Visigothic kingdom of Hispania by the combined Berber and Arab troops of Tarik and Musa in the second decade of the 8th century. But by the middle of the 15th century an important development occurred that would change the course of modern slavery. The traditional slave trade started shifting from an interior route through the Sahara desert, controlled by Arabs and Berbers, toward a maritime route along the Western Atlantic coast of the African continent. Portuguese and Castilian ships started providing new slaves to cities like Lisbon and Seville that soon became, in the early part of the 16th century, the two most important Atlantic cities in Europe. America had created an enormous need for labor to exploit the newly conquered lands, which made the slave trade increasingly profitable.

The introduction of the Atlantic route in the slave trade would have far-reaching consequences. The diaspora of Black Africans, which had started with the Muslim slave trade, was extended, from the 16th century onwards, to the new economic interests of capitalist Europeans. Spain was the first imperial power, together with Portugal, in deciding to consider Africans the main object of the slave trade.[6] The rise of the "Black" as the ideal candidate for slavery coincided with the waning of other sources of slaves, mainly Muslim North Africans.

Black women were, as a group, the most oppressed human collective in Spanish society during the Renaissance. Sex, gender, and race were incorporated to a mode of production in the case of Black women that differed profoundly from that of Black men. In all slave societies the condition of women slaves is radically different from that of men. Anthropologist Gayle Rubin has defined the position of women in society as that of being the object of a transaction between men. All our societies have been organized in a patriarchal system that reduces women to a domestic sphere and excludes them from the more public domain reserved to men in general. Following the example of Gayle Rubin's basic question about what constitutes a "domesticated woman," it is necessary to explore what constituted a Black slave woman during the Spanish Renaissance.[7] In order to do that we have to describe the "sex/gender/race system" that allowed the existence of Black women slaves.

Slavery in Spain was for the most part an urban phenomenon.[8] Although there were some exceptions to the rule, slave women lived in the same household as their masters and their master's family. Slavery in Renaissance Spain was incorporated into the kinship system then operating in Spanish society. A kinship system is not a list of biological relatives but rather a system of categories and statuses (Rubin, 1975, p. 169). Kinship is the culturalization of biological sexuality on the social level (Rubin, 1975, p. 189).[9] According to the anthropologist Lévi-Strauss (1969), the essence of the kinship system is the exchange of women between men. Women are given in marriage as a gift to another man, in exchange for certain goods. Women are not partners in the exchange but rather "conduits" in a relationship between men (Rubin, 1975, p. 174). This phenomenon is not exclusive to "primitive" societies, but rather it transcends geography and history, which renders concepts such as "primitive" rather useless. In order for an exchange of women to exist in a society there must be an equivalent for women: *her worth* (Rubin, 1975, p. 206). Worth takes the form of dowries, brideswealth, or price in the case of a slave woman in Renaissance Spain. Like slave men, a slave woman was sold for a price, but as a woman she acquired an additional value. She could become the price paid by a master to secure the loyalty of a male slave, her future husband. Or she could become the master's concubine.

Slavery developed in Spain in the middle of gradual social changes. Social stratification in a Medieval sense—in which feudal lords could command the allegiance of their subjects—was giving way to a new economic framework. These changes created new social relations among preexisting classes. The growing class of artisans and merchants did not depend for their well-being on the possession of land, but rather on the possession of money and urban rents (houses, businesses, and trade). Land or real estate became important only if it could yield money. Artisans and merchants paid wages to unskilled workers and servants, or owned slaves. Slaves were a commodity that not only produced more money through work and reproduction, but also could be sold, rented, and leased for more money. Thus social relations changed: A petty nobleman was considerably worse off than a plebeian artisan who could use his skill to acquire wealth, and that wealth to acquire a newly developed prestige. Having slaves was not only a good investment but an external sign of one's worth. They were wealth that could be shown walking in the streets. Owners belonged to all sectors of society. An important aristocrat like the Archbishop of Seville could have up to 70 or even 100 slaves in his household, whereas the wife of a painter could boast about owning 2 or 3, sometimes even more. The owners included all sectors of society.

The records used by the main historians on Spanish slavery are those of notary public protocols in major cities. A. N'Damba Kabongo (1975, 1976), in his studies of slavery in Seville and Córdoba, notes how extended the practice was. Slave holders included: artisans, ecclesiastics, noblemen, yeomen, and merchants. As to the people actively involved in the slave trade, we can see a true European Community of *mercaderes* or merchants: from England, Genoa, Florence, France, Germany, and of course from the different peninsular kingdoms of Portugal, Castile, Aragón, Valencia, and Catalonia.[10]

Black Slave Women in Christian Spain

The presence of the Black slave woman in Christian Spanish households continued a pattern in the structure of the family that had its roots in Muslim Spain (711-1492).[11] According to Muslim law and custom, the male offspring of a free man and *his* slave woman could be freed by him and be considered officially his son; not so in Christian Spain. Monogamy on the one hand and the tradition of the Roman law on the other made the children of slave women the property of the latter's master, whether she had had them from him or from another man, free or slave. Black slave women found themselves treated as one more item of property in the household. If a slave woman became pregnant from a free man not her legal owner, her child was still the property of the legal owner unless the free man paid the price to free his offspring. Prices varied and haggling ensued. The owner wanted "his" money in compensation for the "damages" occasioned by the diminution of working capability of the slave woman during her pregnancy.

The value of a slave woman depended on her age, her skills, and, in the course of the 16th century, her race. The price of an "average" Black slave woman in Renaissance Spain was slightly superior to the total earnings of a worker for the whole year—around 10,000 maravedís—same price as a good horse (Franco Silva, 1979, p. 115). The highest price for a slave woman was paid during her fertile years, especially during her twenties. Skills such as fruit preserving and candy making, or an ability in needlework, served as an enticement to prospective buyers. This situation impeded free labor, especially for freed Black women. In the increasingly expensive Spanish cities of the 16th century, free Black women could hardly earn a living in the few activities allowed to them, mostly related to domestic work.[12] The salary earned by an adult slave woman per day—excluding Sundays—was 13 maravedís in the early 16th century. This constituted a yearly earning of less than 4,000 maravedís, of which a hefty 50% if not more went to her owner. Considering the inflated price of self-purchase for a slave (around 15,000 maravedís for a healthy adult woman), a slave woman was expected to consume most of her youth and strength saving for her own freedom.

The sale of a slave was a crucial moment in her life. In addition to the main preoccupation of having to deal with the personality of the new owner, her position and relation to his family and rest of the household—other servants and slaves of both sexes—there were the complications of her sale. The purchase had to be made in public and *almojarifazgo* (sales tax) applied. Cheating on the part of buyers and sellers was not uncommon. If an owner did not pay such sales tax to the officer, the slave was declared *descaminada* (wayward), and the tax officers could apprehend her. This added a burden to the slave, who might find herself in prison through no fault of her own (Franco Silva, 1979, p. 121). Prison at that time, in the words of Miguel de Cervantes, was a place "where every discomfort takes place, and every sad noise is lodged" (*Don Quijote,* Prologue, 1986, p. 1).

The legal code of the *Siete Partidas* recognized certain rights for the slave. A slave could contract marriage, and the owner was supposed to respect that.[13] A non-Christian (Jewish, Muslim) could not own slaves. A slave could buy his or her own freedom only if he or she was a Christian. Expectedly, most Black slaves became part of the religious unification process going on in Spain during the later part of the Middle Ages and all of the Renaissance, with the hope of attaining freedom.

Black Slave Women in the Emerging Capitalist Structure

Slaves were property, with the advantage for the owner of its easy convertibility into money or its equivalent in goods. The most important notion a slave in Spain acquired was that her body was worth value, whether paid in money or in services. Concepts such as "work" and "service," when women are the protagonists, have often been confused by those—generally men—who define the terms. All the production a Black slave woman was capable of was considered "service," that is, an expression of the loyalty she owed to her master (or mistress), which was essentially different from the "loyal service" of a wife or a child. Therein lay the difference with a proper "servant" or a wife, who related to the master or husband by means of a contract. A wife was supposed to "serve" her husband but her service was recognized in different ways, and she obtained certain things in exchange for submitting to her husband's authority and giving him offspring. A servant derived a salary, food, clothes, and lodgings for his or her "service." On the other hand, "work" started being defined at the time in cities like Seville as a money-earning activity outside the domestic domain. Capitalist production was emerging in Southern Spain, with industries such as silk works and other textiles, ceramics, soap making, and different other manufactures, as well as commerce. Black women found this "work" outside the household their best way to earn the money necessary to gain their freedom or that of their relatives—husbands, lovers, and children. Their ability to earn money for their masters and mistresses gave them some bargaining power, recognized in different kinds of public contracts.

Women's work outside the domestic sphere was not considered a legitimate activity, however, and it was subject to different kinds of limitations and prohibitions in the form of city ordinances against their commercial activities.[14] All in all, Black women were protagonists in the emergence of a manufacturing industry in Spain. Documents attest to the presence of two Black women bought by their owner to work at a textile loom: Juana, a 20-year-old, bought for 12,000 maravedís, and another Juana, a 25-year-old Mandinga, bought for 10,000 maravedís.[15]

If the work in store for the slave woman was considered undesirable by the general population, there was no problem. María, a Black slave from Jolof (Wolof) was sold by her owners, who were innkeepers. Women slaves, together with men, were forced to work in potentially life-threatening businesses such as innkeeping, a risky activity due to the frequency of altercations, sometimes bloody, among the patrons (Franco Silva, 1979, p. 308). And there existed a preference for someone recently arrived over a more seasoned slave.[16] This speaks of the hardship of the work and the little personal reward it could offer.[17] The determination of slave women to free themselves by any means came from such situations in some cases.

Sexual Exploitation of Black Slave Women

The theoretical and legal possibility of freedom made a slave as pre-occupied with the acquisition of money as the rest of the urban community was with the acquisition of other commodities. Slaves were allowed to save money destined to buy their own freedom, but nothing else. Any possession of the slave belonged instantly to her owner. Slave women had to negotiate permission to work for a salary outside the owner's household. Because work for salary was scarce and not regular, prostitution was one of the avenues for a Black woman in need of money, but the activity put her immediately on the wrong side of the law. The activity was in itself not illegal, because free White women could resort to it. In fact, cities like Seville had it regulated and under the supervision of Church and local authorities.[18] Black freed women could lose their freedom if caught exercising the profession in an independent manner, and in the case of a slave, her owner could face the confiscation of the slave woman by the City Council. Documents show how the issue became a source of strife between owners and slave women. Owners either consented or protested. In the latter case, they denounced the slave woman to the authorities. Juan Pérez Hurtado sold 25-year-old Catalina, a Black woman born in Portugal, because "she is a whore, a drunk, a thief and prone to escape," for 11,000 maravedís. In spite of her "immoral" ways, this woman commanded the usual high price for a slave woman of her age.[19] A great number of slave women were routinely arrested and imprisoned by the local authorities, which gives us an idea of how extensive prostitution by slave women was.[20] *Mala mujer de su cuerpo* (a bad woman about her body) was a phrase recorded in a document to describe one such slave (in this case a Moorish one) denounced by her former owner and whose freedom was revoked. The "bad use" of her body by a slave woman always coincided with a clash of interest with the (male) owner, who in all probability expected to derive some benefit from the slave woman's activities.

Slavery transformed the urban household in relation to its rural, nonslave counterpart. A system of de facto polygamy occurred in many cases, which was hardly acceptable for Christian Spain although not new in Muslim Seville, Córdoba, and Granada. Cases of concubinage were frequent and only rarely denounced. One such case concerned a priest, Cristóbal Martínez de Sanjuán, sanctioned for maintaining sexual relations with a slave woman who belonged to someone else (Franco Silva, 1979, p. 139). Another case involving an ecclesiastic and a Black slave woman illustrates the common assumption of the multiple services the latter was supposed to render a master. A soldier was tried by the Spanish Inquisition after he tried to sell a Black slave woman to the priest:

> [the soldier] offered her to him [the priest], that she was pretty, and she would
> serve him as a lover also, and when he replied that it was a sin, he said: let God
> suffer it and take her home; you'll screw her to your heart's content and yet you
> will not be guilty of sin.[21]

The soldier's crime was his proclamation that fornication with a Black slave was not a sin, not the fact that he was trying to sell the slave woman to a priest for the purpose of the new owner's sexual gratification.

Sexual intercourse with Black women was not particularly discouraged, in spite of protestations and calls to morality by authorities and owners alike. The Black woman slave became more valuable than ever as a means of reproduction. Between 10% and 25% of female slaves sold and bought in Seville during the period from 1453 to 1525 were either pregnant or had a child less than 10 years of age. Should the mother die, the owner's wife continued raising the child, but as a slave, as is testified in many wills (Franco Silva, 1979, p. 156).

Resistance, Rebellion, and Escape

Although the means of resistance to the slave condition were constantly repressed by owners and the authorities, slaves did rebel and escape in many cases. There was no proper antislavery sentiment at the time, with the exception of some timid protestations about the "method" of enslaving (cases like the moralists Alonso de Albornoz and Tomás de Mercado), or indirect calls for a humane treatment such as that of Saint Teresa of Avila.[22] But in general, the institution of slavery as such was taken for granted.

The most definitive form of resistance was escape, but it was the most difficult one, too. Success was unlikely for a Black woman. Yet there arc cases, like Felipa, *lora* (mixed-race), who escaped from the Council jail itself with her 18-month-old baby daughter Juana, together with Juan, another *loro* slave. All were apprehended in Fregenal, a nearby town.[23] The persecution of runaway slaves was entrusted to people by special documents (*cartas de poder*) so they could legally apprehend them. Punishment of recaptured slaves was harsh: flogging, branding, and the infamous *pringado* (larding), which consisted in pouring hot lard on the open sores left by the whipping. Such punishment left permanent and disfiguring marks. Women were the victims of branding less often than men, but certainly did not escape the practice. Because branding was connected in many cases to light skinned slaves who had tried to escape, the practice of branding Black women slaves seems to have a different meaning, namely, that of being marks of property of important owners, such as aristocrats (Fernández Martín, 1988, p. 135). Mutilation was also practiced, like cutting the slave's ears (Franco Silva, 1979, p. 209).[24] Fleeing was so badly taken by the owners that they routinely excluded former fugitive slaves from freedom in their wills (Franco Silva, 1979, p. 210).

Between 1470 and 1525 the number of escapees in Seville alone was 297, of which 123 were Black (31 were women). These Black women must have felt the desperation of their situation quite acutely, as was the case of Juana, a pregnant Black woman of 30 who in 1512 escaped from her master, an ecclesiastic named Alonso de Morales (Franco Silva, 1979, p. 205).[25] Probably in anger or exasperation, one slave owner sold 40-year-old Catalina, a fugitive at the time, for 3,000 maravedís to the person who wanted to find her.[26] A *lora*, also named Catalina, escaped from her master when she was going to be sold for 10,000 maravedís, taking a donkey in her flight.[27]

The flight of slaves tells us something about the formation of a concept of solidarity among Blacks in Spain. Black slaves of both sexes tended to flee to Portugal. There were cases of Portuguese owners who claimed slaves who had fled from Lisbon to Seville. Both cities had large communities of Blacks where these fugitive slaves hoped to find shelter and asylum. On the other side of the coin, there were cases of fraud, as in Valencia, involving free people who promised help in exchange for money to the slave, only to betray them later on (Cortés Alonso, 1964, p. 77; Miret y Sans, 1917, p. 45).

Drinking was an activity that rendered the slave incapable of working. Alcoholism was an endemic problem in Spain, and it affected the Black population, free and slave, men and women. Alfonso Franco Silva (1979) gives very high figures: 20% of the freed slaves and 10% of the slaves were alcoholic. This appears in documents of sale as one of the slave's *tachas* (blemishes) (p. 267). What documents cannot hide is that the so-called defects denounced traits of an individual form of resistance that at times the owner could only check with the help of the authorities. Cities such as Valladolid banned the presence of Blacks in taverns. Their free circulation after dark was equally forbidden. Theft accompanied alcoholism, and the authorities were particularly stern in their punishment: floggings, imprisonment, and even amputation of hands. Twenty-five-year-old Isabel ran into trouble for being *"brava, bravía, borracha e que no quiere hacer lo que le mandan"* ("harsh, a shrew, a drunk who on top of that does not want to do what is asked of her").[28]

Historical documents do not offer many direct examples of rebellion and resistance among slaves, yet owners lived in fear, which is shown indirectly by certain situations. In Valencia, in the late Middle Ages, there were insurance policies to cover owners against the crimes of their slaves. But such crimes proved more costly in court than the profit the owner could gain from the slave's work, so the practice was abandoned by the next century (Gual Camerana, 1953, p. 248). Against other forms of resistance and rebellion, like murder, aggression, theft, arson, or self-mutilation, penalties were harsh.

Any activity deemed strange or suspect by some neighbor could land a Black woman in jail. Such was the case of Beatriz (no last name given), a free woman, executed for having "given some powders" to another slave woman who wanted them for her mistress. The suspicion was enough to send her to the gallows, although the criminality of the action was never determined (de León, 1981, p. 548).

Buying and Securing Freedom

Following the Medieval practice of slavery, freedom was always a hope for a slave in Spain. The practice of *ahorramiento* (manumission) is frequently cited in legal documents of the time. There was even a legal format for the so-called *cartas de ahorramiento* (letters of manumission), which stated that the owner granted freedom to the slave in recognition of loyalty and good service. Certain conditions made the act of freeing slaves more a calculated business operation than an act of generosity. Among them is the price the slave must pay for herself and her children, or the conditions of such payment. Owners bequeathed freedom to their loyal slaves in their wills. This gave rise to a common situation: A Black man or woman could be half-free and half-slave at one point in her or his life. This could be the result of a will in which a husband freed his "part" of the slave owned by him and his spouse, or when the slave was bequeathed in parts to the children of a married couple. Such "largesse" did not come without attachments. In many cases the conditions prior to the final emancipation included years of service to the family of the deceased. In some others, the former slave had to pay weekly or monthly "rent" to the survivors, and so on. Such was frequently the case of those who were half free or even one-third free.

The letter of *ahorramiento* was a true identity document for the slave, who was always in danger of being apprehended and declared a runaway slave, as happened to Ana López, a Black servant of a priest in Portugal. After she was imprisoned her employer left for Seville and did not help her to disentangle the imbroglio, for which she had to spend a considerable sum of money in order to prove her free condition. Therefore, a freed slave depended on the testimony of her former owner to establish her newly gained social identity. Freed did not mean free.

The life of freed slaves was precarious. In the case of Black women it was especially so. Their first task was to find gainful employment in cities plagued by endemic unemployment. They suffered the competition of slave women, who could perform for much less than a free woman asked. Then there was the problem of housing. In Seville, for instance, Black women tended to live in groups of four and five to a small apartment, each of them contributing to the rent. Free and half-free

Black people tended to concentrate their dwelling in some neighbor-hoods, in conditions similar to those of today's large cities in the United States. Many freed Black women decided to continue living in their former owner's household. Imprisonment for debt was also common for freed slaves. Women had the worst part in this latter case, because debts reduced them to their former position of domestic servants in exchange for a very scanty salary (Franco Silva, 1979, p. 268).

Religious Life

Religion occupied a central part in both public and private Spanish life. Slaves were to be included in the project of a Catholic and Imperial Spain at all costs. Propaganda was exercised to convert Black slaves, who for the most part had little alternative. The Church also set up guilds, called *cofradías*, for the organization and regulation of the relig-ious practice of Blacks, both free and slave. Cities such as Seville, Jaén, Valencia, Barcelona, and Cádiz had *cofradías de negros* (Black religious guilds).[29] Membership in the *cofradías* was only for men. In this re-spect, Black women were excluded from active participation and di-rect decision power. Religious expression in Black women was at the mercy of White male authorities, who constricted Black women in differ-ent ways. The Inquisition was the main instrument in that society against deviant or heterodox religious practices by Black women. Black women were dubbed witches on several occasions. One very impor-tant case took place during the *Guerras de las Comunidades* (Civil Wars, from 1519-1521). María de Padilla, the wife of an important leader of the revolt against Charles V, was known to have a *lora* slave woman in her service. This woman was said to have divinatory powers, having convinced her mistress of the success of the revolt against the King. In a letter from Antonio de Guevara, a famous moralist of the time, María de Padilla is warned against the services of such a slave:

> Also, Lady, they accuse you of having a mulatto woman, or rather a crazy mule, at your service who is a notorious witch. They say that she has told you and sustained that in a few days you will be addressed by the title of Your Grace, and your husband by the one of Highness.[30]

Witchcraft was associated with those who rebelled against the insti-tuted authority of the king. This sudden position of power and ascen-dancy in a Black woman over her mistress could be explained by Father Antonio de Guevara only as the direct work of the devil, as he ex-plained to Juan de Padilla, the *Comunero* leader and María de Padilla's husband:

> Also, Sir, I asked you to give to the devil the prophecies, witchcraft and nigro-
> mancy they tell me My Lady María, your wife, and one slave of hers practice.
> Because talking and dealing with the devil cannot result but in her going to
> hell and you, sir, may lose your life.[31]

If some Black women were accused of witchcraft, others were forced to a life of religious observance by the fact of being slaves in convents of nuns. On the other hand, there existed discrimination against Black women who wanted to enter the convent life as regular nuns. Not only did most of them lack the economic means to do so (the entrance dowry being the primary cost), but the prickly issue of *limpieza de sangre* (purity of blood) was at stake. All those of "tainted" blood—descendants from Jews, Moors, Blacks, and later, Indians—were generally excluded from religious life in Spain.

Black women were the object of persecution by the Inquisition for a variety of reasons. One was connected with sexuality. Marriage was a difficult proposition for a Black woman, because she was either unfree or unable to afford housing. There are several cases recorded in which Black women declared in public that there was no sin in maintaining sexual relations outside marriage (fornication) or even in being a prostitute. A telling story is the one of Juana, who explained that, "they put chains around her body in spite of the fact that she was pregnant, and that she did not believe that, that she said it out of rage" (Cortés López, 1989, p. 119). In another case of persecution, a mulatto woman was accused of having expressed her desire to become a "lutheran." This was after she also complained of being mistreated by her owner (Cortés López, 1989, pp. 224-225).

The Inquisition also processed cases of slaves who tried to escape to North Africa, because this was interpreted as a sign of their desire to abandon Christianity. Escape in itself was a civil crime. But the place chosen, North Africa, made the crime a religious one, because it indicated an option for the religious enemy. Escape was in such cases an act of heresy against the Faith.

Golden Age of Literature and the Representations of Black Women

Spanish literature during the 16th and 17th centuries presented a less than flattering image of Black women, as could be expected. Starting with popular songs that ridiculed the speech of slaves and their troubles, popular theater soon developed the stereotypical figure of the *negra*. Characterized by her bad temper, "Black" speech, illusions of grandeur, and "loose" sexual morals, these stereotypical *negras* nevertheless revealed the other side of any stereotype: difficult relations between the free population and the slave communities in big cities, along with the constant threat to the stability and "honor" of the families that owned them.

Stereotypes are simplifications and reductions formed out of complex systems of representation (Bhabha, 1983, p. 27). A White playwright or poet, when presenting a Black woman in a ridiculous and unflattering light, was moved by a desire to please his audience of other White people. This audience was not homogeneous either, yet the artist who reproduced the stereotype of the Black woman had equally to stereotype the audience/reading public as "one" and uniform, in contrast with the reality: a public that was "plural" and diverse. In the Spanish case, the literary representation of Black slave women was reduced to a series of commonplaces, with little change throughout time but with one detail of evolution: the emergence of the mulatto woman on the stage.

One of the earliest creations of a dramatic Black woman for comic effect was Lope de Rueda's character of Eulalla, who was preoccupied by her social class and decided to whiten her face with bleach in order to get married like a lady of means.[32] A White male servant was her suitor, but this ruffian was trying to help her escape only to sell her in another town. Interestingly, the ridiculousness of Eulalla's pretensions to act "White" reads like a list of preoccupations in Spanish society to avoid being connected with Moors or Jews. Acculturation, the acquisition of Spanish customs by newly arrived Black slaves, was a must for any degree of integration in a generally hostile society. The response to this hostile attitude, namely, the bad-tempered Black woman, became another trait. Such is the case of Guiomar, another *negra* of Lope de Rueda's vintage, who is always fussing and arguing with younger White servants.[33] Guiomar is one of the most pathetic figures of the Black woman in Spanish theater. After being the butt of the usual jokes about her color, her bad temper, and her "bad Spanish," her suffering rings more true than that experienced by the main characters. A mother, she breaks up in tears when she receives a letter from her son, separated from her and living in San Juan, Puerto Rico. Slavery—not fantastic pirates or storms—will impede their seeing each other again.[34]

As a corollary to the alienation of her body and its representation, the stereotypical Black woman in Spanish literature is the exponent of constant and dangerous sexual desire. A Black woman was usually presented *pursuing* a man, rather than being sought. When the object of her "desire" was the White man, punishment for the Black woman was almost certain. That is the case, for instance, of *El Santo Negro Rosambuco* (*Rosambuco, the Black Saint*), by the extraordinarily prolific Lope de Vega, author of at least three comedies with Black saints as protagonists (all male). In this play a Black woman tries to seduce the Black saintly man, and later she is involved with a White servant. She meets her punishment at the hands of her White owner, who acts in defense of the "honor of his household."

The "honor of the household" was invoked several times in Spanish theater when it came to the physical punishment of a Black slave woman. Miguel de Cervantes seems to take issue with the theme in his novella *El Coloquio de los Perros* (*The Dialogue of the Dogs*), in which a house dog tries to stop a Black slave woman from receiving the nightly visits of her Black boyfriend, also a slave. The dog fights with the woman, badly biting her, all to make her understand that she does not have the liberty to use her night, her bed, and her body without the permission and knowledge of her owner. Cervantes's irony explores issues of race, gender, and sexuality seemingly from the perspective of the member of another species, but one that is not impartial. The dog Berganza is, after all, upset at his condition: Being intelligent, he is nevertheless treated by all "humans"—Whites—as an inferior, less than a Black slave.

Color and sex mixed in a very curious way on the Spanish stage of the Renaissance. The development in the theater of the type of the *mulata* was a significant change. If the *negra* was marked by her ignorance, bad temper, and childishness, the *mulata* was characterized by her wits, her beauty, and a happy ending to her quest. *Mulatas* also pursued (or were pursued) by White men, generally servants, but they married them in the end. The magnificent *mulata* Elvira, in *Servir a Señor Discreto* (*To Serve a Wise Master*), by Lope de Vega, has quick words for her White lover, a servant, who amorously tells her: "your black pepper burns my mouth." She replies: "my love, why don't you drink cold water?" to let him know that sex is not the only thing on her mind. Light skin, service to and identification with the interests of her mistress will pay off in this woman's social aspirations of upward mobility.

The mulatto woman of the theater seems to represent an anxiety of belonging that spread all over society. A mulatto erased the clear-cut distinctions between who were the ones supposed to be slaves and who were not. This happened in a country that for 800 years had been ruled—at least in its southern half—by peoples coming from Africa. The presence of the *mulata* type on the stage was subversive by itself and by the fact that they avoided punishment for their deals—for mulatto women were always scheming, that was their trademark. In real life mulattoes were living proof of illicit relations between masters and slaves. White male playwrights decided to idealize the picture by exalting the "exoticism" of these women, praising their intelligence but making them objects of illicit desire. These theatrical stereotypes reproduced the image that White society had of itself. On one hand, the *mulata's* intelligence was "due" to her lighter skin color, on the basis of her "approximation" to the ideal of whiteness. Her darkness, however, was a reminder not only of an "inferior" nature and ascendancy, but also of a desire on the part of White men for that which represented inferiority: the Black woman.

Renaissance poetry inherited from the earlier period the theme of the "prisoner of love." The existence of slavery made it acceptable for poets to add variants to the theme, transforming it into the "slave of love." In that fashion, the branding of slaves in real life with the marks *S* and *I* was utilized by male poets as a metaphor for the "enthralling" powers of the (White) lady over her male lover. Similarly, chains, shackles, and other instruments of enslavement became vehicles for a conception of love relations that would have ample reverberations up to the present day (i.e., James Brown's "The Prisoner of Love"). Even mystical poetry (e.g., Saint John of the Cross and Saint Teresa of Avila) expressed the relation between the soul and the Divinity as one of a slave woman, a Black woman, with her master.

But the most harrowing image of the Black woman slave appears in one of the novellas written by María de Zayas in her collection of *Desengaños Amorosos* (*Love's Rude Awakenings*), "Tarde Llega el Desengaño" ("Belated Awakening"). The confrontation between a Black woman and a White one for preference at the table of a powerful nobleman, master, husband, and lover, is quite symptomatic of what occurred on a daily basis. In this novella Don Jaime, a jealous husband, is punishing his (White) wife for having committed adultery, a slander invented by the (Black) slave woman. His revenge is to make the two women change positions, giving the Black woman all the jewels, clothes, and even the marital bed, while his estranged White wife can witness day after day what she has just lost. She is placed in a dungeon, under the table where husband and Black slave eat every day. But the Black woman falls ill and before dying confesses the truth, upon which she is murdered by her furious master. The innocent White wife also dies on the same night, and the husband loses his mind. The story, told from the perspective of the innocent White wife, is remarkable in its vehement attack on the character of the Black woman, presented as a liar, a devil figure, and a usurper. The exchange of social positions in the story is underscored by details such as the wife's having to eat under the table the bones her husband throws to her, while the Black woman is fed by him from his own plate "the best morsels." Usurpation is the ultimate crime of the Black woman and the fear of a White woman, perhaps María de Zayas herself.

Conclusion

Velázquez, as he did later on with his more famous painting *Las Meninas*, makes an issue of central and marginal characters in his composition technique of *The Supper at Emmaus*. Servant women, dwarf women, a Black slave woman, all are given prominence in his paintings over the more "important" subjects, such as the King and the Queen of Spain, or Jesus and his disciples. The people at the margins of history become the central characters, whereas the "protagonists" of official history become a mere pretext, a detail in the background.

Black women in Spain cooked for others, washed for others, and made soap for other people's bodies and sense of cleanliness. Black women did everything except own their destinies. The body of the slave became a writing surface where the owner inscribed his power, literally—that is, with actual letters. The mark left on the Black slave woman's body signaled the alienation of that body, the fact that it belonged to someone else, someone who wanted his or her power and social status to be known by all *through* the body of this slave.

Even a writer like María de Zayas, a feminist for her time who denounced the status of women in Spain, utilized the Black woman as a symbol of evil, in this case the evil of the husband and owner who could do as he pleased in the household. Gayle Rubin's concept of the traffic of women throughout history—that women become objects to be exchanged between men and therefore acquire a value, like currency—is even more poignant in the case of Black women slaves. Spanish society discovered that these women could not only be bought, sold, bequeathed, mortgaged, or hired, but also used as "women," that is, as objects of exchange between men.

In the documents consulted, the Black woman is silent. Her actions are always interpreted by others, her words are never quoted directly. The presence of Black women in these documents is always connected with exceptionality. She is mentioned because she has committed a crime or is the victim of one. In literature she is not allowed to have an individual presence beyond the stereotype that portrays her as an anomaly, and the few times she appears in painting, she is the image of exclusion.

The significant presence of Black women in Spanish society declined rapidly after 1650. The competition of the Spanish-American slave market was too strong for cities like Seville or Valencia, which alone could not command a demand for Black slaves sufficiently strong to attract slave traders. Black women and their value as workers and merchandise became part of the new world being organized on the other side of the Atlantic Ocean. The Black population that remained in Spain started a slow process of integration with the rest of the large underclass of Spaniards, sharing the common fate of dispossession.

Notes

1. Names like *gelofe* (*jolof* or *Wolof*), *biafara, benin, angola, mandinga, carabali,* to mention just a few, distinguished those slaves captured along the coastal line of the Gulf of Guinea. If the Black slaves were Muslim, the word *moro* was added, either as noun or an adjective.

2. The Spanish word *mulato* refers to the mule, that is, a hybrid of horse and donkey. The application of such a term to the child of a Black woman and a White man was clearly derogatory. A common racial epithet used against Blacks was *perro* (dog).

3. The *Siete Partidas* became the rule of thumb for the legislation of Black slaves in the Spanish Colonies. New legislation was compiled for the Indian populations, whereas such need was not felt in the case of Black slaves (Doering, 1966, p. 340).

4. Charles Verlinden, in his studies of late Medieval slavery in Europe, is of the opinion that the origins of the European colonial empires in America had rehearsal grounds in territories such as the Canary Islands, the Madeira Islands, and the Levantine region of Southern Spain, in which relatively large numbers of slaves were employed in sugarcane fields and mills.

5. Even after the war of 1568 to 1570 against the *Moriscos* of Granada, when many of them where reduced to slavery and sold elsewhere, the number of Black slaves largely outnumbered that of White slaves. The city of Valladolid in northern Castile is an example: of 178 registered cases of slaves in official documents, 78 are Black, 60 are *loros* (meaning of mixed Black and White ancestry), and only 40 "White," 39 of which are *moriscos* from Granada, and one is Jewish (Fernández Martín, 1988, pp. 130-131).

6. Spain and Portugal were united during the period from 1580 to 1640 under kings Philip II, Philip III, and Philip IV of Spain, yet both crowns developed separate colonial empires.

7. In her influential essay "The Traffic in Women," Gayle Rubin (1975) asks the question: What is a domesticated woman?, following the example of Karl Marx, who asked the same kind of question about what constituted "a Negro." The answer is extremely simple: "a female of the species . . . she only becomes a domestic, a wife, a chattel . . . in certain relations" (p. 158).

8. Albert N'Damba Kabongo, in his study of slavery in the city of Córdoba during the early part of the 17th century, found only a minority of slaves owned by farmers.

9. These statuses can actually contradict actual genetic relationships. Kinship is a social system that takes precedence over biology. Kinship ordains "economic, political, ceremonial as well as sexual, activity" (Rubin, 1975, p. 169).

10. Historians Alfonso Franco Silva and Vicenta Cortes Alonso offer an interesting list with names of slave owners and traders from different points of Europe who did business in Seville and Valencia in the crucial years before and after the discovery of America.

11. In Muslim Spain and Morocco the word *khadem* meant Black slave, slave woman, and concubine at the same time (Lewis, 1979, p. 64), giving us a good idea of a Black woman slave's position with respect to her master.

12. A churchman, Luis Ordóñez, promises a certain amount of good and clean wheat to a certain Beatriz Bernal so she will teach his slave Isabel to "sew, embroider and iron shirts." All this concern to give a slave marketable skills indicated the wish to free her, either because the slave was the churchman's daughter or he was fulfilling the disposition of someone's death will.

13. Data corresponding to cities like Seville, Valencia, Córdoba, or Valladolid indicate that the demography of Black slaves was more or less equal for men and women. Marriage, however, was a difficult proposition for a slave of either sex. Parish books of neighborhoods in the city of Seville where there were large concentrations of Blacks, both free and slave, indicate a low percentage of marriages (N'Damba Kabongo, 1976, Appendices).

14. Madrid, Málaga, Jerez, and other cities established prohibitions against buying things (especially gold, silver, and jewels) from "unknown" slaves, whatever their color—apparently to prevent theft. The village of Moguer, in Andalucía, makes the prohibition complete (Cortés López, 1989, pp. 90-91).

15. Of. 3, year 1514, leg. 1, fol. 74 and Of. 3, year 1518, leg. 1 n.d.

16. Newly arrived slaves were called *bozales*, meaning someone who does not speak the language and does not know the culture and the customs of the land. On the contrary, those who knew were called *ladinos*. The term *bozal* was applied exclusively to Blacks, and it carried with it the connotation of stupidity. The term *ladino*, from the Latin *latinus*, originally meant someone who understood Latin. The term *ladino* also came to mean "deceitful."

17. Same case is that of another woman from Guinea (Archivo de Protocolos de Sevilla, Of. 3, 1517, leg. 2, fol 288v. and Of. 10, 1514, n.d.).

18. Regulated prostitutes lived together in special houses under the command of a man called "padre de la mancebía" or "father of the brothel," appointed by the authorities and responsible before them (Perry, 1990, p. 139). Moralists, following St. Augustine, justified the existence of public brothels as a defense of the institution of marriage "like the stable, or latrine for the house" (Perry, 1990, p. 47).

19. Archivo de Protocolos de Sevilla Of. 15, year 1515, Leg. 2, fol. 179.

20. In 1503, 21 slaves are in the Council jail, of which 5 are Black women accused of drunkenness and prostitution: Bárbola, Catalina, Catalina de Cádiz, Catalina Fernández, and Isabel (221, Of. 4, year 1503, Leg 2. fol. 253v).

21. This process took place in Córdoba between 1569 and 1570. Archivo Histórico Nacional, Inquisición, leg. 1856, doc. 3, fol. 6. (Cortés López, 1989, p. 96).

22. In the *Book of Her Life* she tells about her father being against slavery in an anecdote. Jewish people and *Moriscos* (descendants from the Moors) were forbidden to own slaves. Saint Teresa was the architect of the reformation of her religious order of the Discalced Carmelites, and one of the provisions was that no servants or slaves would be employed in Carmelite convents. All sisters had to be equals.

23. Of. 15, year 1521, Leg. 2, fol. 24.

24. Archivo de Protocolos, Of. 1, year 1515, leg. 1, fol. 371v and Of. 4, year 1521, leg. 1, fol. 1171v.

25. Archivo de Protocolos de Sevilla, Of. 1, year 1512, leg. 2, fol. 324v, 23 August.

26. Archivo de Protocolos, Of. 5, year 1520, leg. 2, fol. 674v.

27. Archivo de Protocolos, Of. 3, year 1501, fol. 701, 3 October.

28. Archivo de Protocolos de Sevilla, Of. 5, 1522, leg. 1, fol. 332.

29. The history of the religious organizations for Blacks is an old one. These seem to have started in Catalonia, Valencia, and Majorca, all part of the Kingdom of Aragón, in the 14th and 15th centuries. Some were constituted exclusively by freed Blacks, some were mixed associations of free Whites and freed Blacks. Slaves needed their owners' consent to belong (Miret y Sans, 1917; Gual Camerana, 1953). In the kingdom of Castile, they also appeared in Seville during the 15th century (Domínguez Ortiz, 1953, p. 394), as well as in Cádiz and in Jaén.

30. *"También, señora, os levantan que tenéis una esclava lora o loca, la cual es muy grande hechicera, y dicen que os ha dicho y afirmado que en breves días os llamarán Señoría, y a vuestro marido Alteza"* (Guevara, 1942, Part I, letter 47).

31. *"También, señor, os dije diéredes al diablo las profecías y hechicerías y nigromancias de la Sra. Dña. María, vuestra mujer, que me dicen que hace ella y una esclava suya, porque de hablar y tratar con el demonio, no puede resultar sino que ella se infierne, y vos, señor, perdáis la vida"* (Guevara, 1942, Part I, letter 45).

32. *Comedia Eufemia*, Scene 7. Lope de Rueda himself was reputed to be an excellent actor in the roles of Black women, according to Miguel de Cervantes, the author of *Don Quijote*. Thus an early example of the blackface minstrel.

33. The image of the irate Black woman became typical, and the enticement of such wrath was nearly always the racial insult. The list of insults addressed to Blacks, and especially to women, runs long. The generic one was *perra* (dog) and derivates, such as *galga* (greyhound) and *lebrel* (hunting dog). Allusions to the Black woman's skin color became "de rigueur": *carbón* (coal), *escarabajo* (beetle), *alquitrán* (tar). When the author felt the need to be poetic and positive, the coals became *azabache* (jet), the body *ébano* (ebony), and the face the pure image of the night, and so on. Another racial joke was the habit of other characters in a play to pretend they were sneezing, to mark that they were in the presence of black pepper (*pimienta*).

34. The tragedy of separation in this slave family is set in contrast with the main plot of the play, *Los Engañados (Mistaken Ones)*, in which a rich man suffers the loss of his twin children to pirates, only to find them alive and safe some 20 years later. Guiomar, the slave woman, knows where her son is, but there is no hope of reunion. This is one of the earliest literary testimonies of the trans-Atlantic connection of slavery in Modern Europe.

References

Bhaba, Homi K. (1983). The other question. The stereotype and colonial discourse. *Screen, 24(6), 18-36.*

Brown, James (Performer). (1963).Prisoner of love. *Star Time* (Compact Disc Recording, Polydor No. 849 108-2; 4-disc set).

Cervantes Saavedra, Miguel de. (1986). *El ingenioso hildalfo don Quijote de la Mancha* (Ed. by L. A. Murillo) (3 vols.). Madrid: Castalia.

Cortes Alonso, Vicenta. (1964). *La esclavitud en Valencia durante el reinado do los Reyes Católicos.* Valencia: Exelentísimo Ayuntamiento de Valencia.

Cortés López, José Luis. (1989). *La esclavitud negra en la España peninsular del siglo XVI.* Salamanca: Publicaciones de la Universidad de Salamanca.

Doering, J. A. (1966). La situación de los esclavos a partir de las Site Partidas de Alfonso el Sabio (Estudio histórico-crítico). *Folia Humanística, 4-40,* 337-361.

Domínguez Ortiz, Antonio. (1953). La esclavitud en Castilla durante la Edad Moderna. *La Sociedad española en al siglo XVII.* Tomo I. Madrid, C.S.I.C.

Fernández Martín, Luis. (1988). *Comediantes, esclavos y moriscos en Valladolid, siglos XVI y XVII.* Valladolid, Spain: Secretariado de Publicaciones, Universidad de Valladolid.

Franco Silva, Alfonso. (1979). *La esclavitud en Sevilla y su tierra a fines de la Edad Media.* Seville: Diputación Provincial de Sevilla.

Greenfield, Sidney M. (1979). Plantations, sugar cane and slavery. In Michael Craton (Ed.), *Roots and branches: Current directions in slave studies* (pp. 85-119). Toronto: Pergamon.

Gual Camerana, Miguel. (1953). Un seguro contra crímenes en esclavos en el siglo XV. *Anuario de Historia del Derecho Español, 23,* 247-258.

Guevara, Antonio de. (1942). *Epístolas familiares.* Buenos Aires: Espasa-Calpe Argentina.

León, Pedro de, S.I. (1981). *Grandeza y miseria en Andalucía. Testimonio de una encrucijada histórica* [Original title: *Compendio de algunas experiencias en los ministerios que usa la Compañía de Jesús*]. Granada: Facultad de Teología.

Lévi-Strauss, Claude. (1969). *The elementary structure of kinship* (Ed. and Trans. by James Harle Bell, John Richard von Sturmer, & Roney Needham) (Rev. ed.). Boston: Beacon.

Lewis, Bernard. (1979). *Race and color in Islam.* New York: Octagon Books.

Miret y Sans, J. (1917). La esclavitud en Cataluña en los últimos tiempos de la Edad Media. *Revue Hispanique, 99.*

N'Damba Kabongo, Albert. (1975). *Les esclaves à Cordoue au debut du XVIIe siècle, 1600-1621: Provenance et condition sociale.* Thesis. Université de Toulouse-le-Mirail. Microfiche. Paris: Micro Editions Hachette.

N'Damba Kabongo, Albert. (1976). *Les esclave à Seville au debut du XVIIe siècle: Approche de leurs origines et de leur condition.* Memoire de Mâitrisse. Université de Toulouse-le-Mirail. Microfiche. Paris: Micro Editions Hachette.

Perry, Mary Elizabeth. (1990). *Gender and disorder in early modern Seville.* Princeton, NJ: Princeton University Press.

Pike, Ruth. (1967). Sevillian society in the 16th. century: Slaves and freedmen. *Hispanic American Historical Review, 47,* 344-359.

Pike, Ruth. (1972). *Aristocrats and traders: Sevillian society in the sixteenth century.* Ithaca and London: Cornell University Press.

Rubin, Gayle. (1975). The traffic in women: Notes on the "political economy" of sex. In Rayna R. Reiter (Ed.), *Toward an anthropology of women* (pp. 157-210). New York: Monthly Review Press.

Rueda, Lope de. (1976). *Teatro completo.* Edición de Angeles Cardona de Gibert. Barcelona: Bruguera.

Vega y Carpio, Lope Félix de. (1916-1930). *Obras de Lope de Vega publicadas por la Real Academia Española (nueva edición): Obras dramáticas.* Editadas por Emilio Cotarelo y Mori. 13 tomos. Madrid: Tipografia de la Revista de Archivos y Bibliotecas.

Verlinden, Charles. (1955). *L'esclavage dans l'Europe Médiévale: Vol. I. Peninsule Iberique. France.* Bruge: De Tempel.

Zayas y Sotomayor, María de. (1950). *Desengaños amorosos: Parte segunda del sarao y entretenemiento honesto.* Madrid: Real Academia Española.

9. The Rape Complex in the Postbellum South

MADELIN JOAN OLDS

The White South has long had an "obsession" with interracial sex.[1] In the antebellum South, interracial sex, though nominally prohibited, occurred especially between the White master and the Black female slave. In the postbellum South, the overriding concern among Whites, particularly White men, was to prevent sexual advances by Black men toward White women. As one interpreter explained, "[A]ny assertion of any kind on the part of the Negro constituted in a perfectly real manner an attack on the Southern White woman."[2]

The fear of Black rape of White women became a consuming one in the White South in the years following Reconstruction. Whites attributed enormous sexual drive to freed Blacks and perceived Black women as temptresses and Black men as rapists. Many White Southerners considered rape the "usual" crime of Blacks—"committed every month, every week, frequently every day," declared one Southern White man.[3] The "protection of white womanhood" from alleged Black rapists justified a wide range of aggressive behavior by Whites toward Blacks.

The White dread of Black rapers was irrational and excessive, however, an "imaginary danger."[4] Sexual assaults of White women failed to constitute a major cause for either Black imprisonments or lynchings in the postbellum era.[5] To account for this disparity, a number of historians and social scientists have concluded that White apprehensions regarding Black rapers stemmed from a guilt reaction based on the White man's sexual exploitation of the Black woman. According to this interpretation, Southern Whites anticipated Black revenge in kind.[6]

EDITOR'S NOTE: This chapter is excerpted from *The Rape Complex and the Postbellum South*, an unpublished doctoral dissertation (Carnegie-Mellon University, 1989) by Madelin Olds (1937-1989), B.A., English, University of Texas, Austin, 1960; M.A., government, University of Texas, Austin, 1965; D.A., history, Carnegie-Mellon University, 1989. It has been edited by her brother, Greg Olds.

Unlike previous studies of race relations in the South, we shall focus here on the rape complex and on evaluating the explanations Whites offered for their fears of Black rapists.[7] More particularly, in order to explore the origins and development of the rape complex, White Southern perceptions of Black sexuality and aggressions—singly and combined as rape—have been traced from the end of Reconstruction in 1876 through the first decade of the 20th century. In these years, as in no other period, White Southerners created and enlarged on the reasons for their rape fears and presented justifications for harboring such anxieties.[8]

This study considers numerous articles written by White Southerners in the major magazines of the postbellum period, mostly non-Southern,[9] and books written by them, published by firms outside of the South. No single White Southerner was responsible for defining the content of postbellum racism.[10] Instead, a number of Whites, usually representing the upper classes, penned a defense of their section against criticisms, arising from the victorious North, that often centered on the "Negro question." Many of the writers were former slaveholders or their heirs and were active as politicians, lawyers, ministers, educators, journalists, novelists, or physicians. They usually spoke for the South as a section, although surges of responses arose from a specific state following some local act of racial violence. Two Southern periodicals—*Sewanee Review* and *South Atlantic Quarterly*—are employed in this study. They were founded by educators in the 1890s and the early 20th century, respectively, to counter the narrow and virulent racism dominant in their section.

Modern historians, such as C. Vann Woodward, George M. Fredrickson, I. A. Newby, and Joel Williamson, have used many of these same sources in their studies of the postbellum South, because White Southerners were discovering and rationalizing a new caste system and racist ideology to encompass emancipated Blacks.[11] A major component of postbellum racism, and Southern writings, was the purported propensity of Black men to rape White women. Southern Whites endorsed the view that Blacks needed to be controlled by Whites—some for paternalistic reasons, but more out of a perception of Black aggression, usually sexual. Most acknowledged an immorality in Blacks and, on the record at least, blamed the rapes of White women on Black equality in economic, political, and social areas rather than on that miscegenation instigated by White men.

The Southern rape complex evolved in three general periods in the postbellum era. In the first period, from 1877 to the late 1880s, Black rapists were a source of apprehension for some White Southerners, but rape was not yet associated with Black rights nor incorporated in racist doctrine. The more common fear was that Black civil rights would encourage miscegenation. Whites viewed Blacks as sexual and, at least in the early years of this period, claimed that Blacks were passive in their relations with Whites. By the late 1880s, however, Whites increasingly detected aggression in Black behavior, and in 1889 the White fear surfaced that Black men wanted to rape White women.

In the 1890s, the "new Negro," or the Black raised free from the beneficial controls of slavery, emerged and was labeled the raper of White women. Contacts between Black men and White women were often branded as "rape" on the grounds that the womanhood of the South resisted any Black overtures. Moreover, the political equality of Blacks to Whites was targeted as a cause of Black rapes, and Black disfranchisement proceeded for one reason, to curtail such rapes.

Finally, in the first decade of the 20th century, all activities of Blacks—whether economic, political, educational, or social—facilitated the Black rapes of White women, according to many Southern Whites. As a result, Whites expanded and finalized that segregationist and racist ideology that held, for the most part, until the middle of the 20th century. Despite this achievement, some Whites in the early 1900s were disturbed by the existence of White male-Black female concubinage arrangements. Such Southerners argued that these sexual relationships affected White racial purity by producing offspring who could "pass" as White. In addition, some Whites charged that such interracial sex caused Black men, in retribution, to rape White women, a view that had long been held by Black leaders and some Northerners.

In each of these three distinctive periods, variations existed in the intensity of White fears regarding Black rapists.[12] For reasons difficult to trace, months or years of heightened apprehensions would pass, broken by months or years of relative calm.

Northern Racial Attitudes

By the 20th century, the intellectual climate had evolved in the North so that a number of Yankees repudiated the Reconstruction policies implemented by the federal government in the 1860s and 1870s. As the rancor of the Civil War and Reconstruction periods abated gradually, non-Southerners began to regard Whites of the old Confederacy with more sympathy. Interest in the South was apparent in those magazines that sponsored articles by Northerners touring the South[13] or ran articles on the Civil War written by participants North and South.[14] The romantic image of the plantation of the Old South with its hierarchical and harmonious race relations had an appeal for Yankees "in this leveling age," as one Northern commentator noted.[15]

The conciliation trend was encouraged by industrial development and general economic change in the United States, which discouraged sectional division. By the turn of the century, Northern interest in "reconstructing" the South had waned. Proposed legislation to offer federal aid to education regardless of race and to protect Black voting

rights had failed in Congress.[16] The Supreme Court decision in 1896 up-
holding segregation in *Plessy v. Ferguson* reflected the general sentiment.

By the 20th century, non-Southern scholars and academicians were
providing support for racism in their studies. For example, the psychologist G. Stanley Hall reported the following in 1905 to an audience at
the University of Virginia:

> No two races in history, taken as a whole, differ so much in their traits, both
> physical and psychic, than the Caucasian and the African. The color of the skin
> and the crookedness of the hair are only the outward signs of many far deeper
> differences, including cranial and thoracic capacity, proportions of body, nervous
> system, glands and secretions, vita sexualis, food, temperament, disposition,
> character, longevity, instincts, customs, emotional traits and diseases.[17]

Some Northerners even upheld the sexual fears that White men
had of Black men. At Columbia in 1907, the historian William Archibald
Dunning published his study of the Reconstruction era, which lent
scholarly support to the allegation of leading White Southerners that
Black equality during those years had caused Black rapes of White women.[18] During Reconstruction in the 1860s, the majority of federal
officials had been acting on democratic theory, specifically the tenet
that citizenship entailed the guarantee of rights even to Blacks. Like
Southern Whites, they recognized that rights were indivisible in the
sense that social rights arose from the attainment of political rights.
Nonetheless, many Northerners had not expected that the possession
of political rights by Blacks would assure their equality nor pose any
threat to Whites, because they felt that Blacks were inferior and, in the
mass, incapable of achieving the social status of Whites.[19]

For most Northerners, however, neither miscegenation or Black
rapes of White women arose from any Black rights, actual or potential.
Although largely silent on the issue of Black rape unless discussing the
South, Northerners probably accepted the notion that Blacks, representing an inferior race, were prone to rape. The race riot in Springfield, IL, in 1908, which was based on White claims of defending White
women from Black rapists, attested to the potency of that fear above
the Mason-Dixon line. The historian Jacquelyn Dowd Hall explains the
non-Southern attitude by stating:

> This southern obsession with rape touched a responsive chord in the nation
> at large. It was rooted in the deepest of American communal preoccupations:
> the conflict between "civilization" and "savagery," historically acted out in the
> destruction of the Indians and the subjugation of African slaves.[20]

Despite this empathy, Black rape fears did not consume the North.
Indeed, Northerners traveling in the South expressed amazement at
the depth of these fears among the Whites.[21]

What was reflected most of all in non-Southern writings as a cause of rape was the charge that concubinal arrangements between White men and Black women in the South led Black men, in revenge, to rape White women. For example, Ray Stannard Baker found such arrangements so prevalent during his tour of the South in 1906 that he exclaimed:

> And yet the South, permitting such training in vice, wonders at Negro immorality and is convulsed over the crime of rape. Demanding that the Negro be self-restrained, white men set the example in every way from concubinage down, of immorality and lack of restraint. They sow the whirlwind and look for no crop![22]

From the abolitionists in the antebellum era through the Social Darwinists in the postbellum era, the North sustained a fascination with the sexual mores of the South and generally tolerated the Southern rape complex unless lynchings or race riots resulted.

In summary, Northern attitudes toward Southern racial practices and the differing views of the sections on the meaning of Black equality led White Southerners to explain their conviction that Black men wanted to rape White women, justifications that were based largely on the concept of Black equality. The evolution of White Southern fears of Black rapists rests on two features of the White South bearing on the rape complex: sexual ideology, and the leading role of those postbellum Southern Whites who promoted the ideas of the antebellum or Old South civilization. Let us consider each in turn.

Sexual Ideology in the South

The acceptance of the Southern rape complex by the non-South and its emergence in the White South was conditioned by the prevailing sexual ideology, or the attitudes and values held by people regarding sex. Generally, the sexual ideology of Victorian America promoted individual sexual control, or more specifically, "male continence and female purity." The sectional variations regarding sexual ideology and behavior arose from two sources. First, the White South—the home to 90% of the nation's Blacks during this period, 8- to 9-million Blacks who were perceived as sexual—feared for its racial purity. Although the White Southern disdain for the alleged sexual promiscuity of Blacks compared to that which the North felt toward immigrants, the issue of sexual control permeated economic, political, and social issues in a manner alien to the rest of the United States. In addition, because White Southern women were the guardians of racial purity and thus of White Southern civilization, they were more idealized and more rigidly confined to their "place"—home and family—than their non-Southern sisters.

Southern Whites and Sexual Blacks

The discussion of sex by White Southerners in the postbellum era centered on Blacks. Southern Whites continually compared themselves to Blacks to the disadvantage of the latter and in the process defined the ideal for White sexual behavior. For example, the physician Robert Bean of Virginia, after stating that the two races were "antipodal," explained that Whites were "domineering, but having great self-control," and Blacks were "meek and submissive, but violent and lacking self-control when the passions were aroused."[23] The Black personality was commanded by its "procreative instinct" and, as Philip Alexander Bruce of Virginia wrote: "Before it all the barriers which society has raised in the instance of the white race, and with which it also endeavors to restrain the negro, go down as if they had no power of thwarting his determination to gratify it."[24]

This striking contrast between the races regarding sexual restraint was largely explained by a developmental theory promoted by Whites that held that, although Black and White children were similar in many respects, at puberty Blacks became "less intellectual" than Whites. At that time, as one Southern White wrote of Blacks, "the passions cloud and do not irradiate the mind."[25] This developmental theory supported the popular belief of Whites that adult Blacks had "the intelligence of children and the instincts of savages."[26]

Most Southern White writers, save a few physicians, resisted dwelling on the assumed anatomical and physiological differences between the races. Instead, they contended that the White race surpassed the Black based on "moral qualities."[27] Blacks were variously described as immune to religious precepts despite their religiosity and as "nonmoral" or "unmoral."[28] As the historian Jack Temple Kirby points out, Whites in the postbellum era associated "color and morality," and black skin signified a potential, if not actual, lack of sexual restraint in its bearer.[29]

The preoccupation of White Southerners with Black immorality betrayed, to a large extent, their apprehensions regarding interracial sex, especially between Black men and White women. The preservation of the Caucasian race was at stake, and, as the Englishman James Bryce observed of the South, Whites felt it was their "supreme duty" to prevent "sexual relations between the races."[30] Whites claimed that slavery had prevented the mongrelization of the White race in the antebellum years; once Blacks were freed and endowed with constitutional rights, "race purity" had to be "safeguarded by other methods."[31] Thus, Whites wanted a new control system enabling them to exercise sexual restraint; in promoting controls on Blacks, Whites perpetuated the fear that Black sexuality endangered Whites.

The racism of the South, as the psychohistorian Joel Kovel points out, "intimately connected" sexuality with "issues of power and dominance."[32] Because antebellum Whites thought they had absolute control over Blacks as property, a distinction between the "public and private, domestic as well as civil" rights of Blacks were largely inconceivable to postbellum Whites.[33] Rights were indivisible, or, more specifically, political equality inevitably led to social equality or miscegenation, or by the 1890s to the rapes by Black men of White women. Democracy countenanced the sexual assimilation of people endowed with civil rights, yet power and women could not be shared by the races, as one White Southerner wrote.[34] As a result, the elimination of Black rights became central to curbing miscegenation and the Black sexual threat to Whites.

Throughout the postbellum era, racial segregation and Black disenfranchisement, supplemented by White terrorist acts against Blacks, evolved to replace slavery and reestablish White control over Blacks. Despite increasing White dominance, however, Whites continually felt vulnerable and unprotected from Black eroticism or, more to the point, their own sexual implications. As the historian John G. Mencke remarks, "Negroes were not dangerous because they were going to force racial mixing on the white man, but because they threatened, by their own apparently passionate natures, to arouse inner desires which whites were striving so hard to control or suppress within themselves."[35]

Dr. J. Wellington Byers, a physician in Charlotte, NC, writing in 1888 of the Black problem with sexual restraint, revealed a White problem as well. For Byers, "The negro is peculiarly unfortunate; he has not only the inherent frailties of his nature to war against—instincts, passions and appetites; but also those nocuous, seductive, destroying influences that emanate from free institutions in a country of civil liberty."[36]

As in the antebellum era, the control system elevating one race as superior and demeaning the other failed to eliminate tensions regarding interracial sex.[37] Instead, the White controls in the postbellum era promoted, rather than relieved, miscegenation, especially between White men and Black women. As the Northerner Charles B. Spahr stated following his tour of the South in 1899: "So long . . . as an exalted caste lives side by side with a degraded one, a thoroughly healthful social morality cannot be secured for either."[38]

Although a few moderate White Southerners saw that, in order to prevent miscegenation, both races needed "self-respect,"[39] more Whites accepted the notion that, because of "self-loathing," Blacks wanted to become White and sought White mates.[40] Interracial contacts were maintained in the postbellum years, and Blacks still, as one Southern White wrote, "belong to us" and "are our people."[41] Increasingly in the years following emancipation, however, Whites expressed distress regarding Black behavior and debated whether their association with Blacks morally contaminated Whites, especially White children. In the 1880s, most White writers stressed that the superior race could not be contaminated because "the finer nature always maintains the ascendancy over the coarser."[42] As Lewis Blair of Virginia queried, "For centuries the Southern Whites have been intimately associated with the Blacks, and have we become demoralized?"[43] In the late 19th century, however, some White parents expressed their fears by curtailing the use of Black wet nurses for their children, despite the White refrain that the adored mammies taught White children their morals.[44] The Northerner A. B. Hart made the distinction regarding White children that, "The girls, by some miracle, grow up fresh and pure as though there were no such contamination, but it is demoralizing to the boys."[45]

Black women were more frequently criticized by Southern Whites than Black men throughout the postbellum period, even after the 1880s when Whites believed that bestial and fiendish Black men menaced White women. For one reason, Black women were held responsible for that race's immorality. Whites believed that, "A race never rises in integrity above the morality and virtue of the mothers of the race,"[46] a standard applied to White women as well. Black mothers produced unchaste daughters, lustful sons, and the dreaded mulattoes, according to many Whites. Moreover, Black women were seducing or sexually tempting to White men, an admission only reluctantly acknowledged by some White men and women.[47] The Northern educator A. D. Mayo concluded that, "This profound skepticism concerning the possible virtue of the Negro woman is an important element in the violent resistance, especially of Southern women, to social contact."[48]

White Southerners, like Northerners, were devoted to idyllic depictions of antebellum race relations, especially involving mammies. Records from the postbellum era as well as the antebellum era, however, offer little support for any widespread existence of mammies.[49] The historian Catherine Clinton, writing of the slavery period, suggests that the mammy developed as "a counterpoint to the octoroon concubine." She explains: "Mammy was created by white southerners to redeem the relationship between black women and white men within the slave society in response to the anti-slavery attack from the North during the antebellum era, and to embellish it with nostalgia in the post-bellum period."[50] White references to mammies in the postbellum era also established at least a pretense of upper-class standing and generally advanced White denials that Blacks were mistreated in the South.

Along with structural inequality, elements of traditional White attitudes toward Blacks enlivened White notions that Blacks sought miscegenation. In the first place, many Whites boasted that Blacks loved Whites or White children more than persons of their own race. For example, Thomas Nelson Page of Virginia, in describing antebellum race relations, commented that "the affection of the slaves was stronger toward the Whites than toward their own offspring."[51] Such boasts fed White assumptions that Black women wanted children fathered by White men rather than Black men.[52] Similarly, although White guidance of Blacks supposedly facilitated Black imitation of Whites and thus Black progress,[53] some Whites confessed that Blacks absorbed White "vices" as well as some White virtues.[54] In addition, Whites considered thievery a trait of the Black race, one that had been encouraged by Yankees during the Reconstruction years. As one Alabamian decried: "The negro race was then taught a lesson that was easily learned and has never been forgotten, that the property in the South was produced by negro labor and therefore by right much of it should belong to the blacks."[55]

The superior White womanhood of the South had also been a product of the antebellum period,[56] and some Whites linked Black thievery and the Black rages to White women. As Philip Alexander Bruce wrote: "This thieving disposition would be overlooked if the lawlessness of the blacks stopped there. It has, however, taken a form [rape] the least likely to be tolerated by the white people, its victims."[57]

Mulattoes were especially despised by Southern Whites because their existence provided graphic evidence of White sexual transgressions. As one White wrote, mulattoes "have all the sensuality of the aboriginal African, and all the savage nature of the primitives from the wilds of Europe, without the self-control of the caucasian or the amiability of the negro."[58]

Other Whites feared the negative influence mulattoes had on pure Blacks in urging them to act on their rights or in abetting general Black criminality; female mulattoes were labeled "yellow Jezebels."[59] Mixed bloods defied the logic of a racially separate society, and Alfred Holt Stone of Mississippi sought to give them more legal recognition than pure Blacks—but less than Whites—in order to dilute their mischief as leaders of the Black masses.[60] Whites feared mulattoes "passing" as Whites, and, in the early 20th century, some Whites expressed outrage regarding the White male-Black female sexual relationships.[61] Moreover, such relationships, according to some Whites, gave Black men cause to pursue, that is, to rape, White women.

Although some White men struggled for sexual restraint, other White men covered for each other and accepted interracial philandering. The musician Lehman Engel, who was born in Mississippi in 1910, recalled from his childhood a summer evening as he sat on the front porch with his family. A young Black woman, walking home from work, was stopped by two young White men who, in spite of her struggle and screams, carried her away. Engel wrote:

> I was emotionally upset, not understanding anything except that the girl was being forced to do something against her will. I yelled at my uncle and my father, who did nothing. They said simply that I did not understand. Then I peered up and down the dimly lit street, and as far as I could see, other men sat on the other front porches. All were rocking peacefully, some fanning themselves.[62]

Most White Southerners believed that rape of the immoral Black woman was not possible. As Fredrick Douglass pointed out in *North American Review* in 1892, sexual assaults alarmed few White people until the "reversal of colors in the participants," a development Douglass disclaimed.[63]

The Southern rape complex emerged in the late 1880s because Whites felt that the controls on Black sexuality had in some manner weakened or in some manner needed to be strengthened. Precedent existed for such fears from the antebellum years, when rumors of slave unrest aroused terror in Whites not only for the safety of their lives but for the protection of their women from sexual assault.[64] In the late 1880s the arousal of White rape fears coincided with widespread economic and political changes.

The values associated with modernization and the "New South"— which gained in acceptance in the 1880s despite meager economic development—called for increasing White sexual restraint. Moreover, Southern politics was in turmoil as poor Whites sought to unite with poor Blacks in the Farmer's Alliance and the Populist party. At the national level, Republicans had recaptured the presidency in 1888 following a Democratic incumbency, and Congress began again pressuring the White South to protect Black rights. In addition, White Southerners in the late 1880s had reason to question their conviction, developed in the antebellum years, that Blacks would become extinct without the White supervision and protection provided by the slavery system.[65]

In the census of 1870, White Southern beliefs regarding Black extinction had been buttressed by a Black increase in population of only 9% compared to a White increase of 24%. The 1880 census, however, reported a Black gain of 34% compared to a White gain of only 29%. In 1882, a Northerner traveling in the South reported the following in the *Atlantic Monthly*:

> In some parts of the South I found many people, even among the more intelligent classes, who believed that the negro race was rapidly decreasing in numbers. . . . None of these people had heard of the revelations of the last census regarding the increase of the negroes, and they regarded the information as astounding and incredible.[66]

Some White Southerners who were informed of the 1880 census downplayed or dismissed those findings. Nathaniel Shaler stated that the 1870 census had underreported Blacks. The 1880 census, he claimed, had been administered with care and, therefore, "doubtless gave us the first accurate knowledge" of the ratio of Blacks to Whites.[67] At a public health conference in Louisville, KY, in 1888, one participant stated that the Black increase shown in the 1880 census would not continue because "there is no longer an intelligent class which has direct pecuniary interest in the health of the negroes." He also predicted further Black decline because Blacks were moving into towns and cities and living in unhealthy environments.[68]

Despite such reassurances, other informed White Southerners viewed the 1880 census as an ominous sign. In the early 1890s, according to Thomas Nelson Page, Whites were apprehensive about the "Negro problem" because the results of the 1890 census were not yet known and Republicans in Congress were pushing legislation to protect Black voting rights.[69] The White fear of Black rapists emerged in 1889, most notably in *The Plantation Negro as a Freeman* by Philip Alexander Bruce, who also was troubled by the 1880 census results. Regarding Black growth, Bruce stated in his introductory chapter:

> It is difficult to understand how any one can contemplate in a narrow and illiberal way the questions involved in their numerical increase in the South, for these questions in reality touch every citizen, affect directly or remotely the interests of every community, and are as wide in their scope as the republic itself.[70]

Throughout his book Bruce accepted the traditional view that Blacks, in freedom, were reverting to the "original physical type," but he questioned the inevitability of Black extinction. Moreover, because a large and growing Black population threatened the stability of government, he considered the removal of Blacks from the United States "if nothing shall intervene to check their numerical growth."[71]

Significantly, Bruce failed to connect the rapes by Black men of White women with the failure of Black extinction; instead, he attributed them, most of all, to Black revenge against Whites for past bondage and continuing oppression. The Black man, as he then wrote, raped the White woman because she was "the representative of that race which had always overawed him."[72] Ten years later, in 1899, Bruce had abandoned the revenge thesis, however, and he, along with many other White Southerners, adapted the extinction thesis to postbellum conditions. By the mid-1890s at least, many White Southerners argued that such rapes were the work of the "new Negro," who had been raised in freedom without White attention and the discipline provided by slavery.[73]

The belief of Whites in some form of Black degeneration had become crucial to the defense of the nobility and virtue of their ancestors and the Old South civilization, which had prevented Black extinction, if not contributed to Black progress, through the slavery system. Though postbellum Whites bemoaned the lack of Black "gratitude" for White selflessness, they insisted that Blacks were not "vindictive."[74] The extinction thesis also shifted the responsibility for alleged Black savagery to the North, which by emancipating Blacks and granting them rights had precipitated the ruination of a weaker race.

The census of 1890, of 1900, and of 1910 showed a greater growth rate for Whites than Blacks, and some White optimism regarding Black extinction returned,[75] although probably not to its 1870 level. Many Southern Whites realized that Black extinction would not occur in their lifetime, only Black degeneration. Although a belief in Black revenge as a cause of rape could have resulted in some conscious guilt among Whites and some reforms, the belief in degeneration or extinction justified White dominance over Blacks. At the same time, it stimulated White fears concerning continuing Black aggression.

In the early 20th century some Whites anticipated race wars as Blacks competed economically with Whites, a fate that one Northerner held haunted Southern Whites like "the day of Judgment in the minds of primitive Christians."[76] Most Whites continued to accept Black "bestiality" as the cause of the rapes of White women rather than Black "diabolism" or revenge against Whites, and few questioned that a single Black man could rape a number of White women in the course of one day.[77] Black regression into savagery—"as the dog to the wolf"—meant the proliferation of the rapes of White women as Blacks struggled to survive as a race or succumbed to lust.[78]

The Postbellum Triumph of Old South Racism

In the postbellum years those Southern Whites who closely identified with the antebellum White planter class and the civilization established by slavery—Old South Whites—insisted that Black sexual aggression threatened White racial purity. Precedent existed for such White anxieties. In the antebellum period, during perceived threats of slave unrest or rebellion, masters had prophesied that Blacks would rape White women.[79] Moreover, the proslavery argument before the Civil War had predicted that Black emancipation would lead to miscegenation, or Black extinction through miscegenation, or Black regression.[80]

From 1876 to the early years of the 20th century, the main challenges to the racial views of Old South Whites came from members of the younger generation and, more specifically, from the New South movement, Populism, and a turn-of-the-century group of intellectual reformers. To counter the challengers, adherents of the Old South embraced Lost Cause mythology, elevated White womanhood, co-opted White racial moderates, and saw their view of Black sexual aggression erupt into popular expression by demagogic politicians. As the historian George M. Fredrickson points out, a "submerged link" existed between the antebellum attitudes of Whites toward freed Blacks and the Negrophobia of the late 19th and early 20th centuries.[81] The incorporation of the fears of Black rapers into White racist ideology by the

1890s in effect authenticated the racial views as well as the status of Old South Whites.

The Lost Cause and the Old South

Following the Civil War, many White Southerners became increasingly committed to, indeed obsessed with, a defense of their past. Both the Lost Cause and the Old South traditions proclaimed the past as precedent, as the model for the present and future South. Initially in the post-Reconstruction years, however, these traditions were somewhat distinct. The Lost Cause stressed rationalizations for secession from the Union and defeat by the North, whereas the Old South emphasized justifications for slavery and for antebellum White civilization. Moreover, racism was not as central to the Lost Cause as it was to Old South beliefs.

The Lost Cause evolved soon after Robert E. Lee surrendered at Appomattox as "a byword for the perpetuation of the Confederate ideal,"[82] and became a broad-based movement in the postbellum South. Lost Cause beliefs were propagated especially by preachers in the White Protestant churches, which were heavily attended throughout the South.[83] In addition, the activities of organizations such as the Southern Historical Society, the United Confederate Veterans, the United Daughters of the Confederacy, and the United Sons of Confederate Veterans kept the Cause alive.

According to the historian Charles Reagan Wilson, the Lost Cause was the "civil religion" of the postbellum South.[84] It provided cohesion for a society demoralized by defeat, and it celebrated the valor of noble Confederates who had lost to the greater strength of arms held by their foes.[85] The former Confederate President, Jefferson Davis, typified the attitude of Lost Cause adherents in addressing the Mississippi legislature in 1884: "Remembering, as I must, all which has been suffered, all which has been lost, disappointed hopes and crushed aspirations, yet I deliberately say, if it were to do over again, I would again do just as I did in 1861."[86]

White Southerners insisted that they were "better men"—more moral and virtuous—than the materialistic and atheistic Yankees.[87] Moreover, Northern actions toward the South after the war had shown the world, as Jefferson Davis wrote, "how faithless, dishonest, and barbarous our enemies were."[88]

The race issue, according to the historian Charles Reagan Wilson, was not an integral part of the Lost Cause mentality. Its proponents denied that the secession of the South from the Union had been caused by the institution of slavery.[89] Instead, Lost Cause advocates declared that secession and the war had been meant to serve the purpose of "noninterference" or "civil liberty."[90] Jefferson Davis justified the

South's withdrawal from the Union by comparing that action to the revolt by the American colonies against England in the 18th century.[91]

Nevertheless, the racial views promoted by Lost Cause supporters were compatible with the development of the Southern rape complex in several respects. In the first place, the Lost Cause accepted the view that slavery had been a divinely ordained institution, and that the racial inferiority of Blacks to Whites stemmed from "the eternal law of God."[92] Moreover, promoters of the Cause stressed the loyalty of the slaves during the war in protecting White women, a notion that in the writings and speeches of some meant that the slaves had not raped those women in their care. Because the Lost Cause emphasized Confederate morality, some expressed fears that freed Blacks, especially the "new Negro," would taint Whites, a danger often expressed in sexual terms.[93] Perhaps most important of all, however, the Lost Cause myth, as the historian Joel Williamson points out, increasingly in the late 19th century unified the White masses of Southerners and the Old South elites.[94]

The Old South ethos, although similar to the Lost Cause, was more of a class movement espoused by former slaveowners and their heirs. Northern educator A. D. Mayo reported on this movement in 1892:

> A considerable class of socially exclusive heads of families even in their own decay hold stoutly to the faith that the ancient social regime was the grandest on earth and in its revival is the only hope of social upbuilding in the South of the future.[95]

The Old South movement served to maintain and perpetuate class distinctions among Whites as well as the traditional racist views. This upper class deplored the "leveling tendencies" of the age and feared a loss of "caste" if its members socialized with or labored in occupations held by lower-class Whites or Blacks.[96] From habit, however, if not from respect, many of the poorer Whites looked to the former masters to provide leadership following the war.[97] Because slaves and much of the wealth were lost as a means of signifying membership in the elite, many Whites of the upper classes turned to family history to demonstrate such status.[98] The lower classes of Whites valued the ancestral claims of the elite—the "white pillar crowd"—to the extent that the number of pretenders to high descent increased in the late 19th and early 20th centuries.[99] Much of this higher class status—or pretense—was effected by recalling ancestral military heroes; by citing affectionate relationships with loyal Black retainers, especially mammies; and by praising White Southern womanhood. Unity between the Lost Cause and the Old South supporters was also established by the complementary visions regarding the role of White women. The validity of the Lost Cause was reaffirmed when White Southern men acclaimed the wartime bravery of their women and labeled them "unreconstructed" in the postbellum years.[100] A number of Southern women, perhaps in part deflecting anger from Southern men to Yankees, obligingly portrayed an intransigent loyalty to the Confederacy.[101] For example, Northerners noted the "hostile feeling" of Southern women and complained that they were teaching their children to "hate Yankees."[102] One Southern woman defended her behavior, however, by explaining, "it is not loyalty which makes us proud; it is pride which makes us loyal."[103] Even in the early years of the 20th century some White women donned black in mourning for their dead and for the Lost Cause.[104]

To the benefit of the Old South's position, the postbellum White woman was modeled on the antebellum White woman. As W. F. Tillett of Vanderbilt University explained in 1891, "The virtues that adorn and ennoble the Southern woman of today find their explanation and origin largely in that womanhood which for the last fifty years and more has been the product and pride of the Southern people."[105]

This model defined women's "sphere" as the home and the family. It promoted the superiority of antebellum civilization because the Southern woman had been produced by the slavery system and by White male chivalry.[106] Thus, while the Lost Cause made White Southern women the "highest symbol" of Confederate virtue because of their endurance during the war and in defeat, the Old South clung to that female purity that in a biracial society was crucial to the maintenance of White supremacy.[107] The Southern rape complex originated more from the Old South attitudes and beliefs than from those of any other class, faction, or movement. According to some writers, lower-class Whites in the South harbored less of a "theory of race" than upper-class Whites but were alarmed by the rivalry or competition from freed Blacks.[108] These differing class concerns were emphasized by Philip Alexander Bruce of Virginia in an article in *Sewanee Review* in 1911. In arguing for racially separate schools he suggested that poorer Whites were more apprehensive about "social equality" than "moral contamination," which was the manor fear of the upper-class Whites.[109] Bruce defined "social equality" as that which would exist, "should the intermarriage of the races, their coeducation, and indiscriminate commingling in public conveyances and in residential sections of the cities, be permitted."[110]

The "moral contamination" of Blacks—the dread of upper-class Whites—was based on "the indifference to chastity in the females, the lewdness in the males, the physical uncleanliness, the unrefined manners, and the generally careless habits of life distinguishing so many of both sexes alike."[111] Based on Bruce's analysis, the Southern rape complex emerged in most Whites, regardless of class, when the "moral contamination" from Blacks was believed possible because Blacks were perceived as seeking "social equality" with Whites.

In the postbellum years, Old South Whites persisted in expressing their fears of miscegenation. In 1904, the Northerner Ernest Hamlin

Abbott wrote in *The Outlook* that the planter class agitated the issue of
"Black domination" to keep race animosities alive lest poorer Whites
marry comely or wealthy Blacks. He reported an "imaginable case" that
had been told to him several times "in almost identical terms" as he
toured the South. Abbott quoted a North Carolina lawyer as follows:

> You see, people are afraid of the first hole in the dike. In this town there are
> two or three families of mulattoes who are well-to-do. The children are educated
> and attractive. A poor white man, enticed by the beauty of one of these
> mulatto girls, and by the chance of comfort and the pleasure of travel which
> her money would afford, might be tempted to marry into the family. The girl
> and her people might be tempted in turn by the chance of a white alliance. The
> only thing that stands in the way of such a marriage is public opinion.[112]

Although interracial marriages were illegal in all the Southern states,
such miscegenation was apparently considered too inevitable to be
impeded by law.

In the postbellum years, the miscegenation fears of the Old South
Whites accelerated—and were exacerbated by—their feelings of diminished mastery. As the historian Bertram Wyatt-Brown observes:
"Fear of the contamination of blood lineage was not a purely sexual
fear, but was a dread of loss of race command, the nightmare of impo-
tence, both physical and social."[113]

The identity of the slaveowners had been formed in the antebellum
era, in many respects, by the institution of slavery. Because they were
masters, slavery had provided the temptation or the opportunity for
miscegenation. At the same time, slavery had bestowed on White owners
that "instinct for command,"[114] a characteristic that postbellum Whites
of the Old South considered almost innate. According to South Caro-
linian Isaac DuBose Seabrook in 1892:

> By the laws of the land the whites of every rising generation were born
> masters of the other race. They were reared in the habit of exercising the
> powers and the duties of the ruler as an inherited and inalienable right. The
> immense and subtle influence which this inherited and unquestioned power
> has upon the minds and feelings of the master race cannot be overestimated.
> They were rulers from their birth.[115]

A Southern White woman commented that, in the postbellum years,
the men suffered from "the lack of something to govern."[116]

Black behavior in the postbellum years compounded the Old
South's feelings of lost power as well as their fears of miscegenation.
Masters had expressed anger and hurt at the elation Blacks displayed
upon emancipation and felt demoralized by the failure of freedmen to
honor the traditional racial rituals, such as deference to Whites.[117] The
historian Leon F. Litwack points out that, "To those long accustomed
to absolute control, even the smallest exercise of personal freedom by

a former slave, no matter how innocently intended, could have an unsettling effect."[118]

Reconstruction, in which allegedly the "bottom rail" had been on "top," aroused in Whites enduring feelings of humiliation.[119] The resentment Whites initially felt toward the Yankees was transferred to the freed slaves because, as Joel Chandler Harris wrote, "In a manner, we held the poor blacks responsible for the shock that their emancipation gave to our social system."[120]

More specifically, former masters were dismayed by the diminished trust between the races in the postbellum years as compared to the antebellum years. The ideal of such trust, according to a number of Whites, had existed in the war period when the White women and children had been safe on the plantations in the care of their slaves.[121] Moreover, Whites were stunned by the lack of gratitude Blacks showed their former masters and mistresses. For example, one Southern White woman presented Black ingratitude as "this patent and ubiquitous fact." She rationalized that gratitude was "a late development in the progress of any race from barbarism" and that several generations would pass before it emerged.[122] It was something of an adage among Old South Whites that the Black "owes no gratitude, bears no malice."[123] Claims of paternal feelings abated in the face of the Blacks' quest for independence from White controls.[124]

Adherents to the Old South ideology seemed to move in several directions, consciously or unconsciously trying to compensate for those feelings of powerlessness wrought by Black emancipation and Black citizenship. The White Southern gentleman became a prominent figure, more so than in the antebellum era. Katherine DuPre Lumpkin felt that her father, a former slaveowner, had been raised to be a master and a gentleman, and that the loss of the former role seemed to strengthen the latter one.[125] Gentlemanly behavior was evidenced by genteel manners, concern with personal honor, patience toward inferiors, and obeisance toward White women.[126] One Texan insisted that Black men raped White women because, under freedom, they associated with lower-class White men who lacked that gentlemanly respect for White women that had been exhibited by antebellum masters.[127]

Gentlemanly behavior, however, was not transgressed when White men sought sexual enjoyment from Black women.[128] In 1899, Mrs. L. H. Harris, a White woman from Georgia, wrote several articles on White Southerners for *The Independent*. In response to editorial criticism that she neglected accounting for that miscegenation encouraged by White men, Mrs. Harris explained the White Southern man as follows:

> There is one thing he believes more steadfastly than any other doctrine, human or divine—this that he was born a gentleman, is a gentleman, and always will be one. If every other man comes to despise him, he never despises himself; nor, in the midst of any dishonor, does he lose the sublime confidence in his

possible integrity. If he discovers himself debauched, he reforms, turns over a
new leaf, and forgets the past. No other man has such confidence in the clean
page as he.[129]

Debauchery aside, the Southern gentleman was esteemed as the product of the slavery system because the care and responsibility for savage
and inferior Blacks had developed the "moral nature" of the master.[130]

In addition, members of the Old South launched a defense of
slavery to prove that Blacks suffered or regressed without White controls comparable to slavery. As the Northerner Albion W. Tourgee
stated in *The Forum* in 1888, many Whites in the South believed that the
slave had "loved his chains and was all the better physically and
morally for wearing them."[131] Whites argued that slavery had been a
burden—not an economic boon nor a harem, as the Yankees claimed.
Because of the sacrifices of the stronger race, the argument ran, the institution of slavery had been a civilizing agency—a "positive good"—
in disciplining and controlling barbaric Blacks.[132] Moreover, the Black
rapes of White women had been rare in the antebellum years because
Blacks had been under the "restraining influence" of White masters
and mistresses.[133] According to one Old South advocate, the master
class should be given the credit for the absence of Black violence during
the war toward the White women and children left on the plantation.[134]

In summary, the postbellum attitudes of many supporters of the
Old South traditions tended to encourage rather than relieve those
racial views culminating in the Southern rape complex. The Old South
Whites could not relinquish the ideology of slavery because, as one
White Southerner wrote, the freed slaves were reminders of "defeat
and humiliation and the passing of the old order of things."[135] Such
Whites felt betrayed by Blacks, and increasingly insisted that their
worst prognostications in the antebellum era regarding the danger of
uncontrolled Blacks had been true.

In the postbellum years Old South Whites used the antebellum or
proslavery argument regarding Black extinction that, as adapted to
postbellum conditions, fed White fears that Black men wanted to rape
White women. According to some Whites, usually those with a scientific background, Black men, freed of controls, regressed into savagery
and raped White women in an effort to fend off the inevitable extinction of their race.[136] Most Southern Whites, however, claimed that the
"new Negro," raised in freedom and not by Whites in slavery, raped
White women.[137] Revenge as a motive for Black rapes was largely
rejected, at least until the early 20th century, because it implied White
mistreatment of Blacks. The defense by Old South Whites of their
institution of slavery, and the influence of these elites over the White
society, made the Southern rape complex inescapable.

Black Equality—A Legal and
a Sexual Construct in the White South

In summary, from 1889 through the first decade of the 20th century, leading White Southerners explained their fear that Black men would rape White women in the context of that equality extended Blacks by the 14th and 15th Amendments to the Federal Constitution. The 14th Amendment granted citizenship to freed Blacks and guaranteed them the "equal protection of the laws," and the 15th Amendment gave Black men the right to vote. In the view of many White Southerners, this legal equality unleashed sexual Blacks from White controls. Whites considered Blacks to be inherently sexual and aggressive toward Whites when not controlled by a system such as slavery. Black rapes resulted because pure White womanhood resisted Black sexual advances.

In the antebellum years, equality had been seen by Whites and Blacks alike as the probable outcome of Black emancipation.[138] The association between Black equality and the Black rapes of White women developed gradually following the Civil War and Reconstruction, however, striking in the 1890s at Black political equality and extending in the first decade of the 20th century to any kind of Black equality. The moderate White Southerner Edgar Gardner Murphy, who deplored this progression, described it as moving

> by easy stages from an undiscriminating attack upon the negro's ballot to a like attack upon his schools, his labor, his life;—from the contention that no negro shall vote, to the contentions that no negro shall learn, that no negro shall labor, and (by implication) that no negro shall live.[139]

The White charge that Black equality caused the rape of White women was more than an effective tactic for oppressing Blacks: Many White Southerners were convinced of a link between equality and rape. As envisioned by many Southern Whites, bearers of constitutional rights were within the political, economic, and social circle forming the civilization with the family as its basic unit. Black equality with Whites would result in miscegenation and the debasing of the superior Anglo-Saxons. Furthermore, many Whites argued that Black elevation made Blacks appear closer to White standards, increasing the likelihood of interracial unions, especially between Black women and lower-class White men.

The elements of the Southern rape complex—in particular, the glorification of White womanhood and the fear of sexual aggression when Blacks were freed from White controls—had existed in the antebellum era. Nevertheless, White Southern racism was largely silent regarding Black rapists in the early years following Reconstruction. In the late 1870s and most of the 1880s, Whites abhorred miscegenation and most predicted that Blacks would seek sexual union within their own race. Partly, such White optimism was designed to forestall any resumption of Reconstruction policies and to attract Northern investments in the South. In addition, some White Southerners clung to the antebellum tenet that Blacks freed from the White supervision offered during slavery would become extinct. By the early 1890s, as Whites grew alarmed by Black political participation and were dismayed by the lack of Black deference to Whites, Black political equality provided by the 15th Amendment was deplored and connected with the alleged Black rapes of White women.

Joel Chandler Harris of Georgia found no "Negro problem" in the postbellum South, only Yankees with unrealistic remedies to imagined conditions and White Southerners who feared the reestablishment of Reconstruction, that "wretched experiment" when Blacks supposedly exercised dominance over Whites. In 1901 Harris predicted that, "No doubt the historians who rise up in the future will examine with amazement the records which contain the discussions of the negro question during the past thirty years."[140] The amazement for modern historians is that the Black adaptation to freedom—what Harris described as the "efforts and movements of a race slowly and painfully feeling its way to a higher destiny"[141]—threatened postbellum White Southerners, who perceived it as Black sexual aggression.

Clearly, the postbellum years were tumultuous ones for Southern Whites who had lost a civil war and, seemingly, that social system based on slavery. The racial moderation that held sway in the early post-Reconstruction years failed to compensate the White patriarchy for feelings of powerlessness. Instead, the Lost Cause movement grew and bonded White Southerners of all classes in praise of the sacrifices in the South made during the Civil War. In this climate of nostalgia, the racial views of the Old South elite emerged—in particular, the belief that freed Blacks endangered White racial purity.

The Old South Whites were influential, and the story of the Southern rape complex from the late 1880s on concerned the role played by these elites in undermining and co-opting the racial moderates, whether the New South Whites, the Populists, or the educated reformers of the early 20th century. The Old South traditionalists demanded and won respect for the antebellum patriarchy and its institution of slavery. The main proof given of the superiority of the civilization was White Southern womanhood and the absence of Black sexual violence. The Old South position aroused White anxieties regarding Black sexual aggression in the postbellum years that were too compelling to be countered by the arguments of White racial reformers. Amid the economic, political, and social turbulence of those years the belief that Blacks wanted Whites sexually, and would use force to that end, became part of White racism and justified White oppression of Blacks.

Modern historians and social scientists have at times suggested that the Southern rape complex resulted from an anticipation in Whites that

Blacks sought revenge because White men sexually abused Black women. This contention, however, can be neither confirmed nor discounted with any finality by a reading of postbellum accounts. Clearly, many White Southerners were preoccupied with Black sexuality and immorality to such an extent that constitutional equality for Blacks was laden with sexual meaning. The rapes by Black men of White women in revenge for the sexual abuse of Black women by White men was, however, not aired by many Southern Whites until the first decade of the 1900s.

In 1889, when the rape fears of Whites first emerged in the writing of Philip Alexander Bruce of Virginia, Black revenge against the general oppression of Whites was cited as the main motive for Black rapes of White women. Then, in the 1890s under the influence of Old South thinking, most White Southerners denied that Blacks felt vengeance toward them. Whites insisted that they had not mistreated Blacks, whether in slavery or in freedom, and that Blacks therefore had no motive to rape White women in revenge. Instead, according to Whites, the "new Negro," born in freedom and endowed with constitutional rights, raped White women. Equality freed immoral Blacks from White controls, unleashing the bestiality inherent in that race. Whenever forced to acknowledge voluntary miscegenation, Southern Whites usually faulted the passionate Black females and the basest White males.

In the early 20th century, however, the rationale used by Whites to deny Black revenge unraveled. A number of White Southerners expressed outrage at the White man's sexual use of Black women, often arguing that Black men raped White women in retaliation. In effect, in the first decade of the new century Southern Whites were fighting on two fronts: to raise the moral behavior of Whites and, still more importantly, to counter any Black equality with Whites.

Toward the end of the first decade of the 20th century, the quantity of White Southern writings on the "Negro problem" diminished, and the explanations for the rape fears of Whites largely faded from print. The question of whether the Black rapes of White women were caused by Black equality or Black revenge was neither resolved nor effectively confronted. The rape complex persisted in the White South as more recent histories have shown, but such assaults were apparently no longer phenomena that needed justification or explanation. The nation was racist, including most of its academics, and the North became riled at the White South only when racial violence, such as lynchings or riots, occurred. In the South the extreme racists became quiet, apparently feeling that Blacks were by then sufficiently controlled by Whites, whereas the moderates ignored Blacks to focus on reforms benefiting poor Whites. The discussion of the "Negro problem," according to the White educated elite, merely roused White fears and too often led to racial violence. In *World's Work*, the Southerner Walter Hines Page called for the formation of a "Society to Suppress Theories About the

Race Problem" with membership open, no doubt, to Southerners and Northerners alike.[142]

As the Southern novelist, Ellen Glasgow, wrote: "For as long as the human race remains virtually, and perhaps essentially, barbarian, all the social orders invented by man will be merely the mirrors of his favourite imperfections."[143]

A variety of personal, class, and historical interests converged and were served by the Black rapist theme. The rape complex functioned in the South to safeguard the dominance of Whites over Blacks, to reinforce the status of upper-class Whites over lower-class Whites, and to assure White male authority over women, White or Black. Although resolving some of the sexual and power needs of the White patriarchy, the rape complex aggravated those needs as well.

Notes

1. Gunnar Myrdal, *An American Dilemma*, 2d ed. (New York, NY: Harper & Row, 1962), p. 562; Richard H. King, *A Southern Renaissance* (New York: Oxford University Press, 1980), p. 166; Joel Kovel, *White Racism* (New York: Random House, 1970), pp. 56-57, 67-68.

2. Wilbur J. Cash, *The Mind of the South* (New York: Knopf, 1941; reprint ed., New York: Vintage Books, 1969), p. 119.

3. George T. Winston, "The Relation of the Whites to the Negroes," *American Academy of Political and Social Science Annals*, 18 (1901), p. 109. For an example of Black rape of White women as the "usual" crime, see Ellen Glasgow, *The Voice of the People* (New York: A. L. Burt, 1900), p. 423.

4. I. A. Newby, *Jim Crow's Defense* (Baton Rouge: Louisiana State University Press, 1965), p. 131.

5. Myrdal, *An American Dilemma*, pp. 972, 560-561; Frances A. Kellor, "The Criminal Negro. VIII. Environmental Influences," *Arena*, 26 (1901), pp. 525-526.

6. See, for example, David C. Roller and Robert W. Twyman, eds., *The Encyclopedia of Southern History* (Baton Rouge: Louisiana State University Press, 1979), s.v. "Rape Complex, Southern," by Lawrence J. Friedman; Jacquelyn Dowd Hall, *Revolt Against Chivalry* (New York: Columbia University Press, 1979), pp. 148-149; Oscar Handlin, *Race and Nationality in American Life* (Boston: Little, Brown, 1950; reprint ed., Garden City, NY: Doubleday, Anchor, 1957), pp. 123-124, 126-127; John G. Mencke, *Mulattoes and Race Mixture* (Ann Arbor: UMI Research Press, 1979), p. 7; Myrdal, *An American Dilemma*, pp. 562, 591; Newby, *Jim Crow's Defense*, pp. 135-138; Hortense Powdermaker, *After Freedom: A Cultural Study in the Deep South* (New York: Viking, 1939), p. 52; Allen W. Trelease, *White Terror: The Ku Klux Klan Conspiracy and Southern Reconstruction* (New York: Harper & Row, 1971), pp. xx-xxi; John D. Weaver, *The Brownsville Raid* (New York: Norton, 1973), pp. 269-270; Joel Williamson, *The Crucible of Race* (New York: Oxford University Press, 1984), p. 307; Forrest G. Wood, *The Black Scare: The Racist Response to Emancipation and Reconstruction* (Berkeley: University of California Press, 1970), pp. 143-145, 148, 151.

7. Laurence Alan Baughman, *Southern Rape Complex, Hundred Year Psychosis* (Atlanta, GA: Pendulum Books, 1966) relies heavily on Wilbur Cash, John Douard, Lillian Smith, and others. From the 1890s into the 20th century, many White Southerners claimed that Reconstruction had been an era characterized by numerous Black rapes of White women, a charge accepted by early 20th-century historians, especially the Dunning School at Columbia. See Newby, *Jim Crow's Defense*, pp. 66-67. Later historians have revised this interpretation because they found that most racial violence originated with Whites, directed most often at politically active Blacks. See Trelease, *White Terror*, p. xliv. The charges of Black sexual assaults during Reconstruction, such as those depicted in the novels of Thomas Dixon, Jr., were "baseless." See Bernard A. Weisberger, "The Dark and Bloody Ground of Reconstruction Historiography," *Journal of Southern History*, 25 (1959), p. 432.

8. Baughman, *Southern Rape Complex*.

9. Non-Southern magazines include *The American Magazine, The Arena, Atlantic Monthly, The Century Magazine, The Forum, Harper's New Monthly Magazine, The Independent, Lippincott's Magazine, Literary Digest, McClure's, The Nation, North American Review, The Outlook, Popular Science Monthly, Scribner's Magazine,* and *World's Work.*

10. Newby, *Jim Crow's Defense,* p. 115.

11. C. Vann Woodward, *The Strange Career of Jim Crow,* 3rd ed. (New York: Oxford University Press, 1974); George M. Fredrickson, *The Black Image in the White Mind* (New York: Harper & Row, 1971); Newby, *Jim Crow's Defense;* and Williamson, *The Crucible of Race.*

12. Williamson, *The Crucible of Race,* pp. 6, 181.

13. Edward King, "The Great South," *Scribner's* (1873-1874), reprinted in *The Great South,* W. Magruder Drake and Robert R. Jones, eds. (Baton Rouge: Louisiana State University Press, 1972); "Studies in the South, I-XI," *Atlantic Monthly, 49-51* (1882-1883).

14. Frank Luther Mott, *A History of American Magazines* (Cambridge, MA: Harvard University Press, 1938; reprint ed., Cambridge, MA: Belknap Press, 1957), vol. II, p. 253; vol. III, pp. 460, 468-469, 376.

15. Charles Dudley Warner, "Society in the New South," *New Princeton Review, I* (1886), p. 3. See also Paul M. Gaston, *The New South Creed* (New York: Knopf, 1970), p. 178.

16. The Blair bill and the Lodge bill, respectively.

17. Stanley Hall, "The Negro in Africa and America," *Pedagogical Seminary, 12* (1905), p. 358. Hall told this same audience that although he had been "an abolitionist both by conviction and descent" he wished "to confess" his "error of opinion in those days" (p. 364).

18. Newby, *Jim Crow's Defense,* pp. 66-67.

19. J. R. Pole, *The Pursuit of Equality in American History* (Berkeley: University of California Press, 1978), p. 147.

20. Hall, *Revolt Against Chivalry,* p. 147.

21. Baker, *Following the Color Line,* p. 7; Albert Bushnell Hart, "The Outcome of the Southern Race Question," *North American Review, 188* (1908), p. 56.

22. Baker, *Following the Color Line,* p. 169.

23. Robert Bennett Bean, "The Negro Brain," *Century, 72* (1906), p. 784.

24. Philip Alexander Bruce, *The Plantation Negro as a Freeman* (New York: G. P. Putnam, 1889; reprint ed., Williamstown, MA: Corner House, 1970), p. 16.

25. Shaler, "The Negro Problem," p. 701. See also Bailey, *Race Orthodoxy,* p. 319; E. H. Randle, *Characteristics of the Southern Negro* (New York: Neale Publishing, 1910), p. 61; William B. Smith, *The Color Line* (New York: McClure, Phillips, 1905), p. 48.

26. Thomas Dixon, Jr., *The Clansman* (New York: Doubleday, Page, 1905), p. 294.

27. Bruce, *The Plantation Negro,* p. 144.

28. Bruce, *The Plantation Negro,* p. 101; Smith, *The Color Line,* p. 55; William Baxter Poe, "Negro Life in Two Generations. The Observations of a Southern Farmer," *Outlook, 75* (1903), p. 496; Wade Hampton, "Ought the Negro to Be Disfranchised? Ought He to Have Been Franchised?" Symposium in *North American Review, 268* (1879), p. 240.

29. Jack Temple Kirby, *Darkness at the Dawning* (Philadelphia: J. B. Lippincott, 1972), p. 5.

30. James Bryce, "America Revisited: The Changes of a Quarter-Century," *Outlook, 79* (1905), p. 853.

31. Poe, "Negro Life in Two Generations," p. 494.

32. Joel Kovel, *White Racism* (New York: Random House, 1970), p. 68.

33. George Washington Cable, "The Freedman's Case in Equity," *Century, 29* (1884-1885), pp. 409 ff., reprinted in *The Silent South* (New York: Scribner, 1889; reprint ed., Montclair, NJ: Patterson Smith, 1969), p. 10.

34. Charles Gayarre, "The Southern Question," *North American Review, 125* (1877), p. 496.

35. John G. Mencke, *Mulattoes and Race Mixture* (Ann Arbor: UMI Research Press, 1979), p. 107.

36. J. Wellington Byers, "Diseases of the Southern Negro," *Medical & Surgical Reporter, 58* (1888), p. 735.

37. Winthrop D. Jordan, *White Over Black: American Attitudes Toward the Negro, 1550-1812* (New York: Norton, 1968), p. 136.

38. Charles B. Spahr, "The Negro as a Citizen," *Outlook, 62* (1899), p. 494.

39. Edgar Gardner Murphy, *The Basis of Ascendancy* (New York: Longmans, Green, 1909), p. 55. See also Lewis H. Blair, *A Southern Prophecy,* C. Vann Woodward, ed. (Boston: Little, Brown, 1964), p. 74.

40. Myrta Lockett Avary, *Dixie After the War* (New York: Doubleday, Page, 1906; reprint ed., Boston: Houghton Mifflin, 1937), p. 397.

41. Noah K. Davis, "The Negro in the South," *Forum, 1* (1886), p. 132.

42. Wilbur Fiske Tillett, "Southern Womanhood as Affected by the War," *Century, 43* (1891), pp. 11, 14.

43. Blair, *A Southern Prophecy*, p. 144.

44. Leon F. Litwack, *Been in the Storm so Long* (New York: Knopf, 1979), p. 264; Julia R. Tutwiler, "Mammy," *Atlantic Monthly, 91* (1903), p. 62; Thomas Nelson Page, "On the Decay of Manners," *Century, 81* (1910-1911), p. 881.

45. Albert Bushnell Hart, "A Cross-Section Through North Carolina," *Nation, 54* (1892), p. 208.

46. Mrs. L. H. Harris, "Negro Womanhood," *Independent, 51* (1899), p. 1687. See also Murphy, *The Basis of Ascendancy*, p. 58; Bruce, *The Plantation Negro*, p. 11; Avary, *Dixie After the War*, p. 395; T. W. Higginson, "Some War Scenes Revisited," *Atlantic Monthly, 42* (1878), p. 5; Eleanor Tayleur, "The Negro Woman. I. Social and Moral Decadence," *Outlook, 76* (1904), pp. 267, 270.

47. John Roach Straton, "Will Education Solve the Race Problem?" *North American Review, 170* (1900), p. 790; Walter Hines Page, *The Southerner* (New York: Doubleday, Page, 1909), p. 211.

48. A. D. Mayo, *Southern Women in the Recent Educational Movement in the South*, Dan T. Carter and Amy Friedlander, eds. (Baton Rouge: Louisiana State University Press, 1978), p. 108.

49. Herbert G. Gutman, *The Black Family in Slavery and Freedom, 1750-1925* (New York: Pantheon, 1976), p. 443; Catherine Clinton, *The Plantation Mistress* (New York: Pantheon, 1982), p. 202.

50. Clinton, *The Plantation Mistress*, p. 202.

51. Thomas Nelson Page, *The Negro: The Southerner's Problem* (New York: Scribner, 1904), p. 174. See also Sherwood Bonner, *Suwanee River Tales* (Boston: Robert Brothers, 1884), p. 3; James Branch Cabell, *Let Me Lie* (New York: Farrar, Straus, 1947), p. 191; Harry Stillwell Edwards, *Two Runaways and Other Stories* (New York: Garrett, 1889), pp. 198-199; Walter L. Fleming, "The Servant Problem in a Black Belt Village," *Sewanee Review, 13* (1905), p. 6.

52. Murphy, *The Basis of Ascendancy*, p. 59; Spahr, "The Negro as a Citizen," p. 494.

53. Nathaniel Shaler, "The Nature of the Negro," *Arena, 3* (1890), p. 28; Alfred Holt Stone, *Studies in the American Race Problem* (New York: Doubleday, Page, 1908), pp. 234-235.

54. Mrs. L. H. Harris, "A Southern Woman's View," *Independent, 51* (1899), p. 1354. See also E. M. DeJarnette, "Cream-White and Crow Black," *Atlantic Monthly, 52* (1883), p. 472; John C. Kilgo, "Our Duty to the Negro," *South Atlantic Quarterly, 2* (1903), p. 371; *Joel Chandler Harris, Editor and Essayist*, Julia C. Harris, ed. (Chapel Hill: University of North Carolina Press, 1931), pp. 128-129.

55. Fleming, "The Servant Problem," p. 12. See also Belle Kearney, *A Slaveholder's Daughter* (New York: Abbey Press, 1900; reprint ed., New York: Negro Universities Press, 1969), p. 106; Katherine DuPre Lumpkin, *Making of a Southerner* (New York: Knopf, 1947), p. 135.

56. Tillett, "Southern Womanhood," p. 9; Frank Clayton [pseud.], "A Sketch in Black and White," *Atlantic Monthly, 97* (1906), p. 608.

57. Philip Alexander Bruce, "The Negro Population of the South," *Conservative Review, 2* (1899), p. 232.

58. Bean, "The Negro Brain," p. 780.

59. Alfred Holt Stone, "The Mulatto Factor in the Race Problem," *Atlantic Monthly, 91* (1903), p. 661; Smith, *The Color Line*, p. 255; "Experiences of the Race Problem," *Independent, 56* (1904), p. 593.

60. Stone, *Studies in the American Race Problem*, pp. 397-398.

61. Ray Stannard Baker, *Following the Color Line* (New York: Doubleday, Page, 1908; reprint ed., Williamstown, MA: Corner House, 1973), pp. 165-169.

62. Lehman Engel, "This Bright Day," reprinted in Dorothy Abbott, ed., *Mississippi Writers, Reflections of Childhood and Youth, Vol. II* (Jackson: University Press of Mississippi, 1986), p. 192. See also Walter Hines Page, *The Southerner*, p. 262.

63. Frederick Douglass, "Lynch Law in the South," *North American Review, 155* (1892), p. 19.

64. Jordan, *White Over Black*, p. 398; Stephen B. Oates, *The Fires of Jubilee: Nat Turner's Fierce Rebellion* (New York: Harper & Row, 1975), pp. 20, 50-51.

65. George M. Fredrickson, *The Black Image in the White Mind* (New York: Harper & Row, 1971), pp. 49, 155; Litwack, *Been in the Storm so Long*, pp. 361-362, 275.

66. "Studies in the South. IX," *Atlantic Monthly, 50* (1882), p. 630.

67. Nathaniel Shaler, "Nature and Man in America. Part III," *Scribner's, 8* (1890), p. 655.

68. "Sanitation Among the Negroes," *Popular Science Monthly, 33* (1888), p. 715.

69. Thomas Nelson Page, "A Southerner on the Negro Question," *North American Review, 154* (1892), p. 401.

70. Bruce, *The Plantation Negro,* p. vii.

71. Bruce, *The Plantation Negro,* pp. 129-130, 261.

72. Bruce, *The Plantation Negro,* p. 84.

73. Bruce, "The Negro Population of the South," p. 272.

74. Mrs. L. H. Hammond, "A Southern View of the Negro," *Outlook, 73* (1903), p. 620; *The Hammonds of Redcliffe,* Carol Bleser, ed. (New York: Oxford University Press, 1981), p. 324; E. E. Breckenridge, "The Race Question," p. 478; Lumpkin, *Making of a Southerner,* p. 74; William Lee Howard, "The Negro as a Distinct Ethnic Factor in Civilization," *Medicine, 9* (1903), p. 426.

75. George F. Milton, "The Material Advancement of the Negro," *Sewanee Review, 3* (1894), pp. 44, 46; Thomas Nelson Page, "A Southerner on the Negro Question," pp. 411-412; Wallace Putnam Reed, "The Old South on Deck," *Independent, 50* (1898), p. 1497.

76. Ernest Hamlin Abbott, "The South and the Negro. VI. Diversities of Burdens," *Outlook, 77* (1904), p. 693; Albert Bushnell Hart, "The Outcome of the Southern Race Question," *North American Review, 188* (1908), p. 60.

77. Smith, *The Color Line,* p. 257; Straton, "Will Education Solve the Race Problem?" p. 787.

78. Hilary A. Herbert, "The Problems That Present Themselves," *Race Problems of the South,* Proceedings of the 1st Annual Conference of the Southern Society for the Promotion of the Study of Race Conditions and Problems in the South (Richmond, VA: B. F. Johnson Publishing, 1900), p. 28.

79. Jordan, *White Over Black,* p. 398.

80. Jordan, *White Over Black,* p. 542; George M. Fredrickson, *The Black Image in the White Mind* (New York: Harper & Row, 1971), pp. 49, 155.

81. Fredrickson, *The Black Image in the White Mind,* p. 221.

82. Thomas L. Connelly and Barbara L. Bellows, *God and General Longstreet: The Lost Cause and the Southern Mind* (Baton Rouge: Louisiana State University Press, 1982), p. 2.

83. "Studies in the South, VIII," *Atlantic Monthly, 50* (1882), p. 484; William P. Trent, "Tendencies of Higher Life in the South," *Atlantic Monthly, 79* (1897), p. 777; Charles Reagan Wilson, *Baptized in Blood: The Religion of the Lost Cause, 1865-1920* (Athens: University of Georgia Press, 1980), p. 11.

84. Wilson, *Baptized in Blood,* p. 13.

85. Wilson, *Baptized in Blood,* p. 15; Connelly and Bellows, *God and General Longstreet,* p. 25.

86. Hudson Strode, *Jefferson Davis: Tragic Hero, 1864-1899* (New York: Harcourt, Brace & World, 1964), p. 469.

87. Connelly and Bellows, *God and General Longstreet,* p. 22; Wilson, *Baptized in Blood,* p. 8.

86. Jefferson Davis, *Private Letters, 1823-1889,* Hudson Strode, ed. (New York: Harcourt, Brace, 1966), p. 483.

89. Wilson, *Baptized in Blood,* pp. 12, 100.

90. Noah K. Davis, "The Negro in the South," *Forum, 1* (1886), p. 132; B. L. Gildersleeve, "The Creed of the Old South," *Atlantic Monthly, 69* (1892), p. 87.

91. Strode, *Jefferson Davis,* pp. 485-486.

92. E. H. Abbott, "The South and the Negro. I. The Confusion of Tongues," *Outlook, 77* (1904), p. 226; H. Shelton Smith, *In His Image, But . . . : Racism in Southern Religion, 1780-1910* (Durham, NC: Duke University Press, 1972), p. 208.

93. Wilson, *Baptized in Blood,* pp. 104, 106-107.

94. Joel Williamson, *The Crucible of Race* (New York: Oxford University Press, 1984), p. 517.

95. A. D. Mayo, *Southern Women in the Recent Educational Movement in the South,* Dan T. Carter and Amy Friedlander, eds. (Baton Rouge: Louisiana State University Press, 1978), p. 162.

96. Paul Hamilton Hayne, *A Man of Letters in the 19th Century,* Rayburn S. Moore, ed. (Baton Rouge: Louisiana State University Press, 1982), p. 218; "Studies in the South, III," *Atlantic Monthly, 49* (1882), p. 683; Shields McIlwaine, *The Southern Poor-Whiter From Lubberland to Tobacco Road* (Norman: University of Oklahoma Press, 1929), pp. 186-187.

97. John Spencer Bassett, "The Reign of Passion," *South Atlantic Quarterly, 1* (1902), pp. 302-307; Litwack, *Been in the Storm so Long* p. 364.

98. "Studies in the South, I," *Atlantic Monthly, 49* (1882), p. 81; Walter Hines Page, "Story of an Old Southern Borough," *Atlantic Monthly, 47* (1881), p. 656; John Spencer Bassett, "Stirring Up Fires of Racial Antipathy," *South Atlantic Quarterly, 2* (1903), p. 300.

99. Joan Givner, *Katherine Anne Porter: A Life* (New York: Simon & Schuster, 1982), p. 18; Walter Hines Page, "The Last Hold of the Southern Bully," *Forum, 16* (1893), p. 313; Hollinger F. Barnard, ed., *Outside the Magic Circle, the Autobiography of Virginia Foster Durr* (University: University of Alabama Press, 1986), p. 10.

100. Thomas Nelson Page, *Red Rock* (New York: Scribner, 1898), pp. 49-50, 173; Hayne, *A Man of Letters in the 19th Century*, p. 243; Henry Watterson, "Oddities of Southern Life," *Century, 23* (1881-1882), p. 894; Thomas Dixon, Jr., *The Leopard's Spots* (New York: Doubleday, Page, 1902), pp. 51, 81.

101. Grace King, "Bayou L'Ombre: An Incident of the War," in *Grace King of New Orleans, A Selection of Her Writings*, Robert Bush, ed. (Baton Rouge: Louisiana State University Press, 1973), p. 125; Mrs. L. H. Harris, "The Southern White Woman," *Independent, 52* (1900), p. 431.

102. Charles Dudley Warner, "Impressions of the South," *Harper's, 71* (1885), p. 549; Atticus Haygood, *Our Brother in Black* (Nashville, TN: Southern Methodist Publishing House, 1881; reprint ed., Freeport, NY: Books for Libraries Press, 1970), p. 95.

103. Elizabeth McCracken, "The Women of America. Third Paper, The Southern Woman and Reconstruction," *Outlook, 75* (1903), p. 701.

104. Henry James, *The American Scene* (London, England: Chapman & Hall, 1907; reprint ed. Bloomington: University of Indiana Press, 1968), p. 414.

105. Wilbur Fiske Tillett, "Southern Womanhood as Affected by the War," *Century, 43* (1891), p. 9.

106. Tillett, "Southern Womanhood as Affected by the War," p. 9; John C. Kilgo, "An Inquiry Concerning Lynching," *South Atlantic Quarterly, I* (1902), p. 6; J.L.M. Curry, "Popular Education," *Race Problems of the South*, Proceedings of the 1st Annual Conference of the Southern Society for the Promotion of the Study of Race Conditions and Problems in the South (Richmond, VA: B. F. Johnson Publishing, 1900), pp. 112-113.

107. Wilson, *Baptized in Blood*, pp. 46-48; W. Cabell Bruce, "Lynch Law in the South," *North American Review, 155* (1892), p. 379.

108. Mayo, *Southern Women in the Recent Educational Movement*, p. 280; Isaac DuBose Seabrook, *Before and After, or The Relations of the Races at the South*, John Hammond Moore, ed. (Baton Rouge: Louisiana State University Press, 1967), p. 90; Alexander C. King, "The Punishment of Crimes Against Women, Existing Legal Remedies and Their Sufficiency," in *Race Problems of the South*, p. 162.

109. Philip Alexander Bruce, "Evolution of the Negro Problem," *Sewanee Review, 19* (1911), p. 391.

110. Bruce, "Evolution of the Negro Problem," p. 386.

111. Bruce, "Evolution of the Negro Problem," p. 391.

112. E. H. Abbott, "The South and the Negro. V. Social Equality Versus Social Service," *Outlook, 77* (1904), p. 590. See also Abbott, "The South and the Negro. II. The Confusion of Tongues," pp. 228-229.

113. Bertram Wyatt-Brown, "W. J. Cash and Southern Culture," in *From the Old South to the New*, Walter J. Fraser, Jr., and Winfred B. Moore, Jr., eds. (Westport, CT: Greenwood Press, 1981), p. 209.

114. Thomas Nelson Page, *The Negro: The Southerner's Problem* (New York: Scribner, 1904), p. 24.

115. Seabrook, *Before and After*, p. 128.

116. Mrs. L. H. Harris, "The White Man in the South," *Independent, 51* (1899), p. 3475.

117. Grace King, "Bayou L'Ombre," p. 117.

118. Litwack, *Been In the Storm So Long*, p. 227.

119. Thomas Nelson Page, *Red Rock*, p. 322; Dixon, *The Leopard's Spots*, pp. 146-147; Alfred H. Colquitt, "Is the Negro Vote Suppressed?" *Forum, 4* (1887), p. 274; William Garrott Brown, "The Ku Klux Movement," *Atlantic Monthly, 87* (1901), pp. 635-636; Alfred Holt Stone, *Studies in the American Race Problem* (New York: Doubleday, Page, 1908), pp. 268-269; Walter Hines Page, *The Southerner* (New York: Doubleday, Page, 1909), p. 211.

120. W. M. Beckner, "Shall the Negro Be Educated or Suppressed?" *Independent, 41* (1889), p. 226; *Joel Chandler Harris, Educator and Essayist*, Julia C. Harris, ed. (Chapel Hill: University of North Carolina Press, 1931), p. 61.

121. Francis A. Shoup, "Uncle Tom's Cabin Forty Years After," *Sewanee Review, 2* (1893), p. 96; Nathaniel S. Shaler, "The Nature of the Negro," *Arena, 3* (1890), p. 31; W. Cabell Bruce, "Lynch Law in the South," p. 381; Haygood, *Brother in Black*, p. 37; Thomas Nelson Page, *The Negro*, p. 22.

122. Mrs. L. H. Hammond, "A Southern View of the Negro," *Outlook, 73* (1903), p. 620.

123. *The Hammonds of Redcliffe,* Carol Bleser, ed. (New York: Oxford University Press, 1981), p. 324. See also E. E. Breckenridge, "The Race Question," *Independent, 43* (1891), p. 478; Katherine DuPre Lumpkin, *The Making of a Southerner* (New York: Knopf, 1947), p. 74; E. H. Randle, *Characteristics of the Southern Negro* (New York: Neale Publishing, 1910), p. 69.

124. Seabrook, *Before and After,* p. 67.

125. Lumpkin, *The Making of a Southerner,* pp. 37, 39.

126. Thomas Nelson Page, "On the Decay of Manners," *Century, 81* (1910-1911), p. 885; Francis Hopkinson Smith, *Colonel Carter of Cartersville* (New York: P. F. Collier, 1891), pp. 7, 15, 94, 208.

127. Granville Jones, *The Saloon and The Race Problem* (North Waco, TX: B. H. Simpson, Printer, 1903), p. 9.

128. Walter Hines Page, *The Southerner,* p. 262; William B. Smith, *The Color Line* (New York: McClure, Phillips, 1905), p. 9.

129. Mrs. L. H. Harris, "The White Man in the South," p. 3476.

130. James C. Austin, *Bill Arp* (New York: Twayne Publishers, 1969), p. 32. See also Jefferson Davis, *Private Letters,* p. 483.

131. Albion W. Tourgee, "The South as a Field of Fiction," *Forum, 6* (1888), p. 411.

132. Thomas Nelson Page, *The Negro,* p. 57.

133. Randle, *Characteristics of the Southern Negro,* p. 74.

134. Gildersleeve, "The Creed of the Old South," p. 86.

135. Walter Hines Page, *The Southerner,* p. 268.

136. William B. Smith, *The Color Line,* pp. 256-257; Thomas W. Murrell, "Syphilis in the Negro: Its Bearing on the Race Problem," *American Journal of Dermatology, 10* (1906), p. 305.

137. Philip Alexander Bruce, "The Negro Population of the South," *Conservative Review, 2* (1899), p. 272; Atticus G. Haygood, "The Black Shadow in the South," *Forum, 16* (1893), p. 173; W. P. Lovejoy, "Georgia's Record of Blood," *Independent, 51* (1899), pp. 1299-1300; George F. Milton, "The Material Advancement of the Negro," *Sewanee Review, 3* (1894), p. 42; Thomas Nelson Page, *The Negro,* pp. 95-97; Walter Hines Page, "The Last Hold of the Southern Bully," p. 303; Charles H. Smith, "Have American Negroes Too Much Liberty?" *Forum, 16* (1893), p. 179.

138. Stephen B. Oates, *The Fires of Jubilee: Nat Turner's Fierce Rebellion* (New York: Harper & Row, 1975), pp. 18-19, 49, 55; Edgar Gardner Murphy, *The Basis of Ascendancy* (New York: Longmans, Green, 1909), pp. 15-16.

139. Murphy, *The Basis,* pp. 29-30.

140. *New York Journal.* November 3, 1901, reprinted in Julia C. Harris, *The Life and Letters of Joel Chandler Harris* (Boston: Houghton Mifflin, 1918), p. 500.

141. Harris, *The Life and Letters of Joel Chandler Harris,* pp. 500-502.

142. Walter Hines Page, "A Rest Cure," *World's Work, 6* (1903), p. 3942.

143. Ellen Glasgow, *A Certain Measure* (New York: Harcourt, Brace, 1938), p. 144.

10. On the Use of Medical Diagnosis as Name-Calling
Anita F. Hill and the Rediscovery of "Erotomania"

BRIDGET A. ALDARACA

> *The Black female . . . is caught in the tripartite crossfire of masculine prejudice,*
> *white illogical hate and Black lack of power.*
>
> Maya Angelou,
> *I Know Why the Caged Bird Sings*

> *Speaking out is not easy. To speak out is to look into the face of power.*
> Anita F. Hill, University
> of Pennsylvania (April 16, 1992)

Those of us who had the opportunity to watch, in February 1991, the televised Senate hearings that reviewed the qualifications of Judge Clarence Thomas for the position of Supreme Court Justice will have been struck by the ease with which many witnesses employed diagnostic terms usually used by professionals in the mental health field, by psychiatrists, psychologists, or psychiatric social workers. Medical terms such as *schizophrenia* and *dual personality*, references to delusion and fantasy, and especially the recently revived early 19th-century diagnosis of "erotomania" were all used to categorize the behavior of Professor Anita F. Hill, who was testifying against Judge Clarence Thomas's suitability for the Supreme Court position. Professor Hill maintained that Judge Thomas had repeatedly sexually harassed her over the period of time when she was employed by him and under his supervision at two different federal government agencies. Judge Thomas implied that Professor Hill was lying and his supporters insinuated that she was mentally ill.

The Contemporary Reconstruction of "Erotomania"

The naming of psychiatric illnesses and the use of diagnostic categories serve a legitimate function in the world of medicine and mental health care. The branch of medicine referred to as nosology—the classification of illnesses and disease according to symptoms, causes, and prognosis—is necessary for facilitating communication among health care practitioners and between them and their patients. Although symptoms can be treated without defining the illness or the cause of the symptom, naming an illness is a necessary step prior to making it an object of systematic research. Correct diagnosis of an illness or mental disorder, rather than the simple identification of a symptom, also goes hand in hand with prescribing proper treatment and the potential cure of the illness.

Most mental health practitioners are aware of the potential abuse of labeling a patient rather than diagnosing the patient's specific problem or illness. People labeled mentally ill are still often perceived as "out of control" and consequently a danger to the public welfare because they transgress conventional codes of behavior. Words like *hysterical, paranoid, schizo,* or *loony*—we may now need to add *erotomaniac* to the list—express fear, disgust, and even hatred. The name-caller seeks to eliminate the targeted individual or group from certain areas of social life. For example, homophobic slurs disguised as the medicalization of sexual preference—homosexuality as aberrant behavior or mental illness—seek to shut out gay men and women from specific job sectors, housing, and so forth. As a community, we pay recognition to the potentially destructive power of name-calling by codifying medical and legal concepts such as psychological abuse, verbal harassment, slander, and defamation of character.

Nevertheless, the distinction between name-calling and legitimate medical diagnosis is not always clear cut. One area for consideration by feminist health professionals, both men and women, is the very process by which diagnostic criteria are written and codified. In the United States, the source book for this codification is the *Diagnostic and Statistical Manual,* known familiarly as the *DSM,* which is written and published by the American Psychiatric Association. The first edition of the *DSM* appeared in the 1950s and was followed in 1968 by a somewhat extended version. In 1980, medical diagnosis took an enormous quantitative leap with the publication of the *DSM III,* listing more than 100 mental disorders in a volume almost four times the length of the second edition's 119 pages. The revised edition (*DSM-III-R*) appeared in 1987, and has now been supplanted by the *DSM-IV,* which finally appeared—after much fanfare—in June 1994.

The adjective *erotomanic* appeared for the first time in the 1987 *DSM-III-R* to describe a sub-type of the category called Delusional Disorder. (The writers of this section seemed to have made an effort to avoid the more antiquated term *erotomania,* nor does the term *de Clérambault's syndrome,* also used to describe erotomania, appear in the index.) The term Delusional Disorder has itself undergone a name change, because the previous reference in the 1980 *DSM-III* was to Paranoid Disorder.

If we employ the more familiar vocabulary, then, we would say that erotomania is a sub-type of paranoia. The erotomaniac is not a neurotic. She would be described as a functioning psychotic, functioning to the extent that her delusion does not interfere with her work or daily living. In the area of her delusion, however, the erotomaniac has completely lost touch with reality. The authors of this normative diagnostic manual maintain that erotomania is diagnosed predominantly in females (American Psychiatric Association [APA], 1987, p. 199). Males tend to act out erotic delusions violently and are more likely to end up in a court of law than a psychiatric hospital, reinforcing today's growing consensus that whereas women are sick, men tend to be criminal (Slavney, 1984; Warner, 1978). The *DSM-III-R* description of erotomania reads as follows:

> The central theme of an erotic delusion is that one is loved by another. The delusion usually concerns idealized romantic love and spiritual union rather than sexual attraction. The person about whom this conviction is held is usually of higher status, such as a famous person or a superior at work, and may even be a complete stranger. Efforts to contact the object of the delusion, through telephone calls, letters, gifts, visits, and even surveillance and stalking are common, though occasionally the person keeps the illusion secret. (APA, 1987, p. 199)

The Historical Genesis of "Lovesickness"

The earliest description of erotomania, by Etienne Esquirol (1838/ 1965), disciple of Philippe Pinel and leading clinician at the Parisian hospital of the Salpêtrière in the early part of the 19th century, emphasizes the asexual content of the delusion and the purity of the erotomaniac's desire. In his work *Des Maladies Mentales* (*Concerning Mental Illnesses*), published in French in 1838 and translated into English a decade later, Esquirol writes this definition of Erotomania.

> Erotomania lies within the province of medicine. It is a chronic cerebral affection, characterized by an excessive love, be it for a known object or an imaginary one. In this disorder, only the imagination is damaged: the understanding is at fault. It is a mental illness in which amorous ideas are fixed and dominant, in the same way that religious ideas are fixed and dominant in theomania, that is, in religious lypemania (melancholia or depression with religious ideation.) (Esquirol, 1838, p. 32) (present trans. by B.A.A.)

Esquirol insists on this distinction between mind and body, citing the imagination (a function of the brain) as the site of the illness, because he has in mind the etiology of another more horrifying disease, *furor uterinus*, a term that appears in English texts of the period as uterine fury or nymphomania, and that was believed to originate as a lesion on the diseased female reproductive organs. In 19th-century medical literature the insatiable and disgusting sexual desire of the nympho-maniac is abhorred, in accordance with the belief that the only pure love of a woman is nonsexual maternal love. Nevertheless, excessive love uncontaminated by bodily lust can still fit within the paradigm of the 19th-century bourgeois image of the good woman. Esquirol's ero-tomaniac, although perceived as sick, is presented with sympathy and tolerance as an example of a woman or man who simply loves too much, who is, so to speak, in love with being in love. Esquirol tells us: "In erotomania, the eyes are animated, the gaze passionate, speech is tender and action expansive but the erotomane never goes beyond the limits of propriety" (Esquirol, 1838, p. 33; present trans. by B.A.A.). What is being idealized is love, and it is important to note that in Esquirol's nosology, erotomania is not yet classified as a female obses-sion, men may also fall under the spell of a chaste love.

At the turn of the century, the renowned German psychiatrist Emil Kraepelin wrote a new taxonomy of symptoms, replacing Esquirol's term *monomania* (*idée fixe* or partial ideational insanity) with *paranoia*, a term that continued to emphasize an intellectual disorder rather than an emotional (affective or mood) disorder such as depression. Kraepelin (1856-1926) was an early contemporary of Freud who remained at odds with Freud's psychodynamic conception of neurotic disorders as the manifestation of repressed sexual desire, and particularly with Freud's theory that the delusions of the erotomaniac are a defense against repressed and latent homosexual desire (Kraepelin, 1921/1976, p. 265; Segal, 1984, p. 1262). Kraepelin's description of erotomania is of particular interest to us in light of the so-called neo-Kraepelinian revival that influences the writing of the *DSM* since 1980 (Andreasen, 1985, pp. 150-161).

According to Kraepelin, erotomania is a form of paranoid delusion of grandeur, of "paranoic megalomania" in which: "The patient per-ceives that a person of the other sex, distinguished really or presumably by high position, is kindly disposed to him and shows him by atten-tion which cannot be misunderstood" (Kraepelin, 1921/1976, pp. 245, 247). Kraepelin details the course of this delusion, insisting that the goal of the deluded sufferer is usually some form of participation in the life of the renowned person, generally marriage. There is a notable absence of sexual desire expressed by the sufferer: Kraepelin main-tains that, "The whole colouring of the love is at the same time vision-ary and romantic; the real sexual instinct in the patient is often slightly developed or developed in an unwholesome way (onanism or mastur-bation)" (Kraepelin, 1921/1976, p. 248).

Our discussion of erotomania's historical genesis shows a general consensus on various points. First, the essence of the erotic delusion is not that the woman loves, but that she feels herself *to be loved*. One could say that erotomania is the socially constructed feminine version of the male's delusion of grandeur. Rather than imagining that she *is*

Napoleon, Prince Charles, or Lee Iacocca, the female erotomaniac believes that a powerful male within her purview, perhaps the president of the company for which she is a poorly paid clerical worker, longs to share his higher status with her. The woman conforms to her feminine role by remaining passive. In her imagination, her social superior falls in love with her. She cannot control him or his desire. It is she who is pursued by him, secretly (romantically) through coded messages. The female erotomaniac satisfies narcissistic needs by choosing someone whose superior status will enable her to participate vicariously in the social power that she herself lacks. Contemporary case histories of erotomania all share one important element: The fantasy of being loved chastely by a superior man almost always ends in the fantasy of marriage, the traditional means by which women share in patriarchal power (Hollender & Callahan, 1975; Segal, 1989; Rudden, Gilmore, & Frances, 1980; Taylor, Mahendra, & Gunn, 1983).

The Use of "Erotomania" as a Political Weapon

The Clarence Thomas-Anita Hill confrontation has been compared repeatedly to the William Kennedy Smith rape trial, as well as to the rape trial of heavyweight boxer Mike Tyson. Leaving aside the important differences among the three cases, two similarities stand out. In all three, the issue was a man's sexual exploitation of a woman against her will, and in all three cases the outcome would be decided by weighing his testimony against hers. To use the phrase coined by the journalists, the search for truth would be reduced to a he said/she said duel between the two antagonists. In a February 2 interview on the television program *60 Minutes*, and subsequently reported in *The New York Times*, Professor Hill commented on this when she maintained that the hearings were essentially unfair because the rules of procedure and evidence that structure a trial setting were absent ("Constitutional Test," 1992, p. A9).

"He said/she said" is a catchy phrase that has the effect of dismissing out of hand any possibility of knowing who is right and who has been wronged. The reduction of sexual harassment and rape to "he said/she said" seeks to dismiss the importance and the reality of sexual abuse as an abuse of power by men in the workplace or in the public ritual of dating. "He said/she said" implies that what takes place in any intimate male/female relationship is so open to subjective interpretation that real events by definition become unknowable. This phrase, with its well-balanced formula of equal components, also seeks to give credence to another more dangerous myth, that all women have equal access with all men to public discourse. "He said/she said" covers up and denies any gender or racial inequality, any power gap between the wealthy and the economically disenfranchised, between heterosexual and gay or lesbian.

Given the lack of scandal in Anita Hill's personal history and her public demeanor as a witness, as well as the credibility of the character witnesses who testified in her defense, the Republican senators in support of Clarence Thomas decided that it was necessary to impeach Professor Hill's testimony. To do this, they planned to establish that she was not a reliable witness because she was acting out a fantasy of unrequited love for a man who was her superior, an ideal future husband who would protect her and allow her to share in his power but who had provoked in her a desire for revenge when he married another woman, a White woman, and definitively rejected her. (The committee's strategy meeting is recorded in detail in "At Hearings, the Tide Shifts With the Testimony," 1991, pp. A1, A11). Senator Arlen Specter brought out into the open their determination to attack Anita Hill's mental health status when he introduced the idea of fantasy as an alternative to the opposition truth/nontruth (CNN Live Broadcast, October 14, 1991). The possibility that Anita Hill had fantasized her experience provided an escape route from the confrontation between she and he, truth and lies, good and evil. At worst, she was mentally ill, victim of a falsely remembered delusion. At best, she was innocent of lying because she was still under the influence of her mental aberration. In other words, Anita Hill's diagnosis of temporary and/or partial insanity became Clarence Thomas's defense against sexual harassment.

The idea that truth = memory = distortion of reality was reinforced in *The New York Times* by various psychology experts specializing in such subjects as memory, lying, and delusional disorders. One psychologist hypothesized that the substance of Anita Hill's testimony might have had its source in something she had heard or read ("Psychologists Try," 1991, p. A11). (Those of us who were able to watch the live television broadcast will recall the rather frantic waving around of the novel, *The Exorcist*, as Thomas's defenders attempted to utilize this line of defense.) Because Anita Hill had passed a lengthy lie detector test (even though this information was not publicized widely), it became essential to educate the public in the equation of truth = memory = distortion of reality.

The strategy of a concerted attack on Professor Hill's mental status was made even more apparent in the testimony of Thomas's supporters, notably that of Ms. J. C. Alvarez, who criticized Anita Hill's behavior as suffering from an exaggerated self-confidence that appeared schizophrenic because such self-confidence had no basis in reality ("At Hearings," 1991, p. A11). This *ad feminam* argument directly attacked the person (or personality) of Anita Hill. This is to say, her very manner of being, her calm, unemotional (non-hysterical) rational comportment was itself cited as evidence of mental delusion. But such an argument needed an official seal of approval from the psychiatric establishment.

The labeling of Professor Anita Hill as suffering from erotomania, that is, the paranoid delusion that she was the love object of Clarence Thomas, was accomplished through the gratuitous use of psychiatric terms by co-workers such as Ms. Alvarez, by insistent questions concerning the number of contacts that Hill had maintained with Thomas after her resignation, and by the medical expertise provided to the Republican senators by Dr. Park Dietz, a forensic psychiatrist and former FBI employee who went to Washington and conferred with Senators Arlen Specter, Alan Simpson, and Orrin Hatch as they planned their attack on Professor Hill's credibility ("Use of Psychiatry," 1991, p. A11). (Dr. Dietz reappeared in the news as an expert witness for the prosecution of the bizarre murderer Jeffrey Dahmer, testifying that Dahmer was sane when he killed and ate his victims.) But the key witness against Professor Hill was the self-proclaimed victim of Professor Hill's erotomaniacal tendencies, Yale-graduated lawyer, John Doggett III.

At the hearings, Mr. Doggett testified that Professor Hill found him so attractive that he became the object of her romantic fixation. To bolster his affirmation that Hill had a problem with being rejected by men, Doggett went on to relate having witnessed behavior he felt was symptomatic of Hill's problematic relationship with *all* males. Describing one of the networking parties attended by the tight group of Yale law school graduates, Doggett relates how he observed Anita Hill in friendly conversation with men, taking the initiative and prolonging contact with men, and he states he also observed that the men that she talked to would at some point walk away from her (CNN Broadcast of Senate Hearings, October 14, 1991).

Doggett would like to insinuate that this apparently quite normal pattern of cocktail party circulation is really the desperate attempt of a man-starved female to unsuccessfully catch unwary men in her conversational net. (His testimony also constitutes an unwitting admission on Doggett's part that he evidently spent a fair amount of time at this particular party observing Ms. Hill's behavior from a distance.) Doggett goes on to provide his listeners with more supposedly objective facts that purport to bolster his argument that Anita Hill is delusional. As further evidence, he reveals to the Senate Committee and his television audience that the first time he went to visit Clarence Thomas in his office, Anita Hill actually stopped him and attempted to talk to him. Indeed, she appeared to expect that they would go in together and talk to Ms. Hill's employer, Mr. Thomas (CNN Live Broadcast, October 14, 1991).

From Doggett's perspective, the bizarre behavior that demonstrates that Anita Hill is out of touch with reality is the "fact" that she takes the initiative in social interaction with men. At a professional gathering, she initiates conversation with men. At her workplace as Doggett walks toward the office of her supervisor, Clarence Thomas, she attempts to stop him and to speak with him. Doggett's anger appears to be directed primarily at Anita Hill's uppity behavior with men. She doesn't wait to be spoken to by men, she speaks to them first. She goes where she isn't invited. In a word, she presumes membership in what is primarily a male fraternity, the Washington political scene personified by the group of male senators who are questioning Doggett with such gentle care. Anita Hill has made the fantastical assumption that because she and Doggett are both Black Yale law school graduates, she is Doggett's equal. A very strange fantasy indeed.

And Doggett goes on to predict that dire consequences will result from Anita Hill's public stand against sexual harassment. He fears that men may no longer be able to act like human beings if the people they are with happen to be women (CNN Live Broadcasts of Senate Hearings, October 14, 1991). Doggett's underlying argument is that Anita Hill's behavior is symptomatic of a delusional state because she is behaving as if she were "one of us" when in reality she is "one of them." The implied sub-text of Doggett's testimony is an unshaken belief in a world that is constructed precariously along a fault line; on the one side—his side—the male "us," and on the other a very dangerous female "them."

Doggett's breakdown of the public work world into a gendered and linguistically nonracial "them" and "us" helps to clarify the confrontation between Anita Hill and Clarence Thomas by momentarily erasing the issue of race and its potential to polarize the question of job discrimination along the more familiar and historically recognized axis of a Black "them" and a White "us." We will see this gendered version of them and us discussed in articles such as the one that appeared 6 months later in the widely circulated magazine, *Jet*, with the headline: "Experts Tell Ways Men Can Avoid Sex Harassment Charges" (Hare & Hare, 1992). As the banner headline indicates, sexual harassment has now become a danger to the (Black) male in the workforce, thus neatly reversing the roles of female victim and male predator. Examples given by Nathan and Julia Hare imply that sexual harassment is essentially impolite, rude, or inappropriate male behavior that can be used against him by any female co-worker out for revenge. New rules of etiquette need to be drawn, together with a more precise line between the public and the private. Certain vocabulary and sexual allusions, certain gestures or kinds of touching are no longer acceptable in the public workplace.

From this particular Black perspective, sexual harassment is essentially a White Emily Post problem of proper workplace etiquette. Nathan Hare reminds his (Black male) readers that in the workplace even innocent compliments are dangerous, since flattery is unacceptable (Hare & Hare, 1992, p. 15). By mixing together *all* levels of sexual comportment—for example, asking women to share male pleasure in pornographic material, or soliciting sexual favors in exchange for career advancement, with lesser offenses such as "lustful glances" or calling a co-worker "Mama" or "Babe"—the Hares establish a context that defines sexual harassment simply as rude behavior rather than a form of male aggression or coercion against women.

But of course the idea that certain kinds of behavior are not permissible in the workplace carries with it the implied corollary that this same behavior *is* permissible in private. This argument has been refined in an issue of *The Black Scholar*, dedicated to the Hill-Thomas confrontation, in which authors such as the sociologist Orlando Patterson and the ubiquitous Hares maintain that the concept itself of sexual harassment between Black men and women in the workplace is a form of cultural colonialism by the cabal of prissy (hysterical) White bourgeois feminists who seek to impose their own moral code of sexual repression upon the more liberated and natural Black man (Hare & Hare, 1991-1992; Patterson, 1991-1992). According to Patterson (1991-1992), Clarence Thomas was guilty of nothing more than a "down-home style of courting" (p. 79), and, in fact, he was perfectly justified in denying his behavior (lying) on the "utilitarian moral grounds" (p. 78) that the punishment—the derailing of his appointment to the Supreme Court— did not fit the crime.

What links the article in *Jet* magazine to Doggett's diatribe against Anita Hill is not the idea of delusion or "erotomania," however, but rather the idea that Black women can and will use false charges of sexual harassment, whether lies *or* fantasies, to seek revenge for either real or imagined rejection. The barrier to success for the ambitious Black male no longer consists solely of White men (and women). There is a new, more insidious enemy, the Black woman who works by his side and who can use this proximity and the potential trust that he places in her to betray him more successfully. The Hares's bottom-line message is that the Black career woman is dangerous. She cannot and should not be trusted by her Black brother.

Alessandra Stanley (1991, p. E2), in her Op-Ed piece in *The New York Times* titled "Erotomania: A Rare Disorder Runs Riot—in Men's Minds," analyzes this burgeoning form of male paranoia as an insidious consequence of male narcissism. Stanley gives Doggett credit for discovering a uniquely male disorder called erotomonomania. The main symptom is the sufferer's belief that he is being pursued by beautiful young females filled with an uncontrollable erotic desire of which he is the target. And certainly, throughout Doggett's testimony one can hear sotto voce the petulant complaint that he was a victim of an aggressive female who was, as we say in the vernacular, "hitting on him."

What Doggett would have us believe is that Anita Hill became obsessed with both himself and with Thomas, desired both men sexually, and made advances toward them that were rejected, hence her longing for revenge. This description of erotomania leads us much farther away from the *DSM-III-R* definition of an obsessive but chaste love for one man and closer to the traditional image of the out-of-control nymphomaniac who suffers from a promiscuous compulsion to engage in sexual activity. (Although the image of the sexually insatiable nymphomaniac has survived the 19th century and lives on in contemporary mythology, nymphomania is still not an official *DSM* diagnosis.)

Today's Erotomaniac: A New Version of an Old Myth?

The idea that men are the victims of emotionally unstable erotomaniacs who will arbitrarily attack them and take away their power, wealth, and social status is now becoming a commonplace defense against female accusations of sexual abuse. Mike Tyson's rape victim was condemned by his defense lawyer as a woman of the world, motivated by his client's wealth ("Jury Begins," 1992, p. B11). Patricia Bowman was portrayed successfully as a "scorned woman" out for revenge, who brought rape charges against the aspiring young doctor William Kennedy Smith because he called her by another woman's name during consensual sex and then sent her home without giving her his phone number. We are witnessing the contemporary refurbishing of a powerful and long-standing myth—the man, White *and* Black, as victim of feminine wiles, of an evil and exploitive female who disguises her voracious emotional and sexual needs behind the facade of a youthful seductive appearance.

The inclusion of erotomania in the 1987 *DSM-III-R* legitimizes this new version of the stereotypic castrating woman. Whether Black or White she is still a black widow spider who uses her sex to lure her victim into a trap where she can consume him. The new Male Victims' Club may even have found its president in John Doggett III, who resurfaced again in February at a campaign rally for then-Governor Bill Clinton in order to defend the democratic presidential candidate against the attack of another supposed erotomaniac, Gennifer Flowers, a cabaret singer who maintains that she had a 12-year love affair with Mr. Clinton ("From Nixon," 1992, p. A14).

During Clarence Thomas's testimony, one of the most dramatic moments, and certainly the most strategically successful on Thomas's part, was the depiction of his experience as a metaphorical lynching, engineered by an unnamed White liberal-conservative cabal. With this accusation of racism against the White senators, Thomas was able to erase the distinction between liberal and conservative as well as his own proven ultraconservative allegiance and to call into question the post-1960s post-Civil Rights tacit agreement that references to race will be eliminated from public discourse. Outside the African-American community racial references are now seen as gauche and rude, a throwback to the racist attitudes of the pre-Civil Rights days. And logically, the deracializing of public discourse implies an absence of racist attitudes in the White community. As Toni Morrison reminds us in her essay *Playing in the Dark*, "the habit of ignoring race is understood to be a graceful, even generous, liberal gesture. To notice is to recognize an already discredited difference" (Morrison, 1992, pp. 9-10).

Thomas's reintroduction of the issue of race was tactically brilliant because he forced the White male senators to choose between one of their two historic roles in Black history: the White mob that lynches the innocent Black male victim, or the White male who protects (White) women against the aggression of the Black male. What is missing, of course, is any historic White male role as protector of the Black woman. Certainly, one of the most persuasive media images during the hearing was the long table filled with righteously angry, even tearful African-American women who refused to collaborate in the supposed "hi-tech lynching" of their brother. By crying "lynch mob," Thomas effectively maintained that for Black women to support Anita Hill in her charges of sexual harassment was to play the role of the White woman who cries "rape" and provokes the lynch mob into action. Thomas, then, sought to establish a moral imperative of the choice of race over gender, for the survival of the race.

Conclusion: African-American Women Speak Out

Approximately 4 weeks after Anita Hill's appearance in front of the all-White male Senate Judiciary Committee, on November 17, 1992, a group called "African American Women in Defense of Ourselves" took out an ad in *The New York Times* signed by 1,603 American women of African descent in support of Anita Hill. African-American women affirmed themselves as the collective subject of their own history with the following words: "We want to make clear that the media have ignored or distorted many African American voices. . . . We will not be silenced" (African American Women in Defense of Ourselves [paid advertisement, reprinted in *The Black Scholar*, 1991-1992, p. 155]). It was an historic moment in which White feminists in sympathy with Anita Hill were required by the political circumstances to stand on the sidelines in quiet admiration as Black women across the nation publicly raised their voice in defense of their Black sister. And we listened as Black women, transcending the partisanship of gender, class, and race, spoke for all of us:

> Further, the consolidation of a conservative majority on the Supreme Court seriously endangers the rights of all women, poor and working class people and the elderly. The seating of Clarence Thomas is an affront not only to African American women and men, but to all people concerned with social justice. (African-American Women in Defense of Ourselves [paid advertisement, reprinted in *The Black Scholar*, 1991-1992, p. 155])

Since that moment, many events have taken place. The indignation of both Black and White women as well as an important segment of the male population has had, and continues to have, important repercussions in electoral politics and in the public consciousness. A Gallup Poll taken one year later found that Anita Hill's credibility had increased by 14% and that an estimated 43% of the American public now believed Professor Hill, in comparison to the 39% who sided with Judge Thomas. Viewed from another perspective, 61% of the American public do not believe or are not sure that Supreme Court Justice Thomas told the truth when he maintained that he was not guilty of sexual harassment (McAneny, 1992).

Also of great significance is the impact of Anita Hill's public pillorying on the issue of sexual harassment in general and on the current critical debate on race-gender issues such as job discrimination, workfare versus welfare, as well as the long-ignored subject of spouse abuse and domestic violence. It is possible that we may see the issue of sexual harassment and sexual abuse become the bridge that unites, at least politically, White women and women of color in the workplace. The significance of the stand taken by African-American women against the political/ideological cul-de-sac that forced them to choose between humiliating silence or race betrayal cannot be overestimated. In a word, African-American women have positioned themselves at the center of political discourse concerning the hitherto forbidden or secret theme of gender relationships in both the public and the private spheres.

The image of Anita Hill, sitting alone at the same long table that would be filled with Clarence Thomas's Black women supporters, her family behind her but still alone as she looked into the White male "face of power" has produced, I believe, a lasting impression upon the American psyche. Some Black women commentators, refusing to censor themselves, described the spectacle as a "hi-tech gang rape" and it is very difficult not to agree with them (Boyd, 1992; Ransby, 1991-1992). But as the ensuing debate over the confrontation between these two Black professionals has made clear, the face of power is not only White. A common thread that runs through the essays of African-American feminists is their disillusionment with Black male leadership. Some Black writers take this critique of Black leadership a step further, to argue against the psychological damage inflicted upon African-American women who may, for example, experience the assault of such demeaning epithets as "bitch" and "ho" on a regular basis. In one writer's words: "The brothers too often forget about the daily challenges African American women face in order to maintain self confidence and strong egos. These women struggle in a nation that renders brown and black skinned women invisible at best. African American men join the oppressors when they label and degrade their sisters" (Pope, 1991-1992). Clearly, one of the effects of the Hill-Thomas confrontation has been to bring out into the open the issue of misogyny in the Black community.

More than 2 months after Doggett testified before the Senate Judiciary Committee, Anita Hill appeared with Gloria Steinem as principal speaker at the Conference on Parity, Power and Sexual Harassment at Hunter College in New York. Relating sexual harassment to issues of power, Professor Hill insisted that sexual harassment must be understood as something other than spontaneous and crude behavior brought about by the individual male response to a woman's short skirt or large breasts. Sexual harassment cannot be dismissed as anecdotal. Rather it is purposeful directed activity, often planned in concert by other male employees and having as its goal the exclusion of women from the work site and from the hierarchy of power. Professor Hill underlined the analogy between racism and sexism, insisting that if sexual harassment is considered in terms of access to or exclusion from power in the workplace, sexual harassment is the equivalent of a sign saying "Men Only" (CNN Live Broadcast, April 26, 1992).

The different points under discussion—female sexual abuse, the ideological power of the official institutions of American psychiatry, and the question of access to public discourse—can be tied together by underlining some events that did not take place at the Senate hearings. Questions concerning what was said and what information was withheld have been asked from the very beginning. For example, why were available witnesses from Judge Thomas's Yale law school period not called to testify concerning his well-known predilection for discussing pornography? And why did the Democratic Chair, Senator Joseph Biden, persuade Angela Wright not to testify, after she had expressed her willingness to give testimony that would support Anita Hill's description of Justice Thomas's office behavior? (Many of these questions have been addressed in Jill Abramson and Jane Mayer's lengthy review article published in the May 24, 1993 issue of *The New Yorker*, in which the authors take apart, argument by argument, David Brock's scandalous book, *The Real Anita Hill: The Untold Story.*) The American public did eventually have access to Angela Wright's testimony through the political satire of Gary Trudeau and his widely circulated comic strip, *Doonesbury.* Given the blurred line between fiction and fact, popular culture and legal affidavits, his readers may not be aware that Trudeau's comic material was in fact based on Angela Wright's sworn deposition in which she maintained that Clarence Thomas constantly pressured her to date him, that he frequently made personal comments about women's anatomy, and that in her opinion Clarence Thomas was capable of behaving in the ways that Anita Hill described in her testimony (CNN Interview, October 14, 1991).

Likewise, the American public is almost certainly unaware of the fact that Dr. Robert Spitzer, member of the American Psychiatric Association and chairman of the committee that wrote *DSM-III* and the revised edition that includes the description of erotomania, was called to give his opinion on the relevance of erotomania to Professor Hill's accusation of sexual harassment. According to Dr. Spitzer, Anita Hill's behavior was not symptomatic of any mental disorder, but her behavior did fit the profile of sexual harassment victims. (Some of these symptoms would be the attempt to repress the emotional reactions of fear and disgust provoked by the harasser, conscious and/or unconscious attempts to deny that the behavior is happening, and somatic complaints that develop as a result of this process of repression and denial. In this case, Spitzer may be referring to the fact that Anita Hill was at one point hospitalized with a gastric complaint, during the period in which she was working under Thomas's supervision.) According to *The New York Times*'s report, Dr. Spitzer was ready to testify in public before the Judiciary Committee, but he was not called by the Democratic senators nor were his opinions referred to during the hearings ("Use of Psychiatry," 1991, p. A11).

Authentic cases of erotomania have been documented in the pages of reputable psychiatric journals (Hollender & Callahan, 1975; Rudden et al., 1980; Segal, 1989). The misuse of this diagnosis for political purposes does not take away from its validity. But we are also witnessing the construction of a popular version of erotomania that has no more to do with the clinical model of this delusional disorder than the glamorous movie star Glen Close of the movie *Fatal Attraction* has to do with the real-life experience of the average Black or White female worker in today's low-salaried pink-collar ghetto. The new stereotype of the young seductive erotomaniac who entraps her innocent victim, is, I believe, a male defense tactic as women begin to speak out in the courts against sexual harassment and date rape.

Since the resurgence of feminism in the late 1960s and early 1970s, mental health practitioners and social workers are much more informed concerning the parallel reactions that exist between victims of incest, rape, and sexual harassment: feelings of intense shame and humiliation, depression, feelings of helplessness, loss of a sense of self-worth, the repression of details that at times may only surface years later (Herman, 1981; Morrison, 1989). Because of the televised Senate Judiciary hearings as well as the televised rape trial of William Kennedy Smith, we have all been made aware, men and women alike, of the courage that it takes for a woman to face her tormentor in the public arena of a court of law, or, in the case of Anita Hill, in the legally unprotected setting of the Senate hearings. I have no doubt that many women who watched the Senate hearings attempted to imagine themselves, as I did, in Anita Hill's place. Certainly many women have wondered how we would have responded. Could we have stood up under the questioning, the innuendos, the implied threats, such as Senator Specter's suggestion that Anita Hill was criminally liable for perjury?

Sexual harassment in the workplace is pandemic in American culture. All women pay for discrimination in the workplace with loss of wages and lack of promotions, but they also pay for being forced to work in an unsafe environment with psychological stress, depression, and loss of self-esteem. No one who saw Anita Hill's face after the hearings can doubt that if she lost the battle of the hearings, she won a personal tug of war with herself and her need to reclaim what she had lost during her experience of sexual harassment. By daring to speak out and to insist on her right to have access to public discourse, she has given a gift of her courage to all of us.

References

Abramson, Jill, & Mayer, Jane. (1993, May 24). Review of *The real Anita Hill: The untold story* by David Brock. *The New Yorker, 69*(14), pp. 90-97.

African American women in defense of ourselves. (1991-1992). *The Black Scholar, 22*(1 & 2), 155. [Reprinted from a paid advertisement in *The New York Times*, November 17, 1992]

Andreasen, Nancy C. (1985). *The broken brain: The biological revolution in psychiatry*. New York: Harper & Row.

American Psychiatric Association. (1987). *Diagnostic and statistical manual of mental disorders* (3rd. ed., rev.). Washington, DC: Author.

At hearings, the tide shifts with the testimony. (1991, October 14). *The New York Times*, pp. A1, A11.

Boyd, Melba Joyce. (1992). Collard greens, Clarence Thomas, and the high-tech rape of Anita Hill. *The Black Scholar, 22*(1 & 2), 25-27.

Constitutional test is seen in inquiry on leak to press. (1992, February 3). *The New York Times*, p. A9.

Esquirol, J.E.D. (1965). *Mental maladies: A treatise on insanity*. New York: Hafner Publishing. [Original work published in French (*Des Maladies Mentales*) 1838; trans. by E. K. Hunt in 1845]

From Nixon, predictions on the presidential race. (1992, February 6). *The New York Times*, p. A. 14.

Hare, Nathan, & Hare, Julia. (1991-1992). The Clarence Thomas hearings. *The Black Scholar, 22*(1 & 2), 37-41.

Hare, Nathan, & Hare, Julia. (1992, March 30). Experts tell ways men can avoid sex harassment charges. *Jet*, pp. 14-17.

Herman, Judith Lewis. (1981). *Father-daughter incest*. Cambridge, MA, & London: Harvard University Press.

Hollender, Marc, & Callahan, Alfred. (1975). Erotomania or de Clérambault syndrome. *Archives of General Psychiatry, 32*, 1574-1576.

Jury begins deliberations in rape case against Tyson. (1992, February 11). *The New York Times*, p. B11.

Kraepelin, Emil. (1976). *Manic-depressive insanity and paranoia*. New York: Arno Press. [Original work published 1921; trans. by Mary Barclay from *Psychiatrie*, eighth German ed., Vols. 3 & 4]

McAneny, Leslie. (1992, October). One year later: Anita Hill now deemed more believable than Justice Thomas (Clarence Thomas). *The Gallup Poll Monthly*, no. 325, p. 34.

Morrison, James. (1989). Childhood sexual histories of women with somatization disorder. *American Journal of Psychiatry, 146*(2), 239-241.

Patterson, Orlando. (1991-1992). Race, gender and liberal fallacies. *The Black Scholar, 22*(1 & 2), 77-80.

Pope, Jaqueline. (1991-1992). The Clarence Thomas confirmation: Facing race and gender issues. *The Black Scholar, 22*(1 & 2), pp. 80-81.

Psychologists try to explain reason for opposing views. (1991, October 14). *The New York Times*, p. A11.

Ransby, Barbara. (1991-1992). The gang rape of Anita Hill and the assault upon all women of African descent. *The Black Scholar, 22*(1 & 2), 82-85.

Rudden, Marie, Gilmore, Margaret, & Frances, Allen. (1980). Erotomania: A separate entity. *American Journal of Psychiatry, 137*(10), 1262-1263.

Segal, Jonathan H. (1989). Erotomania revisited: From Kraepelin to *DSM-III-R*. *American Journal of Psychiatry, 146*(10), 1261-1266.

Slavney, Philip R. (1984). Histrionic personality and antisocial personality: Caricatures of stereotypes? *Comprehensive Psychiatry, 25*, 129-141.

Spitzer, Robert. L., & Williams, Janet. (1983). The issue of sex bias in DSM-III: A critique of "A woman's view of DSM-III" by Marcie Kaplan. *American Psychologist, 38*, 793-798.

Stanley, Alessandra. (1991, November 10). Erotomania: A rare disorder runs riot—In men's minds. *The New York Times*, p. E2.

Taylor, Pamela, Mahendra, B., & Gunn, John. (1983). Erotomania in males. *Psychological Medicine, 13*, 645-650.

Use of psychiatry in Thomas battle raises ethics issue. (1991, October 20). *The New York Times*, p. A11.

Warner, Richard. (1978). The diagnosis of antisocial and hysterical personality disorders: An example of sex bias. *Journal of Nervous and Mental Disease, 166*, 839-845.

11. Sapphires, Spitfires, Sluts, and Superbitches
Aframericans and Latinas in Contemporary American Film

ELIZABETH HADLEY FREYDBERG

The American film industry continues to produce films in which Aframericans and Latinas are cast in degrading roles, irrespective of the vehement protests of these two groups. The roles to which it most often relegates members of the two largest minority groups in America are unquestionably negative stereotypes. *Stereotype* as defined here "is an imitation, a copy of something or someone that is, by means of the media machinery, held up first as THE symbol or symbols to the exclusion of others; and then repeatedly channeled out to viewers so often that in time it becomes a 'common' representation of something or someone in the minds of viewers" (Blackwood, 1986, p. 205).

Stereotypes may be either positive or negative; for example, *some* Black people are excellent singers and dancers, but not *all* Black people are endowed with these talents. Whether the image a stereotype projects is positive or negative, however, it always limits the range of human behaviors and emotions that viewers are willing to ascribe to a stereotyped group. In the language of fictive or imaginative media, stereotype creates "flat" characters.

Stereotypes in many contemporary films reinforce preconceived notions of the status quo about people outside mainstream society. Moreover, the majority of stereotyping found in films is negative: It portrays the individuals in the stereotyped group as having personal qualities that are undesirable. This negative stereotyping fulfills a social function: it is through stereotype that the ruling majority rationalizes its maltreatment of people it has designated as inferior.

Images of Aframericans and Latinas have a long history of deformation and distortion because of racism—a byproduct of colonialism, and sexism. "Racism is the subjugation of a cultural group by another for the purpose of gaining economic advantage, of mastering and having power over that group—the result being harm done, consciously or unconsciously, to its members" (Anzaldúa, 1990, p. 225). Sexism in many ways resembles racism in that its dynamic can be expressed largely in terms of social and economic power. Although racism may create social structures in which the dominator and dominated can be almost entirely separate in terms of social contact, sexism requires contact between dominator and dominated. In addition, dominating cultural groups have long used sexism in the service of racism by using the sexual terrorism of rape as a weapon to punish and control both genders of the subjugated group.

The "exaggerated images" depicted in film as representative of Blacks and Latinas are those of prostitutes—women who sell their bodies for monetary profit; concubines—women who are kept, usually by a White male; whores—sexually promiscuous women who do not profit financially but who appear to enjoy sleeping around; and bitches—sexually emasculating, razor-tongued and razor-toting, hostile, aggressive women who will fight man or woman at the slightest provocation. A critical analysis of films and the use of historical and sociological data demonstrate some rationale for why these stereotypes persist in American society. Such analysis also reveals that these stereotypes originate with and are maintained by the racism and sexism of those who control America's film industry specifically and media in general.

Aframerican and Latina women have historically been treated as demoralized sex objects by White men. Black women were brought by White men to America to work in the agrarian South and to breed a larger slave population to supplement the workforce with free labor. White men not only appropriated the labor and the children of Black women under slavery, they also appropriated Black women's bodies through rape. And, when the color of their mulatto offspring bore silent witness to rape, these men profited from the unholy harvest by selling their own children and justified their violent subordination of Black women by labeling them promiscuous seducers. White women to some extent accepted the rationale offered by their husbands and brothers. Although their acceptance of the rationale of promiscuous Black women may have been motivated by the need to repress an unpleasant truth, White women had an even more compelling reason to believe: profit. Like White men, White women profited from the economics of slavery. After Emancipation and the failure of Reconstruction, White women as well as White men retained a system of beliefs about Black people that was fundamentally identical to what they had maintained during the slave era—for the same reason, profit.

Although Latina women were not brought to America for breeding, they were perceived as members of a "conquered" people, and as such were accorded the same lack of respect by Anglo men. (The term *Anglo*, in Latina discourse, refers to Caucasians not of Hispanic descent;

although context can create a negative connotation, it is not used in this chapter derogatorily). Mexicans were defeated by the United States first in battle at San Jacinto in 1836, then their final ruination was precipitated by the loss of the majority of their land to the United States with the annexation of Texas in 1845; the signing of the Treaty of Guadalupé Hidalgo in 1848—the acquisition of California, Nevada, Utah, Arizona, New Mexico, and even parts of Colorado and Wyoming; and finally the Gadsden Purchase of 1853 (Brinton, Christopher, & Wolff, 1964, p. 510). The attitude of Whites toward Hispanics was infused with biological and militaristic superiority based upon the same pseudo-scientific rationalizations that had nurtured the most sophist defenses of slavery. Such ethnocentricity is manifest in Arthur G. Pettit's (1980) observation that:

> The issue by the early 1840's was not whether the Mexicans were inferior to the north Americans but whether the Mexicans *as* inferiors ought to be left alone or conquered. Southerners, speaking with the "voice of experience" in dealing with another dark skinned race, were simultaneously loudest in asserting brown inferiority and strongest in affirming the risks of racial pollution. John C. Calhoun, standing firm on the Old Testament conviction of Ham's degeneracy, argued that the true misfortunes of Spanish America involved the fatal error of placing colored races on an equal footing with white men and maintained that the alternative to racial separation was economic stagnation, political chaos, and genetic pollution. (p. 12)

And in reference to Anglo attitudes regarding the Puerto Ricans, Luis Mercado (1974) states that, "Puerto Rico was governed through the U.S. Department of Interior and the U.S. Navy and Army Departments. The ruling officials usually were men who strongly reflected the plantation mentality, customs, and folkways of the Deep South, with its preoccupation with race, class, and religion" (p. 153). Puerto Rico was annexed in 1898 with the signing of the Paris Treaty, and its people became United States citizens with the enactment of the Jones Act in 1917 (Kelley, 1986, pp. 443, 568).

The dehumanization of Black and Latina women was maintained in stereotypes in literature created by White people that were eventually to surface in film during the early 20th century and that continue in contemporary film as the century draws to a close. The images of Latinas have their origins in the dimestore novels of the 19th century, but the images of African American women are derivatives of sentimental apologists for slavery in the plantation novel genre and their successors in the wave of nostalgia for a way of life "gone with the wind" after 1865. Even D. W. Griffith consulted the rabidly racist novels of Southerner Thomas Dixon to "authenticate" the controversial images of Black people reflected in *The Birth of a Nation* (1915). All the *Black* characters, male and female, are abnormally lustful and are preformed by white men in "black face," except the "tragic mulatto'" played by Madame Sul-Te-Wan.

Similarly, the Latina of conquest fiction is portrayed as the half-breed harlot whose purpose is to pique the male sexual appetite and whose mixed blood elicits similar behavior to that of her Black counterpart the mulatto. Both Black and Latina women may be used as White men's sexual playmates, as concubines or prostitutes, but neither possess the necessary matrimonial attributes assigned to the characters of virtuous White women. Their "colored" blood precludes such unions because it activates capricious behavior (also characteristic of the "tragic mulatto").[1] These stereotypes are conceptualized according to a racial hierarchy in which purity, chastity, and moral virtue are equated with light skin, and lustful debauchery is equated with darker coloring. The Latin "dark lady" is often a promiscuous, short-tempered, miscegenated bitch who will curse, stab, or poison her love interest in a jealous rage; whereas her Castilian sister, of aristocratic ancestry, is the lady. The well-bred Castilian lady of literature and film is permitted these characteristics not because Anglos respect her ancestry, but because she is usually cast as whiter than her darker Latina sisters of Mexican, Puerto Rican, or Brazilian descent.

Before turning to analysis of specific films it is important to acknowledge that stereotypes of Black and Latina women do have their counterparts in images of White women in film. White women have been maligned, stereotyped, and derogated. White women, however, have the privilege of a more diverse palette of images. In some cases, White women have exercised the prerogative to change their images through the Hollywood "star" system, through "power behind the throne" roles offscreen; and finally through their own work as filmmakers, producers, directors, and writers. Black and Latina women have had nominal access to the informal routes to genuine power; thus they have had less opportunity to redefine their own images.

African American women continued to appear in films as maids and mammies throughout the 1930s, which culminated in Hattie McDaniels receiving an Oscar for her role as a mammy in *Gone With the Wind* (1939). Hollywood musicals became the popular fare of the 1940s because they were a necessary diversion from World War II. Hollywood musicals that launched the careers of both African American and Latin women (leading many to believe that this was their chance to escape the traditional stereotypes in entertainment), were short-lived and spawned new stereotypes.

Lena Horne, initially mistaken for a Latina in her film debut in which she briefly sings and dances in *Panama Hattie* (1942), received accolades for her singing of a Latin song. She subsequently appeared in *Thousands Cheer* (1943); the all-Black *Cabin in the Sky* (1943) as seductress Georgia Brown; and in the all-Black *Stormy Weather* (1943) as Selina, whose rendition of "Stormy Weather" is renowned. MGM, however, did not know what to do with a beautiful African American woman who refused to pass and who rejected scripts that she considered negative to African American images. Although the studio attempted to make her a sex object even in the latter two films, her poise and sophistication transcend the stereotype. Horne was continually cast in limited musical scenes "that Southern distributors, who objected to seeing a black woman on the screen could neatly excise from the films" (Kakutani, 1981, p. 24D).

Although her Latin sisters may have been cast in more films, the 1930s and 1940s images were either zany caricatures or carnal playmates for Anglos. Mexicana, Lupé Velez (1908-1944; née Maria Guadalupe Velez de Villalobos) and Brazilian, Carmen Miranda (1909-1955; née Maria do Carmo Miranda da Cunha) exemplify the former, and Del Río, discussed later, represents the latter. Velez, whose fiery harlot depiction began with the silent film *The Gaucho* (1928), became famous as the zany Latina in *Hot Pepper* (1933), *Strictly Dynamite* (1934), *The Girl From Mexico* (1939), *The Mexican Spitfire's Baby* (1941), *The Mexican Spitfire's Elephant* (1942), and *The Mexican Spitfire's Blessed Event* (1943). Miranda's Hollywood musical films include *That Night in Rio* (1941), *Weekend in Havana* (1941), *Springtime in the Rockies* (1942), and *Copacabana* (1947).

Characterizations of women generally became more derelict after the Hollywood Production Codes, established during the 1930s, were relaxed around 1951. White women played the harlot, the heroine, and also during this era and successive eras appeared as African American and Latina women. But the African American and Latina women were limited to the injurious images—frequently used to demonstrate the contrast between them and the superior White women on the screen. The focus here is on African American and Latina women who have had a reasonable amount of longevity in film and those who have starred in films that are financial successes.[2]

Black people have arduously opposed the demeaning images of their race presented in films since the appearance of D. W. Griffith's *Birth of a Nation* (1915). Now, as then, representatives of the commercial film industry respond to criticism through the assertion that they are reflecting "real life" (Dempsey & Gupta, 1982, p. 68). During the 1950s, however, Black people in "real life" were engaged in the struggle for racial equality and Civil Rights in every American institution. Although African American women such as Rosa Parks, Ella Baker, Daisy Bates, and Autherine Lucy[3] were at the forefront of the struggle for integration, the most publicized image of the African American woman on the movie screen was that of a whore played by Dorothy Dandridge in *Carmen Jones*.[4]

Dorothy Dandridge, an entertainer on the vaudeville circuit from age five, began her film career with performances in *A Day at the Races* (1937) and *Going Places* (1939) and continued through several 1940s musicals up through the 1950s when she appeared in *Tarzan's Peril* (1951) as an abducted African princess. Her performance as Carmen made her a celebrity. *Carmen Jones* (1954) was "the 1950's most lavish, most publicized, and most successful all-Black spectacle" (Bogle, 1988, p. 169). The film's release coincided with the revival of the musical *Porgy and Bess* (1953) featuring Leontyne Price in a highly acclaimed production on international theater tour. Dandridge went on to play Price's filmic counterpart. *Carmen Jones* is a loose interpretation of Bizet's 19th-century opera, which was based on a work by French novelist Prosper Merimée about a Spanish Gypsy peasant girl (Carmen) who works in a tobacco factory in Seville, Spain. In the opera, Carmen is a promiscuous woman who accords toreador Escamillo her sexual favors after having professed her love for the sergeant, don Jose. The screenplay *Carmen Jones*, written by Harry Kleiner, produced and directed by Otto Preminger, with incredibly stereotyped lyrics conceived and perceived to be "Black dialect" (replete with "dese," "dat's," and "dis's") by Oscar Hammerstein II, is transplanted to a parachute factory in the American South during 1943. After "hair-pulling fights between black females, the inevitable barroom brawl, the exaggerated dialect, the animalistic passions and furies of the leads" (Bogle, 1988, p. 169), Carmen Jones meets her demise, provoked by her whorish nature, at the hands of Joe, a student air force pilot whom she has rejected for Husky Miller, a prize fighter. Dandridge's character Carmen Jones embodies two stereotypes of African American women—those of whore and bitch.[5] She is sexually promiscuous, emasculating, and foul-mouthed, and she carries a razor that she uses on one of her co-workers. Pauline Kael's description of Dandridge as "fiery and petulant, with whiplash hips" (Kael, 1982, p. 93) and Donald Bogle's as "animalistic and elemental" (Bogle, 1988, p. 169) are indicative of what critics said of Dandridge's portrayal of Carmen Jones.

The role garnered Dandridge an Academy Award nomination for Best Actress—the first time a Black woman was so honored.[6] Dandridge received a 3-year contract with Twentieth Century Fox Studios under Darryl F. Zanuck that stipulated she would star in one movie a year with a starting salary of $75,000 per picture (Robinson, 1966, p. 74). Several achieved notoriety for their controversial implications of interracial love rather than for her acting ability. In *Island in the Sun* (1957), Dandridge became the first African American actress to be cast opposite a White actor (John Justin) as a serious romantic interest. The cast included James Mason, Joan Fontaine, Joan Collins, and Michael Rennie, and co-starred Harry Belafonte. This was the first of at least three films in which she was so cast. Dandridge was the first African American woman contracted as a leading lady in an American film; as such, according to the formula, she would have to kiss or indicate romantic intimacy with her leading man. The producer vacillated because, according to her manager Earl Mills, he "could not decide how to handle the Caucasian-Negro relationship" (quoted in Robinson, 1966, p. 75). The producers were unwilling to break the stereotypical mold even for the acclaimed actress and legendary beauty. In *Tamango* (1959), for example, she was cast as a scantily clad African slave opposite Curt Jurgens as a sea captain who falls in love with her. The kissing scenes remained in the French release but were removed for the English release. Nevertheless, distribution was hampered in the United States because of a section in the Motion Picture Production Code that prohibited miscegenation on screen. Dandridge completed her three films cast opposite a White actor in each of them, but did not receive further acclaim for her acting until she again played a whore (Bess) in *Porgy and Bess* (1959), for which she received the Golden Globe Award as Best Actress in a Musical. By today's standards Carmen and Bess seem to exemplify characteristics of the liberated woman, but according to the moral expectations of the African American community these women were sexually promiscuous.[7]

In 1965, the first African American actress to grace the cover of *Life* magazine (1954) was found dead from an overdose of antidepressant pills. Dandridge was dedicated to achieving recognition as a dramatic actress. After talking with director Rouben Mamoulian she believed that she would play Cleopatra, but the role went to Elizabeth Taylor. After the many years she had struggled in her career, and after achieving acclaim, there is no doubt that Dandridge was disappointed and perhaps depressed regarding her career. When the Hollywood offers subsided she exclaimed, "I could play the part of an Egyptian or an Indian or a Mexican, and I'm certainly not the only one . . . there are other Negro actors and actresses who can do the same thing" (quoted in Robinson, 1966, p. 80). Dandridge had confidence in herself as an actress—of the roles proffered by Hollywood's movie moguls she said, "more often than not—and more often than I would like—the role calls for a creature of abandon whose desires are stronger than their sense of morality" (quoted in Robinson, 1966, p. 80).

Latinas in commercial films were treated no more equitably than their Black sisters. Hollywood filmmakers projected the same images of the Latinas as those that Pettit (1980) maintains are manifested in the conquest fiction of Anglos. He asserts that:

> Authors of conquest fiction tend to divide all Spanish Mexican women into two categories: A majority of dark-skinned half-breed harlots and a minority of Castilian dark ladies who are actually no darker than the American heroines, and may or may not be virtuous. . . . The one similarity between these two types of women is that both are "naturally" sexual. However, their sexuality takes different forms, each based on color. The sexual behavior of the Castilian dark ladies is carefully programmed and controlled. The sexual behavior of the half-breed women is spontaneous, constant, and entirely lacking in control, if not design. (p. 20)

Hollywood applies this "natural sexual" image to all Latin women—the only distinction is through a false verisimilitude that implies that all Latinas in urban settings are *Puertorriqueña*, and all Latinas in rural settings are Mexicana. White actresses playing Latinas are also limited to the same stereotypes as in the case with Jane Russell as Rio in *The Outlaw* (1943), release delayed until 1947 because of publicized censorship feuds; and Linda Darnell as Chihuchua in *My Darling Clementine* (1946); Jennifer Jones as Pearl Chavez, a half-breed whorish wretch in *Duel in the Sun* (1946); and even with Lena Horne's character Claire Quintana in *Death of a Gunfighter* (1969); they were women of easy virtue, prostitutes, madames, or concubines. Latina actresses should have had little trouble securing roles that would permit them to play a greater latitude of minority roles as well as White or "generic" women's roles, because they could "pass" for women of other nationalities. As George Hadley-Garcia wrote in 1990, negative film images of Latinas continue to persist because of "the sexism which overlaps the standard racism and xenophobia" (Hadley-Garcia, 1990, p. 111). Moreover, when Latina actresses are cast in roles depicting other nationalities, although these roles imply diversity, frequently they are characterizations of members of another outcast minority group. Mexican actress Lupé Velez once said in reference to roles in which she had been cast, that "she had portrayed Chinese, Eskimos, Japanese, squaws, Hindus . . . Malays, and Javanese" (Woll, 1980, p. 60).

The roles designated to Delores Del Río, one of Hollywood's first Latina stars, exemplifies this practice. Although she occasionally played the aristocratic Castilian, she was more frequently stereotyped. She, too, began as an actress during the silent screen era in the 1920s, playing "exotic heroines." Throughout the 1920s, 1930s, and into the 1940s, Del Río portrayed a French peasant in *What Price Glory* (1926), a Russian peasant in *Resurrection* (1927), a half-Indian in *Ramona* (1928), and a Polynesian in *Bird of Paradise* (1932) (Gaiter, 1983, p. 23D). She also played the role of Carmen in *Loves of Carmen* (1927), of which critic Mordaunt Hall (1927) wrote: "The alluring Ms. Del Río with her bright eyes, pretty lips and lithe figure, gives a decidedly unrestrained portrait of the faithless creature." Between 1925 and 1943, Del Río was featured in at least 14 Hollywood films. During the 1930s and 1940s she appeared in *The Girl of the Rio* (1932) as a cantina dancer in this successful film that raised the ire of the Mexican government, which leveled a formal protest for its derogatory representation of Mexican law; and in *In Caliente* (1935) a sequel to *The Girl of the Rio* with the same cast and the same opposition from the Mexican government. *Flying Down to Rio* (1932) features Del Río as a Brazilian once again generating controversy because she sports a two-piece bikini; and African American actress Etta Moten as a dark-skinned South American who sang "The Carioca." Del Río, who insisted upon being recognized as a

Mexican in her publicity releases, tired of these stereotypical roles and returned to Mexico during the 1940s where she continued to perform on stage and screen and was instrumental in the founding of the Mexican film industry (Gaiter, 1983, p. 23D). She starred in John Ford's *The Fugitive* (1947), filmed in Mexico, as a Chicana mother of an illegitimate child who sacrifices her life to save the Anglo priest (Henry Fonda); and resurfaced in Hollywood in two roles as a Native American. The first, as the mother of Elvis Presley in *Flaming Star* (1960) and in *Cheyenne Autumn* (1964), John Ford's "apology to the Indians" in which Native Americans are decimated but in a more "sympathetic" manner.

Rita Moreno, a *Puertorriqueña* and who, like Dandridge, also appeared on the cover of *Life* in 1954, began her career as a film actress in *So Young, So Brave* (1950) and continued to play stereotyped roles similar to those of Del Río's. Her film credits include *Pagan Love Song* (1950), *Latin Lovers* (1953), and *Untamed* (1955); in 1956 she received critical recognition as a talented actress for her role as the Siamese Princess Tuptim in *The King and I.* During this period of her acting career, Moreno says that she portrayed "the Indian lady with feathers in her head or the Latin lady who's always demeaned and never winds up with a man, especially if he's a white man" (Bermel, 1965, p. 38). Moreno's comment reverberates with the Anglos' fear of "genetic pollution" referenced above; the same fear they have of the African Americans intermingling with White women.[8]

After a 4-year hiatus, during which Moreno performed on the legitimate stage, she returned to Hollywood in 1961 in the role of Anita in *West Side Story.* As Anita, Moreno portrays a *Puertorriqueña* who is the razor-tongued, street-wise friend of Maria (a suntanned Natalie Wood!) The story focuses on Maria, a *Puertorriqueña* who has just arrived in Spanish Harlem from Puerto Rico. Anita warns Maria of the dangers of falling in love with a White boy, which Maria promptly does when she falls in love with Tony's close friend Riff, the leader of the Jets. Their relationship ignites the fermenting feud between rival street gangs, the Jets (White boys) and the Sharks (*Puertorriqueño*), advancing the conflict in the film.

There are both overt and subliminal messages of ubiquitous promiscuity regarding the character of the *Puertorriqueña* in the film. The constancy of derogatory lyrics with pretentious accents (as in *Carmen Jones* and *Porgy and Bess*; this time in conceived Puerto Rican lyrics by Stephen Sondheim), compounded with decidedly risqué costumes for the era in which the film was produced, heighten this promiscuity. The lyrics of "America," a duet sung by Rosalia and Anita, contain both positive and negative descriptions of Puerto Rico but the negative descriptions prevail. The introduction to this song implies that the long Hispanic names are ridiculous and continues in the following pejorative manner: "Always the population growin'/And the money owing/

And the babies crying/Hundreds of people in each room!" The diffuse dialogue in negative reference to large Hispanic families subliminally reinforces the stereotyped beliefs held by mainstream America. The image of the promiscuous Latina is effectively buttressed by placing Anita on the side of her bed skimpily clad in undergarments as she suggestively sings: "Anita's gonna get her kicks/Tonight/We'll have our private little mix /Tonight/He'll walk in hot and tired,/poor dear./ Don't matter if he's tired,/As long as he's here/Tonight!"

Costuming women in red in both theater and film productions is universally synonymous with "loose women" (see Note 5) and there is certainly a proliferation of red in the costumes of the Latinas in this film. Presumably red is reflecting the fire smoldering inside of the character wearing it. Maria's virtuous White "coming out" dress flaunts a red waist sash; the majority of the *Puertorriqueña* wear red; and the lavish crinoline slips underneath Anita's black "mourning" skirt are red (which are revealed when some of the Jets attempt to rape her); and Maria wears a red dress in the final scene of the film. The color red combined with low-cut, suggestive blouses and tight skirts exemplifies the attire of the whore, and its repeated use implies that this mode of dress is indigenous to Latinas. And finally, the conclusion pays homage to all of the earlier prototypes of films containing interracial relationships—the Latina cannot wed the Anglo—she or he in this case must die.

Costumes and lyrics are only two of the negative images presented in this film, but they are two of the strongest subliminal production elements that serve to lull an audience into a false sense of reality. In both film and theater, music and color are utilized to manipulate moods and attitudes. The majority of the Anglo critics hailed this film as a masterpiece, with one notable dissenter—Pauline Kael (1966). They did not comment on the negative stereotypes; perhaps because they believed—as critic Stanley Kaufman believed—that "we are seeing street gangs for the first time as they really are" and by extension Latinas (quoted in Kael, 1966, p. 131). A positive statement such as this can be made without any personal knowledge of Puerto Ricans or gang members because the stereotyped images are imprinted in the spectator's subconscious. The people whose images were negatively affected did complain, however. Although "The Puerto Rican Action Coalition" implored Paramount to remove the "racist" film, *West Side Story*, from circulation, Paramount President Frank Yablans refused. The film continued to play throughout the United States, and Hollywood honored it with 10 Academy Awards, including one for Best Color Costume Design. Rita Moreno received an Oscar for Best Supporting Actress for her role as Anita (Pickard, 1977, pp. 175-176). Moreno subsequently played a stripper in *Marlowe* (1969) and Alan Arkin's mistress in *Poppi* (1969), while simultaneously continuing her illustrious stage career.

Moreno is the only woman to have received an award in every media—the Academy Award, the Emmy, and the Tony.

American cinema has presented a similarly distorted picture of the African American family[9] structure, bolstered by "documentation" from sociological studies. This distortion has led to a corresponding distortion of the depiction of African American women. From the latter half of the 1960s through the 1970s many Black Americans gradually shifted from an integrationist to a separatist ideology. The separatist ideology is sometimes referred to as the "Black Power Movement," which "meant rejection of the white man's images of fun, beauty, profit, and virtue, replacing them with black images . . . was cultural, political, social, religious, and economic" (Berry & Blassingame, 1982, p. 419). The contemporary feminist movement evolved almost simultaneously, and African American women were involved in both movements. These activities coincided with a spate of sociologically based studies that argue that the Black family is dominated by women and that this domination is responsible for the deterioration of the Black family in America. Although many Black men and women verbally denounced these assertions, many embraced them. Paula Giddings (1984) explains:

> Some Black intellectuals of the time were not content merely to relegate Black women to the political—or biological—back seat of the movement. Sociologists, psychiatrists, and the male literati accused Black women of castrating not only their men but their sons; of having low self-esteem; of faring badly when compared to the virtues of white women. Black women were unfeminine, they said; how could they expect the unflagging loyalty and protection of Black men? (p. 319)

These seeds of derision sown among African American men and women blossomed on the silver screen during the late 1960s through the mid-1970s and have resurfaced to haunt us in the ongoing heated debates about the Steven Spielberg adaptation of Alice Walker's novel *The Color Purple* (1984).[10] The sociological theories provided both Black and White males with justification for their maltreatment of Black women. African American men such as Amiri Baraka, Eldridge Cleaver, and Malcolm X espoused male domination of women (albeit the latter's attitude was tempered by his religious beliefs). These attitudes were reflected in film through the exploitation of African American women by both Black and White males. White males more often than not cast Black women primarily as concubines, prostitutes and superbitches, achieving monetary success from the films. Black men, portraying pimps and pushers, exploited, brutalized, and destroyed their Black women on the silver screen for all to see, even though for many it was a one-film deal.

Lena Horne, just as Del Río, returned to Hollywood film during this era, after a 12-year hiatus from the medium. Horne resurfaced in

Universal Pictures' *Death of a Gunfighter* (1969) as Claire Quintana, a Latina and Frank Patch's (Richard Widmark) concubine. Claire Quintana runs a brothel, wants to run away with Patch, and insists that he does not have to marry her. Patch, despised by the townspeople, decides to marry her but (in concert with its filmic predecessors) is killed just before the wedding. Horne plays the role with dignity, as she had in earlier films that depicted her as a sex object. Bogle has said of Horne that "she always proved herself too much the lady to be believable as the slut" (Bogle, 1989, p. 127). Horne, whose beauty established her as "the first Negro sex symbol," said that because people saw her perform in cabarets as well as film, the audience could vicariously "entertain the possibility of involving themselves imaginatively in miscegenation" (Kakutani, 1981, p. D1). Twenty years later, as Claire Quintana, Horne's first serious dramatic role, she appears to be fulfilling the same function.

This film was followed by *Slaves* (1969), a remake of *Uncle Tom's Cabin*, in which vocalist Dionne Warwick made her debut as Cassy, the malevolent slavemaster, MacKay's (Stephen Boyd), concubine. MacKay collects African Art and spouts African History and dresses his African concubine in the finest African gowns and jewelry. Cassy, adorned in African gowns and jewelry, stumbles around drunk from imbibing rum continually, while hissing hostile remarks at her master MacKay, whom she appears to despise. The characterization vaguely implies that although she appears to enjoy her status, she despises MacKay as a White man and all that he represents. These scenes suggest that African American co-writer, novelist John O. Killens, was in conflict with what he wanted to write versus what was expected. The concubine character, however, remains intact.

The *Liberation of L. B. Jones* (Columbia, 1970), was the vehicle that launched Lola Falana, a vocalist and dancer, into film. Falana starred as Emma Jones, wife of the wealthiest Black man in Somerset, TN, Lord Byron Jones (Roscoe Lee Browne), who publicly humiliates her husband by becoming the concubine of Willie Joe Worth (Anthony Zerbe), a red-neck cop. She discontentedly lounges around (like Cassy) in her own bourgeois home half-clad in sexy lingerie, reading movie magazines. Canby refers to Falana as being "like an all-black Jean Harlow . . . an admirable, not entirely conventional slut" (Canby, 1970, 6C: 1).

Melinda (Vonetta McGee) in the film *Melinda* (Metro-Goldwyn-Mayer, 1972) is the concubine of a White Mafia boss (Paul Stevens). She is slashed to death early in the film, providing the motivation for narcissistic Frankie J. Parker (Calvin Lockhart) to avenge her murder by karate kicking and chopping his way through hoodlums for the remainder of the film. Although Lonne Elder III (an accomplished playwright and screenwriter for the Oscar-nominated *Sounder*) wrote the screenplay and Hugh A. Robertson was the director, the two Black men alleged that the White movie moguls "kept pushing for all sex and violence" (Mitchener, 1975, p. 243). Veteran actress Rosalind Cash (Terry

Davis) who played a respectable business executive, contends that she vigorously fought to develop a character that was more than a "black whore" (Ward, 1977, p. 223). The Terry Davis character indicated that African American women are business women also. This film was popular among African Americans who had complained about the "blaxploitation" fare. It grossed $1,560,000 in domestic film rentals (Parish & Hill, 1989, p. 216).

In each of these early blaxploitation films it is apparent that the writers were in a quandary as to what to do with women. The shallow characters are more illustrative of Barbie Dolls (her first appearance was in 1959)—engaged in nothing more than maintaining their beauty, revealing flesh while changing their clothes, and developing variations of seductive poses—rather than complex, loving human beings. Manifestly, the filmmakers of these films recognized the marketability of beautiful Black women on the screen and that their beauty had to be combined with sex. After several decades of mammies, maids, tragic mulattoes, and matriarchs, however, they did not know quite what to do with this combination. The subsequent phase of blaxploitation temporarily resolved this confusion.

Blaxploitation refers to films that feature predominantly Black casts, are sometimes authored by Black writers and guided by Black directors, but always hastily produced on a shoestring budget by White-owned Hollywood studios that earn millions of dollars from their enterprise. Earlier films in this genre featured Black men in the leading roles functioning in a male metier (e.g., *Shaft*, 1971; *Superfly*, 1972; *Across 110th Street*, 1972; and *The Mack*, 1973). Women in these films were incidental; they created the "ambience" of the ghetto as prostitutes, whores, and drug addicts. With the arrival of *Coffy* (1973) starring Pam Grier, however, women became the focal point and the next phase of blaxploitation combined beauty and sex with violence that engendered sexploitation films and the arrival of the "superbitch."

The superbitch embodies characteristics similar to those ascribed to the matriarch (dominating woman) combined with the description of the bitch delineated above. Pam Grier achieved stardom as the superbitch supreme throughout the first half of the 1970s. She appeared on the covers of both *Ms.*—which celebrated her as a liberated woman—and *New York*, which exalted her as a sex goddess (Bogle, 1989, p. 399). Grier, initially a switchboard operator for American International Pictures, eventually grossed millions for this company after becoming their contract star. She was featured in more than a dozen films, the majority of which were produced by AIP, brandishing such titles as *Coffy* (1973), *Black Mama, White Mama* (1973), *Foxy Brown* (1974), *Sheba, Baby* (1975), and *Friday Foster* (1975). Grier starred as a nurse, a prostitute, a private investigator, and a glamour magazine photographer who sports very sexy attire and literally castrates men on the screen. In *Foxy Brown* alone, Grier thrashes a call girl in a bar, slashes the throat of another woman, cremates two men to death, and castrates a third and delivers his genitals in a pickle jar to his womanfriend as a warning. She strutted her sexiness through the decadent ghetto world of pimps, pushers, and prostitutes, variously armed with profanity, a spear gun, and a sawed-off shotgun, the tools of her trade that facilitated her cleansing the community of these seedy elements. It didn't matter what Grier's slated role was, her character type remained the same—whorish superbitch who bedded with anyone including her professed enemies. When AIP's box-office dollars for Grier movies began to dwindle in 1975, her contract was not renewed (Parish & Hill, 1989, p. 145).

The Pam Grier movies exploited sex and women during the era of the contemporary women's liberation movement. The creation of this machisma character provided soft pornography for men and a vicarious pleasure and satisfaction for some feminists who believed these images were positive examples of equitable casting. These films represented the female counterparts to the popular male films such as *Shaft* (1971), *Superfly* (1972), and *The Mack* (1973); the audience is told in the latter that "a pimp is only as good as his product—and his product is women." This statement is visually reinforced as the audience is bombarded with the display of Black women as whores and prostitutes who are referred to and addressed as "bitches." Fortunately, the popularity of these films was ephemeral. Unfortunately, with the death of blaxploitation films, Black actresses became unemployed. They were no longer in demand because the industry was unwilling to cast them in any but the dehumanized sex-object roles.

Indeed, commercial films of the 1980s have neglected to provide alternatives to these images as evidenced in the film *Fort Apache, the Bronx* (1981), where men refer to women as "bitches" and "fuckin' sluts," and that features Pam Grier, who received critical praise for her role as Charlotte, a drugged-out prostitute who wanders through a decadent community populated with pushers, pimps, prostitutes, and arsonists in the South Bronx, where she shoots two cops at close range during the film's opening—and randomly slits the jugulars of men with a razor blade concealed under her tongue for no apparent reason, until the middle of the film when she blunders and is killed by her would-be victim. Grier's absence is inconsequential to the community as well as to the film's progression.

Rachel Ticotin stars as Isabelle, a *Puertorriqueña* nurse with whom Murphy (Paul Newman) falls in love—Isabelle, an intelligent, clean-cut nurse who could have become a doctor if racial discrimination had not aborted her education. Upon her initial encounter with Murphy he flirts—she responds with an assertive "I'm not that kind of woman" monologue. By 12 midnight, however, dressed in a red outfit, she not only goes to dinner with him (upon her request), but to bed as well. Isabelle's character further declines when Murphy discovers that she is a heroin addict. When Murphy confronts her with his discovery, Isabelle replies, "I get high every once in awhile, just like everybody else—smack is like a vacation for me." She dies from an overdose of pure heroin supplied by an *Puertorriqueño* pusher angry because Isabelle is dating a cop. In a superfluous macabre scene, she wanders in a heroin stupor down the street in her pajamas, providing the audience with gratuitous sex until she arrives at the hospital and dies. Isabelle's performance does not end, however, until grief-stricken Murphy pulls her off the examining table and drags her corpse around the emergency room rejecting her death. The parading of her body in pajamas by Murphy reinforces his image as the good guy and Isabelle's as the bad girl responsible for her own ruin. The conclusion, once again, resonates with the fear of miscegenation—Murphy or Isabelle had to leave or die, thus eliminating any possibility of validating their relationship. And of course, the Anglo is conscience-free.

In addition to depicting a Black woman as a castrating, addicted prostitute (Grier), a Latina as an addict, whore (Ticotin), *Fort Apache, the Bronx* sustains the stereotype of the promiscuous Latina who produces large families that are crammed into small apartments. Whereas it was stated in the lyrics of *West Side Story*, here it is expressed visually in one scene in which Murphy and Corelli (Ken Wahl) arrive at an apartment to deliver a baby. During this scene, the camera tracks Murphy and Corelli through a railroad flat, where in each room there are men and women cavorting on a bed with a crucifix (icon used repeatedly in film to indicate Latin religiosity) prominently displayed above each bed, until finally they arrive in the end room where they discover a 14-year-old Puertorriqueña with rosary beads wrapped around her fingers who has kept her coat on for 9 months to conceal her pregnancy from her mother.

The producers provided copies of the script to community groups and leaders in the South Bronx and although this group objected to several scenes in the script, just as with *West Side Story*, it was released unaltered (Raab, 1981, p. C6). Black and Hispanic people formed a coalition (Committee Against Fort Apache) initially to abort the filming project and later to halt the showing of the film in movie theaters. Critics such as Vincent Canby (1981), however, found the film to be "entertaining and very moving" (p. 6C); and Pauline Kael stated that the accusation made by the opposition that the film is "exploitative and stereotypes Blacks and Puerto Ricans as 'savages, criminals, and degenerates'—seem way off the beam. The movie is clearly an expression of disgust at racism" (Kael, 1982, p. 105).

The 1980s film season for African American and Latina women concluded almost as it began with a sexploitation bill-of-fare launched by *She's Gotta Have It* (1986), a Spike Lee enterprise featuring Tracy Camila Johns as Nola Darling who—under Lee's interpretation of a sexually liberated female (she chooses multiple sex partners)—is prone throughout the film, and Opal the lesbian with all of the homophobic stereotyped characteristics;[11] and continued in Lee's *School Daze* (1988); *Action Jackson* (Lorimar, 1988), with vocalist Vanity as Sydney Ash a heroin-addicted-concubine to the sinister White male Peter Dellaplane, who shoots her up before he "fucks" her; *Harlem Nights* (1989), an Eddie Murphy enterprise in which women were addressed as bitches in almost every scene, with veteran vocalist and actress Della Reese as a boisterous, foul-mouthed brothel madame who among other sense-less antics engages in fisticuffs with Murphy in a vicious fight-to-finish; and finally hearkening back to vestiges of the 19th-century "good old days," the talented Whoopi Goldberg (who won the 1991 Oscar for Best Supporting Actress for *Ghost*; as a contemporary mammy, minus the headrag) appeared as Clara, a Jamaican "maid/mammy" in *Clara's Heart* (1988).

Latina actresses were more difficult to ascertain in the contempo-rary film industry because their numbers are scant and because some are cross-cast. Presumably there is a younger generation of Latina actresses who like their predecessors have changed their names, and there are many women who are not easily identifiable as Latinas. The women who attained celebrity status were white-skinned; Rita Hayworth (née Margarita Cansino), and Racquel Welch (née Raquel Tejada), whose anonymity permitted them a "greater variety of screen roles and iden-tities" (Cortés, 1985, pp. 99, 100; Hadley-Garcia, 1990, p. 178).

Although Rachel Ticotin continues in roles that are non-generic regarding race, she continues as nothing more than a male appendage. She was Melina, a prostitute in *Total Recall* (1990); Kim Brandon, single mother and woman-friend of Rollie (Bryan Brown) in *The Deadly Art of Illusion* (1991); Grace, concubine to the dope-pusher, but actually an undercover detective in *One Good Cop* (1991). Incidentally, the popu-lar 1986 science fiction film *Aliens* featured Private Vasquez, a fierce machine-gun-toting Latina (possibly a flirtation with gender-bending?) who was very impressive as being equal to the boys when it came to combat. The role, however, was played by a suntanned White actress (Jenette Goldstein). It is still not clear as to why this character had to be Latina, and since she was, considering the paucity of roles, why was a Latina not cast?

The 1990s do not envisage brighter horizons for Aframerican and Latina women. The options of roles that Aframerican and Latina ac-tresses are offered continue to illustrate what James Baldwin (1975) said of the intentional misrepresentations in *Carmen Jones* 40 years ago:

> *Carmen Jones* has Negro bodies before the camera and Negroes are associated in the public mind with sex. Since to lighter races, darker races always seem to have an aura of sexuality, this fact is not distressing in itself. What is distressing is the conjecture this movie leaves one with as what Americans take sex to be. (p. 93)

Commercially successful films continue to manifest this ignorance. Spike Lee's *Do the Right Thing* (Universal, 1989), in which Latina Rosie Perez ("all you do is curse," Tina) is used only as a sex object (as women are continually used in his subsequent films); *A Rage in Harlem* (1991) features Robin Givens—replete with red dress—as Imabelle, a prostitute (whose rendition has been compared to Dorothy Dandridge in *Carmen Jones*) redeemed by Forrest Whitaker; *New Jack City* (1991), where Africamericans in addition to fulfilling their sexual expectations are accorded parity with males through their ability to unblinkingly blow someone's head off at close range with an Uzi (reminiscent of Pam Grier's 1970s' characters); to name a few.

The same year that Black and Hispanic people formed the Committee Against Fort Apache, the NAACP announced that, "1980 had been the worst year for black actors and actresses since 1970" (Sterritt, 1983, p. 12), and withheld the Image Awards (Black version of the Oscar) for Best Actress after it was realized that Cicely Tyson was the only actress who played in a role large enough to qualify for nomination (*Bustin' Loose*, 1981). There were no Black actresses in a leading role in 1982, and in 1983, in an act of desperation, the Image Award was bestowed on Jennifer Beals—an actress whose African American heritage was publicly ambiguous—for her part in *Flashdance* (certainly not a Black film). Her nomination was accompanied by an explanation from Willis Edwards, then-president of the NAACP's Hollywood Beverly Hills branch, who maintained "that the Image Awards were created to honor individuals—black or white—who present a positive image for minorities" (London, 1983, p. 1). The 1990 Image Award for the category of Best Actress was suspended because there were not enough leading performances to adjudicate (Givens, 1991, p. 38). Although 29% of the feature films cast women, only 10% of principal roles in both film and television were awarded to African American women (Givens, 1991, p. 36).

There is a glimmer of hope in Matty Rich's *Straight Out of Brooklyn* (1991) and John Singleton's *Boyz N the Hood* (Columbia, 1991), two films that, although focused on men, portray African American women realistically. The former sensitively addresses the complexities surrounding wife battering and child abuse; the latter presents diverse images of Africamericans. Among the characters represented in *Boyz N the Hood* are the responsible single mother who recognizes the necessity of a father-son relationship and delivers the adolescent to his father, completes her master's degree, and opens her own business; the single mother who attempts to raise two sons but errs in lavishing affection on one to the neglect of the other; the "crackhead" mother who's toddler is frequently wandering the street in traffic; and finally a refreshing young high school woman who verbalizes that she will not become sexually active because of her man-friend's demands but that she will determine when she is ready. The latter character is contrasted with a young woman of the same age who hangs with the "Boyz" but nevertheless articulates her malcontent with the way in which they reference women when she asks "why we always gotta be bitches, hoes and hootches?" Rae Dawn Chong and Jennifer Beals are at least two African American actresses frequently cross-cast. And although cross-casting on the one hand is positive, on the other, cross-casting solely light-skinned actresses hearkens back to earlier filmic practices that exclude the darker skinned sisters. The same is true for Latina actresses. Del Río, Miranda, and Velez were vocal about their Latin heritage, there were darker Latinas whose careers were truncated because of their color, and finally there were those who could pass.

For the most part, attention to the plight of the image of Black women in film has been precipitated by Black women, such as Ruby Dee and Alice Childress who long ago published articles addressing the issue of the Black women's image in literature and the visual arts; and Saundra Sharp who maintained in 1982 that young Black actresses were still being offered "four or five lines on a stupid comedy show, a bit part as a prostitute or a dope addict, or straight T and A" (Dempsey & Gupta, 1982, p. 69). Her words continue to be echoed in 1991 by a new generation of actresses who lament the absence of diverse roles for women of color: "when you are an ethnic woman of color, you play the hooker or you don't work" (Givens, 1991, p. 40).

Africamerican and Latina actresses continue to struggle alone—making achievements, winning awards, but alone—there is no support system, and "Hollyweird" allows only one "success" at a time. Like their foremothers Nina Mae McKinney, Freddie Washington, Lena Horne, Dorothy Dandridge, Cicely Tyson, Delores Del Río, Carmen Miranda, Lupé Velez, and Maria Montez (to whom Pam Grier has been compared) whose beauty is renowned, a prerequisite for Hollywood films, and who have won numerous accolades against all odds, to maintain gainful employment in the motion picture industry. There is a paucity of roles for women in general, but there are even fewer for African American and Latina actresses. Whereas White women have taken the opportunity to portray African American and Latina women—among them Jeanne Crain, Janet Leigh, Linda Darnell, Jennifer Jones, Susan Kohner, and recently Jenette Goldstein—"women of color" are not offered the option to play themselves and certainly not to play a White women or even a role believed to be a White woman's. Finally, while White Hollywood simultaneously celebrates Meryl Streep, Demi Moore, Julia Roberts, Melanie Griffith, Jodie Foster, and others, only one African American actress at a time is considered a "box-office attraction." "Hollyweird" currently recognizes Whoopi Goldberg (who has had an uphill battle in "tinsel town"), but remains ignorant of Sheryl Lee Ralph, Lynn Whitfield, Vanessa Bell Calloway, and Kimberly Russell.

Today when Black women writers are acclaimed for literary works (Alice Walker, Toni Morrison, and Terry McMillan—all three appeared on *The New York Times* Best Seller's List simultaneously in 1992), and when women of color own their own publishing houses (e.g., Kitchen Table: Women of Color Press), are publishing books internationally and multiculturally (*Charting the Journey: Writings by Black and Third World Women; Women's Fiction From Latin America: Selections From Twelve Contemporary Authors;* and *Bridges of Power,* among many other titles), there is no indication from the Hollywood film industry that complex stories about Africamericans and Latinas are imminent.

Films have long ceased to be innocuous entertainment. In fact, when dealing with Africamericans and Latinas, Hollywood has never been apolitical.[12] Hollywood designs and distributes entertainment for the dominant culture. Art has been abused for the sake of maintaining the status quo. After all, the business of Hollywood is illusion. Lamentably there is no distinction made between mythology and actuality. Films that have been released irrespective of opposition from minorities impart a clear message that the White-controlled studios, distribution centers, and critics don't give a damn about the derogatory images of minorities if there is a profit to be made in those images. The film industry can no longer be permitted to be irresponsible; they must be held culpable for their decision making. The reason stereotypes continue to abound is, as Gordon W. Allport (1981) states, "they are socially supported, continually revived and hammered in, by our media of mass-communication—by novels, short stories, newspaper items, movies, stage, radio and television" (p. 200). Western society continually espouses the need for universality in art. But this has become an excuse to give the public a homogenized universality that appeals solely to White people—if it deviates from their cultural understanding, then it has no validity. This is a prime example of cultural genocide. American film has buttressed institutional teachings of mainstream America to invalidate all that is different, as well as to convince the "different" that they and their culture are invalid.

Although White Hollywood exercises the luxury of remakes (often of bad films), the diverse stories of African American and Latin women have not been told even once. There are African American and Latina independent filmmakers telling those stories. Women such as Julie Dash, Michelle Parkerson, Allile Sharon Larkin, Ayoka Chenzira, the late Kathleen Collins, Leslie Harris, Marta N. Bautis, Sylvia Morales, Pilar Rodriguez, Teresa 'Osa', and many others have been recording the African American women's experiences for more than a decade, without acknowledgment from Hollywood—and with nominal acknowledgment from critics.[13] And their stories will survive just as their cultures have survived in spite of the multifarious means employed by Anglos to nullify them.

Notes

1. Films featuring the half-breed Latina character include *The Outlaw* (1943) and *My Darling Clementine* (1946); films on the "tragic mulatto" include *The Debt* (1912), *The Octoroon* (1913), *Imitation of Life* (1934 & 1959), and *Pinky* (1949).

2. For an indication of box-office returns on contemporary Black films see Parish and Hill (1989). It is important to note that with the advent of videotapes some of these films are still reaping profits. Pam Grier's films are excellent examples; released in 1988, the package was promoted as "sex for the price of five."

3. Rosa Parks refused to relinquish her bus seat to a White man, precipitating the Montgomery Bus Boycott and the beginning of the Civil Rights Movement; Ella Baker, an activist and Coordinator of Dr. Martin Luther King, Jr.'s, Southern Christian Leadership Conference (SCLC); Daisy Bates, president of the Arkansas National Association for the Advancement of Colored People (NAACP) chapter and publisher of the *Arkansas State Press*, led the integration of Central High School during the 1957 school integration crisis in Little Rock, AR; and Autherine Lucy, the first African American to desegregate the University of Alabama at Tuscaloosa.

4. Dorothy Dandridge had been in films since the early 1940s, but the role that gained her recognition as a movie star was that of Carmen Jones in the film of the same title.

5. Indeed, Donald Bogle describes how Dandridge outfitted herself and altered her behavior in Otto Preminger's office to convince him that the role belonged to her, because Preminger believed Dandridge was "too sleek and sophisticated for the role of a whore" (Bogle, 1988, p. 168).

6. Hattie McDaniel won an Academy Award for Best Supporting Actress of 1939, for her "mammy" performance in *Gone With the Wind*. Beah Richards was nominated in 1967 for Best Supporting Actress in *Guess Who's Coming to Dinner*. The second African American woman to receive an award in the history of the Academy is Whoopie Goldberg, who won for Best Supporting Actress in 1991. Incidentally, Goldberg plays an intermediary to the White stars in the film *Ghost*.

7. Other films characterizing Black women in this manner were the remake of *Imitation of Life* (1959), in which a White actress portrays the irrepressibly sexual and fiery, tragic mulatto Sarah Jane whose Black blood lures her to degraded occupations and compels her to hide in her room engaged in licentious gyrations to African American jazz. Juanita Moore, who plays Sarah Jane's mother, won an Oscar nomination for Best Supporting Actress for her subservient performance to Claudette Colbert in this 1959 remake of the 1934 classic based on the novel by Fannie Hurst, a White woman. Although the stereotypical names have been changed from Aunt Delilah to Annie and from Peola to Sarah Jane, the negative stereotypes remain unchanged. *Sapphire* (1959), a British-made film scripted by Janet Green, a White woman, also features the tragic mulatto theme in which the murdered Sapphire is found dead at the film's beginning, dressed in a red petticoat that does not match the rest of her luxurious lingerie. During the ensuing investigation by White detectives to establish the murderer, it is determined that Sapphire was a Negro passing for White and engaged to be married to a White man; she clandestinely frequented Black hangouts and had secret friendships with Black men. *Melinda* (MGM, 1972), *The Liberation of L. B. Jones* (1970).

8. The rationale for the lynching of Black men that occurred in the United States during the 19th and up until the mid-20th century was predicated on this fear.

9. Independent Black filmmakers have made some positive and realistic family films, most notably *The Learning Tree* (1969), by Gordon Parks (a Hollywood exception, based on Park's childhood); *The Sky is Grey* (1972), by Stan Lathan; *The Killer of Sheep* (1977); *Bless Their Little Hearts* (1984), by Billy Woodberry; *To Sleep With Anger* (1990), by Charles Burnett; *Daughters of the Dust* (1991), by Julie Dash; and *Nothing But A Man* (1963), a White independent film by Michael Roemer. Also see the special issue of *The Nation: Scapegoating the Black Family, Black Women Speak* (1989, July 24/31). A diverse group of Black women, including educators, legislators, and other professional women, address issues concerning the Black family.

10. Although there were many, Tony Brown's articles and Minister Louis Farrakahn's tapes were perhaps the most critically severe in their attacks (see Tony Brown, 1986). This syndicate column, in addition to thanking the Academy of Motion Picture Arts and Sciences "for not rewarding Purple People for their lack of self-love," levels scurrilous personal attacks against Whoopi Goldberg, Oprah Winfrey, and Margaret Avery. In addition, Minister Louis Farrakahn took time out of his busy schedule to produce a long-running commercial audiotape that derides *The Color Purple* and also levels personal attacks against the artists.

11. Masculine lesbians, only meaner, had already been presented in Pam Grier's earlier films, *The Big Doll House* (1971), and *Black Mama, White Mama* (1973).

12. Nor, for that matter, films depicting any group of color—including Indians, Asians, and others. For an introduction to this issue see Miller (1980).

13. For a more comprehensive listing see Michelle Parkerson (1990).

References

Allport, Gordon W. (1981). *The nature of prejudice* [25th anniv. ed.]. Reading, MA: Addison-Wesley.

Anzaldúa, Gloria. (1990). Bridge, drawbridge, sandbar or island: Lesbians-of-color Hacienda Alianzas. In Lisa Albrecht & Rose M. Brewer (Eds.), *Bridges of power: Women's multicultural alliances* (pp. 216-231). Philadelphia: New Society Publishers.

Atille, Martina, & Blackwood, Maureen. (1986). Black women and representation. In Charlotte Brunsdon (Ed.), *Films for women* (pp. 202-208). London: British Film Institute.

Baldwin, James. (1975). Carmen Jones: The dark is light enough. In Lindsay Patterson (Ed.), *Black films and film-makers: A comprehensive anthology from stereotype to superhero* (pp. 235-246). New York: Dodd, Mead.

Bates, Karen Grigsby. (1991, July 14). "They've gotta have us." *The New York Times Magazine*, pp. 15+.

Bermal, Albert. (1965, April). Getting out from under an image. *Harper's Magazine*, pp. 38+.

Berry, Mary Frances, & Blassingame, John W. (1982). *Long memory: The Black experience in America.* New York: Oxford University Press.

Blackwood, Maureen. (1986). Stereotypes: Beyond the "mammie." In Charlotte Brunsdon (Ed.), *Films for women.* London: British Film Institute.

Bogle, Donald. (1988). *Blacks in American films and television: An illustrated encyclopedia.* New York: Garland.

Bogle, Donald. (1989). *Toms, coons, mulattoes, mammies, and bucks: An interpretive history of Blacks in American films* (Expanded ed.). New York: Continuum.

Brinton, Crane, Christopher, John B., & Wolff, Robert Lee. (1964). *Civilization in the west.* Englewood Cliffs, NJ: Prentice Hall.

Brown, Tony. (1986, April 5). Whoopi for the Academy Awards. *The Indianapolis Recorder*, p. 11.

Canby, Vincent. (1970, March 19). The liberation of L. B. Jones. *The New York Times*, p. 60:1.

Canby, Vincent. (1981, February 6). Screen: "Fort Apache, the Bronx," with Paul Newman. *The New York Times*, p. 6C.

Corliss, Richard. (1984, October 1). Blues for Black actors. *Time*, pp. 75-76.

Cortés, Carlos E. (1985). Chicanas in film: History of an image. In *Chicano cinema: Research, reviews, and resources* (pp. 98-100). Binghamton, NY: Bilingual Review/Press.

Dempsey, Michael, & Gupta, Udayan. (1982, April). Hollywood's color problem. *American Film*, pp. 66-70.

Gaiter, Dorothy J. (1983, April 13). Dolores Del Rio, 77, is dead; Film star in U. S. and Mexico. *The New York Times*, p. 23D.

Giddings, Paula. (1984). *When and where I enter: The impact of Black women on race and sex in America.* New York: William Morrow.

Givens, Robin. (1991, June). Why are Black actresses having such a hard time in Hollywood? *Ebony*, pp. 36-40.

Hadley-Garcia, George. (1990). *Hispanic Hollywood: The Latins in motion pictures.* New York: Citadel.

Hall, Mordaunt. (1927, September 27). *The New York Times.*

Horne, Lena. (1990, November). 45 years in movies and entertainment. *Ebony*, pp. 88+.

Kael, Pauline. (1966). West Side story. In *I lost it at the movies* (pp. 127-133). New York: Bantam.

Kael, Pauline. (1981, February 23). The itch to act. *The New Yorker*, p. 105.

Kael, Pauline. (1982). *5001 nights at the movies: A guide from A to Z*. New York: Holt, Rinehart & Winston.

Kakutani, Michiko. (1981, May 3). Lena Horne: Aloofness hid the pain, until time cooled her anger. *The New York Times*, sec. 2, pp. D1+.

Kelley, Robert. (1986). *The shaping of the American past*. Englewood Cliffs, NJ: Prentice Hall.

London, Michael. (1983, November 9). Beals named as NAACP image awards nominee. *Los Angeles Times*, Sec. 6, p. 1 col. 1.

Mercado, Luis. (1974). A Puerto Rican American speaks. In Edward Mapp (Ed.), *Puerto Rican perspectives* (pp. 150-157). Methuen, NJ: Scarecrow Press.

Miller, Randall M. (1980). *Kaleidoscopic lens: How Hollywood views ethnic groups*. Englewood, NJ: Jerome S. Ozer.

Mitchener, Charles. (1975). Black movies. In Lindsay Patterson (Ed.), *Black films and film-makers: A comprehensive anthology for stereotype to superhero* (pp. 235-246). New York: Dodd, Mead.

Parish, James Robert, & Hill, George H. (1989). *Black action films*. Jefferson, NC: McFarland.

Parkerson, Michelle. (1990). Did you say the mirror talks? In Lisa Albrecht & Rose M. Brewer (Eds.), *Bridges of power: Women's multicultural alliances* (pp. 108-117). Philadelphia: New Society Publishers.

Pettit, Arthur G. (1980). *Images of the Mexican American in fiction and film*. College Station: Texas A&M University Press.

Pickard, Roy. (1977). *The Oscar movies from A-Z*. London: Frederick Muller.

Raab, Selwyn. (1981, February 6). Film image provokes outcry in South Bronx. *The New York Times*, p. 6C.

Robinson, Louie. (1966, March). Hollywood's tragic enigma. *Ebony*, pp. 70+.

Sterritt, David. (1983, May 9). In film, progress is obvious but not enough and affects only certain groups. *Christian Science Monitor*, pp. 11-13.

Ward, Francis. (1977). Black male images in films. In Ernest Kaiser (Ed.), *A freedomways reader: Afro-America in the seventies*. New York: International Publishers.

Woll, Allen L. (1980). Bandits and lovers: Hispanic images in American film. In Randal M. Miller (Ed.), *The kaleidoscopic lens: How Hollywood views ethnic groups* (pp. 54-72). Englewood, NJ: Jerome S. Ozer.

Woll, Allen L. (1981, March 1). How Hollywood has portrayed Hispanics. *The New York Times*, Sec D: 17+.

12. African-American Single Mothers
Public Perceptions and Public Policies

SHIRLEY M. GEIGER

🖎 Although African-American female-headed families are usually portrayed as being social problems or presenting social problems, there is no necessary connection between the number of parents in a family and the presence of problems or difficulties (Caples, 1988). Similarly, although their 1987 poverty rate was twice that of Black male heads of household, and more than seven times that of White male heads of household, there is no inherent reason why half of all Black female-headed household should be poor. Their poverty is best understood as a political and economic issue: It is the result of conscious human action and inaction. The persistent poverty Black women heads of household face is inherent in a society organized along hierarchical racial, gender, class, and ideological lines (Arendell, 1988). The confluence of these factors may result in a kind of negative synergy—where the interactive effect of the variables together is greater than the sum of the variables taken individually. The impact of this negative synergistic force hits Black solo mothers not with a double whammy of racism and sexism, but with a quadruple whammy as classism and ideological bias are added to the equation.

The effects of the whammy are most evident in the public policy responses to the economic problems faced by Black solo mothers. Efforts to translate their problems into effective public policies are shaped by attitudes toward Black single mothers and the disapproval of the way they choose to organize their reproductive and conjugal activity (Reed, 1988). In this chapter I explore the political influences on public policy affecting Black single mothers. I raise questions about the utility of analytical frameworks that ignore the role of ideological and other factors on public policy decision making. I begin with an assessment of the validity and reliability of the currently dominant characterization of Black solo mothers. Next, I identify their major public policy concerns and some of the ways their needs are being addressed. Finally, using the example of public housing, I discuss the workings of the quadruple whammy and the evolution of federal housing policy in this country.

Public Policy Process

Public policy has to do with how problems are defined in government; decisions about how to address those problems reflect sets of value priorities and causal assumptions about how to reach them (Sabatier, 1991). Such sets of value priorities represent political ideologies that provide justification for public policy decisions affecting people's lives (Hoover, 1987). That some possible alternatives are never given serious consideration by political elites reflects the "mobilization of bias" that Schattschneider (1960/1971) defines as a set of predominant values, beliefs, rituals, and institutional procedures that operates systematically and consistently to the benefit of certain groups at the expense of others. Given the distribution of power in this country, that bias is upper-class, White, male, and conservative. When policies must be made affecting those perceived to be outside the system, they are often made on the basis of little information about either the problems or the solutions as defined by those experiencing them. The result is public policy that is safely within the parameters defined by the mobilization of bias and, with regard to social welfare policy, reflects a conservative ideological view.

Preferences and Power

Boulding (1985) observes that conservatives tend to know what they like, which is what they have now; whereas persons to the left of conservatives tend to be convinced of what they do not like but are unable to specify what they prefer in place of the conservative status quo. In their analysis of poverty and power, Bachrach and Baratz (1970) point to the strong limits that are placed on the total range of decisions possible in the system because of the shared values and assumptions of participants. They argue that certain societal problems and certain alternative means of addressing them are simply never discussed, debated, or put on the agenda because decision makers share the fundamental belief that these problems or solutions are not legitimate topics for political debate. Such restrictions on the range of policy options have often worked to the disadvantage of Black solo mothers.

Female Heads of Household

The rising number of female-headed families is neither unique to the African-American community nor limited to the United States. Women are heading an increasing number of families in all advanced Western industrialized countries, including Canada, Australia, the Netherlands, Sweden, France, Great Britain, and New Zealand, as well as the Soviet Union and Poland (Kamerman & Kahn, 1988). Single mothers head approximately 40% of families in some places in Africa and Latin America, one third of families in Jamaica, and one fifth of families in Peru, Honduras, and Cuba (Caples, 1988). Possible explanations for this trend include changing attitudes toward marriage and divorce, increased migration of fathers in search of work, premature death of males, and economic hardship (Mollison, 1991).

What is disturbing about the trend in the United States is the high incidence of poverty in Black female-headed families and the long-term effects of poverty on the children raised by their mothers alone. Since 1960, the percentage of Black children living with their mother below the poverty level increased nearly 300%, up from 29.4% in 1960 to 79% in 1987 (U.S. Bureau of the Census, 1988b). That percentage exceeds the 47.2% of Hispanic children and 46% of White children living in poverty stricken female-headed households. The fact that more than two thirds of all children living in female-headed households have incomes below the poverty level has led some researchers to describe the phenomenon as the feminization of poverty.

Although the term suggests an increase in the incidence of poverty among female-headed households, statistics show that the poverty rate of women who head families has actually been moving down over the past 30 years. The rate of poverty in female-headed Black families dropped 23.1% between 1960 and 1987. For White female heads of household a decrease of 37.6% occurred, and for Black males a decline of 66%. More significantly, during the 1980s the downward trend stopped and the poverty rate headed upward for Black single mothers. What happened to Black solo mothers during the 1980s seems to be directly related to the Reagan budget cuts of 1981. A study by the Congressional Research Service (U.S. Congress, 1984) indicates that more than 550,000 persons were pushed into poverty by the policy changes of the Omnibus Budget Reconciliation Act of 1981, with Black women and children among the hardest hit. Families headed by Black women lost 3.6% in real disposable income between 1980 and 1984 (Simms, 1983).

In addition to the direct impact of the Reagan budget cuts, Black solo mothers have also faced indirect barriers in changed eligibility guidelines and increased bureaucratic red tape that limit their access to welfare assistance or delay receipt of benefits. Between 1972 and 1984 the percentage of White recipients of Aid to Families with Dependent Children (AFDC) increased by 22%, up from 32.2% to 41.3%, whereas the percentage of Black AFDC recipients declined 15% during the same period. The decline occurred even though the number of Black children in female-headed families rose 25% (Ellwood, 1988). The lower number of Black solo mothers receiving AFDC may be the result of the renewed use of regulations to limit their access, rather than a decline in their need for assistance.

Like Black women, the economic situation of Black male heads of household also declined in the 1980s after dramatic reductions in the poverty rate between 1960 and 1978—down from 50.7% in 1960 to 15.1% in 1978 (U.S. Bureau of the Census, 1988b). That factors other than race are at work here is suggested by the widening gap between Black women and Black men heads of household between 1960 and 1987 from a difference of 19.3 percentage points in 1960 to a gap of 36.6 points in 1987. In 1960, around 70% of Black female-headed households were in poverty versus 50.7% of households headed by Black males; in 1987 the poverty rate for Black male householders was 17.2% compared with 53.8% of Black female-headed households. African-American women fared even worse when compared to White men. The poverty rate gap between Black female heads of household and White male householders was 51.5 percentage points in 1960 and 45.6 in 1987, narrowing only by 5.9 points between 1960 and 1987.

That the Reagan policies, which made things worse for already disadvantaged groups, generated no widespread opposition shows the hegemony of the ruling conservative ideology that draws on classism, racism, and sexism to influence American social policy adoption and implementation. Spakes (1991) argues that under the conservative ideology, welfare policy is made by legislative bodies consisting of middle- and upper-class White men who have no experience and little understanding of the problems that face solo mothers and their children. Further, women's groups have generally not been outspoken supporters of the problems of poor women. Welfare has not typically been regarded as a women's issue, and women's organizations have focused their attention on the constituency concerns of middle- and upper-class women, adopting what is essentially a trickle-down approach to the problems of low-income women. Black policy advocates have focused considerable attention on the unemployment concerns of Black men even though the unemployment of Black solo mothers is just as high. West (1981) notes that for many Whites, including women, welfare is a Black issue and for many Blacks, including women, it is a class issue.

In some of the countries experiencing an increase in female-headed families, the problems of solo mothers are treated as problems that can be alleviated with policies designed to remedy economic and social hardship. Others, however, like the United States, have responded to the phenomenon with policies designed less to remedy inequities than to try to control behavior and demonstrate dominant attitudes about the relationship between home, family, and government.

Perceptions of AFDC Mothers

In talking about the perceptions of Black single mothers whose poverty forces them to become welfare recipients, welfare activist Johnnie Tillmon observed in 1972: "There are a lot of . . . lies that male society tells about welfare mothers. . . . If people are willing to believe these lies, it's partly because they're just special versions of the lies that society tells about all women" (quoted in Amott, 1990, p. 289).

Distortion, myth, and outright lies have been part and parcel of the currently dominant characterization of Black solo mothers, especially the 53.8% who live below the poverty level. Researchers have noted the persistence of many old and false stereotypes about Black single mothers, some of which have come from within the academic community (for criticism, see Gresham, 1989; Jackson, 1988; Malveaux, 1988; McAdoo, 1991; Pope, 1988; Reed, 1988). For example: that most poor people are on welfare, that AFDC mothers have more children to collect greater benefits, that AFDC is draining the national treasury, that Black welfare dependency is transmitted intergenerationally, that most single mothers are Black, that most welfare recipients are Black, and that fraud and cheating are rampant among welfare recipients.

The truth is: In 1987 almost two thirds of the 32.4 million poor people in this country did not receive AFDC. Federal expenditures on the poor are not draining the federal treasury. The main government cash assistance program for the poor, AFDC, cost about $8 billion in 1984. That equated to about 7% of the $111 billion spent to service the interest on the national debt, about 5% of the amount spent on Social Security, and less than 4% of the $227 billion spent on defense in 1984 (O'Hare, 1986). In 1980 the money spent on AFDC represented about 4% of all the costs of major public assistance and social insurance programs for the elderly and disabled (Katz, 1988). Women on AFDC have an average of 1.9 children and nearly 75% of them have just one or two children. Only 8% have five or more children; almost 68% have only one child. Researchers have found no link between the welfare dependency of Black single mothers and their children; such youngsters are no more likely than any other children to be on welfare when they grow up. Two thirds of the single mothers in this country are White and the majority (56.4%) of AFDC recipients are not Black. Finally, a study by the Department of Health and Human Services found that fraud or misrepresentation occurred in less than four tenths of one percent of the total national caseload (Karger & Stoesz, 1990).

Even though scholarly evidence points to the falsity of the myths, some politicians and policy makers continue to endorse these untruths.

Particularly with regard to Black solo mothers, the misrepresented public image grows out of and contributes to the tendency to focus on that family style as deviant, amoral, or pathological (Reed, 1988). The rise in the percentage of Black single parents is largely a function of the decrease in the number of children born to Black married women and, to some extent, to the increasing number of employed Black men between the ages of 16 and 34 who are not married (Amott, 1990).

Income Differences

The income problems of Black single mothers are rooted in the reality that in this country, men earn more than women, Whites earn more than Blacks, and many two-parent families must rely on the earnings of two working adults. The average family income of households headed by White single mothers was $17,018 compared with $26,230 for White single fathers. Black single fathers averaged $17,455, but Black single mothers were lowest of all with an average income of $9,710 (U.S. Bureau of the Census, 1988b). Also influencing the income of Black single mothers are historically high levels of unemployment and underemployment, lower levels of education, lack of work experience, and discrimination based on race and sex (Sawhill, 1978).

Although Black married mothers have a higher labor force participation rate than White married mothers, unmarried Black mothers have had a higher unemployment rate than other groups since detailed statistics on women's labor force participation began being kept in the 1940s (Zalokar, 1990). For Black women generally, the unemployment rates have been higher than those of White women and White men, and as high as or higher than those of Black men. Because this pattern of high rates of unemployment was evident for at least two decades before the broader access of Black women to AFDC, welfare is not a plausible cause for their lower force participation rates.

Other Public Policies

In addition to unemployment, Black single mothers are affected by public policies concerning child support, child care, health care, pay equity, welfare reform, social services, affordable housing, and family-workplace issues such as maternity leave and parental leave. Child support provides an example of an issue where policies intended to help one target group may not address the needs of another group. Although White single mothers may benefit from strengthened child support legislation, such laws offer little hope to Black single mothers. A 1984 study found that only one third of Black mothers were granted child support payments compared with two thirds of White mothers and 41% of Hispanic mothers (Schafran, 1988). Only 11% of never-married mothers had an award. Among those Black solo mothers to whom courts awarded child support, the award amount was about 18% lower than for non-Blacks, and high levels of Black male unemployment make wage garnishment a less effective remedy for Black mothers (Beller & Graham, 1986; Radigan, 1988).

Policy Options

In some countries policies have been adopted that have benefited single-mother families: flexible working hours, child care at the workplace, liberal dependent care leave policies, paid maternity leaves, better coordination of the school day with the workday, and linkage of a housing subsidy with income assistance. Kamerman and Kahn (1988) point to several policy strategies that other countries have adopted depending on their definition of the problem. First, the antipoverty strategy in which government adopts policies to meet the general needs of the poor. Second, the categorical strategy of providing special financial assistance to single mothers, supporting them so that they can remain at home with their children. Third, the universal young-child strategy under which cash benefits are provided to all families with children under a certain age. The fourth strategy involves a combination of cash benefits and policy supports for families with young children. Advocacy efforts to move similar alternatives onto the American political agenda have not yet been successful. In general, those who would benefit the most from addressing the issue are absent from the debate.

Some might argue that the dismal record of federal housing policy was not purposely established; that neither liberals nor conservatives are satisfied with it, but neither side sees any alternative. Bachrach and Baratz (1970), however, would argue that the apparent lack of alternatives is caused not by the absence of alternatives but by the shared assumptions that some alternatives cannot be placed on the political agenda by those in the mainstream, whether they call themselves liberals or conservatives. Ideological debates over the proper role of government have always been at the heart of federal housing policy, whether or not policy makers have been willing to acknowledge it (Hays, 1985, 1990). Housing policy alternatives encompass views on the appropriate role of government, the role of women, and the form and amount of assistance that should be provided by government to women without husbands. In the United States the poor comprise the population with the greatest housing need and no one is poorer in this country than Black solo mothers and their children. Female-headed households live disproportionately in inferior housing with extremely limited financial resources for improving their housing (Schwartz, Ferlauto, & Hoffman, 1988). Some conservatives have advocated policies that would deny lone mothers who are unable to support their children federal assistance sufficient to allow them to set up an independent household (Murray, 1984). Thus the evolution of public housing policy provides a focal point for examining the kind of public policy that emerges at the nexus of race, gender, class, and ideology in American politics. The examination of housing policy is also important because the lack of linkage between housing assistance and welfare subsidies to single mothers may be a primary factor in the failure of social welfare assistance to lift people out of poverty in the United States.

Twenty percent of all female heads of household cannot afford to pay anything for rent and still meet other basic needs. So, although they are not generally thought of as such, both the conventional public housing (also called housing projects) and the Section 8 program (where the government provides a rental subsidy to make up the difference between 30% of the recipient's income and a federally established maximum rent) are programs predominantly used by women (National Low Income Housing Coalition, 1980). Only 28% of low-income renters lived in subsidized housing in 1985 (Dolbeare & Stone, 1990), however. In the past decade the growth in the number of poor households has exceeded the growth in subsidized housing as housing costs have risen faster than the incomes of poverty households (Apgar, Masnick, & McArdle, 1991).

Conservatives tend to see the public housing program as an encroachment on the private sector and as an endlessly expensive social program (Harney, 1976). The truth is that low-income housing programs have always been underfunded and inadequate to the needs. Direct federal spending for low-income housing has never been more than a tiny fraction—less than 1.5%—of the total federal budget (Dolbeare & Stone, 1990). The number of units authorized to be built under the Housing Act of 1949 (810,000 units by 1955) still had not been built by the 1970s (Jones, 1977). Richard Nixon's 1973 cutback in housing funds was ideologically consistent with his vote against the Housing Act of 1949. Similarly, Gerald Ford voted against the 1949 legislation and, like Nixon, advocated only minimal involvement in housing and other urban matters (Caves, 1989). Few were surprised by Ronald Reagan's embrace of Britain's conservative Prime Minister Margaret Thatcher's proposal to sell off their public housing stock and his subsequent support for a similar proposal in the United States. His administration advocated federal withdrawal from housing matters, and during the first 3 years of the Reagan presidency there was a net reduction of 68% in the federal housing budget.

The recently adopted Cranston-Gonzalez National Affordable Housing Act of 1990, hailed as the best housing legislation in a decade, still reflects the conservative, pro-producer, private sector bias (Upchurch, 1991). In fact, housing advocates contend that then-Secretary of Housing and Urban Development (HUD) Jack Kemp was acting on a not-so-hidden agenda to promote his own conservative approach to housing policy aimed at drastically reducing the role of the federal government and stressing private ownership over federally financed and supported construction of low-income apartments and single-family homes (Frisby, 1991; Ifill, 1990).

Secretary Kemp's commitment to privatization was exemplified by HUD's exclusive reliance upon housing vouchers and existing private-sector housing and his plan to sell more than 20,000 units of public housing to tenants during his tenure (McWilliams, 1991). Neither policy represented additions to the existing inventory, even as the growth in the number of poor households in need outstripped the available subsidized housing. The private sector, mainly interested in constructing housing for wealthier homeowners, has shown little or no interest in low-income housing.

The majority of the 4.6 million welfare recipients do not receive housing assistance and live in physically deficient or overcrowded housing. An example of the lack of federal response was the 1992 Bush budget proposal to provide rental assistance vouchers to 87,000 new households nationally, although housing specialists indicate that in that year New York City alone needed at least 500,000 new vouchers or certificates to assist low-income renters.

The real beneficiaries of federal housing policy have been middle- and upper-income homeowners, with the largest amounts going to the wealthiest households. The tax benefits that these owners receive as an entitlement totaled more than $52 billion in 1988 alone, more than all of the housing assistance paid in the 50 years since the inception of the public housing program and more than double the estimated cost of providing a housing subsidy to all eligible low-income households. Because 70% of Black solo mothers are renters, most do not benefit from tax subsidies to homeowners (U.S. Bureau of the Census, 1988a). Renters typically pay a higher percentage of their income for housing than owners and tend to be more vulnerable to forces they cannot control, such as rising rents, inadequate housing maintenance, displacement, and discrimination. Although discrimination against families with children was outlawed in the 1988 fair housing legislation, discrimination persists (Leigh, 1989; Mariano, 1990). A considerable body of evidence also points to the reality that Black female heads of household encounter serious and persistent discrimination in the housing market. Galster and Constantine (1991) write:

> Female-headed households with a child were treated less courteously, they were asked for prior landlord references more often, and they were more likely to be told the apartment was not immediately available for occupancy. [They] were quizzed about their employment and financial circumstances significantly more often than were males. (p. 94)

Unfortunately the law provides no safeguards against discrimination based on source of income, and women on welfare or who receive federal rental assistance certificates or housing vouchers report difficulty finding landlords willing to accept holders of certificates or vouchers as tenants (Mulroy, 1988). Such discrimination contributes to the high number of Black women who surrendered their Section 8 certificates and vouchers unused because they were unable to find suitable housing in the allotted time (U.S. House Committee on Banking, Finance, & Urban Affairs, 1990). In New York City, 65% of families receiving a certificate or voucher failed in their housing search, in Cambridge 52%, and in San Francisco 50%. Research by Cahan (1987) and Fuentes and Miller (1989) provides compelling evidence that women without realistic housing alternatives may also be victims of sexual harassment by their landlords, against whom they are reluctant to press charges for fear of eviction or other retaliation.

In setting federal housing policy, policy makers have focused more on the preferences of the private sector than on the needs of the recipients of housing assistance. Those most affected by the policies have lacked the political resources to compel greater attention to their housing needs. A study by the National Council of Negro Women concluded that some of the problems with housing policy exist because "women do not share the inner circle of interest groups which persistently and systematically help shape housing policies and budget proposals" (Skinner, 1978, p. 229). Similarly, except for the brief period of advocacy by the National Welfare Rights Organization in the 1960s, Black women's influence on federal welfare programs has been negligible (Gordon, 1991; West, 1981).

The first federally funded involvement with public housing was justified as an economic stimulus and to protect banks from massive losses, not as part of a comprehensive national policy to address the acute housing shortages among the poorest class. Key provider interest groups that supported the adoption of legislation providing federal housing subsidies to homeowners were at the same time vehemently opposed to the construction of public rental housing (Lilley, 1980). The compromise worked out with this powerful economic lobby—which included the homebuilders, mortgage bankers, and real estate brokers—sowed the seeds that would lead some 30 years later to the negative image of public housing. By agreement with this lobby, federal public housing was to be built so that it would be inferior in all respects to housing provided by the private sector. Its construction was to ensure a short building life, it would be located in the most undesirable areas, and its design and appearance would have no aesthetic appeal (Bratt, 1989).

When the great Black migration brought millions of Blacks from the rural South to the urban centers of the North, they increasingly became tenants in public housing as Whites moved to the suburbs with federal mortgage guarantees. Later, as middle-class Blacks became homeowners and the clientele for public housing narrowed to Black single mothers, the reservoir of political support for housing programs shrank. Despite the recent surges of sympathy for the homeless, only a few voices were raised in or out of Congress against the deep reductions in housing subsidies in the past two decades (Rubin & Zuckman, 1991). The decline in support is linked to the widespread perception that the public housing program is a failure, despite the fact that there is no evidence that the program has failed and considerable evidence that public housing has succeeded in many communities (Meehan, 1979; Schill, 1990). Negative assessments of public housing may be based less on the objective facts than on attitudes toward the non-elderly occupants of public housing.

Federal housing policy reflects, as does welfare policy, our national unwillingness to come to grips with the problems of poverty and racism. Conservatives tend to argue that the federal government should intervene in the housing market only to the extent that it enhances the free market. Although liberals may attempt to push government to do more, on the issue of housing policy, they—like the conservatives—remain firmly within the parameters of a dominant capitalist political economy (Gordon, 1977).

Because Black single mothers are more likely to be poor, they are disproportionately affected by the way the issues of poverty, race, and gender are dealt with in the political arena. Even a cursory review of the lack of sensitivity to their needs, which has typified public policy in the past, is disheartening, and the future also looks bleak. As this society ages, more of its future resources must be allocated to the social welfare of the elderly, who will need more income support, health services, and nursing home care in the coming decades. Unlike poor children in female-headed households, the elderly have the political clout to assure that their needs will be met.

Even though viewed in negative terms, the household headed by a Black single mother is a viable family form that has the potential for nurturing and strengthening individual family members if there are supportive—not antagonistic—public and private institutional structures through which it can meet its basic human needs (Mulroy, 1988). Understanding that public policy decisions do not just happen reinforces the need for sustained advocacy and political pressure by and with Black single mothers to address their needs and concerns. In pointing to the pervasive influence of racial, gender, class, and ideological bias I have argued that the public policies that affect the lives of Black solo mothers are not simply the benign, befuddled results of well-intentioned politicians. Such a recognition is an essential step in understanding why there has been so limited a range of alternatives perceived as legitimate approaches to address the needs of Black single mothers.

The power of ideology and the myths of AFDC determine the agenda for public policy responses in ways that are damaging to all poor families, including the 40% headed by White males. They are particularly devastating to Black single mothers and their children. Future research should focus on how Black solo mothers are coping in various communities and identify those public policy strategies that might be successful for a majority of their families. Attention should also focus on the political activities of Black women, especially single mothers, and the degree to which they are able to use the political arena to increase their sense of efficacy and make public officials and bureaucrats respond to their needs. Rather than being overwhelmed by the power of the myths, it is incumbent upon Black women to participate in the political process. Part of the research agenda should involve scorekeeping on the voting record of politicians representing communities with substantial numbers of Black single mothers. Expanded political involvement is one way that Black single mothers can find their own voices to promote their political interests in a political system that seems bent on excluding them almost entirely except where they can be used as scapegoats for social problems. Countering the quadruple whammy will not be easy.

References

Amott, Teresa L. (1990). Black women and AFDC: Making entitlement out of necessity. In Linda Gordon (Ed.), *Women, the state, and welfare* (pp. 280-298). Madison: University of Wisconsin Press.

Apgar, William C., Masnick, George S., & McArdle, Nancy. (1991). *Housing in America: 1970-2000: The nation's housing needs for the balance of the 20th century* (draft copy). Cambridge, MA: The Joint Center for Housing Studies.

Arendell, Teresa. (1988). Unmarried women in a patriarchal society: Impoverishment and access to health care across the life cycle. In Donald Tomaskovic-Devey (Ed.), *Poverty and social welfare in the United States* (pp. 53-81). Boulder, CO: Westview.

Bachrach, Peter, & Baratz, Morton S. (1970). *Power and poverty: Theory and practice.* New York: Oxford University Press.

Beller, Andrea J., & Graham, J. W. (1986). Child support awards: Differentials and trends by race and marital status. *Demography, 23*(2), 231-245.

Boulding, Kenneth B. (1985). *Human betterment.* Beverly Hills, CA: Sage.

Bratt, Rachel G. (1989). *Rebuilding a low income housing policy.* Philadelphia: Temple University Press.

Cahan, Regina. (1987). Home is no haven: An analysis of sexual harassment in housing. *Wisconsin Law Review, 6,* 1061-1097.

Caples, Frances Small. (1988). Restructuring family life. In Elizabeth A. Mulroy (Ed.), *Women as single parents: Confronting institutional barriers in the courts, the workplace and the housing market* (pp. 73-98). Dover, MA: Auburn House.

Caves, Roger W. (1989). An historical analysis of federal housing policy from the presidential perspective: An intergovernmental focus. *Urban Studies, 26,* 59-76.

Dolbeare, Cushing, & Stone, Anne J. (1990). Women and affordable housing. In Sara E. Rix (Ed.), *American woman 1990-1991: A status report* (pp. 94-131). New York: Norton.

Ellwood, David T. (1988). *Poor support: Poverty in the American family*. New York: Basic Books.

Frisby, Michael K. (1991, April 30). Kemp is fought on bid to sell public housing. *Boston Globe*, p. 1-A.

Fuentes, Annette, & Miller, Madelyn. (1989). Unreasonable access: Sexual harassment comes home. In Willem van Vliet (Ed.), *Women, housing, and community* (pp. 153-160). Aldershot, UK: Avebury.

Galster, George, & Constantine, Peter. (1991). Discrimination against female-headed households in rental housing: Theory and exploratory evidence. *Review of Political Economy, 69*(3), 76-100.

Gordon, D. M. (1977). *Problems in political economy* (2nd ed.). Lexington, MA: D. C. Heath.

Gordon, Linda. (1991, September). Black and White visions of welfare: Women's welfare activism, 1890-1945. *The Journal of American History*, pp. 559-590.

Gresham, Jewell Handy. (1989, July 24). White patriarchal supremacy: The politics of family in America. *The Nation*, pp. 116-122.

Harney, Kenneth R. (1976, September). Changes may be in store for federal housing policy. *National Journal*, pp. 1270-1278.

Hays, R. Allen. (1985). *The federal government and urban housing: Ideology and change in public policy*. Albany: SUNY Press.

Hays, R. Allen. (1990). The president, congress, and the formation of the housing policy: A re-examination of redistributive policy-making. *Policy Studies Journal, 18*(4), 847-869.

Hoover, Kenneth R. (1987). *Ideology and political life*. Belmont, CA: Brooks/Cole.

Ifill, Gwen. (1990, July 6). HUD's "clear deck" assailed as empty: Kemp cancelling programs but not replacing services, critics say. *The Washington Post*, p. 6-A.

Jackson, Jacqueline Johnson. (1988). Aging Black women and public policies. *The Black Scholar, 19*(May/June), 31-43.

Jones, Charles O. (1977). *An introduction to the study of public policy* (2nd ed.). North Scituate, MA: Duxbury Press.

Kamerman, Sheila B., & Kahn, Alfred J. (1988). What Europe does for single parent families. *The Public Interest, 93*(Fall), 70-86.

Karger, Howard J., & Stoesz, David. (1990). *American social welfare policy*. New York: Longman.

Katz, Michael. (1988). *The undeserving poor: From the war on poverty to the war on welfare*. New York: Pantheon.

Leigh, Wilhelmina A. (1989). Barriers to fair housing for Black women. *Sex Roles, 21*(1/2), 69-84.

Lilley, William, III. (1980). The homebuilders lobby. In Jon Pynoos, Robert Schafer, & Chester W. Hartman (Eds.), *Housing urban America* (pp. 30-49). Hawthorne, NY: Aldine de Gruyter.

Malveaux, Julianne. (1988). Race, class, and Black poverty. *The Black Scholar, 19*(May/June), 18-21.

Mariano, Ann. (1990, September 22). Reports of bias against families on rise. *The Washington Post*, p. 19-A.

McAdoo, Harriett Pipes. (1991). A portrait of African American families in the United States. In Sara E. Rix (Ed.), *The American woman 1990-1991: A status report* (pp. 71-93). New York: Norton.

McWilliams, Rita. (1991). Dream houses for the poor. *Governing, 4*(10), 54-59.

Meehan, Eugene J. (1979). *The quality of federal policy making: Programmed failure in public housing*. Columbia: University of Missouri Press.

Mollison, Andrew. (1991, September 9). A tidal wave of poverty is rolling through rich nations, experts warn. *The Atlanta Journal Constitution*, p. 1.

Mulroy, Elizabeth A. (Ed.). (1988). *Women as single parents: Confronting institutional barriers in the courts, the workplace, and the housing market*. Dover, MA: Auburn House.

Murray, Charles. (1984). *Losing ground: American social policy, 1950-1980*. New York: Basic Books.

National Low Income Housing Coalition. (1980, October). *Triple jeopardy: A report on low income women and their housing problems*. Washington, DC: Author.

O'Hare, William. (1986, May). Eight myths of poverty. *Demographics*, pp. 23-25.

Pope, Jacqueline. (1988). Women and welfare reform. *The Black Scholar, 19*(May/June), 22-29.

Radigan, Anne L. (1988). Federal policy making and family issues. In Elizabeth A. Mulroy (Ed.), *Women as single parents* (pp. 203-226). Dover, MA: Auburn House.

Reed, Adolph, Jr. (1988, February 6). The liberal technocrat [Review of *The truly disadvantaged: The inner city, the underclass, and public policy*]. *The Nation, 246*(5), 167-170.

Rubin, Alissa J., & Zuckman, Jill. (1991, June 8). House revives space station with cuts to housing. *Congressional Quarterly Weekly Report*, pp. 1492-1494.

Sabatier, Paul. (1991). Towards better theories of the policy process. *P.S.: Political Science and Politics, 24*(2), 146-156.

Sawhill, Isabel V. (1978, April). Black women who head families: Economic needs and economic resources. In *Research papers: Conference on the Educational and Occupational Needs of Black Women*, Vol. 2. Washington, DC: U.S. Department of Health, Education and Welfare.

Schafran, Lynn Hecht. (1988). Gender bias in the courts. In Elizabeth A. Mulroy (Ed.), *Women as single parents* (pp. 39-72). Dover, MA: Auburn House.

Schattschneider, E. E. (1971). *The semi-sovereign people*. New York: Holt, Rinehart & Winston. (Original work published 1960)

Schill, Michael A. (1990). Privatizing federal low income housing assistance: The case of public housing. *Cornell Law Review, 75*, 878-948.

Schwartz, David C., Ferlauto, Richard C., & Hoffman, Daniel. (1988). *A new housing policy for America: Recapturing the American dream*. Philadelphia: Temple University Press.

Simms, Margaret C. (1983). Women and housing: The impact of government housing policy. In Irene Diamond (Ed.), *Families, politics, and public policy*. New York: Longman.

Skinner, Allene Joyce. (1978, May). Women consumers, women professionals: Their roles and problems in housing and community development. *Journal of Housing*, pp. 228-230.

Spakes, Patricia. (1991). A feminist approach to national family policy. In Elaine A. Anderson & Richard C. Hula (Eds.), *The reconstruction of family policy* (pp. 23-42). Westport, CT: Greenwood Press.

U.S. Bureau of the Census. (1988a). *Current population reports* (Series P-20, No. 424). *Household and family characteristics: March 1987*. Washington, DC: Government Printing Office.

U.S. Bureau of the Census. (1988b). Table 1—Money income and poverty status in the United States: 1987. In *Current population reports* (Series P-60, No. 161). Washington, DC: Government Printing Office.

U.S. Congress. (1984). *The impact of OBRA changes on poverty in the United States*. Washington, DC: Government Printing Office.

U.S. House Committee on Banking, Finance, and Urban Affairs. (1990). *Hearings on the Public Housing and Section 8 Programs* [101st Congress. Subcommittee on Housing and Community Development]. Washington, DC: Government Printing Office.

Upchurch, James. (1991, May-June). Housing policy: An international perspective. *Journal of Housing*, pp. 105-106.

West, Guida. (1981). *The national welfare rights movement: The social protest of poor women*. New York: Praeger.

Zalokar, Nadja. (1990, October). *The economic status of Black women: An exploratory investigation* [Staff Report. U.S. Commission on Civil Rights]. Washington, DC: U.S. Commission on Civil Rights.

PART III

Performing Their Visions

13. "Oh, What I Think I Must Tell This World!"
Oratory and Public Address of African-American Women

CHARLES I. NERO

🗿 Lorraine Hansberry[1] wrote the words that form the first part of the title of this chapter while preparing the manuscript that would become the 1959 hit Broadway drama *A Raisin in the Sun*. In that play Hansberry sought to depict African Americans who possessed, she stated, "the essence of human dignity." In the historical context in which Hansberry lived no African-American woman had ever had a drama produced on Broadway. In fact, very few dramas by African Americans had appeared on the Broadway stage, and when they did the shows were often butchered for the consumption of White audiences as in the case of Langston Hughes's 1935 drama *Mulatto*.[2] African Americans were more often seen on Broadway in the musical revue or in stereotypical roles of servants—formulas that would not offend White patrons.

To tell the world that Africans Americans possessed "the essence of human dignity" within the context of a financially and critically successful drama was a remarkable feat, which Hansberry accomplished with aplomb.[3] More to the point of this chapter, Hansberry's musings about *A Raisin in the Sun* as expressed in her query, "Oh, what I think I must tell this world," reveals an intention on her part to speak to the world via the form of drama, and, in this sense, Hansberry's work can be considered a public address. Drama, however, is not the discursive form studied most often by critics of public address. Usually, public address is confined to studies of oratory. In this chapter I discuss the public address and oratory of African-American women. First, I present an historical overview of African-American women's oratory and I focus primarily on African-American women's struggle to gain access to the masculine-defined space of the speaker's platform. Second, I discuss the paucity of texts by African-American women as a central problematic for the study of their oratory. Third, I argue for enlarging the scope of public address so that it includes forms other than oratory. The study of oratory tends to produce studies of leadership, which invariably excludes ordinary women. I use naming practices as an example of enlarging the study of public address and creating a more inclusive discipline.

The Struggle for the Speaker's Platform

African-American women along with White women entered the speaking platform in the early 19th century. One critic has dubbed them "pioneer women" because they were the first to enter the male terrain of the speaker's platform.[4] But before discussing African-American women on the speaker's platform, it is necessary to give background about the importance of public speaking in 19th-century America.

It is difficult for many to imagine the prominence that public speaking held in the 19th century, but it was a major form in both politics and mass entertainment. In politics, oratory became widespread as Jacksonian democracy removed property as a criterion for male suffrage, which ironically expanded the vote among White men but removed Black men from the electorate. The importance of oratory in politics is superbly documented in Robert Gunderson's *The Log Cabin Campaign*, a study of the efforts of the Whigs to capture the 1836 election from the Jacksonian Democrats. Those efforts included feats such as the South Carolina politician and linguist Hugh Swinton Legare teaching himself the patois spoken in the Western states, donning leather and a coonskin cap, and taking to the stump (literally, a tree stump in a clearing in the woods) in order to address White male frontiersmen.

Outside of electoral politics, oratory became a central means of advancing the causes of the numerous reform movements that characterized the antebellum United States. Reforms of every kind conceivable at the time, sponsored in earlier years by individuals, "evolved into well-organized movements for peace, communistic experimentation, care of the poor and of the insane, temperance, universal equality and suffrage, and free inquiry."[5] Blacks, especially, had opportunities in antislavery societies. John A. Collins, an agent of the American Anti-Slavery Society, stated in the *Liberator* in 1842 that "the public have itching ears to hear a colored man speak, and particularly a *slave*."[6]

In the arena of entertainment, "Oratory filled the ears of the city as resonantly as the church bells on Sunday."[7] The subject matter of this oratory was quite broad. For example, Doris Yoakam noted that, "During the 1852 lecturing season alone, New Yorkers might listen to at least thirteen different courses of lectures, ranging from those of Professor Adolphus L. Koeppen, 'of Kentucky Cave memory,' and of Mrs. E. Oakes Smith on women, down to the 'Polyglot Lectures' in Italian, Spanish, French and German."[8] Lecture halls, usually associated with the Lyceum Movement, were a nearly universal phenomenon. The Lyceum Movement had as its purpose the diffusion of knowledge, the promotion of schools, the creation of libraries, and the establishment of lecture halls.[9] By 1835 there were more than 3,000 Lyceums in 15 states, and by 1840 they were found even at the edges of the frontier, as far west as Iowa and Minnesota.[10]

Lecturing was also quite lucrative. Mark Twain remarks that some lecturers charged as much as $250 when they spoke in towns and $400 when they spoke in cities.[11] With fees such as those mentioned by Twain, lecturing could become a career choice that, in the case of women, could provide a means of independence. Lucy Stone, for example, taught school for 9 years while saving funds to enter Oberlin College in order to become a professional speaker.[12]

Oratory was a phenomenon, thus, popular on the frontier and in the city. It could be financially rewarding, and it was a major form in politics, in the many organized reform movements, and in entertainment. Despite its widespread popularity, women were generally not allowed to speak publicly in the United States. By the 1830s, however, the speaker's platform had become a site of struggle and contestation because women wanted access to it. African Americans were instrumental in women gaining access to the platform.

An African American was the first woman to speak before a "promiscuous audience," that is, one composed of men and women, and leave extant copies of her text.[13] In September 1832, in Boston, Maria W. Stewart mounted a lecture platform and spoke out against the colonization movement, a controversial plan endorsed by many prominent Whites (such as Thomas Jefferson and James Monroe) to expatriate free and freed Blacks to West Africa. Her public career spanned barely 3 years—from 1831 to 1834—but she left four extant public lectures that were published in *The Liberator*.[14] In those four addresses, Stewart moves from protégé of David Walker, who had published the incendiary antislavery 1829 pamphlet *David Walker's Appeal*, to proto-feminist. Walker's influence on Stewart can be seen in several recurring themes in her speeches, notably, deep religiosity, that education would help Blacks reverse their fortunes in this country, that American slavery was the most vicious form of bondage known to history, and that Blacks had a great past in Egypt. By the time of her farewell address in 1834, however, Stewart had surpassed Walker and was "urging women to strike out on their own, pursuing education as a means of fulfilling their individual and collective destinies," states Marilyn Richardson in her superbly edited collection of Stewart's works.[15]

Stewart's entry to the platform was not easy. Like other 19th-century women, Stewart's public activities were greatly constrained by restrictive gender expectations for women. A public activity such as speaking, according to one historian, "was outside a mystic geometrical entity called 'women's sphere.' "[16] Because of custom, religion, and law, many politically active women closely adhered to the "women's sphere" ideal, according to Lillian O'Connor. Mary Lyons, in her efforts to raise funds for Mount Holyoke Seminary, avoided the platform in favor of sewing circles and went from house to house gathering contributions.[17] In securing funds for their schools, educators Emma Willard and Catherine Beecher wrote speeches but had them read by men from the public platform.[18] According to Willard, it was "too great a strain on the properties for a woman to read her own address before such an assemblage" of citizens meeting in behalf of the common schools.[19] Dorothea Dix, noted primarily for her activities for the reform of asylums, prisons, and hospitals, also refused to speak in public to further her causes. In 1848 and 1850 she met the members of Congress privately and individually, for, as she said, she "laid great stress on preserving her womanly dignity" and did not want to "vulgarize a cause and its representative by a pushing and teasing demeanor."[20] The Stone family was deeply divided in regard to Lucy's interest in public speaking. Her mother urged her to go back to teaching or, if she must lecture, to do so "from house to house rather than in public;" Lucy's sister, Sarah, expressed the hope that if Lucy did speak in public, she would "not come into this state [Massachusetts];" ironically, her brothers Bowman and Frank supported her endeavors, encouraging Lucy to do what she felt was her duty.[21]

Opposition to women who violated the ideals of their sphere by speaking in public took various forms. Ministers delivered sermons to congregations against these violators of Pauline doctrine. In July 1837 the General Association of Congregational Ministers decided to make the usual annual pastoral letter the vehicle of an assault on women who dared lead public lives. The letter stated, "The power of woman is her dependence, flowing from the consciousness of that weakness which God has given her in those departments of life that form the character of individuals, and of the nation," and it asserted that when women assume the place of men as public reformers, public lecturers, and teachers, their characters become unnatural, and they sever themselves from the protection and care that are their right.[22]

Women speakers were also subject to more direct, physical harassment than edicts from pulpits. It was not unusual for mobs to gather, according to Yoakam, when women were scheduled to speak and for them to shout threats, hurl showers of rocks, brickbats, and rotten eggs at the speakers.[23] One such mob, which had been rowdy at Frances Harper's lecture, sabotaged her wagon.[24] The 1840s antislavery speaker Abby Kelley reported that she learned "how to dodge every kind of missile, from rotten eggs on down to tobacco quids."[25] Maria W. Stewart was pelted with tomatoes by Black men for criticizing them for failing to follow Christian principles of thrift, sobriety, and hard work.[26]

The efforts of Black women to speak in public were an especially sensitive issue to embattled and stigmatized African-American communities. Women's rights, Shirley Yee has contended, "seemed to contradict a central goal of Black activism, which was to adopt separate sex roles."[27] Men such as the influential Samuel Cornish regularly denounced Black and White women speakers in the pages of his newspaper, *Freedom's Journal*. Yet, men such as Frederick Douglass and Charles Lenox Remond wholeheartedly supported women lecturers. They saw these women as assets in the campaign to promote race pride as well as allies in creating public opposition to slavery and racism.[28]

In addition to support from influential male allies, other reasons accounted for Black women's ascension to the platform and their eventual acceptance as lecturers. The appeal to race pride by Black women helped to justify their participation in public activities, and, as Shirley Yee has noted, it may "have made it more acceptable for Black women than for White women to engage in non-traditional activities such as public speaking."[29] Black women like Frances Harper, Sojourner Truth, Sarah Remond, Harriet Tubman, and the contentious Mary Ann Shadd were skilled orators and received considerable praise for their abilities from the African-American and the White presses. On one occasion, for example, Tubman "created such a sensation at the Massachusetts Anti-Slavery Society that James Yerrington [the recorder] was a bit paralyzed and . . . did not give her words."[30] Mary Webb was dubbed "the Black Siddons" in recognition of her considerable skills as an elocutionist.[31] The fact that Black women were praised, Yee states, for exuding "feminine qualities" helped make them more acceptable to their audiences, and such praise must have soothed the concerns of many in the Black community about White attributions of more stigma to their race.

Economics could permit African-American women to participate in public activities, also. Because Black women often worked outside the home—unlike middle-class White women—they could participate in public activities because their lives did not mirror the ideals of "women's sphere" or the aims of the reigning 19th-century ideology of true womanhood—piety, purity, submissiveness, and domesticity.[32]

African-American women's ascent to the speaker's platform was a dramatic struggle. They encountered opposition and open hostility from their home communities as well as from the dominant White communities. Their ascent to the speaker's platform is a remarkable story of courage. In the next sections, I discuss the status of African-American women's oratory.

The Study of African-American Women's Oratory

In her 1990 work *Invisibility Blues*, feminist cultural critic Michele Wallace suggested that Black women be represented by "X," the radical sign of negation; that designation seems appropriate for the study of

African-American women's oratory.[33] Generally, Black women have been excluded from anthologies of orations. The handful of studies of their oratory seem perpetually bogged down by issues such as the degree to which Black women are either "women" or "persons."

The Public Address Anthology

The public address anthology is perhaps the most important vehicle for establishing the canon of American oratory. These anthologies tend to be the orations of "great leaders" who have influenced the so-called sweep of history. Carole Spitzak and Kathryn Carter's observation that within this model "female experience is restricted and excluded" is also quite true for African Americans in general.[34] An early work like *Oratory of the South: From the Civil War to the Present Time* (1908) contained no speeches by African Americans. Ernest Wrage and Barnet Baskerville's *American Forum: Speeches on Historic Issues, 1788-1900*, "based on issues underlying the American experience," not surprisingly includes no speeches by either African Americans or White women.[35] The only speech by an African American in Charles Hurd's *A Treasury of Great American Speeches: Our Countries [sic] Life and History in the Words of Its Great Men* is Booker T. Washington's acceptance speech on receiving an honorary Master of Arts degree from Harvard University in 1896.

More recent anthologies are only slightly more inclusive of women and African Americans than earlier ones. Ronald Reid's *Three Centuries of American Rhetorical Discourse* (1988) contained five works by African Americans, one of which is by a woman: Frederick Douglass's "What to the Slave Is the Fourth of July?," Sojourner Truth's "Speech to the Anniversary Convention of the American Equal Rights Association," Booker T. Washington's 1895 "Cotton States Exposition Address," W.E.B. DuBois's "Of Mr. B. T. Washington and Others," and Martin Luther King, Jr.'s "I Have A Dream." Reid's selection of African-American orations is all the more peculiar because of its inclusion of DuBois and Washington. The two are included as counterpoints to each other. DuBois's work is not a speech, however, but an excerpt from *The Souls of Black Folk*. Moreover, no reason is given for the absence of counterpoints for the other selections. For example, King's rhetoric is not contrasted with someone of the caliber of Malcolm X, Fannie Lou Hamer, or Stokeley Carmichael. Johannesen, Allen, and Linkugel's *Contemporary American Speeches* (1988) includes speeches by three African-American men—John E. Jacob (former head of the National Urban League), Martin Luther King, Jr. ("I Have A Dream"), and Jesse Jackson ("The Rainbow Coalition"), as well as Barbara Jordan's Keynote Address to the Democratic Party. King's "I Have a Dream," Jackson's "The Rainbow Coalition," and Jordan's "Keynote Address" are the entries by African Americans in Ryan's *American Rhetoric from Roosevelt to*

Reagan. Ryan's collection seems to strive for some sort of African-American gender parity because by including Shirley Chisholm's "For the Equal Rights Amendment," it's two for two.

"Tokenism" is the problem with these anthologies of American public address. When speeches by African Americans are included at all, they are the ones that Whites know and that have influenced "White society" in some direct, palpable way. That usually means that the works have been included in other anthologies and are reprinted again. It means that the speech was probably given before a White American audience and probably published in *Vital Speeches of the Day*, a weekly periodical that reprints contemporary speeches by figures of national importance.

The model of "great leaders" established by White men is replicated in anthologies that specialize in orations by African Americans or women. From these anthologies it is not clear, however, to what degree Black women are in the ranks of either "great African-American leaders" or "great women leaders." The inclusion or exclusion of African-American women in these anthologies is a shifting terrain.

The status of African-American women as leaders and worthy of inclusion has been unstable since the three anthologies of African-American public addresses published in the first quarter of this century. The first anthology of African-American public address, *Masterpieces of Negro Eloquence* (1914), was edited by Alice Moore Dunbar, a noted African-American scholar, teacher, and writer of fiction and short stories. *Masterpieces of Negro Eloquence* was published to coincide with the 50th anniversary of the Proclamation of Emancipation, an event that Dunbar called "the birth of the Negro into manhood."[36] Unlike future anthologists, Dunbar seems to view "manhood" as metaphorical for she includes addresses by herself, Frances Ellen Watkins Harper, Josephine St. Pierre Ruffin, and Fanny Jackson Coppin among the 49 works in *Masterpieces of Negro Eloquence*. Given the fact that Dunbar had access to a vast network of African-American middle-class activist women, it is not unreasonable to assume that she may have wanted to include more works by them in the anthology. In prefatory remarks to the anthology, Dunbar seems to be referring to the dearth of women in the anthology when she states, "Sometimes it has been difficult to obtain good speeches from those who are living because of their innate modesty, either in not desiring to appear in print, or in having thought so little of their efforts as to have lost them."[37] In *The Dunbar Speaker and Entertainer* (1920), a resource book for orators and commemorative occasions, Dunbar (-Nelson) includes prose and poetry (including orations) by African-American and White men and women.

In 1925 Carter G. Woodson edited what would be the largest anthology of African-American public addresses for almost 50 years. *Negro Orators and Their Orations* contained 75 entries. *Negro Orators and Their Orations* reflected Woodson's superb academic training in history and included, he stated, "practically all of the extant speeches of consequence delivered by Negroes of the United States" (Foreword). Unlike Dunbar's pioneering anthologies, Woodson's contained no works by African-American women. An important clue to this absence can be found in Woodson's phrase "of consequence." In praxis, "of consequence," with its debt to causitry, is the model of the "sweep of history" and, as has already been stated, is inherently male. Many of the speeches "of consequence" occurred either in contexts in which women were excluded by law or that were at the very least inimical to their presence. Nineteen of the speeches, for example, were delivered by African-American Congressmen elected during Reconstruction.

This exclusion of African-American women repeated itself in the anthologies that emerged from the upsurge of publication due to the Civil Rights Movement. In general, Black women fared better in anthologies that attempted greater spans of time than those focused on the Civil Rights Movement, although Arthur L. Smith [Molefi Kete Asante] and Stephen Robb's *The Voice of Black Rhetoric* (1971) contained no women's voices. Women were absent in Haig and Hamida Bosmajian's *The Rhetoric of the Civil-Rights Movement* (1969), and Robert L. Scott and Wayne Brockriede's *The Rhetoric of Black Power* (1969) but were included (albeit marginally) in Golden and Rieke's *The Rhetoric of Black Americans* (1971), Borman's *Forerunners of Black Power: The Rhetoric of Abolition* (1971), and Foner's *The Voice of Black America* (1972).

Foner's *The Voice of Black America* (1972) warrants special mention for it surpassed all other anthologies in breadth and scope. It contained 198 entries, thus surpassing in number Woodson's *Negro Orators and Their Orations*. Despite its enormous number of entries, only 8 were by women. In other words, little over 4% of the entries were by African-American women. That is also a 4% decline if compared to Alice Dunbar's 1914 *Masterpieces of Negro Eloquence*.

One of the most refreshing works to emerge during this period was Gerda Lerner's *Black Women in White America: A Documentary History* (1972). *Black Women in White America* was a path-finding anthology.[38] Still in print, it contains an enormous amount of texts in varied forms. Many of the entries were given as speeches, but, unfortunately, it is not always clear from Lerner's annotations which ones were.

Contemporary anthologies are bringing many more texts by African American women into existence. Karlyn Kohrs Campbell's *Man Cannot Speak for Her: Key Texts of the Early Feminists* (1989) includes speeches by Maria W. Stewart, Sojourner Truth, Ida B. Wells, and Mary Church Terrell. Marilyn Richardson has splendidly edited *Maria W. Stewart, America's First Black Woman Political Writer*. Richardson includes the four known speeches by Stewart and an extremely informative introduction. One of the highlights of the introduction is her textual analysis of Stewart's addresses showing the influence of David Walker's *Appeal* on her work. Robbie Jean Walker's *The Rhetoric of*

Struggle: Public Address by African American Women contains 36 entries. Although Robbie's anthology is problematic, it is the first time that so many speeches by African-American women have been in the same anthology.[39]

Finally, the largest collection of public addresses by African-American women is in Robert Branham's forthcoming anthology, *Lift Every Voice*.[40] It is a significant revision of Foner's earlier *The Voice of Black America*. *Lift Every Voice* will contain at least 237 entries, 60 of which are by women. I note as well that Branham's collection contains more speeches *by women* than any other published anthology in English in the United States to date, a fact that suggests, it seems to me, that African-American women should occupy a central space in the study of women's oratory. Moreover, Branham's method of compilation should serve as a model for future anthologies. Many of the excerpts in *Lift Every Voice* have never been anthologized, and some have never been published before. So, it will be the first time that we encounter in one anthology speeches by seldom studied or almost forgotten African-American women leaders such as Maggie Lena Walker, Mary Ann Shadd, Sara Staley, Sarah Parker Remond, Sara J. Woodson, Fannie Barrier Williams, Mary Church Terrell, Lucy Craft Laney, Mary A. Lynch, Nannie Helen Burroughs, Coralie F. Cook, Henrietta Vinton Davis, Charlotte Hawkins Brown, and Mary McLeod Bethune. The breadth of *Lift Every Voice* makes possible comparisons across gender as well as the continuity of ideas in African-American oratory. Using *Lift Every Voice*, greater possibilities exist for the study of how African-American women have read, heard, and revised the ideas of other African-American women. *Lift Every Voice* will be a significant contribution to contemporary scholarship.

The Study of African-American Women's Oratory

"Are 'Black women' women?" and "Are 'Black women' persons?" seem to be the two questions that dominate the study of African-American women's oratory. Early studies of women's oratory and their participation in women's rights movements consistently excluded or consigned African-American women to the margins of her-/history. Doris Yoakam's originary essay, "Women's Introduction to the American Platform," completely ignored Maria W. Stewart. This omission is incredible when one considers Stewart's role in American women's oratory as the first woman to leave extant texts of her public lectures. More appalling is that Yoakam's omission of Stewart must be deliberate. Four of Stewart's lectures were published in *The Liberator*, and referring to that journal's importance, Yoakam states, "If the bibliography of the first chapter of women's speaking were limited to one source, it would be the famous abolition weekly, *The Liberator*." In fact, *The Liberator* is so central to Yoakam's study that it accounts for 38 of its 99 references. One wonders how Yoakam explained away to herself Maria W. Stewart's addresses in *The Liberator*. If Yoakam referred to them in her study, one wonders if William Brigance, an editor of the volume in which Yoakam's essay appeared, suggested that Yoakam delete all references to Stewart?

Whatever the case may be about Yoakam's erasure of Stewart, it foreshadows future studies of African-American women's oratory. In the preface to the 1989 *Man Cannot Speak for Her: A Critical Study of Early Feminist Rhetoric*, Karlyn Kohrs Campbell claims that talking to Black women from the Kansas Association of Colored Women's and Girl's Clubs has "enlarged . . . [her] understanding of feminism, past and present."[41] With this enlarged understanding, Campbell begins a discussion of the oratory of Mary Church Terrell and Ida B. Wells in the following manner:

> Given commonalities as well as differences arising from the special conditions confronting Afro-American women, their rhetoric requires special treatment. This chapter examines the ways in which, if at all, it resembled the rhetoric of other women activists, and the degree to which the activities of Afro-American women were related to the woman's rights and woman suffrage movement.[42]

Assertions such as this one by Campbell seem "designed to erase the blackness" from Black women, states Black feminist scholar Marsha Houston.[43] Campbell is unable to think outside of platonist additive concepts of women: women are women (and exist in an ideal [White] body) except some have property x, y, and/or z. The problem with this kind of scholarship is that it almost invariably finds African-American women deficient or lacking. For example, Campbell contends that from women's experience of sexism there emerged a uniquely feminine style of oratory, but she cannot locate or name a style that Black women created that permitted them to talk to White women who were admittedly and avowedly racist. Campbell also cannot conceive that this "feminine style" might be related, in any way, to African-American forms of address such as "call-response." Thus, African-American women are always deficient or on the periphery of the [White] women's movement and Campbell can only conclude that women like Wells and Terrell "felt that the problems of race were more compelling than the grievances of women."[44]

This conclusion by Campbell is patently false, for it suggests somehow that Wells and Terrell did not consider themselves women. This could not be further from the truth, of course. When studying the oratory of African-American women, Houston's suggestions about communication practices in general are appropriate. First, we should have a commitment to "[m]aking women's ethnic culture the central organizing concept for feminist theory and research," which "means thinking of women as enculturated to a gendered communication ideal *within* specific ethnic groups an organizing concept."[45] Second, we must earn the right to speak about them "by learning who they are as they communicate in their own ethnic cultural contexts, *their* world, not simply ours."[46] In this type of research, women's ethnicity and culture does not disappear.

I also put forth an idea for which Ernest Wrage argued 45 years ago, namely, that oratory is a repository of ideas.[47] Studying oratory from this "angle of vision" can provide some unique insights.[48] Notably, several scholars outside of the discipline of public address have used oratory and language fruitfully in superb studies of the concept of racial and gendered consciousness among Black women.[49]

Finally, one of the problems with studying oratory and public address is its inherent class bias. Seldom are the speeches of working-class or poor people recorded. Inevitably, the study of oratory is confined to a class of leader elites. Public address need not confine itself only to leader elites, however. A clearly avant-garde 1973 essay by Lucia S. Hawthorne—an African-American critic, teacher, and a founder of the Black Caucus of the Speech Communication Association—implies a way out of the bind created by class bias in public address. Hawthorne argued that the public address of African Americans be "any recorded statement of a Black American in an attempt to speak to an overt or covert audience."[50]

Hawthorne's redefinition of public address has several important implications. First, Hawthorne clearly means for language, and specifically language *designed* to create change, to be at the center of the study of public address. Second, Hawthorne subordinates form to language, so public address is expanded to include a variety of discursive practices. Poetry and prose, for example, that seek "to inquire, to disseminate information, to find and/or to substantiate truth" are within the province of public address.[51] The third point follows from the second; namely, Hawthorne was advocating interdisciplinarity. Hawthorne envisioned a study of public address that crossed disciplines and redefined the boundaries of intellectual inquiry within the discipline. Hawthorne's essay itself examined recurring *topoi* or themes in diverse forms that included speeches, poetry, newspaper editorials, letters, and fiction by African Americans. Her essay, thus, examined the disciplines of speech communication, history, literature, and journalism. In this pro-interdisciplinary sense, Hawthorne's redefinition of public address was a predecessor of contemporary developments in the study of public address.

Following the implications of Hawthorne's essay, one could begin to study, for example, naming practices of and by African-American women as a form of public address. Clearly, naming has been a locus of oppositional praxis for African Americans since their enslavement. The term *African* as an ethnic indicator and the maintenance of West African personal names in the slave community are particularly

Table 13.1   Correspondence of West African Names With the Days of the Week

	Male	Female
Sunday	Quashee	Quasheba
Monday	Cudjo	Juba
Tuesday	Cubbenah	Benaba
Wednesday	Quaco	Cuba
Thursday	Quao	Abby
Friday	Cuffy	Pheba
Saturday	Quame (Kwame)	Mimba

interesting cases of this form of public address. In the late 18th century *African* became the term North American free Blacks most often used to name their institutions. Geneva Smitherman has suggested that, "This early preference for 'African' was logical since the African experience was still very immediate for many blacks, and the tantalizing possibility of returning there haunted them constantly."[52] Interestingly, the return to the use of *African* in the late 20th century to designate the group was suggested by an African-American woman, Ramona Edelin, who in a 1989 speech identified the change as a necessary "cultural offensive" against the debilitating effects on Blacks of White racism.[53]

Naming has played a significant role in maintaining African culture within the slave community. In his study of the enslavement of African Americans in 17th- and 18th-century South Carolina, the historian Peter Wood found numerous cases of Blacks with West African names. One South Carolina master who died before the Revolutionary War listed the following among his slaves: Allahay, Assey, Benyky, Bungey, Colley, Cumbo, Cush, Dusue, Esher, Into, Jehu, Meminah, Matillah, Meynell, Minto, Quamino, Quash, Quashey, Rinah, Sambo, Satirah, Sibbey, Tehe, Temboy, Tiffey, Yeabow, and Yeakney.[54] Linguists J. L. Dillard, Lorenzo Turner, and N. N. Puckett have found the West African practice of naming children after days of the week in slave communities throughout North America and the Caribbean.[55] The most common names and the days to which they correspond are shown in Table 13.1. Scholars such as Wood, Dillard, and Turner argue quite convincingly that maintaining these names was a means of resistance by Blacks to the onslaught of Euro-American culture.

In contemporary U.S. society, it is estimated that 86% of Black children will spend some time in a mother-only household and that 60% of all Black children will be born to unmarried women.[56] To the degree that women have control over the naming of their children, it becomes important to know the names and the reasons that African-American women name their children. This child's name is recorded and pronounced to the world each time the child says its name or someone calls the child and in this sense fulfills Hawthorne's requirements for a public address. To paraphrase Lorraine Hansberry's words, in the names of their sons and daughters, what is it that these women are trying to tell the world?

Notes

1. Lorraine Hansberry, *To Be Young, Gifted and Black* (New York: New American Library, 1969), p. 107.

2. In *The Life of Langston Hughes*, Arnold Rampersad records Hughes as writing about *Mulatto*: "I Sat and watched my first play—which I had conceived as a poetic tragedy—being turned into what the producer hoped would be a commercial hit" (p. 312). According to Rampersad, the producer of *Mulatto* was so anxious for another hit show that, "Soon the actors were reciting lines Hughes would not have written, and playing at least one scene he would not have conceived, the rape of the hero's sister by a White overseer ('Rape is for sex,' Martin Jones [the show's producer] explained. 'You have to have sex in a Broadway show')" (pp. 312-313).

3. *A Raisin in the Sun* ran for more than a year on Broadway, won a New York Drama Critics Award, became a movie, and showcased the talents of Sidney Poitier, Ivan Dixon, Ruby Dee, Ossie Davis, Louis Gossett, Claudia McNeil, Glenn Turman, and Diana Sands. Accorded the status of a classic, *A Raisin in the Sun* has been revived in performances around the world, has been translated into languages other than English, has appeared in numerous literary anthologies, and has continued to inspire scholars of literature.

4. Lillian O'Connor, *Pioneer Women Orators: Rhetoric in the Antebellum Reform Movement* (New York: Columbia University Press, 1954).

5. Doris G. Yoakam, "Women's Introduction to the American Platform," in William N. Brigance, ed., *A History and Criticism of American Public Address* (New York: Russell & Russell, 1960; originally printed 1943), pp. 155-156.

6. Quoted in John W. Blassingame, ed., *Slave Testimony: Two Centuries of Letters, Speeches, Interviews, and Autobiographies* (Baton Rouge: Louisiana State University Press, 1977), p. 123.

7. Yoakam, p. 155.

8. Yoakam, p. 155.

9. Neil Postman, *Amusing Ourselves to Death: Public Discourse in the Age of Show Business* (New York: Penguin, 1986), p. 40.

10. Postman, p. 40.

11. Postman, p. 40.

12. O'Connor, p. 70.

13. Olga Idriss Davis, "Maria W. Stewart: A Stalwart Figure of Black American Oratory," Paper presented at the Speech Communication Association (November 1986), p. 2; Benjamin Quarles, *The Black Abolitionists* (New York: Oxford University Press, 1969), p. 7; Marilyn Richardson, ed., *Maria W. Stewart, America's First Black Woman Political Writer: Essays and Speeches* (Bloomington: Indiana University Press, 1987), p. xiii.

14. Those lectures are: Lecture Delivered at the Franklin Hall (Boston, September 21, 1832); An Address Delivered Before the Afric-American Female Intelligence Society of America (Spring 1832; *Liberator* April 28, 1832); An Address Delivered at the African Masonic Hall (Boston, February 27, 1833); and Mrs. Stewart's Farewell Address to Her Friends in the City of Boston (September 21, 1833).

15. Richardson, *Maria W. Stewart*, p. 20.

16. Frances J. Horsford, quoted in O'Connor, p. 24.

17. O'Connor, p. 25.

18. O'Connor, pp. 25-26.

19. O'Connor, p. 27.

20. Quoted in O'Connor, p. 28.

21. O'Connor, p. 71.

22. Quoted in Yoakam, p. 163.

23. Yoakam, p. 164.

24. Shirley Yee, *Black Women Abolitionists: A Study of Activism, 1828-1860* (University of Tennessee Press, 1992), p. 113.

25. Quoted in Yoakam, p. 166.

26. Yee, p. 115.

27. Yee, p. 139.

28. Yee, p. 117.

29. Yee, p. 118.

30. O'Connor, *Pioneer Women*, p. 96.

31. O'Connor, *Pioneer Women*, p. 185.

32. Barbara Welty, *Dimity Convictions: The American Woman in the Nineteenth Century* (Athens: The Ohio University Press, 1976), p. 21.

33. Michele Wallace, "Who Owns Zora Neale Hurston?" in *Invisibility Blues: From Pop to Theory* (London: Verso, 1990), p. 182.

34. Carole Spitzak and Kathryn Carter, "Women in Communication Studies: A Typology for Revision," *The Quarterly Journal of Speech, 73* (1987), p. 401.

35. Ernest Wrage and Barnet Baskerville, *American Forum: Speeches on Historic Issues, 1788-1900* (New York: Harper & Brothers, 1960), p. ix.

36. Alice Moore Dunbar, *Masterpieces of Negro Eloquence: The Best Speeches Delivered by the Negro From the Days of Slavery to the Present Time* (1914; reprinted, New York: Johnson Reprint, 1970), "Preface."

37. Dunbar, *Masterpieces*, "Preface."

38. For example, it was a significant source for Delindus R. Brown and Wanda F. Anderson, "A Survey of the Black Woman and the Persuasion Process: The Study of Strategies of Identification and Resistance," *Journal of Black Studies, 9* (December 1978), pp. 233-248.

39. Walker's anthology is impressive. Included are addresses by: Maria Stewart, Frances Harper, Sarah Parker Remond, Anna J. Cooper, Mary Church Terrell, Ida B. Wells-Barnett, Fannie Lee Chaney, Constance Baker Motley, Mary Church Terrell, Alice Walker, Audre Lorde, Sojourner Truth, Lucy C. Laney, Georgia Washington, Fannie Barrier Williams, Mary McLeod Bethune, Shirley Chisholm, Angela Davis, Sadie T. Alexander, Patricia Roberts Harris, Edith S. Sampson, Margaret Walker Alexander, Coretta Scott King, and Barbara Jordan. Many of these addresses have been published and some of the 20th-century speeches are not the most interesting or representative of the speakers. One wishes that Robbie had unearthed more unpublished works for an anthology with such an auspicious title. One also wishes that Walker had devoted less attention to textual analysis; 70 pages are a pedantic discussion of Black women's oratory as a genre. Included in the discussion are uninteresting data such as number of words in sentences, the speaker's word choices, and recurring *topoi*.

40. Robert Branham, *Lift Every Voice: African American Oratory From 1787 to the Present* (University: University of Alabama Press, in press).

41. Karlyn Kohrs Campbell, *Man Cannot Speak for Her: A Critical Study of Early Feminist Rhetoric*, Vol. 1 (Westport, CT: Greenwood Press, 1989), p. vii.

42. Campbell, *Man Cannot Speak*, p. 145.

43. Marsha Houston, "Follow Us Into Our World: Feminist Scholarship on the Communication of Women of Color," ERIC ED 337 816/CS 507 510 (April 1991), p. 10.

44. Campbell, *Man Cannot Speak*, p. 155.

45. Houston, "Follow Us," p. 14.

46. Houston, "Follow Us," p. 16.

47. Ernest J. Wrage, "Public Address: A Study in Social and Intellectual History," *Quarterly Journal of Speech, 33* (1947), pp. 451-457.

48. Patricia Hill Collins, *Black Feminist Thought: Knowledge, Consciousness, and the Politics of Empowerment* (Boston: Unwin Hyman, 1990); Lynda F. Dickson, "Toward a Broader Angle of Vision in Uncovering Women's History: Black Women's Clubs Revisited," *Frontiers, 9*(2) (1987), pp. 62-68; Darlene Clark Hine, *Organization of American History's Magazine of History, 3*(1) (Winter 1988), pp. 7-13; Gerda Lerner, "A New Angle of Vision," in G. Lerner, ed., *The Creation of Patriarchy* (New York: Oxford University Press, 1986), pp. 11-14.

49. Elsa Barkley Brown, "Womanist Consciousness: Maggie Lena Walker and the Independent Order of St. Luke," *Signs: Journal of Women in Culture and Society, 14* (1989), pp. 610-633; Hazel V. Carby, *Reconstructing Womanhood: The Emergence of the Afro-American Woman Novelist* (New York: Oxford University Press, 1987); Patricia Hill Collins, *Black Feminist Thought: Knowledge, Consciousness, and the Politics of Empowerment* (Boston: Unwin Hyman, 1990); Darlene Clark Hine, "Rape and the Inner Lives of Black Women in the Middle West: Preliminary Thoughts on the Culture of Dissemblance," *Signs: Journal of Women in Culture and Society, 14* (1989), pp. 912-920; Marsha Stanback Houston, "Language and Black Woman's Place: Evidence From the Black

Middle Class," in P. A. Treichler, C. Kramarae, and B. Stafford, eds., *For Alma Mater: Theory and Practice in Feminist Scholarship* (Champaign: University of Illinois Press, 1985); Bernice Johnson Reagon, "Women as Culture Carriers in the Civil Rights Movements: Fannie Lou Hamer," in Darlene Clark Hine, ed., *Black Women in United States History* (New York: Carlson Publishing, 1990), Vol. 16, pp. 203-218.

50. Lucia S. Hawthorne, "The Public Address of Black America," in Jack L. Daniel, ed., *Black Communication: Dimensions of Research and Instruction* (New York: Speech Communication Association, 1974), p. 54.

51. Hawthorne, "The Public Address of Black America," p. 54.

52. Geneva Smitherman, *Talkin and Testifyin: The Language of Black America* (1977; reprinted Wayne State University Press, 1986), p. 36.

53. Ramona Hoage Edelin, "Address to the National Conference on the Infusion of African American Content in the School Curriculum: 'Curriculum and Cultural Identity,' " [October 7, 1989], *Vital Issues: The Journal of African American Speeches*, 1 (Winter, 1991), pp. 25-29. Of course, Edelin was not the only person using the term *African American*, but the conference at which she spoke was widely covered by the United States media. For a good discussion of the group names that people of African descent in the United States have used, see the chapter "Black Nationalism" in Mary F. Berry and John Blassingame, *Long Memory* (New York: Oxford University Press, 1982).

54. Peter H. Wood, *Black Majority: Negroes in Colonial South Carolina From 1670 Through the Stono Rebellion* (New York: Norton, 1974), p. 181.

55. J. L. Dillard, *Black English: Its History and Usage in the United States* (New York: Vintage, 1973), p. 124; N. N. Puckett, "Names of American Negro Slaves," in George P. Murdoch, ed., *Studies in the Science of Society* (New Haven, CT: Yale University Press, 1937); Lorenzo D. Turner, *Africanisms in the Gullah Dialect* (Chicago: University of Chicago Press, 1949).

56. National Research Council, *A Common Destiny: Blacks and American Society* (Washington, DC: National Academy Press, 1989), pp. 512, 522.

14. Before Althea and Wilma
African-American Women in Sports, 1924-1948

LINDA D. WILLIAMS

⚏ Tens of thousands of African-American women have participated in numerous sporting events during the first half of the 20th century, yet only the names of Althea Gibson and Wilma Rudolph are brought forward as examples of African-American women athletes who won fame before the Black and Women's Liberation Movements. Before Althea and Wilma, Black women, often working with their male counterparts, created numerous opportunities to participate in elite, collegiate, and recreational athletics. The African-American press, which was dedicated to building community pride, racial dignity, and racial equality, supported and promoted women's efforts in sports.

Table 14.1 briefly illustrates the breadth and depth of opportunities African-American women created and exercised. These individuals and women's teams were culled from the sports pages of the *Pittsburgh Courier* and the *Chicago Defender*, two of the most influential African-American weeklies.

African-American women participated in elite contests as well as in friendly and informal matches. They participated in the "common" sports of basketball and track as well as the "upper-crust" sports of golf and tennis. African-American women also found their way into managerial and ownership positions.

Scholars have been reluctant to examine the role of the African-American female athlete and her participation in various sport activities. Plagued by the "double burden" of racism and sexism, African-American sportswomen generally have been ignored or given only token attention in historical works (Williams, 1994). Studies of women's

AUTHOR'S NOTE: I wish to thank Peg Fabbro and Robert Kilpatrick for their comments, suggestions, and insight on the draft of this chapter.

Table 14.1 A Brief Listing Of African-American Women Athletes and Teams For Selected Sports

Sport	Clubs	High School	Collegiate	Elite/ National Athletes	Management/ Leadership

BASKETBALL	Blue Belt
	Brown Buddies
	Chicago Romas
	Mysterious Five
	Paramount
	Peerless Five
	Philadelphia
	Tribune
		Athens
		Bordentown
		Booker T.
		  Washington
		Downington
		Elkhorn
		Lincoln
		Southern
			Alabama State
			  Normal
			Barber-Scotia
			Bennett College
			Clafin College
			Paine College
			Shaw University
			Talladega College
			Tillotson College
				Eloise Burch
				Isadora Channels
				Ruby Crenshaw
				Ruth Glover
				Hattie Lindsay
				Inez Patterson
				Lula Porter
				Ora Washington
					Lenoir Cook
					Willette Goodlette Hill
					Jean Murrell
					Inez Patterson
					Ameila Roberts
					Fannie N. Scott
					Blanche Winston

MEN'S BASEBALL		Cleveland Giants[1] New Orleans Creoles[1] Newark Eagles[1]		Isabelle Baxter Lucille Gloria Dymond Laura Johnson	Lucille Herbert Clara Muree Jones Effa Manley
SOFTBALL	Sailor's Club Hi Speed Girls	McDonogh	Xavier University Southern University	Fabiola Wilson Lucille Gloria Dymond	
TRACK	Highland Park Athletic Club (A.C.) Mercury A.C. Olde Tymers A.C. Onteora Track Club	Mckees Rock Keith School	Fort Valley Normal Prairie View A & M Tennessee State Tuskegee Institute Wilberforce	Alice Coachman Jean Lane Audrey Patterson Estelle Pearson Tydie Pickett Louise Stokes	Jean Lane Christine Evans Petty Ameila Roberts Florence Wright

SWIMMING	Neptune Aquatic
	  Club
	Midwest Athletic
	  Club
		Carter Playground[2]
		Harlem Branch YWCA[2]
		Wabash YMCA[2]
		Washington Park[2]
			Hampton Institute
			Howard University
			North Carolina
			  College (NCCU)
				Pauline Jackson
				Edith Jeter
				Inez Patterson
				Ellen Ray
					Florence Allen
					Maxine Morrison
					Inez Patterson
					Natalie Pollock

Table 14.1 A BRIEF LISTING OF AFRICAN-AMERICAN WOMEN ATHLETES AND TEAMS FOR SELECTED SPORTS

Sport	Clubs	High School	Collegiate	Elite/ National Athletes	Management/ Leadership
TENNIS	Algonquin Tennis Club (T.C.) Ameita T.C. Germantown T.C. Keystone T.C. Lincoln T.C. Monumental T.C. Mother Seames T.C. Oriole T.C. Pacific Coast T.C. Prairie Tennis T.C. Shady Rest T.C. St. Louis T.C.		Hampton Institute Howard University Shaw University Tuskegee Institute Shaw University	Lula Ballard Eunice Brown Isadore Channels Elsie Conick Dorothy Ewell Juliette Harris Kathryn Jones Evelta Marcellus Margaret Peters Romounia Peters Mrs. C.O. Seames Ora Washington	Dorothy Ewell Laura V. Junior Inez Patterson Mrs. C.O. Seames
GOLF	Chicago Women's Golf Club (G.C.) Cosmopolitan G.C. Fairview G.C. Monumental G.C. Paramount G.C. Pioneer G.C. Royal G.C. St. Nicholas G.C. Wake Robin G.C.			Ella Able Cleo Ball Mel Moye Julia Siler Marie Thompson Sarah Smith Lucy Williams Geneva Wilson	Anna Black Paris Brown Ethel Harris Marie Thompson Lucy Williams
TRAP-SHOOTING	Circle X Merit & Gun Rod Present Day Gun Triangle Day Gun			Margaret Carter Ethel M. Haywood Bobbie Offord Mrs. Glenn V. Porter	

BOWLING	Aboriginee	Portland Cleaners[2]	Isabelle Baxter	Jean Dorsey
	Bowling Club (B.C.)	Westfield Beauty Salon[2]	Gladys Chesnut	Marge McAbee
	Chicago Termites	Woodlawn Alcumes[2]	Virginia Dolphin	Zelda Hines
	Pala-Ette		Faye Kersey	Rosilee Simmons
			Sara Sturdivant	

NOTE: This represents only a brief glance of African-American sportswomen and teams/organizations. It is neither complete nor extensive, but it does document the presence of participants and some opportunities.

1. Professional Men's Baseball Team
2. Recreational Teams

athletics ignored the Black experience, and studies of African-American sports minimized women's efforts. These works, written primarily from a White perspective, alleged that African-American women's participation in competitive sports was perceived less favorably than men's, and that participation was limited to only a few elite athletes. In a word, the historical commonplace of African-American women athletes is that Althea Gibson in tennis and Wilma Rudolph in track were the first and only African-American sportswomen to compete among elite athletes and that athletic stars who followed them received these opportunities through *Brown v. the Board of Education* and Title IX.

In contrast, African-American historians of Black sporting heritage make reference to an active sport milieu for African-American women. Edwin B. Henderson (1939) identified several women sports figures from the 1920s and 1930s in *Negro First in Sport*. He highlighted the achievements of sportswomen in basketball, tennis, track, golf, and swimming. Ora Washington, Mrs. C. O. Seames, Anita Gant, Lula Hymes, Ivy Wilson, Marie Thompson, Lucy Williams, Sarah Smith, Ethel Webb, and Inez Patterson were among some of the earliest Black women acknowledged. Unfortunately, contemporary writers rely exclusively on Henderson's work and fail to utilize newspapers or other primary sources to enhance the information available on the participation of Black women in sports before the 1950s. Additional information about these women, their opponents, rivalries, and sporting events remains locked in newsprint and eyewitness accounts.

There are many partial explanations for the lack of extensive historical description, analysis, and criticism concerning African-American sportswomen. Primary sources are scarce, difficult to find, and, because of inadequate indexing, extremely time-consuming to manipulate. Furthermore, there is an infinitesimally small number of scholars who are willing to do research in this area, even though the scholarship is well received as an important contribution to understanding American culture. The data that researchers do compile are often limited to chronological description, because the lack of sources is so great and the existing theoretical frameworks are so imbued with racist and sexist obstacles that their application to the data is impossible or farcical.

In this study I offer a description of the extent and influence of African-American women's athletic opportunities and endeavors. I examine the important convergence of the African-American press and its women's sporting heritage. Finally, I suggest a few themes that further feminist and African-American analysis and criticism might address in the expansion of their respective bodies of knowledge.

Table 14.1 indicates that African-American women, working within the confines and supportive structures of their racial community, created a vital sport milieu for themselves. Stories of their triumphs and challenges not only provide an important compensatory description of African-American women's sporting foremothers, they also provide the fundamental material upon which thoughtful historical analysis and theoretical construction must be based.

Opportunities for Participation

Recreational, amateur, interscholastic, and collegiate teams provided opportunities for women to compete within the community. Local YMCAs, YWCAs, churches, settlement houses, playgrounds, and other community agencies provided the basis for recreational and competitive sports. Girls and women also engaged in "play days" and competitive sports while attending high schools, training schools, and colleges. Several factors, including discrimination, the popularity of a sport, and a need for social affiliations and interactions, led to the establishment of Negro amateur clubs and governing agencies for sport. Many amateur teams featured the cities' best athletes, and others sponsored sporting activities through athletic and social clubs. Employment units including hospitals and colleges organized teams for women. Both the *Chicago Defender* and the *Pittsburgh Courier* sponsored tournament play for women.

Coverage of women in sports never equalled that of men, but Negro newspapers acknowledged and recognized women's sport participation. The *Courier* published 1,408 newspaper items on sportswomen between 1924 and 1948. Articles and photographs in both the Pittsburgh and Chicago papers displayed women in local, regional, and national competitions. The Chicago paper provided a greater number of photographs and narratives on women's sporting activities. Accounts published in the *Defender* from 1932 through 1948 more than doubled those appearing in the Pittsburgh paper during the same time frame.[1] The number of stories on women in the *Defender* exceeded the *Courier's* 25-year coverage by 331. Basketball, tennis, and track stories constituted the largest number of articles published in both papers.

Top Sports

Basketball

Women's basketball teams existed in both the North and the South. News on women's basketball appeared more frequently than on any other sport. Competition in the South was restricted by racism and societal attitudes about women. Stories about Southern amateur, recreational, or church basketball teams rarely appeared in either the Chicago or Pittsburgh paper, but competition at historically Black colleges and universities was very visible.[2] African-American sportswomen at these Southern colleges, training schools, and high schools participated among themselves and against other Black institutions. Tuskegee

Institute dominated basketball in the deep South. Clafin University and Paine College emerged as winning teams in South Carolina, and Shaw University and Bennett College represented the top round-ball teams in North Carolina. Summaries and scores of games from Florida, Georgia, Texas, Kentucky, and other Southern states were also published.

Similar to their White counterparts, these Southern institutions mostly played six-on-six, using girl's rules. Some of their leaders and coaches had been trained at White colleges, including Sargent's Training School and Oberlin College, whereas others had been influenced by educators who believed that competition and boy's rules were undesirable for women. Basketball for women at these Southern institutions extended beyond "play days." Many African-American colleges engaged in a regular basketball season from early January through March to determine state and league champions.[3] Similar to male basketball competitors, females at Tuskegee Institute, Shaw University, and other Black colleges received letter awards for their participation in the sport.[4]

African-American athletes in the North had several more avenues for participation and competition in basketball than their sisters in the South, even though only a few Black colleges or universities existed north of the Mason-Dixon Line. Churches, YMCAs, YWCAs, clubs, high schools, training schools, and employment units such as hospitals offered competition and leagues. Many Northern teams, which were coached by men or former players, used the same rules as boys. They played five members on each team. Some northern African-Americans competed against White teams or played on an interracial team. On some occasions, females competed against males.

African-American newspapers also supported and sponsored basketball for women's participation. Urged by lovers of the sport in an amateur way, and with the hope of really bringing the game home to the girls and young women in a sense to emphasize its worth (cited in Williams, 1988, p. 84), the *Courier* sponsored a girls' basketball league in 1925. The *Defender* also sponsored a girls' basketball team, the Bessye Bearden's Defender Crackerjacks, which played out of New York City. A featured column, entitled "Women in Athletics" or "Women in Sports," appeared in both papers and regularly highlighted basketball in the *Defender* (Williams, 1988, p. 84).

Under the leadership of Otto Bridges, the *Philadelphia Tribune* Girls were known as the "National Colored Champions of the World." Led by Miss Ora Washington, this team competed under boys' rules and dominated other African-American quintets. During their first 3 years (1931-1934), they compiled a 97-12 record. The 1934 *Tribune* Girls' team, composed of Washington, Rose Wilson, Louise Hill, Ruth Lockley, Lillie Berry, Helen Davis, Lillian Fontaine, Odessa Johnson, Catherine Thomas, and Evelyn Mann, toured the South ("Philly Girls," 1934). Another Southern Tour was scheduled in 1938. Miss Washington, the team's captain, was also a tennis standout.[5] The Chicago Romas, a quintet from Chicago, also featured two tennis standouts, Miss Isadore Channels and Miss Lula Porter.

Tennis

Tennis, which annually ranked first or second among the top sports, appeared to be the most desirable and popular amateur sport for Negroes in both papers. In 1916 the National American Tennis Association (ATA) was established as the governing body for this sport among African Americans, because the United States Lawn Tennis Association (USLTA) prohibited Negro clubs from joining its association. The USLTA also banned African Americans from participation in any of its sanctioned matches or tournaments. The ATA held its first national championships in 1917. Lucy Slowe of Baltimore won the first women's singles crown.

Arthur Francis (1928), the tennis and basketball expert of a New York-based Negro paper, promoted the ATA Championship as the "blue ribbon of American sporting endeavor" (p. 10) among Negroes, drawing "men and women from all walks of life, the rich and the poor, the famous and the unsung" (p. 10). Francis (1928) explicated that the ATA Nationals were more than an athletic event:

> It is an important part of our racial educational system, for it gives opportunity during its one week duration for people of one State to meet, get acquainted with, and study others from other States. It is a common ground of good fellowship, amiability and high class sporting idealism, it is an annual test of clean living, character building and tennis athletic ability. (p. 10)

W. Rollo Wilson (1928b), a writer for the Pittsburgh paper, criticized the ATA publicity staff for a 1928 press release that neglected the athletic aspects of the Nationals, while overemphasizing the social activities. This press release, "Nationals at Bordentown Gala Event" (1928), which was sent to various media sources, failed to publish names of athletic participants or information about the actual competition. Wilson (1928b) contended that writers frequently placed too much emphasis on the social aspects of our sports classics and neglected the athletic component. He insisted that true tennis fans desired to know the names of male and female stars and other participants entered in the tournament.

Both the Pittsburgh and the Chicago papers published media hype prior to, during, and after the Nationals. Narratives about the event, national rankings, and photographs of leading players also appeared.[6] News pertaining to regional tournaments such as the Southeastern Tennis Tournament and the Cockburn Cup; several state tournaments including North Carolina, Virginia, New Jersey, Pennsylvania, New

York and New England; and local and interstate rivalries were reported, regularly.

Miss Ora Washington was by far the most dominant African-American female player prior to Gibson, but "Mother Seames" was a role model for both young and old tennis players. Mrs. Seames of Chicago was known throughout the country as "Mother Seames" or as Mrs. C. O. Seames. Her first name, Mary Anne, rarely appeared in either the *Courier* or the *Defender*. Mrs. Seames learned the game of tennis in 1906 at the age of 38 and participated actively until her death in 1940. She traveled throughout the country to various interstate, regional, and national tournaments to achieve national rating in both singles and mixed doubles. Paired with Dr. L. C. Downing of Virginia, she won the national mixed doubles title in 1925 (Williams, 1989a). In 1927, Mother Seames purchased a house with an adjacent tennis court and donated it to the Midwestern Tennis Association, so that African-American girls and boys would have a facility of their own where they could play and dress ("Mrs. Seames Buys," 1927). She promoted the development of the sport in Chicago, throughout the Midwest, and on a national level.

Track

Track provided the most accessible avenue through sports for Negro women to break down racial prejudices. Its governing body, the Amateur Athletic Union (AAU), did not openly ban competition against African Americans. A story written by Chester Washington, a.k.a. "Ches," of the Pittsburgh paper, subtitled "Track Glory Has No Color Line," urged girls to participate in sporting activities approved by their school, because athletics provides a means for individual achievement, physical fitness, and fame for one's school (Ches, 1927). The opportunity to compete against Whites, the success of African-American athletes in interracial competition, and the recognition gained through both the Negro press and the daily press probably contributed to the prevalence and popularity of track in the African-American community.

The development and tradition of Tuskegee Institute Women's Track and Field Program, initiated in 1929, clearly illustrated the abilities and achievements of African-American women. Following a second place finish at the National Amateur Athletic Union (AAU) meet in 1936, these women returned in 1937 to capture the National crown. Tuskegee's triumph marked the first national championship won by an African-American institution, of either men or women. Unlike many of their male counterparts who gained fame in 1932 and 1936, Tuskegee's women demonstrated that an African-American institution could produce athletes who could obtain an American national team championship. Tuskegee's women retained the National track crown every year between 1937 and 1948, with the exception of 1943 when they finished second.

The prestige of being an Olympian and representing the United States in track and field started in 1932. Tydie Pickett and Louise Stokes became the first African-American women to win berths on the U.S. Olympic team, even though neither of these women actually participated in the 1932 Los Angeles Games. The Pittsburgh paper attributed their absence to their qualifying times, but the Chicago paper alleged racism. Both Pickett and Stokes earned berths on the 1936 Olympic Team, however. Miss Pickett, who competed in the finals of the 80 meter hurdles, hit the second hurdle and was unable to finish the race (Williams, 1987). Although these women did not obtain a medal, they were hailed as Olympic heroes. Fay Young's (1939) article, "What Has Become of Our U.S. Olympic Heroes?", mentioned these women, and he reported that both Pickett and Stokes were unemployed in 1939.

African-American women captured their first Olympic medals during the London Games. Miss Alice Coachman, a former Tuskegee Institute athlete, became the only U.S. female track athlete and the first African-American female to win a gold medal. Coachman, who represented Albany State University at the time, established an Olympic record in the high jump in 1948. It was Miss Audrey Patterson of Tennessee State University, however, a bronze medalist in the 200 meters, who was the first African-American woman to win a medal in the Olympic Games. A total of nine African-American women made the 1948 United States Olympic Team. Lillian Young, Bernice Robinson, Mae Faggs, Nell Jackson, Theresa Manuel, Mabel Walker, and Emma Reed were the remaining members.

The Negro community recognized the magnitude of the Olympic Games and opportunities available through track and field much earlier than the 1960s. Following the success of Jesse Owens and other Negroes during the 1936 Olympic Games, several Black writers urged Black colleges to spend more money in track and less in men's football. Park, a former track coach, insisted that these segregated competitions limited opportunities for the national exposure of achievements by Black college athletes. He urged college presidents to earmark more resources for track and field because the development of one superstar, such as Jesse Owens or Ralph Metacalfe, would generate far more national and international visibility and fame for Black colleges and African Americans than would the football classics ("Have Never," 1936).

Much of track's coverage focused on the Tuskegee Relays, the Women's National Amateur Athletic Union Championships, and potential Olympians. Interest in track appeared to be closely associated with success in the AAU National Championship and Olympic competition rather than the most widely reported sport in either the Chicago or Pittsburgh paper. Scholars maintain that track is the most prevalent sport among Blacks, and especially Black women, but they have failed to recognize that it was the only sport that did not openly ban African Americans from competition with Whites. As a result, the mass media reported African-American achievements in track in which they competed against Whites, while ignoring those sports activities featuring African Americans only. Thus, the perception of racial dominance in track may have emerged and been reinforced because African Americans frequently gained visibility and recognition in both the daily press and Negro newspapers.

Golf and Swimming

In addition to the sports already discussed, the Pittsburgh and Chicago papers covered a variety of activities, including golf and swimming, that are not believed to be popular or common among African Americans. Several men's golf clubs had a women's auxiliary, including Monumental, Fairview, St. Nicholas, Royal, and Pioneer, to name a few. African-American men and women demonstrated a "united division" in their efforts to gain access to tournaments and to all public courses, because only a few Negro-owned courses existed (Williams, 1989b). The United Golfers Association (UGA), the national governing body for African-American golfers, initiated an open national championship for men in 1926, one for amateurs in 1928, and a women's division in 1930. Unlike its White counterpart, the UGA allowed non-Black golfers to compete in its championship.

Female golfers from the Midwest dominated the women's division of the UGA champion during its first decade, but most of its men's open and amateur champions hailed from the East and the South. Women from the Midwest captured 9 of these 10 national titles between 1930 and 1939. The first woman champion, Miss Marie Thompson of Chicago and the Pioneer Golf Club, won in 1930. She successfully defended her title in 1931. In 1933 Miss Julia Siler of Paramount Golf Club (St. Louis, MO) defeated Mrs. Lucy Williams of Indianapolis, the defending champion. Douglass Park Course golfers Mrs. Ella Able and Mrs. Lucy Williams each won two consecutive titles during the following years.

Mrs. Williams became the first UGA golf champion, man or woman, to obtain three UGA titles. She gained permanent possession of the three-legged trophy for women when she retained her crown from 1936. Mrs. Williams annexed her first championship in 1932. During the first 8 years of the women's golf championship, Mrs. Williams finished second during the years in which she failed to capture the title. Mrs. Mel Moye, a Southerner from Atlanta, was the only person outside of the Midwest to surpass the talents of these Midwestern golfers during the first decade of the event (Williams, 1991).

Competition among cities extended beyond gender to the "bragging rights" of a city. One *Indianapolis Recorder* sportswriter, Lee

Johnson (1934), proclaimed, "Indianapolis can certainly be proud of its women golfers. For several years our women have dominated the upper brackets in golf circles in the nation" (p. 7), following Mrs. Ella Able's victory at the 1934 UGA Nationals. Women's achievements in sport contributed to the prestige and bragging rights of a city. Oftentimes, women competitors represented their cities well even when men failed. A Chicago writer's remarks following a tournament in Indianapolis during 1937 revealed the importance and value of women competitors to the city. He declared that though Chicago's seven men competitors stumbled to allow John Green of Indianapolis to capture the title, Mrs. Cleo Ball preserved Chicago's reputation by defeating the national champion, Miss Lucy Williams of Indianapolis (Mrs. Ball's, 1937). Mrs. Ball's win was more than an individual victory: It brought honor to the city of Chicago.

The Chicago paper published golf stories pertaining primarily to local golfers, the Mid-west Tournament, and the nationals, whereas the Pittsburgh paper reported mostly on the Eastern Golf Association Tournaments, activities in Eastern cities such as Philadelphia, Baltimore, and Washington, DC, and the nationals. East Coast female golfers played regularly and secured titles at the local, club, state, and regional levels, even though they failed to acquire national titles during the first decade of the UGA Women's Tournament. Mrs. Marguerite Brown, Mrs. Eloise Wright, Mrs. Ethel Terrell, Mrs. Laura Thoroughgood, and Miss Sarah Smith were among the top East Coast golfers (Williams, 1989a, 1989b).

In 1937 Mrs. Helen W. Harris organized the first African-American women's golf club, the Wake Robin Golf Club, with the intent of developing women golfers to capture the national title. During the late 1930s and the 1940s, Wake Robin golfers become perennial leaders in the sport and in the UGA. Working collectively with the men of the Royal Golf Club, these women helped to obtain the support of the Secretary of the Interior, Harold L. Ickes, in establishing a suitable course for African Americans in the nation's capital. Today, Wake Robin golfers continue to combat discrimination, to produce national champions, and to promote the sport of golf among women and youth (Williams, 1989b).

The establishment of a second African-American women's golf, the Chicago Women's Golf Club, occurred approximately 6 months later (Williams, 1989b, 1991). These Chicago women became the first women's club to join the UGA, in 1939. They also were the first women's club to host the UGA National Championships. Chicago Women's Golf Club received the support of both the *Chicago Defender* and the president of the Amateur Golf Association (AGA) when the newly formed AGA held a national golf championship for amateurs one week prior to the UGA championships on the same course in 1940 (Williams, 1989a). The presence of two national championships for African Americans within one week of each other illustrates not only dissension among amateur and professional golfers, but the popularity of the sport and the desire for an event exclusively for amateurs. Like the members of the Wake Robin Golf Club, the Chicago Women's Golf Club has also had its struggles and has maintained its existence and programs into the 1990s.

Similar to tennis and golf, swimming also banned African Americans from its national championships, but YMCAs, YWCAs, playgrounds, high schools, and colleges provided opportunities for participation and competition in aquatic activities by means of recreational and amateur water carnivals. Interest in and growth of professional swimming were also promoted in the community.

Gertrude Erderle's record-breaking swim of the English Channel sparked interest and opportunities for long-distance swims by women of all races and nationalities. This enthusiasm extended into the Negro community and the Pittsburgh paper. Under the direction of the Reverend Samuel P. W. Drew, pastor of the National Cosmopolitan Baptist Institutional Church, the White Cross Bureau held a contest to identify a Negro woman who would train to cross the Channel. The contest was opened to all Negro girls and women regardless of religious affiliation, and the organization was willing to support and finance the training of an athlete for a year ("Washington Organization," 1926). In 1927 the *Courier* also started a campaign to generate attention and interest in long-distance swimming. Floyd J. Calvin, a writer for the *Courier*, proclaimed that the paper recognized that race women were capable of achieving success in marathon swims and urged them to compete in the sport (Calvin, 1927). That same year a New York City swimmer, Ellen Ray, who aspired to swim the English Channel, was selected as Miss *Pittsburgh Courier* and wore the colors of the paper in her swim across the Hudson.

The Pittsburgh paper also published a couple of articles on Pauline Jackson, another Negro from New York City, who competed in two of the Wrigley Marathons and who planned to swim the English Channel.[7] During the Second Annual Marathon in 1927, she dropped out of the Wrigley Toronto swim due to exhaustion. Nevertheless, the following year the paper printed a story to solicit funds to finance her training for a swim across the English Channel (Wilson, 1928a, 1928c). Of the 75 male and female entries in the Third Wrigley Marathon, only 16 "survived" the elements to complete the swim. Jackson had a respectable finish despite dropping out of the 10-mile swim after completing 6½ miles. Her performance surpassed several other international and national female swimmers (Wilson, 1928d). She continued to train, but she was unable to achieve her quest to capture the women's world championship. Again in 1931 she was forced to abandon the race one-half mile from the finish due to chills and exhaustion ("Guard Seeks," 1931).

Bowling

Consistent with other White sport organizations, the American Bowling Congress (ABC) prohibited interracial competition. Organized in 1939, the National Negro Bowling Association (NBA) provided both contests and esprit de corps among African-American bowlers ("Indianapolis Site," 1947). Interest in and growth of bowling among women and men led to the sponsorship of the Sea Ferguson Annual Bowling Classic. In 1946, this event, sanctioned by the National Bowling Association, was the only all-female tournament with an array of events for women that drew entrants nationwide ("Indianapolis Site," 1947). The total prize money for women was $600; the sum for men was $750. Miss Gladys Chestnut of Indianapolis rolled the highest series among the more than 100 female Midwestern and Eastern bowlers. She received $125 cash and a diamond-studded medal for the victory. The runner-up was awarded $100. Miss Chestnut retained the individual women's champion in 1947 ("Gladys Chestnut," 1947).

Other organizations provided competition for African-American men and women. Efforts by the UAW-CIO to combat racial bias in bowling led to the establishment of a bowling association and an open championship in 1947 ("Auto Workers," 1947). During the same year, the *Defender* initiated the first bowling championship exclusively for women. The winner, Daisy Glenn, captured a first place trophy and received $100 in cash and a diamond medal for her victory in the first *Chicago Defender's* Annual Women's Diamond Singles Sweepstakes ("*Defender's* Diamond," 1947).

Leadership

African-American women not only participated in a variety of sports, they experienced a wide range of leadership roles in athletics. Prominent female owners in baseball were Mrs. C. O. Taylor, the Indianapolis ABC; and Mrs. Effa Manley, co-owner with her husband of the Newark Eagles. Mrs. Effa Manley served as the business manager of the Newark Eagles, and she influenced decisions within the National Negro League. In 1976, she coauthored *Negro Baseball . . . Before Integration*, a history of Negro Baseball, which also reveals her roles and activities for the team and Negro baseball.

The national pastime of baseball provided other opportunities for sportswomen to supervise and participate with men. The Boston ABC established a precedent in 1935 when they elected Mrs. Clara Muree Jones as president of the baseball team ("Boston ABC," 1935). Allen Page, the innovative owner of the New Orleans Creoles, a "true" businessman who had enterprises outside of baseball and sports, hired Lucille Herbert as a coach in 1947 (Jones, 1948; "Woman Coach," 1947).

Page also acquired players who were bona fide athletes with experience in softball and with ties to the city. The New Orleans Creoles featured Fabiola Wilson—who attended Xavier University—in the outfield and recruited a second female, Lucille Gloria Dymond—of Southern University—in 1948. Both women had graduated from McDonogh High School in New Orleans (Jones, 1948).

Leadership roles of women extended beyond baseball to other sports. Laura Junior, a New Jersey tennis player, became the first female vice president in the ATA. Although most women trained and coached members of their own sex, a few women worked with men, as mentioned earlier. The women's basketball coach at Tennessee State University, Mrs. Willette (Goodlette) Hill, also coached the men's basketball team of the university. Women also held management positions in horse racing and boxing (Williams, 1988).

Both the *Courier* and the *Defender* documented that the whole family might be involved in a business venture. For example, Mrs. Ann Booker owned at least two horses, Shadowdale and Pleasant Smiles, which were ridden by her son, F. Booker, and trained by her husband, Hudson ("Pleasant Smiles Ridden," 1927; " 'Pleasant Smiles' Owned," 1927; " 'Shadowdale,' Carrying" 1927). A similar situation existed in boxing. Mrs. Priscilla Anderson, the trainer of Floyd Williams, a middleweight boxer, held licenses in Ohio, Indiana, and the District of Columbia. Her father managed her boxers, and her husband, who worked on the railroad, recruited fighters to work with his wife and father-in-law. Her boxers valued her knowledge and welcomed her presence at ringside ("Now the New Look," 1948).

Even this cursory storytelling reveals just how much additional fundamental research is required in order to appreciate fully the sport experiences of African-American women and to analyze their role in African-American, American, and world culture. Nevertheless, even these few descriptions illuminate the mutually productive relationships among the world of the African-American sportswomen, the African-American press, and the African-American community.

A poll conducted by the *Pittsburgh Courier* reaffirmed the prevalence of male sports figures, even though these experts acknowledged several female tennis participants. In 1943, during World War II, an overseas soldier wrote Lucius Jones, a columnist for the Pittsburgh paper, inquiring: "Who Are the Greatest Colored Athletes of All Time?" (Jones, 1943a). A group of 10 veteran sportsmen—including athletes, sportswriters, club owners, promoters, and trained observers—cast votes to select the winner. Experts ranked the top three people in these sports: boxing, baseball, indoor track, tennis, golf, football, basketball, colored football players at White institutions, and colored basketball players at White institutions. Each expert nominated the following athletes by sport: Jack Johnson and Joe Louis (boxing); Jesse Owens (track); Dolly King (college basketball); Johnny Borican (indoor track);

and Ora Washington and Lula Ballard and Nathaniel and Franklin Jackson (tennis-doubles teams).

The winner of this poll, Joe Louis, received 100 points and was the unanimous choice of these 10 experts. Washington and Ballard, who received 80 points, tied the Jackson brothers for third place honors in the poll. This female pair captured 9 of the 12 National American Tennis Association (ATA) doubles titles between 1925 and 1936 and a host of state and local titles. Jack Johnson, Jesse Owens, Dolly King, and John Borican captured second place honors. Each of these athletes received 90 points (Jones, 1943b).

Men identified in "The Greatest Colored Athletes of All Time" poll represented a variety of sports, but the only women acknowledged were former national women's tennis champions. Experts perceived tennis players as more visible and worthy than Tuskegee's women who amassed both individual and team titles in track and field at the AAU Nationals. Jean Lane of Wilberforce, who received two votes for Women Athlete of the Year in the Associated Press, was also ignored. Were track participants perceived less favorably than other women athletes or did the abundance of outstanding male heroes eliminate their names?

The presence of African Americans in tennis is particularly odd for several reasons. Certainly, tennis is an "acceptable" sport for women, but it did not provide an outlet for interracial competition. African-American women's participation in the sport prior to Althea Gibson has seldom been told or acknowledged. It is possible that these experts' selection reaffirmed the significance of "appropriate" sport activities for women rather than acknowledging the presence and achievements of African-American female tennis players. Tennis has been perceived as a "country club" sport. We have thus been lead to believe that African Americans had neither the time, facilities, nor dollars to engage in this activity, even if they had the knowledge or the desire to learn and to play the game. Finally, the inclusion of an amateur sport, especially one that was played among African-American participants, illustrated the significance of the sport within the Negro community.

Ora Washington, who excelled in both tennis and basketball, garnered the greatest number of points among women in the poll to determine "The Greatest Colored Athletes of All Time." She captured 8 of 10 national ATA ladies' singles tennis championships between 1929 and 1937. Her point total, 65, surpassed those of several male sports figures who are widely known today, including Fritz Pollard, Satchel Paige, Henry Armstrong, Paul Robeson, and DeHart Hubbard. Miss Washington received fifth place honors and was among the top 11 athletes named. Helen Wills Moody, the top American White tennis player, refused to play Miss Washington, even in exhibition matches. Unfortunately, there was no Alice Marble to be a champion for the integration of tennis. Flora Lomax of Detroit and Isadore Channels of Chicago constituted the remaining women tennis players.

Women were among the top vote-getters in other polls sponsored by the *Pittsburgh Courier*. A female track star rather than a tennis player was honored. Alice Coachman, a Tuskegee Institute high jumper and sprinter, earned 10 first place points to tie for third place honors in a selection recognizing outstanding athletes of 1946 (Smith, 1947). Coachman's achievements tied her with Joe Louis, who previously had been selected as "The Greatest Colored Athlete of All Time" in 1943 and with Bill Willis, a football star. Judges named first and second choices in the following sports: baseball, Negro baseball, college football, basketball, track, boxing, golf, tennis, and bowling. Jackie Robinson received the most votes. L. Jackson and M. Motley, two football players, tied for second with 20 first place votes.

Both sporting activities and the selection process for these polls by the *Courier* favored men, because they established categories and criteria for selection. "The Greatest Colored Athletes of All Time" included all colored athletes, whether male or female, in both professional and amateur sports through 1943. In spite of these biases some sportswomen's achievements were deemed comparable with those of men. Accomplishments by Ora Washington and the doubles duo of Washington and Ballard placed each higher in some instances than some of their male counterparts and than men in other amateur and professional sports. Coachman's ranking in the 1946 *Courier* poll reaffirmed the support for women athletes and the success of African-American women in track on a yearly basis. Incidently, this honor was awarded to Coachman prior to her competition and success at the 1948 Olympic Games. This acknowledgment and recognition of her achievements tied her with Joe Louis for third place honors.

An amateur contest conducted by the *Chicago Defender* revealed that amateur women athletes were more popular than amateur men. On May 21, 1927, the *Defender* asked its readers to clip out and submit a coupon from the newspaper identifying their favorite Chicago amateur athlete. Each coupon was worth 10 points; it cost 2 cents to mail the entry. This contest, which was jointly sponsored by Universal Pictures and the *Chicago Defender*, ran from May 21 to July 22, 1927. All nominees had to be amateurs and the coupon had to be used for submission. At the end of the first week, there was a four-way tie for first place between Mrs. C. O. Seames and three men: Mother Seames played a major role in the development of tennis in Chicago and the Midwest; Thomas Verdell and Robert Colin were collegiate athletes at Northwestern University; and Hansel Jones was a Wendell Phillips High School athlete. Each amateur had 20 points ("Popularity Contest," 1927; "Mrs. Seames' Name Entered," 1927).

In mid-June one writer suggested that female athletes were more popular than male athletes, or at least they received more support from their friends than the men did ("Mrs. Seames Still Leads," 1927). Hansel Jones's 500 points ranked him third behind two women athletes. Mrs. Seames tallied 540 points to rank first, and her nearest opponent, Miss Virginia Willis, the captain of the Olivet Baptist Church Basketball Team, received 510. The writer's comment alone is significant for several reasons. It suggests not only that women amateur athletes were more popular than men, but that their friends, both men and women, read the sports section. The contest coupon appeared in the sports pages rather than in another section of the paper. Finally, the popularity of these women demonstrated that their achievements were well known and recognized in Chicago.

Readers responded to the writer's remarks, but the results were only temporary. Standings published for the following week revealed that Hansel Jones emerged as the top vote-getter to become the first man to lead the contest. His stay at the top was brief, however, because Irma Mohr, a medal winner in the *Chicago Tribune* golf tournament and member of Olivet Baptist Church quintet basketball team, became the new leader.

An interesting battle for the title developed among the women. Writers for the paper expected the winner of the contest to garner about 3,000 points. Mohr, who was a chiropractor, and Mrs. Seames achieved this mark by mid-July. Irma Mohr, the contest winner, received almost 18,000 points. Her nearest opponent, Mrs. Seames, earned 10,730. Corrine Robinson, an all-around athlete in basketball, track, and tennis, received slightly more than 5,000 points. Virginia Willis, captain of the Olivet Baptist Church quintet basketball, edged Hansel Jones out by 130 points to capture fourth place with 1,400 points ("Last Minute Rally," 1927).

This contest, which tallied coupons submitted by readers to determine the winner, provides some generalizations and raises some questions. First, readers submitted coupons recognizing and honoring sportswomen. Second, amateur women athletes appeared to be more popular than men. Women represented one third of the 21 nominees. Women claimed the top four positions in the contest; only two men received 1,200 or more points. Third, African-American women competed in activities beyond track. Two of the top three women finishers were recognized for their participation in basketball, whereas Mrs. Seames's activity was tennis. Some African-American women competed in more than one sport. Mohr participated in at least three sports with success: basketball, golf, and tennis.

Although the aforementioned polls in both the *Courier* and the *Defender* illustrated the popularity of women in sports and recognition of these women by experts, they also revealed some problems associated with compiling an accurate history of Negro sportswomen. I find it disturbing that a basketball teammate who received little more than a name in the box results obtained more votes than two of the leading

Chicago women athletes who appeared frequently on the sport pages. Miss Mohr's victory over Virginia Willis, the captain of Olivet's basketball team, and Mrs. Seames raises some questions about criteria for recognition and acknowledgment. Why did a teammate receive more support, as indicated by coupons submitted, than the leading performer and captain of the same team? What actually determines the recognition of female athletes? Is it the sporting event, the woman's social status, her athletic ability, her physical attributes, or her popularity within the community? Women's participation at local and regional levels must be compiled to provide a better understanding of activities offered, the levels of competition, and availability of facilities, as well as participants, coaches, and other administrators.

It should be quite evident that historians such as Arthur R. Ashe, Jr., who allege that women did not participate in sports are wrong. Ashe (1988) states:

> Most black women spent very little time engaged in competitive, organized sport. They worked in the home with few appliances of convenience. In the South, two-thirds of all women who worked outside their own homes did so as domestics in homes of whites. The only times for recreation were Saturday and Sunday afternoons. The percentage of black college women heavily involved in sport was probably less than five percent. (p. 75)

This is simply incorrect. Because it is inconceivable that he and other scholars with the same assertions would deliberately lie or conceal information about African-American women's participation in sports, a deeper and more critical examination of the fundamental theoretical presuppositions are in order. One of the most insidious effects of the oppression of racism and sexism is the development of the ideology that certain "rights" or "opportunities" are or even can be *given* to the oppressed by the oppressors.

These stories of African-American sporting experiences make it quite clear that these women themselves, often working with their male counterparts and using other institutions of the African-American community, created their own sporting opportunities. No Supreme Court decision or Congressional action by a benevolent oppressor created the opportunities for them. The myth that African-American women did not participate in sports because they were too poor, tired, or deprived highlights the sense of helplessness that oppression both feeds on and creates. Theorists in women's studies and sports will eventually have to recognize and explain that African-American women of ordinary, national, and international calibre participated in sports before Althea and Wilma, despite the obstacles of racism and sexism in society.

Notes

1. The national edition of the *Pittsburgh Courier* was read for a 25-year span, and the national edition of the *Chicago Defender* was read from 1932 through 1948.

2. Although the national edition of the *Courier* and the *Defender* failed to publish sports stories of southern YWCAs and women's clubs, articles and photographs of these sportswomen appeared in the *Atlanta Daily World* during the brief years read, 1930-1936, and in the *Norfolk Journal and Guide.*

3. For regular season and conference play, see: "Presenting Carolina's Clever Cage Champ" (1937); "Shaw Quintets in Double Win" (1938); White (1939); "Shaw Bearettes Floor Champ" (1939); "Tuskegee Team Champs" (1939); Smith (1939); "Shaw Quintette Beats West Virginia" (1947); "S.C. State Win" (1947).

4. For letter awards see: "49 Receive Shaw Awards" (1938); "28 Girls Receive Awards" (1938); "Letters Awarded to Forty-Three at Shaw" (1940).

5. Writers for the Negro press generally used the terms *Miss* and *Mrs.* to denote status for African-American women. Whites seldom if ever acknowledged or assigned these terms to women of color, even though *Miss* or *Mrs.* were frequently assigned to White women. The use of the contemporary term *Ms.* is inappropriate for this time period.

6. Similar news items about the ATA National Championships appeared in prominent Negro magazines such as *Crisis* and *Opportunity.*

7. W. Rollo Wilson (1928a) reported that Pauline Jackson lived in Baltimore rather than in New York City. Articles published during 1927 as well as a later article by Wilson (1928d) confirm that she resides in New York City.

References

Ashe, Arthur, Jr. (1988). *A hard road to glory: A history of the African-American athlete 1919-1945.* New York: Warner Books.

Auto workers set to fight bias. (1947, September 27). *Pittsburgh Courier* (National ed.), p. 13.

Boston ABC has woman president. (1935, March 9). *Pittsburgh Courier* (National ed.), p. 4.

Calvin, Floyd J. (1927, February 5). Ellen Ray to attempt 17-mile swim as "Miss Courier" now member of Red Cross Life Saving Corps, she will try to set new record for Race women. *Pittsburgh Courier* (National ed.), p. 4.

"Ches." (1927, June 18). As cinders flew in Pitt stadium. *Pittsburgh Courier* (National ed.), p. 5.

Defender's diamond medal and $100 to Chicagoan. (1947, May 24). *Chicago Defender* (National ed.), p. 20.

49 receive Shaw awards. (1938, May 28). *Pittsburgh Courier* (National ed.), p. 16.

Francis, Arthur. (1928, August 15). On the courts. *New York Amsterdam News*, p. 10.

Gladys Chestnut is pin queen. (1947, February 8). *Pittsburgh Courier* (National ed.), p. 17.

Guard seeks swim title; girl near-victory. (1931, September 12). *Pittsburgh Courier* (National ed.), p. 5.

Hansel Jones grabs lead in popularity vote contest. Mrs. Seames drops to 3rd. (1927, June 25). *Chicago Defender* (City ed.), p. 5.

Have never produced star on track, columnist says. (1936, May 9). *Chicago Defender* (National ed.), p. 14.

Henderson, Edwin B. (1939). *The Negro in sports.* Washington, DC: Associated Publishers.

Indianapolis site of women's pin class. (1947, January 18). *Pittsburgh Courier* (National ed.), p. 17.

Johnson, Lee A. (1934, September 8). Shooting the works. *Indianapolis Recorder*, p. 7.

Jones, Lucius. (1943a, April 17). The sports round-up. *Pittsburgh Courier* (National ed.), p. 19.

Jones, Lucius. (1943b, April 24). The sports round-up. *Pittsburgh Courier* (National ed.), p. 19.

Jones, Lucius. (1948, July 17). Girls featured on crack New Orleans ball team. *Pittsburgh Courier* (National ed.), p. 10.

Last minute rally brings victor in most popular athlete contest; vote large. (1927, July 23). *Chicago Defender* (City ed.), p. 4.

Letters awarded to forty-three at Shaw. (1940, May 25). *Pittsburgh Courier* (National ed.), p. 17.

Manley, Effa, & Hardwich, Leon H. (1976). *Negro baseball . . . before integration*. Chicago: Adams Press.

Mrs. Ball's 93 wins in gold meet. (1937, August 7). *Chicago Defender* (National ed.), p. 21.

Mrs. Seames buys ground for tennis at 32nd and Vernon. (1927, July 16). *Chicago Defender* (City ed.), p. 5.

Mrs. Seames' name entered for silver cup. (1927, May 28). *Chicago Defender* (City ed.), p. 5.

Mrs. Seames still leads in contest; Others made gains. (1927, June 18). *Chicago Defender* (City ed.), p. 4.

Nationals at Bordentown gala event. (1928, August 11). *Pittsburgh Courier* (National ed.), p. 4.

Now the "new look" is in the fight game. (1948, May 15). *Pittsburgh Courier* (National ed.), p. 14.

Philly girls win 97 out of 109 games (ANP). (1934, March 3). *Pittsburgh Courier* (National ed.), p. 5.

"Pleasant Smiles," owned by race woman, trained by her husband and ridden by her son, wins before 12,000 fans. (1927, April 9). *Pittsburgh Courier* (National ed.), p. 4.

Pleasant Smiles ridden by owner's son wins at Bowie. (1927, April 9). *Chicago Defender* (City ed.), p. 4.

Popularity contest. (1927, May 21). *Chicago Defender* (City ed.), p. 5.

Presenting Carolina's clever cage champ [Photo]. (1937, March 27). *Pittsburgh Courier* (National ed.), p. 16.

S.C. State win. (1947, March 1). *Pittsburgh Courier* (National ed.), p. 17.

"Shadowdale," carrying Booker colors finishes first at Harve de Grave. (1927, October 8). *Pittsburgh Courier* (National ed.), p. 4.

Shaw Bearettes floor champ. (1939, March 25). *Pittsburgh Courier* (National ed.), p. 16.

Shaw quintets in double win. (1938, January 15). *Pittsburgh Courier* (National ed.), p. 16.

Shaw quintette beats West Virginia. (1947, March 1). *Pittsburgh Courier* (National ed.), p. 16.

Smith, Wendell. (1939, March 25). Smitty's sports spurts. *Pittsburgh Courier* (National ed.), p. 16.

Smith, Wendell. (1947, January 4). Brooklyn prospects tops *Courier* poll. *Pittsburgh Courier* (National ed.), p. 12.

Tuskegee team champs. (1939, March 25). *Pittsburgh Courier* (National ed.), p. 16.

28 girls receive awards. (1938, June 18). *Pittsburgh Courier* (National ed.), p. 17.

Washington organization ready to back training of girl selected in tryouts. (1926, September 11). *Pittsburgh Courier* (National ed.), p. 5.

White, Bill. (1939, March 9). Claim S.A.C. title. *Pittsburgh Courier* (National ed.), p. 16.

Williams, Linda D. (1987, May). *The coverage of women in sports in the Negro press: The Pittsburgh Courier, 1924-1948 and the Chicago Defender, 1937-1941*. Paper presented at North American Society for Sport History Conference, Columbus, OH.

Williams, Linda D. (1988). *Analysis of American sportswomen in two Negro newspapers: The Pittsburgh Courier, 1924-1948, and the Chicago Defender, 1932-1948*. Eugene: University of Oregon, College of Human Development and Performance, Microforms Publications.

Williams, Linda D. (1989a, April). *Bridging the gap: The Negro press and the invisible athlete, female and Black.* Paper presented at Women's Studies Colloquium, Chapel Hill, NC.

Williams, Linda D. (1989b, March). *Striving for par: Wake Robin Golf Club and Black women in golf.* Paper presented at North American Society for the Sociology of Sport, Washington, DC.

Williams, Linda D. (1991, May). *"Not only do we cook greens, we play on them, too.": Chicago Black female golfers, 1930 through 1937.* Paper presented at North American Society for Sport History Conference, Chicago.

Williams, Linda D. (1994). Sportswomen in Black and White: Sport history from an Afro-American perspective. In Pamela J. Creedon (Ed.), *Women, media and sport: Challenging gender values* (pp. 45-66). Thousand Oaks, CA: Sage.

Wilson, W. Rollo. (1928a, February 11). Sports shots. *Pittsburgh Courier* (National ed.), p. 5.

Wilson, W. Rollo. (1928b, August 18). Sports shots. *Pittsburgh Courier* (National ed.), p. 6.

Wilson, W. Rollo. (1928c, September 1). Sports shots. *Pittsburgh Courier* (National ed.), p. 6.

Wilson, W. Rollo. (1928d, September 15). Sports shots. *Pittsburgh Courier* (National ed.), p. 6

Woman coach for Creoles (NNPA). (1947, July 26). *Pittsburgh Courier* (National ed.), p. 14.

Young, Fay. (1939, September 9). What has become of our U.S. Olympic heroes? *Chicago Defender* (National ed.), p. 13.

15. Black Women in Concert Dance
The Philadelphia Divas

MELANYE WHITE-DIXON

𝕤 This chapter will present profiles of four African-American women dancers who established careers as performing artists between 1950 and 1980: Judith Jamison (Alvin Ailey American Dance Theatre), Delores Brown Abelson (New York Negro Ballet), China White [formerly Melva Murray White] (Dance Theatre of Harlem), and Donna Lowe Warren (Philadelphia Grand Opera Company). All were trained by Marion Cuyjet at the Judimar School in Black Philadelphia. They took advantage of the opportunities that emerged because of the pioneering work of Marion Cuyjet, Katherine Dunham, and Pearl Primus and became members of an elite group of Black female dancers who achieved noteworthy status in the concert dance world.

The chapter will be divided into three sections: Cuyjet and the Judimar School, profiles of the dancers, and strategies for survival.

Background and Orientation

My interest in concert dance in Black Philadelphia stems from my experiences as a young dancer in New York during the 1970s. Many of the most accomplished dancers on the scene and those I most admired were from Philadelphia's Black community. When I began conducting research on concert dance in 1982, I was able to turn my curiosity into a formal investigation about the training that these dancers received. Who were the dance educators responsible for nurturing their talent? My preliminary investigation revealed the work of Marion Cuyjet.

Cuyjet established the Judimar School in 1948 in order to provide increased opportunities in concert dance preparation and performance for African-American youth in Philadelphia. Her initial vision was to produce America's first Black ballerina. Early in the development of Judimar, her vision expanded to offering dance as a means of social, educational, recreational, and cultural development.

There was a thriving dance education community in Black Philadelphia from the late 1940s to the early 1970s. Dance students who were prepared during this period were fortunate to have dance teachers who were unconditionally committed to developing proficient artists. Cuyjet's school was a prime catalyst in promoting and developing dance education in Black Philadelphia. Several of her students pursued performing careers with dance companies such as the Alvin Ailey American Dance Theatre, Jerome Robbins's Ballet USA, Harkness Ballet, the Katherine Dunham Dance Company, the Rod Rodgers Dance Company, the Arthur Hall Afro-American Dance Ensemble, the Philadelphia Civic Ballet, and the Philadelphia Grand Ballet Company.

Methodology

This chapter provides historical and biographical documentation of Marion Cuyjet and the Judimar School and four of her former students: Delores Brown Abelson, Donna Lowe Warren, Judith Jamison, and China White. The dancers profiled were chosen because of their pioneering achievements in concert dance and because they have maintained close personal ties with Cuyjet. Methods of gathering data included interviews with Marion Cuyjet, the dancers profiled in this chapter (Delores Brown Abelson, Donna Lowe Warren, Judith Jamison, and China White), Cuyjet's family, her colleagues, and former students. I also consulted dissertations, books, periodicals, newspaper articles, Cuyjet's photo collection, scrapbooks, recital programs, and Judith Jamison's autobiography, *Dancing Spirit*. Special research collections consulted included the Charles Blockson Afro-American Collection at Temple University; two research collections of the New York City Public Library: The Schomburg Collection and The Joe Nash Dance Archives; and the Dance Collection at Lincoln Center Library of the Performing Arts.

Cuyjet and the Judimar School

Marion Cuyjet was born on July 29, 1920. Her parents, Alonzo and Frances Durham, relocated to Philadelphia from Cheswold, DE, in the early 1900s. The family descended from a community referred to as Delaware Moors.[1] Cuyjet's initial interest in dance was recreational. She began formal dance studies at age 14 in the mid-1930s with dance education pioneer Essie Marie Dorsey. Cuyjet fondly remembers the event in the following account:

> Some friends of mine from Sunday School [First Church] told me that Essie
> Marie was to reopen her studio. All my friends had invitations to the opening
> except me. I asked to go with them. I did not let my mother know about it because
> she would not let me go if I did not have a invitation. Classes were 25 cents. I
> only had enough money for "car fare" home. My friend "Wheedie" [Edith]
> Daniels loaned me the money for class. When I got to the school Mrs. Dorsey
> invited me to join the class.[2]

Opening in 1926, Dorsey's school offered courses in ballet, Spanish,
and tap dancing. During this era most Americans were more familiar
with and accepting of show dancing (e.g., Broadway, Vaudeville, night
clubs) than with concert dance forms and techniques. Dorsey's lavish
recitals became popular events, and she is responsible for providing
the groundwork for the acceptance of concert dance and formal dance
studies in Black Philadelphia.[3] Dorsey was a crusader for providing
opportunities for Black children to study dance, especially ballet. The
late dancer, choreographer, and teacher William Dollar once remarked:
"Essie Marie Dorsey deserves a place in history as a pioneer spirit for
the advancement of the Black dancer in American ballet."[4] In order to
learn her craft, Dorsey studied with many renowned ballet instructors
in New York City. Because ballet studios were closed to African Americans, Dorsey passed for Latino so that she could enroll in leading
dance schools in the 1920s and 1930s. She also studied privately with
White dance pioneers Ruth St. Denis, Ted Shawn, and William Dollar.

The emphasis at the Dorsey School was ballet. There Cuyjet discovered a codified system of dance movement that required a great deal
of physical and mental discipline. Her desire and initiative exceeded
her technical ability, but she was a diligent student and promising novice
teacher. Dorsey had a positive vision of Cuyjet's capabilities and provided her with a tremendous amount of support and encouragement.
Because Cuyjet's family could not afford to pay for classes, Dorsey put
her on scholarship. She eventually became Cuyjet's mentor, and they
cultivated a cherished friendship.

Cuyjet was in her late twenties and had discontinued her studies
and teaching responsibilities with Dorsey when she renewed her interest in dance. In 1944 she married Stephen Cuyjet, and he supported her
desire to establish a school. She began by offering ballet classes at home
for her daughter and neighborhood children. This venture served as a
trial run for Cuyjet's career aspirations, and its success encouraged her
to enter a partnership with colleague Sydney King.[5] Cuyjet and King
opened the Sydney-Marion School of Dance in 1946. Their mission was
to continue the work begun by Dorsey in the late 1920s. The partnership lasted only 2 years, but it enabled both women to establish
themselves as emerging dance educators in Black Philadelphia.

Cuyjet knew her limits as a dancer and she often says that her
unrelenting passion for teaching was probably the results of wanting
to make her students achieve the technical proficiency that she lacked.

During the beginning of her independent career, Cuyjet propelled herself into a substantive quest to improve her teaching skills. Philadelphia dance educators Thomas Cannon and John Hines assisted Cuyjet in her efforts to become a master teacher. Cannon tutored her in theory and studio work, and Hines advised her to travel to New York City for advanced training at the Katherine Dunham School and Ballet Arts at Carnegie Hall.[6] She developed her capabilities as an advanced-level ballet teacher and augmented her technical training with independent research in dance history and pedagogy.

In 1948 Cuyjet began her independent teaching career by establishing the Judimar School of Dance, and she received tremendous support from Black Philadelphia. During this post-World War II era, Black Philadelphians publicly addressed the need for better economic and educational opportunities, increased political power, racial harmony, and adequate social and cultural outlets. Several self-help organizations emerged as advocacy factions that campaigned for an improved quality of life for Black Philadelphia. The prevailing climate was one of formulating an agenda for survival that supported establishing institutions and organizations devoted to meeting the needs of the community. Cultural arts, along with economics, education, politics, and race relations, took priority. The Judimar School emerged as a noteworthy educational institution that contributed to the cultural arts enrichment of Black Philadelphia.[7]

Cuyjet's primary motivation for continuing to operate a dance studio after she dissolved her partnership with King was to provide increased opportunities in dance training and performance for youth in Black Philadelphia. Few dance schools existed and most of the established schools in the larger Philadelphia community would not admit Black students. Cuyjet's initial vision was to nurture America's first Black ballerina. She comments:

> My goal was to make the first Black ballerina on pointe, in New York, performing in a meaningful situation. It may not have been with a company. Janet Collins got there first at age 38, dancing with the New York Metropolitan Opera. I was happy she got there.[8]

In the early 1950s, Cuyjet's goal began to shift. She states:

> Then I wanted to make as many ballerinas as possible, but they had to be brown-skinned. They had to look Negro. We were not calling ourselves Black back then. If she could pass for White, forget it. That would not give me anything. Her picture had to tell the whole story. I never worried about the light-skinned girls. It was the brown-skinned girls I had to open doors for.[9]

Cuyjet groomed brown-skinned ballerinas during an era in which Black dancers were excluded from the mainstream concert dance arena. She aspired to change the Philadelphia community attitude about the ability of Blacks to perform ballet technique on a professional level. She was also concerned with changing Black dancers' attitudes about their potential for successfully executing dance techniques beyond the realm of "show dancing." Philadelphia Dance Company director Joan Myers Brown once aspired to a career in ballet. In the 1950s she studied at the Philadelphia Ballet Guild with noted dance choreographer Anthony Tudor and later in New York at the Katherine Dunham School. She excelled in ballet but discovered that there were few opportunities for Black dancers. Brown comments:

> Anthony Tudor put me in his production of Les Sylphides, which made quite a stir. But there was no future for a black dancer in classical ballet and I needed to make some money. I toured with Cab Calloway, Sammy Davis Jr., and Pearl Bailey, then worked with Larry Steele in Smart Affairs, an Atlantic City revue.[10]

Though we can trace trained Black ballet dancers to the 1930s, their performance opportunities were limited until the establishment of the Dance Theatre of Harlem (DTH) by Arthur Mitchell in the late 1960s. Dancers who were not members of DTH, like Sandra Fortune of the Jones-Haywood Capital Ballet and Anna Benna Sims of the Frankford Ballet, showcased their talents in Europe. During the time that Cuyjet was nurturing her students, Raven Wilkinson made a breakthrough by becoming the first Black ballerina to perform with the famous Ballet Russe de Monte Carlo (based in New York City). She danced with the company for 6 years, but it was a troubled tenure. It took her ballet teachers and the director of the company 2 years to decide to admit her; she entered the company in 1954, the year civil rights legislation declared public school segregation illegal. In 1955, during the company's second tour of the South, racial hatred marred their performances. Theaters that were booked and hotels they stayed in received bomb threats, and there were several Klan confrontations. Because of these incidents she was required to stay in New York City whenever the company toured the Southern United States.[11]

Early in the development of Judimar, Cuyjet's vision expanded to include offering dance as a means of social, educational, recreational, and cultural development. Although Cuyjet aspired to direct her dancers toward professional status, she never suggested that they pursue dance careers. Instead, she provided training experiences that would enable them to realize their full potential. Above all, she wanted them to become achievers.

According to Cuyjet's family and colleagues, Judimar was in its heyday during the 1950s. Its popularity was fueled by Black Philadelphia's cultural renaissance, spearheaded by Dr. Eugene W. Jones.[12] This was a period in U.S. history when the struggle for equality for Black Americans began to gain momentum. The mainstream dance world's acceptance of African-American dancers Janet Collins, Alvin Ailey,

Carmen de Lavallade, and Mary Hinkson (a Philadelphian) inspired Cuyjet's vision. Collins's professional ballet debut was a symbol of hope for Black dancers who aspired to enter the ballet world. The prospect of desegregating the concert stage became a possibility. Cuyjet, however, was not preoccupied with challenging the entire concert dance culture. Her priority was making dance preparation available to youth in Black Philadelphia, regardless of their level of technical proficiency.

Assertive, goal oriented, enthusiastic, courageous, and savvy are personality traits that distinguished Cuyjet among her colleagues. Her most dominant trait was her determined spirit. Delores Brown Abelson, a former student, referred to Cuyjet as a "gutsy lady," because of her tendency to pursue ambitious production projects. She was constantly amazed that Cuyjet staged successful classical ballet pieces with student dancers and limited financial assistance.[13] Colleague Joe Nash remarked of Cuyjet's infectious enthusiasm and energy: "The zest with which she approached her work influenced everyone around her, and it was a key ingredient to the success of her school."[14] Cuyjet's courageous and savvy attributes were exemplified when she desegregated an all-White business district in downtown Philadelphia by opening her first independent school in 1948 at 1310 Walnut Street.

During her career, Cuyjet had to contend with several forces that tested her spirit. One of the most critical obstacles during Judimar's first decade was securing permanent studio space in downtown Philadelphia. The average length of residence for the school's first four studios was 1 to 2 years. Most of the landlords assumed that Cuyjet was White because of her fair skin, but when they realized that she was Black they began to complain about the "dancing sounds" coming from her busy studio and issued notices for her to leave.[15]

Throughout Judimar's existence economic survival was a prime concern. Even during the height of its popularity, tuition and profits generated by recitals and the Mothers' Club were never enough to cover expenses when due. Regardless of the school's financial instability, Cuyjet always managed to provide scholarships to gifted students.

Cuyjet's precarious physical health constantly challenged her determined spirit. A spinal problem caused by a fall down the cellar steps, and a foot injury, the result of a fall she incurred while teaching, caused considerable physical stress. She coped with the spinal injury, yet neglected to curtail her strenuous teaching schedule. As a result, the condition deteriorated. The foot injury finally persuaded Cuyjet to proceed with caution. Her relentless quest for building a tradition of excellence in dance education, regardless of her physical health, threatened her teaching endurance and caused the temporary demise of her career in the early 1970s.

Numerous student performances for the public schools, the Heritage House's Philadelphia Cotillion Society, guest appearances with the Philadelphia Concert Orchestra, and the Dra Mu Opera company enhanced Cuyjet's popularity and influential standing in the cultural arts community.[16] Her collaborations with New York dancer-educators such as Joe Nash, Ernest Parham, George Chaffe, and Luigi undoubtedly impressed the local community. Her friendship and professional relationship with Jay Dash, a dance educator in the larger Philadelphia community, enabled her to impact the White dance education community. From the late 1950s to the early 1970s she was in constant demand as a teacher for tri-state dance conventions sponsored by Dash. In addition, Cuyjet's ability consistently to produce dancers who gained professional status bolstered her reputation.

Cuyjet's contribution toward social change in the Philadelphia dance community was manifested in her school's interracial policy. Judimar's "open door" was a vehicle for promoting cooperation between Black and White dancers. In the 1960s, Cuyjet's association with Dash conventions and her invitation to leading Philadelphia dance educators to teach seminars at Judimar, spurred joint projects between Black and White dance education communities.[17]

Although her forte was ballet, Cuyjet valued contemporary and ethnic dance techniques. During her teaching career she studied jazz, modern, and Afro-Caribbean dance forms. As a result she emerged as a versatile and marketable dance educator. Her active teaching schedule included teaching at her own school, local dance studios, recreation and community centers, and three predominantly Black colleges in the tri-state area.[18]

Cuyjet was known as a strict disciplinarian and a thorough teacher. In retrospect, many of her former students view her stern disposition in class as positive because it influenced them to approach their studies with a serious attitude. Her teaching method stressed performance and an academic knowledge of the theory and craft of ballet. She knew that proficiency in these areas would distinguish her students from the average dancer. According to former students who pursued professional dance careers, Cuyjet's pedagogical approach prepared them for a dance world in which African Americans had to be technically superior in order to achieve minimal success.

Cuyjet was concerned with educating the whole person. She sponsored cultural field trips during the summer school session and social gatherings during the regular school year. Because of her attitude toward formal education, she persistently reminded students of the significance of continuing their education after high school. The exposure to Africentric dance forms such as Dunham Technique, encouraged them to take caution with Euro-American aesthetic assimilation and maintain an appreciation for their African heritage. The "homey" atmosphere created by the involved presence of Cuyjet's immediate family gave the studio an environment conducive to a sense of community.[19] The school promoted an extended family orientation common to traditional African-American communities.

　　　Cuyjet's commitment to artistic integrity permeated her work. She advocated standards established by the New York concert dance community. She invited African-American dancers from that community to Judimar as role models and for artistic inspiration and direction. Her students were guided to be expressive communicators in the classroom and on the stage. They developed performing sensibilities often associated with seasoned professionals.[20]

　　　In the early 1950s Cuyjet began taking her advanced students to study dance in selected studios in New York City. During the summers and on selected holidays they studied at the Katherine Dunham School, Ballet Arts at Carnegie Hall, and the George Chaffe studio.[21] The Dunham school was predominantly Black and the Chaffe studio accepted African-American students, but Ballet Arts received Cuyjet's students only because they assumed she was White. Because of their preconceived ideas about the ballet aptitude of African Americans, the teachers and students were not welcoming of Cuyjet's students. Their exceptional performance in the classes proved that it is talent and training, not skin color, that make a ballet dancer. The teachers at the school eventually accepted Cuyjet's students, but the student body always kept their distance. Delores Brown Abelson comments: "The students were dreadful, the teachers were wonderful. In Vladimir Dokoudovsky's partnering class, the men had refused to dance with any of the women of color. Miss Cuyjet said, 'OK, girls we'll partner each other.' Finally one man extended his hand to me."[22]

　　　Judimar's unique feature was that its emphasis was ballet. Very few Black dance schools during this era, with the exception of the Sydney School of Dance in Philadelphia and the Jones-Haywood School in Washington, DC, specialized in ballet. Cuyjet strongly believed that ballet was an essential technique. She states:

> No matter what type of dancer you are going to be, you are never going to be up to your full capacity unless you also study ballet. You don't have to perform classical ballet, but ballet is going to refine a lot of your work so that you can be versatile.[23]

　　　Although the school's focus was ballet, students were required to take other dance techniques. The curriculum included modern dance, jazz dance, tap, "primitive" (African and Caribbean dance forms), and interpretive (a combination of Afro-Caribbean dance forms and modern dance technique). Cuyjet had the desire to develop versatile dancers. Joe Nash, former Judimar instructor, praised Cuyjet's interest in nurturing well-rounded dancers:

> They [the students] were so flexible. Those students were amazing. They could move from one dance style to the other. That was valuable training they received with Marion. I applaud her for what she did, she prepared them to

be ballet dancers or modern. The students were introduced to the full spectrum of dance.[24]

The primary Judimar faculty consisted of Cuyjet, John Hines, and Ann Hughes.[25] Hines taught ballet, interpretive, and primitive dance, and Hughes was in charge of tap. Advanced students would serve as student teachers for the beginning-level classes, and Cuyjet guided their development just as her mentor, Essie Marie Dorsey, had done for her. She observed while they taught and afterward offered constructive criticism. Some eventually graduated to the status of apprentice teachers and senior teachers.

Judimar was coeducational and served two types of students. There were children who came for recreational, educational, and cultural enrichment, and there were the "dancers," the advanced students who quietly aspired to dance professionally. Many of the advanced dancers received full scholarships. Stephen Cuyjet, Jr., believes that his mother's practice of granting scholarships to talented students evolved from her experiences with Dorsey. "Mother could not afford dance classes and Aunt Essie put her on scholarship. If a student wants to dance, make a way for them. That was the atmosphere."[26]

The school boasted an array of female advanced dancers. Every few years a group of young women would emerge as school "stars." Cuyjet refers to periods in Judimar's development according to the female dancers who were the most accomplished at the time. Judimar's first era, 1948 to 1953, was marked by a group of dancers Cuyjet refers to as the "big three," Delores Brown Abelson, Alice Mays, and Juanita Jones. Judy Cuyjet, Gloria Higdon, Gwendolyn Riley, and Penny Vaden reigned from 1953 to 1955. Judith Jamison, Joyce Graves, and Donna Lowe Warren emerged between 1955 and 1958. China White and Salley Anne Richardson took the forefront from 1959 to 1963. In the mid-1960s Renee Wadley, Robby Green, Tina Johnson, and Myrna Munchus were lead dancers; and Debra Bland, Tawny Turner, and Carol Treherne were promising dancers from the mid-1960s to 1971.[27] According to Judith Jamison, a friendly competitive spirit existed among the Judimar female lead dancers, and the desire to be recognized as the best never became a destructive force that endangered friendships. The advanced women dancers were important role models for the younger students. Donna Lowe Warren recalls: "Delores Brown was my idol, and many of the dancers wanted to be like her."[28]

Performance was a significant aspect of the Judimar experience. Students performed in school recitals, for elementary and high schools, social clubs, civic organizations, and cabarets. Cuyjet was a firm believer that you cannot confine your training to a dance studio; a dancer learns to dance by performing as much as possible. In the 1950s Judimar students began to perform for musical organizations, colleges, and citywide arts events, and they participated in the annual Philadelphia

Cotillion Society's Christmas Ball. The event always featured a ballet production that showcased students and teachers from selected dance schools in Black Philadelphia.[29] In 1952 an ensemble performed in the Dra Mu Opera's production of *Carmen* and in 1954 in *Samson and Delilah.* That same year they performed with the National Negro Opera Company and the Pittsburgh Symphony in *Aida* at the Syria Mosque in Pittsburgh. In the early 1950s selected advanced students appeared on the *Today Show,* hosted by Dave Garroway, on location at the Philadelphia Museum of Art.[30]

Cuyjet's daughter Judy refers to the 1960s as the beginning of the end. Enrollment decreased because of competition created by newly desegregated dance academies and dance schools being established by former students. In 1971, family obligations, faltering health, and an exhausting teaching schedule caused Cuyjet to discontinue her school and teaching activity.[31] Her pedagogical legacy continues in Philadelphia and selected cities in the United States through the work of former students.[32] Four Judimar women who are ramifications of Cuyjet's legacy and who emerged as divas in the dance world are Delores Brown Abelson, Donna Lowe Warren, Judith Jamison, and China White. Black Philadelphia embraced their talent and the Judimar school primed them for success.

The Philadelphia Divas

Delores Brown Abelson

Abelson's initial interest in dance was spurred at the age of nine by the Hollywood dance movies of the mid-1940s. She briefly discusses the circumstances under which she sought dance training:

> My family could not afford to give me dance lessons. That was totally out of our reach. My aunt said that if I found a school that would take me that she would pay for my lessons. This was the late 1940s. I went to every school that was established in center city. I lived at 22nd and Ordain [South Philadelphia], so at that time I could walk to everywhere in the general center city area. They put me on a waiting list. I was too young to understand what that meant. I was never called.[33]

When the time came for Abelson to choose a junior high school, she chose Barratt because it had an established dance program. Her dream of receiving formal dance training came to fruition when she joined the ballet club. She states: "When I got that opportunity, that was one in a million."[34] While at Barratt Junior High School, Abelson was discovered by Marion Cuyjet who subsequently gave her a scholarship to study at Judimar in 1948. Her recollection of the occasion is as follows:

Cuyjet had just broken up (the partnership) with Sydney King. She was starting out on her own and wanted some advanced students when she started. She visited Barratt Junior High School. She contacted Virginia Lingenfelder, the director of the dance club. She requested two of the top students in the club—Alice Mays and Juanita Jones. The teacher [Lingenfelder] asked Cuyjet if she would take one more, a student who was a hard worker, that was me. I had been studying just about six months. I was a year younger than the other two girls. She took all three of us on full scholarship.[35]

Her Judimar experience began at the age of 14 and she progressed at an astounding rate. In 6 months' time she was chosen for the lead role in *Sleeping Beauty*. In retrospect, Abelson is amazed at Cuyjet's ability to work miracles with young people who began their ballet training at what was considered a late age.

During the initial stages of her training Abelson attended Judimar twice a week, and by the time she was 17 she was there every day. She studied ballet (including pointe and partnering) with Cuyjet and Dunham Technique with John Hines.[36] She studied tap but admits that her aptitude was low. She studied ballet with the guest teachers who frequented the school, and she was always included on the New York City trips to Ballet Arts and the Dunham school during the early 1950s.[37] Abelson recalls the circumstances surrounding her enrollment at the all-White Ballet Arts dance studio at Carnegie Hall:

The day I went to pay my tuition the woman at the registration desk told me that there had been a mistake and that I was to take my classes at the annex. [We found out later African-American children were shuttled off to another area to take class.] Well, Marion had "schooled" us and told us what to expect and what to do. She told us what [ballet level] our classes were and who our teachers were supposed to be. I told the woman that if she did not let me enter the classes I would have to ask for the tuition back that my father had paid. I was then allowed to enter. I believe we were the only Blacks at the school during that time.[38]

Abelson's parents were supportive of her dance endeavors and frequently allowed her to get a head start on the New York trips by arriving early to begin classes. "My father paid extra for me to go early and I stayed at the 'Y.' John Hines and George Mills (Judimar associates) were in New York at that time, so I had people to look out for me."[39]

Abelson's teacher/pupil relationship with Cuyjet was special. She states that Cuyjet saw something special in her and helped her develop it. Cuyjet's desire to produce Black ballerinas during an era when there were few came to fruition through Abelson. She was Cuyjet's first student to dance professionally.

One of the most attractive features of Judimar was the opportunity to perform. Abelson danced for recitals, cotillions, and numerous community performances. She was chosen to perform with the Dra Mu Opera Company for their production of *Carmen* and with the National

Negro Opera Company in *Aida*. Her most memorable performing experience was the 1955 Christmas Cotillion production of the *Blue Venus*. Brown states: "I was the Pearl. It was thrilling, the whole production was exhilarating."[40]

In addition to her performance activity with Judimar, Abelson danced with the Philadelphia Ballet Dance Guild under the direction of Anthony Tudor. She danced along with Philadelphia dancers Joan Myers Brown and John Jones, and according to Abelson their residency with the company was hampered by the fact that the White dancers were unhappy with the presence of African Americans. "There were many unpleasant experiences. I was 16 at the time and I was there because I was a good dancer. Tudor was supportive of our presence and he chose us because he wanted the best dancers for his company."[41]

Abelson left Judimar in 1953 to go to New York to pursue professional dance preparation. She was 17 years of age and had just graduated from West Philadelphia High School. The Judimar Mothers' Club offered her financial assistance for her studies. Abelson comments on the support she received from Judimar:

> The Mothers' Club was strong then. Judy's [Judith Jamison] mother was one of the leaders in that club. They gave me the money to go to the School of American Ballet and they said if I got through the audition that they would pay my tuition for a year. They did just that. I got into the advanced class and they paid the tuition for the first year in New York. That was the kind of support I started out with.[42]

In order to gain admission to the School of American Ballet, each dancer was required to audition. Brown passed the audition and was placed in Level C for advanced dancers. She was excited to be there because it was the training school for George Balanchine's New York City Ballet Company (NYCB). When she arrived, there were six other African-American dancers: Georgia Collins, Barbara Wright, Michaelyn Jones, Bernard Johnson, Arthur Mitchell, and Louis Johnson. She remembers that Louis Johnson made a special effort to reach out to her and always included her in his school-based choreographic projects. She received strong support from her teachers, but she was disappointed that she was never invited to take class with Level D, the company class. She comments:

> At the audition we were told if you were an older student (over 14) we had to place at Level C in order to be admitted to the school. There were four levels: A, B, C, D, and C and D were the highest. I was placed in C, the next to highest level. Level D was the company class of the New York City Ballet and at that time Arthur Mitchell and Louis Johnson were the only African Americans in that level. Arthur Mitchell was eventually chosen as the first Black dancer for NYCB. Louis danced with the company for selected pieces but never was admitted as a permanent member. The heartbreak for me was that I was always chosen by my teachers to demonstrate and I was always placed in the front

line in class [a mark of excellence], but I was never moved up to Level D. The thing that hurts the most is that I excelled on my own merit and I was still passed over for a place in the company class. I agree with Louis Johnson's recent comment in *The New York Times* that African-American ballet dancers had to be better than the best—to get nothing![43]

Abelson returned to Philadelphia after the first year. She decided to return to New York a few years later (around 1956) and enrolled at the Ballet Theatre School. During that period she joined the New York Negro Ballet Company (Ballet Americana).[44] She embarked on a performing career that would last until the late 1960s. She performed and toured with the New York Negro Ballet company for 2 years; during that time they toured England and Scotland. The company received excellent reviews, and the general public was very receptive. "They thought we were going to be 'exotics' and were surprised that our repertory was classical ballet."[45] Brown was singled out by many British dance critics for her performance in the Bluebird Pas de Deux from *Sleeping Beauty*. She states that the ability to perform this selection was a mark of excellence for a ballet dancer. Because of lack of funds, the London performance and tour of France were canceled. The company returned to the United States and then disbanded.

She then performed with noted choreographers Talley Beatty, Geoffrey Holder, Louis Johnson, and Billy Wilson. She was chosen to appear in Cuba with Alicia Alonso's Ballet Alonso, and she had a brief residency with the dance company of the National Center for Afro-American Artists in Boston, under the direction of Elma Lewis and Billy Wilson. In the early 1960s she was chosen by Alvin Ailey to dance in the musical play, *Dark of the Moon*. "The play was directed by Vinette Carrol and choreographed by Alvin. We had a wonderful cast that included James Earl Jones, Isabel Sanford and Roscoe Lee Brown.

"At that time they did not have dance companies like we have today. There were no years of employment. We did concerts and tours. You were employed and then [you were] out of work."[46] During this time she continued her dance studies with Karel Shook (cofounder of the Dance Theatre of Harlem) at night after rehearsals. In between her performance work Abelson taught ballet. She states:

> I had always taught and liked it. It was a way to earn money and stay in the business. I taught ballet for Syvilla Fort [former lead dancer and ballet mistress of the Katherine Dunham Dance Company]. I was capable of teaching Dunham but I had moved away from it. I decided to stay with ballet.[47]

Abelson eventually established a strong reputation as a ballet teacher, and in the early 1970s she joined the staff of the newly established Alvin Ailey American Dance Center in New York City. She assumed the post of scholarship director and taught advanced ballet for the school and the company until the late 1970s. In the mid-1970s she began teaching for Philadanco (Philadelphia Dance Company) and states that Marion Cuyjet had a profound influence on her teaching style and approach. She briefly discusses that influence:

> I am also very specific about being on time for classes, training the whole person, stressing the importance of knowing your craft. I'm pretty tough about those things. I don't think that when you are taking class that you should take a frivolous attitude about it. Its too important even if it is for you own amusement. I've taught adult ballet and when I teach these classes I teach them as if I feel they are going to do something with it.[48]

She commuted to Philadelphia once a week to teach company ballet class for Philadanco from the late 1970s to the late 1980s. Abelson is married, and up until the early 1990s she devoted her full-time energies to operating a successful Native American art gallery on Park Avenue in New York City.

Donna Lowe Warren

Donna Lowe Warren is a native of Brooklyn, NY, but was reared in Philadelphia by her maternal aunt. Lowe's aunt enrolled her in Judimar for formal dance preparation at the age of five. She began by attending class once a week on Saturdays; then as she advanced in level she was in attendance several days a week. She studied ballet with Delores Brown Abelson, selected guest teachers, and tap with Ann Bernadino Hughes and John Hines. Her advanced ballet classes were taken with Cuyjet. According to Warren, although Cuyjet's stern teaching manner was sometimes intimidating, she enjoyed her classes regardless. She states: "She scared us a bit but we loved her classes. She made us want to dance."[49]

She speaks of her Judimar experience as the highlight of her childhood and teenage years. "I remember being so very happy there. It was one big family and we all knew we were there for one purpose—to dance."[50] Warren participated in all of the Judimar performance events and enrichment activities except for the trips to New York City. She studied in New York with George Chaffe during her annual summer vacation with her parents. Warren emerged as a leading dancer in the mid-1950s and was given her debut at age 15. She comments: "Cuyjet staged *Giselle* for me. That was my most memorable experience. It was quite an honor to have my first classic role in a ballet of note. I received roses afterwards."[51]

Warren left Judimar in the late 1950s. Cuyjet advised her to study with Thomas Cannon, a colleague and close friend who was at that time ballet master for the Philadelphia Grand Opera Company. Cannon chose Lowe to be a member of the opera's ballet unit in 1958. During an era when Philadelphia's professional ballet arena remained closed to African Americans, Warren's fair complexion enabled Cannon to pass her off as White. She performed in the corps, then graduated to soloist. Warren reflects on her experiences with the company:

> I toured many cities with the opera company. New York, Boston, Miami, and Tulsa were a few. It was an exciting time for me. We worked with the great singers of the day like Richard Tucker and Roberta Peters. This was a new aspect of theater for me. Still, because I had been exposed to Judimar's elaborate productions at an early age, I was not flabbergasted when I arrived in the professional world.[52]

In the early 1960s Warren decided to continue her education. She auditioned for the Julliard School's (in New York City) ballet program, was accepted, and received a partial scholarship for her first year. Although her major emphasis was ballet she was also required to study modern dance. She recalls studying with modern dance pioneers Martha Graham and José Límon. In addition, there were classes in composition, Labanotation (a system of notating dances using signs and symbols), and kinesiology. She discontinued her studies after the first year because her parents were unable to afford full tuition, and the commute from Brooklyn was taking its toll on her physically.[53]

Warren returned to Philadelphia and enrolled in Joseph University with a major in social studies. She resumed her position with the Philadelphia Grand Opera Company and moved up the ranks to prima ballerina status and remained with the company until 1971.

She married a childhood friend from Brooklyn and they moved to Florida in the late 1970s. In 1982 Warren opened the Philadelphia School of Dance in Lehigh Acres, FL. She comments: "I feel like a pioneer bringing dance to this area. Most have not been exposed to ballet. The community has responded positively. The 'Y' is no longer in existence so the parents were glad to have a place for their children to go."[54]

Warren invited Cuyjet to Florida as a guest speaker for the opening of the school. She states: "I wanted her to share this special occasion with me. She is extremely instrumental in my development."[55] The school is expanding and now offers instruction in ballet (with pointe), tap, jazz, baton, and gymnastics. Warren envisions establishing a regional ballet company.

Judith Jamison

Judith Jamison entered Judimar in 1950s at the age of six. Her mother strongly believed that dance was an essential artistic experience for children. Her father, an accomplished musician, and her mother, an avid theatergoer and collector of graphic art, played an important role in her all-around artistic development.[56]

According to Marion Cuyjet, Jamison displayed natural dance ability from the start of her studies. She was viewed as a prodigy. When Jamison entered Judimar, Cuyjet recalls having a heated argument with colleague John Hines because he wanted to place her in the second grade (level).[57] Jamison traveled to Judimar several times a week from her home in the Germantown section of Philadelphia. She studied ballet, tap, primitive, jazz, and acrobatics. Although she loathed acrobatics, she applauded the school's policy of requiring students to take a variety of movement techniques. "Cuyjet made well-rounded dancers."[58] Jamison's teachers included Cuyjet, Delores Brown Abelson, John Jones, the late Elmer Ball (ballet), John Hines (Dunham Technique), Ann Bernadino Hughes (tap), and Dunham dancer Leigh Parham (modern and jazz).

Jamison was impressed with the manner in which Judimar was managed. She states: "The school was very professional—the recitals and the way in which classes were conducted. She prepared me for a professional life even before I knew I was going to dance."[59] According to Jamison, Judimar possessed a unique environment. She comments: "We learned how to dance and to teach. In addition, Cuyjet created a world within the school, social as well as educational. She'd give these little parties—quite formal and polite, you know—and she'd match the right gentleman with the right lady."[60]

Jamison participated in recitals, community performances, and Christmas Cotillions. Just before she graduated from high school she received the Cotillions Society's dance award. Her formal debut was in 1959—at the age of 15—in which she danced the role Myrtha in *Giselle.* Cuyjet comments on Jamison's performance savvy in a 1974 *Philadelphia Inquirer* article: "She stuck to the choreography, but she added her artistry to it, which astounded me because the role always came off looking like something different than I planned . . . and usually better."[61]

After graduating from Germantown High School, Jamison decided to pursue a college degree. Cuyjet assisted her in securing admission and a partial scholarship at Fisk University in Nashville, TN. Her goal of becoming a psychologist became less important than her desire to dance, so she left the school after her freshman year. She returned to Philadelphia in the early 1960s to continue her dance training and entered the Philadelphia Dance Academy (presently a division of the University of the Arts). In 1964 Agnes de Mille discovered her in a master class at the Academy and invited her to come to New York to perform in the *Four Marys.* That initial exposure paved the way for her entrance to the professional dance world. She comments:

> I wanted to be a fine dancer. I had been performing since I was six and I wanted to perform more. New York was a mecca. All I thought about was getting better at what I was doing and performing more. So whoever heard of getting your job in New York with ABT [American Ballet Theatre]—understudying

Carmen de Lavallade! I've been blessed. But the perseverance was instilled in me by my parents and Marion Cuyjet.[62]

When her work with ABT was over Jamison decided to stay in New York. She found work at the World's Fair selling tickets and dispatching boat rides at one of the pavilions. When her job at the World's Fair ended she auditioned for choreographer Donald McKayle for a Harry Belafonte television special. The experience was a turning point in her quest for a dance career:

I went to the audition but I wasn't very good. In fact, I was dreadful. I hadn't danced the entire summer and I was in very bad shape. . . . Donald McKayle was so sweet and gentle that he kept me until the last. . . . However, I left the audition in tears. On the way out I passed a friend of Mr. McKayle's on the stairs, whom I barely saw because I was so upset. . . . I was very sad and walked outside to call my mother from a pay phone on the street and told her that I did not make the audition but wished to stay in New York because I felt that there was something that I had to do here. I wasn't quite sure what that was. . . . Three days later, still out of work, the man I'd passed on my way out of the audition called me and asked me to join his company. His name was Alvin Ailey. Without hesitation I said yes.[63]

In 1965 Jamison joined the Alvin Ailey American Dance Theater and remained with the company for 15 years. Ailey created many roles for Jamison; the most notable was *Cry* (dedicated to all Black women). She emerged as the lead female dancer and established herself as an international dance star. She left the company in 1980 to assume the starring role in the Broadway musical, *Sophisticated Ladies*.

Jamison began developing her skills as a choreographer and teacher in the mid-1980s. In 1984 the Ailey company premiered her first dance work, *Divining*. She began devoting a great deal of time to teaching master workshops nationwide and teaching advanced students at the Alvin Ailey American Dance Center. Jamison admits that her teaching disposition is firm and direct. She says that her manner has been influenced by Cuyjet. She comments: "Cuyjet was very strict. I believe that is why she turned out so many serious students. It [Cuyjet's disciplinary teaching style] carried over to my teaching."[64]

Performance savvy was a vital aspect of the Judimar school. Jamison continues to perpetuate the school's emphasis on nurturing expressive dancers. She elaborates:

In my coaching sessions at the Ailey School, I'm trying to make advanced students blossom beyond only technique. Technical dancers are boring. I try to get them closer to their uniqueness. The most gratifying moments when I was with Ailey were to see a dancer figure our that there's only one of him. When that happens, the flood gates open. You get depth.[65]

In the late 1980s Jamison formed her own dance company, the Jamison Project. After the death of Alvin Ailey in December 1989, she was selected as the artistic director of the Alvin Ailey American Dance Theater. Jamison will lead the company into its fourth decade. "Though I'll be taking the Ailey company into the next decade, I will still be Judith Jamison. I'm simply helping to keep Alvin Ailey's dream alive"[66] [Paid advertisement, "The Magic of the Spirit," designed by Jamison & Leary Advertising, Inc., written by Andrea Davis, concept by Katheryn D. Leary, editorial development by Marie Sutton Brown. Appeared in *Essence Magazine* (December 1990), pp. 69-70. Used with permission.].

Since taking the helm of the company, Jamison has begun to develop a national outreach program for children. Dance camps have been established in Kansas City, MO, and Baltimore, MD, so that each summer children ages 11 to 14 can study modern dance, ballet, jazz, improvisation, and creative writing. Jamison speaks adamantly about the program:

> The program is saying to our young ones, "There's no one else like you in the world. Look what you can create. Look what you can share." We want to fill our children with the spirit of self-worth that will change their lives for the better!"[67] [Paid advertisement, "The Magic of the Spirit," designed by Jamison & Leary Advertising, Inc., written by Andrea Davis, concept by Katheryn D. Leary, editorial development by Marie Sutton Brown. Appeared in *Essence Magazine* (December 1990), pp. 69-70. Used with permission.]

China White

China White was born in Philadelphia and was reared by her maternal grandmother. She was introduced to dance by her neighbor, Aisha Carol Davis, an older sisterly companion. At the age of two, White went along with Davis to watch dance classes at a local recreation center. She eventually entered a talent contest sponsored by the center and won third prize. This experience served as the initial impetus for her interest in dance. During her elementary school years at Pratt Arnold Elementary School, she danced annually in the school's Christmas musical.

At the age of nine, White began her formal dance training at the Sydney School of Dance. Soon after, Sharmaine Thomas, a neighbor and friend of the family, recommended that she attend Cuyjet's Judimar School of Dance. White visited Judimar and immediately transferred to the school. She states, "I always wanted to be a ballerina, and after I visited Judimar, I knew that is where I wanted to be."[68] White received a great deal of support from her family to study dance. Her mother had always wanted to take ballet but had never had the chance because of the lack of schools in the African-American community and the discrimination policies of the White dance studios. White was now receiving opportunities that did not exist for her mother.

When White entered Judimar she remembers receiving a great deal of special attention from Cuyjet. She states:

> She would come over and help me with my barre work, and sometimes she would take me aside to offer help with steps or movements. She was strict and stern. I was scared to death of her. Eventually we became very close and I began to call her mommy Marion.[69]

White remembers moving quickly through the grade levels. Each week she moved on to more advanced ballet work. When she arrived at Judimar, Delores Brown Abelson, one of the school's earliest role models, had graduated, but White recalls Judith Jamison and Donna Lowe Warren as part of the older group. Her first teacher was Frances Jiminez, a first-generation Judimar dancer. She also studied with Judith Jamison. "Judy Jamison was nice, a good teacher, and had a crazy sense of humor."[70]

White quietly aspired to be a professional dancer. "I always wanted to be a ballerina."[71] Cuyjet recognized White's potential and desire to dance and she gave her the encouragement she needed. She provided her with the opportunity to take advanced-level ballet classes in New York City, and at 16 she received the traditional Judimar debut. White states:

> Mrs. Cuyjet never told me that I should pursue a professional career in dance. She never said it directly. She did say many times: "When you get to Broadway you'll need to know tap dance." This statement must have meant that she thought I had what it took to dance professionally.[72]

White studied at Judimar until she graduated from West Philadelphia High School in 1963. During her last year at Judimar, Cuyjet took White to audition at the school of the newly organized Pennsylvania Ballet Company. White won one of the two full scholarships offered and became the company's first African-American dancer. She was chosen to perform in the company's first public performance in Philadelphia. White became an apprentice with the company and danced in a few performances before she entered college.

Although White made a breakthrough in the Philadelphia ballet community, barriers still existed for Black ballet dancers. Her experiences with racial discrimination were fewer than Delores Brown Abelson's, yet she remembers one specific incident:

> One of my teachers at the school of the Pennsylvania Ballet, David McClain, wrote the Joffrey Ballet in New York about me. He felt that I had a great deal of talent and wanted the Joffrey to assess my potential for becoming a professional dancer. I went to the school one summer for classes. I was the only African American in my class. No one ever mentioned the letter from my teacher and I did not receive any encouragement from the teachers there. In fact, I was placed in a lower level ballet class and I had to ask to be moved up. They did

but I was basically ignored. I'll never forget how one teacher treated me. She
carefully placed all of the students in the center of the floor by leading them
to a space, but when it was my turn she pointed at me and said in a flat tone
"and you go right there." After that incident I never went back.[73]

In 1963 Cuyjet arranged for White to enter Maryland State College,
in Princess Anne, MD (now University of Maryland at Eastern Shore).
White comments:

> Around 1963 Mommy Marion took me to college. She encouraged all of her
> students to get a college education. She got the college application, brought it
> to the house, and helped me fill it out. She did this with many students. She
> also helped me cut through a lot of "red" tape.
>
> My freshman year I became involved in the civil rights demonstrations
> and sit-ins to desegregate the lunch-stands and eating establishments in
> Princess Anne, Maryland. I was becoming involved in the struggle for equal
> rights. My actions upset my mother. She was afraid for me.[74]

Bettye Robinson, White's aunt, suggested to her mother that she
attend Ohio State University in Columbus because there were more opportunities in dance than at Maryland State. Robinson was the director
of a well-known dance school in Black Columbus and a close friend
and colleague of Cuyjet's. Cuyjet and Robinson collaborated, and with
the consent of White's mother brought White to Columbus. The first
year she lived with Robinson and eventually began to teach at her school.

Ohio State's dance department was within the Physical Education
department. White majored in health and physical education with a
concentration in dance. While there she was introduced to modern
dance technique in addition to taking classes in choreography, dance
notation, dance history, ballet, and lighting for dance, and emerged as
a leading dancer with the University Dance Company. In her final year
Viola Farber, a guest teacher from New York City and dancer with the
Merce Cunningham Dance Company (a leading modern dance company at the time), quickly recognized White's talent. White knew she
wanted to go to New York and dance professionally even before Farber
talked to her. Farber's interest in her development served to solidify
her desire to dance even more. She describes the circumstances:

> Farber told Maggie Patton [a faculty member] that she thought I was special
> and Maggie told me. Farber requested to have lunch with me to talk about my
> future. She advised me to work a while and save my money before going to
> New York. I did not want to wait, I wanted to go straight to New York. I had
> relatives there that I could stay with so housing was not going to be a problem.[75]

After graduating in 1969 White decided to teach dance for the Columbus Parks and Recreation Department. She began to perform with
a local group of dancers and her urge to pursue a performing career
was rekindled. During this time she met and married her husband

Bob White, who was also employed as an athletic coach in the same department. She continued to teach dance for the city and rejoined the faculty at her aunt's dance school.

In 1970 Robinson took White and some of her advanced students to Cincinnati to see a performance given by the newly organized Dance Theatre of Harlem (DTH). She also arranged for them to take a master class with the company's founder and artistic director, Arthur Mitchell. White was mesmerized by the company's performance. She states:

> I loved what I saw. I had given up the idea of performing professionally but when I saw this all-Black ballet company I knew that was what I wanted to do. I wanted to do ballet.
>
> I took the master class with Arthur Mitchell, and after class he invited me to come to New York to take classes with the company during Thanksgiving break. I had to wait until Christmas because the company went to the Virgin Islands. I followed through and went in December. After I took my first class with the company, Mr. Mitchell offered me a job.[76]

White joined the company in January 1971 and remained with the Dance Theatre of Harlem as one of its principal dancers until 1980. She went on tour with the company to Europe, Mexico, the Virgin Islands, and throughout the United States. Even though the company had to lay off dancers temporarily during the late 1970s because of financial difficulties, White remained loyal and did not seek opportunities to dance with other companies. Based on a recommendation from Judith Jamison, Alvin Ailey offered her a place in his company when she arrived in New York, but she never considered the offer because of her devotion to ballet and Dance Theatre of Harlem.[77] White has fond memories of performing with DTH, and she states that she feels privileged and very lucky to have been chosen for the company. "It was a dream come true."[78]

White and her husband decided to relocate to Columbus, OH, in 1980. She became the first dance specialist for the Columbus public schools and established a dance school in the Black community (Theatre Street Dance Academy). Her mentor Robinson retired, and White acquired her dance studio. Presently, she maintains a full-time teaching position in the preprofessional dance program at Fort Hayes Metropolitan Education Center. Her teaching disposition has been shaped by her experiences at Judimar with Cuyjet and with Arthur Mitchell at DTH. She views herself as an educator who guides her students to value performance savvy, self-motivation, and self-discipline.[79]

Strategies for Survival

Cuyjet and the Judimar School of Dance made a significant impact on the lives of Abelson, Warren, Jamison, and White. Cuyjet provided them with a positive vision of their capabilities, and they were given professional-level dance preparation that distinguished them in the dance world. All four women acknowledge that Cuyjet never directly told them that they should pursue professional dance careers. She was realistic about the tremendous racial discrimination that existed for African-American dancers. Still, Cuyjet opened doors for them and steadfastly guided their development.

In examining the career paths of the dancers, Dolores Brown Abelson, Judimar's first diva, received the least visibility but she emerged as the key role model for Warren and Jamison. Their success in the dance world was fueled by the inspiration that Abelson provided. She entered the dance world in the 1950s, a period in which the modern dance community was beginning to welcome Black dancers but the American ballet arena remained closed. In order to remain in the dance field she eventually sought opportunities to work with modern dance groups. She maintained her ties with ballet through continuing her studies and sharing her adept knowledge of the craft of classical ballet through teaching.

All of the divas, with the exception of Jamison, actively sought careers in ballet. This arena has traditionally been extremely difficult for African Americans to enter. The resounding attitude in the American ballet establishment is that ballet is a "White" domain and that African-American dancers are not physically suited to perform the technique. This stereotypical view of the abilities of Black dancers has been disputed by the success of Black ballerinas such as Janet Collins (Metropolitan Opera-1955), Anna Benna Simms (American Ballet Theatre-1980s), Debra Austin (Pennsylvania Ballet-1980s), and the myriad women dancers who have been groomed by the Dance Theatre of Harlem (DTH). Arthur Mitchell, its founder, is extremely vocal in dispelling the myths that plague many African-American ballet dancers:

> Ballet is the noble way of dancing; is nobility a virtue of the white dancer alone, and not of the black? . . . Ballet is the classical theatre dance, but have you ever seen African dancers—what could be more classic than a Watusi dancer? . . . there is no difference, except color, between a black ballet dancer and a white ballet dancer.[80] [Copyright © 1994, *Dance Magazine*. Used with permission.]

The ballet world's treatment of Black women dancers can be described as "violent." Before the establishment of DTH in the late 1960s many either left ballet entirely, passed for White as Warren did, or traveled to Europe where the color of one's skin did not matter in the ballet world. One of the core elements of ballet is the celebration of feminine beauty, and in the United States that has been viewed in Eurocentric terms. With the advent of the Dance Theatre of Harlem the general public was exposed to women of African descent whose brown skin, vibrant energy, and fluid dancing style challenged this standard. White, who joined the Dance Theatre of Harlem in 1971, emerged on the dance scene during a period in civil rights history when the African-American arts community was involved in a national movement to create an agenda for survival. She benefited from the establishment of an African-American dance institution that was dedicated to developing Black ballet dancers, and she became one of the few Judimar "stars" who achieved longevity in the ballet world.

Jamison found a "home" in the modern dance world in 1965. During this time the popularity of modern dance was being bolstered by the Alvin Ailey American Dance Theatre. This interracial company was known for its universality and its celebration of the human spirit. Jamison was in the right place at the right time when she was discovered by Alvin Ailey. He saw her auditioning for a TV special starring Harry Belafonte and offered her a place in his company. A special liaison developed between Ailey and Jamison. She was given the opportunity to develop her talent and became one of the most well-known modern dancers of the 20th century.

It is important to acknowledge the support that Abelson, Warren, Jamison, and White received from family, friends, colleagues, and African-American dance institutions. They were nurtured by a community that supported their aspirations to dance. The encouragement they received enabled them to hold fast to their dreams and they entered the professional dance world with confidence. Their survival depended in part on the manner in which they utilized the foundation they received at the Judimar School. Their Philadelphia dance preparation enabled them to travel throughout the world as technically proficient, versatile, and self-motivated performers. They inherited a determined spirit from Cuyjet that allowed them to emerge as change agents and role models for dancers in Black America. Their continued involvement perpetuates a positive vision for African-American women in concert dance.

Notes

1. See C. A. Weslager's *Delaware's Forgotten Folk* (Philadelphia: University of Pennsylvania Press, 1943) for detailed information on the history of the Delaware Moors. According to Cuyjet, the community has a multiethnic heritage—West African, Spanish, and Native American.

2. Marion Cuyjet, interview with author, Philadelphia, November 29, 1985.

3. Melanye White-Dixon, "Marion Cuyjet: Visionary of Dance Education in Black Philadelphia" (Doctoral dissertation, Temple University, 1987), pp. 18-24.

4. Joan Myers Brown's "Essie Marie Dorsey," *Philadelphia Tribune* (February 12, 1977), p. 12.

5. King and Cuyjet met while students at the Dorsey School. King established the Sydney School of Dance in 1948 and it has remained in existence since that time.

6. Philadelphia dance studios that offered professional level training, discriminated against African Americans until the late 1960s. In the 1940s and 1950s several Black dancers resorted to studying at the Dunham School and Ballet Arts.

7. White-Dixon, pp. 110-161.

8. Marion Cuyjet, interview with author, Philadelphia, November 29, 1985.

9. Marion Cuyjet, interview with author, Philadelphia, February 13, 1986.

10. Margaret A. Robinson, "A Dancer Grooms Students for Greatness—Joan Myers Brown," *Essence Magazine* (July, 1981), p. 15.

11. Zita Allen, "Blacks in Ballet," *Dance Magazine* (July, 1976) p. 66.

12. Jones was a prominent community activist who was a champion for the cultural and educational advancement of Black Philadelphia. See Nancy L. Giddens, "Black History Salute to Dr. Eugene W. Jones," *The Philadelphia New Observer* (February 20, 1986), p. 6.

13. Delores Brown Abelson, interview with author, New York City, August 23, 1985.

14. Joe Nash, interview with author, New York City, August 16, 1985.

15. Melanye White-Dixon, "Marion Cuyjet: Dance Educator," *Sage, A Scholarly Journal on Black Women,* 2(2) (1988), p. 66.

16. The Heritage House, founded by Dr. Eugene W. Jones, was the leading cultural institution in Black Philadelphia from 1954 to the mid-1970s. The Philadelphia concert orchestra and the Dra Mu Opera were established in the 1940s by Raymond Smith in order to provide Black Philadelphia with performance opportunities in classical music. Max de Schaunensee's "Fine Performances Feature Dra Mu Opera Festival," *Philadelphia Bulletin* (May 9, 1948) is a source for information regarding the Philadelphia Concert Orchestra and the Dra Mu Opera.

17. White-Dixon, "Marion Cuyjet: Dance Educator," p. 67.

18. It was a rare occurrence that a studio-based dance educator received the opportunity to teach in a college or university setting. Cuyjet held part-time positions at Cheyney State College (Cheyney University) and Delaware State College, 1958-1960 and Maryland State College (University of Maryland at Eastern Shore) 1957-1971.

19. Mark, Judy, and Stephen, Jr. (Cuyjet's children) assisted with the operation of Judimar in addition to dancing in the performing groups and teaching. According to Judy Cuyjet Colvin, her mother and father were almost surrogate parents for some of the students.

20. White-Dixon, "Marion Cuyjet: Dance Educator," p. 67.

21. White-Dixon, "Marion Cuyjet: Visionary of Dance Education in Black Philadelphia," pp. 122-123.

22. Judith Jamison with Howard Kaplan, *Dancing Spirit* (Garden City, NY: Doubleday, 1993), p. 33.

23. Cuyjet, interview with author, Philadelphia, February 13, 1986.

24. Joe Nash, interview with author, New York City, August 23, 1985.

25. White-Dixon, "Marion Cuyjet: Visionary of Dance Education in Black Philadelphia," p. 124.

26. Stephen Cuyjet, Jr., interview with author, Philadelphia, March 1, 1986.

27. White-Dixon, "Marion Cuyjet: Visionary of Dance Education in Black Philadelphia," pp. 134-135.

28. Donna Lowe Warren, telephone interview with author, Philadelphia to Lehigh Acres, FL, September 28, 1985.

29. White-Dixon, "Marion Cuyjet: Visionary of Dance Education in Black Philadelphia," pp. 84-85.

30. White-Dixon, "Marion Cuyjet: Visionary of Dance Education in Black Philadelphia," p. 142.

31. The significance of Cuyjet's contribution was not recognized until after the Judimar School closed. She has been honored by the Philadelphia Urban League (1982), Juba Contemporary Dance Company (1985), Philadelphia Dance Company-Philadanco (1982), the Women's Way of Philadelphia (1986), and the Afro One Dance Company, Camden, NJ (1990). She remains an active member of Black Philadelphia's dance community and she teaches children's professional classes and serves as an advisor for Philadanco.

32. White-Dixon, "Marion Cuyjet: Visionary of Dance Education in Black Philadelphia," pp. 100-106.

33. Delores Brown Abelson, interview with author, New York City, August 23, 1985.

34. Abelson, interview with author, New York City, August 23, 1985.

35. Abelson, interview with author, New York City, August 23, 1985.

36. Dunham Technique was developed in the mid-1940s by dancer, choreographer, and anthropologist Katherine Dunham. It is a combination of African and Afro-Caribbean dance

technique with ballet and modern dance as additional components. It is the official technique of the Katherine Dunham Dance Company.

37. Abelson, interview with author, New York City, August 23, 1985.

38. Delores Brown Abelson, telephone interview with author, Columbus, OH, to Long Beach, NY, February 17, 1994.

39. Abelson, interview with author, New York City, August 23, 1985.

40. Abelson, interview with author, New York City, August 23, 1985.

41. Abelson, interview with author, Columbus, OH, to Long Beach, NY, February 17, 1994.

42. Abelson, interview with author, New York City, August 23, 1985.

43. Abelson, interview with author, Columbus, OH, to Long Beach, NY, February 17, 1994.

44. For detailed information about the establishment of the New York Negro Ballet company see Zita Allen's "Blacks in Ballet," *Dance Magazine* (July 1976), pp. 68-69.

45. Abelson, interview with author, Columbus, OH, to Long Beach,NY, February 17, 1994.

46. Abelson, interview with author, Columbus, OH, to Long Beach, NY, February 17, 1994.

47. Abelson, interview with author, New York City, August 23, 1985.

48. Abelson, interview with author, New York City, August 23, 1985.

49. Donna Lowe Warren, telephone interview with author, Philadelphia to Lehigh Acres, FL, September 28, 1985.

50. Warren, interview with author, Philadelphia to Lehigh Acres, FL, September, 28, 1985.

51. Warren, interview with author, Philadelphia to Lehigh Acres, FL, September 28, 1985.

52. Warren, interview with author, Philadelphia to Lehigh Acres, FL, September, 38, 1985.

53. Warren, interview with author, Philadelphia to Lehigh Acres, FL, September 28, 1985.

54. Warren, interview with author, Philadelphia to Lehigh Acres, FL, September 28, 1985.

55. Warren, interview with author, Philadelphia to Lehigh Acres, FL, September 28, 1985.

56. Olga Maynard, *Judith Jamison: Aspects of a Dancer* (Garden City, NY: Doubleday, 1982), p. 16.

57. Barbara Faggins, "Judith Jamison, More Than a Dancer." *Philadelphia Tribune*, weekend portfolio (February 8, 1985), pp. 1 & 8.

58. Judith Jamison, interview with author, Philadelphia, May 16, 1985.

59. Jamison, interview with author, Philadelphia, May 16, 1985.

60. Nancy Goldner, "She Has Danced Far From Philadelphia, but Tomorrow Is a Homecoming." *Philadelphia Inquirer* (February 9, 1985), pp. 1-D, 3-D.

61. Patsy Sims, "Marion Cuyjet Couldn't Dance So She Produced Judith Jamison," *Philadelphia Inquirer*, clipping, Marion Cuyjet, private collection, no date.

62. Goldner, p. 3-D.

63. Jamison, *Dancing Spirit*, pp. 64-66.

64. Jamison, interview with author, Philadelphia, May 16, 1985.

65. Goldner, p. 3-D.

66. "Judith Jamison, The Magic of the Spirit," *Essence Magazine* (December 1990), pp. 69-70.

67. "Judith Jamison, The Magic of the Spirit," pp. 69-70.

68. China White, telephone interview with author, Columbus, OH, October 17, 1992.

69. White, interview with author, Columbus, OH, October 17, 1992.

70. White, interview with author, Columbus, OH, October 17, 1992.

71. White, interview with author, Columbus, OH, October 17, 1992.

72. White, interview with author, Columbus, OH, October 17, 1992.

73. China White, interview with author, Columbus, OH, February 2, 1994

74. White, interview with author, Columbus, OH, October 17, 1992.

75. White, interview with author, Columbus, OH, October 17, 1992.

76. China White, telephone interview with author, Columbus, OH, October 26, 1992.

77. White, interview with author, Columbus, OH, October 26, 1992.

78. White, interview with author, Columbus, OH, October 26, 1992.

79. White, interview with author, Columbus, OH, October, 26, 1992.

80. Olga Maynard, "Arthur Mitchell and the Dance Theatre of Harlem," *Dance Magazine* (March 1970), p. 54. [Copyright © 1994, *Dance Magazine.*]

16. Sisters in the Name of Rap
Rapping for Women's Lives

ROBIN ROBERTS

So much of what has been written about rap has proclaimed the genre's misogyny that no one who has heard of artists like Public Enemy or 2 Live Crew or N.W.A. would expect rap to also contain feminist performers like M. C. Lyte, Queen Latifah, or Salt 'n Pepa. Yet although Michele Wallace (1990) can write that, "Like many black feminists I look on sexism in rap as a necessary evil" (p. C11), she can also acknowledge that the answer to "the tensions between the sexes in the black community . . . may lie with women [rappers]" (p. C11). Rap music, like all other forms of music, is not innately feminist or political; nevertheless, female performers have excelled in using rap's specific generic qualities to promote feminist messages of self-assertion for women, the necessity of a strong identity for women, the legitimacy of women's sexual desires, and explicit criticism of sexism. Feminist rap should be considered and evaluated as a demonstration of practical feminist criticism.

There are specific generic qualities of rap that enable female performers to use the genre effectively. Rap is noted for its strong rhythm—often only a percussive beat—and its emphasis on lyrics that usually rhyme and involve linguistic plays on meaning and sound. It is a highly political genre with a history of lyrics of explicit protest against racism. As Houston Baker (n.d.) describes it, "in its very structure, rap interrogates the politics and technologies of record production in the United States (p. 11). As Baker (1990) also points out, "rap is the form of audition in our present era that utterly refuses to sing anthems of, say, whitemale hegemony" (p. 182). Baker does not discuss feminist rappers but they perhaps best exemplify what he sees as a quality intrinsic to rap. He calls upon "today's critic" to "understand the rap artist as critic" (Baker, 1990, p. 185). This chapter is an answer to that demand.

Baker (1990) insists that rap is "destabilizing in its synergistic collagings of performative sounds and images" (p. 180). I would argue that Baker is right, but I would add that no where is rap more destabilizing than in feminist rap. Because it is a form that is already associated with the political, female rappers readily add an attack on sexism to the genre's critique of racism. Furthermore, because many prominent male rappers (like 2 Live Crew) are overtly hostile to women, women respond to sexist raps by rapping in defense of women. Through their lyrics, female rappers call for the treatment of women with respect and equality.

Rap also intrinsically enables the promotion of a strong performer. The rap performer is the focus of the group, rather than the instrumentalists or record scratchers (the disc jockeys who manipulate records to produce that sound unique to rap of a record being moved back and forth rapidly). If the rapper is female, the emphasis on her promotes a depiction of a strong female image. In rap, particular emphasis is placed upon the performer's personality and name. Because rap revolves around self-promotion, female rappers are able to use the form without facing accusations of being self-centered or narcissistic. Salim Muwakkil (1988) claims, "The rap motif—rapping about being the best at saying you're the best—evolved out of black youth's search for an affirmation they rarely find in this society" (p. 10). What is true for Black youth is also true for young African-American women (most female rappers, like their male counterparts, are in their late teens or early twenties). Yet when women rappers put themselves center stage, they do so with a difference. As Jon Pareles (1989) notes, "unlike male rappers, most of these women don't dwell on their sexual prowess or cast themselves at the center of violent escapades; they're more likely to be sober observers . . . they're neither naive nor self-effacing" (p. 29).

Because of its specific qualities and because of its tremendous popularity, rap provides a unique forum for African-American feminists. What Barbara Christian (1986) suggests about blues singers can be applied to rap: "Perhaps because the blues was seen as 'race music' and catered to a black audience, black women were better able to articulate themselves as individuals and as part of a racial group in that art form" (p. 122). In an article on Black female sexuality, Hortense Spillers (1984) discusses blues singers, but her argument applies equally well to female rappers: "The singer is likely closer to the poetry of black female experience than we might think . . . in the sense of dramatic confrontation between ego and the world that the vocalist herself embodies" (p. 86). African-American women have a tradition to draw on—a tradition in which, as Spillers notes, the singer's "sexuality is precisely the physical expression of the highest self-regard and often the sheer pleasure she takes in her own powers" (p. 88). Daphne Duval Harrison (1989) explains that "women began to use the blues as a positive means of retaliation" (p. 89), and that blues singers "introduced a new, different model of black women—more assertive, sexy, sexually aware, independent, realistic, complex, alive" (p. 111). This transformation is occurring again, this time under the aegis of rap.

Rap, or hip hop, as "the culture of clothes, slang, dances, and philosophies that sprang up in the '80s" (p. 40) is sometimes called, has been described as "music shaped by the most pervasive instrument of American popular culture—commercial television," but rappers, especially female rappers, are fulfilling Pareles's (1990) description of rap "turning television's rhythm's to their own ends" (p. 1). Through music videos, female performers can use the televisual mechanisms to promote and strengthen their feminist messages (Roberts, 1991). Through clothes, camera address, and visual images, female rappers add to their depictions of female power and healthy and appropriate depictions of female sexual desire.

Because so much of contemporary performance is visual, music videos and long-form music videos such as filmed concerts provide a perfect opportunity to discuss and analyze rap. Music videos have also provided the mechanism for rap artists to reach a wide and varied audience. Through shows like "Pump It Up," on Fox Television hosted by Dee Barnes, "Rap City" on Black Entertainment Television, and "Yo MTV Raps," (on MTV, of course), rappers have extended their influence and communicated their sense of style, and in the case of female rappers, their feminist message. Although not every female rapper is feminist, and certainly the degree and explicitness of their feminism varies, by virtue of their appearance in a male-dominated and misogynist genre, female rappers militate against sexism and for women.

A recent pay-per-view special (that cost $19.95) titled *Sisters in the Name of Rap* provides an excellent overview of the contributions of women in rap. This special emphasizes the degree to which a large number of women artists are turning rap to their own ends. Both music videos and pay-per-view customarily bombard the viewer with depictions of women as sexual objects for a male gaze—rap music videos by men frequently feature scantily clad, gyrating female dancers, and the most popular events on pay-per-view are soft porn movies. In this context, then, a 2-hour concert performed by women, which might seem unremarkable in and of itself, creates a radical discontinuity in the televisual text.

To appreciate the messages of television, a viewer must redefine the idea of a "text," expanding it to include nonverbal signs such as a performer's dress, gestures, enunciation, and style. Redefining a text also requires redefining an "author." The female performer creates meaning through her delivery, her look, her gestures, and her use of lyrics and music. Nowhere is the centrality of the performer clearer than in rap, and *Sisters in the Name of Rap* demonstrates how this positioning can be used for feminist messages.

Sisters in the Name of Rap could really be considered a long-form music video. It contains performances by more than 22 artists, and even though the film depicts a concert, it is one edited and clearly played for the cameras. It includes a touching tribute to MC Trouble, who was scheduled to perform at this show but who died suddenly and unexpectedly. In addition to the tributes to their deceased sister, the program is connected by the use of two female video jockeys, Dee Barnes (well known for filing a suit against a male rapper who assaulted her) and backstage, interviewing performers, Dutchezz. Although this framing of female video jockeys is in and of itself empowering to women because women are in charge of the show, the real connection to feminism lies in the commitment to women that undergirds each performance.

Many of the performers echo Nikki? Nicole!, who announces that she is dedicating her song, "to all the black females who came here tonight." Her rap "I Believe in Me" makes the feminist inclinations of the show clear. She espouses female self-affirmation and strength. Attired in a shiny black patent leather coat and backed by a wall of video monitors depicting her visage, Nikki Nicole proclaims, "I will achieve for the fact I believe in me." She points to herself as a role model and explains "the perfect example is me . . . a female rapper . . . I feel I can make a change . . . I paved the way." The visual images reinforce her message of self-assurance and autonomy. The backdrop first depicts an immense image of her, and then two columns of her image—facing and singing to herself. This refraction is then directed to the audience when the lyrics switch to "just say to yourself I believe in me." She also explains "many say you can't, but I say take a chance." Nikki Nicole's self-assertion is perfectly consonant with the conventions of rap, but in its switch to promoting the listener, it moves toward the women in the audience to whom she dedicates the song. In her inclusiveness and attentiveness to women listeners, Nikki Nicole reflects an attitude taken by many female rappers. For example, Harmony proclaims "power to the mothers and the sisters." Nikki Nicole's self-promotion and confidence is echoed later in the program when Tam Tam proclaims, "There's no limit to the things I can do." Her self-promotion is shored up by the performers' attire—in Tam Tam's act, her musicians and dancers wear T-shirts that proclaim "Tam Tam." In her strong, energetic performance, she persuades the viewers that, as she says, "I won't stop until I'm number one." Her ascendancy is created in part through the vigorous dance that she leads her backup dancers through. M. C. Lyte similarly asserts her preeminence when she announces, "I'm the toughest female you ever saw," as male dancers on either side of her—attired exactly like her in a wild print jacket, red short overalls, and black boots—follow her dance moves. A male chorus supports her, imploring, "Do it Lyte—make them stop and listen." The video screens behind her and the camera cuts reinforce her multiplicity. Like several other performers, Lyte appears to be multitudinous as images of her—first gigantic and then numerous—appear in the large video screens. In between these shots, the camera moves four times to a group of women in the audience, their faces reflecting their rapt attention to Lyte. She asserts her control through sexual innuendo: "It'll only get as wet as I let it."

Like Lyte and Nikki Nicole, Roxanne Shante directs her male dancers through their gyrations and uses Grand Daddy IU, a male rapper, to describe her as, "the originator, the first female." She herself declares "I'm the Queen of Rap and I've mastered it." She declares "I stand tall" and that she's "making her way to the top." Aggressively, she blurts out "no bitch in the house can fuck with this." More tactfully, Shelley Thunder declares "I do what I want. I answer to no one."

Shante's use of the word *bitch* contrasts with the reclamation elsewhere of the word *lady* by other feminist rappers. Both terms, however, function as a repositioning of loaded terms by female rappers. Although Queen Latifah and other female rappers chose what might be called a high-road strategy, Shante chooses, as some African-American males have done, to turn a word of opprobrium around. As *nigger* used by African-American males becomes their word and thus loses its power over them, so Shante's use of *bitch* is an attempt to reclaim the word as an in-group term. How successful this strategy is, is debatable. Using *bitch* also brings up the competitive nature of rap, in which the rapper denigrates his or her colleagues' abilities. Furthermore, Shante's approach is, both in terms of *Sisters in the Name of Rap* and feminism in general, an exception. More common is Queen Latifah's forthright rejection of the term in "U.N.I.T.Y.," a cut from her third CD: "who you callin a bitch?"

As the female rappers promote themselves, in the words of Roxanne Shante, they advise the audience, "do whatever you do best." This apparently contradictory stance characterizes female rap. Each female rapper asserts herself as the best, but then invariably turns to inspire and motivate her female fans.

Perhaps no one has done more for women than Yo-Yo. Described as "hip hop's first self-proclaimed feminist activist" (Morgan, 1991, p. 75), Yo-Yo repeats the strong assertions of competency and worth when she declares "I'm intelligent—I know it," as she also insists "don't call me baby." Her strong feminist pronouncements are supported by her activism. She founded the Intelligent Black Woman's Coalition (IBWC), "dedicated to raising self-esteem and dealing with issues like teen pregnancy and drug use among young women. Yo-Yo started the IBWC because she wanted to extend the peer-counseling work she did in her South Central Los Angeles high school to her rap career" (McDonnell, 1991, pp. 32-33). Yo-Yo appears several times throughout the concert, and in her first appearance, with Deb B, Yo-Yo and her fellow rapper are introduced by Dee Barnes who explains, "IBWC is definitely in effect." Deb B immediately makes the familiar dedication, "This is for all the sisters in the house," as she begins a rap that criticizes men's inattentiveness to women. In this rap, Deb B throws out her unworthy male partner. "Pack your bags Jake, it's time to get out" she announces. Yo-Yo joins her on stage and with an allusion to Aretha Franklin, demands "give me r-e-s-p-e-c-t." (Later on in the show, a new rapper, Dazha, continues the allusion when she declares "all I want is a little respect"). The way female rappers work together is through both indirect allusion and dialogue, and overtly, as Deb B and Yo-Yo together declare, "I'm sincere when I tell you that you're out of here. Get the fuck out of here."

Yo-Yo's attire proclaims her emphasis on a self beyond sexual posturing. Even though female rappers may wear bustiers and stretch pants and point their posteriors toward the audience, their costumes are characterized by large, loose-fitting jackets that cover up or mini-mize the exposure of their flesh. Their clothes look comfortable and practical for the strenuous dancing they perform as they rap. Dazha makes this aspect of female rappers clear when she declares without humor, "I'm a heavyweight." They seem to reify the idea that weight literally gives women substance and does so symbolically, too. Their bodies are not compartmentalized or fetishized as they are in so many rap videos by male performers (or for that matter, music videos by male and female rock performers). Their dress, then, accentuates the lyrics and their assertion of a self beyond sexual appeal. Yo-Yo and Nikki Nicole in particular are large women, quite unlike the more cus-tomary female rock performers—say, for example, the self-exposing and body-exploiting Madonna.

Although these performers downplay their sexuality, Salt 'n Pepa represent another, more specific manifestation of female strength and energy. Yet they, too, are taken to represent feminism, for as Dee Barnes introduces Salt 'n Pepa, she begins the introduction by asking, "How many sisters out there are independent?" Through their lyrics, style, and dance, these female rappers emphasize "uses of the erotic; the erotic as power" (Lorde, 1984, p. 53). What Lorde describes is how the erotic can be developed as a strength rather than as a liability for women. She describes the erotic as, "an assertion of the lifeforce of women; of that creative energy empowered, the knowledge and use of which we are now reclaiming in our language, our history, our dancing, our loving, our work, our lives" (Lorde, 1984, p. 55). If women are in control of their own sexuality and attractiveness, the erotic can be empowering. Although all music video performers allude to or use sexuality to pro-mote themselves, Salt 'n Pepa are explicit and overt but without de-meaning themselves or their viewers. They take great relish in depict-ing a healthy and attractive female desire for sex through both lyrics and performance.

In "Most Men are Tramps," for example, Salt 'n Pepa ask "have you ever seen a man who's stupid and rude . . . who thinks he's God's gift to women?" They gesture to the male dancers and demand "don't hand me a line." The rap is highlighted by a group of male dancers wearing black trench coats. As Salt 'n Pepa repeat "tramp," the dancers flash open their coats to reveal that they are wearing nothing but minuscule red G-strings. Through a clever playful role reversal, Salt 'n Pepa point to the ways in which male sexuality can be corrupt and unappealing. The male dancers are only exposed for a split second, so they are not trying to exploit the male body, except to make a point. To the same effect, when they are saying, "ride it like a horse," Salt 'n Pepa playfully pretend to be riding the male dancers. The exposé of male dominance is further emphasized by the band that backs up the group. In a startling contrast to most rap bands, the musicians are all female and they are attired in jeans and T-shirts. The emphasis is on their musicianship rather than their bodies. In "Do You Really Want Me?" they press the male characters for an honest answer to that question and in the process, assert the right of a woman to say no to sex and to her right to control the time and place and circumstances of sexual relations. They advise the audience, "Get to know each other" and then direct the lyric to themselves, "be my friend, not just my lover . . . know my mind, not just my body." A male rapper feeds her lines as he pretends to seduce Salt. He describes that they've been kissing and hugging and then he asks is anything going to happen and she says "Nothing." As they explain, "Please understand how I feel. I must have trust or it's no deal." Through these narratives, Salt 'n Pepa allow women viewers to act out and experience self-assertion. In a segue into "Let's Talk About Sex," they call again for open, honest discussion of sexuality between men and women. They depict the conflict as one between sex and love, and call for a combination for men and women. Pepa asserts her right to talk about sex, even on television, because "everybody has sex." This point in the dialogue prepares for the words of the rap, in which they declare "people who think it's dirty have a choice to change the station." Salt insists "everybody should be making love." Pepa agrees, but asks, "How many fellows you know make love?" Her intonation and expression make it clear that this is a rhetorical question—that a general failing of men is their attitudes toward sex and women. The performance directs the viewers' attention toward Salt 'n Pepa's sexual assertiveness. They caress themselves symbolically as male dancers then imitate the motions.

As Salt 'n Pepa assert their right to a healthy, vibrant sexuality under their control, later in the show Yo-Yo also elicits the image of a woman with desires she considers appropriate. Raising an issue about status that is very much a part of feminist rap, she declares, "You may say I'm not ladylike, but I'm a lady." The assertion functions as a reclamation of that term, *lady*, in a way that asserts that women are ladies even if they express sexual desire. The determination of *lady* is to be decided not by others, but by the woman herself.

The word *lady* appears frequently in feminist rap, but nowhere more effectively than in Queen Latifah's rap, "Ladies First." Queen Latifah uses the plural, *ladies,* emphasizing female solidarity and sisterhood. In her introduction of Queen Latifah, Dee Barnes identifies "Ladies First" as, "the anthem for all the sisters out there." Latifah's version of this song appropriately ends the concert, for it is a song about female solidarity. On her compact disc and music video, Queen Latifah's collaborative work with Monie Love and a group of female rappers including Antoinette, Ms. Melodie, Ice Cream Tee, and Shelly Thunder, emphasizes the feminism of the female rappers' project. They rap together, in contrast to the single male performers who spend most of their raps "dissing" each other. As Tricia Rose (1990) comments, "her decision to collaborate on her debut album is as surprising as it is ambitious; it suggests that being a solo rap artist does not mean isolating yourself from your peers" (p. 16). Rose's comments about Queen Latifah's debut album should also be applied to *Sisters in the Name of Rap,* for this concert proves that women rappers want to work together.

In her performance here, Queen Latifah directs her attention to the women in the audience. She calls the women to join her in the refrain— "Sing it with me girls," she requests—and the camera stresses her relationship with the women in the audience as it zooms in for close-ups of four or five women in the front row, not once, but three times. Like Salt 'n Pepa, Queen Latifah calls for a new type of relationship between men and women. Queen Latifah also endorses Afrocentrism. Queen Latifah's name, dress, music, and lyrics are a synergistic synthesis of a Pan-African and feminist sensibility. Like many male rappers, Latifah believes that Black North Americans should look to Africa to create their identities. "To me Afrocentricity is a way of living," she says. "It's about being into yourself and your people and being proud of your origins" (Dafoe, 1990, p. D8).

"Ladies First" reveals that Queen Latifah is also proud of being a woman. Queen Latifah has been shy about identifying herself as feminist, but she is quite explicit about her goals in writing "Ladies First." She created the rap to "lift females up . . . I wanted female rappers in to show a unified thing" (Much Music, 1990). In "Ladies First," Latifah shares with African-American women writers what Michael Awkward has described as "the figure of a common (female) tongue, of a shared Afro-American woman's authorial voice" (Awkward, 1989, p. 13).

"Ladies First" plays on the chivalric phrase, *ladies first.* In the 19th century, the phrase would not have been applied to African-American women. Its reclamation here by Latifah (and elsewhere by other female rappers) positions the female rapper as a lady, a rank underscored by Latifah's assumption of the title of "queen." The irony of the phrase in the rap "Ladies First" is that though ladies were supposed to be first, their status was completely titular. Ladies had no legal rights or powers. As Queen Latifah says about the music video of "Ladies First," "I wanted to show the strength of black women in history—strong black women . . . I wanted to show what we've done. Sisters have been in the midst of these things [activism] for a long time, but we just don't get to see it that much" (Rose, 1990, p. 19). *Sisters in the Name of Rap* provides many examples of strong African-American women.

Queen Latifah presents only an abbreviated version of "Ladies First" in this concert, perhaps because her fellow rapper Monie Love, with whom she raps on the CD, could not participate in the concert. The lines she does sing and her demeanor throughout carry the message of feminism loud and clear. The rap includes the adjuration, "stereotypes they got to go." She declares, "a woman can bear you, break you, take you." In a phrase that aptly describes *Sisters in the Name of Rap*, she proclaims, "Queens of civilization are on the mike." Describing herself, she explains that in her, the audience "sees a woman standing up on her own two. Sloppy slouching is something I never do," a description certainly corroborated by her own energetic, stalwart performance. Her rap is primarily directed to women, but she does emphasize "a footnote for the opposite sex . . . you get the drift it's 'ladies first.' " This lively and unabashedly pro-female stance is received with delight by the crowd, especially the women in the front row, to whom she directs the mike.

Before her next rap, "Fly Girl," she asks the women in the audience: "How many girls out here have gone into a club or something and passed some guys who said hey baby come here?" She describes her riposte to situations like that, but then sympathizes briefly with men. She explains that sexist behavior hurts them, too. "I know a lot of guys who are sick of looking bad and getting no place because girls expect them to say stupid nonsense like that." The rap, though, emphasizes women's oppression in dating situations, but at the same time she stresses female strength through her posture. Responding to a hypothetical pass in a scene she depicts as at a club, she raps, "No my name ain't 'yo,' and I'm not your baby." "It's hard to keep a good woman down, so I keep coming." As she explains, "But I'm not the type of girl that you think I am; I don't jump into the cars of just any man." She insists, "I don't need your money," and demands, "treat me like a lady." And echoing Salt 'n Pepa's line, she too asks: "I want a friend, not just a lover."

The emphasis on respect and equality appears repeatedly in rap by women. Their demands are clear and unequivocal. The stress on friendship and the emphasis on an equal relationship rather than sex is underscored by Queen Latifah's attire, which, like other female rap performers', is modest, especially by the standards of the women who appear with male rappers. She sports a black turban, a large thigh-length beige jacket, and black stretch pants. A large woman, Queen Latifah is elegant with a commanding presence. She doesn't need to exploit her body to sell her music. Instead, her message itself is sufficient. "Ladies First" can be considered the message of the show, for the credits roll with this song, and the viewer is treated to brief images of each of the performers.

Queen Latifah, Salt 'n Pepa, Yo-Yo, and other female rappers are quite clear about the feminism of their image and rap. As Salt 'n Pepa said in an MTV interview, "you could call what we do feminist." They stress that they "dress the way we want to dress and say what we want to say" (*Rockumentary*, 1991). Yo-Yo explains in the same MTV Rocku-mentary on rap that, "I get to tell the women's side—you know of how women feel and disagree on some things that males say." Perhaps the most explicit and eloquent of all is Queen Latifah, who in the same documentary explains: "Of course, I think we can act as an instrument of change. I think it's important that we do try to change people's concept of how male-female relationships should be." She and the other feminist rappers are doing a superb job of communicating the idea that men and women should interact as equals, that women deserve respect, and that women have a right to sexual desire and gratification.

Sisters in the Name of Rap, then, provides a nice synecdoche of the feminism expressed in women's rap. There are many different ways of expressing feminism, but even though the emphases may vary, the central concern of female autonomy and respect for women does not vary. This brief survey of female rappers begins, I hope, to suggest that popular culture, even an overtly misogynist genre like rap, can pro-vide a place for feminist sentiments to flourish. Female rappers can be seen as yet another triumph for African-American women, who in popular music as well as in the written word express unparalleled creativity. This concert video also suggests ways in which dress and style can be used to augment and underscore a message delivered in words. Most importantly, the cumulative effect of seeing dozens of women rappers in concert emphasizes African-American women's strength and power.

References

Awkward, Michael. (1989). *Inspiriting influences: Tradition, revision, and Afro-American women's novels*. New York: Columbia University Press.

Baker, Houston. (1990). Handling "Crisis": Great books, rap music, and the end of western homogeneity (Reflections on the humanities in America). *Callaloo, 13,* 173-194.

Baker, Houston. (n.d.). *Practical philosophy and vernacular openings: The poetry project and the American mind*. Unpublished manuscript.

Christian, Barbara. (1986). *Black feminist criticism: Perspectives on Black women writers*. Elmsford, NY: Pergamon.

Dafoe, Chris. (1990, May 18). Rapping Latifah rules new tribes. *Toronto Star*, p. D8.

Harrison, Daphne Duval. (1989). *Black pearls*. New Brunswick, NJ: Rutgers University Press.

Lorde, Audre. (1984). The uses of the erotic: The erotic as power. In *Sister/Outsider.* Trumansburg, NY: Crossing Press.

McDonnell, Evelyn. (1991, January 1). I, Yo-Yo. *The Village Voice,* p. 75.

Morgan, Joan. (1990, June 11). Throw the "F." *The Village Voice,* pp. 32-33.

Much Music. (1990). (Canada). 19 May.

Muwakkil, Salim. (1988, January 22). *The Reader,* p. 10.

Pareles, Jon. (1989, November 5). Female rappers strut their stuff in a male domain. *The New York Times,* p. 29.

Pareles, Jon. (1990, January 14). How rap moves to television's beat. *The New York Times,* sec. 2, p. 1.

Roberts, Robin. (1991). Music videos, performance, resistance: Feminist rappers. *Journal of Popular Culture, 25,* 141-152.

Rockumentary on rap. (1991). MTV.

Rose, Tricia. (1990, Spring). One queen, one tribe, one destiny. *The Village Voice, Rock and Roll Quarterly,* pp. 10, 16, 19.

Spillers, Hortense. (1984). Interstices: A small drama of words. In *Pleasure and danger* (pp. 75-90). Boston: Routledge.

Wallace, Michele. (1990, July 29). *The New York Times,* (p. C11).

PART IV

Contemporary Psychosocial Challenges

17. Life Satisfaction and the Older African-American Woman

BERNITA C. BERRY

Jacquelyn J. Jackson (1988), the eminent scholar on older (65 years plus) African-American women, tells us that there is no "average old Black woman," even though groups such as The National Caucus and Center on Black Aged and the American Association for Retired Persons continue to present the public with this image. Older African-American women are characterized in two main ways: being great or extraordinary (see, for example, *Black Women Oral History Project*, 1978; Jones, 1973) and as victims of racism, sexism, ageism, and classism (Daly, 1976; Jackson, 1972; McLaughlin, 1983; Taylor & Taylor, 1982). The latter description is given greater emphasis for older African-American women as a group (Jackson, 1988) due to the meanings attached to their ascribed social statuses of race, sex, and age.

My research interest in older African-American women developed along a two-pronged focus. First, my informal interactions with and observations of older African-American women in a variety of settings such as gatherings at neighborhood and community events, church meetings, educational institutions, and general conversations presented me with a level of heterogeneity of this segment of the population. Second, this heterogeneity was lacking in my study of the more formal written research on aged African Americans in general and in older African-American women in particular. This persistent "gap" coupled with research that took a problem-centered approach (Gibson, 1989) led me to embark on an investigation of older African-American women.

AUTHOR'S NOTE: An earlier version of this chapter was presented at the Fourth Annual Women's Studies Conference at Western Kentucky University, Bowling Green, KY, 1990. I have benefited from comments, criticisms, and encouragement from Tina Pippin, Martha W. Rees, Suzanne Hall, and anonymous reviewers.

Equally important was the fact that I (given longevity) will eventually become a member of this group.

Empirical research on the aged addresses the question of how persons 65 and older get by or adapt to old age. Usually examined are relationships among certain demographic variables—primarily race, sex, age, and income—and outcomes such as well-being or life satisfaction, social support networks, and health. The data show that the aged population is as diverse as the non-aged population and that this diversity also applies to each aged subgroup (e.g., African-American women, African-American men, White women, White men, etc.) in spite of popular generalizations.

Contradictory findings have been reported in prior research on the aged, especially regarding the relationship between subjective well-being (see Neugarten, Havighurst, & Tobin, 1961, for life satisfaction scales) and race, age, and sex. Subjective well-being is the umbrella concept that takes into account life satisfaction, quality of life, morale, happiness, and contentment. Some researchers (Markides, 1983; McKenzie & Campbell, 1987; Rao & Rao, 1981-1982) have questioned the reliability and validity of life satisfaction scales for aged minority groups. Aged African Americans tend to score lower than aged White Americans, leading to the conclusion that aged African Americans are less satisfied with their lives. Two factors have complicated investigations of ethnicity and its importance to life satisfaction: (a) whether life satisfaction variables are similar across ethnic groups and (b) whether socioeconomic status variables are confounded by minority status (McKenzie & Campbell, 1987).

Larson's (1978) review of the research covering a 30-year period on subjective well-being of the aged concluded that, "Level of education, occupational status, marital status, availability of transportation, housing, and non-amorous forms of social interaction ... appear to be related to subjective well-being" (p. 116). These variables are considered to be positively related to life satisfaction whereas poor health, lack of social interaction, and low income are negatively associated. This conclusion takes on added significance, especially regarding low income, when we study older African-American women.

Empirical research on aged African-American women and life satisfaction is minimal. This group may be included in studies that include race, age, and gender as independent variables. Not very much is known, however, about older African-American women. I essentially wanted to know how aged African-American women perceive themselves—the lives they have lived in the past and the lives they live now: Are they happy grandmothers, are they extremely religious, what kinds of discrimination have they experienced and what are their reactions to them, are they satisfied with their lives or do they feel old and helpless? By having older African-American women "speak for themselves" this study will fill some gaps in our knowledge about this group in our society.

Patricia Hill Collins (1990), in developing her theory of Black feminist thought, deconstructs the concept "intellectual" by moving it beyond the walls of academia to encompass the everyday ideas and experiences of Black women. Collins asserts that, "At the core of black feminist thought lie theories created by African American women which clarify a black women's standpoint—in essence, an interpretation of black women's experiences and ideas by those who participate in them" (p. 15). The Black feminist approach gives the African-American woman the opportunity to "speak for herself"; to verbalize those factors that contribute positively to her life and indicate her satisfaction (or dissatisfaction) with her life.

The aged African-American women who participated in this research, just as their other aged cohorts, have lived through the Depression, periods of economic recession, and periods of economic and social segregation. These women are now in their old age and are described by Jackson (1972, 1985) as members of an elite group of aged African Americans who have survived to reach old age. What kinds of lives have these women had? Do their present lives have meaning for them? This study investigated whether older African-American women's lives have meaning for them from their perception and, if so, to determine the source(s) of meaning in their lives. An integral part of this research was whether older African-American women are satisfied with their lives. Little scientific research has investigated whether older African-American women have meaningful lives in spite of structural and social constraints. Older African-American women possess three dominant social statuses that are evaluated negatively by the larger society, namely: being African American, being old, and being female.

Statistics and other census data demonstrate that African Americans in general in the United States have lower incomes than White Americans (Farley, 1988). Research on the aged that utilizes life satisfaction scales reports that there is a relationship between income and well-being: Low income is negatively related to life satisfaction. The scales do not distinguish between actual dollar amount and perception of income adequacy. This, I believe, can be important, particularly with groups that have historically received less pay for their labor (Jackson, 1988). Given that these aged African-American women have held jobs that Blacks in general have held in this country, how did they reconcile the fact of differential pay?

In this research I combined a case study and a Black feminist approach, whereby in-depth interviews were conducted with each participant in order to describe and analyze the lives of older African-American women based on how they view themselves. Major stages of the life cycle were tapped in order to gain as complete a picture as possible of each woman. These were: childhood and adolescent years, early and middle adult years, later life and present adult years. Included under these major areas of life were family relationships; marriage and children; education; employment; discrimination experiences, particularly in the areas of sex, age, and race; physical health; social activities; general life satisfaction; and personal philosophy.

Data and Methods

A convenience sample of 38 women participated in this research. Participants were recruited primarily by the researcher, some were referred by individuals who knew of my research, by key persons in community and church groups, by personnel of social service agencies, and by the participants themselves.

The women's ages ranged from 65 to 89 with the majority (63.2%) between the ages of 70 and 79. The sample was homogeneous in terms of age (minimally 65), sex (female), race (African American), relative independent personal functioning (able to take of herself through personal hygiene), and independent living status (living in her own home or apartment) (see Table 17.1). These women were not nationally known or public figures. I was not looking for a special type of woman or a woman who had accomplished "great things" during her lifetime. These women may be described as "sturdy Black bridges" (Bell, Parker, & Guy-Sheftall, 1979) who worked to keep family and hearth together. The women in this study are the ones one is likely to see in the grocery store with a pushcart, sitting in church on Sunday morning, or perhaps one's next-door neighbor.

Variables and Measures

In this study respondents were asked directly their age, marital status, level of education, present employment and occupation, source of income, current residence, place of birth, and number of children. Variables and measures central to this research are included in Appendix B to this chapter.

The data were collected through tape-recorded, face-to-face, in-depth individual interviews conducted with each participant. I interviewed all participants. With few exceptions each interview was mostly conversational. This style freed the participant to elaborate on what she considered to be significant points about her life as well as eliminated the need to probe in some areas or ask questions for others. For example, when asked about childhood and place of birth, most of the participants extended their answers by elaborating on special friendships, unpleasant experiences, kindnesses extended by parents, or relations with siblings. This style was also important because these women's narratives articulated their view of their lives' meaning.[1]

Table 17.1 Selected Demographics of the Sample of Older African-American Women at the Time of Interview

	N	Percentage
Age Distribution		
65-69	8	21.1
70-79	24	63.2
80-89	6	15.7
Total	38	100.0
Marital Status		
Never married	0	0.0
Married	15	39.5
Divorced	3	7.9
Widowed	20	52.6
Total	38	100.0
Estimated Family Income		
Less than $5,000	2	6.1
5,000-9,000	12	36.4
9,000-13,000	9	27.3
13,000-17,000	5	15.3
17,000-21,000	2	6.1
More than $21,000	3	9.0
Total	33*	100.0
Level of Education		
8th grade or less	10	26.3
Some high school	4	10.5
High school graduate	10	26.3
Technical (high school plus)	6	15.8
Some college	4	10.5
College degree	2	5.3
Master's degree	2	5.3
Total	38	100.00
Number of Children		
1	4	10.5
2-3	15	39.5
4-5	10	26.3
6 or more	6	15.8
Total	38	100.0

NOTE: * Missing cases = 5

Findings

Demographics

At the time of the study all of the participants were residents of cities, townships, or villages in northeastern Ohio. Marriages were long-lived for most, whether currently married, widowed, or divorced. Of the 25 women who had married only once, 19 had marriages that lasted 30 or more years with the remaining 6 averaging 18 years. Although most of the respondents married for the first time between the traditional ages of 18 and 22, 7 did so later in life (e.g., late twenties, thirties, forties, and fifties). One woman married for the first time at age 51 and had been married for 25 years. The primary reason for late first marriage was pursuit of educational and career interests.

Most (n = 29) of the 38 older African-American women who were interviewed for this study were born and/or partially reared in the South. These women have, however, lived most of their adult lives in northeastern Ohio, either migrating there with their families due to the pull of economic opportunities and the push of segregation or following their husbands for similar reasons. Marriage and family obligations did not prevent these aged African-American women from seeking employment themselves. Day work in private homes or laundries and custodial work were their primary sources of employment. Marriage and employment were not mutually exclusive or an "either/or" choice for the majority of these women.

One woman mentioned that she had contemplated leaving her husband because the responsibilities of home and paid labor were becoming too burdensome for her. She realized she had no place to go because her mother was staying with them (running home to her mother was her logical choice), so she abandoned the idea. Her husband died just before they celebrated their 50th wedding anniversary.

These women expressed pride in their children and the job they had done in rearing them. One married respondent who did not have the opportunity to complete high school stated she is happy that all five of her children are college graduates. The respondents reported having daily (73.5%) and weekly (20.6%) contact with their children through visits and/or telephone calls. For women whose children lived in other states, visits and telephone calls were a two-way affair.

Thirty-five of the women have been in the paid labor force in a variety of job classifications (see Table 17.2). At the time of the interview, 33 (94.3%) had retired. Two respondents were still employed: a 72-year-old part-time domestic and a 72-year-old college professor. The 72-year-old part-time domestic said she helps "an old [96-year-old] woman clean her house every now and then." On average the kinds of jobs these women have had are traditional jobs that women have held or African Americans have held.

When asked, "How do you feel about aging or getting old?" none of the respondents indicated they are worried about aging. Overall, the respondents were thankful and proud to have lived long enough to reach their present age. One respondent stated:

> You know I'm just as happy as I can be. I love my age. I'll be 75 next January. I love my age. I heard them talk about that on television the other day and honey, I wouldn't give my life to go back there. I like where I'm at now. I love it. I love my age.

Other women made similar statements. One explanation as to why these women were not worried about aging but, rather, feel good about it

Table 17.2 Jobs Held by Older African-American Women Before Retirement

	N	Percentage
Semi-professional		
Director of community agency	1	
Public school teacher	4	
Nurse	3	
Total	8	24.2
Semi-skilled		
Factory worker	3	
Bus driver	1	
Seamstress	2	
Nurse's aide	1	
Health clinic worker	1	
Food service worker	1	
Total	9	27.2
Clerk/Sales		
Postal worker	1	
Secretary	2	
Teaching assistant	1	
Library aide	1	
Bookkeeper	1	
Insurance worker	1	
Government worker	1	
Total	8	24.2
Domestic	7	21.2
Unskilled		
Laundry room worker	1	3.0
Total	33	100.0

SOURCE: Percentages do not always add to 100 due to rounding.

may be that they, as indicated by one respondent, "never think about it." That is, their focus is not on *being old* even though they are aware they are getting older, but on doing what they can regardless of their chronological age. One respondent summed up these feeling when she said:

> I don't feel 78. In fact, it doesn't bother me; some of my friends it bothers. I don't have time to think about aging. That's not what it's about. I'm just busy trying to do and I enjoy doing. No, I don't have any problem with age.

The primary sources of income for the respondents were social security and pension. The annual family incomes ranged from less than $5,000 to more than $30,000. Of the 33 respondents who reported their incomes, most (*n* = 30) have incomes at or below $21,000. In terms of economic status most of the women are low income. Of concern to this research, however, was the respondent's perception of her financial well-being.

When asked how well they were coping financially—whether the money they received was adequate or inadequate—three of the respondents felt their incomes were inadequate. One widowed respondent who has an annual income under $5,000 and lives alone stated:

> I don't eat much. I come from poor people. Have to make ends meet. I know how to do that. It's hard sometimes but what can you say.

Another respondent—widowed for 3 years, with an annual income between $9,000 and $11,000—stated she is still paying medical bills from her husband's illness. Insurance covered a large portion of hospital and doctor fees, but it did not take care of everything.

Respondents who stated monies received were adequate reported annual family incomes that ranged from less than $5,000 to more than $30,000. A married respondent stated:

> I could use a little bit more, but I can manage. It doesn't always take money—a little bit of ingenuity, a little of know-how-to-make-it. I don't have a lot of money but I've learned how to manage my money so I can get the most out of it.

Another married respondent commented, "I take this little bit I got and it go everywhere." This woman started working at the age of nine as a baby-sitter at the rate of $1.00 a week. She said she saved a part of this pay and developed a habit of saving and money management.

The women say their lives today are enjoyable with a lot less worry than when they were younger. They do not have the burdens of the early and middle adult years of family responsibility (i.e., rearing children), employment, bills, and other stresses in life. They are free to pursue personal interests. One respondent made this comment when comparing her life now with her life in the early and middle adult years. She was widowed and 80 years old.

> Oh yes, I'm free. I can go anytime I feel like it. They said you should have a dog or cat and I said "Oh no." I get ready to go any place I just have my little suitcases and things and I lock my door and off I go. I don't have to worry about putting a dog in a kennel or something like that. No, I don't want any animals to take care of.

One woman said her daughter asked her why she was so happy. She said, "Because I don't have the worry of children and husband that you have, working."

Social Involvement

The respondents reported involvement in a wide variety of activities (see Appendix A in this chapter). One respondent said, "I'm not a sitter or a complainer. I'm always active, always doing something." Another respondent volunteers her time to do marketing and other errands such as paying bills for elderly people in her community. She was 78 years old. A 79-year-old respondent does quite a bit of traveling. She said:

> I been to Hawaii. I've been to Israel. I've been to California a couple of times. My one daughter lives in Washington. I was just up there last week. Kansas City, I've been there. During back in the twenties and thirties I never would have dreamed that I'd a went over there. Jerusalem. I never would have dreamed I'd a went over there. But we did and we had a wonderful time. And right now my life, I'm at the peak of my life right now.

Participation in church activity was expressed by slightly more than half (51.4%) of the respondents. Participation in church activity, however, does not necessarily reflect one's faith or belief or level of religiosity or spirituality. As indicated by one respondent:

> I'm not one of those super religious people. Don't misunderstand me. I just enjoy working in the church and working with the people in the church because they're nice people to work with.

She also commented that going to church "was an activity" when she was growing up because there were few recreational outlets for young people and the church filled that void. It is well documented (Blackwell, 1991; Cone, 1970; Pinkney, 1993) that for African Americans in the past the church served as an all-encompassing entity, that is, a place for educational, economic, political, and social, as well as religious, functions. There are sacred sentiments attached to the church; however, it is also a social environment. One respondent said the church is a good place to meet people.

The respondents also visit and telephone neighbors and friends. One respondent said she has a telephone hour every Saturday during which she calls friends. Some of the respondents stated they try to make contact especially with the sick and shut-in. One woman who had a heart attack more than a year ago expressed it this way:

> If I don't get to see somebody in spite of my not suppose to be running around seeing, once or twice a week visiting, I just feel lost. So, well, then I start to sit down and go to phone calls or get the [greeting] cards out.

Health Assessment

In response to self-assessment of their health ("Overall, how would you describe your health?"), 48.6% rated their health as good, 21.6% said excellent, and 29.7% gave a rating of fair. A more objective measure of health was taken by asking the women if they had any physical ailments, and if so, the seriousness of the problem (i.e., under a doctor's care, taking medication, etc.). Some of these women experienced health problems such as arthritis, high blood pressure, heart disease, and diabetes with varying degrees of seriousness.

Health is a factor in the life satisfaction of these older African Americans. Less than three fourths (72.7%) of the women who think their physical well-being is fair are very satisfied with their lives, whereas 94.4% of those who access their physical well-being as good are very satisfied. Many (87.9%) of those who rated themselves as excellent are very satisfied with their lives. Being under a doctor's care has influence, as well: A smaller proportion of those under a doctor's care (81.0%) compared to those not under a doctor's care (93.8%) are very satisfied with their lives. One respondent who rated her health as excellent commented:

> I have no pains. I don't even have a doctor. I don't go to no doctor. If you have the proper intake and the proper elimination you have no problem. When you have your health you've got everything.

Another respondent who has experienced quite a bit of sickness over her lifetime and has had several operations, stated:

> I look at life as something special. You blessed when you got a portion of your health. You really blessed. At one point I never thought I would make it to see 30 years.

Overall the mental well-being of the respondents was good. In response to the question "How often are you happy?, Sad?, Lonely?, Depressed?" (measured by rarely, sometimes, often, and always), 83.8% ($n = 31$) indicated they were often happy and 13.5% ($n = 5$) said they were always happy. Some of the respondents, however, did say they were sometimes sad (21.6%), depressed (40.5%), or lonely (5.4%). It is important to note that feeling sad, depressed, or lonely did not diminish general life satisfaction for these women. Some of their comments were:

> Oh yeah, I get disappointment but I don't let them take over. I wasn't depressed when I went to the hospital. My friend was telling me "I come running to see how you reacting. Ready to cry and here you are just as nice and everything." And I get over to the hospital and this nurse was feeling sorry for me. I said "Never mind that." I said "You don't need to feel sorry for me." I said "the only thing I could say God said I better slow down and this is the only way he could get me to do it."

Race, Sex, and Age Discrimination

Racial discrimination was reported by more (52.9%) of the respondents than either gender (5.4%) or age (0%) discrimination. Some respondents, however, did report discrimination of a combination of these variables. Primary sources of discrimination were work and school. One of the respondents whose physical features were quite similar to White Americans (i.e., very light skin color and straight, long hair) was asked if she ever thought of "passing." She was asked this by a White male physician at the hospital where she was employed. The exchange continued:

> She said, "Pass for what?"
>
> He said, "Pass, you know, pass for White."
>
> She said, "No. Why would there be an advantage for me passing for White?"
>
> He said, "Maybe your advantages would have been so much better."
>
> She said, "What are you trying to say to me? I should be a little frog in a big pool? I'd rather be a big frog in my pool."

Some of the respondents indicated they had experienced discrimination in their travels to the South or while living in the South—incidents such as having to sit in the "colored" section on a bus or train or being served from the back door of a restaurant. A small percentage (5.4%) of the women reported experiencing discrimination due to their gender. One woman described an incident where she was overcharged for work done on her house, "just because I'm a woman and don't know any better." Another respondent stated that she and her husband were performing the same job duties but her husband was paid higher wages. She said she did not complain because the money was coming to their needy household. She said she does not believe it is right for men and women to receive differential pay when they are both performing the same job duties.

A respondent who was an ordained minister reported experiencing race and gender discrimination. When asked, "Have you ever experienced discrimination because of your race, sex, or age?" she answered:

> Only in the church. Now that's a strange place. Well that's a strange place for discrimination to be period. But to be Black and a woman and in the church . . . so yes, I am discriminated against because I'm Black and because I'm a woman and because I know how to write my name.

Another woman stated she had experienced discrimination because of her age and gender, and this also happened in the church.

Sixteen (47.1%) of the respondents stated they had not had any personal experiences with discrimination because of their race, sex, or age or any combination of these three variables. These women are aware that discrimination, particularly racial discrimination, is a fact of life in this society. As one respondent commented:

I'm sure there has been some but I'd rather ignore it. I think about it for a minute. Then, I know that's how this society is set up.

Perhaps these respondents who say they have not experienced any discrimination have chosen, as did this respondent, to ignore it. They did not ignore discrimination in the sense of burying their heads in the sand and saying, "if it doesn't happen to me then it doesn't exist." Rather, they deliberately chose to engage in some worthwhile activity that would make them feel good about themselves. In other words, given the structural constraints associated with age, race, and sex, which these women do not and cannot control, they have chosen instead to involve themselves in pursuits they can control.

For example, a 78-year-old retired school teacher stated that as a high school student she was discouraged from preparing a report on the accomplishments of Black people. She said the librarian told her that there were not any books on that subject, and "besides, no one was interested in that." This woman said this made her so angry that she found and memorized the titles and authors of every book about and by Blacks that the library had at that time.

One respondent summarized discrimination this way:

Oh, I think most of us have [experienced discrimination]. But learning how to deal with them is the important thing. I've met people who . . . I've always felt that if people didn't want to be with me it was their loss because I wasn't going to hurt them and I've always been willing to work cooperatively with people. There is some [discrimination], you can always find some. But I just ignore it because life is too short for that.

Gender discrimination for most of these women may not be as evident as racial discrimination—a phenomenon they are aware of and can relate to personally. The Civil Rights era raised everyone's consciousness about racial discrimination, including the aged respondents in this study. Gender discrimination may not be thought of as relating to them personally but to other women. The Women's Liberation Movement apparently did not speak to these women.

Life Satisfaction

When asked, "Overall, are you satisfied with your life?" (somewhat satisfied, satisfied, very satisfied), a very high proportion (86.5%) of the respondents stated they were very satisfied with their lives in general, 2.7% indicated satisfied, and 10.8% said they were somewhat satisfied. Some level of satisfaction with life was expressed by all of the respondents with *none* of the respondents reporting being dissatisfied with life. One 74-year-old widow who was somewhat satisfied with her life stated: "I've had some good times, I've had some hard times, but more good than bad." Another commented, "Maybe I don't have

much but I get along. I just don't worry. I'm satisfied with my life."
Comments by other respondents were:

> Basically, I think its been a pretty good life. I don't know anything I really
> wanted to do badly enough to wish that I had done that.

> I couldn't ask for any better. I don't want to be a rich woman. I know I'm not
> going to be. And the Lord has truly been good to be. So what more can you ask.

> Generally, I feel I've had a good life. I've had a good life. I had . . . I never been
> hungry, I had a family, I had the love and care of a good man, home. What else
> could you want?

Respondents were asked to share their personal philosophy of life,
if they had one. A *personal philosophy* is a motto or creed that one
believes in and uses as a guide for one's life. Each respondent's personal philosophy was coded as self-oriented only (focused primarily
on the respondent), other-oriented (focused primarily on others), and
self- and other-oriented (focused on both the respondent and others).
Slightly more than two thirds (67.7%) of the respondents' personal
philosophy of life is self- and other-oriented.

One respondent whose personal philosophy is more self-oriented
stated: "I don't get into anything that I know is against me. I don't ask
for much help. I just do things myself." A respondent whose philosophy is more other-oriented said:

> I always go around people that other people overlook. Now I don't have to
> do what they do but if there is any way I can help them I will. Now that's the
> way I feel about religion. I tell [others] if that don't get me in heaven I'm lost.
> Help people that other people overlook.

Nearly all of the respondents whose personal philosophy is self-
and other-oriented quoted the golden rule as part of their philosophy.
The following are some excerpts:

> Living a Christian life and a clean life. Do unto others as you would have
> them do unto you. For God sake, eat right! When I help somebody it makes
> me feel good.

> I've always felt that always do unto others as you would have them do unto
> you. So whatever you wouldn't want somebody to do to you then don't you do
> that to somebody. I never believed what anybody would tell me. I just didn't
> accept that. I would always try to think things out for myself. And that's very
> important. Do your own thinking.

> Each day—now I won't say that I'm a religious fanatic, but you know, I truly
> believe in God—and each morning when I wake up I just usually, it's another
> day, and I thank God for it. And my philosophy is to just go through this day

as if this is the last day. But by doing good things. And I just can't see stepping
on anyone else or doing something just to gain for yourself. Consider other
people, their feelings. And that old saying that "he that soweth thorns shall
never expect to gather roses." In other words, you reap what you sow one way
or another. If I don't, maybe my children or grandchildren.

I think trying to live a clean life and do unto others as you would have them
do unto you. I think maybe don't do anything to anything or anyone you
wouldn't want them to do to you. Try to think of other people. Put yourself
in their place and try to treat them like you want to be treated.

Discussion

The older African-American women in this study reported that they
are satisfied with their lives. Contrary to multiple jeopardy found in
some survey studies, low income, low education, menial employment,
retirement, and marital status did not diminish the life satisfaction of
these women. Past studies have concluded that low income contributes to low levels of satisfaction whereas, conversely, high income
enhances one's satisfaction with life. This finding was not supported
by the data of this research.

Symbolic interaction emphasizes (a) central meanings an individual uses to define her identity, and (b) the individual's control over her
life situation that is compatible with her felt identity (Marshall, 1978-
1979). From the symbolic interactionist approach to aging and the aged
it is evident these older African-American women give meaning to
their lives, construct their identities, and seek to direct their interactions
with others in ways compatible with their sense of identity. In contrast,
multiple jeopardy describes the older African-American woman as
being controlled by structural constraints and therefore unable to have
a meaningful life. The use of multiple jeopardy with minority groups
imposes a reality, as in the case of older African-American women, that
may not correspond to how they see themselves.

An important concern of this research was these older African-
American women's perceptions of income. Perceiving one's income as
adequate—whether the actual dollar amount was under $5,000 or
above $30,000—was critical to life satisfaction. Padgett (1989) states
that aging minority women "have spent their lives as strategists, mar-
shalling scarce resources to cope with everyday demands and these
coping strategies 'pay off' later on in self-reliance" (p. 219). According
to Padgett, applying an adaptive perspective to aging minority groups
will help to identify factors that may enhance survival. Throughout
their lives, these women have learned to manage with low incomes.
Now that they have reached old age and their income levels are more
or less fixed, they have the necessary skills to manage how their money
is spent and have "some left over."

Aging as a status passage is not problematic for these older African-American women, because their focus is not on being old but on doing what they can regardless of the objective fact of chronological age. These women live their lives as they see fit.

They control this passage of life as much as they can and enact the kind of freedom addressed by symbolic interaction theory on aging. These older African-American women are free from rearing children, but they enjoy having contact with their adult children and grandchildren. They are relatively free from financial worries associated with rearing children and other family responsibilities as well as major household expenses even though they must still pay monthly bills. Aging for these women is not a process of being old but of having the freedom to do what they want. One of the women said a friend asked her how it is that she can stay in her house all day now that she is retired from working. This woman responded: "If you had stood on your legs for as many years as I have stood on mine from working you'd be glad to stay home, too."

Multiple jeopardy describes race, sex, and age as objective factors producing processes of racism, sexism, and ageism for older African-American women. These women are aware that discrimination exists. This is especially the case for race, with less certainty for sex and age. Societal constraints associated with race, sex, and age do not seem to have prevented these women from creating meaningful and satisfying lives. This is not to say that aged African-American women may not be in need of federal assistance and other professional services. Aged African-American women are not a homogeneous group; assumptions should not be made about their needs. They should be asked. In fact, they need to be asked.

These women's words show us the intersection of race, sex, age, and class. They tell us something about academic theories of race, class, and gender: that each is embedded in the other. Collins (1990) contends that Black women intellectuals have a critical vantage point as female members of the African-American community and as academics wherein they can ask the right questions and investigate all dimensions of "the taken-for-granted knowledge shared by African-American women as a group" and "produce a more specialized type of knowledge," thus rearticulating an African-American women's standpoint (p. 30). The aged African-American women in this research do not need me or other intellectuals to expound upon the difficulties of oppressed groups in this society. We can, however, began to develop a more realistic portrayal of characteristics and skills that enhance survival.

These women are active in a variety of activities, they have contact with their families, and they state that religion is important to their lives. The religious faith of these women was presented by them as a way of life. That is, it is a part of how they view themselves. For example, most of the women's personal philosophy of life is the golden rule: Do to others as you would have others do to you. The golden rule is based on principles of ethical conduct and religious teachings. Based on their statements, these women try to live what they believe: They believe it is right to treat other people the way they would like other people to treat them. They recognize that this may not always happen in reality, but they continue to hold to this belief and align their actions accordingly.

The reality is that African Americans as a group have less opportunity and more burdens because of a number of factors that are primarily related to race. But in spite of constraints placed on them, these older African-American women have done something with their lives: Some have completed high school, others have advanced their education to the master's degree level; they have maintained relatively stable marriages and family relations; they have bought and owned homes and are established in their communities; they have volunteered their time and energy for various causes; they have helped others less fortunate themselves; and they did all this and more while working various jobs outside the home where they experienced some horizontal and vertical mobility.

Note

1. Some of the women expressed concern about whether they would have "something to say." Each woman did have something to say; most interviews lasted 2 hours. One interview was particularly stressful for me because the participant, a widow who lives alone, seemed to need someone to talk to and used the interview for this purpose. This interview lasted for 5½ hours without covering all of the information needed.

References

Bell, Roseann P., Parker, Bettye J., & Guy-Sheftall, Beverly. (Eds.). (1979). *Sturdy Black bridges: Visions of Black women in literature.* Garden City, NY: Anchor Books.

Blackwell, James E. (1991). *The Black community: Diversity and unity* (3rd ed.). New York: HarperCollins.

Black Women Oral History Project. (1978). Cambridge, MA: Radcliff College, Schlesinger Library.

Collins, Patricia Hill. (1990). *Black feminist thought: Knowledge, consciousness and the politics of empowerment.* Boston: Unwin Hyman.

Cone, James H. (1970). *A Black theology of liberation.* Philadelphia: J. B. Lippincott.

Daly, Frederica V. (1976). To be Black, poor, female, and old. *Freedomways, 16,* 222-229.

Farley, John E. (1988). *Majority-minority relations.* Englewood Cliffs, NJ: Prentice Hall.

Gibson, Rose C. (1989). Minority aging research: Opportunity and challenge. *Journal of Gerontology: Social Sciences, 44,* s2-s3.

Jackson, Jacquelyn J. (1972). Black aged: In quest of the Phoenix. In *Triple jeopardy . . . Myth or reality* (pp. 27-40). Washington, DC: National Council on Aging.

Jackson, Jacquelyn J. (1985). Race, national origin, ethnicity, and aging. In Robert H. Binstock & Ethel Shanas (Eds.), *Handbook of aging and the social sciences* (2nd ed. pp. 264-303). New York: Van Nostrand Reinhold.

Jackson, Jacquelyn Johnson. (1988, May/June). Aging Black women and public policies. *The Black Scholar,* pp. 31-43.

Jones, Faustine C. (1973). The lofty role of the Black grandmother. *The Crisis, 80,* 19-21.

Larson, Reed. (1978). Thirty years of research on the subjective well-being of older Americans. *Journal of Gerontology, 33,* 109-125.

Markides, Kyriakos S. (1983). Minority aging. In M. W. Riley, B. B. Hess, & K. Bond (Eds.), *Aging in society: Selected reviews of recent research* (pp. 115-137). Hillsdale, NJ: Lawrence Erlbaum.

Marshall, Victor W. (1978-1979). No exit: A symbolic interactionist perspective on aging. *International Journal on Aging and Human Development, 9,* 345-358.

McKenzie, Brad, & Campbell, James. (1987). Race, socioeconomic status, and the subjective well-being of older Americans. *International Journal of Aging and Human Development, 25,* 43-61.

McLaughlin, Lillie. (1983). Still invisible: Poor Black women and the feminization of poverty. *Women of Color Organizing, 11,* 14-16.

Neugarten, B. L., Havighurst, R. J., & Tobin, S. S. (1961). The measurement of life satisfaction. *Journal of Gerontology, 16,* 134-143.

Padgett, Deborah. (1989). Aging minority women: Issues in research and health policy. *Women and Health, 14,* 213-225.

Pinkney, Alphonso. (1993). *Black Americans* (4th ed.). Englewood Cliffs, NJ: Prentice Hall.

Rao, V. Nandini, & Prasko Rao, V. V. (1981-1982). Life satisfaction in the Black elderly: An exploratory study. *International Journal of Aging and Human Development, 14,* 55-65.

Taylor, Robert, & Taylor, Willie H. (1982). The social and economic status of the elderly. *Phylon, 43,* 295-306.

APPENDIX A
ACTIVITIES OF RESPONDENTS

1. Helping others or volunteering
2. Public speaking or listening to a good speaker
3. Calling and/or visiting family and friends
4. Traveling
5. Entertaining or being entertained
   a. Playing bridge
   b. Attending ballets, operas, shows
6. Physical exercising
   a. Visiting the spa
   b. Bowling
   c. Playing golf
   d. Swimming
   e. Walking
7. Education and religion
   a. Completing requirements for GED
   b. Bible study
   c. Working in the church
   d. Prison ministry
8. Gardening
9. Collecting
10. Television viewing
11. Playing or listening to music
12. Sewing or quilting
13. Rug making
14. Reading
15. Meditation
16. Cooking and baking

APPENDIX B
VARIABLES AND MEASURES

Coping Mentally:

"Do you ever (0) rarely (1) sometimes (3) often or (4) always feel happy, sad, depressed, or lonely?"

Coping Financially:

"Is amount of income (1) inadequate or (2) adequate?"

Adequate is defined as monies received cover living expenses with modest discretionary funds available. *Inadequate* is defined as monies received cover only living expenses.

Coping Physically:

Subjective measure = Self-assessed health is (1) poor (2) fair (3) average (4) excellent.

Objective measure = Physical problem seriousness

(0) no problem (1) problem not serious (2) problem somewhat serious (3) problem very serious.

Feelings About Aging:

"How do you feel about aging?" (0) not worried at all (1) worried to a degree (2) worried quite a bit.

Discrimination:

"Have you ever experienced discrimination because of your race, sex, or age?"

Personal Philosophy:

"Do you have a personal philosophy or personal motto that you live by?" (1) self-oriented (2) other-oriented (3) self- and other-oriented.

General Life Satisfaction:

"Overall, how satisfied are you with your life?" (1) not at all satisfied (2) somewhat satisfied (3) satisfied (4) very satisfied.

Keeps Going:

"Tell me what a typical day is like for you?"

18. Sisterhood Among African-American Mothers of Daughters Addicted to Crack Cocaine

AARON A. SMITH

Introduction and Literature Review

🌀 In this chapter I describe the development of a self-help, mutual-aid support group, Grandmothers United, Inc., that was organized by and for African-American grandmothers rearing their addicted daughters' children. In 1990, three grandmothers discovered each other and their mutual trials and tribulations as caregivers during their regular visits to medical and social service agencies seeking help for their grandchildren. These women also discovered that the mutual sharing of their life situations provided an outlet for relieving some of the frustrations and pressures they experienced as older women rearing infants and young children, many of whom required special treatments for their physical and emotional problems.

Eventually these women began to explore the idea of expanding the group to include other women with the same or similar concerns about their role as caregiver grandmothers. They were rapidly recognizing that their own lives were consumed by problems centered around their solitary efforts to provide full-time caregiving and "parenting" to their addicted daughters' children.

African-American women of all ages—and their families—are suffering greatly from the devastating effects of the crack cocaine epidemic that has besieged African-American and other minority communities throughout the United States (Koppelman, 1989). When African-American women who are addicts become pregnant—and continue to use the drug—they pass their addiction and its effects to their unborn children (Chasnoff, 1989; MacGregor, Keith, & Chasnoff, 1987). Women of childbearing age (15 years to 44 years) make up about 3 million of the regular 10 million drug users (Silverman, 1989). The vast majority of this group are disproportionately poor, African-American women (Chasnoff, Landress, & Barnett, 1990).

In recent years, medical researchers have intensified their efforts to investigate the mortality and morbidity problems of infants born to African-American women using crack cocaine. Their findings reveal a variety of medical problems and conditions found in these infants and their mothers (Baker, 1990; Bingol et al., 1986; Chasnoff, Burns, & Burns, 1985; Harpring, 1991; Hodgkinson, 1991; Toufexis, 1991).

Some mothers may respond to the use of crack cocaine with violent, erratic behavior, subjecting their infants to possible physical abuse and injury (Berger et al., 1990). Some mothers possess an intense primary commitment to the drug rather than to their children (Harpring, 1991). Consequently, some infants and children may become the innocent victims of their mother's neglect and possible abandonment.

Nationwide, medical social workers in hospital neonatal intensive care nurseries and social workers in child welfare placement agencies are greatly challenged by the increasing demand for out-of-home placement of these infants. Some infants are abandoned by their mothers, who cannot or chose not to be responsible for their care. Some mothers are allowed to take their infants home, provided they enter drug treatment programs and attend supervised parenting classes.

The care required for the well-being of these infants can be exhausting and quite stressful for anyone providing for their present and ongoing needs. Young, inexperienced drug-traumatized mothers are overwhelmed by the care required by these children. Many infants remain hospitalized for several months before they are either discharged home with some of their more capable and responsible mothers, or placed in foster homes. Due to the shortage of licensed African-American foster homes, however, there are those rare instances when other relatives or extended family members or friends take the children into their homes, but not for long periods of time.

The purpose of this chapter is to describe the development of a self-help, mutual-aid support group of women who discovered their individual and group strengths and in the process established a connectedness that empowered them to approach their caregiving from a more adaptive, enlightened perspective. As African-American women, these grandmothers encountered their collective frustrations and stresses, combined their meager resources, and became strengthened by their oneness of purpose and their dedication to their grandchildren's well-being and survival.

The impressions and analysis identified in this chapter emerged from my interactions with this particular group of women; it is not intended to speak about all grandmother caregivers, only the women who founded Grandmothers United, Inc. I changed the actual names of the women to protect their integrity and privacy.

There is considerable literature on grandparenthood and the recognition of the increased number of children in the United States who now live with their grandparents. Creighton (1991) states that 4% of all Caucasian children and 12% of African-American children in the United States live with grandparents. Half of these children live with both grandparents; most of the others live with only the grandmother.

An extensive review of the literature did not indicate any references to African-American grandmothers as primary caregivers to their crack cocaine exposed grandchildren. The limited literature that does exist has focused primarily on grandparents assuming parenting responsibilities for daughters who are adolescent mothers (Colletta & Lee, 1983; Flaherty, 1988; Pearson, Hunter, Ensminger, & Kellam, 1990; Stevens, 1984).

Burton (1989), however, states that grandmothers taking care of grandchildren is not new because they have historically been primary caretakers in African-American family life and structure. What is new, as acknowledged by the grandmothers in this support group, are the conditions of drug addiction and alcoholism in their daughters that lead to their assumption of "parenting" responsibilities in their later years. Moreover, Dressler (1985) broadens Burton's perspective by defining the role of the extended family kinship system within African-American communities. This support system provides links within individual family units to induce a larger network of family and friends to provide emotional as well as financial support (Billingsley, 1968; McAdoo, 1978; Stack, 1975). The sharing of resources and the ability to depend upon family in times of trouble binds individuals into a protective network that crosses intergenerational lines. These binding ties are inclusive, and they provide a supportive as well as a survival base for all members.

Frazier (1939) identified grandmothers as "guardians of the generations" who, in their role as heads of the maternal family household, somehow kept generations together and tenaciously watched over the destiny of their family members. Hill-Lubin (1986) identified the grandmothers in both Africa and America as having been significant forces in the stability and continuity of the family and the community. Grandmothers were seen as the traditional preservers of the family, the sources of folk wisdom, and the instillers of values within the African-American community.

Campbell (1987) states that, historically, African-American women have always been responsible for the care and nurturance of their families. Ladner and Gourdine (1984) viewed the role of grandmothers as surrogate mothers for others' infants as a role that is assumed with minimal reservations. With changing times, Burton's (1989) contention that some grandmothers do not readily accept becoming primary surrogates for these children may be characterizing increasing numbers of African-American women.

African-American grandmothers and their grandchildren should be understood within the broader context of the family and how its limited resources are brought into action whenever family crises occur (Billingsley, 1968; McAdoo, 1980; Martin & Martin, 1978). Hines and Boyd-Franklin (1982) identify the links that connect these families with their extended relatives into an adaptive mode that sustains them even in the midst of extreme deprivation and hardships. These studies indicate that in spite of poverty, oppression, racism, and other threats to its stability and survival, the African-American family survives because of its strengths (Hill, 1972; Littlejohn-Blake & Darling, 1993) and its ability to utilize its active extended kinship resources, especially dedicated grandparents and nonrelative friends with strong family connections (Stack, 1975).

Staples (1973) stated that African-American women have always been known for two basic qualities: their mothering and their caregiving abilities. When the crack cocaine epidemic draws young African-American women away from their children and their families, however, these grandmothers experience the loss of their daughters to crack cocaine as a major statement about their capacities as mothers. For a child or children to need care (mothering and caregiving) outside its own home is the ultimate acknowledgment that they have lost total control over their lives and the lives of their significant family members. Even though this traditional caregiver role of African-American grandmothers is respected and acknowledged for its value in linking and rescuing generations, not much attention has been given to what really happens to these women when they take on this role, especially in the absence of traditional, extended family supports.

Formation of the Grandmother's Group: The Participants

Grandmothers United, Inc., is an effort on the part of some African-American women to cope with the drug culture that has ensnared their families through their daughters' addiction to crack cocaine. I joined the three original grandparents as a volunteer group facilitator, and we met for 3 months until they were able to attract nine other women. Four other women joined the group and attended group meetings for approximately 3 months; three of those women died, and one Caucasian grandmother rearing her 16-year-old daughter's three African-American children left the group due to chronic and disabling diabetes.

Three women were married living with their husbands, and nine were single, widowed, or divorced. Collectively, they were parenting 35 children ranging in age from 2 months to 16 years. All of the women in the group were the mothers of female addicts; only one grandmother was caregiver to her son's children. Two grandmothers were great-grandmothers. None of the three grandfathers living in the homes ever attended the meetings even though they were invited. All of the grand-mothers received some form of public assistance—including AFDC (Aid to Families with Dependant Children), food stamps, and Medi-care—and only two grandmothers were employed full time. Seven of the grandmothers were high school graduates; two of them had taken some junior college courses. All of the grandmothers reported a vari-ety of chronic health problems including severe hypertension, diabe-tes, and cardiovascular problems. Two grandmothers had sustained strokes and massive heart attacks since taking their grandchildren into their homes.

Support Group Sessions

The grandmothers were encouraged to attend the weekly, 2-hour group sessions for the purpose of being able to share with each other their feelings and concerns as caregivers. As the social worker, I inter-viewed each new grandmother by phone before she attended the first meeting, discussing the goals and objectives of the group and encour-aging each woman to use the group as a means of helping her cope with her role as caregiver and "parent" to her grandchildren. The sessions were held in a neighborhood health center, and those grand-mothers who did not have someone to baby-sit their children brought them to the center, where teenagers were hired for that purpose.

The grandmothers listened to each other's concerns, complaints, and confusions. As each shared her feelings and experiences, they all received support, acknowledgment, and affirmation that their feelings were valid and worthy of the group's consideration. As some grand-mothers struggled to express their inner feelings, I was able to guide the discussion back into the group experience. The grandmothers were very careful with each other. They recognized the pain each woman felt as she shared her feelings about her addicted daughter, her grand-children's future, and her own changed life once she assumed primary responsibility for her grandchildren. My primary focus was to assist the grandmothers in maintaining their commitment to supporting and nurturing each other as they discovered each others' frustrations and stresses.

One of the most beneficial components of the grandmothers' group sessions was their development of relationships that extended outside the group. Several grandmothers "visited" each other by telephone on a daily basis; occasionally several together would take their grandchil-dren to McDonald's, for example, or to shopping malls during Christ-mas and other holidays. Each of these activities would be initiated and carried out by the women themselves. The more often they did these and other activities, the more positive their individual perspectives became.

Most of the group sessions involved excursions into painful areas of the grandmothers' life histories. They did acknowledge, however, that as they discussed their individual life situations they experienced some major relief and some awareness and clarity concerning the real issues and feelings they had as caregivers to their grandchildren.

Many of these women also encountered their unconscious feelings of anger toward and disappointment in their daughters' lifestyles and their abandonment of the children that their mothers must now parent. Though such sessions were very painful for these women to experience, they eventually relished the idea of getting in touch with the whole range of their feelings.

Grandmothers' Support Group Experiences

The support group provided the women with a place where they verbalized their feelings and identified their concerns and needs. The relating of shared experiences and feelings validated their efforts and created an atmosphere in which they could express themselves without fear of retribution, rejection, ridicule, or guilt.

These women spoke freely and openly to each other about their life circumstances and the burdens they carried in their everyday living situation. Initially, several of the grandmothers were somewhat embarrassed to talk about family problems with outsiders. Eventually they were convinced by each others' caring and concern that they could trust each other to care and to understand. This feeling of connectedness extended beyond the weekly group sessions; Mrs. Knox relates a phone conversation she had one evening with Mrs. Mack:

> When she calls, I can tell by her voice that she needed to talk; the first words out of her mouth, "Hey, it's me. You busy?" We are that close. This tells me to stop what I'm doing because we got to talk. We are there for each other, because I know that my time is coming and I want her and the others to hear me out. We know where we are coming from. We are connected even when you don't see us together. That has been a big turn-on for us. Now we have our own group, it isn't big yet but at least we have it.

Mrs. Knox and Mrs. Mack have established a trusting relationship that continues outside the group. Both women acknowledged not having related too well in the past with other women, but through interacting in the support group where they share each others' pain and frustrations they began to trust each other openly.

The grandmothers often conveyed skepticism concerning their daughters' abilities to recover from their drug addiction and resume responsibility for their dependent children. Mrs. Knox expressed strong feelings of doubt about her daughter's chances of becoming well again:

> We might as well face it, our daughters might not come back. They improve a little, but that crack thing is vicious, our daughters become less than human, they lose their motherly instincts and crack cocaine becomes their god. She looks like the walking dead, the spirit's gone out of her. We might not want to admit it but they are gone, never to come back the way we want them to. But I don't know, so we better face it. (Several of the women begin to cry, including Mrs. Knox.)

Mrs. Knox verbalized the feelings of desperation that all of the mothers had expressed at some point: Their daughters will never resume their responsibilities as mothers. What is to be gained by all of the sacrifices that they make in order to rescue their grandchildren? Mrs. Knox often defined taking her grandchildren into her home as a "life sentence, we will have these kids until we die, we are held prisoners by our daughters and their kids." This is a grim perspective, and it accounts for some of the original depression, anger, and sadness that these women felt and expressed when they entered the group.

Mrs. Knox had come to an acceptance of their situation and the lives of their addicted daughters. Some grandmothers had great difficulty accepting some of these blunt realities that were articulated by women like Mrs. Knox. Mrs. Jones struggled with some of the perspectives offered by the other women. The following is a statement that she made during her first and last visit to the group:

> This is my first visit here and I am scared by what you say about your daughters. I'm new at this. My 18-year-old daughter just had a baby who is now one year old. I did not know my daughter was on drugs. I was the last to know. She left home at 16, but she started leaving at age 15. We did everything possible to make her happy. When she left, we didn't know where she was for almost 8 months. Friends would tell us they saw her certain places but we never saw her. I worried all the time about her, never knowing if she was dead or alive. All of a sudden she shows up, pregnant, but she said she was not on drugs. When she went into labor she told the nurse about taking drugs and when the baby was born, it had seizures and it shook all the time. The judge made her go to a residential drug program and we took the baby home. I'm only 40 years old. I don't want her baby. I want her to come get her baby. My husband is angry with me because he said that I brought the baby home against his wishes. I know he loves the baby, but he's only 42 and we don't need a baby to take care of. I have to look on the bright side, but I would go crazy if I thought that I would have to do this the rest of my life. You people scare me with your attitude.

Several times new group members were overwhelmed by the established members' enthusiastic efforts to communicate the painful realities of their situations. It was necessary to help the established members to understand that not everyone is always able to accept truth as quickly as they would like. New members often saw their caregiving as temporary, until their daughters overcame their addiction. Information to the contrary presented a problem for them. Established group members who had been caregiving for a long time had had a series of realistic encounters with the addiction process and treatment programs. They had acquired an understanding that enabled them to be realistic about their daughters' prospects for recovery. I helped the group recognize that they needed to be more careful so as not to alienate or scare away others who were unready or unprepared for the truths that they had learned to accept.

Stresses and Strains Experienced by Grandmothers

Because of the enormous demands of the caregiving role, the women experienced feelings of intense sadness, a sense of hopelessness and helplessness. Suppressed feelings of anger that typically express themselves through physical illnesses and symptoms of depression and suicidal ideations are common. A majority of these women initially wanted to talk about their feelings but seemed uncomfortable with making these feelings public. Husbands were either unsupportive or too overwhelmed to share fully in the awesome responsibilities of caregiving and sacrificing. Feelings of inadequacy and the questioning of their abilities to "parent" their grandchildren caused some of these women to wonder if they had made a mistake in taking on the caregiver role.

The following excerpt illustrates some of the stresses experienced by the grandmothers as they experienced their caregiving responsibilities to their grandchildren. Mrs. Jacobs and her 80-year-old mother are taking care of her 16-year-old daughter's two children. They have been evicted from two apartments within the past year because of the all-night crying and screaming of the two babies, 13 months and 3 months old.

> We are at the end of our rope. Every day I can see how this is bothering my mother. Neither one of us can sleep at night, both babies are addicted and they have seizures all the time and they cry all the time, too. What's worse, my doctor just told me that I need two operations. Who will take care of my mother, who will be 81 in 2 weeks, and these babies? Some relatives told us to give them to welfare and let them find homes for them, but we won't do that, we can't. It would kill both of us. Sometimes I have wondered what would happen if we just all didn't wake up one morning. What would happen? Don't worry, I want to live, but sometimes I am so tired and frustrated and scared all the time.

All those feelings were most intense when numerous problems converged on them simultaneously and their already challenged resources were stretched to the maximum. A most pressing concern for each was their parenting competence. If they had been unsuccessful in creating healthy daughters, how can they be sure that they would do any better by their grandchildren?

Survival in Sisterhood

In spite of the obstacles, these grandmothers managed to continue to be responsive to the needs of their grandchildren, even when their own support system was deficient and unresponsive to their needs. The group served as a major source of regeneration, becoming a safe, empathic place where they could explore feelings that had been suppressed: Their coping abilities had been built around avoiding the exposure and expression of these emotions. Boyd-Franklin (1986) states that many African-American women in urban areas feel isolated and alone in their struggles and that there is a need for a feeling of sisterhood.

This small group of African-American women became its own surrogate family and support network. The group became an active force in providing emotional support and practical assistance with child custody regulations, the acquisition of food stamps and medical care, AFDC qualifying standards, and public housing regulations.

Audre Lorde (1984) states that African-American women have healed each other's wounds, raised each other's children, and therefore know the possibilities of support and connection. The women in the group stated that they felt stronger because they demonstrated to themselves and each other that they could bring about real changes in their own lives. Mrs. Langford expressed her appreciation to the women for the fresh start they had given her:

> I know I'm going to get emotional as I try to say this. You saved my life. I lost my daughter one year to this day when I joined the group. I really fought coming here. I missed my daughter, and I thought I wanted to die. Even though she was 40 years old, she was my baby. She did me dirty and she made me cry many times but I loved her. I found some relief talking to you other women, but I didn't believe you could help me. How could you? My daughter was dead and you couldn't give her back to me. I tried to fight the feelings you stirred up in me. You all was so angry and sad all at the same time and you were still hopeful that everything would be alright. I saw how you all helped Annabel when she got sick and you all took care of her three grandkids for her. Even though you all were strangers you acted like sisters. What can I say? I still miss my daughter, and I cry a lot but not as much as before. My grandkids still drive me crazy, but I manage better, all because of you all. I feel loved by women who understand and give without taking. That's new for me and it comes from sisters. Thank you.

The women in this self-help support group found that their "habit of surviving" (Scott, 1991), from the past, did not always work when they were confronted by the contemporary reality of crack cocaine. Their strengths were being challenged by something foreign to their experiences. They could no longer draw on an extended kinship network for support. Whenever they turned to their kin for support, they discovered relatives coping with the same problems and with support usually unavailable. Through the group experience they have recognized the importance of conserving and marshaling their personal resources so as to extend their abilities to survive in an adaptive, less stressful manner. It is their hope that they will be able to live long enough to help their grandchildren remain drug free and as emotionally healthy as possible. Every sacrifice they make today is to enhance their chances later on.

The work that these women do with and on behalf of these children exacts an extreme toll on their own quality of life and overall survival. Just as these women are convinced that their grandchildren could not survive unless grandmothers emerge as their caregivers, they too may not survive unless they adopt strategies that enhance their own survival chances. It was the goal of the self-help support group that they initiate strategies to accomplish that.

During one of their group sessions, when the discussion focused on self-esteem and self-image, these women acknowledged their anger when people referred to them as strong women. They did not feel strong, they did not see themselves as heroines; they felt shame, disgust, anger, and self-pity because they felt trapped in situations that offered them no way out. They felt victimized by their own daughters, abandoned by their extended family and close relatives, and the community "admired" them but did not help them. Everyone failed to see or understand how they were literally dying and no one understood what was really happening to them.

In her article, "In Search of Our Mother's Garden," Alice Walker (1974) states that in order to find any part of the truth, women must themselves travel to where they hope to find it. These women in Grandmothers United learned to look to each other for affirmation, validation, and courage. These women continue to learn from each other how to take better care of themselves, each other, and consequently the children in their care. The sisterhood they share helps them adapt to, as well as begin to change, some of the conditions that imperil their survival. The adaptive coping skills of one sister is enhanced when she recognizes herself in the struggle of her other sisters. Such moments of self-discovery strengthen as well as empower the individual woman and the group of women.

References

Baker, M. (1990). HHS report: "Crack babies" [Special issue]. *Children Today, 19*(4), 34-37.

Berger, C. J., et al. (1990). Cocaine and pregnancy: A challenge for health care providers. *Health and Social Work, 15*(4), 310-316.

Billingsley, Andrew. (1968). *Black families in White America*. Englewood Cliffs, NJ: Prentice Hall.

Bingol, N., et al. (1986). Tetrogenicity of cocaine in humans. *Journal of Pediatrics, 110*(1), 93-96.

Boyd-Franklin, Nancy. (1986). Group therapy for Black women: A therapeutic support model. *American Journal of Orthopsychiatry, 37,* 394-401.

Burton, Linda M. (1989). *Early and on-time grandmotherhood in multigenerational Black families.* Unpublished doctoral dissertation, University of Southern California.

Campbell, B. M. (1987). *Successful women, angry men: Backlash in the two career marriage.* New York: Random House.

Chasnoff, I. J. (1989). Drugs and women: Establishing a standard of care. *Annals New York Academy of Obstetrics, 157,* 686-690.

Chasnoff, I. J., Burns, W. J., & Burns, K. A. (1985). Cocaine use in pregnancy. *The New England Journal of Medicine, 313,* 669-679.

Chasnoff, I. J., Landress, H. F., & Barnett, M. E. (1990). The prevalence of illicit drug or alcohol use during pregnancy and discrepancies in mandatory reporting in Pinellas County, Florida. *The New England Journal of Medicine, 332*(17), 1202-1206.

Colletta, N. D., & Lee, D. (1983). The impact of support for Black adolescent mothers. *Journal of Family Issues, 4,* 127-143.

Creighton, L. L. (1991, December 16). Silent survivors. *U.S. News & World Report,* pp. 80-89.

Dressler, W. W. (1985). Extended family relationships, social support, and mental health in a southern Black community. *Journal of Health and Social Behavior, 26,* 39-48.

Flaherty, M. J. (1988). Seven caring functions of Black grandmothers in adolescent mothering. *Maternal-Child Nursing Journal, 17*(3), 191-207.

Frazier, E. Franklin. (1939). *The Negro family in the United States.* Chicago: University of Chicago Press.

Harpring, J. (1991). *Cocaine babies: Florida's substance exposed youth.* Tallahassee, FL: Department of Education, Prevention Center, Office of Policy Research and Improvement.

Hill, Robert (1972). *The strengths of Black families.* New York: Emerson Hall.

Hill-Lubin, M. A. (1986). The grandmother in African and African-American literature: A survivor of the African extended family. In Pauline Denise (Ed.), *Women of tropical Africa: Studies of women in African literature.* Berkeley: University of California Press.

Hines, P., & Boyd-Franklin, N. (1982). Black American families: A clinical perspective. In M. McGoldnick, M. J. Pearce, & J. Giordamo (Eds.), *Ethnicity and family therapy* (pp. 84-107). New York: Guilford.

Hodgkinson, H. (1991). Reform versus reality. *Phi Delta Kappa, 73,* 8.

Koppelman, J. (1989). Crack. It's destroying fragile low-income families. *Public Welfare, 47,* 13-15.

Ladner, Joyce A., & Gourdine, R. (1984). Intergenerational teenage motherhood: Some preliminary findings. *Sage: A Scholarly Journal on Black Women, 1*(2), 22-24.

Littlejohn-Blake, S. M., & Darling, Carol Anderson. (1993). Understanding the strengths of African American families. *Journal of Black Studies, 23,*(4), 460-471.

Lorde, Audre. (1984). *Sister outsider: Essays and speeches.* Watsonville, CA: Crossing Press.

MacGregor, J., Keith, L. C., Chasnoff, I. J., et al. (1987). Cocaine use during pregnancy: Adverse prenatal outcome. *American Journal of Obstetrics and Gynecology, 157,* 686-690.

Martin, E. P., & Martin, J. M. (1978). *The Black extended family.* Chicago: University of Chicago Press.

McAdoo, H. P. (1980). Black mothers and the extended family support network. In L. F. Rodgers-Rose (Ed.), *The Black woman* (pp. 103-114). Beverly Hills, CA: Sage.

McAdoo, H. P. (1978). Factors related to stability in upwardly mobile Black families. *Journal of Marriage and the Family, 40*(4), 761-778.

Pearson, J. P., Hunter, A. G., Ensminger, M. E., & Kellam, S. G. (1990). Black grandmothers in multi-generational households: Diversity in family structure and parenting involvement in The Woodland Community. *Child Development, 61,* 434-442.

Scott, K. Y. (1991). *The habit of surviving.* New York: Ballantine.

Silverman, S. (1989). Scope, specifics of maternal drug use, effects on fetus are beginning to emerge for studies. *Journal of the American Medical Association, 313,* 1688-1689.

Stack, Carol. (1975). *All our kin: Strategies for surviving in a Black community.* New York: Harper.

Staples, R. (1973). *The Black woman in America: Sex, marriage and the family.* Chicago: Nelson-Hall.

Stevens, J. H. (1984). Black grandmothers and Black adolescent mothers' knowledge about parenting. *Developmental Psychology, 20,* 1915-1925.

Toufexis, A. (1991, May 16). *Innocent victims. Time,* pp. 56-60.

Walker, Alice. (1974). In search of our mother's garden. *MS, 105,* 64-70.

APPENDIX

A Brief Guide to Resources By and About African-American Women

Compiled by *GWYNNE L. JENKINS*

African-American women's studies is one of the most dynamic and rapidly growing bodies of literature in contemporary academia. Its writers, filmmakers, researchers, and artists actively challenge and expose White patriarchy and the silence it attempts to impose on African-American women. These cultural workers are bringing African-American women's lives to the forefront of the American consciousness.

This guide is but a brief introduction to this enormous and multifaceted body of literature. It has been coalesced with both students and teachers in mind. Its references sample the "classics" as well as noteworthy bibliographies and resource guides for in-depth research.

Section 1. African-American Feminist Thought

Andolsen, Barbara H. (1986). *Daughters of Jefferson, daughters of bootblacks: Racism and American feminism*. Macon, GA: Mercer University Press.

Bambara, Toni Cade. (Ed.). (1970). *The Black woman: An anthology*. New York: New American Library.

Bell-Scott, Patricia. (Ed.). (1989). Black women's studies [Special issue]. *Sage: A Scholarly Journal on Black Women, 6*(1).

Cole, Johnetta B. (1986). *All American women: Lines that divide, ties that bind*. New York: Free Press.

Collins, Patricia Hill. (1990). *Black feminist thought: Knowledge, consciousness and the politics of empowerment*. Boston: Unwin Hyman.

Combahee River Collective. (1979). A Black feminist statement. In Z. Eisenstein (Ed.), *Capitalist patriarchy and the case for socialist feminism* (pp. 362-372). New York: Monthly Review Press.

Davis, Angela Y. (1981). *Women, race, and class*. New York: Random House.

Hirsch, Marianne, & Keller, Evelyn Fox. (Eds.). (1990). *Conflicts in feminism*. New York: Routledge.

hooks, bell. (1981). *Ain't I a Woman? Black women and feminism*. Boston: South End.

Hull, Gloria T., Smith, B., & Scott, P. B. (Eds.). (1982). *All the women are White, all the Blacks are men, but some of us are brave: Black women's studies*. Old Westbury, NY: Feminist Press.

LaRodgers-Rose, Frances. (Ed.). (1980). *The Black woman*. Beverly Hills, CA: Sage.

Lorde, Audre. (1984). *Sister outsider*. Trumansburg, NY: Crossing Press.

Lorde, Audre. (1986). *I am your sister: Black women organizing across sexualities*. Latham, NY: Kitchen Table Press.

Moraga, Cherrie, & Anzaldua, Gloria. (Eds.). (1981). *This bridge called my back: Writings by radical women of color*. Watertown, MA: Persephone Press.

Smith, Barbara. (Ed.). (1983). *Home girls: A Black feminist anthology*. Latham, NY: Kitchen Table Press.

Walker, Alice. (1983). *In search of our mothers' gardens: Womanist prose*. San Diego, CA: Harcourt Brace Jovanovich.

Section 2. The History of African-American Women

Collier-Thomas, Bettye. (1981). *National council of Negro women, 1935-1980*. Washington, DC: Bethune Museum Archives.

Crawford, Vicki, Rouse, J. A., & Woods, B. (Eds.). (1990). *Women in the civil rights movement: Trailblazers and torchbearers, 1941-1965 (Black Women in United States History*, Vol. 16). Brooklyn, NY: Carlson Publishing.

Davis, Lenwood G. (1975). *Black women in the cities, 1872 to 1975: A bibliography of published works on the life and achievements of Black women in cities in the U.S.* Chicago: CPL Bibliographies.

Giddings, Paula. (1984). *When and where I enter: The impact of Black women on race and sex in America*. New York: Morrow.

Giddings, Paula. (1988). *In search of sisterhood: Delta Sigma Theta and the challenge of the Black sorority movement*. New York: William Morrow.

Guy-Sheftall, Beverly. (1990). *Daughters of sorrow: Attitudes toward Black women, 1880-1920 (Black Women in United States History*, Vol. 11). Brooklyn, NY: Carlson Publishing.

Harley, Sharon, & Terborg-Penn, Rosalyn. (Eds.). (1978). *The Afro-American woman: Struggles and images*. Port Washington, NY: Kennikat Press.

Hine, Darlene Clark. (Ed.). (1990). *Black women's history: Theory and practice (Black Women in United States History*, Vols. 9-10). Brooklyn, NY: Carlson Publishing.

Hine, Darlene Clark. (Ed.). (1990). *Black women in American history: From colonial times through the nineteenth century (Black Women in United States History*, Vols. 1-4). Brooklyn, NY: Carlson Publishing.

Hine, Darlene Clark. (Ed.). (1990). *Black women in American history: The twentieth century (Black Women in United States History*, Vols. 5-8). Brooklyn, NY: Carlson Publishing.

Lerner, Gerda. (1972). *Black women in White America: A documentary history*. New York: Pantheon.

Lerner, Gerda. (1979). *The majority finds its past: Placing women in history*. New York: Oxford University Press.

Morton, Patricia. (1991). *Disfigured images: The historical assault on Afro-American women*. Westport, CT: Greenwood Press.

Noble, Jeanne L. (1978). *Beautiful, also, are the souls of my Black sisters: A history of the Black woman in America*. Englewood Cliffs, NJ: Prentice Hall.

Salem, Dorothy. (1990). *To better our world: Black women in organized reform, 1890-1920 (Black Women in United States History*, Vol. 14). Brooklyn, NY: Carlson Publishing.

Sterling, Dorothy. (Ed.). (1984). *We are your sisters: Black women in the nineteenth century*. New York: Norton.

Terborg-Penn, Rosalyn. (1980). Teaching the history of Black women: A bibliographic essay. *The History Teacher, 13*(2), 245-250.

Walker, Melissa. (1991). *Down from the mountaintop: Black women's writings in the wake of the civil rights movement, 1966-1989*. New Haven, CT: Yale University Press.

Walker, Robbie Jean. (Ed.). (1992). *The rhetoric of struggle: Public address by African-American women*. Hamden, CT: Garland.

Washington, Mary Helen. (1987). *Invented lives: Narratives of Black women 1860-1960*. Garden City, NY: Anchor/Doubleday.

White, Deborah Gray. (1985). *Ar'n't I a woman? Female slaves in the plantation South*. New York: Norton.

White, Deborah Gray. (1987). Mining the forgotten: Manuscript resources for Black women's history. *Journal of American History, 74,* 237-242.

Section 3. Social Conditions of Contemporary African-American Women

A. Career, Education, and Political Economy

Amott, Teresa, & Matthaei, Julie. (1991). *Race, gender, and work*. Boston: South End.

Barnes, Annie S. (1988). *Black women: A sociological study of work, home, and the community*. Bristol, IN: Wyndham Hall.

Bell-Scott, Patricia. (Ed.). (1984). Black women's education [Special issue]. *Sage: A Scholarly Journal on Black Women, 1*(1).

Bell-Scott, Patricia. (Ed.). (1986). Workers [Special issue]. *Sage: A Scholarly Journal on Black Women, 3*(1).

Bell-Scott, Patricia, & Guy-Sheftall, Beverly. (1991). *Black women in higher education: An anthology of essays, studies, and documents, New York, 1987*. New York: Garland.

Brookman, Ann, & Morgen, Sandra. (Eds.). (1988). *Women and the politics of empowerment*. Philadelphia: Temple University Press.

Broussard, Cheryl D. (1991). *Black woman's guide to financial independence: Money management strategies for the 1990s*. Oakland, CA: Hyde Park Publishing.

Collins, Patricia Hill, & Anderson, Margaret L. (Eds.). (1987). *An inclusive curriculum: Race, class, and gender in sociological instruction*. Washington, DC: American Sociological Association Teaching Resource Center.

Higginbotham, Elizabeth. (1984). *Work and survival for Black women*. Tennessee: Memphis State University, Center for Research on Women.

Higginbotham, Elizabeth. (1985). *Employment for professional Black women in the twentieth century*. Tennessee: Memphis State University, Center for Research on Women.

Ihle, Elizabeth L. (1988). *Black girls and women in elementary education* [microfilm]. Washington, DC: U.S. Department of Education, Office of Educational Research & Improvement, Educational Resources Center.

Jones, Jacqueline. (1985). *Labor of love, labor of sorrow: Black women, work, and family, from slavery to present*. New York: Basic Books.

Ladner, Joyce A. (1971). *Tomorrow's tomorrow: The Black woman*. Garden City, NY: Doubleday.

Malson, Micheline R., et al. (Eds.). (1990). *Black women in America: Social science perspectives*. Chicago: University of Chicago Press.

Malveaux, Julianne. (1985). The political economy of Black women. In M. Davis et al. (Eds.), *The year left 2: An American socialist yearbook* (pp. 52-72). New York: Routledge, Chapman & Hall.

Nivens, Beatryce. (1987). *Black women's career guide*. Garden City, NY: Doubleday.

Scott, Kesho Yvonne. (1991). *The habit of surviving: Black women's strategies for life*. New Brunswick, NJ: Rutgers University Press.

Simms, Margaret C., & Malveaux, Julianne. (Eds.). (1986). *Slipping through the cracks: The status of Black women*. New Brunswick, NJ: Transaction Books.

Sims-Wood, Janet. (1986). Black women as workers: A selected listing of masters' theses and doctoral dissertations. *Sage: A Scholarly Journal on Black Women, 3*(1), 64-65.

Spanier, Bonnie, Bloom, A., & Boroviak, D. (Eds.). (1984). *Toward a balanced curriculum: A sourcebook for initiating gender integration projects*. Cambridge, MA: Schenkman.

Swerdlow, Amy, & Lessinger, Hanna. (Eds.). (1983). *Class, race, and sex: The dynamics of control*. Boston: G. K. Hall.

Zalokar, Nadja. (1990). *The economic status of Black women: An exploratory investigation*. Washington, DC: U.S. Commission on Civil Rights.

B. Health and Well-Being

Bell-Scott, Patricia. (Ed.). (1985). Health [Special issue]. *Sage: A Scholarly Journal on Black Women, 2*(2).

Black Women's Liberation Group, Mount Vernon, NY. (1970). Statement on birth control. In R. Morgan (Ed.), *Sisterhood is powerful* (pp. 360-361). New York: Random House.

Coley, Soraya M., & Beckett, Joyce O. (1988). Black battered women: A review of empirical literature. *Journal of Counseling and Development, 66*(6), 266-270.

Davis, Angela Y. (1987). *Violence against women and the ongoing challenge to racism*. Latham, NY: Kitchen Table.

Fried, M. G. (Ed.). (1990). *From abortion to reproductive freedom*. Boston: South End.

Fullilove, Mindy T., Fullilove, R. E., Haynes, K., & Gross, S. (1990). Black women and AIDS prevention: A view towards understanding the gender rules. *Journal of Sex Research, 27*(1), 47-64.

Hall, Christine C. I., Evans, B. J., & Selice, S. (Eds.). (1989). *Black females in the United States: A bibliography from 1967 to 1987*. Washington, DC: American Psychological Association.

Howze, Beverly. (1977). Suicide: Special references to Black women. *Journal of Non-White Concerns in Personnel and Guidance, 5*(2), 65-72.

Kanuha, Valli. (1990). Compounding the triple jeopardy: Battering in lesbian of color relationships. *Women and Psychotherapy, 9*(1/2), 169-184.

Lorde, Audre. (1980). *The cancer journals*. San Francisco: Spinster/Aunt Lute.

Mitchell, Ella P. (Ed.). (1985). *Those preachin' women: Sermons by Black women preachers*. Valley Forge, PA: Judson.

Mitchell, Ella P. (Ed.). (1988). *Those preachin' women: Vol. 2. More sermons by Black women preachers*. Valley Forge, PA: Judson.

Richardson, Marilyn. (1980). *Black women and religion: A bibliography*. Boston: G. K. Hall.

Ruzek, Sheryl, et al. (1986). *Minority women, health and healing in the U.S.: Selected bibliography and resources*. San Francisco: University of California, Women, Health & Healing Program.

Teish, Luisah. (1985). *Jambalaya: The natural woman's book of personal charms and practical rituals*. San Francisco: Harper.

White, Evelyn C. (1985). *Chain, chain, change: For Black women dealing with physical and emotional abuse*. Seattle: Seal Press, New Leaf.

White, Evelyn C. (Ed.). (1990). *The Black women's health book: Speaking for ourselves*. Seattle: Seal Press.

Young, Glenell S., & Sims-Wood, Janet. (1984). *The psychology and mental health of Afro-American women: A selected bibliography*. Temple Hills, MD: Afro Resources.

Young, Glenell S., & Sims-Wood, Janet. (1985). Black women's mental health: A selected listing of recent masters' theses and doctoral dissertations. *Sage: A Scholarly Journal on Black Women, 2*(2), 77-78.

C. Family and Relationships

Aldridge, Delores. (1990). *Focusing: Black male-female relationships*. Chicago: Third World Press.

Allen, Walter R., et al. (Eds.). (1986). *Black American families, 1965-1984: A classified, selectively annotated bibliography*. Westport, CT: Greenwood Press.

Angelou, Maya. (1970). *I know why the caged bird sings*. New York: Random House.

Barnes, Annie S. (1988). *Black women: A sociological study of work, home and the community*. Bristol, IN: Wyndham Hall.

Bell-Scott, Patricia. (1991). *Double stitch: Black women write about mothers and daughters*. Boston: Beacon.

Gibbs, J., & Bennett, S. (Eds.). (1980). *Top ranking: A collection of articles on racism and classism in the lesbian community*. Brooklyn, NY: February Third Press.

Omolade, Barbara. (1987). *It's a family affair: The real lives of Black single mothers*. Latham, NY: Kitchen Table.

Roberts, J. R. (1981). *Black lesbians: An annotated bibliography*. Tallahassee, FL: Naiad Press.

Sims-Wood, Janet, & Staples, Robert E. (1984). Black mother-daughter relationships: A list of related readings. *Sage: A Scholarly Journal on Black Women, 1*(2), 38-39.

Stacks, Carol. (1974). *All our kin: Strategies for survival in a Black community*. New York: Harper & Row.

Staples, Robert. (1986). *The Black woman in America: Sex, marriage and the family*. Belmont, CA: Wadsworth.

Section 4. Literature and Literary Critique of African-American Women

Bell-Scott, Patricia. (Ed.). (1989). Women as writers [Special issue]. *Sage: A Scholarly Journal on Black Women, 2*(1).

Braxton, Joanne M. (1989). *Black women writing autobiography: A tradition within a tradition*. Philadelphia: Temple University Press.

Braxton, Joanne M., & McLaughling, Andree Nicola. (Eds.). (1989). *Wild women in the whirlwind: Afra-American culture and the contemporary literary renaissance*. New Brunswick, NJ: Rutgers University Press.

Brown-Guillory, Elizabeth. (1991). *Wines in the wilderness: Plays by African-American women from the Harlem renaissance to the present*. Westport, CT: Greenwood Press.

Chapman, Dorothy H. (1986). *Index to poetry by Black American women*. Westport, CT: Greenwood Press.

Christian, Barbara. (1985). *Black feminist criticism: Perspectives on Black women writers*. Elmsford, NY: Pergamon.

Gates, Henry Louis, Jr. (Ed.). (1990). *Reading Black, reading feminist: A critical anthology*. New York: Meridian Books.

Honey, Maureen. (1989). *Shadowed dreams: Women's poetry of the Harlem renaissance*. New Brunswick, NJ: Rutgers University Press.

Howard, Sharon M. (1992). *African-American women fiction writers, 1959-1986: An annotated bio-bibliography*. Hamden, CT: Garland.

Jones, Lola E. (Ed.). (1991). *20th century Black American women in print*. Acton, MA: Copley Publishing.

Perkins, Kathy. (Ed.). (1989). *Black female playwrights: An anthology of plays before 1950.* Bloomington: Indiana University Press.

Pryse, Marjorie, & Spillers, Hortense J. (Eds.). (1985). *Conjuring: Black women, fiction, and literary tradition.* Bloomington: Indiana University Press.

Roses, Lorraine Elena, & Randolph, Ruth Elizabeth. (1989). *The Harlem renaissance and beyond: Literary biographies of 100 Black women writers, 1900-1945.* Boston: G. K. Hall.

Sherman, Joan R. (Ed.). (1988). *Collected Black women's poetry* (Vols. 1-4). New York: Oxford University Press.

Shockley, Ann Allen. (1988). *Afro-American women writers, 1744-1933: An anthology and critical guide.* Boston: G. K. Hall.

Sims-Wood, Janet. (1985). African-American women writers: A selected listing of masters' theses and doctoral dissertations. *Sage: A Scholarly Journal on Black Women, 2*(1), 69-70.

Smith, Barbara. (1991). The truth that never hurts: Black lesbians in fiction in the 1980s. In C. T. Mohanty et al. (Eds.), *Third world women and the politics of feminism* (pp. 101-129). Bloomington: Indiana University Press.

Stetson, Erlene. (1982). Black women in and out of print. In J. E. Hartman & E. Messer-Davidow (Eds.), *Women in print: Vol. 1. Opportunities for women's studies research in language and literature* (pp. 87-107). New York: Modern Language Association of America.

Wall, Cheryl A. (Ed.). (1989). *Changing our own words: Essays on criticism, theory, and writing by Black women.* New Brunswick, NJ: Rutgers University Press.

Washington, Mary Helen. (Ed.). (1975). *Black-eyed Susans: Classic stories by and about black women.* Garden City, NY: Anchor.

Washington, Mary Helen. (Ed.). (1980). *Midnight birds: Stories by contemporary Black women writers.* Garden City, NY: Anchor.

Watson, Carole McAlpine. (1985). *Prologue: The novels of Black American women, 1891-1965.* Westport, CT: Greenwood Press.

Yellin, Jean Fagan, & Bond, Cynthia. (Compilers). (1991). *The pen is ours: A listing of writings by and about African-American women before 1910 with a secondary bibliography to the present.* New York: Oxford University Press.

Section 5. African-American Women in the Arts

Bell-Scott, Patricia. (Ed.). (1987). Artists and artisans [Special issue]. *Sage: A Scholarly Journal on Black Women, 4*(1).

Bentley, Kenneth W. (1985). *Beyond a dream: Black women in the arts.* Los Angeles: Carnation.

Brown, Elsa Barkley. (1989). African-American women's quilting: A framework for conceptualizing and teaching African-American women's history. *Signs: Journal of Women in Culture and Society, 14*(4), 921-929.

Campbell, Loretta. (1983). Reinventing our own image: 11 Black women filmmakers. *Heresies, 16,* 58-62.

Green, Mildred Denby. (1983). *Black women composers: A genesis.* Boston: Twayne Publishers.

Handy, D. Antoinette. (1981). *Black women in American big bands and orchestras.* Metuchen, NJ: Scarecrow Press.

Harrison, Daphne Duval. (1988). *Black pearls: Blues queens of the 1920s.* New Brunswick, NJ: Rutgers University Press.

Hill, George H., Raglin, L., & Johnson, C. F. (1990). *Black women in television: An illustrated history and bibliography.* New York: Garland.

LaDuke, Betty. (1987). The grand dame of Afro-American art: Lois Mailou Jones. *Sage: A Scholarly Journal on Black Women, 4*(1), 53-58.

Maynard, Olga. (1986). *Judith Jamison: Aspects of a dancer*. Garden City, NY: Doubleday.

Moutoussamy-Ashe, Jeanne. (1986). *Viewfinders: Black women photographers, 1839-1985*. New York: Dodd, Mead.

Parkersons, Michelle. (Producer & Director). (1983). *Gotta make this journey: Sweet Honey in the Rock* [film]. New York: The Black Filmmaker Foundation.

Roberts, Robin. (1991). Music videos, performance and resistance: Feminist rappers. *Journal of Popular Culture, 25*, 141-152.

Royals, Demetria B., & Diamon, Louise. (Producer). (1988). *Mama's pushcart: Ellen Stewart and 25 years of La Mama ETC* [film]. New York: Women Make Movies.

Story, Rosalyn M. (1990). *And so I sing: African American divas of opera and concert*. New York: Warner Books.

Worteck, Susan Willand. (1982). Forever free: Art by African-American women, 1862-1980: An exhibition. *Feminist Studies, 8*(1), 97-108.

Section 6. Women of African Descent Throughout the Contemporary Diaspora

Afram, Silvana. (Director). (1986). *Black women of Brazil* [film]. New York: Women Make Movies.

Bryan, Beverly, Dadzie, S., & Scafe, S. (1985). *The heart of the race: Black women's lives in Great Britain*. London: Virago.

Clark, Bori S. (Compiler). (1981). *Trinidad women speak out*. Redlands, CA: Libros Latinos.

Essed, Philomena. (1990). *Everyday racism: Reports from women of two cultures*. Claremont, CA: Hunter House.

Morgan, Robin. (Ed.). (1984). *Sisterhood is global: The international women's movement anthology*. Garden City, NY: Anchor.

Nasta, Susheila. (Ed.). (1992). *Motherlands: Black women's writings from Africa, the Caribbean, and South Asia*. New Brunswick, NJ: Rutgers University Press.

Opitz, May, Oguntoye, K., & Schultz, D. (1992). *Showing our colors: Afro-German women speak out*. Amherst: University of Massachusetts Press.

Robertson, Claire, & Berger, Iris. (Eds.). (1986). *Women and class in Africa*. New York: Africana Publishing.

Senior, Olive. (1992). *Working miracles: Women's lives in the English-speaking Caribbean*. Bloomington: Indiana University Press.

Steady, Filomina Chioma. (Ed.). (1981). *The Black woman cross-culturally*. Cambridge, MA: Schenkman.

Terborg-Penn, Rosalyn, Harley, S., & Rushing, A. B. (1987). *Women in Africa and the African diaspora*. Washington, DC: Howard University Press.

Thiam, Awa. (1986). *Black sisters, speak out: Feminism and oppression in Black Africa*. London: Pluto.

Thornhill, E., & Jennings, M. (1987). Black women in Canada: Embattled and battling for empowerment. *Women's Studies International Forum, 10*(5), R59-R60.

Wilentz, Gay. (1992). *Binding cultures: Black women writers in Africa and the diaspora*. Bloomington: Indiana University Press.

Index

377

About the Contributors

Bridget A. Aldaraca received her doctorate in Spanish literature from the University of Washington and a Master's of Social Work from Florida State University. She has published articles on feminism and ideology, women, and medicine in the nineteenth century. Her book, *El Angel del Hogar: Galdos and the Ideology of Domesticity in Spain*, was published in 1991. The Spanish-language version has been published by Siglo XXI (Madrid, 1992). Her work-in-progress is titled *Hysteria and Sexuality: The Medical Construction of Women in Nineteenth Century Spain*, to be published in Spain by Siglo XXI.

Bernita C. Berry received her Ph.D. degree in sociology from Kent State University in 1988. Her special areas of expertise are race and ethnic relations, gender, and aging. She is a powerful motivational speaker and lectures on topics related to women and minorities. She has been on the faculty of sociology at Agnes Scott College and John Carroll University.

Deborah Brown Carter received her doctorate in sociology in 1988. Her dissertation was a case study of Local 282—Furniture Division—International Union of Electrical Workers. She has been on the sociology faculty at Radford University and Johnson C. Smith University. She teaches Deviance, Introduction to Sociology, the Sociology of Work and Occupations, Social Inequality, Social Movements, and the Sociology of Alcohol and Drug Use. Her current research interest concerns alcohol use among African-American women.

Baltasar Fra-Molinero received his doctorate in Spanish literature from Indiana University, Bloomington. He is a Visiting Associate Professor in the Department of Romance Languages at Bates College. His dissertation was a study of the images of Blacks in Spanish Golden Age literature. He obtained his baccalaureate in English from the University of Santiago de Compostela in Spain and a doctorate in English from the University of Seville. His research focuses on the representation of minorities and marginalized groups in Spanish classical literature.

Elizabeth Hadley Freydberg, Ph.D., is Assistant Professor of African American Studies at Northeastern University in Boston where she teaches Film History, Drama and Literature of African-American Women, and African-American Drama/Film. She was a Fulbright Lecturer (1989-1990) in the Department of Literature at Kenyatta University. She has been researching and writing on African-American women pioneers in aviation since 1984 and contributed biographical articles on five aviatrixes to *Black Women in America: An Historical Encyclopedia* (1993). She has been awarded a 1994-1995 Rockefeller Fellow to write a feature filmscript based on her book, *Bessie Coleman: The Brownskin Lady Bird* (1994), the African-American aviatrix who barnstormed the United States during the 1920s. She is concurrently writing a bio-bibliography on Ethel Waters. Her publications include articles on film, feminism, women entertainers, and aviators and appear in *Multiple Voices in Feminist Film Criticism; Spirit, Space and Survival; African American Women: A Biographical Dictionary; Notable Black American Women; Notable Women in The American Theatre: A Biographical Dictionary,* and *Visions Magazine for Film and Television.*

Shirley M. Geiger is on the Political Science faculty at the University of South Carolina in Columbia. She teaches American politics, public policy, and the politics of the budget process. Her research interests include housing and social welfare policy; federal, state, and local budgeting; and women and politics.

Joy James teaches feminist theory and courses on African-American women activists in Women Studies at the University of Massachusetts-Amherst. She has published articles in *Z, Race and Class,* and the *Black Scholar;* and is coeditor with Ruth Farmer of *Sprit, Space, and Survival: African American Women in (White) Academe* (1993). She is currently working on a book on African-American women's radicalism and political thought as well as research on race, representation, and sexual violence in American visual culture.

Gwynne L. Jenkins is a doctoral student at the State University of New York at Albany where she is working toward her doctorate in cultural anthropology. Her research interests include the critical analysis of anthropological fieldwork and theory from a feminist perspective. She has conducted research on midwifery in a Costa Rican community and on the political activism of African-American club women in Albany, NY, from the 1920s to the 1940s.

Barbara A. Moss is Assistant Professor of History at the University of Georgia in Athens. She received her Ph.D. from Indiana University. Research interests include Southern African history, African religious beliefs, passive resistance, and women's studies. She is presently working on a monograph, *Holding Body and Soul Together: Women, Autonomy, and Christianity in Colonial Rhodesia.*

Charles I. Nero is Assistant Professor of Rhetoric and Chair of African American studies at Bates College. He has received research grants from the Ford and Rockefeller Foundations. Research interests about African American conservatism, HIV/AIDS education, gay studies, and the 19th century oratory have appeared in *Brother to Brother: New Writings by Black Gay Men, Howard Journal of Communication, Our Voices: Essays in Communication and Culture, Law and Sexuality: A Journal of Lesbian and Gay Legal Issues,* and *Journal of Counseling and Development.* He is presently completing a book-length work *Reconstructing Manhood: Contemporary Black Gay Literature and film.*

Greg Olds is currently publishing newsletters concerning story ideas for newspaper and TV editors. He has 25-years work experience as a newspaper reporter and editor. He was the editor of *The Texas Observer,* a political journal based in Austin, that covered state affairs in 1966-1970.

Madelin Joan Olds earned a doctorate degree in history from Carnegie-Mellon University in 1989. She was, until her death (fall 1989), a Professor of Political Science at Del Mar College, Corpus Christi, TX, where she had taught since 1966. In 1965-1966 she was on the faculty of Blinn College, Brenham, TX. In addition to her teaching, she was politically active in Corpus Christi and Texas state politics. She took some time off from Del Mar in 1972 to serve as director of research for the gubernatorial campaign of Frances T. "Sissy" Farenthold, a campaign that just barely failed to elect the state's second woman governor. She helped lead the research effort for a dissident group of Texas legislators in 1969—that came to be known as the "Dirty Thirty"—in their efforts to reform the state legislature, particularly its appropriations procedures. She served as a co-chair of a statewide committee appointed by Texas Lt. Governor Bill Hobby on ethics in government. At her death, friends, students, and fellow faculty members established a scholarship at Del Mar College in her name, the proceeds to be used, when possible, to assist women, particularly those beyond usual college age, in undertaking (or resuming interrupted) college studies pursuant to a career outside the home.

M. Rivka Polatnick (Ph.D., Sociology) teaches Women's Studies at San Jose State University. She is the granddaughter of Eastern European Jewish immigrants and the mother of Esta Joy. She has been active for women's liberation since the late 1960s, focusing especially on consciousness-raising, sexual harassment, racism, infant mortality, and other reproductive rights issues. The larger study from which her chapter derives is being revised for publication.

Mary C. Pruitt is a Professor of American Women's History at Minneapolis Community College. She is a cofounder of the Women's Studies Program, which recently celebrated its 20th anniversary. Her current research project, sponsored by the Minnesota Historical Society, is a study of the women of the Farmer-Labor Association (FLA) in Minnesota in the 1930s. Sources include newspapers (from the labor movement, the African-American community, settlement houses, women's clubs, and the FLA) and oral history interviews. The range of women's organizations across the political spectrum, from the moderate League of Women Voters to the far-leftist Rosa Luxemborg Women's League, is what kept the FLA a vital force in Upper Midwest politics for more than a decade.

Robin Roberts is on the faculties of English and Women's Studies at Louisiana State University. She has written numerous articles on women and popular culture, including two on women rappers. Her study of feminist science fiction, *A New Species: Gender and Science in Science Fiction*, was published in 1993.

Dorothy C. Salem, Ph.D., received her degree from Kent State University and is currently a Professor of History at Cuyahoga Community College in Cleveland. Her research and training interests are in African American history, women's history, immigration history, the Progressive Era, and racial and ethnic relations. Her publications include *African American Women: A Biographical Dictionary*; and *To Better Our World: Black Women in Organized Reform, 1890-1920*; chapters in *Encyclopedia of the American West*; *Handbook of American Women's History*; *Women Writing in the United States*; *Great Lives in History II: American Women*; *Black Women in America: An Historical Encyclopedia*, and the forthcoming *Images of Black Women*, and journal articles, including "A White Woman in Black Women's Studies: A Personal Narrative," in *Sage: A Scholarly Journal on Black Women* (April 1990). She has received the American Fellowship from the AAUW, Summer Study Fellowship from NEH, and Gund Foundation Publication Grant for *Women's Equity Issues in Comparative Cultures: A Handbook for Postsecondary Teachers*. She has received the National Teaching Excellence Award from NISOD (1989), Besse Award for Teaching Excellence (1985), and Distinguished Alumnae Award, Cleveland State University (1990). She serves on the board of Children's Support Rights.

Aaron A. Smith is an Associate Professor of Social Work at the University of South Florida. He received his doctorate in Medical Sociology from the University of California, San Francisco. He has spent almost 30 years as a medical social worker and psychotherapist, specializing in family and couples work. He is presently involved in research relating to intergenerational issues experienced by the Black family involved with drug and substance abuse. He is also interested in studying the multiple influences of race, class, and gender upon the survival of Black families.

Kim Marie Vaz received her doctorate in Educational Psychology from Indiana University, Bloomington. Currently, she is on the faculty of the Department of Women's Studies at the University of South Florida. She is a co-producer of a video-essay titled *Spirit Murder: Stopping the Violent Deaths of Black Women* (available from USF's Video and Film Distribution Library, Division of Learning Technologies, Tampa, FL 33620). Her book, titled *The Woman With the Artist Brush: A Life History of Yoruba Batik Artist, Nike Olaniyi Davies*, will be published by the Foremother Legacy Series of M. E. Sharpe.

Melanye White-Dixon, dancer, educator, and historian, is an Associate Professor and coordinator of the Teacher Education Program in the Department of Dance at Ohio State University. She graduated from Spelman College and Columbia University and received her doctorate from Temple University. In 1991 she was honored as an Alumni Fellow for her contributions to teacher education in dance. Her research on African-American women in concert dance has been published in the *Philadelphia New Observer; Sage: A Scholarly Journal on Black Women;* and the *Dance Research Journal of CORD* (Congress on Research in Dance). She serves on the board of directors of the American Dance Guild and is on the advisory board of *Talking Drums! The Journal of Black Dance.*

Linda D. Williams completed her undergraduate and master's degrees at the University of North Carolina-Chapel Hill. She holds a Ph.D. from The Ohio State University, where she wrote her dissertation: *An Analysis of American Sportswomen in Two Negro Newspapers: The* Pittsburgh Courier, *1924-1948 and the* Chicago Defender, *1932-1948.* She recently completed a chapter, "Sportswomen in Black and White: Sports History From an Afro-American Perspective," in *Women, Media, and Sport: Challenging Gender Values,* edited by Pamela J. Creedon. She has served as a co-investigator for two major media studies sponsored by The Amateur Athletic Foundation of Los Angeles. The first, *Gender Stereotyping in Televised Sports,* was released in 1990, and the second, *Coverage of Women's Sports in Four Daily Newspapers,* was released in January 1991.

Shirley J. Yee graduated from the University of Scranton in 1981 with a B.A. in History and Communication. She earned her doctorate in History from The Ohio State University in 1987. Since 1988, she has been on the faculty of the Women Studies Program at the University of Washington, with adjunct appointments in the Department of History, American Ethnic Studies Department, and Canadian Studies Program.